Collins
School
Thesaurus

HarperCollins Publishers
Westerhill Road
Bishopbriggs
Glasgow
G64 2QT
Great Britain

Second Edition 2003

Latest Reprint 2005

© HarperCollins Publishers 2001,
2003

ISBN 0-00-720214-8 UK Hardback
ISBN 0-00-719638-5 UK Paperback
ISBN 0-00-713989-6 Australian
ISBN 0-00-714405-9 New Zealand
ISBN 0-00-719786-1 South African

Collins® and Bank of English® are
registered trademarks of
HarperCollins Publishers Limited

www.collins.co.uk

A catalogue record for this book is
available from the British Library

Typeset by Thomas Callan

Printed in Great Britain by Clays
Ltd, St Ives plc

Acknowledgements
We would like to thank those
authors and publishers who kindly
gave permission for copyright
material to be used in the Collins
Word Web. We would also like to
thank Times Newspapers Ltd for
providing valuable data.

Contents

BANK of ENGLISH

This book has been compiled by referring to the Bank of English, a unique database of the English language with examples of over 520 million words enabling Collins lexicographers to analyse how English is actually used and how it is changing. This is the evidence on which the material in this book is based.

The Bank of English was set up as a joint initiative by HarperCollins Publishers and Birmingham University to be a resource for language research and lexicography. It contains a very wide range of material from books, newspapers, radio, TV, magazines, letters, and talks reflecting the whole spectrum of English today. Its size and range make it an unequalled resource and the purpose-built software for its analysis is unique to Collins Dictionaries.

This ensures that Collins Dictionaries accurately reflect English as it is used today in a way that is most helpful to the dictionary or thesaurus user as well as including the full range of rarer and historical words and meanings.

Editorial Staff

Editors
Lorna Gilmour
Imogen Kerr
Jenny Kumar

Contributors
W A Krebs
Elizabeth Gordon
Geoffrey Hughes

Computing Support and Typesetting
Thomas Callan

Publishing Director
Lorna Sinclair Knight

Editorial Director
Jeremy Butterfield

Publishing Manager
Elaine Higgleton

Introduction

When the *Collins New School Thesaurus* was first published in 2001, it proved itself to be a vital language and literacy tool for today's students. It was created to meet their needs and aspirations, and through research among teachers, many samples were tested so Collins could establish exactly what features would be considered most helpful. All those identified were incorporated into its text. This new edition has been revised and expanded to give students even more language and study help.

Collins New School Thesaurus is easy to use. On the outer edge of each page there is a marker highlighting the letter of the alphabet featured on that page. At the top of each page, the first and last words entered on the page are clearly shown.

But what exactly does this book offer that isn't already featured in any other school thesaurus text? Collins' unique approach ensures that each entry word is followed by a short explanation of its meaning, which is then followed by an example of real English showing the context in which the word may be used. Furthermore, each synonym given for the entry word is also accompanied by an example showing context; this makes it clearer for the student to see which synonyms can be directly substituted for the entry word, and which involve a slight shift in sense.

Unlike most thesauruses, *Collins New School Thesaurus* splits the different parts of speech of a word, and its different senses, into separate entries. Therefore, instead of scanning through the synonyms in one single, long entry to find the relevant part of speech or sense, the student will find ❶ **glow** NOUN, as one entry, followed by a second entry, ❷ **glow** VERB. Similarly, literal and figurative senses have been split into separate entries, e.g. ❶ **painful** ADJECTIVE causing emotional pain, and ❷ **painful** ADJECTIVE causing physical pain.

Collins New School Thesaurus has even more ways to help. The *Word Power* features have been specially created to further expand the vocabulary of older or keener students. These items give more advanced synonyms for the entry word, a suitable antonym where appropriate, and related words. For example, at the entry **❶ lying** NOUN, as well as the synonyms *deceit*, *dishonesty*, *fabrication*, *fibbing* and *perjury*, you will find a *Word Power* list showing the more advanced synonyms *dissimulation*, *duplicity*, and *mendacity*. And at the entry **child**, as well as a list of synonyms, you will also find the antonym *adult*, the related word *filial*, and the related prefix *paedo-*.

We occasionally offer themed lists relevant to the entry word, such as different *shades of red* at **red**, or different *types of weather* at **weather**. These lists are specifically intended to expand the students' vocabulary and to enhance their creative writing skills.

Two new features offer students even more language help. The **Word Study** supplements give advice on how to avoid the most over-used words, such as **nice**, and offer detailed groups of alternatives for every context and shade of meaning, illustrated clearly with real examples from the Bank of English. And the **Subject List** supplements provide students with the essential vocabulary relevant to key school subjects, all in one place for easy and instant access.

Also unique to an alphabetically-listed thesaurus is the detailed index at the end of the book. This lists all the synonyms which appear in the thesaurus and shows which headwords each appears under, so the student can see at a glance whether a word is a synonym for more than one entry word.

Another exciting feature is the Wordgames section, designed to expand the students' vocabulary and enhance their appreciation of language.

Collins New School Thesaurus is even more relevant, accessible, and student-friendly than before – in fact, it's exactly what you asked us to make it. And it's an indispensable companion to the *Collins New School Dictionary*.

How To Use The Thesaurus

Collins New School Thesaurus is easy to use and understand. Below are some entries showing the thesaurus's main features, along with an explanation of what they are.

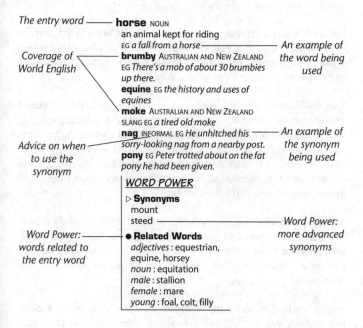

The entry word —— **horse** NOUN
an animal kept for riding
EG *a fall from a horse* —— *An example of the word being used*

Coverage of World English —— **brumby** AUSTRALIAN AND NEW ZEALAND
EG *There's a mob of about 30 brumbies up there.*
equine EG *the history and uses of equines*
moke AUSTRALIAN AND NEW ZEALAND
SLANG EG *a tired old moke*

Advice on when to use the synonym —— **nag** INFORMAL EG *He unhitched his sorry-looking nag from a nearby post.* —— *An example of the synonym being used*
pony EG *Peter trotted about on the fat pony he had been given.*

WORD POWER

▷ **Synonyms**
mount
steed —— *Word Power: more advanced synonyms*

● **Related Words**
adjectives : equestrian, equine, horsey
noun : equitation
male : stallion
female : mare
young : foal, colt, filly

Word Power: words related to the entry word

How To Use The Thesaurus

idle ADJECTIVE ———————————— *The word's*
doing nothing *part of speech*
EG *a popular occupation for idle,*
wealthy young women
jobless EG *One in four people are now*
jobless.
redundant EG *redundant workers*
unemployed EG *jobs for the*
unemployed

WORD POWER

▷ **Synonyms**
inactive
stationary

Word Power: ———— ► **Antonym**
antonyms busy

lake NOUN

Types of lake
lagoon
loch (*Scottish*) ————*Themed list of*
lough (*Irish*) *words connected*
mere *with the entry*
reservoir *word*
tarn

Each sense of ——— **❶ lame** ADJECTIVE
a word is unable to walk properly because of ——— *What the*
shown as a an injured leg *word means*
separate entry EG *She was lame in one leg.*
crippled EG *a woman crippled by*
arthritis
Synonyms **hobbling** EG *a hobbling old man*
limping EG *limping from a hamstring*
injury

nice ADJECTIVE
attractive or enjoyable
EG *Did you have a nice time, dear?*
Cross-reference —— → see Word Study **nice**
to expanded
Word Study
panel in the
supplement

How To Use The Index

The index helps you find any word in the thesaurus. Below is a section showing how the index is arranged.

Look up a word here to find which entry word it appears under as a synonym

The arrow directs you to the entry word

If a word appears as a synonym in more than one entry, there is an index reference for each place where it can be found

If a phrase is given as the synonym's target, you should look under the word shown in bold to find the entry it appears under

abstain → refuse
abstruse → mysterious
abstruse → obscure
absurd → impossible
absurd → incredible
absurd → irrational
absurd → ridiculous
absurd → silly
absurd → stupid
absurdity → stupidity
abundance → a **lot** or lots
abundance → wealth
abundant → ample
abundant → generous
abundant → plentiful
abundant → rich
abuse → **impose** on
abuse → harm
abuse → insult
abuse → mistreat
abuse → wrong
abused → oppressed
abusive → offensive
abutment → support
abysmal → awful
abysmal → terrible
abyss → hell
academic → learned
accelerate → hurry
accelerated → fast
accent → emphasis
accent → emphasize

New
School
Thesaurus

Aa

a b c d e f g h i j k l m n o p q r s t u v w x y z

❶ abandon VERB
to leave someone or something
EG *His parents had abandoned him.*
desert EG *Medical staff have deserted the city's main hospital.*
jilt EG *She was jilted by her first fiancé.*
leave EG *My husband has left me.*
leave behind EG *He walked out and left behind a wife and two young children.*

WORD POWER

▷ **Synonyms**
forsake
leave in the lurch

❷ abandon NOUN
lack of restraint
EG *He began to laugh with abandon.*
recklessness EG *the headstrong recklessness of youth*
wildness EG *Her wildness just needed to be channelled properly.*

WORD POWER

▶ **Antonym**
control

abate VERB
to become less
EG *The four-day flood at last abated.*
decrease EG *The pain had decreased considerably.*
diminish EG *The attacks on the village did not diminish.*
ebb EG *Her strength was ebbing fast.*
lessen EG *After a while, the cramps lessened.*
subside EG *Their enthusiasm was beginning to subside.*
wane EG *His popularity shows no sign of waning.*

ability NOUN
the skill needed to do something
EG *the ability to get on with others*
capability EG *We have the capability of going out and winning.*

competence EG *They have a high level of competence.*
expertise EG *legal expertise*
skill EG *the skill to play at a higher level*
talent EG *a talent for music*

WORD POWER

▷ **Synonyms**
dexterity
proficiency

▶ **Antonym**
inability

able ADJECTIVE
good at doing something
EG *He proved himself to be an able politician.*
accomplished EG *an accomplished pianist*
capable EG *a very capable manager*
efficient EG *a team of efficient workers*
expert EG *My mother was an expert baker.*
first-rate EG *This run is only suitable for first-rate skiers.*
skilled EG *a skilled craftsman*
talented EG *a talented actor*

WORD POWER

▷ **Synonyms**
competent
proficient

abolish VERB
to do away with something
EG *Their objective was to abolish capital gains tax.*
annul EG *The marriage was annulled last month.*
do away with EG *the proposal to do away with nuclear weapons*
overturn EG *criminals seeking to overturn their convictions*

put an end to EG *efforts to put an end to the traffic in drugs*

WORD POWER

▷ **Synonyms**
quash
rescind
revoke

❶ about PREPOSITION
of or concerning
EG *anxiety about his sick son*
concerning EG *documents concerning the estate*
on EG *his book on Picasso*
regarding EG *strict rules regarding the disposal of food*
relating to EG *the rules relating to transfer fees*

❷ about ADVERB
not exactly
EG *The procedure takes about thirty minutes.*
almost EG *Their wages have almost doubled.*
approximately EG *It was approximately three times the size of a domestic cat.*
around EG *The crowd here was around 12,000.*
nearly EG *a tradition going back nearly 20 centuries*
roughly EG *One unit is roughly equivalent to half a pint of beer.*

❶ above PREPOSITION
over or higher than something
EG *above the clouds*
higher than EG *There are no hotels higher than four storeys.*
over EG *the picture over the fireplace*

WORD POWER

▶ **Antonym**
below

● **Related Words**
prefixes : super-, supra-, sur-

❷ above PREPOSITION
greater than a certain level or amount
EG *The death toll will rise above 50.*
beyond EG *I expect to live way beyond 100.*
exceeding EG *a floor area exceeding 50,000 square feet*

❶ abrupt ADJECTIVE
sudden or unexpected
EG *the abrupt resignation of the prime minister*
sudden EG *this week's sudden thaw*
unexpected EG *His career came to an unexpected end.*
unforeseen EG *unforeseen difficulties*

WORD POWER

▷ **Synonyms**
precipitate
unanticipated

❷ abrupt ADJECTIVE
unfriendly and impolite
EG *He was a taken aback by her abrupt manner.*
curt EG *`The matter is closed,' was the curt reply.*
rude EG *He was frequently rude to waiters and servants.*
short EG *She seemed tense and was definitely short with me.*
terse EG *He received a terse one-line rejection from the Ministry.*

WORD POWER

▷ **Synonyms**
brusque
unceremonious

▶ **Antonym**
polite

absent ADJECTIVE
not present
EG *absent from work*
away EG *She is away on a business trip.*

elsewhere EG *Four witnesses can prove he was elsewhere at the time.*
gone EG *I'll only be gone for ten minutes.*
missing EG *Another 44 passengers are still missing.*

WORD POWER

▶ **Antonym**
present

absent-minded ADJECTIVE
forgetful or not paying attention
EG *Her absent-minded stepfather left the camera under the carriage seat.*
distracted EG *He seems distracted, giving the impression of being elsewhere.*
forgetful EG *She's getting rather forgetful, and living mostly in the past.*
random NEW ZEALAND EG *I'm sorry, I'm a bit random these days.*

❶ absolute ADJECTIVE
total and complete
EG *He is talking absolute nonsense.*
complete EG *The operation was a complete success.*
total EG *the total destruction of the city*
downright EG *That's a downright lie!*
pure EG *a work of pure genius*
sheer EG *It would be sheer madness to carry on after this.*
thorough EG *He has a thorough knowledge of the subject.*
utter EG *He stared at me in utter disbelief.*

WORD POWER

▷ **Synonyms**
unmitigated
unqualified

❷ absolute ADJECTIVE
having total power
EG *an absolute ruler*
dictatorial EG *a dictatorial system of government*
supreme EG *humble subjects of her supreme rule*
tyrannical EG *popular uprisings against tyrannical rulers*

absorb VERB
to soak up or take in something
EG *plants absorb carbon dioxide*
digest EG *Fats are hard to digest.*
soak up EG *Stir until the wheat has soaked up all the water.*
take in EG *A growing tree takes in light and processes it for food.*

abstain VERB
to choose not to do something
EG *The patients had to abstain from alcohol.*
avoid EG *Heartburn sufferers should try to avoid fatty foods.*
deny oneself EG *I won't deny myself some celebration tonight.*
forgo EG *My wife and I have to forgo holidays now.*
give up EG *She gave up smoking last year.*
refrain EG *He appealed to all factions to refrain from violence.*

WORD POWER

▷ **Synonyms**
desist
forbear
renounce

absurd ADJECTIVE
ridiculous or nonsensical
EG *an absurd waste of money*
crazy INFORMAL EG *It would be crazy to tinker with a winning team.*
illogical EG *his completely illogical arguments*
ludicrous EG *It was ludicrous to suggest that the visit could be kept secret.*
nonsensical EG *He says many diets are harmful and nonsensical.*
ridiculous EG *The programme is too ridiculous to take seriously.*

a
b
c
d
e
f
g
h
i
j
k
l
m
n
o
p
q
r
s
t
u
v
w
x
y
z

WORD POWER

▷ **Synonyms**
incongruous
preposterous

abundance NOUN
a great amount of something
EG *an abundance of wildlife*
affluence EG *Pockets of affluence coexist with poverty.*
bounty EG *autumn's bounty of fruit, seeds, and berries*
plenty EG *Allow plenty of time to get home.*

WORD POWER

▷ **Synonyms**
cornucopia
plethora

▶ **Antonym**
shortage

abundant ADJECTIVE
present in large quantities
EG *an abundant supply of cheap labour*
ample EG *ample space for a good-sized kitchen*
copious EG *copious amounts of red wine*
full EG *a full tank of petrol*
plentiful EG *a plentiful supply of vegetables*

WORD POWER

▶ **Antonym**
scarce

❶ abuse NOUN
cruel treatment of someone
EG *child abuse*
exploitation EG *Most human life involves the exploitation of animals.*
harm EG *the harm smokers willingly do to their own health*
hurt EG *The victims suffer mental scars as well as physical hurt.*
ill-treatment EG *the ill-treatment of political prisoners*
oppression EG *the oppression of black people throughout history*

❷ abuse NOUN
unkind remarks directed towards someone
EG *I was left shouting abuse as the car sped off.*
censure EG *a controversial policy which has attracted international censure*
derision EG *He was greeted with shouts of derision.*
insults EG *They shouted insults at each other.*
invective EG *A woman had hurled racist invective at the family.*

❸ abuse VERB
to speak insultingly to someone
EG *He was verbally abused by other soldiers.*
curse EG *We started cursing them under our breath.*
insult EG *I did not mean to insult you.*
scold EG *Later she scolded her daughter for having talked to her father like that.*
slate BRITISH; INFORMAL EG *Willis's acting skills have been slated, yet again.*

abusive ADJECTIVE
rude and unkind
EG *abusive language*
disparaging EG *He made some disparaging remarks about the team.*
insulting EG *She was charged with insulting behaviour to a police officer.*
offensive EG *The book was seen by many Muslims as being deeply offensive to Islam.*
rude EG *He is rude to her friends.*
scathing EG *He made some particularly scathing comments about the design.*

WORD POWER

▷ **Synonyms**
censorious
vituperative

abyss NOUN
a very deep hole
EG *He crawled to peer over the edge of the abyss.*
chasm EG *The climbers strung a rope across the chasm and crawled along it.*
fissure EG *The earthquake opened large fissures in the ground.*
gorge EG *The valley narrowed to a gorge with cascading crags.*
pit EG *Eric lost his footing and began to slide into the pit.*
void EG *His feet dangled in the void.*

accelerate VERB
to go faster
EG *She accelerated away from the kerb.*
hurry EG *He shouted at me to hurry.*
quicken EG *Her pulse quickened in alarm.*
speed up EG *It is designed to speed up credit-card transactions.*

WORD POWER

▶ **Antonym**
decelerate

accept VERB
to receive or agree to something
EG *All those invited to next week's conference have accepted.*
acknowledge EG *He was willing to acknowledge her as his child.*
agree to EG *Hours before the deadline, the Chinese agreed to the conditions.*
concur with EG *I concur with her opinion.*
consent to EG *The Russians consented to the peace treaty.*
take EG *He took the job.*

WORD POWER

▶ **Antonym**
refuse

acceptable ADJECTIVE
good enough to be accepted
EG *an acceptable standard of living*
adequate EG *a lack of adequate facilities*
all right EG *The meal was all right for the price.*
fair EG *He is a fair player, but not outstanding.*
good enough EG *I'm afraid that excuse just isn't good enough.*
passable EG *She can speak fluent Spanish and passable French.*
satisfactory EG *The workmen have done a satisfactory job.*
tolerable EG *a tolerable level of noise*

accidental ADJECTIVE
happening by chance
EG *The fire was accidental.*
casual EG *a casual remark*
chance EG *a chance meeting*
inadvertent EG *She giggled at the inadvertent pun.*
random EG *the random nature of death in war*

WORD POWER

▶ **Antonym**
deliberate

accommodate VERB
to provide someone with a place to stay
EG *a hotel built to accommodate guests for the wedding*
house EG *The building will house 12 boys.*
put up EG *I wanted to know if she could put me up for a few days.*
shelter EG *There were no facilities for sheltering the refugees.*

accommodating ADJECTIVE
willing to help
EG *his polite, accommodating manner*

a
b
c
d
e
f
g
h
i
j
k
l
m
n
o
p
q
r
s
t
u
v
w
x
y
z

considerate EG *I try to be considerate to non-smokers.*
helpful EG *The staff in the Newcastle office are very helpful.*
hospitable EG *He was very hospitable to me when I came to New York.*
kind EG *It was very kind of you to come.*
obliging EG *an extremely pleasant and obliging man*

accommodation NOUN
a house or room for living in
EG *Travel and overnight accommodation are included.*
digs BRITISH; INFORMAL EG *I was studying and living in digs all round the country.*
house EG *He sold his house in London and moved to the country.*
housing EG *a serious housing shortage*
lodgings EG *At the moment the house provides lodgings for Oxford students.*
quarters EG *the officers' quarters*

❶ accompany VERB
to go somewhere with someone
EG *Children must be accompanied by an adult.*
conduct FORMAL EG *He asked if he might conduct us to the ball.*
escort EG *They were escorted by police to their plane.*
go with EG *I haven't asked my friend to go with me yet.*
usher EG *I ushered him into the office.*

❷ accompany VERB
to occur with something
EG *severe pain accompanied by fever*
come with EG *Stress comes with this job.*
go together with EG *Poverty and illiteracy go together with high birth rates.*

accomplish VERB
to manage to do something
EG *If we'd all work together, I think*

we'd accomplish our goal.
achieve EG *Achieving our aims makes us feel good.*
bring about EG *the only way to bring about political change*
complete EG *She has just completed her first novel.*
do EG *Have you done it yet?*
fulfil EG *All the necessary conditions were fulfilled.*
manage EG *40% of children managed the required standard in reading.*

> *WORD POWER*
> ▷ **Synonyms**
> effect
> execute
> realize

accurate ADJECTIVE
correct to a detailed level
EG *Quartz watches are very accurate.*
correct EG *The correct answers can be found at the bottom of the page.*
exact EG *an exact copy*
faithful EG *a faithful translation*
precise EG *precise sales figures*
right EG *That clock never tells the right time.*
strict EG *He has never been a playboy in the strict sense of the word.*
true EG *a true account of what happened*

> *WORD POWER*
> ▶ **Antonym**
> inaccurate

accuse VERB
to charge someone with doing something wrong
EG *He accused her of having an affair.*
blame EG *The police blamed the explosion on terrorists.*
censure EG *The Stock Exchange took the unusual step of censuring him in public.*
charge EG *Police have charged Mr Smith with murder.*

cite EG *He was banned for 30 days after being cited for foul play.*
denounce EG *He publicly denounced government nuclear policy.*

WORD POWER

▷ **Synonyms**
impeach
incriminate
indict

---

accustomed ADJECTIVE
used to something
EG *The manager has become accustomed to abuse of late.*
adapted EG *The camel's feet, well adapted for dry sand, are useless on mud.*
familiar EG *He was very familiar with contemporary music.*
used EG *I'm used to having my sleep interrupted.*

WORD POWER

▶ **Antonym**
unaccustomed

---

achieve VERB
to gain by hard work or ability
EG *She has achieved her best tournament result for years.*
accomplish EG *halfway towards accomplishing an important career goal*
carry out EG *debate about how such reforms should be carried out*
complete EG *The commission completed this task in March.*
do EG *I have done what I came here to do.*
fulfil EG *The army has fulfilled its objective.*
perform EG *He has not performed his administrative duties properly.*

achievement NOUN
something which someone has succeeded in doing
EG *His presence here is an achievement in itself.*

accomplishment EG *The list of her accomplishments is staggering.*
deed EG *His heroic deeds were celebrated in every corner of India.*
exploit EG *His wartime exploits were later made into a TV series.*
feat EG *A racing car is an extraordinary feat of engineering.*

acquire VERB
to get something
EG *I have recently acquired a digital camera.*
attain EG *students who attain the required grades*
gain EG *He gained valuable experience from the job.*
get EG *My video's broken - I'll have to get a new one.*
obtain EG *I couldn't obtain a ticket at any price.*
pick up EG *You can pick up some real bargains at the January sales.*
procure EG *It was still difficult to procure food and fuel.*
secure EG *The team have secured a place in the semi-finals.*

❶ act VERB
to do something
EG *The bank acted properly in the best interests of the depositors.*
function EG *All the computer systems functioned properly.*
operate EG *In the first half he operated effectively in defence.*
perform EG *He performed well in a World Cup match last summer.*
work EG *All sides will work towards a political solution.*

❷ act VERB
to perform in a play or film
EG *He acted in 91 films altogether.*
act out EG *It was made using real people to act out the scene.*
perform EG *She performed the role on television twice more.*
play EG *He plays agent Lillian Scully in a spoof of The X-Files.*

a
b
c
d
e
f
g
h
i
j
k
l
m
n
o
p
q
r
s
t
u
v
w
x
y
z

play the part of EG *She agreed to play the part of Evita.*
portray EG *His mean, moody looks are perfect for the cynical anti-hero he portrays.*

WORD POWER

▷ **Synonyms**
characterize
personify

❸ **act** NOUN
a single thing someone does
EG *an act of disloyalty to the King*
accomplishment EG *Winning the tournament would be an incredible accomplishment.*
achievement EG *She was honoured for her achievements as a film-maker.*
deed EG *forgotten deeds of heroism*
feat EG *an outstanding feat of athleticism*
undertaking EG *Organizing the show has been a massive undertaking.*

❶ **action** NOUN
the process of doing something
EG *He had to take evasive action to avoid being hit.*
activity EG *the electrical activity of the brain*
operation EG *It is quite a tricky operation.*
process EG *the peace process*

❷ **action** NOUN
something that is done
EG *He did not like his actions questioned.*
accomplishment EG *sporting accomplishments*
achievement EG *If we can win the league it will be a great achievement for me.*
deed EG *daring and heroic deeds*
exploit EG *the stories of his wartime exploits*
feat EG *prodigious feats of engineering*

❶ **active** ADJECTIVE
full of energy
EG *Having an active child around the house can be exhausting.*
energetic EG *an energetic, happy young girl*
lively EG *a lively and attractive teenager*
restless EG *On Christmas Eve the kids are too restless to sleep.*
sprightly EG *a small, sprightly 60-year-old*
vivacious EG *He was very vivacious and great fun to work with.*

WORD POWER

▷ **Synonyms**
indefatigable

❷ **active** ADJECTIVE
busy and hardworking
EG *people who are active in local politics*
busy EG *My husband lived a full and busy life.*
engaged EG *The contenders are now fully engaged in their campaigns.*
enthusiastic EG *As a student he was an enthusiastic member of the Communist party.*
hardworking EG *a team of hardworking and dedicated volunteers*
industrious EG *It is a happy and industrious community.*
involved EG *She is heavily involved in local fundraising projects.*
occupied EG *A busy social life will keep you fully occupied in February.*

❶ **activity** NOUN
a situation in which lots of things are happening
EG *There is an extraordinary level of activity in the office.*
action EG *a film full of action and excitement*
bustle EG *the hustle and bustle of a busy hospital*

energy EG *I love the energy you find in big cities.*
liveliness EG *a restaurant with a wonderful atmosphere of liveliness*

❷ activity NOUN
something you do for pleasure
EG *sports and other leisure activities*
hobby EG *My hobby is birdwatching.*
interest EG *Amongst his many interests are angling and painting.*
pastime EG *You need a more active pastime than playing computer games.*
pursuit EG *I like art, cooking and outdoor pursuits.*

actual ADJECTIVE
real, rather than imaginary or guessed at
EG *That is the official figure: the actual figure is much higher.*
authentic EG *music played on authentic medieval instruments*
genuine EG *a store selling genuine army clothing*
realistic EG *a realistic picture of Dublin life*
true EG *The film is based on a true story.*
verified EG *verified reports of serious human rights violations*

❶ acute ADJECTIVE
severe or intense
EG *an acute shortage of supplies*
critical EG *suffering from a critical illness*
extreme EG *a crippling disease which causes extreme pain*
grave EG *His country faces grave problems.*
great EG *He died in great agony.*
intense EG *I felt an intense loneliness.*
serious EG *It increases the risk of serious injuries.*
severe EG *Nuts can trigger off a severe allergic reaction.*

❷ acute ADJECTIVE
very intelligent

EG *an acute mind*
alert EG *He is old, but he has a very quick and alert mind.*
astute EG *He has a remarkably astute brain.*
bright EG *You don't need a bright mind to figure that one out.*
keen EG *a competent economist with a keen intellect*
perceptive EG *a perceptive analysis of the situation*
quick EG *a child with an enquiring mind and a quick intelligence*
sharp EG *His gentle manner disguised a sharp mind.*
shrewd EG *He demonstrated a shrewd understanding of human nature.*

WORD POWER

▷ **Synonyms**
discerning

adapt VERB
to alter for a new use
EG *Shelves were built to adapt the library for use as an office.*
adjust EG *He had to adjust the driver's seat.*
alter EG *The government has altered the rules.*
change EG *The law needs to be changed.*
convert EG *a table that converts into an ironing board*
modify EG *Our workshop is busy modifying the tanks for desert conditions.*

❶ add VERB
to put something with something else
EG *Add the grated cheese to the sauce.*
attach EG *Don't forget to attach the completed entry form.*
augment EG *a way to augment the family income*
supplement EG *I suggest*

supplementing your diet with vitamin A.

> ### WORD POWER
>
> ▷ **Synonyms**
> adjoin
> affix
> append

❷ add VERB
to combine numbers or quantities
EG *Banks add all the interest and other charges together.*
add up EG *adding up calories on a calculator*
count up EG *They counted up all the hours the villagers worked.*
total EG *They will compete for prizes totalling nearly £300.*

> ### WORD POWER
>
> ▶ **Antonym**
> subtract

addition NOUN
something that has been added to something else
EG *recent additions to their range of cars*
increase EG *a substantial increase in workload*
supplement EG *a supplement to their basic pension*

> ### WORD POWER
>
> ▷ **Synonyms**
> addendum
> adjunct
> appendage

adequate ADJECTIVE
enough in amount or quality for a purpose
EG *an adequate diet*
acceptable EG *a company which offers an acceptable benefits package*
ample EG *You've had ample time to discuss this matter.*
enough EG *enough money to live on*

satisfactory EG *a satisfactory bid for the company*
sufficient EG *One teaspoon of salt should be sufficient.*

> ### WORD POWER
>
> ▶ **Antonym**
> insufficient

❶ administer VERB
to be responsible for managing something
EG *people who administer large companies*
be in charge of EG *Who is in charge of this division?*
command EG *Who would command the troops in the event of war?*
control EG *He controls the largest publishing house in the country.*
direct EG *Christopher will direct day-to-day operations.*
manage EG *Within two years he was managing the shop.*
run EG *This is no way to run a business.*
supervise EG *the men who supervised the project*

❷ administer VERB
to inflict or impose something on someone
EG *He administered most of the blows.*
carry out EG *You are not authorized to carry out disciplinary action.*
deal EG *His attacker dealt him a severe blow to the face.*
dispense EG *They have set up military courts to dispense swift justice.*
execute EG *She leapt up and executed a spinning kick to his head.*
impose EG *The judge had no choice but to impose a death sentence.*
inflict EG *Inflicting punishment to stop crime is not the answer.*
perform EG *He had to perform emergency surgery.*

WORD POWER

▷ **Synonyms**
mete out

admiration NOUN
a feeling of great liking and respect
EG *I have always had the greatest admiration for him.*
appreciation EG *gifts presented to them in appreciation of their work*
approval EG *His son had an obsessive drive to gain his father's approval.*
esteem EG *Their public esteem has never been lower.*
regard EG *He has always been held in high regard.*
respect EG *We all have so much respect for her.*

admire VERB
to like and respect someone or something
EG *All those who knew him will admire him for his work.*
appreciate EG *the need for children to appreciate their mother tongue*
look up to EG *A lot of the younger girls look up to you.*
respect EG *I want him to respect me as a career woman.*
value EG *She genuinely values his opinion.*

WORD POWER

▷ **Synonyms**
esteem
venerate

▶ **Antonym**
scorn

❶ admit VERB
to agree that something is true
EG *The driver admitted to falling asleep at the wheel.*
accept EG *I accepted the truth of all that Nicola had told me.*
acknowledge EG *Belatedly the government has acknowledged the*

problem.
grant EG *The magistrates granted that the RSPCA was justified in bringing the action.*

WORD POWER

▶ **Antonym**
deny

❷ admit VERB
to allow to enter
EG *He was admitted to university after the war.*
accept EG *Stephen was accepted into the family.*
let in EG *Turnstile operators were accused of letting in fans without tickets.*
receive EG *He was received into the priesthood.*
take in EG *The monastery has taken in 26 refugees.*

WORD POWER

▶ **Antonym**
exclude

adult NOUN
a grown-up person
EG *Becoming a father signified he was now an adult.*
grown-up EG *Las Vegas is the ultimate playground for grown-ups.*
man EG *He is now a man of 42.*
woman EG *A woman of child-bearing age.*

WORD POWER

▶ **Antonym**
child

❶ advance VERB
to move forward or develop
EG *Rebel forces are advancing on the capital.*
make inroads EG *They have made impressive inroads in the movie business.*
press on EG *Poland pressed on with*

a b c d e f g h i j k l m n o p q r s t u v w x y z

economic reform.
proceed EG *He proceeded down the spiral stairway.*
progress EG *the ability to progress from one step to the next*

❷ **advance** NOUN
progress in something
EG *scientific advance*
breakthrough EG *a breakthrough in cancer treatment*
development EG *the development of the car*
gain EG *a gain of nearly 10%*
progress EG *signs of progress in his reading*
step EG *the first step towards peace*

advantage NOUN
a more favourable position or state
EG *We have a competitive advantage.*
ascendancy EG *The extremists are gaining ascendancy.*
benefit EG *For maximum benefit use your treatment every day.*
dominance EG *the battle for high-street dominance*
superiority EG *military superiority*

advertise VERB
to present something to the public in order to sell it
EG *Bookmakers cannot advertise on television.*
plug INFORMAL EG *If I hear another actor plugging his latest book I will scream.*
promote EG *What are you doing to promote your new film?*
publicize EG *He never publicized his plans.*
push EG *a publisher who knows how to push a product*

advertisement NOUN
a public announcement to sell or publicize something
EG *She recently placed an advertisement in the local newspaper.*
ad INFORMAL EG *an ad for a minicab company*
advert BRITISH; INFORMAL EG *She appeared in a coffee advert.*
commercial EG *She has turned down a small fortune to do TV commercials.*
notice EG *The request is published in notices in today's national newspapers.*
plug INFORMAL EG *a shameless plug for his new film*

advice NOUN
a suggestion as to what to do
EG *Take my advice and stay away from him!*
counsel FORMAL EG *He had always been able to count on her wise counsel.*
drum AUSTRALIAN; INFORMAL EG *What's the drum on this?*
guidance EG *The nation looks to them for guidance.*
opinion EG *You should seek a medical opinion.*
suggestion EG *She made suggestions as to how I could improve my diet.*

❶ **advise** VERB
to offer advice to someone
EG *The minister advised him to leave as soon as possible.*
caution EG *The researchers caution against drawing general conclusions from this study.*
counsel EG *My advisers counselled me to do nothing.*
recommend EG *We strongly*

recommend reporting the incident to the police.
suggest EG *He suggested a visit to the Cézanne exhibition.*
urge EG *We urge that vigorous action be taken immediately.*

WORD POWER

▷ **Synonyms**
commend
enjoin
prescribe

②️ advise VERB
to notify someone
EG *I think it best that I advise you of my decision to retire.*
inform EG *My daughter informed me that she was pregnant.*
make known EG *The details will be made known by the end of August.*
notify EG *The skipper notified the coastguard of the tragedy.*

adviser NOUN
a person whose job is to give advice
EG *The President and his advisers spent the day in meetings.*
aide EG *a former aide to Ronald Reagan*
consultant EG *a management consultant*
guru EG *He became Britain's modern design guru after launching Habitat in 1964.*
mentor EG *He is my friend and musical mentor.*
tutor EG *my college tutor*

advocate VERB
to publicly support a plan or course of action
EG *Mr Smith advocates corporal punishment for young offenders.*
back EG *The newspaper is backing the residents' campaign.*
champion EG *He passionately champions our cause.*
endorse EG *We are reluctant to endorse such drastic measures.*

favour EG *judges who favour the death penalty*
promote EG *He promoted the idea of Scottish independence.*
recommend EG *I can't recommend such a course of action.*
support EG *people who supported his policies*
uphold EG *We uphold the capitalist free economy.*

①️ affair NOUN
an event or series of events
EG *The funeral was a sad affair.*
business EG *This business has really upset me.*
event EG *A wedding should be a joyous event.*
issue EG *a major political issue*
matter EG *I never interfere in these business matters.*
question EG *the difficult question of unemployment*
situation EG *The whole situation is now under control.*
subject EG *a subject which had worried him for some time*

②️ affair NOUN
a secret and romantic relationship
EG *He had an affair with someone he met on holiday.*
fling EG *We had a brief fling, but it was nothing serious.*
liaison EG *He denied that he had had a sexual liaison with his secretary.*
relationship EG *She went public on her relationship with a Hollywood star.*
romance EG *Our company discourages office romances.*

affect VERB
to influence something or someone
EG *More than 7 million people have been affected by the drought.*
act on EG *This drug acts very fast on the central nervous system.*
alter EG *The earth's climate appears to have been altered by pollution.*

change EG *It was to change the course of my life.*
impinge on EG *My private life does not impinge on my professional life.*

affection NOUN
a feeling of fondness for someone or something
EG *She thought of him with affection.*
attachment EG *Mother and child form a close attachment.*
fondness EG *his fondness for cats*
liking EG *a liking for flashy cars*
love EG *My love for all my children is unconditional.*
warmth EG *He greeted us both with warmth and affection.*

> ### WORD POWER
> ▶ **Antonym**
> dislike

affectionate ADJECTIVE
full of fondness for someone
EG *She gave me a long and affectionate hug.*
caring EG *a loving, caring husband*
fond EG *She gave him a fond smile.*
loving EG *The children were very loving to me.*
tender EG *a tender kiss*

> ### WORD POWER
> ▶ **Antonym**
> cold

afraid ADJECTIVE
scared of something unpleasant happening
EG *I was afraid of the other boys.*
apprehensive EG *People are still terribly apprehensive about the future.*
fearful EG *Bankers were fearful of a world banking crisis.*
frightened EG *She was frightened of flying.*
nervous EG *Emotionally, he left me a*

wreck, nervous of everyone.
scared EG *I was too scared to move.*

> ### WORD POWER
> ▶ **Antonym**
> unafraid

after ADVERB
at a later time
EG *Shortly after, police arrested five suspects.*
afterwards EG *He was taken to hospital but died soon afterwards.*
following EG *We shared so much, not only during the war, but in the many years following.*
later EG *He resigned ten years later.*
subsequently EG *She subsequently became honorary secretary.*

> ### WORD POWER
> ▶ **Antonym**
> before
>
> ● **Related Words**
> prefix : post-

again ADVERB
happening one more time
EG *He kissed her again.*
afresh EG *The couple moved abroad to start life afresh.*
anew EG *She's ready to start anew.*
once more EG *Rage overcame him once more.*

❶ **against** PREPOSITION
in opposition to
EG *I am against animal cruelty.*
averse to EG *He's not averse to a drink.*
hostile to EG *countries that were once hostile to South Africa*
in opposition to EG *radio stations set up in opposition to the BBC*
versus EG *Portugal versus England*

WORD POWER

● **Related Words**
prefixes : anti-,
contra-, counter-

---

❷ against PREPOSITION
in preparation for or in case of
something
EG *precautions against fire*
in anticipation of EG *His school was
one of several which closed in
anticipation of Arctic conditions.*
in expectation of EG *The hotel was
being renovated in expectation of a
tourist boom.*
in preparation for EG *The army
massed troops and guns in
preparation for a counter-attack.*

aggressive ADJECTIVE
full of hostility and violence
EG *These fish are very aggressive.*
hostile EG *The prisoner eyed him in a
hostile silence.*
quarrelsome EG *He had been a wild
boy and a quarrelsome young man.*

WORD POWER

▷ **Synonyms**
belligerent
pugnacious

▶ **Antonym**
peaceful

---

agile ADJECTIVE
able to move quickly and easily
EG *He is as agile as a cat.*
lithe EG *a lithe young gymnast*
nimble EG *He built his career around
quick reflexes and nimble footwork.*
sprightly EG *She is alert and sprightly
despite her 85 years.*
supple EG *She is as supple as a
dancer.*

WORD POWER

▷ **Synonyms**
limber

lissom *or* lissome

▶ **Antonym**
clumsy

---

❶ agitate VERB
to campaign energetically for
something
EG *The women had begun to agitate
for better conditions.*
campaign EG *an organization which
campaigns for better consumer rights*
demonstrate EG *marchers
demonstrating for political reform*
protest EG *country dwellers who
were protesting for the right to hunt*
push EG *Some board members are
pushing for the merger.*

❷ agitate VERB
to worry or distress someone
EG *Everything she said was beginning
to agitate me.*
bother EG *It really bothers me when
you talk like that.*
distress EG *sudden noises which
distressed the animals*
disturb EG *These dreams disturb me
for days afterwards.*
trouble EG *Are you troubled by
thoughts of the future?*
upset EG *The whole incident upset
me dreadfully.*
worry EG *I didn't want to worry you
with my own problems.*

WORD POWER

▷ **Synonyms**
discompose
faze
perturb

---

❶ agree VERB
to have the same opinion as
someone
EG *So we both agree there's a problem?*
assent EG *I assented to the request of
the publishers to write this book.*
be of the same opinion EG *All the
other players are of the same opinion.*

a b c d e f g h i j k l m n o p q r s t u v w x y z

concur EG *Four other judges concurred.*

see eye to eye EG *He has not always seen eye to eye with his brother.*

WORD POWER

▶ **Antonym**
disagree

❷ agree VERB
to match or be the same as something
EG *His second statement agrees with facts as stated by the other witnesses.*

accord EG *I cannot support policies that no longer accord with my principles.*

conform EG *It doesn't conform with current building regulations.*

match EG *Attendances do not match the ticket sales.*

square EG *Does that explanation square with the facts?*

tally EG *The figures don't seem to tally.*

❶ agreeable ADJECTIVE
pleasant or enjoyable
EG *I found it a most agreeable experience.*

delightful EG *I've had a delightful time.*

enjoyable EG *an enjoyable meal*

lovely EG *I hope you have a lovely holiday.*

nice EG *It would be very nice to get away from it all for a few days.*

pleasant EG *This restaurant offers good food in pleasant surroundings.*

pleasurable EG *the pleasurable task of deciding where to go on holiday*

WORD POWER

▶ **Antonym**
disagreeable

❷ agreeable ADJECTIVE
willing to allow or do something
EG *She said she was agreeable to this plan.*

game EG *Are you game to try something a little bit different?*

happy EG *I'm happy to go along with what everyone else thinks.*

prepared EG *Would you be prepared to queue for hours for a ticket?*

ready EG *I'm ready to take over if he resigns.*

willing EG *Are you willing to take part in a survey?*

WORD POWER

▷ **Synonyms**
amenable
compliant

agreement NOUN
a decision reached by two or more people
EG *The two countries have signed agreements on fishing and oil.*

arrangement EG *Eventually we came to an arrangement that suited us both.*

contract EG *She has signed an exclusive solo-album contract.*

deal INFORMAL EG *The company recently won a five-year deal to build runways.*

pact EG *He ruled out any formal pact with the government.*

settlement EG *She accepted an out-of-court settlement of £4000.*

treaty EG *negotiations over a 1992 treaty on global warming*

WORD POWER

▷ **Synonyms**
compact
covenant

❶ aim VERB
to plan to do something
EG *The company aims to sign 1 million customers within five years.*

aspire EG *people who aspire to public office*

attempt EG *He will attempt to win the title for the second year running.*

intend EG *I intend to remarry.*
plan EG *Mr Beach was planning to sue over injuries he received.*
propose EG *And where do you propose building such a huge thing?*
strive EG *He strives hard to keep himself very fit.*

❷ aim NOUN
what someone intends to achieve
EG *Our main aim is to offer a superior product.*
ambition EG *His ambition is to sail round the world.*
goal EG *I have to keep setting goals for myself.*
intention EG *It was always my intention to stay in Italy.*
objective EG *His objective was to play golf and win.*
plan EG *His plan was to acquire paintings by the best artists in Italy.*
target EG *his target of 20 goals this season*

❶ alarm NOUN
a feeling of fear
EG *The cat sprang back in alarm.*
anxiety EG *anxiety about crime*
apprehension EG *I tensed every muscle in my body in apprehension.*
fright EG *The birds smashed into the top of their cages in fright.*
nervousness EG *I smiled warmly so he wouldn't see my nervousness.*
panic EG *There was panic in the streets of the capital.*
scare EG *Despite the scare there are no plans to withdraw the drug.*

WORD POWER
▷ **Synonyms**
consternation
trepidation

▶ **Antonym**
calm

❷ alarm NOUN
a device used to warn people of something

EG *a burglar alarm*
distress signal EG *The pilot was trying to send a distress signal when the aircraft crashed.*
siren EG *a police siren*
warning EG *A second air raid warning sounded over the capital.*

❸ alarm VERB
to fill with fear
EG *We could not see what had alarmed him.*
distress EG *He is very distressed by what happened.*
frighten EG *The future frightens me.*
panic EG *He was panicked by his wife's behaviour.*
scare EG *Horses scare me.*
startle EG *startled by a gunshot*
unnerve EG *Investors had been unnerved by the country's ailing stockmarket.*

WORD POWER
▶ **Antonym**
calm

alcohol NOUN
a drink that can make you drunk
EG *There wasn't even any alcohol at the party.*
booze INFORMAL EG *clutching a bottle of booze*
drink EG *Too much drink is bad for you.*
grog AUSTRALIAN AND NEW ZEALAND; INFORMAL EG *They demanded a bottle of grog.*
liquor EG *I could smell liquor on his breath.*
spirits EG *a voluntary ban on advertising spirits on TV*

WORD POWER
● **Related Words**
like : dipsomania

❶ alert ADJECTIVE
paying full attention
EG *apprehended by alert security staff*

attentive EG *an attentive audience*
observant EG *an observant policeman*
on guard EG *on guard against the threat of invasion*
vigilant EG *letter bombs intercepted by vigilant post office staff*
wary EG *He kept a wary eye on the dog as he passed the gate.*

WORD POWER

▶ **Antonym**
unaware

❷ alert VERB
to warn of danger
EG *I was hoping he'd alert the police.*
forewarn EG *The guide had forewarned me what to expect.*
inform EG *The patient was not properly informed of the risks.*
notify EG *The passengers were notified of the bomb threat.*
warn EG *They warned him of the dangers of sailing alone.*

❶ alike ADJECTIVE
similar in some way
EG *You and your father are so alike.*
analogous EG *a ritual analogous to those of primitive cultures*
close EG *a creature close in appearance to a panther*
identical EG *Nearly all the houses were identical.*
similar EG *These two wines are very similar in taste.*
the same EG *products which are almost the same in every respect*

WORD POWER

▶ **Antonym**
different

❷ alike ADVERB
in a similar way
EG *I punish all my pupils alike if they misbehave.*
equally EG *Democracy calls for all people to be treated equally.*

in the same way EG *He speaks in the same way to his boss as to his own employees.*
similarly EG *All the children were dressed similarly.*
uniformly EG *The rules apply uniformly to everyone.*

❶ alive ADJECTIVE
having life
EG *They kept her alive on a life support machine.*
animate EG *animate beings*
breathing EG *Not only is he still breathing, but he lives right here in New York.*
living EG *The blue whale is the largest living thing on the planet.*

WORD POWER

▶ **Antonym**
dead

❷ alive ADJECTIVE
lively and active
EG *I never expected to feel so alive in my life again.*
active EG *half an hour's physical activity, five times a week, will keep you active*
alert EG *A brisk walk will make you feel more alert.*
animated EG *He becomes animated when talking about his work.*
energetic EG *a vital and energetic man*
full of life EG *She was so chatty and full of life.*
lively EG *Cheryl was a very lively and attractive girl.*
vivacious EG *a vivacious personality*

WORD POWER

▶ **Antonym**
dull

all PRONOUN
the whole of something
EG *Why did you have to go and say all that?*

each EG *Each of us received a free gift.*
every one EG *Every one of you must take a share of the blame.*
everything EG *Sit down and tell me everything.*
the whole amount EG *Have you paid the whole amount of the fine?*
the (whole) lot EG *The whole lot of you are under arrest.*

WORD POWER

● **Related Words**
prefixes : pan-,
panto-

---

❶ **allow** VERB
to permit someone to do something
EG *Smoking will not be allowed.*
approve EG *The Housing Minister approved the building of the flats.*
authorize EG *authorized to carry weapons*
let EG *They won't let her leave the country.*
permit EG *Unauthorized personnel are not permitted to enter.*
stand for EG *We won't stand for it any more.*
tolerate EG *I won't tolerate sloppiness.*

WORD POWER

▷ **Synonyms**
brook
give leave
sanction

▶ **Antonym**
forbid

---

❷ **allow** VERB
to set aside for a particular purpose
EG *Allow four hours for the paint to dry.*
allocate EG *an efficient method of allocating resources*
allot EG *We were allotted just 15 minutes.*
assign EG *the full amount of economic aid assigned for the year*

grant EG *Funding had been granted for the project.*
set aside EG *money set aside for education*

all right ADJECTIVE
acceptable
EG *It was all right but nothing special.*
acceptable EG *We've made an acceptable start, but it could have been better.*
adequate EG *Our accommodation was adequate.*
average EG *I was only average academically.*
fair EG *The overall standard of the entries was fair.*
okay *or* **OK** INFORMAL EG *The prices here are okay.*

almost ADVERB
very nearly
EG *Over the past decade their wages have almost doubled.*
about EG *I was about nine at the time.*
approximately EG *The family owns approximately 8% of the company.*
close to EG *He spent close to 30 years in prison.*
nearly EG *The beach was very nearly empty.*
not quite EG *It's more than a hill but not quite a mountain.*
practically EG *I've known him practically all my life.*

alone ADJECTIVE
not with other people or things
EG *He was all alone in the middle of the hall.*
detached EG *a `counter-culture' detached from the rest of the world*
isolated EG *Talking things over in a group meant none of us felt isolated.*
separate EG *They were kept separate from the other prisoners.*
single EG *I get depressed on Valentine's Day because I'm still single.*

aloud ADVERB
out loud

EG *Our father read aloud to us.*
audibly EG *Hugh sighed audibly.*
out loud EG *I tried not to laugh out loud.*

also ADVERB
in addition
EG *He is also an army doctor.*
as well EG *She published historical novels as well.*
besides EG *You get to sample lots of baked things and take home masses of cookies besides.*
furthermore EG *Furthermore, they claim that any such interference is completely ineffective.*
into the bargain EG *The machine can play ordinary cassettes into the bargain.*
moreover EG *They have accused the government of corruption. Moreover, they have named names.*
too EG *I was there too.*

always ADVERB
all the time or forever
EG *She's always moaning.*
continually EG *Malcolm was continually changing his mind.*
every time EG *You can't get it right every time.*
forever EG *He was forever attempting to arrange deals.*
invariably EG *Their teamwork was invariably good.*
perpetually EG *The two groups are perpetually at loggerheads.*

amaze VERB
to surprise greatly
EG *He amazed us by his knowledge of Welsh history.*
astonish EG *I was astonished at his stupidity.*
astound EG *I am astounded at the comments made by the Chief Superintendant.*
shock EG *She was shocked by the appalling news.*
stagger EG *He was staggered by the sheer size of the crowd.*
stun EG *Many cinema-goers were stunned by the film's tragic end.*
surprise EG *We'll solve the case ourselves and surprise everyone.*

WORD POWER
▷ **Synonyms**
dumbfound
flabbergast
stupefy

amazement NOUN
complete surprise
EG *Much to my amazement, he arrived on time.*
astonishment EG *They looked at each other in astonishment.*
shock EG *I am still getting over the shock of winning.*
surprise EG *To my surprise, I found I liked it.*
wonder EG *Cross shook his head in wonder.*

WORD POWER
▷ **Synonyms**
perplexity
stupefaction

amazing ADJECTIVE
very surprising or remarkable
EG *some of the most amazing stunts you're ever likely to see*
astonishing EG *an astonishing display of physical strength*
astounding EG *The results are quite astounding.*
staggering EG *a staggering 17% leap in sales*
startling EG *startling new evidence*
stunning EG *a stunning piece of news*
surprising EG *A surprising number of customers order the same sandwich every day.*

❶ among PREPOSITION
surrounded by
EG *The bike lay among piles of chains and pedals.*

amid EG *a tiny bungalow amid clusters of trees*
amidst EG *His parents were found dead amidst the wreckage of the plane.*
in the middle of EG *a tiny island in the middle of the Pacific*
in the thick of EG *a restaurant built on stilts in the thick of a vast mangrove swamp*
surrounded by EG *surrounded by bodyguards*

❷ **among** PREPOSITION
between more than two
EG *The money will be divided among seven charities.*
between EG *Proceeds from the auction will be shared between the artists.*
to each of EG *£2,000 to each of the five winners*

amount NOUN
how much there is of something
EG *I still do a certain amount of work for them.*
expanse EG *a vast expanse of grassland*
quantity EG *vast quantities of food*
volume EG *the sheer volume of traffic and accidents*

ample ADJECTIVE
of an amount: more than enough
EG *There is ample space for a good-sized kitchen.*
abundant EG *providing abundant food for local wildlife*
enough EG *Do you have enough money for a taxi home?*
plenty of EG *You've had plenty of time to make up your mind.*
sufficient EG *The police have sufficient evidence to charge him.*

ancestor NOUN
a person from whom someone is descended
EG *He could trace his ancestors back 700 years.*

forebear EG *our Victorian forebears*
forefather EG *the land of their forefathers*

WORD POWER

▷ **Synonyms**
precursor
progenitor

❶ **anger** NOUN
extreme annoyance
EG *She vented her anger at the umpire.*
fury EG *She screamed, her face distorted in fury.*
outrage EG *The decisions provoked outrage from human rights groups.*
rage EG *An intense rage was burning inside her.*
wrath EG *He incurred the wrath of the referee.*

WORD POWER

▷ **Synonyms**
choler
ire
pique
spleen
vexation

❷ **anger** VERB
to make someone angry
EG *remarks which will anger his critics*
enrage EG *He enraged the government by renouncing the agreement.*
infuriate EG *Peter's presence had infuriated Gordon.*
outrage EG *Customers are outraged by the bank's soaring profits.*

WORD POWER

▶ **Antonym**
calm

angry ADJECTIVE
very annoyed
EG *He gets angry with me if I'm late.*
cross EG *She was rather cross about having to trail across London.*

a
b
c
d
e
f
g
h
i
j
k
l
m
n
o
p
q
r
s
t
u
v
w
x
y
z

A
B C D E F G H I J K L M N O P Q R S T U V W X Y Z

enraged EG *The enraged crowd stoned the car, then set it on fire.*
furious EG *He is furious at the way his wife has been treated.*
mad INFORMAL EG *I'm pretty mad about it, I can tell you.*

animal NOUN
a living creature
EG *He was attacked by wild animals.*
beast EG *the threat our ancestors faced from wild beasts*
creature EG *sea creatures*

WORD POWER
● **Related Words**
prefix : zoo-

animosity NOUN
a feeling of strong dislike towards someone
EG *There is no animosity between these two players.*
antagonism EG *a history of antagonism between the two sides*
antipathy EG *our growing antipathy towards our manager*
dislike EG *She looked at him with dislike.*
hatred EG *He didn't bother to conceal his hatred towards my mother.*
hostility EG *unacceptable hostility toward minority groups*
ill will EG *He didn't bear anyone any ill will.*
malice EG *There was no malice in her voice.*
resentment EG *There is growing resentment towards newcomers.*

announce VERB
to make known something publicly
EG *He will announce tonight that he is resigning from office.*
advertise EG *He did not want to advertise his presence in the town.*
make known EG *Details will be made known tomorrow.*
proclaim EG *He loudly proclaimed his innocence.*

reveal EG *They were now free to reveal the truth.*
tell EG *She was relieved that she'd finally told the full story.*

WORD POWER
▷ **Synonyms**
promulgate
propound

announcement NOUN
a statement giving information about something
EG *There has been no formal announcement by either government.*
advertisement EG *an advertisement placed in the local newspaper*
broadcast EG *In a broadcast on state radio the government announced its plans.*
bulletin EG *At 3.30pm a bulletin was released announcing the decision.*
declaration EG *a public declaration of support*
report EG *Local press reports estimate that at least sixteen people have died.*
statement EG *a short statement by her solicitors*

annoy VERB
to irritate or displease someone
EG *Try making a note of the things which annoy you.*
bother EG *I didn't think it would bother me so much to see Brian again.*
displease EG *Not wishing to displease her, he avoided answering the question.*
get on someone's nerves INFORMAL EG *That song gets on my nerves.*
hack off BRITISH AND NEW ZEALAND; SLANG EG *This will just hack people off more.*
hassle INFORMAL EG *Then my husband started hassling me.*
irritate EG *The flippancy in her voice seemed to irritate him.*

plague EG *We were plagued by mosquitoes.*
vex EG *Cassandra was vexed at not having noticed it herself.*

❶ annoyance NOUN
a feeling of irritation
EG *He made no secret of his annoyance.*
displeasure EG *She voiced her displeasure at her treatment.*
irritation EG *He tried not to let his irritation show.*

❷ annoyance NOUN
something that causes irritation
EG *Snoring can be more than an annoyance.*
bore EG *It's a bore to be off sick.*
drag INFORMAL EG *A dry sandwich is a drag to eat.*
nuisance EG *He could be a bit of a nuisance when he was drunk.*
pain INFORMAL EG *The peacocks are a pain - beautiful but noisy.*
pain in the neck INFORMAL EG *Traffic jams are a pain in the neck.*
pest EG *He climbed on the table, pulled my hair, and was generally a pest.*

❶ answer VERB
to reply to someone
EG *I knew Ben was lying when he answered me.*
reply EG *He replied that this was absolutely impossible.*
respond EG *`Mind your manners, lady!' I responded.*
retort EG *Was he afraid, he was asked. `Afraid of what?' he retorted.*

> *WORD POWER*
>
> ▶ **Antonym**
> ask

❷ answer NOUN
a reply given to someone
EG *Without waiting for an answer, he turned and went in through the door.*
reply EG *I called out a challenge but*

there was no reply.
response EG *There has been no response to his remarks from the government.*
retort EG *His sharp retort clearly made an impact.*

> *WORD POWER*
>
> ▷ **Synonyms**
> rejoinder
> riposte
>
> ▶ **Antonym**
> question

anxiety NOUN
nervousness or worry
EG *our growing anxiety about their safety*
apprehension EG *a feeling of apprehension about the future*
concern EG *growing concern about the environment*
fear EG *His fears might be groundless.*
misgiving EG *She had some misgivings about what she had been asked to do.*
nervousness EG *I smiled, trying to hide my nervousness.*
unease EG *a deep sense of unease about the coming interview*
worry EG *a major source of worry to us all*

> *WORD POWER*
>
> ▷ **Synonyms**
> trepidation

anxious NOUN
nervous or worried
EG *He admitted he was still anxious about the situation.*
apprehensive EG *Their families are apprehensive about the trip.*
bothered EG *I'm still bothered about what she's going to say.*
concerned EG *a phone call from a concerned neighbour*
fearful EG *We are all fearful for the*

A
B
C
D
E
F
G
H
I
J
K
L
M
N
O
P
Q
R
S
T
U
V
W
X
Y
Z

security of our jobs.

nervous EG *I still get nervous before a visit to the dentist's.*

troubled EG *He was troubled about his son's lifestyle.*

uneasy EG *an uneasy feeling that something was wrong*

worried EG *His parents are worried about his lack of progress.*

apathetic ADJECTIVE
not interested in anything
EG *apathetic about politics*

cool EG *The idea met with a cool response.*

indifferent EG *People have become indifferent to the sufferings of others.*

passive EG *His passive attitude made things easier for me.*

uninterested EG *unhelpful and uninterested shop staff*

WORD POWER

▶ **Antonym**
enthusiastic

apologize VERB
to say sorry for something
EG *I apologize for being late.*

ask forgiveness EG *He fell to his knees asking for forgiveness.*

beg someone's pardon EG *I was impolite and I do beg your pardon.*

express regret EG *Mr Galloway expressed regret that he had caused any offence.*

say sorry EG *I wanted to say sorry to her.*

❶ appeal VERB
to make an urgent request for something
EG *The police appealed for witnesses to come forward.*

beg EG *I begged him to leave me alone.*

call upon EG *Frequently he was called upon to resolve conflicts.*

plead EG *I pleaded to be allowed to go.*

request EG *She had requested that the door to her room be left open.*

WORD POWER

▷ **Synonyms**
entreat
implore
pray

❷ appeal VERB
to attract or interest
EG *The idea appealed to him.*

attract EG *What attracted you to research work?*

fascinate EG *Classical music had fascinated him since the age of three.*

interest EG *It was the garden that really interested me.*

please EG *It pleased him to talk to her.*

❸ appeal NOUN
a formal request for something
EG *an appeal for peace*

petition EG *The court rejected their petition.*

plea EG *his emotional plea for help in solving the killing*

request EG *France had agreed to his request for political asylum.*

WORD POWER

▷ **Synonyms**
entreaty
supplication

❶ appear VERB
to become visible or present
EG *A woman appeared at the far end of the street.*

come into view EG *Nearly fifty gliders came into view to the south of the plateau.*

crop up INFORMAL EG *Problems will crop up and hit you before you are ready.*

emerge EG *The postman emerged from his van soaked to the skin.*

show up INFORMAL EG *He failed to show up at the ceremony.*

surface EG *The same old problems*

would surface again.
turn up EG *This is like waiting for a bus that never turns up.*

WORD POWER

▶ **Antonym**
disappear

❷ appear VERB
to begin to exist
EG *small white flowers which appear in early summer*
become available EG *In 1950, legal aid became available in Britain.*
be invented EG *The lawn mower was invented in 1830.*
come into being EG *Fireworks first came into being with the invention of gunpowder.*
come into existence EG *before our solar system came into existence*
come out EG *This book first came out in 1992.*

❸ appear VERB
to take part in a show or play
EG *He is soon to appear in two more films.*
act EG *She has also been acting in a sitcom.*
perform EG *He is currently performing in the West End show "Grease".*
play EG *He played Hamlet to packed houses.*
play a part EG *His ambition is to play the part of Dracula.*

❶ appearance NOUN
the time when something begins to exist
EG *the appearance of computer technology*
advent EG *the advent of satellite and cable channels*
arrival EG *the arrival of modern technologies*
coming EG *the coming of the railways*
debut EG *the debut of the new channel*

emergence EG *the emergence of pay-per-view TV*
introduction EG *the introduction of the minimum wage*

❷ appearance NOUN
the way that a person looks
EG *She used to be so fussy about her appearance.*
bearing EG *a man of iron will and military bearing*
image EG *He urged the rest of the band to update their image.*
look EG *She is so much happier with her new look.*
looks EG *a young woman with wholesome good looks*

WORD POWER

▷ **Synonyms**
demeanour
mien

❶ appointment NOUN
an arrangement to meet someone
EG *She has an appointment with her accountant.*
date EG *I have a date with Wendy.*
interview EG *a job interview*
meeting EG *Can we have a meeting to discuss that?*
rendezvous EG *I had almost decided to keep my rendezvous with Tony.*

❷ appointment NOUN
the choosing of a person to do a job
EG *his appointment as manager*
election EG *the election of the government in 1997*
naming EG *the naming of the new captain*
nomination EG *They opposed the nomination of a junior officer to the position.*
selection EG *his selection as a parliamentary candidate*

❸ appointment NOUN
a job
EG *He applied for an appointment in Russia.*

assignment EG *my first assignment for The New York Times*
job EG *He's trying for a job in the Civil Service.*
place EG *All the candidates won places on the ruling council.*
position EG *She took up a position at the Arts Council.*
post EG *He has held several senior military posts.*

❶ appreciate VERB
to value something highly
EG *He appreciates fine wines.*
admire EG *All those who knew him will admire him for his work.*
prize EG *Military figures made out of lead are prized by collectors.*
rate highly EG *The four-year-old mare is rated highly by her trainer.*
respect EG *I respect his talent as a pianist.*
treasure EG *She treasures her memories of those joyous days.*
value EG *I value the work he gives me.*

WORD POWER
▷ **Antonym**
scorn

❷ appreciate VERB
to understand a situation or problem
EG *I didn't appreciate the seriousness of it at the time.*
be aware of EG *I am well aware of the arguments on the other side.*
perceive EG *to get pupils to perceive for themselves the relationship between success and effort*
realize EG *People don't realize how serious this is.*
recognize EG *They have been slow to recognize it as a problem.*
understand EG *They are too young to understand what is going on.*

appropriate ADJECTIVE
suitable or acceptable for a given situation
EG *Jeans are not appropriate wear for work.*
apt EG *an apt title for his memoirs*
correct EG *the importance of correct behaviour and social niceties*
fitting EG *a fitting tribute to a great man*
proper EG *the proper course for the court to take*
suitable EG *a suitable location*

WORD POWER
▷ **Synonyms**
apposite
appurtenant
congruous
germane

▶ **Antonym**
inappropriate

❶ approval NOUN
agreement given to something
EG *The plan will require approval from the local authority.*
agreement EG *The clubs are seeking agreement for a provisional deal.*
authorization EG *We didn't have authorization to go.*
blessing EG *Mr Ryabov appeared to give his blessing to Mr Yeltsin's plan.*
endorsement EG *His endorsement has been fervently sought by all the main presidential candidates.*
permission EG *They cannot leave the country without permission.*
sanction EG *The King cannot enact laws without the sanction of Parliament.*

WORD POWER
▷ **Synonyms**
assent
imprimatur
mandate
ratification

❷ approval NOUN
liking and admiration of a person or thing

EG *He wanted to gain his father's approval.*
admiration EG *a strategy that is winning admiration from around the world*
esteem EG *Their public esteem has never been lower.*
favour EG *He has won favour with a wide range of groups.*
praise EG *She is full of praise for the range of excellent services available.*
respect EG *We all have so much respect for her.*

WORD POWER

▶ **Antonym**
disapproval

❶ **approve** VERB
to think something or someone is good
EG *Not everyone approves of the festival.*
admire EG *I admire him for his work.*
favour EG *The opposition parties favour constitutional reform.*
praise EG *He praised the fans for their continued support.*
respect EG *I want him to respect me as a career woman.*
think highly of EG *He thought highly of his brother.*

WORD POWER

▶ **Antonym**
disapprove

❷ **approve** VERB
to agree formally to something
EG *The court approved the compensation plan.*
authorize EG *to authorize the use of military force*
consent to EG *His parents consented to an autopsy.*
endorse EG *I can endorse their opinion wholeheartedly.*
permit EG *The doorman is not allowed to permit them entry to the film.*
sanction EG *He may now be ready to sanction the use of force.*

WORD POWER

▶ **Antonym**
veto

approximate ADJECTIVE
close but not exact
EG *We believe that an approximate figure of 20% is nearer the mark.*
estimated EG *Our estimated time of arrival is 3.30.*
inexact EG *Forecasting is an inexact science.*
loose EG *a loose translation*
rough EG *a rough estimate*

WORD POWER

▶ **Antonym**
exact

ardent ADJECTIVE
full of enthusiasm and passion
EG *an ardent supporter of capital punishment*
avid EG *an avid follower of the team*
devoted EG *surrounded by devoted fans*
enthusiastic EG *enthusiastic collectors of Elvis memorabilia*
fervent EG *a fervent admirer of his*
intense EG *his intense love of football*
keen EG *a keen supporter of the cause*
passionate EG *He developed a passionate interest in motor racing.*

WORD POWER

▷ **Synonyms**
zealous

▶ **Antonym**
apathetic

❶ **area** NOUN
a particular part of a place
EG *a built-up area of the city*
district EG *I drove around the business district.*

locality EG *All other factories in the locality went on strike in sympathy.*
neighbourhood EG *She no longer takes evening strolls around her neighbourhood.*
region EG *a remote mountainous region of Afghanistan*
zone EG *a war zone*

❷ area NOUN
the size of a two-dimensional surface
EG *The islands cover a total area of 625 square kilometres.*
expanse EG *a huge expanse of blue-green sea*
extent EG *the extent of the rain forest*
range EG *a driver's range of vision*
size EG *a country nearly three times the size of ours*

❶ argue VERB
to disagree with someone in an angry way
EG *They argued over the cost of the taxi fare.*
bicker EG *They bickered endlessly about procedure.*
disagree EG *They can communicate even when they strongly disagree.*
fall out INFORMAL EG *Mum and I used to fall out a lot.*
feud EG *feuding neighbours*
fight EG *We're always fighting about money.*
quarrel EG *My brother quarrelled with my father.*
row EG *We started rowing about whose turn it was next.*
squabble EG *The children were squabbling over the remote control.*
wrangle EG *Delegates wrangled over the future of the organization.*

❷ argue VERB
to try to prove
EG *She argued that her client had been wrongly accused.*
assert EG *The defendants continue to assert their innocence.*

claim EG *Statisticians claim that the book contains inaccuracies.*
debate EG *Parliament will debate the issue today.*
maintain EG *He had always maintained his innocence.*
reason EG *I reasoned that if he could do it, so could I.*

WORD POWER

▷ **Synonyms**
controvert
expostulate
remonstrate

❶ argument NOUN
an angry disagreement
EG *She got into an argument with one of the marchers.*
barney BRITISH, AUSTRALIAN, AND NEW ZEALAND; INFORMAL EG *We had such a barney that we nearly split up.*
blue AUSTRALIAN; SLANG EG *He gets into more blues with authority than I do.*
clash EG *clashes between police and demonstrators*
dispute EG *a dispute over ticket allocation*
feud EG *a two-year feud between neighbours*
fight EG *We had another fight about money.*
row EG *Maxine and I had a terrible row.*
squabble EG *a family squabble over Sunday lunch*

❷ argument NOUN
a set of reasons presented for something
EG *There's a strong argument for lowering the price.*
case EG *the case for his dismissal*
grounds EG *facts providing grounds for an unfair dismissal complaint*
logic EG *The logic is that, without more growth, the deficit will rise.*
reasoning EG *the reasoning behind the decision*

❶ arrange VERB
to make plans to do something
EG *Why don't you arrange to meet him later?*
fix up EG *I fixed up an appointment to see her.*
organize EG *She organized the trip to the museum.*
plan EG *She planned to leave in August.*
schedule EG *Our appointment is scheduled for Tuesday.*

❷ arrange VERB
to set things out in a particular order
EG *He started to arrange the books in piles.*
classify EG *Weathermen classify clouds into several different groups.*
group EG *The fact sheet is grouped into seven sections.*
order EG *The French order things differently.*
organize EG *He began to organize his materials.*
sort EG *The students are sorted into three ability groups.*

WORD POWER

▷ **Synonyms**
array
systematize

---

❶ arrest VERB
to take someone into custody
EG *Police arrested five men in connection with the attack.*
apprehend EG *Police have not apprehended her killer.*
capture EG *Her accomplice was captured by Dutch police.*
nick BRITISH; SLANG EG *Keep quiet or we'll all get nicked.*
seize EG *Two military observers were seized by rebels yesterday.*
take prisoner EG *He was taken prisoner in 1940 at the fall of Dunkirk.*

❷ arrest NOUN
the act of arresting someone
EG *The police made two arrests.*
apprehension EG *information leading to the apprehension of the killer*
capture EG *He was trying to evade capture by security forces.*
seizure EG *the mass seizure of terrorists*

❶ article NOUN
a piece of writing in a newspaper or magazine
EG *There's an article about it in today's paper.*
feature EG *a feature about Gulf War syndrome*
item EG *I read an item about this only last week.*
piece EG *I disagree with your recent piece about Australia.*
story EG *Most newspapers had a story about the film's premiere.*

❷ article NOUN
a particular item
EG *household articles*
item EG *Various items have gone missing from my desk.*
object EG *everyday objects such as wooden spoons*
thing EG *I have a few things to buy for the trip.*

ashamed ADJECTIVE
feeling embarrassed or guilty
EG *He was not even ashamed of what he had done.*
embarrassed EG *I'm not embarrassed to admit I cried.*
guilty EG *When she realized I was watching, she looked guilty.*
humiliated EG *I felt humiliated at the scene he was causing.*
sheepish EG *"I'm afraid it was my idea," he admitted, looking sheepish.*
sorry EG *She's really sorry for all the trouble she's caused.*

a
b
c
d
e
f
g
h
i
j
k
l
m
n
o
p
q
r
s
t
u
v
w
x
y
z

WORD POWER

▷ **Synonyms**
mortified

▶ **Antonym**
proud

1 ask VERB
to put a question to someone
EG *She asked me if I'd enjoyed my dinner.*
inquire EG *I rang up to inquire about train times.*
interrogate EG *I interrogated everyone even slightly involved.*
query EG *He queried whether sabotage could have been involved.*
question EG *He was questioned by police.*
quiz EG *He was quizzed about his eligibility for benefits.*

WORD POWER

▶ **Antonym**
answer

2 ask VERB
to make a request to someone
EG *We had to ask him to leave.*
appeal EG *The police appealed for witnesses to come forward.*
beg EG *I begged him to leave me alone.*
demand EG *I demanded an explanation from him.*
implore EG *I implored him not to give it up.*
plead EG *She pleaded to be allowed to go.*
seek EG *Always seek legal advice before entering into any agreement.*

WORD POWER

▷ **Synonyms**
beseech
entreat

3 ask VERB
to invite someone

EG *Not everybody had been asked to the wedding.*
bid LITERARY EG *They all smiled at him and bade him eat.*
invite EG *She invited him to her 26th birthday party.*

aspect NOUN
a feature of something
EG *Exam results are only one aspect of a school's success.*
consideration EG *The cost involved will be a chief consideration in our choice.*
element EG *Fitness is now an important element in our lives.*
factor EG *an important factor in a child's development*
feature EG *the most significant feature of his childhood*
part EG *Respect is an important part of any relationship.*
point EG *There is another point to remember when making your decision.*
side EG *He had a darker side to his character.*

1 assemble VERB
to gather together in a group
EG *a convenient place for students to assemble between classes*
collect EG *We all collected round him to listen.*
come together EG *a common room where we can come together and relax*
congregate EG *Youngsters love to congregate here in the evenings.*
convene EG *A grand jury has convened to gather evidence.*
gather EG *We all gathered in the board room.*
mass EG *Troops were massing on both sides of the border.*

2 assemble VERB
to fit the parts of something together
EG *Workers were assembling planes.*
build EG *A carpenter built the shelves*

for us.
construct EG *He had constructed a crude explosive device.*
erect EG *Stagehands are employed to erect the scenery.*
make EG *I like making model aeroplanes.*
put together EG *You can buy the parts and put it together yourself.*

assistant NOUN
a person who helps someone
EG *His assistant took over while he went out.*
aide EG *a presidential aide*
ally EG *her political allies*
colleague EG *a business colleague*
helper EG *volunteer helpers*
right-hand man EG *the resignation of the manager's right-hand man*

❶ associate VERB
to connect one thing with another
EG *Poverty is associated with old age.*
connect EG *a common problem directly connected with stress*
couple EG *The papers coupled the Gulf crisis with the problems facing the former Soviet Union.*
identify EG *Candidates want to identify themselves with reform.*
link EG *Liver cancer is linked to the hepatitis B virus.*

❷ associate VERB
to spend time with a person
EG *I began associating with different crowds of people.*
hang out INFORMAL EG *People want to hang out with you for the wrong reasons.*
mingle EG *reporters who mingled freely with the crowd*
mix EG *local youths who want to mix with the foreign tourists*
run around INFORMAL EG *What's he doing running around with a teenager?*

socialize EG *She made little effort to socialize with other staff.*

WORD POWER
▷ **Synonyms**
consort
fraternize

❸ associate NOUN
a person known through work
EG *the restaurant owner's business associates*
colleague EG *learning from more experienced colleagues*
co-worker EG *Their Chinese co-workers often worked seven days a week.*
workmate EG *employees who expose dishonest workmates*

❶ association NOUN
an organization
EG *a research association*
body EG *the chairman of the policemen's representative body*
club EG *the local Young Conservatives' club*
company EG *a major motor company*
confederation EG *the Confederation of British Industry*
group EG *an environmental group*
institution EG *a member of various financial institutions*
league EG *the World Muslim League*
society EG *the Royal Society for the Protection of Birds*
syndicate EG *a syndicate of international banks*

WORD POWER
▷ **Synonyms**
fraternity

❷ association NOUN
a connection or involvement with a person or group
EG *his association with a terrorist group*
affiliation EG *He has no affiliation with any political party.*

a
b
c
d
e
f
g
h
i
j
k
l
m
n
o
p
q
r
s
t
u
v
w
x
y
z

attachment EG *Mother and child form a close attachment.*
bond EG *There is a special bond between us.*
connection EG *He has denied any connection with the organization.*
relationship EG *Ours was strictly a professional relationship.*
tie EG *I had very close ties with the family.*

WORD POWER

▷ **Synonyms**
affinity
liaison

❶ assume VERB

to accept that something is true
EG *I assumed that he would turn up.*
believe EG *I believe she'll be back next week.*
guess INFORMAL EG *I guess she thought that was pretty smart.*
imagine EG *You tend to imagine that you cannot put a foot wrong.*
suppose EG *I see no reason to suppose that it isn't working.*
think EG *They thought that they had the match won.*

❷ assume VERB

to take responsibility for something
EG *Mr Cross will assume the role of Chief Executive.*
accept EG *He accepted the role of player-captain.*
shoulder EG *He has had to shoulder the responsibility of his father's mistakes.*
take on EG *Don't take on more responsibilities than you can handle.*
undertake EG *He undertook to edit the text himself.*

astute ADJECTIVE

very intelligent or perceptive
EG *an astute judge of character*
alert EG *He is old, but he has a very quick and alert mind.*
clever EG *a clever business move*

keen EG *a keen understanding of politics*
perceptive EG *his perceptive analysis of the situation*
quick EG *He has an enquiring mind and a quick intelligence.*
sharp EG *His gentle manner disguised a sharp mind.*
shrewd EG *He demonstrated a shrewd understanding of human nature.*
smart EG *a very smart move*

WORD POWER

▷ **Synonyms**
discerning

attach VERB

to join or fasten things together
EG *The gadget can be attached to any surface.*
affix EG *His name was affixed to the wall of his cubicle.*
connect EG *Connect the pipe to the tap.*
couple EG *The engine is coupled to a gearbox.*
fasten EG *The shelves are fastened to the wall with screws.*
join EG *two sticks joined together by a chain*
link EG *tree houses linked by ropes*
tie EG *He tied the dog to a post with its leash.*

WORD POWER

▶ **Antonym**
separate

❶ attachment NOUN

a feeling of love and affection
EG *Mother and child form a close attachment.*
affection EG *the affection between a pet and its owner*
bond EG *There has always been a strong bond between us.*
fondness EG *I have a great fondness for all animals.*

liking EG *He has never shown any liking for his colleagues.*
love EG *A deep love gradually developed between them.*

❷ **attachment** NOUN
a part attached to something else
EG *The drill comes with a wide range of attachments.*
accessory EG *a range of accessories for your mobile phone*
fitting EG *bathroom fittings*
fixture EG *The box can be adapted to take a light fixture.*
component EG *Additional components are available as listed.*
part EG *Extra parts can be added later.*
unit EG *The unit plugs into any TV set.*

❶ **attack** VERB
to use violence against someone or something
EG *I thought he was going to attack me.*
assault EG *The gang assaulted him with iron bars.*
charge EG *He ordered us to charge.*
invade EG *The allies invaded the Italian mainland at Anzio.*
raid EG *He was found guilty of raiding a bank.*
set upon EG *As the lorry drove east it was set upon by bandits.*
storm EG *The refugees decided to storm the embassy.*

❷ **attack** VERB
to criticize someone strongly
EG *She attacked the government's economic policies.*
blast EG *He blasted the referee for his inconsistency.*
censure EG *The bank has been censured and fined by the authority.*
criticize EG *The regime has been harshly criticized.*
have a go BRITISH; INFORMAL EG *If they made a mistake the crowd would have a go at them.*

put down INFORMAL EG *He was always putting me down.*
vilify FORMAL EG *He was vilified, hounded, and forced into exile.*

WORD POWER

▷ **Synonyms**
   berate
   lambast *or* lambaste
   revile

❸ **attack** NOUN
violent physical action against someone or something
EG *a vicious attack on an unarmed man*
assault EG *The rebels are poised for a new assault.*
charge EG *a bayonet charge*
invasion EG *the Roman invasion of Britain*
offensive EG *the government's military offensive against the rebels*
onslaught EG *civilians trying to flee from the military onslaught*
raid EG *a raid on a house by armed police*

❶ **attempt** VERB
to try to do something
EG *They attempted to escape.*
endeavour EG *I will endeavour to arrange it.*
seek EG *We have never sought to impose our views.*
strive EG *The school strives to treat pupils as individuals.*
try EG *I tried hard to persuade him to stay.*
try your hand at EG *He'd always wanted to try his hand at writing.*

❷ **attempt** NOUN
an act of trying to do something
EG *one of his rare attempts at humour*
bid EG *a bid to save the newspaper*
crack INFORMAL EG *his third crack at the world heavyweight*
go INFORMAL EG *My mum suggested I should have a go at becoming a*

jockey.

shot INFORMAL EG *We'd like a shot at winning the league.*

stab INFORMAL EG *Several tennis stars have had a stab at acting.*

try EG *That makes the scheme worth a try.*

attitude NOUN
someone's way of thinking and behaving
EG *negative attitudes to work*

outlook EG *behaviour that seems contrary to his whole outlook*

perspective EG *It gave me a new perspective on life.*

point of view EG *Try to look at this from my point of view.*

position EG *What's your position on this issue?*

stance EG *the Church's stance on contraception*

attract VERB
to appeal to or interest
EG *The trials have attracted many leading riders.*

appeal to EG *The idea appealed to him.*

draw EG *The match drew a large crowd.*

entice EG *She resisted attempts to entice her into politics.*

lure EG *They were being lured into a trap.*

pull INFORMAL EG *They have to employ performers to pull a crowd.*

tempt EG *Can I tempt you with some wine?*

WORD POWER

▶ **Antonym**
repel

attractive ADJECTIVE
pleasant, especially to look at
EG *an attractive woman*

appealing EG *a sense of humour that I found very appealing*

charming EG *a charming little village*

fetching EG *a fetching outfit*

handsome EG *a handsome man*

lovely EG *a lovely island*

pretty EG *a shy, pretty girl*

WORD POWER

▷ **Synonyms**
comely
prepossessing
winsome

▶ **Antonym**
unattractive

attribute NOUN
a quality or feature
EG *a normal attribute of human behaviour*

characteristic EG *their physical characteristics*

feature EG *the most striking feature of his music*

property EG *the magnetic properties of iron*

quality EG *His humility is one of his most endearing qualities.*

trait EG *personality traits*

WORD POWER

▷ **Synonyms**
peculiarity

augment VERB
to add something to something else
EG *a good way to augment your basic wage*

add to EG *A fitted kitchen adds to the value of your house.*

boost EG *people who boost their earnings by working part-time from home*

complement EG *an in-work benefit that complements earnings*

increase EG *He is eager to increase his income by any means.*

reinforce EG *measures which will reinforce their current strengths*

supplement EG *I suggest supplementing your diet with vitamin A.*

top up EG *compulsory contributions to top up pension schemes*

authentic ADJECTIVE
real and genuine
EG *an authentic French recipe*
bona fide EG *We are happy to donate to bona fide charities.*
dinkum AUSTRALIAN AND NEW ZEALAND; INFORMAL EG *a place which serves dinkum Aussie tucker*
genuine EG *Experts are convinced the manuscript is genuine.*
real EG *It's a real Rembrandt.*
true EG *Of course she's not a true blonde.*

WORD POWER
▶ **Antonym**
fake

---

❶ **automatic** ADJECTIVE
operating mechanically by itself
EG *Modern trains have automatic doors.*
automated EG *highly automated production lines*
mechanical EG *the oldest working mechanical clock in the world*
robot EG *a robot telescope*
self-propelled EG *self-propelled artillery*

❷ **automatic** ADJECTIVE
without conscious thought
EG *automatic body functions*
instinctive EG *an instinctive reaction*
involuntary EG *involuntary muscle movements*
natural EG *the insect's natural instinct to feed*
reflex EG *Blushing is a reflex action linked to the nervous system.*

automobile NOUN; AMERICAN
a vehicle for carrying a few people
EG *the Japanese automobile manufacturer*
car EG *My dad's promised me a car if I pass my finals.*
motor EG *He's bought himself a flash*

new motor.
vehicle EG *A child ran straight out in front of the vehicle.*

available ADJECTIVE
ready for use
EG *There are three small boats available for hire.*
accessible EG *This information is accessible on the Internet.*
at hand EG *Having the right equipment at hand will be enormously useful.*
at someone's disposal EG *Do you have all the facts at your disposal?*
free EG *There was only one seat free on the train.*
handy EG *Keep your keys handy so you can get into your car quickly.*
to hand EG *Keep your insurance details to hand when driving.*

WORD POWER
▶ **Antonym**
unavailable

---

❶ **average** ADJECTIVE
standard or normal
EG *the average American teenager*
normal EG *I am now back to leading a perfectly normal life.*
regular EG *He's just a regular guy.*
standard EG *the standard price of a CD*
typical EG *A typical day begins at 8.30.*
usual EG *This isn't the usual kind of mail-order catalogue.*

❷ **average** **on average** ADVERB
for the most part
EG *Men are, on average, taller than women.*
as a rule EG *As a rule, the fee is roughly equal to the savings you have made.*
generally EG *A glass of fine wine generally costs about £4.*
normally EG *Normally, the transport system carries 50,000 passengers a*

a b c d e f g h i j k l m n o p q r s t u v w x y z

typically EG *In America, estate agents typically charge 5-6% of the sale price.*
usually EG *In good condition, these models usually fetch up to 300 dollars at auction.*

❶ avoid VERB
to make an effort not to do something
EG *We economists always try to avoid giving a straight answer.*
dodge EG *dodging military service by feigning illness*
duck out of INFORMAL EG *ducking out of the post-match press conference*
fight shy of EG *She fought shy of confronting her critics.*
refrain from EG *Mrs Hardie refrained from making any comment.*
shirk EG *We won't shirk our responsibility.*

> *WORD POWER*
> ▷ **Synonyms**
> circumvent
> give a wide berth to

❷ avoid VERB
to keep away from someone or something
EG *She thought he was trying to avoid her.*
dodge EG *He refuses to dodge his critics.*
elude EG *an attempt to elude photographers*
eschew FORMAL EG *He eschewed publicity and avoided nightclubs.*
evade EG *He managed to evade the police.*
shun EG *Everybody shunned him.*
sidestep EG *Rarely does he sidestep a question.*
steer clear of EG *It would be best to steer clear of her.*

❶ aware aware of ADJECTIVE
conscious of something
EG *She was acutely aware of the noise of the city.*
acquainted with EG *He was well acquainted with American literature.*
conscious of EG *She was very conscious of Max studying her.*
familiar with EG *I am not familiar with your work.*
mindful of EG *Everyone should be mindful of the dangers.*

> *WORD POWER*
> ▶ **Antonym**
> unaware

❷ aware ADJECTIVE
knowing about something
EG *Keep me aware of any developments.*
informed EG *the importance of keeping the public properly informed*
in the picture EG *He's always kept me in the picture.*
knowledgeable EG *He's very knowledgeable about new technology.*

> *WORD POWER*
> ▷ **Synonyms**
> au courant
> in the loop

awful ADJECTIVE
very unpleasant or very bad
EG *the same awful jokes*
appalling EG *living under the most appalling conditions*
dreadful EG *They told us the dreadful news.*
frightful EG *a frightful ordeal*
ghastly EG *a mother accompanied by her ghastly unruly child*
horrendous EG *The violence used was horrendous.*
terrible EG *Her French is terrible.*

> *WORD POWER*
> ▷ **Synonyms**
> abysmal
> deplorable

A
B
C
D
E
F
G
H
I
J
K
L
M
N
O
P
Q
R
S
T
U
V
W
X
Y
Z

Bb

babble VERB
to talk in an excited way
EG *He babbled on and on.*
burble EG *He burbles on about the goals he has scored.*
chatter EG *Jane chattered about the children.*
gabble EG *I started to gabble in the interview.*
prattle EG *Alan is prattling on again.*

baby NOUN
a very young child
EG *I've had this birthmark since I was a baby.*
ankle-biter AUSTRALIAN AND NEW ZEALAND; SLANG EG *I knew him when he was just an ankle-biter.*
bairn SCOTTISH EG *My wife's expecting a bairn.*
child EG *They celebrated the birth of their first child.*
infant EG *young mums with infants in prams*

❶ back NOUN
the part that is behind the front
EG *the back of a postcard*
end EG *the end of the corridor*
rear EG *the rear of the building*
reverse EG *the reverse of the sheet*
stern EG *the stern of a boat*

WORD POWER
▶ **Antonym**
front

❷ back VERB
to support a person or organization
EG *His friends are backing him.*
advocate EG *Mr Jones advocates longer school days.*
encourage EG *The government is encouraging better child care.*
endorse EG *Do you endorse his opinion?*
favour EG *I favour a different approach.*

promote EG *Ann is promoting Alan's ideas.*
support EG *We supported his political campaign.*

WORD POWER
▷ **Synonyms**
champion
espouse
second

▶ **Antonym**
oppose

background NOUN
where you come from
EG *a rich background*
culture EG *people from different cultures*
environment EG *the environment I grew up in*
history EG *She has an interesting history.*
upbringing EG *a strict upbringing*

❶ bad ADJECTIVE
harmful, unpleasant, or upsetting
EG *I have some bad news.*
→ see Word Study **bad**

WORD POWER
▶ **Antonym**
good

❷ bad ADJECTIVE
of poor quality
EG *bad roads*
→ see Word Study **bad**

WORD POWER
▶ **Antonym**
satisfactory

❸ bad ADJECTIVE
evil in character
EG *a bad person*
→ see Word Study **bad**

A
B
C
D
E
F
G
H
I
J
K
L
M
N
O
P
Q
R
S
T
U
V
W
X
Y
Z

WORD POWER

▶ **Antonym**
good

badly ADVERB
in an inferior way
EG *This essay is badly written.*
→ see Word Study **badly**

WORD POWER

▶ **Antonym**
well

bait NOUN
something used to tempt someone
EG *Charles isn't taking the bait.*
bribe EG *a politician who took bribes*
decoy EG *He acted as a decoy to trap the murderer.*
inducement EG *financial inducements to talk to the newspapers*
lure EG *the lure of a huge salary*
temptation EG *the temptation of easy money*

❶ balance VERB
to make or remain steady
EG *Balancing on one leg is difficult.*
level EG *House prices have levelled.*
stabilize EG *attempts to stabilize the economy*
steady EG *He steadied himself and shot at goal.*

❷ balance NOUN
a stable relationship between things
EG *the chemical balance of the brain*
equilibrium EG *the political equilibrium of Europe*
equity EG *plans for greater equity of incomes*
equivalence EG *the lack of equivalence between film and radio*
parity EG *She won pay parity with male colleagues.*

ball NOUN
a round object
EG *a ball of wool*

drop EG *a drop of blood*
globe EG *the globe of the eyeball*
pellet EG *an airgun pellet*
sphere EG *a sphere the size of the Earth*

WORD POWER

▷ **Synonyms**
globule
orb
spheroid

❶ ban VERB
to disallow something
EG *I am banned from taking part.*
bar EG *The press will be barred from the talks.*
disqualify EG *He was disqualified from driving.*
exclude EG *They were excluded from the maths class.*
forbid EG *The rules forbid the use of force.*
outlaw EG *regulations outlawing child labour*
prohibit EG *a law that prohibits alcohol*

WORD POWER

▷ **Synonyms**
banish
proscribe
suppress

▶ **Antonym**
permit

❷ ban NOUN
a rule disallowing something
EG *a ban on smoking*
disqualification EG *a four-year disqualification from athletics*
embargo EG *an embargo on trade with the country*
prohibition EG *a prohibition on tobacco*
suppression EG *the suppression of anti-government protests*

WORD POWER

▶ **Antonym**
permit

1 band NOUN
a group of musicians who play together
EG *a singer in a rock and roll band*
group EG *They formed the group while they were still at school.*
orchestra EG *the National Youth Orchestra*

WORD POWER

▷ **Synonyms**
ensemble

2 band NOUN
a group of people who share a common purpose
EG *a band of rebels*
bunch EG *A bunch of protesters were picketing the factory.*
company EG *a company of actors*
crowd EG *A small crowd of onlookers had gathered.*
gang EG *a gang of criminals*
party EG *a party of sightseers*
troupe EG *She toured with a professional dance troupe.*

1 bang VERB
to hit or put something down hard, with a loud noise
EG *a toddler banging a saucepan with a wooden spoon*
beat EG *They sat in a circle, beating small drums.*
hammer EG *The supporters hammered on the windows of the bus.*
hit EG *They were hitting the sides of the van with sticks.*
knock EG *I knocked on the door for ages, but no-one answered.*
pound EG *We pounded on the walls.*
slam EG *I slammed down the receiver.*
thump EG *The children cheered and thumped on their desks.*

2 bang NOUN
a sudden, short, loud noise
EG *The TV exploded with a bang.*
blast EG *the ear-splitting blast of a cannon*
boom EG *There was a boom and a cloud of smoke.*
crack EG *the crack of a pistol shot*
detonation EG *We heard several loud detonations coming from the building.*
explosion EG *the deafening explosion of gunshots*
thump EG *She dropped her case to the floor with a loud thump.*

3 bang NOUN
a hard or painful bump against something
EG *I got a nasty bang on the elbow.*
blow EG *a blow to the side of the head*
clout INFORMAL EG *She gave him a swift clout on the ear.*
knock EG *Knocks like this can cause damage to the spine.*
thump EG *Ralph got a thump on the chest.*
whack EG *She gave the horse a whack on the rump.*

1 banish VERB
to exile someone
EG *She banished him from the house.*
deport EG *Many fans are being deported from Italy.*
eject EG *He was ejected from the club.*
evict EG *Police evicted ten families from the building.*
exile EG *He was exiled from Russia.*
expel EG *patients expelled from hospitals*
transport EG *He was transported to a prison camp.*

2 banish VERB
to get rid of something or someone
EG *to banish illness*
discard EG *Read the instructions before discarding the box.*
dismiss EG *I dismissed the idea from*

A
B
C
D
E
F
G
H
I
J
K
L
M
N
O
P
Q
R
S
T
U
V
W
X
Y
Z

my mind.
dispel EG *The myths are being dispelled.*
eliminate EG *They eliminated him from their enquiries.*
eradicate EG *projects to eradicate certain diseases*
remove EG *talks to remove the last obstacles to the deal*

❶ bank NOUN
a store of something
EG *a blood bank*
fund EG *a pension fund*
hoard EG *a hoard of treasure*
reserve EG *the world's oil reserves*
stock EG *stocks of paper and ink*
store EG *a secret store of sweets*

WORD POWER

▷ **Synonyms**
reservoir
stockpile

❷ bank NOUN
the edge of a river or lake
EG *He sat fishing on the bank.*
brink EG *orchards near the brink of the sea cliffs*
edge EG *She stood too close to the edge and fell in.*
shore EG *He swam towards the shore.*
side EG *a picnic by the side of the river*

❶ bar NOUN
a piece of metal
EG *bars across the windows*
pole EG *He was tied to a pole.*
rail EG *a curtain rail*
rod EG *a fishing rod*
shaft EG *the shaft of a spear*

❷ bar VERB
to stop someone
EG *His bodyguards barred the way.*
obstruct EG *Vehicles have obstructed the entrance.*
prevent EG *A fence prevents people from entering.*

❶ bare ADJECTIVE
not covered
EG *bare legs*
exposed EG *His whole back is exposed.*
naked EG *a naked body*
nude EG *a nude model*
stripped EG *I got stripped to have a shower.*
uncovered EG *His arms were uncovered.*
undressed EG *She got undressed in the bathroom.*

WORD POWER

▶ **Antonym**
covered

❷ bare ADJECTIVE
with nothing on top or inside
EG *a small bare office*
empty EG *an empty room*
open EG *open country*
spartan EG *spartan accommodation*
vacant EG *a vacant chair*

barely ADVERB
only just
EG *She is barely sixteen.*
almost EG *I almost didn't make it.*
hardly EG *I could hardly believe it.*
just EG *They only just won.*
scarcely EG *I can scarcely hear her.*

❶ barren ADJECTIVE
with nothing growing on it
EG *a barren desert*
arid EG *the arid lands of Botswana*
desert EG *desert regions*
desolate EG *a desolate place*
dry EG *poor, dry countries*
empty EG *the empty desert*
waste EG *waste land*

WORD POWER

▷ **Synonyms**
unfruitful
unproductive

▶ **Antonym**
fertile

❷ **barren** ADJECTIVE
unable to produce babies
EG *women who are barren*
childless EG *childless couples*
infertile EG *infertile women*
sterile EG *sterile females*

WORD POWER

▶ **Antonym**
fertile

❶ **barrier** NOUN
something preventing entry
EG *Demonstrators broke through the barriers.*
barricade EG *a barricade of vehicles*
fence EG *a garden fence*
obstruction EG *Check the exhaust pipe is clear of obstructions.*
wall EG *the huge city walls*

WORD POWER

▷ **Synonyms**
fortification
obstacle
rampart

❷ **barrier** NOUN
something that prevents progress
EG *plans to reduce the barriers to trade*
handicap EG *It is a handicap not knowing a foreign language.*
hindrance EG *a potential hindrance to the peace process*
hurdle EG *the first hurdle in a job search*
impediment EG *a serious impediment to free trade*
obstacle EG *the main obstacle to the takeover*

❶ **base** NOUN
the lowest part of something
EG *the base of the cliffs*
bed EG *the river bed*
bottom EG *the bottom of the lake*
foot EG *the foot of the mountain*

foundation EG *They have laid the foundations for the new building.*
pedestal EG *The statue is back on its pedestal.*
stand EG *a microphone stand*

WORD POWER

▶ **Antonym**
top

❷ **base** NOUN
the place you work from
EG *a military base*
camp EG *refugee camps*
centre EG *a health centre*
headquarters EG *army headquarters in Colombo*
post EG *a military post in the capital*
station EG *the police station*

❸ **base** VERB
to use as a foundation
EG *The film is based on a true story.*
build EG *a reputation built on lies*
derive EG *The name is derived from a Greek word.*
found EG *My hopes were founded on a mistake.*
ground EG *I like a film to be grounded in reality.*
hinge EG *The whole play hinges on one character.*

basic ADJECTIVE
most necessary
EG *the basic requirements for the job*
elementary EG *elementary computer training*
essential EG *essential reading and writing skills*
fundamental EG *fundamental rights*
key EG *key skills such as communication and teamwork*
necessary EG *They lack the necessary resources.*
vital EG *vital supplies*

a
b
c
d
e
f
g
h
i
j
k
l
m
n
o
p
q
r
s
t
u
v
w
x
y
z

A
B
C
D
E
F
G
H
I
J
K
L
M
N
O
P
Q
R
S
T
U
V
W
X
Y
Z

WORD POWER

▷ **Synonyms**
central
indispensable
primary

---

basis NOUN
the main principle of something
EG *The same theme is the basis of several poems.*
core EG *the core of Asia's problems*
fundamental EG *the fundamentals of road safety*
heart EG *the heart of the matter*
premise EG *the premise of his argument*
principle EG *the principles of Buddhism*

❶ bay NOUN
a curve in a coastline
EG *the Bay of Biscay*
cove EG *a sandy cove with white cliffs*
gulf EG *the Gulf of Mexico*
inlet EG *a deep inlet on the west coast*
sound EG *streams that run into the sound*

❷ bay VERB
to make a howling noise
EG *wolves baying in the moonlight*
bark EG *a small dog barking at a seagull*
cry EG *I heard animals cry in the forest.*
howl EG *distant coyotes howling in the night*
yelp EG *A dog snapped and yelped at them.*

beach NOUN
an area beside the sea
EG *making sandcastles on the beach*
coast EG *a day at the coast*
sands EG *the long white sands of Goa*
seashore EG *walks along the seashore*
seaside EG *trips to the seaside*
shore EG *He swam out from the shore.*

strand EG *collecting shells on the strand*

❶ bear VERB
to carry something
EG *The ice wasn't thick enough to bear their weight.*
carry EG *He always carried a gun.*
convey EG *The taxi conveyed us to the centre.*
shoulder EG *He had to shoulder the blame for the mistake.*
support EG *Thick wooden posts support the ceiling.*
take EG *You'd better take an umbrella.*

❷ bear VERB
to have or show something
EG *The room bore the signs of a violent struggle.*
exhibit EG *He began to exhibit symptoms of the disease.*
harbour EG *She still harbours feelings of resentment.*
have EG *I have a grudge against her.*

❸ bear VERB
to accept something
EG *He can't bear to talk about it.*
abide EG *I can't abide arrogant people.*
endure EG *The pain was hard to endure.*
stomach EG *He could not stomach violence.*
suffer EG *I had to suffer his company all day.*
tolerate EG *Women tolerate pain better than men.*

❶ beat VERB
to hit someone or something hard
EG *He threatened to beat her.*
batter EG *The waves kept battering the life raft.*
buffet EG *Their plane was buffeted by storms.*
hit EG *He hit me on the head.*
pound EG *Someone was pounding on the door.*

strike VERB EG *She struck him across the mouth.*

thrash EG *He was thrashed by his father.*

② beat VERB
to defeat
EG *She was easily beaten in the race.*
defeat EG *The team hasn't been defeated all year.*
outdo EG *One man was trying to outdo the other.*
outstrip EG *The company is outstripping its rivals.*
overcome EG *Molly had overcome her fear of flying.*
overwhelm EG *One attack could overwhelm the enemy.*
vanquish EG *the man who helped vanquish Napoleon*

WORD POWER

▷ **Synonyms**
conquer
master
surpass

③ beat NOUN
a rhythm
EG *the thumping beat of rock music*
cadence EG *the pulsing cadences of his music*
metre EG *the strict metre of the poem*
rhythm EG *His foot tapped a rhythm on the floor.*
stress EG *differences of stress in speech*
time EG *a song written in waltz time*

beautiful ADJECTIVE
attractive or pleasing
EG *beautiful music*
attractive EG *an attractive woman*
delightful EG *The perfume is delightful.*
fine EG *a fine summer's day*
gorgeous EG *a gorgeous man*
lovely EG *You look lovely.*
pleasing EG *a pleasing appearance*

WORD POWER

▷ **Synonyms**
exquisite
fair

▶ **Antonym**
ugly

① beauty NOUN
the quality of being beautiful
EG *an area of outstanding beauty*
attractiveness EG *the attractiveness of the region*
charm EG *a woman of great charm*
elegance EG *the elegance of the overall design*
loveliness EG *the loveliness of the scene*

WORD POWER

▶ **Antonym**
ugliness

② beauty NOUN
a good-looking person
EG *a dark-haired beauty*
hunk INFORMAL EG *The Swedish hunk is back again.*
stunner INFORMAL EG *the 23-year-old stunner*

③ beauty NOUN
an attractive feature
EG *The beauty of the fund is its simplicity.*
advantage EG *the advantages of the new system over the old one*
asset EG *The one asset the job provided was contacts.*
attraction EG *The main attraction of the place is the monument.*
benefit EG *Every age has its benefits.*

because CONJUNCTION
for the reason that
EG *I went home because I was tired.*
as EG *Don't cook for me as I'll be home late.*

a
b
c
d
e
f
g
h
i
j
k
l
m
n
o
p
q
r
s
t
u
v
w
x
y
z

A B C D E F G H I J K L M N O P Q R S T U V W X Y Z

since EG *Since you didn't listen, I'll repeat that.*

> ### WORD POWER
>
> ▷ **Synonyms**
> in that
> on account of
> owing to

before ADVERB
at a previous time
EG *Have you been to Greece before?*
earlier EG *Here is a cake I made earlier.*
formerly EG *He had formerly been in the army.*
in advance EG *We booked the room well in advance.*
previously EG *Previously she had little time to work.*
sooner EG *I wish I'd arrived sooner.*

> ### WORD POWER
>
> ▶ **Antonym**
> after
>
> ● **Related Words**
> *prefixes* : ante-, fore-, pre-

beg VERB
to ask anxiously for something
EG *I begged him to leave me alone.*
beseech EG *Her eyes beseeched him to show mercy.*
implore EG *I implore you not to say anything.*
petition EG *He petitioned the Court to let him go free.*
plead EG *She was pleading with me to stay.*

> ### WORD POWER
>
> ▷ **Synonyms**
> entreat
> importune
> solicit

begin VERB
to start or cause to start

EG *She began to move around the room.*
commence FORMAL EG *He commenced his journey.*
inaugurate EG *The committee was inaugurated ten days ago.*
initiate EG *They wanted to initiate a discussion.*
originate EG *Mankind may have originated in Africa.*
set about EG *He set about tackling his problems.*
start EG *The meeting starts at 10 o'clock.*

> ### WORD POWER
>
> ▷ **Synonyms**
> instigate
> institute
>
> ▶ **Antonym**
> end

beginner NOUN
someone learning to do something
EG *a beginner's course*
apprentice EG *an apprentice in a law firm*
learner EG *young learners of French*
novice EG *Many of us are novices on the computer.*
starter EG *new starters at school*
trainee EG *a trainee in a newspaper office*

> ### WORD POWER
>
> ▶ **Antonym**
> expert

beginning NOUN
where something starts
EG *the beginning of the city*
birth EG *the birth of modern art*
commencement FORMAL EG *a date for the commencement of talks*
opening EG *the opening of the trial*
origin EG *the origins of civilization*
outset EG *There were lots of problems*

from the outset.
start EG *the start of all the trouble*

WORD POWER

▷ **Synonyms**
inauguration
initiation
onset

▶ **Antonym**
end

behave VERB
to act in a certain way
EG *They were behaving like animals.*
act EG *He is acting like a spoilt child.*
function EG *They are functioning as a team.*
operate EG *I know how Graham operates.*
work EG *My mind is working well today.*

❶ **belief** NOUN
the certainty something is true
EG *belief in reincarnation*
confidence EG *I have every confidence that you'll do well.*
conviction EG *She speaks with conviction.*
judgment EG *My judgment is that he should leave.*
opinion EG *Robert has strong opinions.*
trust EG *She has complete trust that you'll help her.*
view EG *In my view, he is wrong.*

❷ **belief** NOUN
a principle of a religion or system
EG *the culture and beliefs of ancient times*
creed EG *people of every race and creed*
doctrine EG *Christian doctrine*
dogma EG *religious dogma*
faith EG *Do you practise any faith?*
ideology EG *different political ideologies*
principle EG *the principles of Jewish faith*

tenet EG *the fundamental tenets of Islam*

believable ADJECTIVE
possible or likely to be the case
EG *The book is full of believable characters.*
credible EG *credible witnesses*
imaginable EG *It is scarcely imaginable that it happened here.*
likely EG *It's more likely that she forgot.*
plausible EG *a plausible explanation*
possible EG *It's quite possible that I'm wrong.*
probable EG *the most probable outcome*

WORD POWER

▶ **Antonym**
unbelievable

believe VERB
to accept something is true
EG *Don't believe everything you read in the papers.*
accept EG *He can't accept that he is wrong.*
assume EG *I assume these eggs are fresh.*
presume EG *The missing person is presumed to be dead.*
swallow INFORMAL EG *I found their story hard to swallow.*
trust EG *I trust that you will manage.*

WORD POWER

▶ **Antonym**
doubt

belittle VERB
to make someone or something seem less important
EG *He belittles my opinions.*
deride EG *He is derided as weak and incompetent.*
detract from EG *Her sour comments detracted from Meg's happiness.*
downgrade EG *I fear failure, but I downgrade my successes.*

a
b
c
d
e
f
g
h
i
j
k
l
m
n
o
p
q
r
s
t
u
v
w
x
y
z

scorn EG *Eleanor scorns the work of others.*

undervalue EG *We must never undervalue freedom.*

> ### WORD POWER
>
> ▷ **Synonyms**
> denigrate
> minimize
>
> ▶ **Antonym**
> praise

beloved ADJECTIVE
dearly loved
EG *He lost his beloved wife last year.*
adored EG *an adored father*
cherished EG *his most cherished possession*
darling EG *our darling child*
dearest EG *my dearest Maria*
precious EG *I love my precious cat.*
treasured EG *treasured memories*

> ### WORD POWER
>
> ▶ **Antonym**
> despised

below PREPOSITION OR ADVERB
lower down
EG *six centimetres below soil level*
beneath EG *She hid the letter beneath her mattress.*
down EG *I fell down to the bottom.*
lower EG *The price will fall lower than this.*
under EG *tunnels under the ground*
underneath EG *He crawled underneath the table.*

> ### WORD POWER
>
> ▶ **Antonym**
> above

❶ bend VERB
to make or become curved
EG *Bend the bar into a horseshoe.*
buckle EG *A wave buckled the ship's deck.*
curve EG *The wall curves to the left.*

turn EG *The road turns right at the end.*
twist EG *glass twisted into elaborate patterns*
warp EG *The wood had started to warp.*

❷ bend VERB
to move forwards and downwards
EG *I bent over and kissed her cheek.*
arch EG *Don't arch your back!*
bow EG *He turned and bowed to her.*
crouch EG *We were crouching in the bushes.*
incline EG *The woman inclined her head to one side.*
lean EG *She leant out of the window.*
stoop EG *Stooping down, he picked up a stone.*

❸ bend NOUN
a curve in something
EG *a bend in the road*
arc EG *the full arc of a rainbow*
corner EG *He drove round the corner.*
curve EG *the curve of the stream*
loop EG *The river curves in a loop.*
turn EG *a turn in the path*

> ### WORD POWER
>
> ▷ **Synonyms**
> angle
> arch
> twist

beneficial ADJECTIVE
giving some benefit
EG *Wine in moderation is beneficial to the health.*
advantageous EG *an advantageous arrangement*
good for you EG *Regular exercise is good for you.*
healthy EG *trying to switch to a healthy lifestyle*
helpful EG *This treatment is particularly helpful to hay fever sufferers.*
useful EG *a useful addition to your first aid kit*

wholesome EG *food made with good, wholesome ingredients*

❶ **benefit** NOUN
an advantage
EG *the benefits of relaxation*
advantage EG *The advantages of the new system far outweigh its disadvantages.*
asset EG *A second language is an asset in this job.*
boon EG *a great boon for busy housewives*
gain EG *He used the knowledge for his personal gain.*
good EG *Study for your own good!*
help EG *It's no help to know I was right.*
profit EG *the profits of working hard*
use EG *His training was of no use to him.*

WORD POWER

▶ **Antonym**
disadvantage

❷ **benefit** VERB
to help in something
EG *The experience will benefit you.*
aid EG *measures to aid working mothers*
assist EG *The extra money will assist you.*
enhance EG *His injury does not enhance our chances.*
further EG *His support will further our cause.*
help EG *The new laws won't help the environment.*
profit EG *It won't profit us to complain.*

WORD POWER

▶ **Antonym**
harm

benevolent ADJECTIVE
kind and helpful
EG *a benevolent ruler*
benign EG *a benign and loveable man*
charitable EG *charitable*

organizations
compassionate EG *my compassionate friends*
humane EG *humane treatment of prisoners*
kind EG *You have been kind and helpful to us.*

WORD POWER

▷ **Synonyms**
altruistic
beneficent
philanthropic

beside PREPOSITION
next to
EG *I stood beside my father and my uncle.*
adjacent to EG *a hotel adjacent to the beach*
alongside EG *a house alongside the river*
close to EG *The restaurant is close to their home.*
near EG *He stood very near the front door.*
next to EG *She sat down next to him.*

❶ **best** ADJECTIVE
of the highest standard
EG *the best film I have seen in a long time.*
→ see Word Study **best**

WORD POWER

▶ **Antonym**
worst

❷ **best** NOUN
the preferred thing
EG *Of all my presents, this is the best.*
→ see Word Study **best**

WORD POWER

▶ **Antonym**
worst

❶ **betray** VERB
to do someone harm
EG *I was betrayed by someone I had*

a
b
c
d
e
f
g
h
i
j
k
l
m
n
o
p
q
r
s
t
u
v
w
x
y
z

A
B
C
D
E
F
G
H
I
J
K
L
M
N
O
P
Q
R
S
T
U
V
W
X
Y
Z

thought a friend.
be unfaithful EG *He's been unfaithful to his wife.*
break your promise EG *I broke my promise to help her.*
double-cross INFORMAL EG *I was angry that he double-crossed me.*
inform on EG *people who inform on their colleagues*

❷ **betray** VERB
to show feelings
EG *Jeremy's voice betrayed little emotion.*
expose EG *She never exposed her hostile feelings.*
manifest EG *Fear can manifest itself in many ways.*
reveal EG *Her expression revealed nothing.*
show EG *His eyes showed his unhappiness.*

❶ **better** ADJECTIVE
of more worth than another
EG *Today was much better than yesterday.*
→ see Word Study **better**

WORD POWER
▶ **Antonym**
inferior

❷ **better** ADJECTIVE
well after being ill
EG *I hope you feel better soon.*
→ see Word Study **better**

WORD POWER
▶ **Antonym**
worse

beware VERB
to be cautious
EG *Beware of the dog.*
be careful EG *Be careful what you say to him.*
be cautious EG *Doctors are cautious about using the treatment.*
be wary EG *Michelle is wary of*

marriage.
guard against EG *We have to guard against thieves.*
look out EG *Look out, there's a train coming.*
watch out EG *Watch out for fog and ice.*

bias NOUN
prejudice for or against a person or group
EG *bias against women*
bigotry EG *religious bigotry*
favouritism EG *His promotion was due to favouritism.*
prejudice EG *racial prejudice*

biased ADJECTIVE
showing prejudice
EG *biased attitudes*
one-eyed AUSTRALIAN AND NEW ZEALAND
eg *I may be a bit one-eyed because of the family connection.*
one-sided EG *a one-sided argument*
partial EG *a very partial view of the situation*
prejudiced EG *Don't be prejudiced by what you read.*
slanted EG *a slanted newspaper article*
weighted EG *a scheme weighted towards those in need*

WORD POWER
▶ **Antonym**
neutral

❶ **big** ADJECTIVE
of a large size
EG *a big house*
→ see Word Study **big**

WORD POWER
▶ **Antonym**
small

❷ **big** ADJECTIVE
of great importance

EG *a big name*
→ see Word Study **big**

WORD POWER

▶ **Antonym**
unimportant

bill NOUN
a statement of how much is owed
EG *a huge restaurant bill*
account EG *Please charge it to my account.*
charges EG *charges for eye tests*
invoice EG *They sent an invoice for the damage.*
statement EG *a credit card statement*

bit NOUN
a small amount
EG *a bit of coal*
crumb EG *a crumb of comfort*
fragment EG *glittering fragments of broken glass*
grain EG *His story contains a grain of truth.*
part EG *part of the problem*
piece EG *The vase was smashed to pieces.*
scrap EG *a scrap of evidence*

WORD POWER

▷ **Synonyms**
iota
jot
speck

bite VERB
to cut into something with your teeth
EG *His cat bit me when I tried to pat it.*
chew EG *a video of a man having his leg chewed off by a bear*
gnaw EG *The bones had been gnawed by wild animals.*
nibble EG *She nibbled a biscuit.*
nip EG *There were blotches where the mosquitoes had nipped him.*

❶ **bitter** ADJECTIVE
angry and resentful
EG *a bitter row*
acrimonious EG *an acrimonious discussion*
begrudging EG *He gave me begrudging thanks.*
embittered EG *an embittered old lady*
rancorous EG *the issue that led to rancorous disputes*
resentful EG *She is resentful of others' success.*
sour EG *a sour expression*

❷ **bitter** ADJECTIVE
tasting or smelling sharp
EG *bitter lemons*
acid EG *the acid smell of sweat*
acrid EG *clouds of acrid smoke*
astringent EG *astringent disinfectant*
sharp EG *a clean, sharp taste*
sour EG *a rich, sour stew*
tart EG *the tart qualities of citrus fruit*

WORD POWER

▶ **Antonym**
sweet

bizarre ADJECTIVE
very strange or eccentric
EG *He has some bizarre ideas about women.*
curious EG *a curious mixture of ancient and modern*
eccentric EG *Her eccentric behaviour was beginning to attract attention.*
extraordinary EG *What an extraordinary character he is!*
odd EG *a series of very odd coincidences*
outlandish EG *her outlandish style of dressing*
peculiar EG *a peculiar combination of flavours*
queer EG *A very queer thing happened to me tonight.*
strange EG *She's been behaving in a*

very strange way lately.
weird EG *his weird theories about UFOs*

black NOUN OR ADJECTIVE

> **Shades of black**
> coal-black
> ebony
> inky
> jet
> jet-black
> pitch-black
> raven
> sable
> sooty

❶ blame VERB
to believe someone caused something
EG *Don't blame me for this trouble.*
accuse EG *She accused him of causing the fire.*
charge EG *He will be charged for murder.*
hold responsible EG *I hold you responsible for this mess.*

❷ blame NOUN
the responsibility for something bad
EG *I'm not going to take the blame for that!*
accountability EG *He escaped accountability for his crimes.*
fault EG *The fault was all yours.*
guilt EG *the sole guilt for the outbreak of war*
liability EG *He admitted liability for the crash.*
rap SLANG EG *A maid took the rap for stealing the letters.*
responsibility EG *responsibility for the murder*

❶ blank ADJECTIVE
with nothing on it
EG *a blank sheet of paper*
bare EG *bare walls*
clean EG *a clean sheet of paper*
clear EG *a clear patch of floor*
empty EG *an empty page*
plain EG *a plain envelope*
unmarked EG *an unmarked board*

❷ blank ADJECTIVE
showing no feeling
EG *John just looked blank.*
deadpan EG *a deadpan expression*
dull EG *a dull stare*
empty EG *She saw the empty look in his eyes.*
impassive EG *her impassive smile*
vacant EG *the vacant expression on his face*

❶ blend VERB
to mix things so as to form a single item or substance
EG *Blend the butter with the sugar.*
combine EG *Combine the ingredients in a large bowl.*
merge EG *how to merge the graphics with the text*
mingle EG *the mingled smells of flowers and cigar smoke*
mix EG *Mix the two liquids together with a whisk.*

❷ blend VERB
to combine in a pleasing way
EG *The colours blend with the rest of the decor.*
complement EG *The flavours complement each other perfectly.*
co-ordinate EG *Choose accessories*

which co-ordinate with your outfit.
go well EG *a wine which goes well with fish*
harmonize EG *shades which harmonize with most skin tones*
match EG *Those shoes don't match that dress.*
suit EG *glasses which suit the shape of your face*

❸ blend NOUN
a mixture or combination of things
EG *a blend of wine and sparkling water*
alloy EG *an alloy of copper and tin*
amalgamation EG *Bartók's rich amalgamation of musical styles*
combination EG *a fantastic combination of colours*
compound EG *a compound of water, sugar and enzymes*
fusion EG *a fusion of cooking styles*
mix EG *a delicious mix of exotic spices*
mixture EG *a sticky mixture of flour and water*

bless VERB
to ask God's protection
EG *The bishop blessed the congregation.*
anoint EG *The priest anointed the child with oil.*
consecrate EG *ground that has been consecrated*
dedicate EG *The well was dedicated to saints.*
hallow EG *A building could be hallowed by prayer.*

WORD POWER
▶ **Antonym**
curse

❶ blessing NOUN
something good
EG *Good health is a blessing.*
benefit EG *the benefits of technology*
boon EG *This service is a boon to the elderly.*
gift EG *A cheerful nature is a gift.*
godsend EG *The extra twenty dollars*

was a godsend.
help EG *My computer is a real help in my work.*

WORD POWER
▶ **Antonym**
disadvantage

❷ blessing NOUN
approval or permission to do something
EG *She got married with her parents' blessing.*
approval EG *Does this plan have your approval?*
backing EG *We can't do anything without his backing.*
consent EG *He gave his consent to the article.*
leave EG *She gave us leave to start.*
permission EG *You have my permission to go.*
support EG *My manager has given his full support to my project.*

WORD POWER
▷ **Synonyms**
approbation
sanction

▶ **Antonym**
disapproval

blob NOUN
a small amount of a thick or sticky substance
EG *He had a blob of chocolate mousse on his tie.*
bead EG *Beads of blood spattered the counter.*
dab EG *You've got a dab of glue on your nose.*
drop EG *a few thick drops of fluid*
droplet EG *droplets of congealed fat*

❶ block NOUN
a large piece
EG *a block of wood*
bar EG *a bar of soap*
brick EG *concrete bricks*

a
b
c
d
e
f
g
h
i
j
k
l
m
n
o
p
q
r
s
t
u
v
w
x
y
z

A
B
C
D
E
F
G
H
I
J
K
L
M
N
O
P
Q
R
S
T
U
V
W
X
Y
Z

chunk EG *chunks of meat*
ingot EG *a gold ingot*
lump EG *lumps of metal*
piece EG *a big piece of cake*

❷ block VERB
to close by putting something across
EG *Mud blocked the river.*
choke EG *The town was choked with cars.*
clog EG *Dishes clogged the sink.*
obstruct EG *The crash obstructed the road.*
plug EG *Have you plugged the leaks?*

WORD POWER

▶ **Antonym**
unblock

❸ block VERB
to prevent something happening
EG *The council blocked his plans.*
bar EG *He was barred from entering.*
check EG *a policy to check population growth*
halt EG *attempts to halt the spread of disease*
obstruct EG *Lack of funds obstructed our progress.*
stop EG *measures to stop the rising crime rate*
thwart EG *My plans were thwarted by Taylor.*

blockage NOUN
a thing that clogs something
EG *a blockage in the pipe*
block EG *a block in the blood vessel*
obstruction EG *an obstruction on the track*
stoppage EG *We have to clear the stoppage.*

blot out VERB
to cover and prevent from being seen
EG *The smoke blotted out the sky.*
eclipse EG *The moon eclipsed the sun.*
obliterate EG *Our view was obliterated by mist.*
obscure EG *My way was obscured by*

fog.
shadow EG *Her veil shadowed her face.*

❶ blow VERB
to move or cause to move in the wind
EG *The wind blew his papers away.*
buffet EG *The ship was buffeted by gales.*
drive EG *The strong wind drove us forward.*
flutter EG *The flags are fluttering.*
sweep EG *A sudden blast swept away the cloth.*
waft EG *His hair wafted in the breeze.*
whirl EG *The fallen leaves whirled around.*

❷ blow NOUN
a hit from something
EG *a blow to the head*
bang EG *He suffered some bangs and bumps.*
clout INFORMAL EG *a clout on the head*
knock EG *Knocks can cause damage to the spine.*
smack EG *She gave the child a smack.*
thump EG *Ralph got a thump on the chest.*
whack EG *The horse got a whack from its rider.*

❸ blow NOUN
something disappointing or upsetting
EG *Marc's death was a terrible blow.*
bombshell EG *His departure was a bombshell for the team.*
disappointment EG *My exam results were a real disappointment.*
misfortune EG *a series of misfortunes*
setback EG *We faced many setbacks before we got the house.*
shock EG *The news came as a shock.*
upset EG *The defeat caused an upset.*

WORD POWER

▷ **Synonyms**
calamity
catastrophe
jolt

blue NOUN OR ADJECTIVE

Shades of blue
aqua
aquamarine
azure
cerulean
cobalt
cyan
duck-egg blue
electric blue
gentian
indigo
lapis lazuli
midnight blue
navy
Nile blue
peacock blue
periwinkle
petrol blue
royal blue
sapphire
saxe blue
sky-blue
teal
turquoise
ultramarine

❶ **blunt** ADJECTIVE
having rounded edges
EG *blunt scissors*
dull EG *a dull knife*
rounded EG *rounded edges*
unsharpened EG *an unsharpened pencil*

WORD POWER

▶ **Antonym**
sharp

❷ **blunt** ADJECTIVE
saying what you think
EG *a blunt speaker*

bluff EG *a bluff old man*
brusque EG *His response was brusque.*
forthright EG *a forthright reply*
frank EG *I'll be frank with you.*
outspoken EG *an outspoken critic*
straightforward EG *She has a straightforward manner.*

WORD POWER

▷ **Synonyms**
explicit
trenchant

▶ **Antonym**
tactful

❶ **blush** VERB
to go red in the face
EG *I felt myself blushing.*
colour EG *I found myself colouring as I spoke.*
crimson EG *He looked at her and she crimsoned.*
flush EG *I saw her face flush.*
go red EG *His face went red as a beetroot.*
turn red EG *He turned red with embarrassment.*
turn scarlet EG *She turned scarlet with humiliation.*

❷ **blush** NOUN
a red colour
EG *Ann took the gift with a blush.*
colour EG *The walk will bring colour to your cheeks.*
flush EG *A slow flush spread over the man's face.*
glow EG *a healthy glow*

boast VERB
to talk proudly
EG *Carol boasted about her costume.*
brag EG *I don't mind bragging about my talents.*
crow EG *Stop crowing about your success.*
skite AUSTRALIAN AND NEW ZEALAND; INFORMAL EG *That's nothing to skite about.*

boastful ADJECTIVE
tending to brag about things
EG *a boastful liar*
bragging EG *bragging stories about his time in the navy*
cocky EG *The boxer is cocky and brash.*
conceited EG *Young men tend to be conceited.*
crowing EG *crowing remarks*
egotistical EG *egotistical fibs*
swaggering EG *He has a swaggering arrogance.*

WORD POWER

▶ **Antonym**
modest

❶ body NOUN
all your physical parts
EG *My whole body hurt.*
build EG *He is of medium build.*
figure EG *Janet has a nice figure.*
form EG *clothes that flatter your form*
frame EG *their bony frames*
physique EG *a powerful physique*
shape EG *his trim shape*

WORD POWER

● **Related Words**
adjectives : corporal, physical

❷ body NOUN
a dead body
EG *Police found a body hidden in the forest.*
carcass EG *a sheep's carcass*
corpse EG *the corpse of a young man*
dead body EG *He'd never seen a dead body.*
remains EG *human remains*

❸ body NOUN
an organized group of people
EG *local voluntary bodies*
association EG *the Football Association*
band EG *a band of rebels*
company EG *the Royal Shakespeare Company*
confederation EG *a confederation of workers*
organization EG *student organizations*
society EG *I joined the local opera society.*

WORD POWER

▷ **Synonyms**
bloc
collection
corporation

❶ boil VERB
to bubble
EG *The water is boiling.*
bubble EG *Potatoes bubbled in the pot.*
fizz EG *The liquid fizzed and bubbled.*
foam EG *When the butter foams, add the onions.*
froth EG *The milk frothed over in the pan.*

WORD POWER

▷ **Synonyms**
effervesce
seethe

❷ boil NOUN
a swelling on the skin
EG *five boils on his face*
blister EG *a blister on my index finger*
swelling EG *a swelling under the eye*
tumour EG *The tumours had all disappeared.*

WORD POWER

▷ **Synonyms**
blain
carbuncle
pustule

❶ bold ADJECTIVE
confident and not shy
EG *a bold question*
brash EG *a brash young sergeant*
brazen EG *a brazen young woman*

cheeky EG *a cheeky grin*
confident EG *I felt confident confronting him.*
forward EG *It was forward of you to ask him.*
impudent EG *an impudent child*

WORD POWER

▷ **Synonyms**
barefaced
pert
saucy

▶ **Antonym**
shy

❷ bold ADJECTIVE
unafraid of risk or danger
EG *a bold attempt*
adventurous EG *an adventurous spirit*
brave EG *a brave woman*
courageous EG *courageous firefighters*
daring EG *daring feats*
fearless EG *a fearless warrior*
intrepid EG *an intrepid explorer*

WORD POWER

▷ **Synonyms**
audacious
heroic
valiant

▶ **Antonym**
cowardly

❸ bold ADJECTIVE
clear and noticeable
EG *bold colours*
bright EG *bright light*
flashy EG *flashy clothes*
loud EG *a loud tie*
striking EG *a striking tartan pattern*
strong EG *dressed in strong reds and yellows*
vivid EG *vivid green and purple*

WORD POWER

▷ **Synonyms**
conspicuous
prominent
pronounced

▶ **Antonym**
dull

bolt VERB
to escape or run away
EG *I bolted towards the exit.*
dash EG *He dashed out of the room in a panic.*
escape EG *They escaped across the frontier.*
flee EG *We fled before the police arrived.*
fly EG *She flew down the stairs with her attacker in hot pursuit.*
run away EG *I called to him but he just ran away.*
run off EG *The children ran off when they spotted me.*
rush EG *They all rushed away as we approached.*

❶ bomb NOUN
an explosive device
EG *The bomb exploded in the centre of the city.*
device EG *Experts defused the device.*
explosive EG *a block of plastic explosive*
missile EG *long-range missiles*
rocket EG *a rocket launcher*
shell EG *Shells began to fall.*
torpedo EG *The torpedo struck the ship.*

WORD POWER

▷ **Synonyms**
grenade
mine
projectile

❷ bomb VERB
to attack with bombs
EG *His house was bombed.*

a
b
c
d
e
f
g
h
i
j
k
l
m
n
o
p
q
r
s
t
u
v
w
x
y
z

attack EG *We are being attacked!*
blow up EG *He attempted to blow up the building.*
bombard EG *Warships began to bombard the coast.*
destroy EG *Helicopters destroyed his village.*
shell EG *They shelled the troops heavily.*
torpedo EG *His ship was torpedoed in the Channel.*

❶ bond NOUN
a close relationship
EG *a special bond between us*
attachment EG *Mother and child form a close attachment.*
connection EG *a family connection*
link EG *the links of friendship*
relation EG *the relation between husband and wife*
tie EG *the ties of blood*
union EG *the union of father and son*

WORD POWER

▷ **Synonyms**
affiliation
affinity

❷ bond NOUN
an obligation to do something
EG *the social bonds of community*
agreement EG *He has broken our agreement.*
contract EG *He signed a two-year contract.*
obligation EG *your obligation to your father*
pledge EG *a pledge of support*
promise EG *You must keep your promises.*
word EG *I give you my word.*

WORD POWER

▷ **Synonyms**
compact
covenant
guarantee

❸ bond VERB
to attach separate things
EG *Strips of wood are bonded together.*
bind EG *Tape was used to bind the files.*
fasten EG *I fastened the picture to the wall.*
fuse EG *The pieces to be joined are melted and fused together.*
glue EG *Glue the pieces together.*
paste EG *He pasted posters to the wall.*

❶ book NOUN
a number of pages in a cover
EG *I'm reading a great book just now.*
publication EG *publications about job hunting*
textbook EG *He wrote a textbook on law.*
title EG *We publish a range of titles.*
tome EG *a heavy tome*
volume EG *small volumes of poetry*
work EG *my favourite work by this author*

Types of book
anthology
atlas
autobiography
biography
dictionary
directory
encyclopedia
gazetteer
glossary
guidebook
manual
novel
phrasebook
thesaurus

Parts of a book
appendix
bibliography
blurb
caption
chapter
contents
cover

footnote
foreword
glossary
heading
illustration
index
introduction
jacket
layout
line
page
preface
title

Religious books
Bible
Book of Mormon
Diamond Scriptures
Guru Granth *or* Adi Granth
I Ching
Mahabharata
Qu'ran *or* Koran
Ramayana
Sutras
Talmud
Tao-te-Ching
Torah
Tripitaka
Veda

❷ book VERB
to arrange to have or use
EG *The tickets are booked.*
charter EG *A plane was chartered for them.*
engage EG *We engaged the services of a plumber.*
organize EG *I have organized our flights.*
reserve EG *Hotel rooms have been reserved.*
schedule EG *A meeting is scheduled for Monday.*

❶ border NOUN
a dividing line between things or places
EG *the border between two countries*
borderline EG *the borderline between health and sickness*

boundary EG *national boundaries*
frontier EG *the American frontier*
line EG *the line between fact and fiction*

❷ border NOUN
an edge of something
EG *plain tiles with a bright border*
bounds EG *the bounds of good taste*
edge EG *the edge of town*
limits EG *the city limits*
margin EG *the western margins of the island*
rim EG *the rim of the lake*

❸ border VERB
to form an edge
EG *Tall trees bordered the fields.*
edge EG *the woods that edge the lake*
fringe EG *Street lights fringe the bay.*
hem EG *dresses hemmed with feathers*
rim EG *the restaurants rimming the harbour*
trim EG *coats trimmed with fur collars*

bored ADJECTIVE
impatient and not interested in something
EG *I am bored with this business.*
fed up EG *He is fed up with this country.*
tired EG *I am tired of this music.*
uninterested EG *He seems uninterested in politics.*
wearied EG *He spoke in a wearied voice.*

WORD POWER

▶ **Antonym**
interested

---

boredom NOUN
a lack of interest
EG *the boredom of long trips*
apathy EG *political apathy*
dullness EG *a period of dullness*
flatness EG *a feeling of flatness*
monotony EG *the monotony of winter*
tedium EG *the tedium of*

unemployment
weariness EG *a sense of weariness*

WORD POWER

▶ **Antonym**
interest

boring ADJECTIVE
dull and uninteresting
EG *a boring job*
dull EG *dull tasks*
flat EG *a flat performance*
humdrum EG *humdrum lives*
monotonous EG *the monotonous prison routine*
tedious EG *The work is tedious.*
tiresome EG *a tiresome old man*

WORD POWER

▷ **Synonyms**
insipid
repetitious
stale

▶ **Antonym**
interesting

boss NOUN
a person in charge of something
EG *He can't stand his boss.*
chief EG *the police chief*
director EG *the directors of the bank*
employer EG *He was sent to Rome by his employer.*
head EG *Heads of government met in New York.*
leader EG *The party's leader has resigned.*
manager EG *the company's marketing manager*

bossy ADJECTIVE
telling people what to do
EG *a rather bossy little girl*
arrogant EG *arrogant behaviour*
authoritarian EG *He has an authoritarian approach to parenthood.*
dictatorial EG *a dictatorial management style*

domineering EG *She is domineering and ruthless.*
imperious EG *He has an imperious manner.*
overbearing EG *an overbearing mother*

botch VERB
to do something badly
EG *a botched operation*
bungle EG *inefficient people who bungled the job*
mar EG *She marred her exit by twisting her ankle.*
mess up EG *He manages to mess up his life.*

❶ bother VERB
to cause worry or concern
EG *His lack of money bothers him.*
annoy EG *the things that annoy me*
concern EG *The future concerns me.*
disturb EG *It disturbs me to see you unhappy.*
get on someone's nerves
INFORMAL EG *This place gets on my nerves.*
trouble EG *Are you troubled by nightmares?*
worry EG *I'm worried by the amount he is drinking.*

WORD POWER

▷ **Synonyms**
harass
inconvenience

❷ bother NOUN
trouble and difficulty
EG *I hate the bother of shopping.*
annoyance EG *Snoring can be an annoyance.*
difficulty EG *The strikes are causing difficulties for commuters.*
inconvenience EG *a minor inconvenience*
irritation EG *Noise is an irritation.*
trouble EG *You've caused me a lot of*

trouble.
worry EG *It was a time of worry for us.*

WORD POWER

▷ **Synonyms**
nuisance
strain

---

❶ bottom NOUN
the lowest part of something
EG *the bottom of the stairs*
base EG *the base of the spine*
bed EG *the river bed*
depths EG *the depths of the earth*
floor EG *the ocean floor*
foot EG *the foot of the bed*

WORD POWER

▶ **Antonym**
top

---

❷ bottom NOUN
the part of the body you sit on
EG *Sit on your bottom!*
backside INFORMAL EG *the muscles in your backside*
behind INFORMAL EG *He kicked me on the behind.*
buttocks EG *exercises for your buttocks*
posterior HUMOROUS EG *He fell on his posterior.*
rear EG *I was thrown out on my rear.*

❸ bottom ADJECTIVE
in the lowest place or position
EG *the bottom drawer*
base EG *the base edge of the curtain*
basement EG *a basement flat*
ground EG *ground level*
lowest EG *the lowest part of the brain*

WORD POWER

▶ **Antonym**
highest

---

bounce VERB
to spring back or move up and down
EG *I bounced a ball against the wall.*
bob EG *The raft bobbed along.*

bound EG *He bounded up the stairway.*
bump EG *My bicycle bumped along the rough ground.*
jump EG *They jumped up and down to keep warm.*
ricochet EG *The bullets ricocheted off the jeep.*

WORD POWER

▷ **Synonyms**
rebound
recoil

---

box NOUN
a container with a firm base and sides
EG *All her possessions were packed in boxes.*
carton EG *cartons full of books*
case EG *It is still in its original case.*
chest EG *She kept her heirlooms in a carved wooden chest.*
container EG *substances kept in heavy metal containers*
trunk EG *a trunk full of toys*

boy NOUN
a male child
EG *I knew him when he was a boy.*
fellow EG *a fine little fellow*
lad EG *I remember being a lad his age.*
schoolboy EG *a group of schoolboys*
youngster EG *I was only a youngster in 1970.*
youth EG *gangs of youths who cause trouble*

boycott VERB
to refuse to have anything to do with
EG *Some parties are boycotting the elections.*
blacklist EG *He has been blacklisted by various societies.*
embargo EG *Imports of fruit were embargoed.*
exclude EG *I exclude animal products from my diet.*
reject EG *She rejected her parents'*

a b c d e f g h i j k l m n o p q r s t u v w x y z

religion.
spurn EG *You spurned his last offer.*

WORD POWER

▷ **Synonyms**
proscribe
refrain from

brag VERB
to boast about something
EG *I hate people who brag about their achievements.*
boast EG *She kept boasting about how many guys she'd been out with.*
crow EG *Stop crowing about your victory.*
skite AUSTRALIAN AND NEW ZEALAND; INFORMAL EG *That's nothing to skite about.*

braggart NOUN
a person who boasts
EG *He was a braggart and a liar.*
bigmouth SLANG EG *He's nothing but a bigmouth.*
boaster EG *an idle boaster looking for the main chance*
bragger EG *He was quite a bragger.*
show-off EG *I've always been a show-off.*
skite *or* **skiter** AUSTRALIAN AND NEW ZEALAND; INFORMAL EG *a bit of a skite*

❶ brave ADJECTIVE
willing to do dangerous things
EG *a brave attempt to stop the attack*
bold EG *Amrita became a bold rebel.*
courageous EG *a courageous decision*
fearless EG *his fearless campaigning for justice*
heroic EG *The heroic sergeant risked his life.*
plucky EG *The plucky schoolgirl amazed the doctors.*
valiant EG *a valiant attempt to keep going*

WORD POWER

▷ **Synonyms**
daring
intrepid
valorous

▶ **Antonym**
cowardly

❷ brave VERB
to face something without fear
EG *Fans braved the rain to hear him sing.*
face EG *I can't face another three years of this.*
stand up to EG *I have tried to stand up to the bullies.*

bravery NOUN
the quality of being courageous
EG *He deserves praise for his bravery.*
boldness EG *an outward display of boldness*
courage EG *They do not have the courage to apologize.*
fortitude EG *He suffered with tremendous fortitude.*
heroism EG *acts of heroism*
pluck EG *He has pluck and presence of mind.*
valour EG *He won a medal for valour.*

WORD POWER

▷ **Synonyms**
fearlessness
mettle

▶ **Antonym**
cowardice

❶ breach NOUN
a breaking of an agreement or law
EG *a breach of contract*
infringement EG *an infringement of the rules*
offence EG *criminal offences*
trespass EG *a campaign of trespasses and demonstrations*

violation EG *a violation of the peace agreement*

WORD POWER

▷ **Synonyms**
contravention
transgression

❷ **breach** NOUN
a gap in something
EG *the breach in the Berlin Wall*
crack EG *a large crack in the ice*
gap EG *a narrow gap in the curtains*
hole EG *We cut holes in the fabric.*
opening EG *an opening in the fence*
rift EG *The earthquake caused a deep rift.*
split EG *There's a split in my mattress.*

WORD POWER

▷ **Synonyms**
chasm
fissure
rupture

❶ **break** VERB
to separate into pieces
EG *I broke a plate.*
→ see Word Study **break**

❷ **break** VERB
to fail to keep a rule or promise
EG *He broke his promise to attend.*
breach EG *breaches of discipline*
contravene EG *His behaviour contravenes our code of conduct.*
infringe EG *The judge ruled that he had infringed no rules.*
violate EG *They violated the peace agreement.*

❸ **break** NOUN
a short period of rest or change
EG *I took a five-minute break from work.*
interlude EG *a happy interlude in my life*
interval EG *a long interval when no-one spoke*
pause EG *After a pause Alex spoke.*

recess EG *The court adjourned for a recess.*
respite EG *They have had no respite from bombing.*
rest EG *I'll start again after a rest.*

❶ **breed** NOUN
a type of animal
EG *rare breeds of cattle*
kind EG *What kind of horse is that?*
species EG *Pandas are an endangered species.*
stock EG *cattle of Highland stock*
strain EG *a special strain of rat*
type EG *What type of dog should we get?*
variety EG *many varieties of birds*

❷ **breed** VERB
to produce and look after
EG *He breeds dogs for the police.*
cultivate EG *She cultivates fruit and vegetables.*
develop EG *A new variety of potato is being developed.*
keep EG *He keeps guinea pigs.*
nurture EG *trimming and nurturing plants and saplings*
raise EG *He raises birds of prey as a hobby.*
rear EG *the difficulties of rearing children*

❸ **breed** VERB
to produce offspring
EG *Frogs can breed in most ponds.*
multiply EG *Rats multiply quickly.*
produce EG *She produced a son.*
propagate EG *This plant is difficult to propagate.*
reproduce EG *the natural desire to reproduce*

WORD POWER

▷ **Synonyms**
engender
procreate

❶ **brief** ADJECTIVE
lasting for a short time
EG *a brief appearance on television*

fleeting EG *a fleeting glimpse*
momentary EG *There was a momentary silence.*
quick EG *a quick look at the newspaper*
short EG *a short holiday*
swift EG *a swift glance at John's face*

WORD POWER

▷ **Synonyms**
ephemeral
temporary
transitory

▶ **Antonym**
long

❷ brief VERB
to give necessary information
EG *A spokesman briefed reporters.*
advise EG *I must advise you of my decision to retire.*
fill in INFORMAL EG *Can you fill me in on Wilbur's visit?*
inform EG *They would inform him of their progress.*
instruct EG *He instructed us in first aid.*
prepare EG *I will prepare you for this exam.*
prime EG *Arnold primed him for his duties.*

❶ bright ADJECTIVE
strong and startling
EG *a bright light*
brilliant EG *brilliant green eyes*
dazzling EG *a dazzling white shirt*
glowing EG *the glowing windows of the Cathedral*
luminous EG *a luminous star*
radiant EG *eyes as radiant as sapphires*
vivid EG *strong, vivid colours*

WORD POWER

▷ **Synonyms**
blazing
illuminated
resplendent

▶ **Antonym**
dull

❷ bright ADJECTIVE
clever and alert
EG *my brightest student*
brainy EG *I don't consider myself brainy.*
brilliant EG *She has a brilliant mind.*
clever EG *a clever child*
ingenious EG *an ingenious idea*
intelligent EG *Dolphins are an intelligent species.*
smart EG *He thinks he's as smart as Sarah.*

WORD POWER

▷ **Synonyms**
acute
astute
sharp

▶ **Antonym**
dim

❸ bright ADJECTIVE
cheerful and lively
EG *a bright smile*
cheerful EG *Jack sounded quite cheerful about the idea.*
happy EG *a confident, happy child*
jolly EG *a jolly nature*
light-hearted EG *They are light-hearted and enjoy life.*
lively EG *He has a lively personality.*
merry EG *bursts of merry laughter*

❶ brilliant ADJECTIVE
very bright
EG *a brilliant light*
bright EG *a bright star*
dazzling EG *a dazzling white shirt*
gleaming EG *gleaming headlights*
glowing EG *glowing colours*
luminous EG *luminous orange paint*
radiant EG *a figure surrounded by a radiant glow*
sparkling EG *a choker of sparkling jewels*

vivid EG *the vivid hues of tropical flowers*

WORD POWER
▶ **Antonym**
dull

② brilliant ADJECTIVE
very clever
EG *a brilliant pupil*
acute EG *His relaxed exterior hides an acute mind.*
brainy INFORMAL EG *You don't have to be too brainy to work that one out.*
bright EG *an exceptionally bright child*
clever EG *What a clever idea!*
intelligent EG *a lively and extremely intelligent woman*
perceptive EG *a perceptive analysis of the situation*
sharp EG *a sharp intellect*
smart EG *He's the smartest student we've ever had.*

WORD POWER
▶ **Antonym**
stupid

③ brilliant ADJECTIVE
wonderful or superb
EG *It's a brilliant film.*
first-class EG *a first-class violinist*
great EG *one of the greatest novels of the century*
magnificent EG *a magnificent display*
marvellous EG *I've had a marvellous time.*
outstanding EG *He's an outstanding actor.*
superb EG *a superb artist*
tremendous EG *a tremendous performance*
wonderful EG *the most wonderful music I've ever heard*

WORD POWER
▶ **Antonym**
terrible

① bring VERB
to take somewhere
EG *Bring a friend to the party.*
bear EG *They bore the box into the kitchen.*
carry EG *She carried her son to the car.*
convey EG *Emergency supplies were conveyed by truck.*
lead EG *She led him into the house.*
take EG *He took cakes to the party.*
transport EG *The troops were transported to Moscow.*

② bring VERB
to cause to happen
EG *Bring the vegetables to the boil.*
cause EG *My mistake caused me some worry.*
create EG *The new factory will create more jobs.*
inflict EG *The attack inflicted heavy casualties.*
produce EG *The drug produces side effects.*
result in EG *Many accidents result in serious injuries.*
wreak EG *Violent storms wreaked havoc.*

WORD POWER
▷ **Synonyms**
effect
occasion

bring about VERB
to cause something to happen
EG *It was his arrogance which brought about his downfall.*
cause EG *This may cause delays.*
create EG *The new scheme will create even more confusion.*
generate EG *the excitement generated by this film*
make happen EG *If you want*

change, you have to make it happen yourself.
produce EG *His comments produced a furious response.*
provoke EG *a move that has provoked a storm of protest*

❶ broad ADJECTIVE
large, especially from side to side
EG *His shoulders were broad and his waist narrow.*
expansive EG *There also are several swing sets and an expansive grassy play area.*
extensive EG *The palace grounds were more extensive than the town itself.*
large EG *He was a large man with a thick square head.*
thick EG *a finger as thick as a sausage*
vast EG *rich families who own vast stretches of land*
wide EG *a sunhat with a wide brim*

WORD POWER

▷ **Synonyms**
ample
spacious

▶ **Antonym**
narrow

❷ broad ADJECTIVE
including or affecting many different things or people
EG *A broad range of issues was discussed.*
wide-ranging EG *The aims of our campaign are wide-ranging but simple.*
comprehensive EG *This book is a comprehensive guide to the region.*
extensive EG *extensive research into public attitudes to science*
general EG *The project should raise general awareness about bullying.*
sweeping EG *sweeping economic reforms*
universal EG *the universal problem of pollution*
wide EG *a major event which brought together a wide range of interest groups*

❸ broad ADJECTIVE
general rather than detailed
EG *These documents provided a broad outline of the Society's development.*
approximate EG *They did not have even an approximate idea of what the word meant.*
general EG *The figures represent a general decline in employment.*
rough EG *I've got a rough idea of what he looks like.*
vague EG *They have only a vague idea of the amount of water available.*
non-specific EG *I intend to use these terms in a deliberately non-specific way.*
sweeping EG *a sweeping statement about women drivers*

❶ broken ADJECTIVE
in pieces
EG *a broken window*
burst EG *a burst pipe*
demolished EG *a demolished house*
fractured EG *He suffered a fractured skull.*
fragmented EG *fragmented images*
shattered EG *shattered glass*
smashed EG *smashed windows*

❷ broken ADJECTIVE
not kept
EG *a broken promise*
infringed EG *a case of infringed human rights*
violated EG *a series of violated agreements*

WORD POWER

▷ **Synonyms**
disobeyed
traduced
transgressed

brown NOUN OR ADJECTIVE

Shades of brown
auburn
bay
beige
bronze
brunette
buff
burnt sienna
burnt umber
café au lait
camel
chestnut
chocolate
cinnamon
coffee
dun
fawn
ginger
hazel
khaki
mahogany
mocha
oatmeal
ochre
putty
russet
rust
sandy
sepia
tan
taupe
tawny
terracotta
umber

❶ build VERB
to make something
EG *The house was built last year.*
assemble EG *Workers were assembling planes.*
construct EG *plans to construct a temple on the site*
erect EG *The building was erected in 1900.*
fabricate EG *All the tools are fabricated from steel.*
form EG *hotels formed from cheap cement*
make EG *a wall made of bricks*

> ### WORD POWER
>
> ▶ **Antonym**
> dismantle

❷ build VERB
to develop gradually
EG *I want to build a relationship with them.*
develop EG *These battles could develop into war.*
extend EG *Three new products extend the range.*
increase EG *The population continues to increase.*
intensify EG *The conflict is bound to intensify.*
strengthen EG *Cycling strengthens the muscles.*

> ### WORD POWER
>
> ▷ **Synonyms**
> augment
> enlarge
> escalate

❸ build NOUN
the size of a body
EG *He is of medium build.*
body EG *a body of average size*
figure EG *Janet has a nice figure.*
form EG *clothes that flatter your form*
frame EG *their bony frames*
physique EG *a powerful physique*
shape EG *his trim shape*

building NOUN
a structure with walls
EG *a glass building*
edifice EG *historic edifices in the area*
structure EG *The museum is an impressive structure.*

❶ bulge VERB
to swell out
EG *He bulges out of his black T-shirt.*
expand EG *The pipes expanded in the heat.*

bulge >> bump

6

protrude EG *His blue eyes protruded from his head.*
stick out EG *His stomach stuck out under his jacket.*
swell EG *My ankles swelled.*

❷ bulge NOUN
a lump in something
EG *My purse made a bulge in my pocket.*
bump EG *a bump in the road*
hump EG *a camel's hump*
lump EG *itchy red lumps on the skin*
protrusion EG *a strange protrusion on his forehead*
swelling EG *a swelling on my foot*

❶ bully NOUN
someone who deliberately frightens or hurts others
EG *I fell victim to the class bully.*
oppressor EG *They were powerless against their oppressors.*
persecutor EG *Eventually he stood up to his persecutors.*

❷ bully VERB
to frighten or hurt someone deliberately and repeatedly
EG *I wasn't going to let him bully me.*
intimidate EG *Jones had set out to intimidate and dominate Paul.*
oppress EG *men who try to dominate and oppress women*
persecute EG *Tom was persecuted by his sisters.*
pick on EG *I don't like to see you pick on younger children.*
tease EG *The boys in the village had set on him, teasing him.*
torment EG *My older brother and sister used to torment me.*

❸ bully VERB
to make someone do something by using force
EG *She used to bully me into doing my schoolwork.*
force EG *I cannot force you in this. You must decide.*
intimidate EG *attempts to intimidate*

people into voting for the governing party
pressurize EG *Do not be pressurized into making your decision immediately.*

WORD POWER

▷ **Synonyms**
coerce
dragoon

❶ bump VERB
to hit something
EG *He bumped his head on the wall.*
bang EG *I banged my shin on the edge of the table.*
collide EG *The car collided with a tree.*
hit EG *She hit the last barrier and fell.*
jolt EG *We hit the wall with a jolt.*
knock EG *He knocked on the door.*
strike EG *His head struck the windscreen.*

❷ bump NOUN
a dull noise
EG *He heard a bump outside.*
bang EG *I heard four or five loud bangs.*
knock EG *They heard a knock at the door.*
thud EG *She tripped and fell with a thud.*
thump EG *There was a loud thump against the house.*

❸ bump NOUN
a raised part of something
EG *a bump in the road*
bulge EG *My purse made a bulge in my pocket.*
hump EG *a camel's hump*
knob EG *a door with a brass knob*
lump EG *itchy red lumps on the skin*
swelling EG *a swelling on my foot*

WORD POWER

▷ **Synonyms**
contusion
node
protuberance

❶ bunch NOUN
a group of people
EG *The players were a great bunch.*
band EG *Bands of criminals have been roaming some neighbourhoods.*
crowd EG *All the old crowd have come out for this occasion.*
gaggle EG *A gaggle of journalists sit in a hotel foyer waiting impatiently.*
gang EG *Come on over - we've got lots of the old gang here.*
group EG *The trouble involved a small group of football supporters.*
lot EG *Future generations are going to think that we were a pretty boring lot.*
multitude EG *surrounded by a noisy multitude*

❷ bunch NOUN
several cut flowers held together
EG *He had left a huge bunch of flowers in her hotel room.*
bouquet EG *She laid a bouquet on his grave.*
posy EG *a posy of wild flowers*
spray EG *a small spray of freesias*

❸ bunch NOUN
a group of things
EG *George took out a bunch of keys and went to work on the lock.*
batch EG *She brought a large batch of newspaper cuttings.*
bundle EG *a bundle of sticks tied together with string*
cluster EG *a cluster of shops, cabins and motels*
heap EG *a heap of old boxes for the bonfire*
load EG *His people came up with a load of embarrassing stories.*
pile EG *I've got a pile of questions afterwards for you.*
set EG *Only she and Mr Cohen had complete sets of keys to the shop.*

❶ burden NOUN
a load that is carried
EG *My wet clothes were an added burden.*

load EG *a big load of hay*
weight EG *straining to lift heavy weights*

❷ burden NOUN
something that worries you
EG *the burden of looking after a sick parent*
anxiety EG *He expressed his anxieties to me.*
care EG *Forget all the cares of the day.*
strain EG *I find the travelling a strain.*
stress EG *the stress of exams*
trouble EG *The Sullivans have money troubles.*
worry EG *My son is a worry to me.*

WORD POWER

▷ **Synonyms**
affliction
millstone
trial

● **Related Words**
adjective : onerous

bureaucracy NOUN
complex rules and procedures
EG *Is there too much bureaucracy in government?*
administration EG *high administration costs*
officialdom EG *Officialdom is against us.*
red tape EG *Our application was delayed by red tape.*
regulations EG *absurd regulations about opening hours*

❶ burn VERB
to be on fire
EG *a fire burning in the fireplace*
be ablaze EG *The houses were ablaze.*
be on fire EG *The ship was on fire.*
blaze EG *The wreckage blazed.*
flame EG *We watched as the house flamed.*
flare EG *The match flared in the dark.*
flicker EG *The fire flickered and crackled.*

a b c d e f g h i j k l m n o p q r s t u v w x y z

A
B
C
D
E
F
G
H
I
J
K
L
M
N
O
P
Q
R
S
T
U
V
W
X
Y
Z

❷ burn VERB
to destroy with fire
EG *They burned the house down.*
char EG *charred bodies*
incinerate EG *Hospitals incinerate waste.*
scorch EG *The bonfire scorched the grass.*
shrivel EG *The papers shrivelled in the flames.*
singe EG *Her hair was singed and her coat burnt.*

❶ burst VERB
to split apart
EG *The balloon burst.*
break EG *He broke the box open.*
crack EG *A water pipe had cracked.*
explode EG *The glass exploded.*
puncture EG *The glass punctured the tyre.*
rupture EG *His appendix ruptured.*
split EG *The seam of my dress split.*

❷ burst VERB
to happen or appear suddenly
EG *to burst into flames*
barge EG *He barged into the room.*
break EG *Her face broke into a smile.*
erupt EG *Violence could erupt soon.*
rush EG *Water rushed out of the hole.*

❸ burst NOUN
a short period of something
EG *a burst of energy*
fit EG *a fit of rage*
outbreak EG *an outbreak of violence*
rush EG *a sudden rush of excitement*
spate EG *a spate of attacks on horses*
surge EG *a surge of emotion*
torrent EG *a torrent of words*

❶ business NOUN
the buying and selling of goods
EG *a career in business*
commerce EG *commerce between Europe and South America*
dealings EG *All dealings with the company were suspended.*
industry EG *the American car industry*

trade EG *French trade with the West Indies*
trading EG *trading between the two countries*
transaction EG *We settled the transaction over lunch.*

❷ business NOUN
an organization selling goods or services
EG *a family business*
company EG *the Ford Motor Company*
corporation EG *international corporations*
enterprise EG *small industrial enterprises*
establishment EG *shops and other commercial establishments*
firm EG *a firm of engineers*
organization EG *a well-run organization*

WORD POWER

▷ **Synonyms**
concern
venture

---

❸ business NOUN
any event or situation
EG *This business has upset me.*
affair EG *He handled the affair badly.*
issue EG *What is your view on this issue?*
matter EG *This is a matter for the police.*
problem EG *solutions to the drug problem*
question EG *the whole question of TV censorship*
subject EG *He raised the subject of money.*

❶ bustle VERB
to move hurriedly
EG *My mother bustled about the room.*
dash EG *We dashed about purposefully.*
fuss EG *Waiters were fussing round the table.*

hurry EG *Claire hurried along the road.*
rush EG *I'm rushing to finish the cooking.*
scurry EG *rats scurrying around*
scuttle EG *Crabs scuttle along the bank.*

❷ bustle NOUN
busy and noisy activity
EG *the bustle of modern life*
activity EG *a burst of activity in the building*
commotion EG *He heard a commotion outside.*
excitement EG *The news created great excitement.*
flurry EG *a flurry of activity*
fuss EG *He works without any fuss.*
hurry EG *the hurry and excitement of the city*

WORD POWER
▶ **Antonym**
peace

❶ busy ADJECTIVE
doing something
EG *What is it? I'm busy.*
active EG *He is active in local politics.*
employed EG *He was employed helping me.*
engaged EG *He was engaged in conversation.*
engrossed EG *She is engrossed in her work.*
occupied EG *He is occupied with the packing.*
working EG *I am working on a novel.*

WORD POWER
▶ **Antonym**
idle

❷ busy ADJECTIVE
full of activity
EG *a busy tourist resort*
active EG *an active, independent country*
full EG *a full life*

hectic EG *my hectic work schedule*
lively EG *a lively restaurant*
restless EG *a restless mind*

❸ busy VERB
to occupy or keep busy
EG *Kathryn busied herself in the kitchen.*
absorb EG *Her career absorbed her completely.*
employ EG *You'd better employed helping me.*
engage EG *He was engaged in a meeting when I called.*
immerse EG *She immersed herself in her book.*
occupy EG *Try to occupy yourself with something.*

❶ but CONJUNCTION
although
EG *Heat the cider until it is very hot but not boiling.*
although EG *He was in love with her, although he had not yet admitted it to himself.*
though EG *He's very attractive, though not exactly handsome.*
while EG *The first two services are free, while the third costs £35.*
yet EG *It is completely waterproof, yet light and comfortable.*

❷ but PREPOSITION
with the exception of
EG *The crew gave them nothing but bread to eat.*
except EG *I don't take any drugs except aspirin.*
except for EG *No-one has complained except for you.*
save EG *The people had no water at all save that brought up from bore holes.*
other than EG *This route is not recommended to anyone other than the most experienced cyclist.*

buy VERB
to obtain with money
EG *I'd like to buy him lunch.*

a
b
c
d
e
f
g
h
i
j
k
l
m
n
o
p
q
r
s
t
u
v
w
x
y
z

A
B
C
D
E
F
G
H
I
J
K
L
M
N
O
P
Q
R
S
T
U
V
W
X
Y
Z

acquire EG *I have acquired a new car.*
invest in EG *I invested in a house.*
obtain EG *She went to obtain a ticket.*
pay for EG *He let me pay for his drink.*
procure EG *attempts to procure more food*

purchase EG *He purchased a sandwich for lunch.*

WORD POWER

▶ **Antonym**
sell

Cc

calculate VERB
to work out a number or amount
EG *how to calculate the cost of setting up a business*
count EG *Shareholders are counting the cost of the slump.*
determine EG *calculations to determine the rate of tax*
reckon EG *an amount reckoned at 140 billion marks*
work out EG *Work out the distance of the journey.*

calculated ADJECTIVE
deliberately planned
EG *Everything they said was calculated to wound.*
aimed EG *The restructuring is aimed at reducing costs.*
designed EG *a scheme designed to help poorer families*
intended EG *the intended effect of the revised guidelines*
planned EG *a carefully planned campaign*

WORD POWER

▶ **Antonym**
unplanned

❶ call VERB
to give a name
EG *a man called Jeffrey*
→ see Word Study **call**

❷ call VERB
to telephone
EG *He called me at my office.*
→ see Word Study **call**

❸ call VERB
to say loudly
EG *I heard someone calling my name.*
→ see Word Study **call**

❹ call NOUN
an instance of someone shouting out
EG *a call for help*
cry EG *the cry of a seagull*

shout EG *I heard a distant shout.*
yell EG *He let out a yell.*

callous ADJECTIVE
not concerned about other people
EG *his callous disregard for human life*
cold EG *What a cold, unfeeling woman she was.*
heartless EG *It was a heartless thing to do.*
indifferent EG *indifferent to the suffering of others*
insensitive EG *insensitive remarks*

WORD POWER

▷ **Synonyms**
hard-bitten
hardhearted
unsympathetic

▶ **Antonym**
caring

❶ calm ADJECTIVE
not worried or excited
EG *Try to keep calm.*
collected EG *She was cool and collected during her interrogation.*
composed EG *a very composed, business-like woman*
cool EG *We have to keep a cool head in this situation.*
impassive EG *He remained impassive as his sentence was passed.*
relaxed EG *a relaxed manner*

WORD POWER

▷ **Synonyms**
imperturbable
unemotional
unruffled

▶ **Antonym**
worried

❷ calm ADJECTIVE
still because there is no wind
EG *Tuesday was a fine, clear and calm day.*

balmy EG *balmy summer evenings*
mild EG *a mild winter climate*
still EG *The air was still.*
tranquil EG *a tranquil lake*

WORD POWER

▶ **Antonym**
rough

---

❸ **calm** NOUN
the state of being peaceful
EG *He liked the calm of the evening.*
calmness EG *an aura of calmness*
peace EG *a wonderful feeling of peace*
peacefulness EG *the peacefulness of the gardens*
quiet EG *a quiet, relaxing holiday*
serenity EG *the peace and serenity of a tropical sunset*
stillness EG *the stillness of the summer night*

❹ **calm** VERB
to make less upset or excited
EG *We were trying to calm him.*
quieten EG *trying to quieten the restless horses*
relax EG *This music is supposed to relax you.*
soothe EG *I think a bath may soothe me.*

WORD POWER

▷ **Synonyms**
mollify
placate

---

campaign NOUN
actions planned to get a certain result
EG *a campaign to educate people*
crusade EG *the crusade for human rights*
movement EG *the human rights movement*
operation EG *a full-scale military operation*
push EG *an all-out push to promote the show*

---

❶ **cancel** VERB
to stop something from happening
EG *We're going to have to cancel our picnic.*
abandon EG *He had to abandon his holiday plans.*
call off EG *The union has called off the strike.*

❷ **cancel** VERB
to stop something from being valid
EG *They were forced to cancel their contract.*
annul EG *The marriage was annulled.*
quash EG *His jail sentence was quashed when new evidence came to light.*
repeal EG *The new law was repealed within the year.*
revoke EG *His licence was immediately revoked.*

WORD POWER

▷ **Synonyms**
abrogate
countermand
rescind

---

candid ADJECTIVE
honest and frank
EG *a candid interview*
blunt EG *She is blunt about his faults.*
frank EG *They had a frank discussion about the issue.*
honest EG *What is your honest opinion?*
open EG *He had always been open with her and she would know if he lied.*
truthful EG *We've all learnt to be fairly truthful about our personal lives.*
straightforward EG *I was impressed by his straightforward manner.*

candidate NOUN
a person being considered for a position
EG *a candidate for the presidency*
applicant EG *one of thirty applicants for the manager's post*
competitor EG *several competitors*

for the contract
contender EG *a strong contender for the chairmanship*

WORD POWER

▷ **Synonyms**
nominee
possibility
runner

---

capable ADJECTIVE
able to do something well
EG *a capable leader*
able EG *a very able businessman*
accomplished EG *an accomplished painter*
adept EG *an adept diplomat*
competent EG *a competent and careful driver*
efficient EG *efficient administration*
proficient EG *proficient with computers*
skilful EG *the country's most skilful politician*

WORD POWER

▶ **Antonym**
incompetent

---

❶ capacity NOUN
the maximum amount that something holds or produces
EG *the vehicle's fuel capacity*
dimensions EG *a car of compact dimensions*
room EG *There wasn't enough room in the baggage compartment for all the gear.*
size EG *My bedroom is half the size of yours.*
space EG *There is space in the back for two people.*
volume EG *a container with a volume of two litres*

❷ capacity NOUN
a person's power or ability to do something
EG *Our capacity for giving care, love and attention is limited.*

ability EG *The public never had faith in his ability to handle the job.*
capability EG *a country with the capability of launching a nuclear attack*
facility EG *Humans have lost the facility to use their sense of smell properly.*
gift EG *As a youth he discovered a gift for making people laugh.*
potential EG *the economic potentials of Eastern and Western Europe*
power EG *Human societies have the power to solve the problems confronting them.*

❶ capture VERB
to take prisoner
EG *He was captured by rebels.*
apprehend EG *Police have not yet apprehended the killer.*
arrest EG *Seven people were arrested.*
catch EG *The thief was caught and the money was returned.*
seize EG *seized by armed police*
take EG *An army unit took the town.*

WORD POWER

▶ **Antonym**
release

---

❷ capture NOUN
the act of capturing
EG *He evaded capture for eight years.*
arrest EG *Police made two arrests.*
seizure EG *the seizure of territory*
taking EG *the taking of hostages*
trapping EG *The trapping of these animals is illegal.*

car NOUN
a vehicle for carrying a few people
EG *I finally left the car at the garage.*
automobile AMERICAN; FORMAL EG *the Japanese automobile manufacturer, Nissan*
motor EG *Patricia's new motor*
vehicle EG *She managed to scramble out of the vehicle.*

① care VERB
to be concerned about something
EG *a company that cares about the environment*
be bothered EG *I am not bothered what others think about me.*
be concerned EG *We are concerned about the problem.*
be interested EG *He's not interested in what anyone else says.*
mind EG *I do not mind who wins.*

② care NOUN
something that causes you to worry
EG *without a care in the world*
anxiety EG *anxieties about money*
concern EG *Their main concern is unemployment.*
stress EG *the stresses of modern life*
trouble EG *She has had her share of troubles.*
woe EG *They blame the government for all their woes.*
worry EG *My biggest worry is how I will cope on my own.*

WORD POWER
▷ **Synonyms**
tribulation
vexation

③ care NOUN
close attention when doing something
EG *We took great care in choosing a location.*
attention EG *medical attention*
caution EG *Proceed with caution.*
pains EG *She takes great pains with her appearance.*

WORD POWER
▷ **Synonyms**
circumspection
forethought

① careful ADJECTIVE
acting with care
EG *Be careful what you say to him.*

cautious EG *a cautious approach*
prudent EG *prudent management*

WORD POWER
▷ **Synonyms**
chary
circumspect
punctilious

▶ **Antonym**
careless

② careful ADJECTIVE
complete and well done
EG *It needs careful planning.*
meticulous EG *meticulous attention to detail*
painstaking EG *a painstaking search*
precise EG *precise instructions*
thorough EG *a thorough examination*

WORD POWER
▶ **Antonym**
careless

① careless ADJECTIVE
not taking enough care
EG *careless driving*
irresponsible EG *an irresponsible attitude*
neglectful EG *neglectful parents*
sloppy INFORMAL EG *sloppy work*

WORD POWER
▷ **Synonyms**
cavalier
lackadaisical
slapdash
slipshod

▶ **Antonym**
careful

② careless ADJECTIVE
relaxed and unconcerned
EG *careless laughter*
casual EG *a casual remark*
nonchalant EG *a nonchalant*

attitude
offhand EG *his usual offhand way*

carry VERB
to hold and take something somewhere
EG *He was carrying a briefcase.*
bear EG *He arrived bearing gifts.*
convey FORMAL EG *The minibus conveyed us to the station.*
lug EG *lugging boxes of books around*
take EG *Don't forget to take your camera.*
transport EG *goods being transported abroad*

carry out VERB
to do and complete something
EG *the surgeon who carried out the operation*
accomplish EG *the desire to accomplish a task*
achieve EG *We have achieved our objective.*
fulfil EG *to fulfil a promise*
perform EG *people who have performed acts of bravery*

WORD POWER

▷ **Synonyms**
execute
implement

carve VERB
to make something by cutting
EG *He carves his figures from pine.*
chisel EG *the mason chiselling his stone*
cut EG *a figure cut from marble*
engrave EG *an engraved crystal goblet*
inscribe EG *the words inscribed on his monument*
sculpt EG *a sculpted clay figure*

WORD POWER

▷ **Synonyms**
hew
whittle

❶ case NOUN
a particular situation or example
EG *a case of mistaken identity*
example EG *an example of what can go wrong*
illustration EG *a clear illustration of this point*
instance EG *a serious instance of corruption*
occasion EG *the last occasion on which he appeared*
occurrence EG *a frequent occurrence*

❷ case NOUN
a container for holding something
EG *a spectacle case*
box EG *a chocolate box*
container EG *a huge plastic container*

WORD POWER

▷ **Synonyms**
holder
receptacle

❸ case NOUN
a trial or inquiry
EG *a libel case*
action EG *a civil action for damages*
lawsuit EG *the rising cost of defending a lawsuit*
proceedings EG *criminal proceedings against the former leader*
trial EG *Police lied at the trial.*

❶ casual ADJECTIVE
happening by chance
EG *a casual remark*
accidental EG *a verdict of accidental death*
chance EG *a chance meeting*
incidental EG *an incidental effect*

WORD POWER

▷ **Synonyms**
fortuitous
serendipitous
unintentional
unpremeditated

► **Antonym**
deliberate

2 casual ADJECTIVE
showing no concern or interest
EG *a casual look over his shoulder*
careless EG *careless remarks*
cursory EG *a cursory glance*
nonchalant EG *his nonchalant attitude to life*
offhand EG *a deceptively offhand style*
relaxed EG *a relaxed manner*

WORD POWER

▷ **Synonyms**
blasé
insouciant
lackadaisical
perfunctory

► **Antonym**
concerned

cat NOUN
a small animal kept as a pet
EG *sharing his flat with four cats*
feline EG *Even the most cuddly feline has claws.*
kitty EG *a kitty stuck up a tree*
moggy or **moggie** BRITISH AND NEW ZEALAND; SLANG EG *a grey, long-haired moggy*
pussy, puss, or **pussycat** INFORMAL EG *a fluffy little pussycat*

WORD POWER

● **Related Words**
adjective : feline
male : tom
female : tabby
young : kitten

1 catch VERB
to capture something
EG *another technique for catching criminals*
apprehend EG *the force necessary to apprehend a suspect*
arrest EG *Police arrested the*

gunman.
capture EG *Poachers had captured a gorilla.*
snare EG *He'd snared a rabbit.*
trap EG *Their aim was to trap drug-dealers.*

2 catch NOUN
a device that fastens something
EG *windows fitted with safety catches*
bolt EG *the sound of a bolt being slid open*
clasp EG *the clasp of her handbag*
clip EG *She took the clip out of her hair.*
latch EG *You left the latch off the gate.*

3 catch NOUN
a hidden difficulty
EG *The catch is that you have to fly via Paris.*
disadvantage EG *The disadvantage is that this plant needs frequent watering.*
drawback EG *The flat's only drawback was its size.*
snag EG *The snag is that you have to pay in advance.*

WORD POWER

▷ **Synonyms**
fly in the ointment
stumbling block

category NOUN
a set of things with something in common
EG *The items were organized into six different categories.*
class EG *dividing the stars into six classes of brightness*
classification EG *There are various classifications of genres or types of book.*
group EG *She is one of the most promising players in her age group.*
set EG *Pupils are divided into sets according to ability.*
sort EG *What sort of school did you go to?*

type EG *The majority of complaints received are of this type.*

1 cause NOUN
what makes something happen
EG *the most common cause of back pain*
origin EG *the origin of the present war*
root EG *We need to get to the root of the problem.*
source EG *the source of the leak*

2 cause NOUN
an aim supported by a group
EG *dedication to the cause of peace*
aim EG *political aims*
ideal EG *socialist ideals*
movement EG *the women's movement*

3 cause NOUN
the reason for something
EG *They gave us no cause to believe that.*
basis EG *There is no basis for this assumption.*
grounds EG *discrimination on the grounds of race or religion*
justification EG *There was no justification for what he was doing.*
motivation EG *the motivation for his actions*
motive EG *Police have ruled out robbery as a motive.*
reason EG *You have every reason to be upset.*

4 cause VERB
to make something happen
EG *This may cause delays.*
bring about EG *We must try to bring about a better world.*
create EG *The scheme may create even more confusion.*
generate EG *the excitement generated by this film*
produce EG *His comments produced a furious response.*

provoke EG *a move that has provoked a storm of protest*

WORD POWER
▷ **Synonyms**
effect
engender
give rise to
lead to
result in

1 caution NOUN
great care taken in order to avoid danger
EG *Drivers are urged to exercise extreme caution in icy weather.*
care EG *Scissors can be safe for young children if used with care.*
prudence EG *A lack of prudence may lead to problems.*

WORD POWER
▷ **Synonyms**
forethought
circumspection

2 caution VERB
to scold or warn someone against doing something
EG *The two men were cautioned but police say they will not be charged.*
reprimand EG *He was reprimanded by a teacher for talking in the corridor.*
tick off INFORMAL EG *Traffic police ticked off a pensioner for jumping a red light.*
warn EG *My mother warned me not to talk to strangers.*

cautious ADJECTIVE
acting very carefully to avoid danger
EG *a cautious approach*
careful EG *Be extremely careful when on holiday abroad.*
guarded EG *a guarded response*
tentative EG *a tentative approach*
wary EG *small firms remain wary of committing themselves to debt*

a b c d e f g h i j k l m n o p q r s t u v w x y z

A
B
C
D
E
F
G
H
I
J
K
L
M
N
O
P
Q
R
S
T
U
V
W
X
Y
Z

WORD POWER

▶ **Antonym**
daring

❶ cease VERB
to stop happening
EG *Almost miraculously, the noise ceased.*
be over EG *The captured planes will be kept until the war is over.*
come to an end EG *The strike came to an end.*
die away EG *The sound died away and silence reigned.*
end EG *The college year ends in March.*
finish EG *The teaching day finished at around four o'clock.*
stop EG *The rain had stopped.*

WORD POWER

▶ **Antonym**
begin

❷ cease VERB
to stop doing something
EG *A small number of firms have ceased trading.*
desist from EG *His wife never desisted from trying to change his mind.*
discontinue EG *Do not discontinue the treatment without consulting your doctor.*
finish EG *As soon as he'd finished eating, he excused himself.*
give up EG *smokers who give up before 30*
stop EG *Stop throwing those stones!*
suspend EG *The union suspended strike action this week.*

WORD POWER

▶ **Antonym**
start

celebrate VERB
to do something special to mark an event
EG *I was in a mood to celebrate.*
commemorate EG *The anniversary of the composer's death was commemorated with a concert.*
party EG *It's your birthday - let's party!*
rejoice EG *My family rejoiced at the happy outcome to events.*

WORD POWER

▶ **Antonym**
mourn

celebration NOUN
an event in honour of a special occasion
EG *his eightieth birthday celebrations*
festival EG *a religious festival*
festivity EG *the wedding festivities*
gala EG *the Olympics' opening gala*
party EG *a housewarming party*

WORD POWER

▷ **Synonyms**
merrymaking
revelry

celebrity NOUN
a famous person
EG *At the age of twelve, he was already a celebrity.*
big name EG *all the big names in rock and pop*
name EG *some of the most famous names in modelling and show business*
personality EG *a well-known radio and television personality*
star EG *Not all football stars are ill-behaved louts.*
superstar EG *a Hollywood superstar*
VIP EG *such VIPs as Prince Charles and the former US President*

❶ censure NOUN
strong disapproval
EG *a controversial policy which has attracted international censure*
blame EG *I'm the one who'll get the blame if things go wrong.*
condemnation EG *There was*

widespread condemnation of
Saturday's killings.
criticism EG *This policy had
repeatedly come under strong
criticism.*
disapproval EG *His action had been
greeted with almost universal
disapproval.*
reproach EG *Those in public life
should be beyond reproach.*

2 censure VERB
to criticize severely
EG *I would not presume to censure him
for his views.*
condemn EG *He condemned the
players for lack of ability and
application.*
criticize EG *The regime has been
harshly criticized for its human rights
violations.*
denounce EG *The letter called for civil
rights, but did not openly denounce
the regime.*
reproach EG *She had not even
reproached him for breaking his
promise.*

WORD POWER
▷ **Synonyms**
castigate

1 centre NOUN
the middle of something
EG *the centre of the room*
core EG *the earth's core*
focus EG *Her children are the main
focus of her life.*
heart EG *the heart of the problem*
hub EG *The kitchen is the hub of most
households.*
middle EG *in the middle of the back
row*

WORD POWER
▶ **Antonym**
edge

2 centre VERB
to have as the main subject

EG *All his thoughts were centred
around himself.*
concentrate EG *Scientists are
concentrating their efforts on finding
a cure.*
focus EG *Attention is likely to focus on
sales growth.*
revolve EG *Since childhood, her life
has revolved around tennis.*

1 ceremony NOUN
formal actions done for a special
occasion
EG *his recent coronation ceremony*
observance EG *a Memorial Day
observance*
pomp EG *His departure was
celebrated with suitable pomp.*
rite EG *a fertility rite*
ritual EG *a Summer Solstice ritual*
service EG *The President attended
the morning service.*

2 ceremony NOUN
formal and polite behaviour
EG *He hung up without ceremony.*
decorum EG *a responsibility to
behave with decorum*
etiquette EG *the rules of diplomatic
etiquette*
formality EG *his lack of stuffy
formality*
niceties EG *social niceties*
protocol EG *minor breaches of
protocol*

1 certain ADJECTIVE
definite or reliable
EG *One thing is certain - they respect
each other.*
definite EG *It's too soon to give a
definite answer.*
established EG *an established
medical fact*
guaranteed EG *Success is not
guaranteed.*
inevitable EG *If she wins her case, it is
inevitable that other people will sue
the company.*
known EG *It is not known when the*

a
b
c
d
e
f
g
h
i
j
k
l
m
n
o
p
q
r
s
t
u
v
w
x
y
z

bomb was planted.

sure EG *Sharpe's leg began to ache, a sure sign of rain.*

undeniable EG *undeniable proof of guilt*

WORD POWER

▶ **Antonym**
uncertain

❷ certain ADJECTIVE
having no doubt in your mind
EG *She's absolutely certain she's going to succeed.*

clear EG *It is important to be clear about what you are doing.*

confident EG *I am confident that everything will come out right.*

convinced EG *He was convinced that I was part of the problem.*

definite EG *Mary is very definite about this fact.*

sure EG *She was no longer sure how she felt about him.*

positive EG *I'm as positive as I can be about it.*

satisfied EG *People must be satisfied that the treatment is safe.*

WORD POWER

▶ **Antonym**
uncertain

certainly ADVERB
without any doubt
EG *I'll certainly do all I can to help.*

definitely EG *Something should definitely be done.*

undeniably EG *Bringing up a baby is undeniably hard work.*

undoubtedly EG *He is undoubtedly a great player.*

unquestionably EG *He is unquestionably a star.*

without doubt EG *The refugees are, without doubt, extremely vulnerable.*

❶ challenge NOUN
a suggestion to try something
EG *They issued a challenge to their*

rivals.

dare EG *He'd do almost anything for a dare.*

invite EG *We were invited to have a try at the limbo.*

❷ challenge VERB
to give someone a challenge
EG *He challenged his rival to a duel.*

dare EG *I dare you to ask him.*

defy EG *He looked at me as if he was defying me to argue.*

❸ challenge VERB
to question the truth or value of something
EG *challenging the authority of the state*

dispute EG *He disputed the charge.*

question EG *questioning the jury's verdict*

❶ champion NOUN
a person who wins a competition
EG *Kasparov became a world chess champion.*

hero EG *the goalscoring hero of the British hockey team*

title holder EG *He became the youngest world title holder at the age of 22.*

victor EG *the British Grand Prix victors*

winner EG *The winner was a horse called Baby Face.*

❷ champion NOUN
someone who supports a group, cause, or principle
EG *He received acclaim as a champion of the oppressed.*

advocate EG *He was a strong advocate of free trade.*

defender EG *a strong defender of human rights*

guardian EG *The party wants to be seen as a guardian of traditional values.*

protector EG *She sees him as a protector and provider.*

❸ champion VERB
to support a group, cause, or

principle
EG *He passionately championed the poor.*
defend EG *his courage in defending religious and civil rights*
fight for EG *Our Government should be fighting for an end to child poverty.*
promote EG *You don't have to sacrifice the environment to promote economic growth.*
stick up for INFORMAL EG *He has shown courage in sticking up for civil liberties.*
support EG *The vice president has always supported the people of New York.*
uphold EG *upholding the artist's right to creative freedom*

WORD POWER

▷ **Synonyms**
espouse

❶ chance NOUN
a possibility of something happening
EG *a good chance of success*
likelihood EG *the likelihood of infection*
odds EG *What are the odds of that happening?*
possibility EG *the possibility of pay cuts*
probability EG *a probability of victory*
prospect EG *There is little prospect of peace.*

❷ chance NOUN
an opportunity to do something
EG *He didn't give me a chance to explain.*
occasion EG *I had no occasion to speak to her that day.*
opening EG *an opening for finding a peaceful outcome to the conflict*
opportunity EG *an opportunity to go abroad to study*
time EG *There was no time to think.*

❸ chance NOUN
the way things happen without being planned
EG *events which were merely the result of chance*
accident EG *a strange accident of fate*
coincidence EG *It was no coincidence that she arrived just then.*
fortune EG *a change of fortune*
luck EG *His injury was just bad luck.*

WORD POWER

● **Related Words**
adjective : fortuitous

❶ change NOUN
an alteration in something
EG *a change in her attitude*
alteration EG *some alterations in your diet*
difference EG *a noticeable difference in his behaviour*
modification EG *Some minor modifications were required.*
transformation EG *the transformation of a wilderness into a garden*

WORD POWER

▷ **Synonyms**
metamorphosis
mutation
transition
transmutation

❷ change VERB
to make or become different
EG *Her views have changed since her husband's death.*
alter EG *There is no prospect of the decision being altered.*
convert EG *a plan to convert his spare room into an office*
moderate EG *They persuaded him to moderate his views.*
modify EG *He refused to modify his behaviour.*
reform EG *his plans to reform the*

a
b
c
d
e
f
g
h
i
j
k
l
m
n
o
p
q
r
s
t
u
v
w
x
y
z

economy
transform EG *The landscape has been transformed.*

WORD POWER

▷ **Synonyms**
metamorphose
mutate
transmute

❸ **change** VERB
to exchange one thing for another
EG *Can I change this sweater for one a size bigger?*
barter EG *bartering wheat for cotton and timber*
exchange EG *the chance to sell back or exchange goods*
interchange EG *Meat can be interchanged with pulses as a source of protein.*
replace EG *His smile was replaced by a frown.*
substitute EG *You can substitute honey for the sugar.*
swap EG *Let's swap places.*
trade EG *They traded land for goods and money.*

changeable ADJECTIVE
likely to change all the time
EG *changeable weather*
erratic EG *erratic driving*
fickle EG *Fashion is a fickle business.*
irregular EG *an irregular heartbeat*
unpredictable EG *unpredictable behaviour*
unstable EG *The political situation is unstable.*
variable EG *a variable rate of interest*
volatile EG *a volatile atmosphere*

WORD POWER

▷ **Synonyms**
mercurial
mutable
protean

▶ **Antonym**
constant

❶ **character** NOUN
the qualities of a person
EG *He has a dark side to his character.*
make-up EG *Determination has always been a part of his make-up.*
nature EG *a sunny nature*
personality EG *an outgoing personality*
temperament EG *his impulsive temperament*

WORD POWER

▷ **Synonyms**
disposition
quality
temper

❷ **character** NOUN
an honourable nature
EG *She showed real character in her attempt to win over the crowd.*
honour EG *He has acted with honour.*
integrity EG *a man of integrity*
strength EG *He had the strength to turn down the offer.*

❶ **characteristic** NOUN
a typical quality
EG *His chief characteristic is honesty.*
attribute EG *a normal attribute of human behaviour*
feature EG *a feature of the local culture*
property EG *This liquid has many unique properties.*
quality EG *leadership qualities*
trait EG *personality traits*

WORD POWER

▷ **Synonyms**
idiosyncrasy
peculiarity
quirk

❷ **characteristic** ADJECTIVE
typical of a person or thing
EG *He responded with characteristic generosity.*
distinctive EG *a distinctive voice*
distinguishing EG *no distinguishing*

marks
typical EG *his typical British modesty*

WORD POWER

▷ **Synonyms**
idiosyncratic
peculiar
singular
symptomatic

▶ **Antonym**
uncharacteristic

❶ **charge** VERB
to ask someone for money as a payment
EG *The majority of producers charged a fair price.*
ask (for) EG *The artist was asking £6,000 for each painting.*
bill EG *Are you going to bill me for this?*
levy EG *Taxes should not be levied without the authority of Parliament.*

❷ **charge** VERB
to rush forward, often to attack someone
EG *He charged into the room.*
dash EG *She dashed in from the garden.*
rush EG *A schoolgirl rushed into the burning flat to help an old man.*
stampede EG *The crowd stampeded.*
storm EG *He stormed into the shop, demanding to see the manager.*

❸ **charge** NOUN
the price you have to pay for something
EG *We can arrange this for a small charge.*
cost EG *Badges are available at a cost of £2.50.*
fee EG *Pay your solicitor's fees.*
payment EG *I'll do it in return for a small payment.*
price EG *We negotiated a price for the service.*

❶ **charm** NOUN
an attractive quality
EG *a man of great personal charm*
allure EG *the allure of Egypt*
appeal EG *confident of his appeal to women*
attraction EG *the attractions of living by the sea*
fascination EG *It is hard to explain the fascination of this place.*
magnetism EG *a man of enormous magnetism*

❷ **charm** VERB
to use charm to please someone
EG *He charmed his 2,000-strong audience.*
bewitch EG *bewitched by her beauty*
captivate EG *The crowd was captivated by her honesty.*
delight EG *a style of music that has delighted audiences*
entrance EG *entranced by her smile*

WORD POWER

▷ **Synonyms**
beguile
enchant
enrapture

❶ **chase** VERB
to try to catch someone or something
EG *She chased the thief for a hundred yards.*
hunt EG *He fled to Portugal after being hunted by police.*
pursue EG *She pursued the man who had snatched her bag.*

❷ **chase** VERB
to force to go somewhere
EG *Angry demonstrators chased him away.*
drive EG *The troops drove the rebels into the jungle.*
hound EG *He was hounded out of his job.*

A
B
C
D
E
F
G
H
I
J
K
L
M
N
O
P
Q
R
S
T
U
V
W
X
Y
Z

WORD POWER
▷ **Synonyms**
expel
put to flight

❶ chat NOUN
a friendly talk
EG *We sat around and had a chat.*
conversation EG *a telephone conversation*
gossip EG *Don't you enjoy a good gossip?*
natter INFORMAL EG *Let's get together for a natter some time.*
talk EG *We will have a talk about it later.*

❷ chat VERB
to talk in a friendly way
EG *He was chatting to his father.*
gossip EG *We gossiped into the night.*
natter INFORMAL EG *His mother would natter to anyone.*
talk EG *She's very easy to talk to.*

❶ cheap ADJECTIVE
costing very little
EG *Cheap flights are available.*
bargain EG *selling at bargain prices*
economical EG *These cars are very economical to run.*
inexpensive EG *an inexpensive wine*
reasonable EG *His fees were quite reasonable.*

WORD POWER
▷ **Synonyms**
cut-price
low-cost
low-priced

▶ **Antonym**
expensive

❷ cheap ADJECTIVE
inexpensive but of poor quality
EG *a suit made of some cheap material*
inferior EG *an inferior imitation*
second-rate EG *second-rate equipment*
tawdry EG *tawdry souvenirs*

cheat VERB
to get something from someone dishonestly
EG *the people he cheated out of their life savings*
con INFORMAL EG *He conned his way into a job.*
deceive EG *Investors were deceived by a scam.*
defraud EG *charges of conspiracy to defraud the government*
dupe EG *Stamp collectors were duped into buying fakes.*
fleece EG *He fleeced her out of thousands of pounds.*
rip off SLANG EG *ticket touts ripping off soccer fans*
swindle EG *two executives who swindled their employer*

WORD POWER
▷ **Synonyms**
bilk
hoodwink

❶ check VERB
to examine something
EG *Check all the details first.*
check out INFORMAL EG *Check out the financial figures.*
examine EG *He examined her passport and stamped it.*
inspect EG *the right to inspect company files*
test EG *The drug must be tested in clinical trials.*

WORD POWER
▷ **Synonyms**
inquire into
look over
scrutinize

❷ check VERB
to reduce or stop something
EG *a policy to check fast population growth*

control EG *a measure to control illegal mining*
curb EG *reforms which aim to curb spending*
halt EG *an attempt to halt the spread of the disease*
inhibit EG *factors which inhibit growth*
restrain EG *the need to restrain wage rises*
stop EG *measures to stop the trade in ivory*

❸ check NOUN
an examination
EG *a thorough check of the equipment*
examination EG *a medical examination*
inspection EG *a routine inspection of the premises*
test EG *a test for cancer*

cheek NOUN
speech or behaviour that is rude or disrespectful
EG *I'm amazed they had the cheek to ask in the first place.*
audacity EG *I was shocked at the audacity of the gangsters.*
gall EG *She had the gall to claim she had been victimized.*
impudence EG *My sister had the impudence to go out wearing my clothes.*
insolence EG *The pupil was excluded for insolence.*
nerve EG *He had the nerve to ask me to prove who I was.*
rudeness EG *Mother was cross at Tom's rudeness.*

WORD POWER

▷ **Synonyms**
temerity

cheeky ADJECTIVE
rude and disrespectful
EG *cheeky teenagers*
impertinent EG *an impertinent question*

impudent EG *his rude and impudent behaviour*
insolent EG *a defiant, almost insolent look*
rude EG *She was often rude to her mother.*

WORD POWER

▶ **Antonym**
polite

cheerful ADJECTIVE
in a happy mood
EG *She was very cheerful despite her illness.*
bright EG *"May I help you?" said a bright voice.*
buoyant EG *in a buoyant mood*
cheery EG *a cheery nature*
happy EG *a confident, happy child*
jaunty EG *a jaunty tune*
jolly EG *a jolly, easy-going man*
light-hearted EG *They were light-hearted and enjoyed life.*
merry EG *a burst of merry laughter*

WORD POWER

▶ **Antonym**
miserable

cheery ADJECTIVE
happy and cheerful
EG *He is loved by everyone for his cheery disposition.*
cheerful EG *They are both very cheerful in spite of their circumstances.*
chirpy EG *She sounded quite chirpy on the phone.*
good-humoured EG *Charles was brave and remarkably good-humoured.*
happy EG *Marina was a confident, happy child.*
jolly EG *She was a jolly, kind-hearted woman.*
upbeat EG *Neil's colleagues said he was in a joking, upbeat mood.*

A
B
C
D
E
F
G
H
I
J
K
L
M
N
O
P
Q
R
S
T
U
V
W
X
Y
Z

sunny EG *a nice lad with a sunny disposition*

WORD POWER

▷ **Synonyms**
jovial

▶ **Antonym**
gloomy

chew VERB
to break food up with the teeth
EG *Eat slowly and chew your food properly.*
crunch EG *She crunched the ice cube loudly.*
gnaw EG *He sat and gnawed at an apple.*
munch EG *Sheep were munching the leaves.*

WORD POWER

▷ **Synonyms**
champ
chomp
masticate

❶ chief NOUN
the leader of a group or organization
EG *the deputy chief of the territory's defence force*
boss EG *He cannot stand his boss.*
chieftain EG *the legendary British chieftain, King Arthur*
director EG *the financial director of the company*
governor EG *The incident was reported to the prison governor.*
head EG *heads of government from 100 countries*
leader EG *the leader of the Conservative Party*
manager EG *a retired bank manager*

❷ chief ADJECTIVE
most important
EG *The job went to one of his chief rivals.*
foremost EG *one of the world's foremost scholars of ancient Indian culture*
key EG *He is expected to be the key witness at the trial.*
main EG *one of the main tourist areas of Amsterdam*
prevailing EG *the prevailing attitude towards women in this society*
primary EG *His language difficulties were the primary cause of his other problems.*
prime EG *The police will see me as the prime suspect!*
principal EG *The principal reason for my change of mind is this.*

WORD POWER

▷ **Synonyms**
pre-eminent

child NOUN
a young person
EG *I lived in France as a child.*
ankle-biter AUSTRALIAN AND NEW ZEALAND; SLANG EG *I knew him when he was just an ankle-biter.*
baby EG *She took care of me when I was a baby.*
bairn SCOTTISH EG *a two-year-old bairn*
infant EG *young mums with infants in prams*
juvenile EG *a prison for juveniles*
kid INFORMAL EG *They've got three kids.*
minor EG *charged with selling cigarettes to minors*
offspring EG *parents choosing shoes for their offspring*
toddler EG *a toddler in a pushchair*
tot EG *The tot was too young to know what was happening.*
youngster EG *I was only a youngster in 1965.*

WORD POWER

▶ **Antonym**
adult

● **Related Words**
adjective : filial
prefix : paedo-

childish ADJECTIVE
immature and foolish
EG *I don't have time for this childish behaviour.*
immature EG *She is emotionally immature.*
infantile EG *infantile jokes*
juvenile EG *juvenile behaviour*
puerile EG *a puerile sense of humour*

WORD POWER

▶ **Antonym**
mature

china NOUN; SOUTH AFRICAN; INFORMAL
a friend
EG *How are you, my old china?*
buddy INFORMAL EG *We've been buddies since we were kids.*
chum INFORMAL EG *He went on holiday with his two best chums.*
crony OLD-FASHIONED EG *She is always surrounded by her cronies.*
friend EG *lifelong friends*
mate BRITISH; INFORMAL EG *Come on mate, things aren't that bad.*
pal INFORMAL EG *He'd never let a pal down.*

❶ **choice** NOUN
a range of things to choose from
EG *available in a choice of colours*
range EG *a range of sun-care products*
selection EG *an interesting selection of recipes*
variety EG *a variety of candidates from which to choose*

❷ **choice** NOUN
the power to choose
EG *They had little choice in the matter.*
alternative EG *He said he could not see any alternative.*
option EG *He was given the option of going to jail or paying a fine.*

say EG *We don't have a say in the company's decisions.*

choose VERB
to decide to have or do something
EG *a number of foods to choose from*
opt for EG *He opted for early retirement.*
pick EG *She was picked for the debating team.*
select EG *She paused to select another cookie from the box.*
take EG *She took the option he offered her.*

WORD POWER

▷ **Synonyms**
elect
fix on
settle on

chop VERB
to cut down or into pieces
EG *I heard him chopping wood in the yard.*
cut EG *Cut the vegetables up.*
fell EG *43,000 square miles of tropical forest are felled each year.*
hack EG *They hacked away at the undergrowth.*
lop EG *Somebody had lopped the heads off our tulips.*

WORD POWER

▷ **Synonyms**
cleave
hew

circulate VERB
to pass around
EG *He circulated rumours about everyone.*
distribute EG *distributing leaflets*
propagate EG *They propagated their political ideas.*
spread EG *spreading malicious gossip*

a
b
c
d
e
f
g
h
i
j
k
l
m
n
o
p
q
r
s
t
u
v
w
x
y
z

A B C D E F G H I J K L M N O P Q R S T U V W X Y Z

> *WORD POWER*
> ▷ **Synonyms**
> disseminate
> promulgate

city NOUN
a large town
EG *the city of London*
metropolis EG *a busy metropolis*
town EG *the oldest town in Europe*

> *WORD POWER*
> ▷ **Synonyms**
> conurbation
> municipality
> ● **Related Words**
> *adjective* : civic

civilized ADJECTIVE
having an advanced society
EG *a highly civilized country*
cultured EG *a mature and cultured nation*
enlightened EG *this enlightened century*

❶ **claim** VERB
to say something is the case
EG *He claims to have lived here all his life.*
allege EG *He is alleged to have killed a man.*
assert EG *The defendants continued to assert their innocence.*
hold EG *She holds that these measures are unnecessary.*
insist EG *They insisted that they had no money.*
maintain EG *I still maintain that I am not guilty.*
profess EG *She professed to hate her nickname.*

❷ **claim** NOUN
a statement that something is the case
EG *He rejected claims that he had taken bribes.*
allegation EG *allegations of theft*

assertion EG *his assertion that he did not plan to remarry*

> *WORD POWER*
> ▷ **Synonyms**
> pretension
> protestation

❶ **clash** VERB
to fight or argue with another person
EG *A group of 400 demonstrators clashed with police.*
battle EG *In one town thousands of people battled with police officers.*
fight EG *two rival gangs fighting in the streets*
quarrel EG *My brother quarrelled with my father.*
wrangle EG *Delegates wrangled over the future of the organization.*

❷ **clash** VERB
of two things: to be so different that they do not go together
EG *Don't make policy decisions which clash with company thinking.*
conflict EG *He held opinions which sometimes conflicted with my own.*
contradict EG *Cut-backs like these surely contradict the Government's commitment to education.*
differ EG *The two leaders differed on several issues.*
disagree EG *Our managers disagreed on several policy issues.*
go against EG *Changes are being made which go against my principles.*
jar EG *They had always been good together and their temperaments seldom jarred.*

❸ **clash** NOUN
a fight or argument
EG *a number of clashes between rival parties*
battle EG *a gun battle between police and drug traffickers*
conflict EG *attempts to prevent a conflict between workers and*

management

confrontation EG *This issue could lead to a military confrontation.*

fight EG *He had had a fight with Smith and bloodied his nose.*

struggle EG *a struggle between competing political factions*

skirmish INFORMAL EG *Border skirmishes between the two countries were common.*

squabble EG *There have been minor squabbles about phone bills.*

❶ clasp VERB
to hold something tightly
EG *Mary clasped the children to her desperately.*

clutch EG *She was clutching a photograph.*

embrace EG *People were crying for joy and embracing each other.*

grip EG *She gripped the rope.*

hold EG *He held the pistol in his right hand.*

hug EG *She hugged her legs tight to her chest.*

press EG *I pressed the child closer to my heart and prayed.*

squeeze EG *He longed to just scoop her up and squeeze her.*

❷ clasp NOUN
a fastening such as a hook or catch
EG *She undid the clasp of her hooded cloak.*

buckle EG *He wore a belt with a large brass buckle.*

catch EG *She fiddled with the catch of her bag.*

clip EG *She took the clip out of her hair.*

fastener EG *a product range which includes nails, woodscrews, and fasteners*

fastening EG *The sundress has a neat back zip fastening.*

❶ class NOUN
a group of a particular type
EG *a new class of vehicle*

category EG *different categories of taxpayer*

genre EG *films of the horror genre*

grade EG *the lowest grade of staff*

group EG *a plan to help people in this group*

kind EG *the biggest prize of its kind in the world*

set EG *The fashionable set all go to this club.*

sort EG *several articles of this sort*

type EG *various types of vegetable*

❷ class VERB
to regard as being in a particular group
EG *They are officially classed as visitors.*

categorize EG *His films are hard to categorize.*

classify EG *Carrots are also classified as a fruit.*

designate EG *The house is designated as a national monument.*

grade EG *This ski-run is graded as easy.*

rank EG *She is ranked in the world's top 50 players.*

rate EG *He rates the film highly.*

classify VERB
to arrange similar things in groups
EG *We can classify the differences into three groups.*

arrange EG *Arrange the books in neat piles.*

categorize EG *This film is hard to categorize.*

grade EG *musical pieces graded according to difficulty*

rank EG *He was ranked among Britain's best-known millionaires.*

sort EG *sorting the material into folders*

WORD POWER

▷ **Synonyms**
pigeonhole
systematize
tabulate

---

a b c d e f g h i j k l m n o p q r s t u v w x y z

A
B
C
D
E
F
G
H
I
J
K
L
M
N
O
P
Q
R
S
T
U
V
W
X
Y
Z

❶ clean ADJECTIVE
free from dirt or marks
EG *clean shoes*
immaculate EG *immaculate white flannels*
impeccable EG *dressed in an impeccable trouser suit*
laundered EG *freshly laundered shirts*
spotless EG *The kitchen was spotless.*
washed EG *newly washed hair*

WORD POWER

▶ **Antonym**
dirty

❷ clean ADJECTIVE
free from germs or infection
EG *a lack of clean water and sanitation*
antiseptic EG *an antiseptic hospital room*
hygienic EG *a hygienic kitchen*
purified EG *Only purified water is used.*
sterilized EG *sterilized milk*
uncontaminated
eg *uncontaminated air*
unpolluted EG *unpolluted beaches*

WORD POWER

▶ **Antonym**
contaminated

❸ clean VERB
to remove dirt from
EG *She cleaned the house from top to bottom.*
cleanse EG *a lotion to cleanse the skin*
dust EG *I vacuumed, dusted and polished the living room.*
scour EG *He scoured the sink.*
scrub EG *I started to scrub off the dirt.*
sponge EG *Sponge your face and body.*
swab EG *an old man swabbing the floor*
wash EG *He got a job washing dishes in a restaurant.*

wipe EG *He wiped the sweat from his face.*

WORD POWER

▶ **Antonym**
soil

❶ clear ADJECTIVE
easy to see or understand
EG *He made it clear he did not want to talk.*
apparent EG *There is no apparent reason for the crime.*
blatant EG *a blatant piece of cheating*
conspicuous EG *one conspicuous difference*
definite EG *a definite advantage*
evident EG *He ate with evident enjoyment.*
explicit EG *He was very explicit about his intentions.*
obvious EG *There are obvious dangers.*
plain EG *The results are plain to see.*

WORD POWER

▷ **Synonyms**
incontrovertible
manifest
palpable
patent
unequivocal

❷ clear ADJECTIVE
easy to see through
EG *a clear liquid*
crystalline EG *crystalline green waters*
glassy EG *The water was a deep glassy blue.*
translucent EG *translucent stones*
transparent EG *transparent glass walls*

WORD POWER

▷ **Synonyms**
limpid
pellucid

see-through

▶ **Antonym**
cloudy

3 clear VERB
to prove someone is not guilty
EG *She was cleared of murder.*
absolve EG *He was absolved of all charges.*
acquit EG *acquitted of disorderly conduct*

WORD POWER

▶ **Antonym**
convict

clever ADJECTIVE
very intelligent
EG *My sister was always a lot cleverer than I was.*
brainy INFORMAL EG *I don't consider myself to be especially brainy.*
bright EG *an exceptionally bright child*
intelligent EG *a lively and intelligent woman*
shrewd EG *a shrewd businessman*
smart EG *a very smart move*

WORD POWER

▷ **Synonyms**
astute
quick-witted
sagacious

▶ **Antonym**
stupid

climb VERB
to move upwards over something
EG *Climbing the first hill took half an hour.*
ascend EG *He ascended the ladder into the loft.*
clamber EG *They clambered up the stone walls.*
mount EG *He mounted the steps.*
scale EG *the first British woman to scale Everest*

1 close VERB
to shut something
EG *Close the gate behind you.*
secure EG *The shed was secured by a padlock.*
shut EG *Someone had forgotten to shut the door.*

WORD POWER

▶ **Antonym**
open

2 close VERB
to block so that nothing can pass
EG *All the roads out are closed.*
bar EG *Protesters barred the way to his car.*
block EG *The road was blocked by debris.*
obstruct EG *buskers obstructing the pavement*
seal EG *Soldiers had sealed the border.*

3 close ADJECTIVE
near to something
EG *a restaurant close to their home*
→ see Word Study **close**

WORD POWER

▶ **Antonym**
distant

4 close ADJECTIVE
friendly and loving
EG *We became close friends.*
→ see Word Study **close**

WORD POWER

▶ **Antonym**
distant

cloth NOUN
woven or knitted fabric
EG *a piece of red cloth*
fabric EG *waterproof fabric*
material EG *This material shrinks badly.*
textiles EG *a trader in clothes and textiles*

a
b
c
d
e
f
g
h
i
j
k
l
m
n
o
p
q
r
s
t
u
v
w
x
y
z

clothes PLURAL NOUN
the things people wear
EG *She spends all her money on clothes.*
attire EG *formal attire*
clothing EG *men's clothing*
costume EG *national costume*
dress EG *traditional dress*
garments EG *winter garments*
gear INFORMAL EG *trendy gear*
outfit EG *a stunning scarlet outfit*
wardrobe EG *next summer's wardrobe*
wear EG *evening wear*

WORD POWER

▷ **Synonyms**
apparel
garb
raiment

❶ **cloud** NOUN
a mass of vapour or smoke
EG *The sky was dark with clouds.*
billow EG *Smoke billowed from the engine.*
fog EG *a fog of cigar smoke*
haze EG *a haze of exhaust fumes*
mist EG *The valley was wrapped in thick mist.*
vapour EG *warm vapour rising from the ground*

❷ **cloud** VERB
to make something confusing
EG *Anger has clouded his judgement.*
confuse EG *You're just confusing the matter by bringing politics into it.*
distort EG *a distorted memory*
muddle EG *The question muddles up two separate issues.*

❶ **cloudy** ADJECTIVE
full of clouds
EG *a cloudy sky*
dull EG *It's always dull and wet here.*
gloomy EG *gloomy weather*
leaden EG *leaden skies*

overcast EG *a damp, overcast morning*

WORD POWER

▶ **Antonym**
clear

❷ **cloudy** ADJECTIVE
difficult to see through
EG *a glass of cloudy liquid*
muddy EG *a muddy duck pond*
murky EG *murky waters*
opaque EG *an opaque glass jar*

WORD POWER

▶ **Antonym**
clear

❶ **club** NOUN
an organization for people with a special interest
EG *a swimming club*
association EG *the Women's Tennis Association*
circle EG *a local painting circle*
group EG *an environmental group*
guild EG *the Screen Writers' Guild*
society EG *a historical society*
union EG *the International Astronomical Union*

❷ **club** NOUN
a heavy stick
EG *armed with knives and clubs*
bat EG *a baseball bat*
stick EG *a crowd carrying sticks and stones*
truncheon EG *a policeman's truncheon*

❸ **club** VERB
to hit with a heavy object
EG *Two thugs clubbed him with baseball bats.*
bash EG *They bashed his head with a spade.*
batter EG *battered to death*
beat EG *beaten with rifle butts*
bludgeon EG *bludgeoning his wife with a hammer*

clumsiness NOUN
awkwardness of movement
EG *The accident was entirely the result of his own clumsiness.*
awkwardness EG *They moved with the awkwardness of mechanical dolls.*
ungainliness EG *his physical ungainliness*

clumsy ADJECTIVE
moving awkwardly
EG *He is big and clumsy in his movements.*
awkward EG *an awkward gesture*
gauche EG *He makes me feel stupid and gauche.*
lumbering EG *a big, lumbering man*
uncoordinated EG *an uncoordinated dancer*
ungainly EG *As a youth he was lanky and ungainly.*

> *WORD POWER*
>
> ▷ **Synonyms**
> accident-prone
> bumbling
> gawky
> maladroit
>
> ▶ **Antonym**
> graceful

coast NOUN
the land next to the sea
EG *a holiday by the coast*
beach EG *a beautiful sandy beach*
border EG *the border of the Black Sea*
coastline EG *the stunning Caribbean coastline*
seaside EG *a day at the seaside*
shore EG *a bleak and rocky shore*
strand EG *boats fishing from the strand*

coat NOUN
an animal's fur or hair
EG *She gave the dog's coat a brush.*
fleece EG *a blanket of lamb's fleece*
fur EG *a kitten with black fur*
hair EG *He's allergic to cat hair.*
hide EG *rhino hide*

pelt EG *a wolf pelt*
skin EG *convicted of attempting to sell the skin of a Siberian tiger*
wool EG *Lanolin comes from sheep's wool.*

coating NOUN
a layer of something
EG *a thin coating of ice*
coat EG *a coat of paint*
covering EG *a covering of dust*
layer EG *a layer of dead leaves*

coax VERB
to persuade gently
EG *We coaxed her into coming with us.*
cajole EG *Her sister cajoled her into playing.*
persuade EG *My husband persuaded me to come.*
talk into EG *They've talked him into getting a new car.*

> *WORD POWER*
>
> ▷ **Synonyms**
> inveigle
> prevail upon
> wheedle

❶ cocky ADJECTIVE
cheeky or too self-confident
EG *He was a bit cocky because he was winning all the time.*
arrogant EG *an air of arrogant indifference*
brash EG *On stage she seems hard and brash.*
conceited EG *I thought him conceited.*
overconfident EG *She couldn't cope with this new generation of noisy, overconfident teenage girls.*

> *WORD POWER*
>
> ▷ **Synonyms**
> swaggering

❷ cocky NOUN; AUSTRALIAN AND NEW ZEALAND
a farmer, especially one whose farm

a
b
c
d
e
f
g
h
i
j
k
l
m
n
o
p
q
r
s
t
u
v
w
x
y
z

A
B
C
D
E
F
G
H
I
J
K
L
M
N
O
P
Q
R
S
T
U
V
W
X
Y
Z

is small
EG *He got some work with the cane cockies on Maroochy River.*
crofter SCOTTISH EG *the financial plight of crofters in the islands*
farmer EG *He was a simple farmer scratching a living from the soil.*

coil VERB
to wind in loops
EG *a coiled spring*
curl EG *dark, curling hair*
loop EG *A rope was looped between his hands.*
spiral EG *vines spiralling up towards the roof*
twine EG *This lily produces twining stems.*
twist EG *She twisted her hair into a bun.*
wind EG *a rope wound round her waist*

❶ cold ADJECTIVE
having a low temperature
EG *the coldest winter for ten years*
arctic EG *arctic conditions*
biting EG *a biting wind*
bitter EG *driven inside by the bitter cold*
bleak EG *The weather can be bleak on the coast.*
chilly EG *It's chilly for June.*
freezing EG *This house is freezing.*
icy EG *the icy north wind*
raw EG *a raw December morning*
wintry EG *wintry showers*

WORD POWER

▶ **Antonym**
hot

❷ cold ADJECTIVE
not showing affection
EG *a cold, unfeeling woman*
aloof EG *He seemed aloof and detached.*
distant EG *She was polite but distant.*
frigid EG *a frigid smile*
lukewarm EG *a lukewarm response*

reserved EG *emotionally reserved*
stony EG *He gave me a stony look.*

WORD POWER

▷ **Synonyms**
standoffish
undemonstrative

▶ **Antonym**
warm

❶ collapse VERB
to fall down
EG *The whole building is about to collapse.*
fall down EG *The ceiling fell down.*
give way EG *The bridge gave way beneath him.*

❷ collapse VERB
to fail
EG *50,000 small businesses collapsed last year.*
fail EG *His hotel business has failed.*
fold EG *We were laid off when the company folded.*
founder EG *a foundering radio station*

❸ collapse NOUN
the failure of something
EG *the collapse of his marriage*
downfall EG *the downfall of the government*
failure EG *the failure of his business empire*

colleague NOUN
a person someone works with
EG *I'll have to consult my colleagues.*
associate EG *business associates*
fellow worker EG *She started going out with a fellow worker.*
partner EG *her business partner*
workmate EG *the nickname his workmates gave him*

collect VERB
to gather together
EG *collecting signatures for a petition*
accumulate EG *Most children enjoy accumulating knowledge.*

assemble EG *trying to assemble a team*
gather EG *gathering information*
raise EG *They've raised over £100 for charity.*

WORD POWER

▷ **Synonyms**
aggregate
amass

▶ **Antonym**
scatter
---

collection NOUN
a group of things collected together
EG *a collection of paintings*
assortment EG *an assortment of pets*
group EG *a group of songs*
store EG *a vast store of knowledge*

colloquial ADJECTIVE
used in conversation
EG *a colloquial expression*
conversational EG *a conversational style*
everyday EG *He used plain, everyday English.*
informal EG *an informal expression*

WORD POWER

▷ **Synonyms**
demotic
idiomatic
vernacular
---

❶ **colony** NOUN
a country controlled by another country
EG *an American colony*
dependency EG *the tiny British dependency of Montserrat*
dominion EG *The Republic is a dominion of Brazil.*
territory EG *territories under Israeli control*

❷ **colony** NOUN
a group of settlers in a place
EG *a colony of Scots*

community EG *the Sikh community in Britain*
outpost EG *a remote outpost*
settlement EG *a Muslim settlement*

colossal ADJECTIVE
very large indeed
EG *a colossal statue*
enormous EG *The main bedroom is enormous.*
gigantic EG *a gigantic task*
huge EG *They are making huge profits.*
immense EG *an immense cloud of smoke*
mammoth EG *This mammoth undertaking was completed in 18 months.*
massive EG *a massive steam boat*
vast EG *farmers who own vast stretches of land*

WORD POWER

▶ **Antonym**
tiny
---

❶ **colour** NOUN
a shade or hue
EG *Her favourite colour is blue.*
hue EG *delicate pastel hues*
pigmentation EG *skin pigmentation*
shade EG *walls painted in two shades of green*
tint EG *a distinct orange tint*

❷ **colour** NOUN
a substance used to give colour
EG *food colour*
dye EG *hair dye*
paint EG *a pot of red paint*
pigment EG *a layer of blue pigment*

❸ **colour** VERB
to give something a colour
EG *Many women colour their hair.*
dye EG *Only dye clean garments.*
paint EG *She paints her toenails red.*
stain EG *Some foods can stain the teeth.*
tint EG *tinted glass*

a
b
c
d
e
f
g
h
i
j
k
l
m
n
o
p
q
r
s
t
u
v
w
x
y
z

A
B
C
D
E
F
G
H
I
J
K
L
M
N
O
P
Q
R
S
T
U
V
W
X
Y
Z

❹ colour VERB
to affect the way you think
EG *Her upbringing has coloured her opinion of marriage.*
bias EG *a biased opinion*
distort EG *The shock of the accident distorted my judgement.*
prejudice EG *Criticism will prejudice the Government's decision.*
slant EG *deliberately slanted news coverage*

❶ colourful ADJECTIVE
full of colour
EG *colourful clothes*
bright EG *a bright green dress*
brilliant EG *The garden has burst into brilliant flower.*
intense EG *an intense shade of blue*
jazzy INFORMAL EG *a jazzy tie*
rich EG *a rich blue glass bowl*
vibrant EG *vibrant orange shades*
vivid EG *vivid hues*

WORD POWER

▷ **Synonyms**
kaleidoscopic
multicoloured
psychedelic

▶ **Antonym**
dull

❷ colourful ADJECTIVE
interesting or exciting
EG *a colourful character*
graphic EG *a graphic account of his career*
interesting EG *He has had an interesting life.*
lively EG *a lively imagination*
rich EG *the rich history of the island*
vivid EG *a vivid description*

WORD POWER

▶ **Antonym**
dull

combination NOUN
a mixture of things

EG *a combination of charm and skill*
amalgamation EG *an amalgamation of two organizations*
blend EG *a blend of wine and spring water*
mix EG *a mix of fantasy and reality*
mixture EG *a mixture of horror, envy and awe*

WORD POWER

▷ **Synonyms**
amalgam
coalescence
composite
meld

combine VERB
to join or mix together
EG *trying to combine motherhood with work*
amalgamate EG *a plan to amalgamate the two parties*
blend EG *The band blends jazz and folk music.*
fuse EG *a performer who fuses magic and dance*
integrate EG *integrating various styles of art*
merge EG *The two countries have merged into one.*
mix EG *mixing business with pleasure*
unite EG *people uniting to fight racism*

WORD POWER

▷ **Synonyms**
meld
synthesize

▶ **Antonym**
separate

❶ come VERB
to move or arrive somewhere
EG *Two men came into the room.*
appear EG *He appeared at about 9 o'clock.*
arrive EG *My brother has just arrived.*
enter EG *The class fell silent as the*

teacher entered.
materialize EG *The car just materialized from nowhere.*
show up INFORMAL EG *He showed up over an hour late.*
turn up INFORMAL EG *I'll call you when she turns up.*

❷ **come** VERB
to happen or take place
EG *Christmas only comes once a year.*
happen EG *Nothing ever happens on a Sunday.*
occur EG *How did the accident occur?*
take place EG *The meeting never took place.*

❶ **comfort** NOUN
a state of ease
EG *He settled back in comfort.*
ease EG *a life of ease*
luxury EG *brought up in an atmosphere of luxury*
wellbeing EG *a wonderful sense of wellbeing*

❷ **comfort** NOUN
relief from worry or unhappiness
EG *Her words gave him some comfort.*
consolation EG *He knew he was right, but it was no consolation.*
help EG *Just talking to you has been a great help.*
relief EG *temporary relief from the pain*
satisfaction EG *At least I have the satisfaction of knowing I tried.*
support EG *His family were a great support to him.*

❸ **comfort** VERB
to give someone comfort
EG *trying to comfort the screaming child*
cheer EG *The thought did nothing to cheer him.*
console EG *"Never mind," he consoled me.*
reassure EG *He did his best to reassure her.*

soothe EG *She took him in his arms and soothed him.*

❶ **comfortable** ADJECTIVE
physically relaxing
EG *a comfortable chair*
cosy EG *a cosy living room*
easy EG *You've had an easy time of it.*
homely EG *a homely atmosphere*
relaxing EG *a relaxing holiday*
restful EG *a restful scene*

WORD POWER

▶ **Antonym**
uncomfortable

❷ **comfortable** ADJECTIVE
feeling at ease
EG *I don't feel comfortable around him.*
at ease EG *He is not at ease in female company.*
at home EG *We soon felt quite at home.*
contented EG *a contented life*
happy EG *I'm not very happy with that idea.*
relaxed EG *a relaxed attitude*

WORD POWER

▶ **Antonym**
uneasy

❶ **command** VERB
to order someone to do something
EG *She commanded me to lie down.*
bid EG *The soldiers bade us turn and go back.*
demand EG *They demanded that he leave.*
direct EG *His doctor has directed him to rest.*
order EG *He ordered his men to cease fire.*

WORD POWER

▷ **Synonyms**
charge
enjoin

a
c
d
e
f
g
h
i
j
k
l
m
n
o
p
q
r
s
t
u
v
w
x
y
z

A B C D E F G H I J K L M N O P Q R S T U V W X Y Z

❷ command VERB
to be in charge of
EG *the general who commanded the UN troops*
control EG *He now controls the whole company.*
head EG *Who heads the firm?*
lead EG *He led the country between 1949 and 1984.*
manage EG *I manage a small team of workers.*
supervise EG *He supervised more than 400 volunteers.*

❸ command NOUN
an order to do something
EG *The execution was carried out at his command.*
bidding EG *They refused to leave at his bidding.*
decree EG *a presidential decree*
directive EG *a government directive*
injunction EG *He left her with the injunction to go to sleep.*
instruction EG *They were just following instructions.*
order EG *I don't take orders from you.*

WORD POWER
▷ **Synonyms**
behest
edict
fiat

❹ command NOUN
knowledge and ability
EG *a good command of English*
grasp EG *a good grasp of foreign languages*
knowledge EG *He has no knowledge of law.*
mastery EG *a mastery of grammar*

commemorate VERB
to do something in memory of
EG *concerts to commemorate the anniversary of his death*
celebrate EG *celebrating their golden wedding*

honour EG *celebrations to honour his memory*

WORD POWER
▷ **Synonyms**
memorialize
pay tribute to

❶ comment VERB
to make a remark
EG *He refused to comment on the rumours.*
mention EG *I mentioned that I didn't like jazz.*
note EG *He noted that some issues remained to be settled.*
observe EG *"You're very pale," he observed.*
point out EG *I should point out that these figures are approximate.*
remark EG *Everyone had remarked on her new hairstyle.*
say EG *"Well done," he said.*

WORD POWER
▷ **Synonyms**
interpose
opine

❷ comment NOUN
something you say
EG *sarcastic comments*
observation EG *a few general observations*
remark EG *snide remarks*
statement EG *That statement puzzled me.*

commit VERB
to do something
EG *A crime has been committed.*
carry out EG *attacks carried out by terrorists*
do EG *They have done a lot of damage.*
perform EG *people who have performed acts of bravery*
perpetrate EG *A fraud has been perpetrated.*

❶ common ADJECTIVE
of many people
EG *a common complaint*
general EG *the general opinion*
popular EG *a popular belief*
prevailing EG *the prevailing atmosphere*
prevalent EG *Smoking is becoming more prevalent among girls.*
universal EG *The desire to look attractive is universal.*
widespread EG *widespread support*

WORD POWER

▶ **Antonym**
rare

❷ common ADJECTIVE
not special
EG *the common man*
average EG *the average teenager*
commonplace EG *a commonplace observation*
everyday EG *your everyday routine*
ordinary EG *an ordinary day*
plain EG *My parents were just plain ordinary folks.*
standard EG *standard practice*
usual EG *In a usual week I watch about 15 hours of television.*

WORD POWER

▷ **Synonyms**
run-of-the-mill
workaday

▶ **Antonym**
special

❸ common ADJECTIVE
having bad taste or manners
EG *a common, rude woman*
coarse EG *coarse humour*
rude EG *It's rude to stare.*
vulgar EG *vulgar remarks*

WORD POWER

▶ **Antonym**
refined

common sense NOUN
the ability to make good judgments
EG *Use your common sense.*
good sense EG *He had the good sense to call me at once.*
judgment EG *I respect your judgment.*
level-headedness EG *He prides himself on his level-headedness.*
prudence EG *His lack of prudence led to financial problems.*
wit EG *They don't have the wit to realize what's happening.*

❶ communicate VERB
to be in touch with someone
EG *We communicate mainly by email.*
be in contact EG *I'll be in contact with him next week.*
be in touch EG *He hasn't been in touch with me yet.*
correspond EG *We correspond regularly.*

❷ communicate VERB
to pass on information
EG *The results will be communicated by post.*
convey EG *They have conveyed their views to the government.*
impart EG *the ability to impart knowledge*
inform EG *Will you inform me of any changes?*
pass on EG *I'll pass on your good wishes.*
spread EG *She has spread the news to everyone.*
transmit EG *He transmitted his enjoyment to the audience.*

WORD POWER

▷ **Synonyms**
disseminate
make known

companion NOUN
someone you travel with or spend time with
EG *He has been her constant companion for the last six years.*

a b c d e f g h i j k l m n o p q r s t u v w x y z

A
B
C
D
E
F
G
H
I
J
K
L
M
N
O
P
Q
R
S
T
U
V
W
X
Y
Z

comrade EG *Unlike so many of his comrades he survived the war.*
crony OLD-FASHIONED EG *a round of golf with his business cronies*
friend EG *Sara's old friend, Charles*
mate EG *A mate of mine used to play soccer for Liverpool.*
pal INFORMAL EG *We've been pals for years.*
partner EG *a partner in crime*

❶ company NOUN
a business
EG *a publishing company*
business EG *a family business*
corporation EG *multi-national corporations*
establishment EG *a commercial establishment*
firm EG *a firm of engineers*
house EG *the world's top fashion houses*

❷ company NOUN
a group of people
EG *the Royal Shakespeare Company*
assembly EG *an assembly of citizens*
band EG *bands of rebels*
circle EG *a large circle of friends*
community EG *a community of believers*
crowd EG *I don't go around with that crowd.*
ensemble EG *an ensemble of young musicians*
group EG *an environmental group*
party EG *a party of sightseers*
troupe EG *a troupe of actors*

WORD POWER

▷ **Synonyms**
concourse
coterie
---

❸ company NOUN
the act of spending time with someone
EG *I could do with some company.*
companionship EG *He keeps a dog for companionship.*

presence EG *Your presence is not welcome here.*

compare VERB
to look at things for similarities or differences
EG *Compare these two illustrations.*
contrast EG *In this section we contrast four possible approaches.*
juxtapose EG *art juxtaposed with reality*
weigh EG *She weighed her options.*

❶ compartment NOUN
a section of a railway carriage
EG *We shared our compartment with a group of businessmen.*
carriage EG *Our carriage was full of drunken football fans.*

❷ compartment NOUN
one of the separate parts of an object
EG *the freezer compartment of the fridge*
bay EG *the cargo bays of the aircraft*
chamber EG *the chambers of the heart*
division EG *Each was further split into several divisions.*
section EG *a toolbox with sections for various items*

compassionate ADJECTIVE
feeling or showing sympathy and pity for others
EG *My father was a deeply compassionate man.*
caring EG *He is a lovely boy, very gentle and caring.*
humane EG *She began to campaign for humane treatment of prisoners and their families.*
kind EG *I must thank you for being so kind to me.*
kind-hearted EG *He was a warm, generous and kind-hearted man.*
merciful EG *a merciful God*
sympathetic EG *She was very sympathetic to their problems.*

tender EG *Her voice was tender, full of pity.*

WORD POWER

▷ **Synonyms**
humanitarian

---

compatible ADJECTIVE
going together
EG *Lifelong partners should be compatible.*
congenial EG *congenial company*
consistent EG *injuries consistent with a car crash*
harmonious EG *a harmonious partnership*
in keeping EG *This behaviour was in keeping with his character.*

WORD POWER

▷ **Synonyms**
accordant
congruent
congruous
consonant

▶ **Antonym**
incompatible

---

❶ compensate VERB
to repay someone for loss or damage
EG *You will be properly compensated for your loss.*
atone EG *He felt he had atoned for what he had done.*
refund EG *The company will refund the full cost.*
repay EG *collateral with which to repay swindled investors*
reward EG *Their patience was finally rewarded.*

WORD POWER

▷ **Synonyms**
make amends
make restitution
recompense
reimburse
remunerate

---

❷ compensate VERB
to cancel out
EG *His lack of skill was compensated for by his enthusiasm.*
balance EG *The pros balance the cons.*
cancel out EG *The two influences cancel each other out.*
counteract EG *pills to counteract high blood pressure*
make up for EG *I'll make up for what I've done.*
offset EG *The loss is being offset by a new tax.*

WORD POWER

▷ **Synonyms**
counterbalance
countervail
redress

---

compensation NOUN
something that makes up for loss or damage
EG *compensation for his injuries*
amends EG *an attempt to make amends for his crime*
atonement EG *an act of atonement for our sins*
damages EG *damages for libel*
payment EG *a redundancy payment*

WORD POWER

▷ **Synonyms**
recompense
reimbursement
remuneration
reparation
restitution

---

compete VERB
to try to win
EG *companies competing for business*
contend EG *two groups contending for power*
contest EG *the candidates contesting in the election*
fight EG *rivals fighting for supremacy*

a
b
c
d
e
f
g
h
i
j
k
l
m
n
o
p
q
r
s
t
u
v
w
x
y
z

A
B
C
D
E
F
G
H
I
J
K
L
M
N
O
P
Q
R
S
T
U
V
W
X
Y
Z

vie EG *The contestants vied to finish first.*

❶ competition NOUN
an attempt to win
EG *There's a lot of competition for places.*
contention EG *contention for the gold medal*
contest EG *the contest between capitalism and socialism*
opposition EG *They are in direct opposition for the job.*
rivalry EG *the rivalry between the two leaders*
struggle EG *a power struggle*

❷ competition NOUN
a contest to find the winner in something
EG *a surfing competition*
championship EG *a swimming championship*
contest EG *a beauty contest*
event EG *major sporting events*
tournament EG *a judo tournament*

competitor NOUN
a person who competes for something
EG *one of the youngest competitors in the event*
adversary EG *his political adversaries*
challenger EG *20 seconds faster than the nearest challenger*
competition EG *staying ahead of the competition*
contestant EG *contestants in the Miss World pageant*
opponent EG *the best opponent I've played all season*
opposition EG *They can outplay the opposition.*
rival EG *a business rival*

complain VERB
to express dissatisfaction
EG *He came round to complain about the noise.*
carp EG *She is constantly carping at*

him.
find fault EG *He's always finding fault with my work.*
grouse EG *You're always grousing about something.*
grumble EG *It's not in her nature to grumble.*
kick up a fuss INFORMAL EG *He kicks up a fuss whenever she goes out.*
moan EG *moaning about the weather*
whine EG *whining children*
whinge INFORMAL EG *Stop whingeing and get on with it.*

WORD POWER

▷ **Synonyms**
bemoan
bewail

complaint NOUN
an instance of complaining about something
EG *There have been a number of complaints about the standard of service.*
criticism EG *The criticism that we do not try hard enough to learn other languages was voiced.*
grievance EG *They had a legitimate grievance against the company.*
grumble EG *Her main grumble is over the long hours she has to work.*
objection EG *I have no objections about the way I have been treated.*
protest EG *Despite our protests, they went ahead anyway.*

❶ complete ADJECTIVE
to the greatest degree possible
EG *a complete transformation*
absolute EG *absolute nonsense*
consummate EG *a consummate professional*
outright EG *an outright victory*
perfect EG *a perfect stranger*
thorough EG *a thorough snob*
total EG *a total failure*
utter EG *an utter shambles*

❷ complete ADJECTIVE
with nothing missing
EG *a complete set of tools*
entire EG *the entire plot*
full EG *a full report*
intact EG *the few buildings which have survived intact*
undivided EG *I want your undivided attention.*
whole EG *I told him the whole story.*

WORD POWER

▶ **Antonym**
incomplete
---

❸ complete VERB
to finish
EG *He has just completed his first novel.*
conclude EG *The judge concluded his summing-up.*
end EG *The crowd was in tears as he ended his speech.*
finish EG *I'll finish my report this week.*

❶ complex ADJECTIVE
having many different parts
EG *complex issues*
complicated EG *a very complicated voting system*
difficult EG *the laborious and difficult process of adopting a child*
intricate EG *intricate patterns*
involved EG *a long, involved explanation*
tangled EG *His personal life has become more tangled than ever.*

WORD POWER

▷ **Synonyms**
convoluted
tortuous

▶ **Antonym**
simple
---

❷ complex NOUN
an emotional problem
EG *I have never had a complex about my weight.*

fixation EG *She has a fixation about men with beards.*
obsession EG *95% of patients know their obsessions are irrational.*
phobia EG *The man had a phobia about flying.*
preoccupation EG *his total preoccupation with neatness*
problem EG *an eating problem*
thing EG *He's got this thing about women's shoes.*

complicated ADJECTIVE
complex and difficult
EG *a complicated situation*
complex EG *a complex issue*
convoluted EG *a convoluted plot*
elaborate EG *an elaborate theory*
intricate EG *an intricate process*
involved EG *a long, involved explanation*

WORD POWER

▷ **Synonyms**
Byzantine
labyrinthine
perplexing

▶ **Antonym**
simple
---

compose VERB
to create or write
EG *He has composed a symphony.*
create EG *He has created a new ballet.*
devise EG *a play devised by the drama company*
invent EG *the man who invented gangsta rap*
produce EG *He has produced a book about the city.*
write EG *I've never been able to write poetry.*

comprehend VERB
to understand or appreciate something
EG *I just cannot comprehend your attitude.*

A
B
C
D
E
F
G
H
I
J
K
L
M
N
O
P
Q
R
S
T
U
V
W
X
Y
Z

appreciate EG *She has never really appreciated the scale of the problem.*
fathom EG *I really couldn't fathom what Steiner was talking about.*
grasp EG *The Government has not yet grasped the seriousness of the crisis.*
see EG *I don't see why you're complaining.*
take in EG *I try to explain, but you can tell she's not taking it in.*
understand EG *They are too young to understand what's going on.*
work out EG *It took me some time to work out what was causing the problem.*

compulsory ADJECTIVE
required by law
EG *School attendance is compulsory.*
mandatory EG *the mandatory retirement age*
obligatory EG *an obligatory medical examination*
required EG *the required reading for this course*
requisite EG *the requisite documents*

WORD POWER
▶ **Antonym**
voluntary

❶ con VERB
to trick someone into doing or believing something
EG *He claimed that the salesman had conned him out of his life savings.*
cheat EG *a deliberate attempt to cheat employees out of their pensions*
deceive EG *She deceived us into giving her a job.*
mislead EG *Ministers must not knowingly mislead the public.*
swindle EG *A City businessman swindled investors out of millions of pounds.*
trick EG *They tricked him into parting with his life savings.*

WORD POWER
▷ **Synonyms**
defraud
dupe

❷ con NOUN
a trick intended to mislead or disadvantage someone
EG *Slimming snacks that offer miraculous weight loss are a con.*
bluff EG *The letter was a bluff.*
deception EG *You've been the victim of a rather cruel deception.*
fraud EG *an investigation into frauds in the world of horseracing*
swindle EG *a tax swindle*
trick EG *a cheap trick to encourage people to switch energy suppliers*

conceit NOUN
excessive pride
EG *his insufferable conceit*
egotism EG *typical showbiz egotism*
pride EG *a blow to his pride*
self-importance EG *his bad manners and self-importance*
vanity EG *her vanity about her long hair*

WORD POWER
▷ **Synonyms**
amour-propre
narcissism
vainglory

conceited ADJECTIVE
too proud
EG *a conceited young idiot*
bigheaded INFORMAL EG *an arrogant, bigheaded man*
cocky EG *I was very cocky as a youngster.*
egotistical EG *an egotistical show-off*
self-important EG *self-important pop stars*
vain EG *a shallow, vain woman*

WORD POWER

▷ **Synonyms**
narcissistic
swollen-headed
vainglorious

▶ **Antonym**
modest

❶ **concentrate** VERB
to give something all your attention
EG *Concentrate on your studies.*
be engrossed in EG *He was engrossed in his work.*
focus your attention on
EG *focusing his attention on the race*
give your attention to EG *I gave my attention to the question.*
put your mind to EG *You could do it if you put your mind to it.*

❷ **concentrate** VERB
to be found in one place
EG *They are mostly concentrated in the urban areas.*
accumulate EG *Cholesterol accumulates in the arteries.*
collect EG *dust collecting in the corners*
gather EG *residents gathered in huddles*

❶ **concern** NOUN
a feeling of worry
EG *public concern about violence*
anxiety EG *anxiety about the economy*
apprehension EG *apprehension about the future*
disquiet EG *a growing sense of disquiet*
worry EG *She has no worries about his health.*

❷ **concern** NOUN
someone's duty or responsibility
EG *His private life is not my concern.*
affair EG *If you want to go, that's your affair.*

business EG *This is none of my business.*
responsibility EG *He's not my responsibility.*

❸ **concern** VERB
to make someone worried
EG *It concerns me that he doesn't want to go.*
bother EG *Nothing bothers me.*
distress EG *They are distressed by the accusations.*
disturb EG *disturbed by the news*
trouble EG *Is anything troubling you?*
worry EG *an issue that had worried him for some time*

WORD POWER

▷ **Synonyms**
disquiet
perturb

❹ **concern** VERB
to affect or involve
EG *This concerns both of us.*
affect EG *the ways in which computers affect our lives*
apply to EG *This rule does not apply to us.*
be relevant to EG *These documents are relevant to the case.*
involve EG *meetings which involve most of the staff*

WORD POWER

▷ **Synonyms**
bear on
pertain to
touch

concise ADJECTIVE
using no unnecessary words
EG *a concise guide*
brief EG *a brief description*
short EG *a short speech*
succinct EG *a succinct explanation*
terse EG *a terse statement*

A
B
C
D
E
F
G
H
I
J
K
L
M
N
O
P
Q
R
S
T
U
V
W
X
Y
Z

WORD POWER

▷ **Synonyms**
epigrammatic
laconic
pithy

▶ **Antonym**
long

❶ **conclude** VERB
to decide something
EG *He concluded that she had been right.*
decide EG *I decided he must be ill.*
deduce EG *She deduced that I had written the letter.*
infer EG *His feelings were easily inferred from his reply.*
judge EG *The doctor judged that he was not fit enough to play.*
reckon INFORMAL EG *I reckon we should wait a while.*
suppose EG *There's no reason to suppose he'll be there.*
surmise EG *It is surmised that he must have known.*

❷ **conclude** VERB
to finish something
EG *He concluded the letter with a postscript.*
close EG *They closed the show with a song.*
end EG *His speech ended with a prayer for peace.*
finish EG *We finished the evening with a walk on the beach.*
round off EG *This rounded the afternoon off perfectly.*
wind up EG *She quickly wound up her conversation.*

WORD POWER

▶ **Antonym**
begin

❶ **conclusion** NOUN
a decision made after thinking carefully about something
EG *I've come to the conclusion that she was lying.*
deduction EG *a shrewd deduction about what was going on*
inference EG *There were two inferences to be drawn from her letter.*
judgment EG *My judgment is that things are going to get worse.*
verdict EG *The doctor's verdict was that he was fine.*

❷ **conclusion** NOUN
the finish or ending of something
EG *the conclusion of the programme*
close EG *bringing the talks to a close*
end EG *The war is coming to an end.*
ending EG *a dramatic ending*
finish EG *the finish of the race*
termination EG *the termination of their marriage*

WORD POWER

▶ **Antonym**
beginning

❶ **condemn** VERB
to say that something is bad or unacceptable
EG *He was condemned for his arrogance.*
blame EG *I blame television for the rise in violence.*
censure EG *a motion censuring the government*
criticize EG *He was criticized for his failure to act.*
damn EG *The report damns the government's handling of the affair.*
denounce EG *He was denounced as a traitor.*

❷ **condemn** VERB
to give a punishment
EG *condemned to death*
damn EG *sinners damned to eternal torment*
doom EG *doomed to die for his crime*
sentence EG *sentenced to ten years in prison*

① condition NOUN
the state of something
EG *The house is in good condition.*
form EG *The team are not in good form this season.*
shape EG *He's in great shape for his age.*
state EG *Look at the state of my car!*

② condition NOUN
something required for something else to be possible
EG *terms and conditions of the contract*
prerequisite EG *A science background is a prerequisite for the job.*
provision EG *a provision in his will forbidding the sale of the house*
proviso EG *The answer is yes, with one proviso.*
qualification EG *He agreed, but with some qualifications.*
requirement EG *The product meets all legal requirements.*
requisite EG *the main requisite for membership*
stipulation EG *The only dress stipulation was "no jeans".*
terms EG *the terms of the agreement*

① conduct VERB
to carry out an activity or task
EG *to conduct an experiment*
carry out EG *carry out a survey*
direct EG *Christopher will direct day-to-day operations.*
do EG *I'm doing a piece of important research right now.*
manage EG *his ability to manage the business*
organize EG *The initial mobilization was well organized.*
perform EG *Several grafts were performed during the operation.*
run EG *Each teacher will run a different workshop.*

WORD POWER

▷ **Synonyms**
execute
implement
orchestrate

---

② conduct NOUN
the way someone behaves
EG *Other people judge you by your conduct.*
attitude EG *His attitude made me angry.*
behaviour EG *Make sure that good behaviour is rewarded.*
manners EG *He dressed well and had impeccable manners.*
ways EG *urged him to alter his ways*

WORD POWER

▷ **Synonyms**
demeanour

---

conduct yourself VERB
to behave in a particular way
EG *The way he conducts himself reflects on the school.*
act EG *a gang of youths who were acting suspiciously*
behave EG *He'd behaved badly.*

WORD POWER

▷ **Synonyms**
acquit yourself

---

conference NOUN
a meeting for discussion
EG *a conference on education*
congress EG *a congress of coal miners*
convention EG *the Geneva convention*
discussion EG *a round of formal discussions*
forum EG *a forum for trade negotiations*
meeting EG *a meeting of shareholders*

a
b
c
d
e
f
g
h
i
j
k
l
m
n
o
p
q
r
s
t
u
v
w
x
y
z

WORD POWER

▷ **Synonyms**
colloquium
convocation
symposium

confess VERB
to admit to something
EG *Your son has confessed to his crimes.*
acknowledge EG *He acknowledged that he was a drug addict.*
admit EG *I admit to feeling jealous.*
own up EG *The headmaster is waiting for someone to own up.*

WORD POWER

▶ **Antonym**
deny

confession NOUN
the act of confessing
EG *a confession of adultery*
acknowledgment EG *an acknowledgment of his mistakes*
admission EG *an admission of guilt*

❶ confidence NOUN
a feeling of trust
EG *I have complete confidence in you.*
belief EG *his belief in his partner*
faith EG *He has great faith in her judgment.*
reliance EG *I don't put much reliance on that idea.*
trust EG *He destroyed my trust in people.*

WORD POWER

▶ **Antonym**
distrust

❷ confidence NOUN
sureness of yourself
EG *I've never had much confidence.*
aplomb EG *She handled the interview with aplomb.*
assurance EG *He led the orchestra with great assurance.*

self-assurance EG *his supreme self-assurance*
self-possession EG *an air of self-possession*

WORD POWER

▶ **Antonym**
shyness

❶ confident ADJECTIVE
sure about something
EG *confident of success*
certain EG *certain of getting a place on the team*
convinced EG *He is convinced it's your fault.*
positive EG *I'm positive it will happen.*
satisfied EG *We must be satisfied that the treatment is safe.*
secure EG *secure about his job prospects*
sure EG *I'm not sure I understand.*

WORD POWER

▶ **Antonym**
uncertain

❷ confident ADJECTIVE
sure of yourself
EG *a confident attitude*
assured EG *His playing became more assured.*
self-assured EG *a self-assured young man*
self-possessed EG *a self-possessed career woman*

WORD POWER

▶ **Antonym**
shy

❶ confine VERB
to limit to something specified
EG *They confined themselves to talking about the weather.*
limit EG *Limit yourself to six units of alcohol a week.*
restrict EG *The patient was restricted to a meagre diet.*

2 confine VERB

to prevent from leaving

EG *confined to bed for two days*

hem in EG *hemmed in by spectators*

imprison EG *imprisoned in a tiny cell*

restrict EG *We were restricted to the building.*

shut up EG *He can't stand being shut up in the house.*

WORD POWER

▷ **Synonyms**
immure
incarcerate
intern

1 confirm VERB

to say or show that something is true

EG *Police confirmed that they had received a call.*

bear out EG *The figures bear out his words.*

endorse EG *This theory has been endorsed by research.*

prove EG *The results prove his point.*

substantiate EG *no evidence to substantiate the claims*

validate EG *It is difficult to validate this belief.*

verify EG *I was asked to verify this statement.*

WORD POWER

▷ **Synonyms**
authenticate
corroborate

2 confirm VERB

to make something definite

EG *Can we confirm the arrangements for tomorrow?*

fix EG *The date for the election was fixed.*

settle EG *I've settled a time to see him.*

1 conflict NOUN

disagreement and argument

EG *conflict between workers and management*

antagonism EG *antagonism within the team*

disagreement EG *The meeting ended in disagreement.*

discord EG *public discord*

friction EG *friction between him and his father*

hostility EG *hostility between parents and teachers*

opposition EG *a wave of opposition*

strife EG *a cause of strife in many marriages*

2 conflict NOUN

a war or battle

EG *the conflict in the Gulf*

battle EG *a battle between two gangs*

combat EG *men who died in combat*

fighting EG *Villagers have left their homes to avoid the fighting.*

strife EG *civil strife*

war EG *the war between Israel and Egypt*

3 conflict VERB

to differ or disagree

EG *conflicting ideas*

be at variance EG *His statements are at variance with the facts.*

be incompatible EG *These two principles are incompatible.*

clash EG *a decision which clashes with official policy*

differ EG *The two leaders differ on several issues.*

disagree EG *Governments disagree over the need for action.*

1 confuse VERB

to mix two things up

EG *confusing fact with fiction*

mistake EG *I mistook you for someone else.*

mix up EG *He sometimes mixes up his words.*

muddle up EG *I keep muddling him up with his brother.*

2 confuse VERB

to puzzle or bewilder

EG *Politics confuse me.*

baffle EG *Police are baffled by the*

murder.
bewilder EG *His silence bewildered her.*
mystify EG *I was mystified by his attitude.*
puzzle EG *One thing still puzzles me.*

WORD POWER

▷ **Synonyms**
bemuse
faze
nonplus
perplex

❶ confused ADJECTIVE
puzzled or bewildered
EG *confused about health risks*
baffled EG *He stared in baffled amazement.*
bewildered EG *bewildered holidaymakers*
muddled EG *She was muddled about the date.*
perplexed EG *perplexed by recent events*
puzzled EG *a puzzled expression*

WORD POWER

▷ **Synonyms**
at a loss
at sea
flummoxed
nonplussed

❷ confused ADJECTIVE
in an untidy mess
EG *They lay in a confused heap.*
chaotic EG *the chaotic mess on his desk*
disordered EG *a disordered pile of papers*
disorganized EG *a disorganized lifestyle*
untidy EG *an untidy room*

WORD POWER

▶ **Antonym**
tidy

confusing ADJECTIVE
puzzling or bewildering
EG *a confusing situation*
baffling EG *a baffling statement*
bewildering EG *a bewildering choice of products*
complicated EG *a complicated voting system*
puzzling EG *a puzzling problem*

confusion NOUN
an untidy mess
EG *My life is in confusion.*
chaos EG *economic chaos*
disarray EG *The nation is in disarray.*
disorder EG *The emergency room was in disorder.*
disorganization EG *scenes of chaos and disorganization*
mess EG *He always leaves the bathroom in a mess.*

WORD POWER

▶ **Antonym**
order

❶ connect VERB
to join together
EG *Connect the pipe to the tap.*
affix EG *His name was affixed to his cubicle.*
attach EG *Attach the curtains to the rods with hooks.*
couple EG *The engine is coupled to a gearbox.*
fasten EG *A hatchet was fastened to his belt.*
join EG *two springs joined together*
link EG *the Channel Tunnel linking Britain with France*

WORD POWER

▶ **Antonym**
separate

❷ connect VERB
to associate one thing with another
EG *evidence connecting him with the robberies*
ally EG *The new government is allied*

with the military.
associate EG *symptoms associated with migraine headaches*
link EG *research which links smoking with cancer*
relate EG *the denial that unemployment is related to crime*

❶ **connection** NOUN
a link or relationship
EG *a connection between drinking and liver disease*
affiliation EG *He has no affiliation with any political party.*
association EG *the association between the two companies*
bond EG *the bond between a mother and child*
correlation EG *the correlation between unemployment and crime*
correspondence EG *the correspondence between Eastern and Western religions*
link EG *a link between smoking and lung cancer*
relation EG *This theory bears no relation to reality.*
relationship EG *the relationship between humans and their environment*

❷ **connection** NOUN
a point where things are joined
EG *The fault was just a loose connection.*
coupling EG *The coupling between the railway carriages snapped.*
fastening EG *a zip fastening*
junction EG *the junction between nerve and muscle*
link EG *a link between the city and the motorway*

conscience NOUN
a sense of right and wrong
EG *He had a guilty conscience.*
principles EG *It's against my principles to eat meat.*
scruples EG *a man with no moral scruples*

sense of right and wrong
EG *children with no sense of right and wrong*

conservative ADJECTIVE
unwilling to change
EG *People get more conservative as they grow older.*
conventional EG *conventional tastes*
traditional EG *a traditional school*

WORD POWER

▷ **Synonyms**
hidebound
reactionary

▶ **Antonym**
radical

❶ **consider** VERB
to think of someone or something as
EG *They do not consider him a suitable candidate.*
believe EG *I believe him to be innocent.*
judge EG *His work was judged unsatisfactory.*
rate EG *The film was rated excellent.*
regard as EG *They regard the tax as unfair.*
think EG *Many people think him arrogant.*

WORD POWER

▷ **Synonyms**
deem
hold to be

❷ **consider** VERB
to think carefully
EG *I will consider your offer.*
contemplate EG *He contemplated his fate.*
deliberate EG *The jury deliberated for three days.*
meditate EG *He meditated on the problem.*
muse EG *She sat musing on how unfair life was.*
ponder EG *pondering how to improve*

a
b
c
d
e
f
g
h
i
j
k
l
m
n
o
p
q
r
s
t
u
v
w
x
y
z

the team
reflect EG *I reflected on the child's future.*
think about EG *I've been thinking about what you said.*

WORD POWER

▷ **Synonyms**
cogitate
mull over
ruminate

❸ **consider** VERB
to take into account
EG *We should consider her feelings.*
bear in mind EG *There are a few points to bear in mind.*
make allowances for
EG *Remember to make allowances for delays.*
respect EG *We will respect your wishes.*
take into account EG *another factor to be taken into account*
think about EG *more important things to think about*

❶ **consideration** NOUN
careful thought about something
EG *a decision requiring careful consideration*
attention EG *I gave the question all my attention.*
contemplation EG *The problem deserves serious contemplation.*
deliberation EG *After much deliberation, he called the police.*
study EG *The proposals need careful study.*
thought EG *I've given the matter a great deal of thought.*

❷ **consideration** NOUN
concern for someone
EG *Show some consideration for other passengers.*
concern EG *concern for the homeless*
kindness EG *We have been treated with great kindness.*
respect EG *no respect for wildlife*

tact EG *a master of tact and diplomacy*

❸ **consideration** NOUN
something to be taken into account
EG *Safety is a major consideration.*
factor EG *an important factor in buying a house*
issue EG *Price is not the only issue.*
point EG *There is another point to remember.*

consist **consist of** VERB
to be made up of
EG *The brain consists of millions of nerve cells.*
be composed of EG *The committee is composed of ten people.*
be made up of EG *The bouquet was made up of roses and carnations.*
comprise EG *The show comprises 50 paintings and sketches.*

conspicuous ADJECTIVE
easy to see or notice
EG *Her conspicuous lack of warmth confirmed her disapproval.*
apparent EG *It has been apparent that someone has been stealing.*
blatant EG *a blatant disregard for rules*
evident EG *He spoke with evident emotion about his ordeal.*
noticeable EG *the most noticeable effect of these changes*
obvious EG *an obvious injustice*
perceptible EG *a perceptible air of neglect*

WORD POWER

▷ **Synonyms**
manifest

❶ **constant** ADJECTIVE
going on all the time
EG *a city under constant attack*
continual EG *continual pain*
continuous EG *continuous gunfire*
eternal EG *an eternal hum in the background*
nonstop EG *nonstop music*

perpetual EG *her perpetual complaints*
relentless EG *relentless pressure*

WORD POWER

▷ **Synonyms**
incessant
interminable
sustained
unremitting

▶ **Antonym**
periodic

❷ **constant** ADJECTIVE
staying the same
EG *a constant temperature*
even EG *an even level of sound*
fixed EG *a fixed salary*
regular EG *a regular beat*
stable EG *a stable condition*
steady EG *travelling at a steady 50 miles per hour*
uniform EG *a uniform thickness*

WORD POWER

▷ **Synonyms**
immutable
invariable

▶ **Antonym**
changeable

construct VERB
to build or make something
EG *The boxes are constructed from rough-sawn timber.*
assemble EG *She had been trying to assemble the bomb when it went off.*
build EG *Workers at the plant build the F-16 jet fighter.*
create EG *We created a makeshift platform for him to stand on.*
erect EG *The building was erected in 1900.*
make EG *The company now makes cars at two plants in Europe.*
put together EG *the mechanic whose job was to put together looms within the plant*

put up EG *He was putting up a new fence.*

consult VERB
to go to for advice
EG *Consult your doctor before undertaking exercise.*
ask for advice EG *Ask your bank manager for advice on mortgages.*
confer with EG *He is conferring with his lawyers.*
refer to EG *I had to refer to the manual.*

❶ **contact** NOUN
the state of being in touch with someone
EG *We must keep in contact.*
communication EG *The leaders were in constant communication.*
touch EG *I've lost touch with her over the years.*

❷ **contact** NOUN
someone you know
EG *a contact in the music business*
acquaintance EG *We met through a mutual acquaintance.*
connection EG *She had a connection in England.*

❸ **contact** VERB
to get in touch with
EG *We contacted the company to complain.*
approach EG *A journalist has approached me for a story.*
communicate with EG *We communicate mostly by email.*
get hold of EG *I've been trying to get hold of you all week.*
get in touch with EG *I will get in touch with my solicitors.*
reach EG *Where can I reach you in an emergency?*

❶ **contain** VERB
to include as a part of
EG *Alcohol contains sugar.*
comprise EG *The band comprises two singers and two guitarists.*
include EG *The price includes VAT.*

A
B
C
D
E
F
G
H
I
J
K
L
M
N
O
P
Q
R
S
T
U
V
W
X
Y
Z

② contain VERB
to keep under control
EG *efforts to contain the disease*
control EG *He could hardly control his rage.*
curb EG *measures to curb inflation*
repress EG *people who repress their emotions*
restrain EG *unable to restrain her anger*
stifle EG *stifling the urge to scream*

container NOUN
something which holds things
EG *a plastic container for food*
holder EG *a cigarette holder*
vessel EG *storage vessels*

WORD POWER

▷ **Synonyms**
receptacle
repository

① contemplate VERB
to think carefully about something
EG *He cried as he contemplated his future.*
consider EG *She paused to consider her options.*
examine EG *I have examined all the possible alternatives.*
muse on EG *Many of the papers muse on the fate of the President.*
ponder EG *He didn't waste time pondering the question.*
reflect on EG *I reflected on the child's future.*
think about EG *Think about how you can improve the situation.*

② contemplate VERB
to consider doing something
EG *He contemplated a career as a doctor.*
consider EG *Watersports enthusiasts should consider hiring a wetsuit.*
envisage EG *He had never envisaged spending the whole of his life in that job.*
plan EG *I had been planning a trip to the West Coast.*
think of EG *Martin was thinking of taking legal action against his employers.*

contempt NOUN
complete lack of respect
EG *I shall treat that remark with the contempt it deserves.*
derision EG *He was greeted with shouts of derision.*
disdain EG *Janet looked at him with disdain.*
disregard EG *total disregard for the safety of the public*
disrespect EG *complete disrespect for authority*
scorn EG *They greeted the proposal with scorn.*

WORD POWER

▶ **Antonym**
respect

① contest NOUN
a competition or game
EG *Few contests in the history of boxing have been as thrilling.*
competition EG *a surfing competition*
game EG *the first game of the season*
match EG *He was watching a football match.*
tournament EG *Here is a player capable of winning a world tournament.*

② contest NOUN
a struggle for power
EG *a bitter contest over who should control the state's future*
battle EG *the eternal battle between good and evil*
fight EG *the fight for the US Presidency*
struggle EG *locked in a power struggle with his Prime Minister*

③ contest VERB
to object formally to a statement or decision

EG *Your former employer has 14 days to contest the case.*

challenge EG *The move was immediately challenged.*

dispute EG *He disputed the allegations.*

oppose EG *Many parents oppose bilingual education in schools.*

question EG *It never occurs to them to question the doctor's decisions.*

WORD POWER

▶ **Antonym**
accept

---

❶ continual ADJECTIVE
happening all the time without stopping
EG *Despite continual pain, he refused all drugs.*

constant EG *She suggests that women are under constant pressure to be abnormally thin.*

continuous EG *a continuous stream of phone calls*

endless EG *her endless demands for attention*

eternal EG *In the background was that eternal hum.*

nagging EG *a nagging pain between his shoulder blades*

perpetual EG *the perpetual thump of music from the flat downstairs*

uninterrupted EG *five years of uninterrupted growth*

WORD POWER

▷ **Synonyms**
incessant
interminable
unremitting

---

❷ continual ADJECTIVE
happening again and again
EG *She suffered continual police harassment.*

frequent EG *He is prone to frequent bouts of depression.*

recurrent EG *buildings in which staff suffer recurrent illness*

regular EG *He is a regular visitor to our house.*

repeated EG *Mr Smith did not return the money, despite repeated reminders.*

WORD POWER

▶ **Antonym**
occasional

---

❶ continue VERB
to keep doing something
EG *Will you continue working after you're married?*

carry on EG *The assistant carried on talking.*

go on EG *Unemployment is likely to go on rising.*

keep on EG *He kept on trying.*

persist EG *She persists in using his nickname.*

❷ continue VERB
to go on existing
EG *The fighting continued after they'd left.*

carry on EG *My work will carry on after I'm gone.*

endure EG *Their friendship has endured for 30 years.*

last EG *Nothing lasts forever.*

persist EG *The problem persists.*

remain EG *The building remains to this day.*

survive EG *companies which survived after the recession*

❸ continue VERB
to start doing again
EG *After a moment, she continued speaking.*

carry on EG *He took a deep breath, then carried on.*

recommence EG *He recommenced work on his novel.*

resume EG *Police will resume the search today.*

continuous ADJECTIVE
going on without stopping

a b c d e f g h i j k l m n o p q r s t u v w x y z

A
B
C
D
E
F
G
H
I
J
K
L
M
N
O
P
Q
R
S
T
U
V
W
X
Y
Z

EG *continuous growth*
constant EG *under constant pressure*
continued EG *a continued improvement*
extended EG *conflict over an extended period*
prolonged EG *a prolonged drought*
uninterrupted EG *uninterrupted rule*

WORD POWER

▶ **Antonym**
periodic

❶ **control** NOUN
power over something
EG *He was forced to give up control of the company.*
authority EG *You have no authority here.*
command EG *He was in command of the ceremony.*
direction EG *The team worked well under his direction.*
government EG *The entire country is under the government of one man.*
management EG *the day-to-day management of the business*
power EG *a position of great power*
rule EG *15 years of Communist rule*
supremacy EG *The party has re-established its supremacy.*

WORD POWER

▷ **Synonyms**
jurisdiction
mastery
superintendence

❷ **control** VERB
to be in charge of
EG *companies fighting to control the Internet*
administer EG *the authorities who administer the island*
be in charge of EG *She is in charge of the project.*
command EG *the general who commanded the troops*

direct EG *He will direct day-to-day operations.*
govern EG *his ability to govern France*
have power over EG *Her husband has total power over her.*
manage EG *the government's ability to manage the economy*
rule EG *the dynasty which ruled China*

convenient ADJECTIVE
helpful or easy to use
EG *a convenient mode of transport*
handy EG *Credit cards can be handy.*
helpful EG *a helpful fact sheet*
useful EG *a useful invention*

WORD POWER

▷ **Synonyms**
labour-saving
serviceable

▶ **Antonym**
inconvenient

❶ **convention** NOUN
an accepted way of behaving or doing something
EG *It's just a social convention that men don't wear skirts.*
code EG *the code of the Shaolin monks*
custom EG *The custom of lighting the Olympic flame goes back centuries.*
etiquette EG *the rules of diplomatic etiquette*
practice EG *It is normal practice not to reveal the sex of the baby.*
tradition EG *different cultural traditions from ours*

WORD POWER

▷ **Synonyms**
protocol

❷ **convention** NOUN
a large meeting of an organization or group
EG *the annual convention of the Parapsychological Association*
assembly EG *an assembly of women*

Olympic gold-medal winners
conference EG *a conference attended by 450 delegates*
congress EG *A lot changed after the party congress.*
meeting EG *the annual meeting of company shareholders*

❶ conventional ADJECTIVE
having or relating to a very ordinary lifestyle
EG *a respectable married woman with conventional opinions*
conformist EG *He may have to become more conformist if he is to prosper.*
conservative EG *The girl was well dressed in a rather conservative style.*
unadventurous EG *He was a strong player, but rather unadventurous.*

WORD POWER
▷ **Synonyms**
bourgeois
staid

❷ conventional ADJECTIVE
familiar, or usually used
EG *These discs hold 400 times as much information as a conventional floppy disk.*
customary EG *the customary one minute's silence*
ordinary EG *It has 25 per cent less fat than ordinary ice cream.*
orthodox EG *Many of these ideas are being incorporated into orthodox medical treatment.*
regular EG *This product looks and tastes like regular margarine.*
standard EG *It was standard practice for untrained clerks to deal with serious cases.*
traditional EG *traditional teaching methods*

convey VERB
to cause information or ideas to be known
EG *I tried to convey the wonder of the*

experience to my husband.
communicate EG *They successfully communicate their knowledge to others.*
express EG *She did her best to express wordless disapproval by scowling.*
get across EG *I wanted to get my message across.*
impart EG *the ability to impart knowledge*

convince VERB
to persuade that something is true
EG *I convinced him of my innocence.*
assure EG *She assured me that there was nothing wrong.*
persuade EG *I had to persuade him of the advantages.*
satisfy EG *He had to satisfy the doctors that he was fit to play.*

convincing ADJECTIVE
persuasive
EG *a convincing argument*
conclusive EG *conclusive proof*
effective EG *an effective speaker*
persuasive EG *persuasive reasons*
plausible EG *a plausible explanation*
powerful EG *a powerful speech*
telling EG *a telling criticism*

WORD POWER
▷ **Synonyms**
cogent
incontrovertible

▶ **Antonym**
unconvincing

cook VERB
to prepare food for eating by heating it in some way
EG *I enjoy cooking for friends.*
bake EG *a machine for baking bread*
barbecue EG *a Korean method of barbecuing meat*
boil EG *Boil the fruit and syrup together for half an hour.*
fry EG *Garnish the rice with thinly sliced fried onion.*

a
b
c
d
e
f
g
h
i
j
k
l
m
n
o
p
q
r
s
t
u
v
w
x
y
z

grill EG *Grill the fish for five minutes.*
microwave EG *Microwaved vegetables have a fresher flavour.*
poach EG *I had ordered poached eggs on toast for breakfast.*
roast EG *Roast the aubergine in the oven for about one hour until soft.*
steam EG *mussels on a bed of steamed cabbage*
stew EG *You can stew the vegetables in oil.*
toast EG *This currant loaf is delicious either fresh or toasted.*

❶ cool ADJECTIVE
having a low temperature
EG *a gust of cool air*
chilled EG *a chilled bottle of wine*
chilly EG *a chilly afternoon*
cold EG *Your dinner's getting cold.*
refreshing EG *a refreshing breeze*

WORD POWER

▶ **Antonym**
warm

❷ cool ADJECTIVE
staying calm
EG *He kept cool through the whole thing.*
calm EG *Try to stay calm.*
collected EG *She was cool and collected throughout the interview.*
composed EG *a composed player*
level-headed EG *Simon is level-headed and practical.*
relaxed EG *a relaxed manner*
serene EG *a serene smile*

WORD POWER

▷ **Synonyms**
dispassionate
imperturbable
unemotional
unexcited
unruffled

▶ **Antonym**
nervous

❸ cool VERB
to make or become cool
EG *Put the cookies on a wire rack to cool.*
chill EG *a glass of chilled champagne*
cool off EG *Dip the carrots in water to cool them off.*
freeze EG *Make double the quantity and freeze half for later.*
refrigerate EG *Refrigerate the dough overnight.*

WORD POWER

▶ **Antonym**
heat

cooperate VERB
to work together
EG *The family cooperated with the author of the book.*
collaborate EG *They collaborated on an album.*
join forces EG *The two political parties are joining forces.*
pull together EG *The staff and management pull together.*
work together EG *industry and government working together*

❶ copy NOUN
something made to look like something else
EG *He had kept a copy of the letter.*
counterfeit EG *This credit card is a counterfeit.*
duplicate EG *I lost my key and had to get a duplicate made.*
fake EG *How do I know this painting isn't a fake?*
forgery EG *The letter was a forgery.*
imitation EG *Beware of cheap imitations.*
replica EG *a replica of the Statue of Liberty*
reproduction EG *a reproduction of a famous painting*

A
B
C
D
E
F
G
H
I
J
K
L
M
N
O
P
Q
R
S
T
U
V
W
X
Y
Z

WORD POWER

▷ **Synonyms**
facsimile
likeness
replication

2 copy VERB
to do the same thing as someone else
EG *My little brother copies everything I do.*
ape EG *Generations of women have aped her style and looks.*
emulate EG *Sons are expected to emulate their fathers.*
follow EG *Where America goes, Britain will surely follow.*
imitate EG *Children imitate what they see on TV.*
mimic EG *He mimicked her accent.*

WORD POWER

▷ **Synonyms**
follow suit
parrot
simulate

3 copy VERB
to make a copy of
EG *documents copied by hand*
counterfeit EG *These banknotes are very easy to counterfeit.*
duplicate EG *Videos are being illicitly duplicated all over the country.*
reproduce EG *a new method of reproducing oil paintings*

corny ADJECTIVE
unoriginal or sentimental
EG *corny old love songs*
banal EG *banal dialogue*
hackneyed EG *a hackneyed plot*
maudlin EG *a maudlin film*
sentimental EG *a sentimental ballad*
stale EG *stale ideas*
stereotyped EG *a stereotyped image of Britain*
trite EG *a trite ending*

WORD POWER

▷ **Synonyms**
mawkish
old hat
unoriginal

1 correct ADJECTIVE
without mistakes
EG *a correct diagnosis*
accurate EG *an accurate description*
exact EG *an exact copy*
faultless EG *Hans's English was faultless.*
flawless EG *a flawless performance*
precise EG *precise calculations*
right EG *That clock never shows the right time.*
true EG *a true account*

2 correct ADJECTIVE
socially acceptable
EG *correct behaviour*
acceptable EG *It is becoming more acceptable for women to drink.*
appropriate EG *appropriate dress*
fitting EG *behaving in a manner not fitting for a lady*
okay or **OK** INFORMAL EG *Is it okay if I bring a friend with me?*
proper EG *In those days it was not proper for women to go on the stage.*
seemly EG *It is not seemly to joke about such things.*

WORD POWER

▶ **Antonym**
wrong

3 correct VERB
to make right
EG *trying to correct his faults*
amend EG *They want to amend the current system.*
cure EG *an operation to cure his limp*
improve EG *We must improve the situation.*
rectify EG *attempts to rectify the problem*
reform EG *He promised to reform his*

A B C
D E F
G H I J K L M N O P Q R S T U V W X Y Z

wicked ways.
remedy EG *What is needed to remedy these deficiencies?*
right EG *I intend to right these wrongs.*

WORD POWER

▷ **Synonyms**
emend
redress

correction NOUN
the act of making something right
EG *the correction of obvious mistakes*
adjustment EG *My car needs a brake adjustment.*
amendment EG *He has made lots of amendments to the script.*
righting EG *the righting of the country's domestic troubles*

WORD POWER

▷ **Synonyms**
emendation
rectification

correspond VERB
to be similar or connected to something else
EG *The two maps correspond closely.*
agree EG *His statement agrees with those of other witnesses.*
be related EG *These philosophical problems are closely related.*
coincide EG *He was delighted to find that her feelings coincided with his own.*
correlate EG *Obesity correlates with increased risk for diabetes.*
fit EG *The punishment must always fit the crime.*
match EG *Our value system does not match with theirs.*
tally EG *This description did not tally with what we saw.*

❶ **corrupt** ADJECTIVE
acting dishonestly or illegally
EG *corrupt politicians*
crooked EG *a crooked cop*

dishonest EG *a dishonest scheme*
fraudulent EG *fraudulent trading*
shady INFORMAL EG *shady deals*
unscrupulous EG *unscrupulous landlords*

WORD POWER

▷ **Synonyms**
unethical
unprincipled
venal

▶ **Antonym**
honest

❷ **corrupt** VERB
to make dishonest
EG *Organized crime has corrupted local government.*
bribe EG *accused of bribing officials*
buy off EG *Police were bought off by drugs dealers.*
fix INFORMAL EG *He fixed the match by bribing the players.*

❸ **corrupt** VERB
to make immoral
EG *TV is corrupting our children.*
deprave EG *material likely to deprave those who watch it*
pervert EG *perverted by their contact with criminals*

corruption NOUN
dishonest and illegal behaviour
EG *charges of corruption*
bribery EG *on trial for bribery*
dishonesty EG *She accused the government of dishonesty and incompetence.*
fraud EG *jailed for fraud*

WORD POWER

▷ **Synonyms**
extortion
profiteering
venality

❶ **cost** NOUN
the amount of money needed
EG *The cost of petrol has increased.*

charge EG *We can arrange this for a small charge.*
expense EG *household expenses*
outlay EG *Buying wine in bulk is well worth the outlay.*
payment EG *an initial payment of just $100*
price EG *House prices are expected to rise.*
rate EG *specially reduced rates*

❷ cost NOUN
loss or damage
EG *the total cost in human misery*
detriment EG *These changes are to the detriment of staff morale.*
expense EG *I supported my husband's career at the expense of my own.*
penalty EG *paying the penalty for someone else's mistakes*

❸ cost VERB
to involve a cost of
EG *The air fares were going to cost a lot.*
come to EG *Lunch came to nearly 15.*
sell at EG *The books are selling at £1 per copy.*
set someone back INFORMAL EG *This wedding will set us back thousands of pounds.*

❶ cosy ADJECTIVE
warm and comfortable
EG *Guests can relax in the cosy bar.*
comfortable EG *a comfortable fireside chair*
snug EG *a snug log cabin*
warm EG *warm blankets*

❷ cosy ADJECTIVE
pleasant and friendly
EG *a cosy chat between friends*
friendly EG *a friendly little get-together*
informal EG *The house has an informal atmosphere.*
intimate EG *an intimate candlelit dinner for two*
relaxed EG *a relaxed evening in*

council NOUN
a governing group of people
EG *the city council*
assembly EG *the National Assembly*
board EG *the Pakistan Cricket Board*
committee EG *the management committee*
panel EG *a panel of judges*

> ### WORD POWER
>
> ▷ **Synonyms**
> conclave
> convocation
> quango
> synod

❶ count VERB
to add up
EG *I counted the money.*
add up EG *Add up the sales figures.*
calculate EG *First, calculate your monthly living expenses.*
tally EG *Computers now tally the votes.*

> ### WORD POWER
>
> ▷ **Synonyms**
> compute
> enumerate
> tot up

❷ count VERB
to be important
EG *Our opinions don't count.*
carry weight EG *a politician whose words carry weight*
matter EG *It doesn't matter what she thinks.*
rate EG *This does not rate as one of my main concerns.*
signify EG *His absence does not signify much.*
weigh EG *This evidence did not weigh with the jury.*

❸ count NOUN
a counting or number counted
EG *The count revealed that our party had the majority.*
calculation EG *I did a quick*

a
b
c
d
e
f
g
h
i
j
k
l
m
n
o
p
q
r
s
t
u
v
w
x
y
z

A
B
C
D
E
F
G
H
I
J
K
L
M
N
O
P
Q
R
S
T
U
V
W
X
Y
Z

calculation in my head.
reckoning EG *By my reckoning we were about two miles from camp.*
sum EG *I've never been good at sums.*
tally EG *They keep a tally of visitors to the castle.*

WORD POWER

▷ **Synonyms**
computation
enumeration

counteract VERB
to reduce the effect of something
EG *pills to counteract high blood pressure*
act against EG *The immune system acts against infection.*
offset EG *The slump was offset by a surge in exports.*

WORD POWER

▷ **Synonyms**
counterbalance
countervail
negate
neutralize

countless ADJECTIVE
too many to count
EG *the star of countless films*
infinite EG *an infinite number of atoms*
innumerable EG *innumerable problems*
myriad EG *pop music in all its myriad forms*
untold EG *untold wealth*

WORD POWER

▷ **Synonyms**
incalculable
limitless
measureless
multitudinous

❶ **country** NOUN
a political area
EG *the boundary between the two*

countries
kingdom EG *The kingdom's power declined.*
land EG *America, land of opportunity*
state EG *a communist state*

❷ **country** NOUN
land away from towns and cities
EG *He lives right out in the country.*
bush NEW ZEALAND AND SOUTH AFRICAN
eg *a trip out to the bush*
countryside EG *surrounded by beautiful countryside*
outback AUSTRALIAN AND NEW ZEALAND
eg *nostalgic paintings of the outback*
outdoors EG *He loves the great outdoors.*

WORD POWER

● **Related Words**
adjectives : pastoral,
rural

courage NOUN
lack of fear
EG *His courage impressed everyone.*
bravery EG *an act of bravery*
daring EG *tales of daring and adventure*
guts INFORMAL EG *He didn't have the guts to admit he was wrong.*
heroism EG *the young soldier's heroism*
nerve EG *I didn't have the nerve to complain.*
pluck EG *You have to admire her pluck.*
valour EG *He was decorated for valour in the war.*

WORD POWER

▷ **Synonyms**
dauntlessness
fearlessness
grit
intrepidity

▶ **Antonym**
fear

❶ course NOUN
a series of lessons
EG *a course in computing*
classes EG *I go to dance classes.*
curriculum EG *the history curriculum*

❷ course NOUN
a policy of action
EG *He took the only course left open to him.*
plan EG *Your best plan is to see your doctor.*
policy EG *She decided the best policy was to wait.*
procedure EG *He did not follow the correct procedure.*

❸ course NOUN
a way taken to get somewhere
EG *She sensed the plane had changed course.*
direction EG *He went off in the opposite direction.*
line EG *the birds' line of flight*
path EG *the path of an oncoming car*
route EG *the most direct route*
trajectory EG *the trajectory of the missile*
way EG *What way do you go home?*

❶ court NOUN
a place where legal matters are decided
EG *He ended up in court for theft.*
bench EG *He was brought before the bench.*
law court EG *prisoners tried by a law court*
tribunal EG *The claim was thrown out by a European tribunal.*

❷ court VERB; OLD-FASHIONED
to intend to marry
EG *I was courting Billy at 19 and married him at 21.*
go steady EG *They've been going steady for six months now.*
woo EG *He wooed and married his first love.*

courtesy NOUN
polite and considerate behaviour
EG *a lack of courtesy to other drivers*
civility EG *Handle customers with tact and civility.*
courteousness EG *his courteousness and kindness*
gallantry EG *He treated me with old-fashioned gallantry.*
good manners EG *the rules of good manners*
grace EG *He didn't even have the grace to apologize.*
graciousness EG *The team displayed graciousness in defeat.*
politeness EG *basic standards of politeness*

❶ cover VERB
to protect or hide
EG *He covered his face.*
cloak EG *a land cloaked in mist*
conceal EG *The hat concealed her hair.*
cover up EG *I covered him up with a blanket.*
hide EG *His sunglasses hid his eyes.*
mask EG *A cloud masked the sun.*
obscure EG *One wall was obscured by a huge banner.*
screen EG *The road was screened by a block of flats.*
shade EG *shading his eyes from the glare*

WORD POWER

▶ **Antonym**
reveal

---

❷ cover VERB
to form a layer over
EG *Tears covered his face.*
coat EG *Coat the fish with batter.*
overlay EG *The floor was overlaid with rugs.*

❸ cover NOUN
something which protects or hides
EG *a duvet cover*
case EG *a spectacle case*
coating EG *steel covered with a coating of zinc*

A B **C** D E F G H I J K L M N O P Q R S T U V W X Y Z

covering EG *a plastic covering*
jacket EG *the jacket of a book*
mask EG *a surgical mask*
screen EG *They put a screen round me.*
wrapper EG *Take the product from its sealed wrapper.*

COW NOUN
a farm animal kept for milk or meat
EG *a herd of dairy cows*
bovine EG *a herd of deranged bovines*
cattle EG *fields where cattle graze*

coward NOUN
someone who is easily scared
EG *He's too much of a coward to fight.*
chicken SLANG EG *We called him a chicken.*
wimp INFORMAL EG *He seems like a wimp to me.*

cowardly ADJECTIVE
easily scared
EG *too cowardly to tell the truth*
chicken SLANG EG *I was too chicken to complain.*
faint-hearted EG *This is no time to be faint-hearted.*
gutless INFORMAL EG *a gutless coward*
sookie NEW ZEALAND EG *a sookie thing to do*

WORD POWER
▷ **Synonyms**
craven
lily-livered
pusillanimous
spineless
timorous

▶ **Antonym**
brave

cower VERB
to bend down with fear
EG *The hostages cowered in their seats.*
cringe EG *I cringed in horror.*
quail EG *She quailed at the sight.*
shrink EG *He shrank back in terror.*

❶ **crack** VERB
to become damaged, with lines on the surface
EG *A gas main has cracked.*
break EG *She broke her leg playing rounders.*
fracture EG *You've fractured a rib.*
snap EG *The mast snapped like a dry twig.*

❷ **crack** VERB
to find the answer to something
EG *We've managed to crack the problem.*
decipher EG *trying to decipher the code*
solve EG *attempts to solve the mystery*
work out EG *I've worked out where I'm going wrong.*

❸ **crack** NOUN
a line or gap caused by damage
EG *a large crack in the wall*
break EG *a train crash caused by a break in the rails*
cleft EG *a cleft in the rocks*
crevice EG *a crevice in the cliff-face*
fracture EG *a hip fracture*

WORD POWER
▷ **Synonyms**
fissure
interstice

crafty ADJECTIVE
clever and rather dishonest
EG *That crafty old devil has taken us for a ride.*
artful EG *the smiles and schemes of an artful woman*
cunning EG *I have a cunning plan to get us out of this mess.*
devious EG *By devious means she obtained the address.*
scheming EG *You're a scheming little devil, aren't you?*
slippery EG *a slippery customer*
sly EG *He is a sly old beggar if ever there was one.*

wily EG *the wily manoeuvring of the President*

cram VERB
to stuff something into a container or place
EG *She crammed her mouth with nuts.*
jam EG *The place was jammed with people.*
pack EG *The drawers were packed with clothes.*
squeeze EG *The two of us were squeezed into one seat.*
stuff EG *wallets stuffed with dollars*

❶ **crash** NOUN
an accident involving a moving vehicle
EG *a plane crash*
accident EG *a serious car accident*
bump EG *I had a bump in the car park.*
collision EG *a head-on collision*
pile-up INFORMAL EG *a 54-car pile-up*
smash EG *He nearly died in a car smash.*

❷ **crash** NOUN
a loud noise
EG *There was a sudden crash outside.*
bang EG *The door slammed with a bang.*
clash EG *the clash of cymbals*
din EG *the din of battle*
smash EG *the smash of falling crockery*

❸ **crash** NOUN
the failure of a business
EG *a stock market crash*
bankruptcy EG *Many firms are now facing bankruptcy.*
collapse EG *The economy is on the edge of collapse.*
depression EG *the Great Depression of the 1930s*
failure EG *a major cause of business failure*
ruin EG *Inflation has driven them to the brink of ruin.*

❹ **crash** VERB
to have an accident

EG *His car crashed into the rear of a van.*
bump EG *I've just bumped my car.*
collide EG *Two trains collided in London today.*
drive into EG *He drove his car into a tree.*
have an accident EG *My brother's had an accident on his moped.*
hurtle into EG *The racing car hurtled into the spectator enclosure.*
plough into EG *The plane had ploughed into the mountainside.*
wreck EG *He's wrecked his van.*

crawl VERB
to be full of
EG *The place is crawling with drunks.*
be alive with EG *The river was alive with frogs.*
be full of EG *The place was full of insects.*
be overrun SLANG EG *The area is overrun with tourists.*
swarm EG *The wood was swarming with police officers.*
teem EG *ponds teeming with fish*

craze NOUN
a brief enthusiasm for something
EG *the latest fitness craze*
fad EG *a new-age fad*
fashion EG *the fashion for Seventies toys*
trend EG *the latest trend among film stars*
vogue EG *a vogue for so-called health drinks*

❶ **crazy** ADJECTIVE; INFORMAL
very strange or foolish
EG *People thought we were crazy when we told them our plans.*
foolish EG *It is foolish to risk skin cancer for the sake of a tan.*
insane EG *If you want my opinion, I think your idea is completely insane.*
mad EG *You'd be mad to work with him again.*
ridiculous EG *It was an absolutely*

ridiculous decision.
wild EG *all sorts of wild ideas*
zany EG *zany humour*

WORD POWER

▶ **Antonym**
sensible

---

2 crazy ADJECTIVE; INFORMAL
very keen on something
EG *He's crazy about football.*
fanatical EG *fanatical about computer games*
mad EG *She's not as mad about sport as I am.*
obsessed EG *He was obsessed with American gangster movies.*
passionate EG *He is passionate about the project.*
smitten EG *They were totally smitten with each other.*
wild EG *I'm just wild about Peter.*

WORD POWER

▷ **Synonyms**
enamoured

---

1 create VERB
to make something happen
EG *His reaction created a bad atmosphere.*
bring about EG *helping to bring about peace*
cause EG *Sugar causes dental decay.*
lead to EG *The takeover led to widespread redundancies.*
occasion EG *the distress occasioned by her dismissal*

2 create VERB
to invent something
EG *creating a new style of painting*
coin EG *the man who coined the term "virtual reality"*
compose EG *Vivaldi composed many concertos.*
devise EG *We devised a scheme to help him.*
formulate EG *He formulated his plan for escape.*

invent EG *He invented the first electric clock.*
originate EG *the designer who originated platform shoes*

creative ADJECTIVE
able to invent
EG *her creative talents*
fertile EG *a fertile imagination*
imaginative EG *an imaginative writer*
inspired EG *his inspired use of colour*
inventive EG *an inventive storyline*

credit NOUN
praise for something
EG *He took all the credit for my idea.*
commendation EG *Both teams deserve commendation.*
glory EG *basking in reflected glory*
praise EG *Praise is due to all concerned.*
recognition EG *She got no recognition for her work.*
thanks EG *He received no thanks for his efforts.*

WORD POWER

▷ **Synonyms**
acclaim
Brownie points
kudos

▶ **Antonym**
disgrace

---

creepy ADJECTIVE; INFORMAL
strange and frightening
EG *This place is really creepy at night.*
disturbing EG *There was something about him she found disturbing.*
eerie EG *I walked down the eerie dark path.*
macabre EG *macabre stories*
scary INFORMAL EG *We watched scary movies.*
sinister EG *There was something sinister about him.*
spooky EG *The whole place has a slightly spooky atmosphere.*

unnatural EG *The altered landscape looks unnatural and weird.*

crime NOUN
an act that breaks the law
EG *the problem of organized crime*
misdemeanour EG *a financial misdemeanour*
offence EG *a serious offence*
violation EG *tax law violations*
wrong EG *I intend to right that wrong.*

WORD POWER
▷ **Synonyms**
felony
malfeasance
misdeed
transgression

1 criminal NOUN
someone who has committed a crime
EG *the country's most dangerous criminals*
crook INFORMAL EG *The man is a crook and a liar.*
culprit EG *the true culprit's identity*
delinquent EG *juvenile delinquents*
offender EG *a first-time offender*
skelm SOUTH AFRICAN EG *a skelm from the city*
villain EG *He tackled an armed villain single-handed.*

WORD POWER
▷ **Synonyms**
evildoer
felon
lawbreaker
malefactor

2 criminal ADJECTIVE
involving crime
EG *criminal activities*
corrupt EG *corrupt practices*
crooked EG *crooked business deals*
illegal EG *an illegal action*
illicit EG *illicit dealings*
unlawful EG *unlawful entry*

WORD POWER
▷ **Synonyms**
culpable
felonious
indictable
iniquitous
nefarious

▶ **Antonym**
legal

1 cripple VERB
to injure severely
EG *crippled in a car accident*
disable EG *disabled by polio*
lame EG *He was lamed for life.*
maim EG *mines maiming and killing civilians*
paralyse EG *paralysed in a riding accident*

2 cripple VERB
to prevent from working
EG *The crisis may cripple the Irish economy.*
bring to a standstill EG *The strike brought France to a standstill.*
impair EG *Their actions will impair France's national interests.*
put out of action EG *The port has been put out of action.*

1 critical ADJECTIVE
very important
EG *a critical point in history*
crucial EG *a crucial election campaign*
deciding EG *Price was a deciding factor.*
decisive EG *a decisive moment in my life*
momentous EG *a momentous decision*
pivotal EG *He played a pivotal role in the match.*
vital EG *vital information*

WORD POWER
▶ **Antonym**
unimportant

a b c d e f g h i j k l m n o p q r s t u v w x y z

❷ critical ADJECTIVE
very serious
EG *a critical illness*
grave EG *grave danger*
precarious EG *a precarious financial situation*
serious EG *His condition is said to be serious.*

❸ critical ADJECTIVE
finding fault with something or someone
EG *critical remarks*
carping EG *carping comments*
derogatory EG *derogatory references to women*
disapproving EG *a disapproving look*
disparaging EG *He spoke in disparaging tones.*
scathing EG *a scathing attack*

> *WORD POWER*
>
> ▷ **Synonyms**
> captious
> cavilling
> censorious
> fault-finding
>
> ▶ **Antonym**
> complimentary

criticism NOUN
expression of disapproval
EG *public criticism of his actions*
censure EG *They deserve praise rather than censure.*
disapproval EG *a chorus of disapproval*
disparagement EG *their disparagement of this book*
fault-finding EG *her husband's constant fault-finding*
flak INFORMAL EG *I got a lot of flak for that idea.*
panning INFORMAL EG *a panning from the critics*

> *WORD POWER*
>
> ▷ **Synonyms**
> animadversion

denigration
stricture

> ▶ **Antonym**
> praise

criticize VERB
to find fault
EG *The regime has been harshly criticized.*
censure EG *a decision for which she was censured*
condemn EG *He refused to condemn their behaviour.*
find fault with EG *She keeps finding fault with my work.*
knock INFORMAL EG *Don't knock it till you've tried it.*
pan INFORMAL EG *Critics panned the show.*
put down EG *She's always putting him down in front of the kids.*

> *WORD POWER*
>
> ▷ **Synonyms**
> disparage
> excoriate
> lambast *or* lambaste
>
> ▶ **Antonym**
> praise

❶ crook NOUN; INFORMAL
a criminal
EG *The man is a crook and a liar.*
cheat EG *a rotten cheat*
rogue EG *Mr Scott wasn't a rogue at all.*
scoundrel OLD-FASHIONED EG *He is a lying scoundrel!*
shark EG *Beware the sharks when you are deciding how to invest.*
swindler EG *Swindlers have cheated investors out of £12 million.*
thief EG *The thieves snatched the camera.*
villain EG *As a copper, I've spent my life putting villains behind bars.*

2 crook ADJECTIVE; AUSTRALIAN AND NEW ZEALAND; INFORMAL
ill
EG *He admitted to feeling a bit crook.*
ill EG *I was feeling ill.*
nauseous EG *The drugs may make the patient feel nauseous.*
poorly EG *Julie's still poorly.*
queasy EG *He was very prone to seasickness and already felt queasy.*
sick EG *The very thought of food made him feel sick.*
under the weather EG *I was still feeling a bit under the weather.*
unwell EG *He felt unwell as he was travelling home this afternoon.*

1 crooked ADJECTIVE
bent or twisted
EG *a crooked tree*
bent EG *a bent back*
deformed EG *born with a deformed right leg*
distorted EG *a distorted image*
irregular EG *irregular and discoloured teeth*
out of shape EG *The wires were bent out of shape.*
twisted EG *bits of twisted metal*
warped EG *warped wooden shutters*

WORD POWER

▶ **Antonym**
straight

2 crooked ADJECTIVE
dishonest or illegal
EG *crooked business practices*
corrupt EG *corrupt police officers*
criminal EG *criminal activities*
dishonest EG *dishonest salespeople*
fraudulent EG *a fraudulent claim*
illegal EG *illegal trading*
shady INFORMAL EG *shady deals*

WORD POWER

▷ **Synonyms**
dishonourable
nefarious

unprincipled

▶ **Antonym**
honest

1 cross VERB
to go across
EG *the bridge which crosses the river*
ford EG *trying to find a safe place to ford the stream*
go across EG *going across the road*
span EG *the iron bridge spanning the railway*
traverse EG *a valley traversed by streams*

2 cross VERB
to meet and go across
EG *the intersection where the roads cross*
crisscross EG *Phone wires criss-cross the street.*
intersect EG *The circles intersect in two places.*

3 cross NOUN
a mixture of two things
EG *a cross between a collie and a retriever*
blend EG *a blend of the old and the new*
combination EG *a combination of fear and anger*
mixture EG *a mixture of two factors*

4 cross ADJECTIVE
rather angry
EG *I'm very cross with him.*
angry EG *Are you angry with me?*
annoyed EG *I'm annoyed with myself for being so stupid.*
fractious EG *The children were getting fractious.*
fretful EG *the fretful expression on her face*
grumpy EG *a grumpy old man*
in a bad mood EG *He's in a bad mood about something.*
irritable EG *She had been restless and irritable all day.*

a
b
c
d
e
f
g
h
i
j
k
l
m
n
o
p
q
r
s
t
u
v
w
x
y
z

A
B
C
D
E
F
G
H
I
J
K
L
M
N
O
P
Q
R
S
T
U
V
W
X
Y
Z

WORD POWER

▷ **Synonyms**
irascible
peevish
splenetic
testy
tetchy

---

crouch VERB
to squat down
EG *A man was crouching behind the car.*
bend down EG *I bent down and touched the grass.*
squat EG *He squatted on his heels to talk to the children.*

❶ crowd NOUN
a large group of people
EG *A huge crowd gathered in the square.*
horde EG *hordes of tourists*
host EG *a host of fans*
mass EG *a heaving mass of people*
mob EG *a mob of demonstrators*
multitude EG *surrounded by a noisy multitude*
swarm EG *swarms of visitors*
throng EG *An official pushed through the throng.*

❷ crowd VERB
to gather close together
EG *Hundreds of fans crowded into the hall.*
congregate EG *A large crowd congregated outside the stadium.*
gather EG *Dozens of people gathered to watch.*
swarm EG *Police swarmed into the area.*
throng EG *The crowds thronged into the mall.*

crowded ADJECTIVE
full of people
EG *a crowded room*
congested EG *congested cities*
full EG *The train was full.*
overflowing EG *buildings*

overflowing with students
packed EG *By 10.30 the shop was packed.*

crucial ADJECTIVE
very important
EG *a crucial moment in his career*
central EG *central to the whole process*
critical EG *a critical point in the campaign*
decisive EG *ready to strike at the decisive moment*
momentous EG *a momentous event*
pivotal EG *He played a pivotal role in the match.*
vital EG *vital information*

❶ crude ADJECTIVE
rough and simple
EG *a crude weapon*
primitive EG *They managed to make a primitive harness.*
rough EG *a rough sketch*
rudimentary EG *some form of rudimentary heating*
simple EG *a simple stringed instrument*

❷ crude ADJECTIVE
rude and offensive
EG *a crude sense of humour*
coarse EG *coarse speech*
dirty EG *a dirty joke*
indecent EG *indecent lyrics*
obscene EG *obscene language*
tasteless EG *a tasteless remark*
vulgar EG *a vulgar phrase*

WORD POWER

▷ **Synonyms**
boorish
crass
smutty

▶ **Antonym**
refined

---

cruel ADJECTIVE
deliberately causing hurt
EG *I hate people who are cruel to*

animals.
barbarous EG *a barbarous attack*
brutal EG *a brutal murder*
callous EG *callous treatment*
cold-blooded EG *a cold-blooded killer*
heartless EG *It was a heartless thing to do.*
inhumane EG *He was kept under inhumane conditions.*
sadistic EG *mistreated by sadistic guards*
vicious EG *a vicious blow*

WORD POWER

▶ **Antonym**
kind

cruelty NOUN
cruel behaviour
EG *an act of unbelievable cruelty*
barbarity EG *the barbarity of war*
brutality EG *police brutality*
callousness EG *the callousness of his murder*
inhumanity EG *man's inhumanity to man*
savagery EG *scenes of unimaginable savagery*
viciousness EG *the viciousness of the attacks*

WORD POWER

▶ **Antonym**
kindness

crumple VERB
to squash and wrinkle
EG *She crumpled the paper in her hand.*
crease EG *Don't crease the material.*
crush EG *Andrew crushed his empty can.*
screw up EG *He screwed the letter up in anger.*
wrinkle EG *trying not to wrinkle her silk skirt*

❶ crush VERB
to destroy the shape of by squeezing
EG *Their car was crushed by an army tank.*
crumble EG *Crumble the stock cubes into a jar.*
crumple EG *She crumpled the note up and threw it away.*
mash EG *Mash the bananas with a fork.*
squash EG *She squashed the wasp under her heel.*

❷ crush VERB
to defeat completely
EG *his bid to crush the uprising*
overcome EG *working to overcome the enemy forces*
put down EG *Soldiers moved in to put down the rebellion.*
quell EG *Troops eventually quelled the unrest.*
stamp out EG *steps to stamp out bullying in schools*
vanquish EG *his vanquished foe*

❶ cry VERB
to have tears coming from your eyes
EG *Stop crying and tell me what's wrong.*
→ see Word Study **cry**

❷ cry VERB
to call out loudly
EG *"See you soon!" they cried.*
call EG *She called to me across the square.*
exclaim EG *'You must be mad!" she exclaimed.*
shout EG *"Over here!" they shouted.*
yell EG *He yelled out of the window.*

❸ cry NOUN
a loud or high shout
EG *a cry of pain*
call EG *the call of a seagull*
exclamation EG *an exclamation of surprise*
shout EG *I heard a distant shout.*
yell EG *Bob let out a yell.*

❶ cunning ADJECTIVE
clever and deceitful
EG *a cunning and ruthless businessman*

a
b
c
d
e
f
g
h
i
j
k
l
m
n
o
p
q
r
s
t
u
v
w
x
y
z

A
B
C
D
E
F
G
H
I
J
K
L
M
N
O
P
Q
R
S
T
U
V
W
X
Y
Z

artful EG *an artful old woman*
crafty EG *a crafty plan*
devious EG *a devious mind*
sly EG *a sly trick*
wily EG *a wily politician*

WORD POWER

▷ **Synonyms**
foxy
Machiavellian

▶ **Antonym**
open

❷ **cunning** NOUN
cleverness and deceit
EG *the cunning of today's criminals*
deviousness EG *the deviousness of drug traffickers*
guile EG *She was without guile or pretence.*

❶ **curb** VERB
to keep something within limits
EG *He must learn to curb that temper of his.*
check EG *an attempt to check the spread of the disease*
contain EG *A hundred firefighters are still trying to contain the fire.*
control EG *the need to control environmental pollution*
limit EG *He limited payments on the country's foreign debt.*
restrain EG *efforts to restrain corruption*
suppress EG *The Government is suppressing inflation by devastating the economy.*

❷ **curb** NOUN
an attempt to keep something within limits
EG *He called for stricter curbs on immigration.*
brake EG *Illness had put a brake on his progress.*
control EG *price controls*
limit EG *limits on government spending*
limitation EG *We need a limitation on*

the powers of the government.
restraint EG *new restraints on trade unions*

❶ **cure** VERB
to make well
EG *a treatment which cures eczema*
heal EG *plants used to heal wounds*
remedy EG *an operation to remedy a blood clot on his brain*

❷ **cure** NOUN
something that makes an illness better
EG *a cure for cancer*
medicine EG *herbal medicines*
remedy EG *a remedy for colds and flu*
treatment EG *the most effective treatment for malaria*

❶ **curiosity** NOUN
the desire to know
EG *a curiosity about the past*
inquisitiveness EG *the inquisitiveness of children*
interest EG *a lively interest in current affairs*

❷ **curiosity** NOUN
something unusual
EG *a museum displaying relics and curiosities*
freak EG *a freak of nature*
marvel EG *a marvel of science*
novelty EG *in the days when a motor car was a novelty*
oddity EG *Tourists are still something of an oddity here.*
rarity EG *Mexican restaurants are a rarity here.*

❶ **curious** ADJECTIVE
wanting to know
EG *He was curious about my family.*
inquiring EG *He gave me an inquiring look.*
inquisitive EG *Cats are very inquisitive.*
interested EG *A crowd of interested*

curious >> custom

villagers gathered.
nosy INFORMAL EG *nosy neighbours*

WORD POWER

▶ **Antonym**
incurious

2 curious ADJECTIVE
strange and unusual
EG *a curious mixture of the old and the new*
bizarre EG *his bizarre behaviour*
extraordinary EG *an extraordinary story*
odd EG *an odd coincidence*
peculiar EG *a peculiar smell*
singular EG *singular talent*
strange EG *a strange taste*
unusual EG *an unusual name*

WORD POWER

▶ **Antonym**
ordinary

1 current NOUN
a strong continuous movement of water
EG *swept away by the strong current*
flow EG *the quiet flow of the olive-green water*
tide EG *We will sail with the tide.*
undertow EG *Dangerous undertows make swimming unsafe along the coastline.*

2 current ADJECTIVE
happening, being done, or being used now
EG *current trends*
contemporary EG *He has adopted a more contemporary style.*
fashionable EG *the fashionable theory about this issue*
ongoing EG *an ongoing debate on inner city problems*
present EG *skilfully renovated by the present owners*
present-day EG *Even by present-day standards these are large aircraft.*
today's EG *In today's America, health*

care is big business.
up-to-the-minute EG *up-to-the-minute information on sales and stocks*

WORD POWER

▶ **Antonym**
past

1 curve NOUN
a bending line
EG *a curve in the road*
arc EG *The ball rose in an arc.*
bend EG *a bend in the river*
trajectory EG *the trajectory of an artillery shell*
turn EG *every turn in the road*

WORD POWER

● **Related Words**
adjective : sinuous

2 curve VERB
to move in a curve
EG *The road curved sharply to the left.*
arc EG *A rainbow arced over the town.*
arch EG *a domed ceiling arching overhead*
bend EG *The path bent to the right.*
swerve EG *His car swerved off the road.*

1 custom NOUN
a traditional activity
EG *an ancient Chinese custom*
convention EG *the conventions of Western art*
practice EG *an old Jewish practice*
ritual EG *an ancient Shintoist ritual*
tradition EG *different cultural traditions*

2 custom NOUN
something a person always does
EG *It was his custom to start work at 8.30.*
habit EG *his habit of making tactless remarks*
practice EG *her usual practice of attending church*

a b c d e f g h i j k l m n o p q r s t u v w x y z

routine EG *his daily routine*
wont EG *Paul woke early, as was his wont.*

customer NOUN
someone who buys something
EG *The shop was filled with customers.*
buyer EG *show homes to tempt potential buyers*
client EG *a solicitor and his client*
consumer EG *the increasing demands of consumers*
patron EG *the restaurant's patrons*
purchaser EG *a prospective purchaser*
shopper EG *late-night shoppers on their way home*

❶ cut VERB
to mark or injure with something sharp
EG *The thieves cut a hole in the fence.*
→ see Word Study **cut**

❷ cut VERB
to reduce something
EG *The department's first priority is to cut costs.*
cut back EG *The Government has decided to cut back on defence spending.*
decrease EG *calls to decrease income tax*
lower EG *The Central Bank has lowered interest rates.*
reduce EG *Gradually reduce the dosage.*
slash EG *Holiday prices have been slashed.*

WORD POWER
▷ **Synonyms**
abridge
downsize
rationalize

▶ **Antonym**
increase

❸ cut NOUN
a mark or injury made by cutting

EG *a cut on his left eyebrow*
gash EG *There was a deep gash across his forehead.*
incision EG *a tiny incision in the skin*
slash EG *jeans with slashes in the knees*
slit EG *Make a slit along the stem.*

❹ cut NOUN
a reduction in something
EG *another cut in interest rates*
cutback EG *cutbacks in funding*
decrease EG *a decrease in foreign investment*
lowering EG *the lowering of taxes*
reduction EG *reductions in staff*
saving EG *household savings on energy use*

WORD POWER
▶ **Antonym**
increase

cute ADJECTIVE
pretty or attractive
EG *You were such a cute baby!*
appealing EG *an appealing kitten*
attractive EG *I thought he was very attractive.*
charming EG *a charming little cottage*
dear EG *Look at their dear little faces!*
good-looking EG *Cassandra noticed him because he was so good-looking.*
gorgeous EG *All the girls think Ryan's gorgeous.*
pretty EG *She's a very pretty girl.*

WORD POWER
▶ **Antonym**
ugly

cynical ADJECTIVE
always thinking the worst of people
EG *a cynical attitude*
distrustful EG *distrustful of all politicians*
sceptical EG *a sceptical response*

Dd

daft ADJECTIVE
extremely silly
EG *Now there's a daft suggestion!*
crazy EG *He has this crazy idea about his neighbours.*
foolish EG *It would be foolish to raise his hopes unnecessarily.*
ludicrous EG *It was ludicrous to suggest that the visit could be kept a secret.*
preposterous EG *their preposterous claim that they had discovered a plot*
ridiculous EG *It was an absolutely ridiculous decision.*
silly EG *That's a silly question.*
stupid EG *I made a stupid mistake.*

WORD POWER

▶ **Antonym**
sensible

❶ damage VERB
to cause harm to something
EG *A fire had severely damaged the school.*
harm EG *a warning that the product may harm the environment*
hurt EG *He had hurt his back in an accident.*
injure EG *Several policemen were injured in the clashes.*

❷ damage NOUN
harm that is done to something
EG *The bomb caused extensive damage to the restaurant.*
harm EG *All dogs are capable of doing harm to human beings.*
injury EG *He escaped without injury.*

❶ damp ADJECTIVE
slightly wet
EG *a damp towel*
clammy EG *clammy hands*
dank EG *The kitchen was dank and cheerless.*
humid EG *Visitors can expect hot and humid conditions.*
moist EG *The soil is reasonably moist*

after the September rain.
sodden EG *We stripped off our sodden clothes.*
soggy EG *soggy cheese sandwiches*
wet EG *My hair was still wet.*

❷ damp NOUN
slight wetness
EG *There was damp all over the walls.*
dampness EG *I could see big circles of dampness under each arm.*
humidity EG *The heat and humidity were intolerable.*
moisture EG *Compost helps the soil retain moisture.*

WORD POWER

▷ **Synonyms**
clamminess
dankness

danger NOUN
the possibility of harm
EG *Your life is in danger.*
hazard EG *a health hazard*
jeopardy EG *A series of setbacks have put the whole project in jeopardy.*
menace EG *In my view you are a menace to the public.*
peril EG *the perils of the sea*
risk EG *There is a small risk of brain damage.*
threat EG *Some couples see single women as a threat to their relationship.*

WORD POWER

▶ **Antonym**
safety

dangerous ADJECTIVE
likely to cause harm
EG *It's dangerous to drive when you're tired.*
hazardous EG *They have no way to dispose of the hazardous waste they produce.*
perilous EG *a perilous journey across*

dark >> dark

the war-zone
risky EG *Investing is risky.*
treacherous EG *Blizzards had made the roads treacherous.*

WORD POWER

▶ **Antonym**
safe

❶ dare VERB
to challenge someone to do something
EG *I dare you to ask him his name.*
challenge EG *He left a note at the scene of the crime, challenging detectives to catch him.*
defy EG *I defy you to watch it on your own.*
throw down the gauntlet
EG *Jaguar has thrown down the gauntlet to competitors by giving the best guarantee on the market.*

❷ dare VERB
to have the courage to do something
EG *Nobody dared to complain.*
risk EG *The skipper was not willing to risk taking his ship through the straits.*
venture EG *the few Europeans who had ventured beyond the Himalayas*

❶ daring ADJECTIVE
willing to take risks
EG *a daring escape by helicopter*
adventurous EG *an adventurous skier*
audacious EG *an audacious plan to win the presidency*
bold EG *bold economic reforms*
brave EG *He was not brave enough to report the loss of the documents.*
fearless EG *They were young and strong and fearless.*

WORD POWER

▷ **Synonyms**
intrepid
valiant

▶ **Antonym**
cautious

❷ daring NOUN
the courage to take risks
EG *His daring may have cost him his life.*
audacity EG *He had the audacity to make a 200-1 bet on himself to win.*
boldness EG *the boldness of his economic programme*
bravery EG *He deserves the highest praise for his bravery.*
courage EG *He impressed everyone with his personal courage.*
guts INFORMAL EG *I haven't got the guts to tell him.*
nerve INFORMAL EG *He didn't have the nerve to meet me.*

WORD POWER

▷ **Synonyms**
fearlessness
intrepidity
temerity

▶ **Antonym**
caution

❶ dark ADJECTIVE
lacking light
EG *It was too dark to see what was happening.*
cloudy EG *a cloudy sky*
dim EG *the dim outline of a small boat*
dingy EG *a dingy bedsit*
murky EG *the murky waters of the loch*
overcast EG *a cold, windy, overcast afternoon*
shadowy EG *a shadowy corner*

WORD POWER

▶ **Antonym**
light

❷ dark ADJECTIVE
dull in colour
EG *a dark suit*

black EG *a black leather coat*
swarthy EG *a broad swarthy face*

❸ **dark** NOUN
lack of light
EG *I've always been afraid of the dark.*
darkness EG *The room was plunged into darkness.*
dimness EG *I squinted to adjust my eyes to the dimness.*
dusk EG *She disappeared into the dusk.*
gloom EG *the gloom of a foggy November morning*

WORD POWER

▷ **Synonyms**
murk
murkiness

▶ **Antonym**
light

---

❶ **dash** VERB
to rush somewhere
EG *Suddenly she dashed out into the garden.*
bolt EG *I bolted for the exit.*
fly EG *She flew downstairs.*
race EG *The hares raced away out of sight.*
run EG *The gunmen ran off into the woods.*
rush EG *Someone rushed out of the building.*
sprint EG *Sergeant Greene sprinted to the car.*
tear EG *He tore off down the road.*

WORD POWER

▷ **Synonyms**
make haste
hasten

---

❷ **dash** VERB
to throw or be thrown violently against something
EG *The waves dashed against the rocks.*
break EG *Danny listened to the waves breaking against the shore.*
crash EG *The door swung inwards and crashed against a cupboard behind it.*
hurl EG *He hurled the vase to the ground in rage.*
slam EG *They slammed me on to the ground.*
smash EG *smashing the bottle against a wall*

❸ **dash** VERB
to ruin or frustrate someone's hopes or ambitions
EG *They had their hopes raised and then dashed.*
crush EG *My dreams of becoming an actor have been crushed.*
destroy EG *Even the most gifted can have their confidence destroyed by the wrong teacher.*
disappoint EG *His hopes have been disappointed many times before.*
foil EG *Our idea of building a water garden was foiled by the planning authorities.*
frustrate EG *The government has deliberately frustrated his efforts.*
shatter EG *A failure would shatter all our hopes.*
thwart EG *Her ambition to be an artist was thwarted by failing eyesight.*

WORD POWER

▷ **Synonyms**
quash

---

❹ **dash** NOUN
a sudden movement or rush
EG *a 160-mile dash to the hospital*
bolt EG *He made a bolt for the door.*
race EG *a race for the finishing line*
run EG *One of the gang made a run for it.*
rush EG *the mad rush not to be late for school*
sprint EG *a last-minute sprint to catch the bus*

a b c **d** e f g h i j k l m n o p q r s t u v w x y z

stampede EG *There was a stampede for the exit.*

⑤ dash NOUN
a small quantity of something
EG *a dash of wine vinegar*
drop EG *I'll have a drop of that milk in my tea.*
pinch EG *a pinch of salt*
splash EG *add a splash of lemon juice*
sprinkling EG *a light sprinkling of sugar*

① daydream NOUN
a series of pleasant thoughts
EG *He learnt to escape into daydreams.*
dream EG *My dream is to have a house in the country.*
fantasy EG *fantasies of romance and true love*

WORD POWER

▷ **Synonyms**
castle in Spain
castle in the air
pipe dream
reverie

② daydream VERB
to think about pleasant things
EG *He daydreams of being a famous journalist.*
dream EG *She used to dream of becoming an actress.*
fantasize EG *I fantasized about writing music.*

dazed ADJECTIVE
unable to think clearly
EG *At the end of the interview I was dazed and exhausted.*
bewildered EG *Some shoppers looked bewildered by the sheer variety.*
confused EG *Things were happening too quickly and Brian was confused.*
dizzy EG *Her head hurt and she felt dizzy.*
light-headed EG *If you miss breakfast, you may feel light-headed.*
numbed EG *I'm so numbed with shock*

that I can hardly think.
stunned EG *a stunned silence*

WORD POWER

▷ **Synonyms**
disorientated
punch-drunk
stupefied

① dead ADJECTIVE
no longer alive
EG *My husband's been dead a year now.*
deceased EG *his recently deceased mother*
departed EG *my dear departed father*
extinct EG *the bones of extinct animals*
late EG *my late husband*

WORD POWER

▶ **Antonym**
alive

② dead ADJECTIVE
no longer functioning
EG *a dead language*
defunct EG *the now defunct Social Democratic Party*
not working EG *The radio is not working.*

deadly ADJECTIVE
causing death
EG *a deadly disease*
destructive EG *the destructive power of nuclear weapons*
fatal EG *a fatal heart attack*
lethal EG *a lethal dose of sleeping pills*
mortal EG *Our lives were in mortal danger.*

deal VERB
to cope successfully with something
EG *He must learn to deal with stress.*
attend to EG *We have business to attend to first.*
cope with EG *She has had to cope with losing all her money.*
handle EG *I have learned how to*

handle pressure.
manage EG *As time passed I learned to manage my grief.*
see to EG *Sarah saw to the packing while Jim fetched the car.*
take care of EG *Malcolm took care of all the arrangements.*

❶ dear NOUN
a person for whom you have affection
EG *What's the matter, dear?*
angel EG *Be an angel and fetch my bag.*
beloved OLD-FASHIONED EG *He took his beloved into his arms.*
darling EG *Thank you, darling.*
treasure INFORMAL EG *Charlie? Oh, he's a treasure.*

❷ dear ADJECTIVE
much loved
EG *a dear friend of mine*
beloved EG *He lost his beloved wife last year.*
cherished EG *his most cherished possession*
darling EG *his darling daughter*
esteemed EG *my esteemed colleagues*
precious EG *Her family's support is very precious to her.*
prized EG *one of the gallery's most prized possessions*
treasured EG *one of my most treasured memories*

❸ dear ADJECTIVE
costing a lot
EG *They're too dear.*
costly EG *Having curtains professionally made can be costly.*
expensive EG *Wine's so expensive in this country.*
pricey INFORMAL EG *Medical insurance is very pricey.*

deceive VERB
to make someone believe something untrue
EG *I was really hurt that he had*

deceived me.
con INFORMAL EG *The British motorist has been conned by the government.*
double-cross EG *They were frightened of being double-crossed.*
dupe EG *a plot to dupe stamp collectors into buying fake rarities*
fool EG *They tried to fool you into coming after us.*
mislead EG *He was furious with his doctors for having misled him.*
take in EG *I wasn't taken in for one moment.*
trick EG *His family tricked him into going to Pakistan.*

WORD POWER

▷ **Synonyms**
bamboozle
beguile
hoodwink

❶ decent ADJECTIVE
of an acceptable standard
EG *He gets a decent pension.*
adequate EG *an adequate diet*
passable EG *She speaks passable French.*
reasonable EG *He couldn't make a reasonable living from his writing.*
respectable EG *investments that offer respectable rates of return*
satisfactory EG *I never got a satisfactory answer.*
tolerable EG *to make life more tolerable*

❷ decent ADJECTIVE
correct and respectable
EG *the decent thing to do*
proper EG *It is right and proper to do this.*
respectable EG *He came from a perfectly respectable middle-class family.*

WORD POWER

▶ **Antonym**
improper

a b c d e f g h i j k l m n o p q r s t u v w x y z

A
B
C
D
E
F
G
H
I
J
K
L
M
N
O
P
Q
R
S
T
U
V
W
X
Y
Z

deceptive ADJECTIVE
likely to make people believe
something untrue
EG *First impressions can be deceptive.*
false EG *'Thank you,' she said with
false enthusiasm.*
fraudulent EG *fraudulent claims
about being a nurse*
illusory EG *They argue that freedom
is illusory.*
misleading EG *It would be
misleading to say that we were friends.*
unreliable EG *His account is quite
unreliable.*

WORD POWER

▷ **Synonyms**
delusive
specious

decide VERB
to choose to do something
EG *She decided to do a secretarial
course.*
choose EG *The council chose to
inform the public about the risks.*
come to a decision EG *Have you
come to a decision about where you're
going tonight?*
determine FORMAL EG *He determined
to rescue his two countrymen.*
elect FORMAL EG *I have elected to stay.*
make up your mind EG *He simply
can't make his mind up whether he
should stay.*
reach a decision EG *He demanded
to know all the facts before reaching
any decision.*
resolve FORMAL EG *She resolved to
report the matter to the authorities.*

decision NOUN
a judgment about something
EG *The editor's decision is final.*
conclusion EG *I've come to the
conclusion that she's a great musician.*
finding EG *It is the finding of this court
that you are guilty.*
judgment EG *a landmark judgment
by the Court of Appeal*

resolution EG *a resolution
condemning violence*
ruling EG *He tried to have the court
ruling overturned.*
verdict EG *The judges will deliver
their verdict in October.*

declaration NOUN
a forceful or official announcement
EG *a declaration of war*
affirmation EG *her first public
affirmation of her decision*
protestation FORMAL EG *his
protestations of innocence*
statement EG *He made a formal
statement to the police.*
testimony EG *His testimony was an
important element in the case.*

WORD POWER

▷ **Synonyms**
assertion
avowal

declare VERB
to state something forcefully or
officially
EG *He declared that he was going to be
famous.*
affirm EG *a speech in which he
affirmed a commitment to lower taxes*
announce EG *She was planning to
announce her engagement.*
assert EG *He asserted his innocence.*
certify EG *The president certified that
the project would receive $650m.*
proclaim EG *He still proclaims himself
a believer in the Revolution.*
profess FORMAL EG *Why do
organisations profess that they care?*
pronounce EG *The authorities took
time to pronounce their verdict.*
state EG *Please state your name.*

WORD POWER

▷ **Synonyms**
attest
aver
avow

❶ decline VERB
to become smaller or weaker
EG *a declining birth rate*
decrease EG *The number of
independent firms decreased from 198
to 96.*
diminish EG *The threat of nuclear war
has diminished.*
drop EG *His blood pressure had
dropped.*
fall EG *Output will fall by six per cent.*
go down EG *Crime has gone down 70
per cent.*
plummet EG *The Prime Minister's
popularity has plummeted to an all-
time low.*
reduce EG *The number of students
fluent in Latin has been steadily
reducing.*

WORD POWER

▷ **Synonyms**
wane

▶ **Antonym**
increase

❷ decline VERB
to refuse politely to accept or do
something
EG *He declined their invitation.*
abstain EG *I will abstain from voting
in the ballot.*
excuse yourself EG *I was invited,
but I excused myself.*
refuse EG *He refused to comment
after the trial.*
turn down EG *I thanked him for the
offer but turned it down.*

WORD POWER

▶ **Antonym**
accept

❸ decline NOUN
a gradual weakening or decrease
EG *economic decline*
decrease EG *a decrease in the
number of young people out of work*

downturn EG *a sharp downturn in
the industry*
drop EG *a drop in support for the
Conservatives*
fall EG *a sharp fall in the value of the
pound*
recession EG *pull the economy out of
recession*
shrinkage EG *a shrinkage in
industrial output*
slump EG *a slump in property prices*

WORD POWER

▶ **Antonym**
increase

❶ decorate VERB
to make more attractive
EG *He decorated his room with
pictures.*
adorn EG *Several oil paintings adorn
the walls.*
deck EG *The house was decked with
flowers.*
ornament EG *a high ceiling,
ornamented with plaster fruits and
flowers*

WORD POWER

▷ **Synonyms**
beautify
bedeck
embellish
festoon

❷ decorate VERB
to put paint or wallpaper on
EG *when they came to decorate the
bedroom*
do up INFORMAL EG *He spent the
summer doing up the barn.*
renovate EG *The couple spent
thousands renovating the house.*

❶ decrease VERB
to become or make less
EG *Population growth is decreasing by
1.4% each year.*
cut down EG *He cut down his coffee
intake.*

A
B
C
D
E
F
G
H
I
J
K
L
M
N
O
P
Q
R
S
T
U
V
W
X
Y
Z

decline EG *The number of staff has declined.*

diminish EG *The threat of nuclear war has diminished.*

drop EG *Temperatures can drop to freezing at night.*

dwindle EG *his dwindling authority*

lessen EG *changes to their diet that would lessen the risk of disease*

lower EG *The Central Bank has lowered interest rates.*

reduce EG *It reduces the risk of heart disease.*

shrink EG *The forests have shrunk to half their size.*

WORD POWER

▷ **Synonyms**
abate
curtail
subside
wane

▶ **Antonym**
increase

2 decrease NOUN
a lessening in the amount of something
EG *a decrease in the number of unemployed*

cutback EG *cutbacks in defence spending*

decline EG *the rate of decline in tobacco consumption*

drop EG *a drop in temperature*

lessening EG *a lessening of tension*

reduction EG *dramatic reductions in staff*

WORD POWER

▷ **Synonyms**
abatement
curtailment
diminution

▶ **Antonym**
increase

1 deep ADJECTIVE
having a long way to the bottom
EG *a deep hole*

bottomless EG *a bottomless pit*

yawning EG *a yawning chasm*

WORD POWER

▶ **Antonym**
shallow

2 deep ADJECTIVE
great or intense
EG *his deep love of Israel*

extreme EG *extreme poverty*

grave EG *a grave crisis*

great EG *the great gulf between the two teams*

intense EG *The pain was intense.*

profound EG *discoveries which had a profound effect on medicine*

serious EG *a serious problem*

3 deep ADJECTIVE
low in sound
EG *a deep voice*

bass EG *a beautiful bass voice*

low EG *Her voice was so low she was sometimes mistaken for a man.*

WORD POWER

▷ **Synonyms**
resonant
sonorous

▶ **Antonym**
high

1 defeat VERB
to win a victory over someone
EG *His guerrillas defeated the colonial army in 1954.*

beat EG *the team that beat us in the final*

conquer EG *During 1936, Mussolini conquered Abyssinia.*

crush EG *in his bid to crush the rebels*

rout EG *the battle at which the Norman army routed the English*

trounce EG *Australia trounced France by 60 points to 4.*

vanquish FORMAL EG *after the hero had vanquished the dragon*

❷ defeat NOUN
a failure to win
EG *a 2-1 defeat by Sweden*
conquest EG *He had led the conquest of southern Poland.*
debacle FORMAL EG *It will be hard for them to recover from this debacle.*
rout EG *The retreat turned into a rout.*
trouncing EG *after a 6-2 trouncing on Sunday*

WORD POWER

▶ **Antonym**
victory

---

defect NOUN
a fault or flaw
EG *A defect in the aircraft caused the crash.*
deficiency EG *the most serious deficiency in NATO's air defence*
failing EG *She blamed the country's failings on its culture of greed.*
fault EG *a minor technical fault*
flaw EG *The only flaw in his character is a short temper.*
imperfection EG *my physical imperfections*
shortcoming EG *The book has its shortcomings.*
weakness EG *His only weakness is his laziness.*

❶ defence NOUN
action to protect something
EG *The flat land offered no scope for defence.*
cover EG *They could not provide adequate air cover for ground operations.*
protection EG *Such a diet is believed to offer protection against cancer.*
resistance EG *Most people have a natural resistance to the disease.*
safeguard EG *legislation that offers safeguards against discrimination*

security EG *Airport security was tightened.*

❷ defence NOUN
an argument in support of something
EG *Chomsky's defence of his approach*
argument EG *There's a strong argument for lowering the price.*
excuse EG *There's no excuse for behaviour like that.*
explanation EG *The authorities have given no explanation for his arrest.*
justification EG *The only justification for a zoo is educational.*
plea EG *a plea of insanity*

❶ defend VERB
to protect from harm
EG *They would have killed him if he hadn't defended himself.*
cover EG *travel insurance covering you against theft*
guard EG *A few men were left outside to guard her.*
protect EG *What can women do to protect themselves from heart disease?*
safeguard EG *action to safeguard the ozone layer*
shelter EG *a wooden house, sheltered by a low roof*
shield EG *He shielded his head from the sun with an old sack.*

❷ defend VERB
to argue in support of
EG *I can't defend what he did.*
endorse EG *I can endorse their opinion wholeheartedly.*
justify EG *No argument can justify a war.*
stick up for INFORMAL EG *Why do you always stick up for her?*
support EG *Would you support such a move?*
uphold EG *upholding the artist's right to creative freedom*

defender NOUN
a person who argues in support of

A
B
C
D
E
F
G
H
I
J
K
L
M
N
O
P
Q
R
S
T
U
V
W
X
Y
Z

something
EG *a committed defender of human rights*
advocate EG *a strong advocate of free market policies*
champion EG *a champion of women's causes*
supporter EG *a major supporter of the tax reform*

deficiency NOUN
a lack of something
EG *signs of vitamin deficiency*
deficit EG *a staffing deficit*
deprivation EG *sleep deprivation*
inadequacy EG *the inadequacies of the current system*
lack EG *a lack of people wanting to start new businesses*
want FORMAL EG *a want of manners and charm*

WORD POWER

▶ **Antonym**
abundance

deficient ADJECTIVE
lacking in something
EG *a diet deficient in vitamins*
inadequate EG *inadequate staffing*
lacking EG *Why was military intelligence so lacking?*
poor EG *soil that is poor in zinc*
short EG *The proposals were short on detail.*
wanting EG *He analysed his game and found it wanting.*

❶ definite ADJECTIVE
unlikely to be changed
EG *It's too soon to give a definite answer.*
assured EG *Victory was still not assured.*
certain EG *Very little in life is certain.*
decided EG *Is anything decided yet?*
fixed EG *a world without fixed laws*
guaranteed EG *Success is not guaranteed.*
settled EG *Nothing is settled yet.*

❷ definite ADJECTIVE
certainly true
EG *The police had nothing definite against her.*
clear EG *It was a clear case of homicide.*
positive EG *We have positive proof that he was a blackmailer.*

WORD POWER

▶ **Synonyms**
black-and-white
clear-cut
cut-and-dried

deformed ADJECTIVE
abnormally shaped
EG *a deformed right leg*
disfigured EG *the scarred, disfigured face*
distorted EG *the distorted image caused by the projector*

degrade VERB
to humiliate someone
EG *the notion that pornography degrades women*
demean EG *I wasn't going to demean myself by acting like a suspicious wife.*
humiliate EG *He enjoyed humiliating me.*

❶ delay VERB
to put something off until later
EG *the decision to delay the launch until tomorrow*
defer EG *Customers often defer payment for as long as possible.*
postpone EG *The visit has been postponed indefinitely.*
put off EG *women who put off having a baby*
shelve EG *The project has now been shelved.*
suspend EG *Relief convoys will be suspended until the fighting stops.*

❷ delay VERB
to slow or hinder something
EG *Various setbacks delayed production.*

check EG *a policy to check fast population growth*
hinder EG *Further investigation was hindered by the loss of all documentation.*
impede EG *Fallen rocks are impeding the progress of rescue workers.*
obstruct EG *The authorities are obstructing a UN investigation.*
set back EG *public protests that could set back reforms*

WORD POWER

▷ **Synonyms**
hold up
retard

▶ **Antonym**
hurry

---

❸ delay NOUN
a time when something is delayed
EG *a 7-hour stoppage that caused delays on most flights*
interruption EG *interruptions in the supply of food*
obstruction EG *Obstruction of justice is a criminal offence.*
setback EG *a setback for the peace process*

delete VERB
to remove something written
EG *The word 'exploded' had been deleted.*
cross out EG *He crossed out the first sentence and wrote it again.*
erase EG *It was unfortunate that she had erased the message.*
rub out EG *She rubbed out the marks in the margin.*

WORD POWER

▷ **Synonyms**
blue-pencil
cancel
edit out
strike out

---

❶ deliberate ADJECTIVE
done on purpose
EG *a deliberate act of sabotage*
calculated EG *a calculated attempt to cover up her crime*
conscious EG *I made a conscious decision not to hide.*
intentional EG *The kick was intentional.*
premeditated EG *a premeditated attack*
studied EG *'It's an interesting match,' he said with studied understatement.*

WORD POWER

▶ **Antonym**
accidental

---

❷ deliberate ADJECTIVE
careful and not hurried
EG *His movements were gentle and deliberate.*
careful EG *The trip needs careful planning.*
cautious EG *a cautious approach*
measured EG *walking at the same measured pace*
methodical EG *Da Vinci was methodical in his research.*

WORD POWER

▶ **Antonym**
casual

---

❸ deliberate VERB
to think carefully about something
EG *The jury deliberated for five days before reaching a verdict.*
debate EG *He was debating whether or not he should tell her.*
meditate EG *She meditated on the uncertainties of his future.*
mull over EG *McLaren had been mulling over an idea to make a movie.*
ponder EG *He was pondering the problem when Phillipson drove up.*
reflect EG *I reflected on the child's future.*

a b c d e f g h i j k l m n o p q r s t u v w x y z

delicious ADJECTIVE
tasting very nice
EG *a wide selection of delicious meals*
appetizing EG *the appetizing smell of freshly baked bread*
delectable EG *delectable wine*
luscious EG *luscious fruit*
tasty EG *The food was very tasty.*

WORD POWER

▷ **Synonyms**
mouthwatering
scrumptious

❶ delight NOUN
great pleasure or joy
EG *To my great delight, it worked.*
glee EG *His victory was greeted with glee by his supporters.*
happiness EG *Our happiness at being reunited knew no bounds.*
joy EG *the joys of being a parent*
pleasure EG *the pleasure of seeing her face*
rapture EG *gasps of rapture*
satisfaction EG *I felt a glow of satisfaction at my achievement.*

❷ delight VERB
to give someone great pleasure
EG *The report has delighted environmentalists.*
amuse EG *a selection of toys to amuse your baby*
captivate EG *captivated the world with her radiant looks*
charm EG *He charmed his landlady, chatting and flirting with her.*
enchant EG *Dena was enchanted by the house.*
please EG *It pleased him to talk to her.*
thrill EG *The electric atmosphere thrilled him.*

demand VERB
to need or require something
EG *This situation demands hard work.*
involve EG *Running a kitchen involves a great deal of discipline.*
need EG *a problem that needs careful handling*
require EG *Then he'll know what's required of him.*
take EG *Walking across the room took all her strength.*
want EG *The windows wanted cleaning.*

WORD POWER

▷ **Synonyms**
call for
entail
necessitate

❶ deny VERB
to say that something is untrue
EG *She denied both accusations.*
contradict EG *Her version contradicted the Government's claim.*
refute EG *He angrily refutes the charge.*

WORD POWER

▷ **Synonyms**
abjure
disavow
disclaim
gainsay
rebut
repudiate

▶ **Antonym**
admit

❷ deny VERB
to refuse to believe something
EG *He denied the existence of God.*
reject EG *children who rejected their parents' religious beliefs*
renounce EG *after she renounced terrorism*

❸ deny VERB
to refuse to give something
EG *His ex-partner denies him access to the children.*
refuse EG *The council had refused permission for the march.*
withhold EG *Financial aid for Russia has been withheld.*

department NOUN
a section of an organization
EG *the marketing department*
division EG *the bank's Latin American division*
office EG *Contact your local tax office.*
section EG *a top-secret section of the Foreign Office*
unit EG *the health services research unit*

❶ depend VERB
to rely on
EG *You can depend on me.*
bank on EG *The government is banking on the Olympics to save the city money.*
count on EG *I can always count on you to cheer me up.*
rely on EG *They can always be relied on to turn up.*
trust EG *I knew I could trust him to meet a tight deadline.*

❷ depend VERB
to be affected by
EG *Success depends on the quality of the workforce.*
be determined by EG *Social status is largely determined by occupation.*
hinge on EG *Victory or defeat hinged on her final putt.*

WORD POWER

▷ **Synonyms**
be subject to
hang on
rest on

---

deposit VERB
to put down or leave somewhere
EG *The barman deposited a bottle in front of him.*
drop EG *He dropped me outside the hotel.*
lay EG *The table was spread with a cloth, and the box was laid on top.*
leave EG *Leave your key with a neighbour.*
place EG *I placed the book on the counter.*
put down EG *Mishka put down her heavy shopping bag.*

derelict ADJECTIVE
abandoned and in poor condition
EG *a derelict warehouse*
abandoned EG *a network of abandoned mines*
dilapidated EG *a dilapidated castle*
neglected EG *a neglected garden*
ruined EG *a ruined church*

descend VERB
to move downwards
EG *as we descend to the cellar*
dip EG *The sun dipped below the horizon.*
dive EG *The shark dived down and under the boat.*
fall EG *Bombs fell in the town.*
go down EG *after the sun has gone down*
plummet EG *as the plane plummeted through the air*
sink EG *A fresh egg will sink and an old egg will float.*

WORD POWER

▶ **Antonym**
ascend

---

describe VERB
to give an account of something
EG *We asked her to describe what she did in her spare time.*
define EG *Culture can be defined in many ways.*
depict EG *a novel depicting a gloomy, futuristic America*
portray EG *a writer who accurately portrays provincial life*

WORD POWER

▷ **Synonyms**
characterize
detail

---

deserve VERB
to have a right to something

A
B
C
D
E
F
G
H
I
J
K
L
M
N
O
P
Q
R
S
T
U
V
W
X
Y
Z

EG *He deserves a rest.*
be entitled to EG *She is entitled to feel proud.*
be worthy of EG *The bank might think you're worthy of a loan.*
earn EG *You've earned this holiday.*
justify EG *The decision was fully justified by economic conditions.*
merit EG *Such ideas merit careful consideration.*
warrant EG *no evidence to warrant a murder investigation*

❶ **design** VERB
to make a plan of something
EG *They wanted to design a machine that was both attractive and practical.*
draft EG *The legislation was drafted by Democrats.*
draw up EG *a working party to draw up a formal agreement*
plan EG *when we plan road construction*

❷ **design** NOUN
a plan or drawing
EG *his design for a new office*
model EG *an architect's model of a wooden house*
plan EG *when you have drawn a plan of the garden*

WORD POWER

▷ **Synonyms**
blueprint
schema

❸ **design** NOUN
the shape or style of something
EG *a new design of clock*
form EG *the form of the human body*
pattern EG *a pattern of coloured dots*
shape EG *a kidney shape*
style EG *Several styles of hat were available.*

❶ **desire** VERB
to want something
EG *We can stay longer if you desire.*
crave EG *I crave her approval.*
fancy EG *She fancied living in Canada.*

long for EG *He longed for the winter to be over.*
want EG *I want a drink.*
wish EG *We wished to return.*
yearn EG *He yearned to sleep.*

WORD POWER

▷ **Synonyms**
ache for
covet

❷ **desire** NOUN
a feeling of wanting something
EG *I had a strong desire to help people.*
appetite EG *She had lost her appetite for air travel.*
craving EG *a craving for sugar*
hankering EG *a hankering to be an actress*
longing EG *her longing to return home*
wish EG *Her wish is to be in films.*
yearning EG *a yearning for a child of my own*
yen INFORMAL EG *Mike had a yen to try cycling.*

❶ **despair** NOUN
a loss of hope
EG *feelings of despair*
dejection EG *There was an air of dejection about her.*
despondency EG *There's a mood of despondency in the country.*
gloom EG *the deepening gloom over the economy*
hopelessness EG *She had a feeling of hopelessness about the future.*

❷ **despair** VERB
to lose hope
EG *I despair at the attitude with which their work is received.*
feel dejected EG *Everyone has days when they feel dejected.*
feel despondent EG *John often felt despondent after visiting the job centre.*
lose heart EG *He appealed to his*

countrymen not to lose heart.
lose hope EG You mustn't lose hope.

despite PREPOSITION
in spite of
EG He fell asleep despite all the coffee he'd drunk.
in spite of EG In spite of all the gossip, Virginia stayed behind.
notwithstanding FORMAL
eg Notwithstanding his age, Sikorski had an important job.
regardless of EG He led from the front, regardless of the danger.

destroy VERB
to ruin something completely
EG The building was completely destroyed.
annihilate EG The lava annihilates everything in its path.
demolish EG A storm moved over the island, demolishing buildings.
devastate EG A fire had devastated large parts of Windsor castle.
obliterate EG Whole villages were obliterated by fire.
raze EG The town was razed to the ground during the occupation.
ruin EG My wife was ruining her health through worry.
wreck EG the injuries which nearly wrecked his career

destruction NOUN
the act of destroying something
EG the destruction of the ozone layer
annihilation EG Leaders fear the annihilation of their people.
demolition EG the demolition of an old bridge
devastation EG A huge bomb blast brought chaos and devastation.
obliteration EG the obliteration of three rainforests

detail NOUN
an individual feature of something
EG We discussed every detail of the performance.
aspect EG Climate affects every

aspect of our lives.
element EG one of the key elements of the peace plan
particular EG You will find all the particulars in Chapter 9.
point EG Many of the points in the report are correct.
respect EG At least in this respect we are equals.

WORD POWER

▷ **Synonyms**
fine point
nicety

---

determination NOUN
a firm decision to do something
EG the government's determination to beat inflation
perseverance EG Adam's perseverance proved worthwhile.
persistence EG She was determined to be a doctor and her persistence paid off.
resolution EG She acted with resolution and courage.
resolve FORMAL EG the American public's resolve to go to war if necessary
tenacity EG Hard work and sheer tenacity are crucial to career success.

WORD POWER

▷ **Synonyms**
doggedness
single-mindedness
steadfastness
willpower

---

❶ **determine** VERB
to cause or control a situation or result
EG The size of the chicken pieces will determine the cooking time.
control EG Scientists may soon be able to control the ageing process.
decide EG The results will decide if he will win a place on the course.
dictate EG A number of factors will

a
b
c
d
e
f
g
h
i
j
k
l
m
n
o
p
q
r
s
t
u
v
w
x
y
z

A
B
C
D
E
F
G
H
I
J
K
L
M
N
O
P
Q
R
S
T
U
V
W
X
Y
Z

dictate how long the tree will survive.
govern EG *the rules governing eligibility for unemployment benefit*
shape EG *the role of key leaders in shaping the future of Europe*

❷ determine VERB
to decide or settle something firmly
EG *The final wording had not yet been determined.*
arrange EG *It was arranged that the party would gather in the Royal Garden Hotel.*
choose EG *Houston was chosen as the site for the convention.*
decide EG *Her age would be taken into account when deciding her sentence.*
fix EG *The date of the election was fixed.*
resolve EG *She resolved to report the matter to the authorities.*
settle EG *That's settled then. We'll do it tomorrow.*

❸ determine VERB
to find out the facts about something
EG *The investigation will determine what really happened.*
ascertain FORMAL EG *We need to ascertain the true facts.*
confirm EG *X-rays have confirmed that he has not broken any bones.*
discover EG *It was difficult for us to discover the reason for the decision.*
establish EG *an autopsy to establish the cause of death*
find out EG *one family's campaign to find out the truth*
verify EG *A clerk verifies that the payment and invoice amount match.*

determined ADJECTIVE
firmly decided
EG *She was determined not to repeat her error.*
bent on EG *They seem bent on destroying the city.*
dogged EG *dogged persistence*

intent on EG *He is intent on repeating his victory.*
persistent EG *He phoned again this morning. He's very persistent.*
purposeful EG *She had a purposeful air.*
resolute FORMAL EG *a decisive and resolute leader*
single-minded EG *a single-minded determination to win*
tenacious EG *a tenacious and persistent interviewer*

WORD POWER

▷ **Synonyms**
steadfast
unflinching
unwavering

---

❶ develop VERB
to grow or become more advanced
EG *Children develop at different rates.*
advance EG *tracing how medical technology has advanced to its present state*
evolve EG *As scientific knowledge evolves, beliefs change.*
grow EG *The boys grew into men.*
mature EG *Other changes occur as the child matures physically.*
progress EG *His disease progressed quickly.*
result EG *Ignore the warnings and illness could result.*
spring EG *His anger sprang from his childhood suffering.*

❷ develop VERB
to become affected by an illness or fault
EG *He developed pneumonia.*
catch EG *catch a cold*
contract FORMAL EG *He contracted AIDS from a blood transfusion.*
fall ill EG *She fell ill with measles.*
get EG *When I was five I got mumps.*
go down with EG *Three members of the band went down with flu.*
pick up EG *They've picked up an*

infection from something they've eaten.
succumb EG *I was determined not to succumb to the virus.*

devious ADJECTIVE
getting what you want by sly methods
EG *a devious politician*
calculating EG *a calculating businessman*
scheming EG *He was branded a "scheming liar".*
underhand EG *He used underhand tactics to win the election.*
wily EG *a wily old statesman*

devoted ADJECTIVE
very loving and loyal
EG *a devoted father*
constant EG *her constant companion*
dedicated EG *dedicated followers of classical music*
doting EG *His doting parents bought him a racing bike.*
faithful EG *I'm very faithful when I love someone.*
loving EG *Jim was a loving husband.*
loyal EG *a loyal friend*
true EG *David was true to his wife.*

dictionary NOUN

> **Parts of a dictionary or thesaurus**
> antonym
> definition
> entry
> example
> homonym
> homophone
> pronunciation
> root word
> synonym
> word derivation

❶ die VERB
to stop living
EG *My mother died of cancer.*
cark it AUSTRALIAN AND NEW ZEALAND;

INFORMAL EG *You think you're about to cark it.*
expire FORMAL EG *before he finally expired*
pass away EG *He passed away last year.*
pass on EG *My mother passed on four years ago.*
perish FORMAL EG *the ferry disaster in which 193 passengers perished*

❷ die VERB
to fade away
EG *My love for you will never die.*
fade away EG *With time, they said, the pain will fade away.*
fade out EG *Thanks to supermarkets, the corner shop is gradually fading out.*
peter out EG *The six-month strike seemed to be petering out.*

die out VERB
to cease to exist
EG *That custom has died out now.*
disappear EG *Huge areas of the countryside are disappearing.*
fade EG *Prospects for peace had already started to fade.*
vanish EG *those species which have vanished*

❶ difference NOUN
a lack of similarity between things
EG *the vast difference in size*
contrast EG *the real contrast between the two poems*
discrepancy EG *discrepancies between their statements*
disparity EG *disparities between poor and wealthy districts*
distinction EG *a distinction between the body and the soul*
divergence EG *There's a substantial divergence of opinion within the party.*
variation EG *a wide variation in the prices charged*

A
B
C
D
E
F
G
H
I
J
K
L
M
N
O
P
Q
R
S
T
U
V
W
X
Y
Z

WORD POWER

▶ **Antonym**
similarity

2 difference NOUN
the amount by which two quantities
differ
EG *The difference is 8532.*
balance EG *They were due to pay the
balance on delivery.*
remainder EG *They own a 75% stake.
The remainder is owned by the bank.*

1 different ADJECTIVE
unlike something else
EG *We have totally different views.*
contrasting EG *painted in
contrasting colours*
disparate FORMAL EG *The republics
are very disparate in size and wealth.*
dissimilar EG *His methods were not
dissimilar to those used by Freud.*
divergent FORMAL EG *divergent
opinions*
opposed EG *two opposed ideologies*
unlike EG *This was a foreign country,
so unlike San Jose.*

WORD POWER

▷ **Synonyms**
at odds
at variance

▶ **Antonym**
similar

2 different ADJECTIVE
unusual and out of the ordinary
EG *The result is interesting and
different.*
special EG *a special variety of
strawberry*
unique EG *Each person's signature is
unique.*

3 different ADJECTIVE
distinct and separate
EG *The lunch supports a different
charity each year.*
another EG *Her doctor referred her to*

another therapist.
discrete FORMAL EG *two discrete sets
of nerves*
distinct EG *A word may have two
quite distinct meanings.*
individual EG *Each family needs
individual attention.*
separate EG *The word 'quarter' has
two completely separate meanings.*

1 difficult ADJECTIVE
not easy to do or solve
EG *a difficult decision to make*
arduous EG *a long, arduous journey*
demanding EG *a demanding job*
hard EG *He found it hard to get work.*
intractable FORMAL EG *an intractable
problem*
laborious EG *a laborious task*
uphill EG *an uphill battle*

WORD POWER

▷ **Synonyms**
knotty
problematic
thorny

▶ **Antonym**
easy

2 difficult ADJECTIVE
not easy to deal with
EG *I hope she isn't going to be difficult.*
demanding EG *a demanding child*
troublesome EG *a troublesome
teenager*
trying EG *The whole business has
been very trying.*

WORD POWER

▷ **Synonyms**
obstreperous
refractory
unmanageable

1 difficulty NOUN
a problem
EG *The central difficulty is his drinking.*
complication EG *An added
complication is the growing concern*

for the environment.
hassle INFORMAL EG *all the usual hassles at the airport*
hurdle EG *preparing a CV, the first hurdle in a job search*
obstacle EG *To succeed, you must learn to overcome obstacles.*
pitfall EG *the pitfalls of working abroad*
problem EG *He left home because of family problems.*
snag EG *The only snag was that he had no transport.*
trouble EG *What seems to be the trouble?*

WORD POWER
▷ **Synonyms**
impediment
stumbling block

❷ difficulty NOUN
the quality of being difficult
EG *the difficulty of the problem*
hardship EG *economic hardship*
strain EG *the stresses and strains of a busy career*
tribulation FORMAL EG *the trials and tribulations of everyday life*

WORD POWER
▷ **Synonyms**
arduousness
laboriousness

❶ dig VERB
to break up soil or sand
EG *He dug a hole in the ground.*
burrow EG *The larvae burrow into cracks in the floor.*
excavate EG *A contractor was hired to excavate soil from the area.*
gouge EG *quarries which have gouged great holes in the hills*
hollow out EG *They hollowed out crude dwellings from the soft rock.*
quarry EG *The caves are quarried for cement.*
till EG *freshly tilled fields*

tunnel EG *The rebels tunnelled out of jail.*

❷ dig VERB
to push something in
EG *He could feel the beads digging into his palm.*
jab EG *A needle was jabbed into the baby's arm.*
poke EG *She poked a fork into the turkey skin.*
thrust EG *She thrust her hand into the sticky mess.*

❸ dig NOUN
a push or poke
EG *She silenced him with a dig in the ribs.*
jab EG *a swift jab in the stomach*
poke EG *a playful poke in the arm*
prod EG *He gave the donkey a prod in the backside.*
thrust EG *knife thrusts*

❶ dim ADJECTIVE
not bright or well-lit
EG *a dim outline of a small boat*
dark EG *a dark corridor*
dull EG *The stamp was a dark, dull blue.*
grey EG *a grey, wet, April Sunday*
murky EG *one murky November afternoon*
poorly lit EG *a poorly lit road*
shadowy EG *a shadowy corner*

❷ dim ADJECTIVE
vague or unclear
EG *a dim memory*
faint EG *a faint recollection*
hazy EG *Many details remain hazy.*
indistinct EG *the indistinct murmur of voices*
obscure EG *The origin of the custom is obscure.*
shadowy EG *the shadowy world of spies*
vague EG *I have a vague memory of shots being fired.*

a b c d e f g h i j k l m n o p q r s t u v w x y z

dim >> direct

154

A B C D E F G H I J K L M N O P Q R S T U V W X Y Z

WORD POWER

▷ **Synonyms**
fuzzy
ill-defined

▶ **Antonym**
clear

❸ dim ADJECTIVE; INFORMAL
slow to understand
EG *He is rather dim.*
dumb INFORMAL EG *I've met a lot of dumb people.*
obtuse EG *I've really been very obtuse.*
slow EG *He got hit on the head and he's been a bit slow since.*
stupid EG *How could I have been so stupid?*
thick INFORMAL EG *I must have seemed incredibly thick.*

WORD POWER

▶ **Antonym**
bright

diminish VERB
to reduce or become reduced
EG *The threat of war has diminished.*
contract EG *Output fell last year and is expected to contract further.*
decrease EG *Gradually decrease the amount of vitamin C you are taking.*
lessen EG *The attention he gets will lessen when the new baby is born.*
lower EG *This drug lowers cholesterol levels.*
reduce EG *It reduces the risk of heart disease.*
shrink EG *the entertainment giant's intention to shrink its interest in the venture*
weaken EG *The Prime Minister's authority has been fatally weakened.*

dinkum ADJECTIVE; AUSTRALIAN AND NEW ZEALAND; INFORMAL
genuine or right
EG *a fair dinkum bloke with no*

pretensions
genuine EG *If this offer is genuine I will gladly accept.*
guileless EG *She was so guileless that he had to believe her.*
honest EG *My dad was the most honest man I ever met.*
sincere EG *a sincere desire to reform*

❶ direct ADJECTIVE
in a straight line or with nothing in between
EG *the direct route*
first-hand EG *She has little first-hand knowledge of Quebec.*
immediate EG *his immediate superior*
personal EG *I have no personal experience of this.*
straight EG *Keep the boat in a straight line.*
uninterrupted EG *an uninterrupted view*

WORD POWER

▶ **Antonym**
indirect

❷ direct ADJECTIVE
open and honest
EG *He can be very direct sometimes.*
blunt EG *She is blunt about her personal life.*
candid EG *I haven't been completely candid with you.*
forthright EG *forthright language*
frank EG *She is always very frank.*
straight EG *He never gives you a straight answer.*
straightforward EG *his straightforward manner*

WORD POWER

▶ **Antonym**
devious

❸ direct VERB
to control and guide something
EG *Christopher will direct day-to-day operations.*

control EG *He now controls the entire company.*
guide EG *He should have let his instinct guide him.*
lead EG *He led the country between 1949 and 1984.*
manage EG *Within two years he was managing the store.*
oversee EG *an architect to oversee the work*
run EG *Is this any way to run a country?*
supervise EG *I supervise the packing of all mail orders.*

❶ direction NOUN
the line in which something is moving
EG *ten miles in the opposite direction*
course EG *The captain altered course.*
path EG *He stepped into the path of a reversing car.*
route EG *We took the wrong route.*
way EG *Does anybody know the way to the bathroom?*

❷ direction NOUN
control and guidance of something
EG *He was chopping vegetables under the chef's direction.*
charge EG *A few years ago he took charge of the company.*
command EG *In 1942 he took command of 108 Squadron.*
control EG *The restructuring involves Ronson giving up control of the company.*
guidance EG *the reports which were produced under his guidance*
leadership EG *The agency doubled in size under her leadership.*
management EG *The zoo needed better management.*

❶ dirt NOUN
dust or mud
EG *I started to scrub off the dirt.*
dust EG *The furniture was covered in dust.*
filth EG *tons of filth and sewage*

grime EG *Kelly got the grime off his hands.*
muck EG *This congealed muck was interfering with the filter.*
mud EG *Their lorry got stuck in the mud.*

❷ dirt NOUN
earth or soil
EG *He drew a circle in the dirt with the stick.*
earth EG *a huge pile of earth*
soil EG *an area with very good soil*

❶ dirty ADJECTIVE
marked with dirt
EG *The kids have got their clothes dirty.*
filthy EG *a pair of filthy jeans*
grimy EG *a grimy industrial city*
grubby EG *kids with grubby faces*
mucky EG *a mucky floor*
muddy EG *his muddy boots*
soiled EG *a soiled white apron*
unclean EG *unclean water*

WORD POWER
▶ **Antonym**
clean

❷ dirty ADJECTIVE
unfair or dishonest
EG *a dirty fight*
corrupt EG *corrupt practices*
crooked EG *crooked business deals*

WORD POWER
▶ **Antonym**
honest

❸ dirty ADJECTIVE
sexually explicit
EG *a dirty joke*
blue EG *a blue movie*
filthy EG *a filthy book*
pornographic EG *pornographic videos*
rude EG *a rude joke*

a
b
c
d
e
f
g
h
i
j
k
l
m
n
o
p
q
r
s
t
u
v
w
x
y
z

A
B
C
D
E
F
G
H
I
J
K
L
M
N
O
P
Q
R
S
T
U
V
W
X
Y
Z

WORD POWER

▷ **Synonyms**
risqué
salacious
smutty

disadvantage NOUN
an unfavourable circumstance
EG *the advantages and disadvantages of allowing their soldiers to marry*
drawback EG *The apartment's only drawback was that it was too small.*
handicap EG *The tax issue was undoubtedly a handicap to Labour.*
minus EG *The plusses and minuses were about equal.*
weakness EG *the strengths and weaknesses of the argument*

WORD POWER

▷ **Synonyms**
downside
hindrance

▶ **Antonym**
advantage

❶ **disagree** VERB
to have a different opinion
EG *They can communicate even when they disagree.*
differ EG *They differ on lots of issues.*
dispute EG *Nobody disputed that Davey was clever.*
dissent EG *dissenting views*

WORD POWER

▶ **Antonym**
agree

❷ **disagree** VERB
to think that something is wrong
EG *I disagree with drug laws in general.*
object EG *We objected strongly but were outvoted.*
oppose EG *protesters opposing nuclear tests*
take issue with EG *I take issue with much of what he said.*

disagreeable ADJECTIVE
unpleasant in some way
EG *a disagreeable odour*
horrible EG *a horrible small boy*
horrid EG *What a horrid smell!*
nasty EG *What a nasty little snob you are!*
objectionable EG *an objectionable, stuck-up young woman*
obnoxious EG *One of the parents was a most obnoxious character.*
unfriendly EG *She spoke in a loud, rather unfriendly voice.*
unpleasant EG *The side-effects can be unpleasant.*

WORD POWER

▶ **Antonym**
agreeable

❶ **disagreement** NOUN
a dispute about something
EG *My driving instructor and I had a brief disagreement.*
altercation FORMAL EG *an altercation with the referee*
argument EG *an argument about money*
difference EG *We have our differences but we get along.*
dispute EG *a pay dispute*
quarrel EG *I had a terrible quarrel with my brother.*
row EG *a major diplomatic row*
squabble EG *minor squabbles about phone bills*
tiff EG *a lovers' tiff*

WORD POWER

▶ **Antonym**
agreement

❷ **disagreement** NOUN
an objection to something
EG *Britain and France have expressed some disagreement with the proposal.*
dissent EG *voices of dissent*
objection EG *I have no objection to banks making money.*

opposition EG *their opposition to the scheme*

❶ disappear VERB
to go out of sight
EG *The aircraft disappeared off the radar.*

be lost to view EG *They observed the comet for 70 days before it was lost to view.*
drop out of sight EG *After his first film he dropped out of sight.*
fade EG *We watched the harbour fade into the mist.*
recede EG *Luke receded into the distance.*
vanish EG *Anne vanished from outside her home the Wednesday before last.*

WORD POWER

▶ **Antonym**
appear

❷ disappear VERB
to stop existing
EG *The pain has finally disappeared.*
cease FORMAL EG *At 1 o'clock the rain ceased.*
die out EG *How did the dinosaurs die out?*
go away EG *All she wanted was for the pain to go away.*
melt away EG *His anger melted away.*
pass EG *He told her the fear would pass.*
vanish EG *species which have vanished*

disappointed ADJECTIVE
sad because something has not happened
EG *I was disappointed that Kluge was not there.*
dejected EG *Her refusal left him feeling dejected.*
despondent EG *After the interview John was despondent.*
disenchanted EG *She has become*

very disenchanted with the marriage.
disillusioned EG *I've become very disillusioned with politics.*
downcast EG *After his defeat Mr Rabin looked downcast.*
saddened EG *He is saddened that they did not win anything.*

WORD POWER

▷ **Synonyms**
disheartened
let down

▶ **Antonym**
satisfied

❶ disappointment NOUN
a feeling of being disappointed
EG *Book early to avoid disappointment.*
dejection EG *There was an air of dejection about her.*
despondency EG *a mood of gloom and despondency*
regret EG *my one great regret in life*

WORD POWER

▷ **Synonyms**
disenchantment
disillusionment

❷ disappointment NOUN
something that disappoints you
EG *The reunion was a bitter disappointment.*
blow EG *It was a terrible blow when he was made redundant.*
setback EG *a setback for the peace process*

disapproval NOUN
the belief that something is wrong
EG *his mother's disapproval of his marriage*
censure EG *He deserves support, not censure.*
condemnation EG *the universal condemnation of French nuclear tests*

a
b
c
d
e
f
g
h
i
j
k
l
m
n
o
p
q
r
s
t
u
v
w
x
y
z

A
B
C
D
E
F
G
H
I
J
K
L
M
N
O
P
Q
R
S
T
U
V
W
X
Y
Z

criticism EG *actions which have attracted fierce criticism*

WORD POWER

▶ **Antonym**
approval

disapprove VERB
to think that something is wrong
EG *Everyone disapproved of their marrying so young.*
condemn EG *Political leaders condemned the speech.*
deplore FORMAL EG *He deplores violence.*
dislike EG *Her father seemed to dislike all her boyfriends.*
find unacceptable EG *I find such behaviour totally unacceptable.*
take a dim view of EG *They took a dim view of local trade unionists.*

WORD POWER

▷ **Synonyms**
frown on
take exception to

▶ **Antonym**
approve

disaster NOUN
a very bad accident
EG *another air disaster*
calamity FORMAL EG *It could only end in calamity.*
catastrophe EG *War would be a catastrophe.*
misfortune EG *She seemed to enjoy the misfortunes of others.*
tragedy EG *They have suffered an enormous personal tragedy.*

discard VERB
to get rid of something
EG *Read the instructions before discarding the box.*
cast aside EG *In America we seem to cast aside our elderly people.*
dispose of EG *how he disposed of the murder weapon*

dump INFORMAL EG *The getaway car was dumped near the motorway.*
jettison EG *The crew jettisoned excess fuel.*
shed EG *a snake that has shed its skin*
throw away EG *I never throw anything away.*
throw out EG *Why don't you throw out all those old magazines?*

discern VERB; FORMAL
to notice or understand something clearly
EG *trying to discern a pattern in his behaviour*
detect EG *Arnold could detect a certain sadness in the old man's face.*
make out EG *I could just make out a shadowy figure through the mist.*
notice EG *Mrs Shedden noticed a bird sitting on the garage roof.*
observe EG *In 1664 Hooke observed a reddish spot on the planet's surface.*
perceive EG *Get pupils to perceive the relationship between success and effort.*
see EG *Supporters saw in him a champion of the oppressed.*
spot EG *I've spotted an error in your calculations.*

❶ discharge VERB
to send something out
EG *The resulting salty water will be discharged at sea.*
emit EG *the amount of greenhouse gases emitted*
empty EG *companies which enpty toxic by-products into rivers*
expel EG *Poisonous gas is expelled into the atmosphere.*
flush EG *Flush out all the sewage.*
give off EG *natural gas, which gives off less carbon dioxide than coal*
release EG *a weapon which releases toxic nerve gas*

❷ discharge VERB
to allow someone to leave hospital or prison

EG *He has a broken nose but may be discharged today.*
free EG *The country is set to free more prisoners.*
let go EG *They held him for three hours and then let him go.*
liberate EG *They promised to liberate prisoners held in detention camps.*
release EG *He was released on bail.*
set free EG *More than ninety prisoners have been set free.*

❸ **discharge** VERB
to dismiss someone from a job
EG *He was discharged from the military.*
dismiss EG *The military commander has been dismissed.*
eject EG *He was ejected from his first job for persistent latecoming.*
fire INFORMAL EG *If he wasn't so good at his job, I'd fire him.*
sack INFORMAL EG *The teacher was sacked for slapping a schoolboy.*

❹ **discharge** NOUN
a sending away from a job or institution
EG *They face a dishonourable discharge from the Army.*
dismissal EG *shock at the director's dismissal from his post*
ejection EG *These actions led to his ejection from office.*
expulsion EG *his expulsion from the party in 1955*
the sack INFORMAL EG *People who make mistakes can be given the sack.*

discourage VERB
to make someone lose enthusiasm
EG *Don't let these problems discourage you.*
daunt EG *He was not the type of man to be daunted by adversity.*
deter EG *Tougher sentences would do nothing to deter crime.*
dissuade EG *He considered emigrating, but his family managed to dissuade him.*

put off EG *I wouldn't let it put you off applying.*

WORD POWER

▷ **Synonyms**
demoralize
dishearten

▶ **Antonym**
encourage

discover VERB
to find something or find out about something
EG *He discovered that she had a brilliant mind.*
come across EG *He came across the jawbone of a carnivorous dinosaur.*
find EG *The police also found a pistol.*
find out EG *Watch the next episode to find out what happens.*
learn EG *The Admiral, on learning who I was, wanted to meet me.*
realize EG *As soon as we realized something was wrong, we took action.*
stumble on *or* **across** EG *They stumbled on a magnificent waterfall.*
unearth EG *Researchers have unearthed documents implicating her in the crime.*

discuss VERB
to talk about something
EG *I will be discussing the situation with colleagues tomorrow.*
debate EG *The UN Security Council will debate the issue today.*
exchange views on EG *They exchanged views on a wide range of subjects.*
go into EG *We didn't go into that.*
talk about EG *What did you talk about?*

discussion NOUN
a talk about something
EG *informal discussions*
consultation EG *consultations between lawyers*
conversation EG *I struck up a conversation with him.*

A
B
C
D
E
F
G
H
I
J
K
L
M
N
O
P
Q
R
S
T
U
V
W
X
Y
Z

debate EG *There has been a lot of debate among scholars about this.*
dialogue EG *a direct dialogue between the two nations*
discourse EG *a long tradition of political discourse*
talk EG *We had a long talk about it.*

❶ disgrace NOUN
lack of respect
EG *She has brought disgrace upon the whole team.*
scandal EG *They often abandoned their children because of fear of scandal.*
shame EG *I don't want to bring shame on the family name.*

> ### WORD POWER
> ▷ **Synonyms**
>   discredit
>   dishonour
>
> ► **Antonym**
>   credit

❷ disgrace VERB
to bring shame upon
EG *I have disgraced my family's name.*
discredit EG *He said such methods discredited the communist fight worldwide.*
shame EG *I wouldn't shame my father by doing that.*

disgraceful ADJECTIVE
deserving of shame
EG *disgraceful behaviour*
scandalous EG *a scandalous waste of money*
shameful EG *the most shameful episode in US naval history*
shocking EG *a shocking invasion of privacy*

> ### WORD POWER
> ▷ **Synonyms**
>   discreditable
>   dishonourable

❶ disgust NOUN
a strong feeling of dislike
EG *his disgust at the incident*
nausea EG *I was overcome with a feeling of nausea.*
repulsion EG *a shudder of repulsion*
revulsion EG *They expressed their shock and revulsion at his death.*

❷ disgust VERB
to cause someone to feel disgust
EG *He disgusted many with his behaviour.*
repel EG *a violent excitement that frightened and repelled her*
revolt EG *The smell revolted him.*
sicken EG *What he saw there sickened him.*

> ### WORD POWER
> ▷ **Synonyms**
>   nauseate
>   turn your stomach

disgusting ADJECTIVE
very unpleasant or unacceptable
EG *one of the most disgusting sights I had ever seen*
foul EG *a foul stench*
gross EG *Don't be so gross!*
obnoxious EG *a most obnoxious character*
repellent EG *a very large, repellent toad*
revolting EG *The smell was revolting.*
sickening EG *a sickening attack on a pregnant woman*
vile EG *a vile odour*

> ### WORD POWER
> ▷ **Synonyms**
>   nauseating
>   repugnant

dishonest ADJECTIVE
not truthful
EG *It would be dishonest to mislead people.*
corrupt EG *corrupt police officers*
crooked EG *crooked business deals*

deceitful EG *The ambassador called the report deceitful and misleading.*
fraudulent EG *fraudulent claims about being a nurse*
lying EG *He called her 'a lying little twit'.*

WORD POWER

▷ **Synonyms**
mendacious
untruthful

▶ **Antonym**
honest

dishonesty NOUN
dishonest behaviour
EG *She accused the government of dishonesty.*
cheating EG *He was accused of cheating.*
corruption EG *The President faces 54 charges of corruption.*
deceit EG *the deceit and lies of the past*
trickery EG *They resorted to trickery in order to impress their clients.*

WORD POWER

▷ **Synonyms**
duplicity
fraudulence
mendacity

▶ **Antonym**
honesty

disintegrate VERB
to break into many pieces
EG *At 420 mph the windscreen disintegrated.*
break up EG *There was a danger of the ship breaking up completely.*
crumble EG *The flint crumbled into fragments.*
fall apart EG *Bit by bit the building fell apart.*
fall to pieces EG *The radio handset fell to pieces.*

fragment EG *The clouds fragmented and out came the sun.*

❶ dislike VERB
to consider something unpleasant
EG *We don't serve it often because many people dislike it.*
abhor FORMAL EG *a man who abhorred violence*
be averse to EG *He's not averse to a little publicity.*
detest EG *Jean detested being photographed.*
hate EG *Most people hate him.*
loathe EG *a play loathed by the critics*
not be able to abide EG *I can't abide liars.*
not be able to bear EG *I can't bear people who speak like that.*
not be able to stand EG *He can't stand the sound of her voice.*

WORD POWER

▶ **Antonym**
like

❷ dislike NOUN
a feeling of not liking something
EG *She looked at him with dislike.*
animosity EG *The animosity between the two men grew.*
antipathy EG *their antipathy to my smoking*
aversion EG *I've always had an aversion to being part of a group.*
distaste EG *Roger looked at her with distaste.*
hatred EG *her hatred of authority*
hostility EG *hostility to ethnic groups*
loathing EG *He made no secret of his loathing of her.*

WORD POWER

▶ **Antonym**
liking

disobey VERB
to deliberately refuse to follow instructions
EG *He was forever disobeying the rules.*

a b c d e f g h i j k l m n o p q r s t u v w x y z

A
B
C
D
E
F
G
H
I
J
K
L
M
N
O
P
Q
R
S
T
U
V
W
X
Y
Z

break EG *drivers breaking speed limits*
defy EG *the first time that I dared to defy my mother*
flout EG *illegal campers who persist in flouting the law*
infringe EG *He was adamant that he had infringed no rules.*
violate EG *They violated the ceasefire agreement.*

WORD POWER

▷ **Synonyms**
contravene (FORMAL)

► **Antonym**
obey

❶ disorder NOUN
a state of untidiness
EG *Inside, all was disorder.*
clutter EG *She prefers the worktop to be free of clutter.*
disarray EG *Her clothes were in disarray.*
muddle EG *a general muddle of pencils and boxes*

WORD POWER

► **Antonym**
order

❷ disorder NOUN
a lack of organization
EG *The men fled in disorder.*
chaos EG *Their concerts often ended in chaos.*
confusion EG *There was confusion when a man fired shots.*
disarray EG *The nation is in disarray following rioting.*
turmoil EG *the political turmoil of 1989*

❸ disorder NOUN
a disease or illness
EG *a rare nerve disorder*
affliction EG *an affliction which can ruin a young man's life*
complaint EG *a common skin complaint*
condition EG *a heart condition*
disease EG *heart disease*
illness EG *mental illness*

dispose of VERB
to get rid of something
EG *Fold up the nappy and dispose of it.*
discard EG *Read the instructions before discarding the box.*
dispense with EG *We got a CD-player and dispensed with our old-fashioned record-player.*
dump EG *The government declared that it did not dump radioactive waste at sea.*
get rid of EG *The owner needs to get rid of the car for financial reasons.*
jettison EG *The crew jettisoned excess fuel and made an emergency landing.*
throw away EG *I never throw anything away.*

disprove VERB
to show that something is not true
EG *the statistics that will prove or disprove the hypothesis*
discredit EG *There would be difficulties in discrediting the evidence.*
give the lie to EG *This survey gives the lie to the idea that the economy is recovering.*
invalidate EG *Some of the other criticisms were invalidated years ago.*
prove false EG *It is hard to prove such claims false.*
refute EG *the kind of rumour that is impossible to refute*

WORD POWER

► **Antonym**
prove

❶ dispute NOUN
an argument
EG *The dispute between them is settled.*
argument EG *a heated argument*
clash EG *the clash between trade union leaders and the government*

conflict EG *Avoid any conflict between yourself and your ex-partner.*
disagreement EG *disagreements among the member states*
feud EG *a bitter feud between the state government and the villagers*
row EG *a major diplomatic row with France*
wrangle EG *a legal wrangle*

2 dispute VERB
to question something's truth or wisdom
EG *He disputed the allegations.*
challenge EG *I challenge the wisdom of this decision.*
contest EG *Your former employer wants to contest the case.*
contradict EG *Her version contradicted the Government's claim.*
deny EG *She denied both accusations.*
query EG *No one queried my decision.*
question EG *It never occurred to me to question the doctor's diagnosis.*

WORD POWER

▶ **Antonym**
accept

1 distant ADJECTIVE
far away in space or time
EG *a distant land*
far EG *Is it very far?*
outlying EG *outlying districts*
out-of-the-way EG *an out-of-the-way spot*
remote EG *a remote village*

WORD POWER

▷ **Synonyms**
faraway
far-flung
far-off

▶ **Antonym**
close

2 distant ADJECTIVE
cold and unfriendly
EG *He is polite but distant.*

aloof EG *He seemed aloof and detached.*
detached EG *He observed me with a detached curiosity.*
reserved EG *She's quite a reserved person.*
withdrawn EG *Her husband had become withdrawn and moody.*

WORD POWER

▷ **Synonyms**
standoffish
unapproachable

▶ **Antonym**
friendly

1 distinguish VERB
to see the difference between things
EG *Could he distinguish right from wrong?*
differentiate EG *At this age your baby cannot differentiate one person from another.*
discriminate EG *He is unable to discriminate a good idea from a terrible one.*
tell EG *How do you tell one from another?*
tell apart EG *I can only tell them apart by the colour of their shoes.*
tell the difference EG *I can't tell the difference between their policies and ours.*

2 distinguish VERB
to recognize something
EG *I heard shouting but was unable to distinguish the words.*
discern EG *We could just discern a narrow ditch.*
make out EG *He couldn't make out what she was saying.*
pick out EG *Through my binoculars I picked out a group of figures.*
recognize EG *He did not think she could recognize his car in the snow.*

distract VERB
to stop someone from concentrating

a b c d e f g h i j k l m n o p q r s t u v w x y z

EG *Playing video games distracts him from his homework.*

divert EG *They want to divert our attention from the real issues.*

draw away EG *to draw attention away from the crime*

WORD POWER

▷ **Synonyms**
sidetrack
turn aside

---

❶ distress NOUN
great suffering
EG *Jealousy causes distress and painful emotions.*

heartache EG *the heartache of her divorce*

pain EG *eyes that seemed filled with pain*

sorrow EG *a time of great sorrow*

suffering EG *to put an end to his suffering*

❷ distress NOUN
the state of needing help
EG *The ship might be in distress.*

difficulty EG *rumours about banks being in difficulty*

need EG *When you were in need, I loaned you money.*

straits EG *The company's closure left them in desperate financial straits.*

trouble EG *a charity that helps women in trouble*

❸ distress VERB
to cause someone unhappiness
EG *Her death had profoundly distressed me.*

bother EG *It bothered me that boys weren't interested in me.*

disturb EG *dreams so vivid that they disturb me for days*

grieve EG *It grieved her to be separated from her son.*

pain EG *It pains me to think of you struggling all alone.*

sadden EG *The cruelty in the world saddens me deeply.*

trouble EG *He was troubled by the lifestyle of his son.*

upset EG *I'm sorry if I've upset you.*

worry EG *I didn't want to worry you.*

❶ distribute VERB
to hand something out
EG *They publish and distribute brochures.*

circulate EG *He has circulated a discussion document.*

hand out EG *One of my jobs was to hand out the prizes.*

pass around EG *Sweets were being passed around.*

pass round EG *She passed her holiday photos round.*

❷ distribute VERB
to spread something through an area
EG *Distribute the topping evenly over the fruit.*

diffuse EG *Interest in books is more widely diffused than ever.*

disperse EG *The leaflets were dispersed throughout the country.*

scatter EG *She scattered the petals over the grave.*

spread EG *A thick layer of wax was spread over the surface.*

❸ distribute VERB
to divide and share something
EG *Distribute chores evenly among all family members.*

allocate EG *funds allocated for nursery education*

allot EG *The seats are allotted to the candidates who have won the most votes.*

dispense FORMAL EG *The Union had already dispensed £400 in grants.*

divide EG *Paul divides his spare time between the bedroom and the study.*

dole out EG *I got out my wallet and began to dole out the money.*

share out EG *You could share out the money a bit more equally.*

WORD POWER

▷ **Synonyms**
apportion
mete out

1 disturb VERB
to intrude on someone's peace
EG *She slept in a separate room so as not to disturb him.*
bother EG *I'm sorry to bother you.*
disrupt EG *Protesters disrupted the debate.*
intrude on EG *I don't want to intrude on your parents.*

2 disturb VERB
to upset or worry someone
EG *Some scenes may disturb you.*
agitate EG *The thought agitated her.*
distress EG *Her death had profoundly distressed me.*
shake EG *Well, it shook me quite a bit.*
trouble EG *He was troubled by the lifestyle of his son.*
unsettle EG *The presence of the two policemen unsettled her.*
upset EG *I'm sorry if I've upset you.*
worry EG *I didn't want to worry you.*

dive VERB
to jump or fall into water
EG *She was standing by the pool, about to dive in.*
jump EG *He ran along the board and jumped in.*
leap EG *as she leapt into the water*
submerge EG *Hippos are unable to submerge in the few remaining water holes.*

1 divide VERB
to split something up
EG *The idea is to divide the country into four sectors.*
cut up EG *Halve the tomatoes, then cut them up.*
partition EG *a plan to partition the country*
segregate EG *Police were used to segregate the two rival camps.*

separate EG *Fluff the rice with a fork to separate the grains.*
split EG *Split the chicken in half.*
split up EG *He split up the company.*

WORD POWER

▶ **Antonym**
join

2 divide VERB
to form a barrier between things
EG *the frontier dividing Mexico from the USA*
bisect EG *The main street bisects the town.*
separate EG *the fence that separated the yard from the paddock*

3 divide VERB
to cause people to disagree
EG *the enormous differences that still divide them*
come between EG *It's difficult to imagine anything coming between them.*
set against one another EG *The case has set neighbours against one another in the village.*
split EG *Women priests are accused of splitting the church.*

1 division NOUN
separation into parts
EG *the unification of Germany after its division into two states*
partition EG *fighting which followed the partition of India*
separation EG *the separation of church and state*

2 division NOUN
a disagreement
EG *There were divisions in the Party on economic policy.*
breach EG *a serious breach in relations between the two countries*
difference of opinion EG *Was there a difference of opinion over what to do with the money?*
rupture EG *a rupture of the family unit*

a b c d e f g h i j k l m n o p q r s t u v w x y z

A B C D E F G H I J K L M N O P Q R S T U V W X Y Z

split EG *They accused both sides of trying to provoke a split in the party.*

❸ division NOUN
a section of something
EG *the Research Division*
department EG *the company's chemicals department*
section EG *a top-secret section of the Foreign Office*
sector EG *the nation's manufacturing sector*

dizzy ADJECTIVE
about to lose your balance
EG *He kept getting dizzy spells.*
giddy EG *She felt slightly giddy.*
light-headed EG *If you skip breakfast, you may feel light-headed.*

❶ do VERB
to carry out a task
EG *He just didn't want to do any work.*
carry out EG *Police believe the attacks were carried out by nationalists.*
execute FORMAL EG *The landing was skillfully executed.*
perform EG *people who have performed outstanding acts of bravery*
undertake EG *She undertook the arduous task of monitoring the elections.*

❷ do VERB
to be sufficient
EG *Home-made stock is best, but cubes will do.*
be adequate EG *The western diet should be perfectly adequate for most people.*
be sufficient EG *One teaspoon of sugar should be sufficient.*
suffice FORMAL EG *Often a far shorter letter will suffice.*

❸ do VERB
to perform well or badly
EG *Connie did well at school.*
fare EG *Some later expeditions fared better.*

get on EG *I asked him how he had got on.*
manage EG *How did your mother manage after your father died?*

❶ dodge VERB
to move out of the way
EG *We dodged behind a pillar out of sight of the tourists.*
duck EG *I wanted to duck down and slip past but they saw me.*
swerve EG *He swerved to avoid a truck.*

❷ dodge VERB
to avoid doing something
EG *dodging military service by feigning illness*
avoid EG *They managed to avoid paying their fares.*
elude EG *He eluded the police for 13 years.*
evade EG *by evading taxes*
get out of EG *He'll do almost anything to get out of paying his share.*
shirk EG *We can't shirk our responsibility.*
sidestep EG *Rarely, if ever, does he sidestep a question.*

dog NOUN
an animal often kept as a pet
EG *a children's book about dogs*
brak SOUTH AFRICAN EG *a rabid brak*
canine EG *a new canine was needed*
mongrel EG *a rescued mongrel called Chips*
mutt SLANG EG *the most famous mutts in the western world*
pooch SLANG EG *Julian's pet pooch*

WORD POWER

● **Related Words**
adjective : canine
female : bitch
young : pup, puppy

doomed ADJECTIVE
certain to fail
EG *a doomed attempt to rescue the*

children
condemned EG *Many women are condemned to poverty.*
hopeless EG *I don't believe your situation is as hopeless as you think.*
ill-fated EG *his ill-fated attempt on the world record*

① double ADJECTIVE
twice the usual size
EG *a double whisky*
twice EG *Unemployment in Northern Ireland is twice the national average.*
twofold EG *a twofold risk*

② double ADJECTIVE
consisting of two parts
EG *a double album*
dual EG *dual nationality*
twin EG *twin beds*
twofold EG *Their concern was twofold: personal and political.*

① doubt NOUN
a feeling of uncertainty
EG *This raises doubts about the point of advertising.*
misgiving EG *I had misgivings about his methods.*
qualm EG *I have no qualms about recommending this approach.*
scepticism EG *The report has been greeted with scepticism.*
uncertainty EG *the uncertainties regarding the future funding of the company*

> *WORD POWER*
>
> ▶ **Antonym**
> certainty

② doubt VERB
to feel uncertain about something
EG *No one doubted his ability.*
be dubious EG *I was dubious about the entire proposition.*
be sceptical EG *Other archaeologists are sceptical about his findings.*
query EG *No one queried my decision.*

question EG *It never occurs to them to question the doctor's decisions.*

> *WORD POWER*
>
> ▶ **Antonym**
> believe

doubtful ADJECTIVE
unlikely or uncertain
EG *It is doubtful whether he will appear again.*
debatable EG *Whether the Bank of England would do any better is highly debatable.*
dubious EG *This claim seems to us rather dubious.*
questionable EG *It is questionable whether the expenditure is justified.*
uncertain EG *It's uncertain whether they will accept the plan.*

> *WORD POWER*
>
> ▶ **Antonym**
> certain

① down ADVERB
towards the ground, or in a lower place
EG *We went down in the lift.*
downwards EG *She gazed downwards.*
downstairs EG *Denise went downstairs and made some tea.*

> *WORD POWER*
>
> ▶ **Antonym**
> up

② down ADJECTIVE
depressed
EG *He sounded really down.*
dejected EG *Everyone has days when they feel dejected.*
depressed EG *She's been very depressed about this situation.*
dispirited EG *I left feeling utterly dispirited.*
fed up INFORMAL EG *I'm just fed up and I don't know what to do.*

a b c d e f g h i j k l m n o p q r s t u v w x y z

A
B
C
D
E
F
G
H
I
J
K
L
M
N
O
P
Q
R
S
T
U
V
W
X
Y
Z

glum EG *She was very glum and was missing her children.*
melancholy EG *It was in the afternoon that Tom felt most melancholy.*
miserable EG *My work was making me really miserable.*

WORD POWER

▷ **Synonyms**
despondent
morose

downfall NOUN
the failure of a person or thing
EG *His lack of experience had led to his downfall.*
collapse EG *The medical system is facing collapse.*
fall EG *the fall of the military dictator*
ruin EG *Inflation has driven them to the brink of ruin.*

drab ADJECTIVE
dull and unattractive
EG *the same drab grey dress*
dingy EG *his rather dingy office*
dismal EG *a dark dismal day*
dreary EG *a dreary little town*
gloomy EG *the gloomy days of winter*
grey EG *a New Year that will be grey and cheerless*
sombre EG *a worried official in sombre black*

WORD POWER

▷ **Synonyms**
cheerless
lacklustre

▶ **Antonym**
bright

drag VERB
to pull something along the ground
EG *He dragged his chair towards the table.*
draw EG *He drew his chair nearer the fire.*
haul EG *A crane was used to haul the car out of the stream.*
lug EG *Nobody wants to lug around huge suitcases.*
tow EG *They threatened to tow away my car.*
trail EG *She came down the stairs slowly, trailing the coat behind her.*

❶ drain VERB
to cause a liquid to flow somewhere
EG *Miners built the tunnel to drain water out of the lakes.*
draw off EG *The fluid can be drawn off with a syringe.*
pump EG *to get rid of raw sewage by pumping it out to sea*

❷ drain VERB
to flow somewhere
EG *rivers that drain into lakes*
discharge EG *Blood was discharging from its nostrils.*
empty EG *The Washougal empties into the Columbia River.*
flow EG *The waters of Lake Erie now flow into the Niagara River.*
seep EG *Radioactive water has seeped into underground reservoirs.*

❸ drain VERB
to use something up
EG *The prolonged boardroom battle drained him of energy and money.*
consume EG *plans which will consume hours of time*
exhaust EG *People are now living longer and exhausting natural resources.*
sap EG *The illness sapped his strength.*
tax EG *Overcrowding has taxed the city's ability to deal with waste.*
use up EG *They aren't the ones who use up the world's resources.*

drastic ADJECTIVE
severe and urgent
EG *It's time for drastic action.*
extreme EG *I would rather die than do anything so extreme.*
harsh EG *harsh new measures to combat drink-driving*

draw >> dream

radical EG *radical economic reforms*
severe EG *a severe shortage of drinking water*

❶ draw VERB
to make a picture
EG *He starts a drawing by painting simplified shapes.*
paint EG *He is painting a huge volcano.*
sketch EG *He sketched a map on the back of a menu.*
trace EG *She learned to draw by tracing pictures out of old storybooks.*

❷ draw VERB
to move somewhere
EG *as the car drew away*
move EG *She moved away from the window.*
pull EG *He pulled into the driveway.*

❸ draw VERB
to pull something
EG *He drew his chair nearer the fire.*
drag EG *He dragged his chair towards the table.*
haul EG *A crane was used to haul the car out of the stream.*
pull EG *a freight train pulling waggons*

drawback NOUN
a problem that makes something less than perfect
EG *The only drawback was that the apartment was too small.*
difficulty EG *There is only one difficulty - I don't have the key.*
hitch EG *It's a great idea but I can see a serious hitch.*
problem EG *The main problem with the house is its inaccessibility.*
snag EG *It's a great school - the snag is the fees are £9,000 a year.*
trouble EG *The trouble is that he might not agree with our plans.*

dreadful ADJECTIVE
very bad or unpleasant
EG *He told us the dreadful news*
appalling EG *living under the most appalling conditions*
atrocious EG *The food here is atrocious.*
awful EG *Jeans look awful on me.*
frightful EG *The war had been so frightful he couldn't talk about it.*
ghastly EG *a ghastly pair of shoes*
horrendous EG *the most horrendous experience of his life*
terrible EG *Thousands more people suffered terrible injuries.*

WORD POWER
▶ **Antonym**
wonderful

❶ dream NOUN
mental pictures while sleeping
EG *He had a dream about Claire.*
hallucination EG *The drug induces hallucinations at high doses.*
trance EG *She seemed to be in a trance.*
vision EG *seeing the Virgin Mary in a vision*

WORD POWER
▷ **Synonyms**
delusion
reverie

❷ dream NOUN
something that you want very much
EG *his dream of winning the lottery*
ambition EG *His ambition is to sail round the world.*
aspiration EG *one of his greatest aspirations*
daydream EG *He learned to escape into daydreams of becoming a writer.*
fantasy EG *fantasies of romance and true love*

WORD POWER
▷ **Synonyms**
Holy Grail
pipe dream

dreary ADJECTIVE
dull or boring
EG *the dreary winter months*
boring EG *a boring job*
drab EG *The rest of the day's activities often seem drab.*
dull EG *There was scarcely a dull moment.*
humdrum EG *The new government seemed rather humdrum.*
monotonous EG *It's monotonous work, like most factory jobs.*
tedious EG *Such lists are tedious to read.*
uneventful EG *her dull, uneventful life*

WORD POWER
▶ **Antonym**
exciting

❶ dress NOUN
a piece of clothing
EG *a black dress*
frock EG *a party frock*
gown EG *wedding gowns*
robe EG *a fur-lined robe*

❷ dress NOUN
clothing in general
EG *evening dress*
attire FORMAL EG *women dressed in their finest attire*
clothes EG *casual clothes*
clothing EG *protective clothing*
costume EG *women in traditional costume*
garb FORMAL EG *his usual garb of a dark suit*

WORD POWER
▷ **Synonyms**
apparel
raiment

❸ dress VERB
to put on clothes
EG *a tall woman dressed in black*
attire EG *He was attired in a smart blue suit.*

clothe EG *He lay down on the bed fully clothed.*
garb FORMAL EG *He was garbed in sweater, jacket and boots.*

WORD POWER
▶ **Antonym**
undress

❶ drink VERB
to swallow liquid
EG *He drank some tea.*
gulp EG *She quickly gulped her coffee.*
guzzle EG *She guzzled gin and tonics like they were lemonade.*
sip EG *She sipped from her coffee mug.*
swig INFORMAL EG *I swigged down two white wines.*

WORD POWER
▷ **Synonyms**
imbibe
quaff
sup

❷ drink VERB
to drink alcohol
EG *He drinks little and eats carefully.*
booze INFORMAL EG *drunken businessmen who had been boozing all afternoon*
tipple EG *We saw a woman tippling from the sherry bottle.*

❶ drip VERB
to fall in small drops
EG *Rain dripped from the brim of his cap.*
dribble EG *Sweat dribbled down his face.*
splash EG *Tears splashed into her hands.*
trickle EG *A tear trickled down the old man's cheek.*

❷ drip NOUN
a small amount of a liquid
EG *drips of water*
bead EG *beads of sweat*

drop EG *a drop of blue ink*
droplet EG *water droplets*

WORD POWER

▷ **Synonyms**
dribble
globule

---

❶ drive VERB
to operate or power a machine or
vehicle
EG *Don't drive a car or operate heavy
machinery after taking this
medication .*
operate EG *A rock fall trapped the
men as they operated a tunnelling
machine.*
pilot EG *He piloted his own plane to
Washington.*
power EG *The flywheel's battery could
be used to power an electric car.*
propel EG *Attached is a tiny rocket
designed to propel the spacecraft
towards Mars.*
run EG *I ran a Rover 100 from 1977
until 1983.*
steer EG *What is it like to steer a ship
this size?*
work EG *I learned how to work the
forklift.*

❷ drive VERB
to force someone to do something
EG *Depression drove him to self-harm.*
compel EG *He felt compelled to speak
out against their actions.*
force EG *A back injury forced her to
withdraw from the tournament.*
lead EG *His abhorrence of racism led
him to write his first book.*
motivate EG *What motivates people
to behave like this?*
prompt EG *The recession has
prompted consumers to cut back on
spending.*
push EG *James did not push her into
stealing the money.*
spur EG *It's the money that spurs
these fishermen to take such risks.*

❸ drive VERB
to force something pointed into a
surface
EG *I used the sledgehammer to drive
the pegs in.*
hammer EG *Hammer a wooden peg
into the hole.*
knock EG *He knocked a couple of nails
into the wall.*
ram EG *He rammed the stake with all
his strength into the creature's heart.*
sink EG *He sinks the needle into my
arm.*
thrust EG *thrusting a knife into his
ribs*

❹ drive NOUN
a journey in a vehicle
EG *We might go for a drive on Sunday.*
excursion EG *an excursion to a local
vineyard*
jaunt EG *Let's take a jaunt down to the
beach.*
journey EG *The journey from
Manchester to Plymouth took a few
hours.*
ride EG *We took some friends for a ride
in the family car.*
run EG *We went for a run in the new
car to try it out.*
spin EG *I was thinking about going for
a spin.*
trip EG *We went on a coach trip to the
seaside.*

❺ drive NOUN
energy and determination
EG *He is best remembered for his drive
and enthusiasm.*
ambition EG *When I was young I
never had any ambition.*
determination EG *her natural
determination to succeed*
energy EG *At 54 years old, her energy
is magnificent.*
enterprise EG *the group's lack of
enterprise*
initiative EG *We were disappointed
by his lack of initiative.*
motivation EG *His poor performance*

a b c d e f g h i j k l m n o p q r s t u v w x y z

may be attributed to lack of
motivation.
vigour EG *He played with great
vigour.*

❶ drop VERB
to fall downwards
EG *She let her head drop.*
descend EG *as the aircraft descended*
fall EG *Bombs fell in the town.*
plummet EG *His parachute failed to
open and he plummeted to the
ground.*
sink EG *She sank to her knees.*
tumble EG *The gun tumbled out of his
hand.*

❷ drop VERB
to become less
EG *Temperatures can drop to freezing
at night.*
decline EG *The number of staff has
declined.*
decrease EG *Population growth is
decreasing by 1.4% each year.*
diminish EG *diminishing resources*
fall EG *Her weight fell to under seven
stone.*
plummet EG *Share prices have
plummeted.*
sink EG *Pay increases have sunk to
around 7%.*
slump EG *Net profits slumped by 41%.*
tumble EG *House prices have
tumbled by almost 30%.*

WORD POWER

▶ **Antonym**
rise

❸ drop NOUN
a small amount of a liquid
EG *a drop of blue ink*
bead EG *beads of sweat*
drip EG *drips of water*
droplet EG *water droplets*

WORD POWER

▷ **Synonyms**
dribble
globule

❶ drug NOUN
a treatment for disease
EG *a new drug in the fight against AIDS*
medication EG *She is not on any
medication.*
medicine EG *herbal medicines*

WORD POWER

● **Related Words**
combining form :
pharmaco-

❷ drug NOUN
an illegal substance
EG *She was sure Leo was taking drugs.*
narcotic EG *He was indicted for
dealing in narcotics.*
stimulant EG *the use of stimulants in
sport*

❶ drunk ADJECTIVE
having consumed too much alcohol
EG *I got drunk.*
babalas SOUTH AFRICAN EG *He was
babalas again last night.*
intoxicated FORMAL EG *He appeared
intoxicated.*
tipsy EG *I'm feeling a bit tipsy.*

WORD POWER

▷ **Synonyms**
bacchic
inebriated

▶ **Antonym**
sober

❷ drunk NOUN
someone who consumes too much
alcohol
EG *A drunk lay in the alley.*
alcoholic EG *after admitting that he
was an alcoholic*
boozer INFORMAL EG *He's a bit of a
boozer.*

❶ dry ADJECTIVE
without any liquid
EG *The path was dry after the sunshine.*
arid EG *arid conditions*
dried-up EG *a dried-up river bed*
parched EG *parched brown grass*

WORD POWER

▶ **Antonym**
wet

❷ dry VERB
to remove liquid from something
EG *Wash and dry the lettuce.*
dehydrate EG *Avoid alcohol, which dehydrates the body.*
drain EG *The authorities have mobilized vast numbers of people to drain flooded land.*

WORD POWER

▷ **Synonyms**
dehumidify
desiccate

▶ **Antonym**
moisten

❶ dubious ADJECTIVE
not entirely honest or reliable
EG *a rather dubious claim*
crooked EG *expose his crooked business deals*
dishonest EG *He had become rich by dishonest means.*
questionable EG *allegations of questionable business practices*
suspect EG *The whole affair is highly suspect.*
suspicious EG *two characters who looked suspicious*
unreliable EG *a notoriously unreliable source of information*

❷ dubious ADJECTIVE
doubtful about something
EG *My parents were a bit dubious about it all.*
doubtful EG *I was still very doubtful about our chances for success.*

nervous EG *The party has become nervous about its prospects of winning.*
sceptical EG *Other archaeologists are sceptical about his findings.*
suspicious EG *I'm a little suspicious about his motives.*
unconvinced EG *Most consumers seem unconvinced that the recession is over.*
undecided EG *After university she was still undecided as to what career she wanted.*
unsure EG *Fifty-two per cent were unsure about the idea.*

❶ dull ADJECTIVE
not interesting
EG *I found him rather dull.*
boring EG *a boring job*
drab EG *The rest of the day's activities often seem drab.*
humdrum EG *The new government seemed rather humdrum.*
monotonous EG *It's monotonous work, like most factory jobs.*
tedious EG *Such lists are tedious to read.*
uninteresting EG *Their media has a reputation for being dull and uninteresting.*

WORD POWER

▶ **Antonym**
interesting

❷ dull ADJECTIVE
not bright or clear
EG *a dark, dull blue colour*
drab EG *the same drab grey dress*
gloomy EG *Inside it's gloomy after all that sunshine.*
muted EG *He likes sombre, muted colours.*
sombre EG *an official in sombre black*
subdued EG *subdued lighting*

a
b
c
d
e
f
g
h
i
j
k
l
m
n
o
p
q
r
s
t
u
v
w
x
y
z

3 dull ADJECTIVE
covered with clouds
EG *It's always dull and raining.*
cloudy EG *In the morning it was cloudy.*
leaden EG *a leaden sky*
murky EG *one murky November afternoon*
overcast EG *For three days it was overcast.*

WORD POWER
▶ **Antonym**
bright

1 dumb ADJECTIVE
unable to speak
EG *We were all struck dumb for a minute.*
mute EG *a mute look of appeal*
silent EG *Suddenly they both fell silent.*
speechless EG *Alex was almost speechless with rage.*

2 dumb ADJECTIVE; INFORMAL
slow to understand
EG *I've met a lot of pretty dumb people.*
dim EG *He is rather dim.*
obtuse FORMAL EG *I've really been very obtuse.*
stupid EG *How could I have been so stupid?*
thick INFORMAL EG *I must have seemed incredibly thick.*

WORD POWER
▶ **Antonym**
smart

1 dump VERB
to get rid of something
EG *The getaway car was dumped near the motorway.*
discharge EG *The resulting salty*

water will eventually be discharged at sea.
dispose of EG *how he disposed of the murder weapon*
get rid of EG *The cat had kittens, which they got rid of.*
jettison EG *The crew jettisoned their excess fuel.*
throw away EG *You should have thrown the letter away.*
throw out EG *You ought to throw out those empty bottles.*

2 dump VERB
to put something down
EG *We dumped our bags at the hotel and went for a walk.*
deposit EG *Imagine if you were suddenly deposited on a desert island.*
drop EG *Many children had been dropped outside the stadium by their parents.*

dupe VERB
to trick someone
EG *Some of the offenders duped the psychologists.*
cheat EG *Many brokers were charged with cheating customers.*
con INFORMAL EG *The British people have been conned by the government.*
deceive EG *He has deceived us all.*
delude EG *Television deludes you into thinking you are experiencing reality.*
fool EG *Art dealers fool a lot of people.*
play a trick on EG *She realized he had played a trick on her.*
trick EG *He'll be upset when he finds out you tricked him.*

1 duty NOUN
something that you ought to do
EG *We have a duty as adults to listen to children.*
obligation EG *He had not felt an obligation to help save his old friend.*
responsibility EG *work and family responsibilities*

2 duty NOUN
a task associated with a job

A
B
C
D
E
F
G
H
I
J
K
L
M
N
O
P
Q
R
S
T
U
V
W
X
Y
Z

EG *He carried out his duties conscientiously and with considerable skill.*

assignment EG *dangerous assignments*

job EG *One of my jobs was to make the tea.*

responsibility EG *He handled his responsibilities as a counsellor very well.*

role EG *Both sides had important roles to play.*

❸ **duty** NOUN
tax paid to the government
EG *customs duties*

excise EG *These products are excused VAT and excise.*

levy FORMAL EG *An annual motorway levy is imposed on all drivers.*

tariff EG *America wants to eliminate tariffs on such items as electronics.*

tax EG *the tax on new cars and motorcycles*

dying be dying for VERB
to want something very much
EG *I'm dying for a breath of fresh air.*

ache for EG *She still ached for the lost intimacy of marriage.*

hunger for EG *Jules hungered for adventure.*

long for EG *He longed for the winter to be over.*

pine for EG *I pine for the countryside.*

yearn for EG *He yearned for freedom.*

a
b
c
d
e
f
g
h
i
j
k
l
m
n
o
p
q
r
s
t
u
v
w
x
y
z

Ee

eager ADJECTIVE
wanting very much to do or have
something
EG *Robert is eager to earn some extra
money.*
anxious EG *She was anxious to leave
early.*
ardent EG *one of the government's
most ardent supporters*
avid EG *He's always been an avid
reader.*
enthusiastic EG *Tom usually seems
very enthusiastic.*
keen EG *Kirsty has always been a keen
swimmer.*
raring to go INFORMAL EG *They're all
ready and raring to go.*

WORD POWER

▷ **Synonyms**
fervent
hungry
zealous

❶ early ADJECTIVE
before the arranged or expected
time
EG *You're not late - I'm early!*
advance EG *We got an advance copy
of her new book.*
premature EG *The injury put a
premature end to his sporting career.*
untimely EG *her untimely death in a
car crash at the age of 21*

WORD POWER

▶ **Antonym**
late

❷ early ADJECTIVE
near the beginning of a period of
time
EG *the early 1970's*
primeval EG *These insects first
appeared in the primeval forests of
Europe.*
primitive EG *We found a fossil of a
primitive bird-like creature.*

❸ early ADVERB
before the arranged or expected
time
EG *We left early so we wouldn't have to
queue.*
ahead of time EG *The bus always
arrives ahead of time.*
beforehand EG *If you'd let me know
beforehand, you could have come
with us.*
in advance EG *You need to book in
advance to get a good seat.*
in good time EG *We arrived at the
airport in good time.*
prematurely EG *men who go
prematurely bald*

❶ earn VERB
to get money in return for doing
work
EG *He earns a lot more than I do.*
bring in EG *My job brings in just
enough to pay the bills.*
draw EG *I draw a salary, so I can
afford to run a car.*
get EG *How much do you get if you're
a lorry driver?*
make EG *She makes a lot of money.*
obtain EG *the profits obtained from
buying and selling shares*

WORD POWER

▷ **Synonyms**
net
reap

❷ earn VERB
to receive something that you
deserve
EG *He earned the respect of his troops.*
acquire EG *She has acquired a
reputation as a liar and a cheat.*
attain FORMAL EG *He finally attained
his pilot's licence.*
win EG *She won the admiration of all
her colleagues.*

❶ earth NOUN
the planet on which we live

EG *the tallest mountain on earth*
globe EG *from every corner of the globe*
planet EG *the effects of pollution on the atmosphere of our planet*
world EG *the first person to cycle round the world*

WORD POWER

● **Related Words**
adjective : terrestrial

❷ **earth** NOUN
soil from the ground
EG *He filled a pot with earth and popped the seeds in it.*
clay EG *lumps of clay that stuck to his boots*
dirt EG *kneeling in the dirt*
ground EG *digging potatoes out of the ground*
soil EG *We planted some bulbs in the soil around the pond.*

WORD POWER

▷ **Synonyms**
loam
topsoil
turf

❶ **ease** NOUN
lack of difficulty or worry
EG *He passed his driving test with ease.*
leisure EG *living a life of leisure*
relaxation EG *The town has a feeling of relaxation and tranquillity about it.*
simplicity EG *The simplicity of the new scheme has made it popular with motorists.*

❷ **ease** VERB
to make or become less severe or intense
EG *The doctor gave him another injection to ease the pain.*
abate EG *By morning the storms had abated.*
calm EG *The government is taking steps to calm the situation.*

relax EG *He relaxed his grip on the axe and smiled.*
relieve EG *The pills will help relieve the pain for a while.*
slacken EG *Her grip on the rope slackened and she fell back.*

WORD POWER

▷ **Synonyms**
allay
alleviate
assuage

❸ **ease** VERB
to move slowly or carefully
EG *He eased the door open and peered outside.*
creep EG *The car crept down the ramp.*
edge EG *I edged the van slowly back into the garage.*
guide EG *Bob guided the plane out onto the tarmac.*
inch EG *The ambulance inched its way through the crowds of shoppers.*
lower EG *He lowered himself into the armchair.*
manoeuvre EG *We attempted to manoeuvre his canoe towards the shore.*
squeeze EG *They squeezed him into his seat and strapped him in.*

❶ **easy** ADJECTIVE
able to be done without difficulty
EG *The software is very easy to install.*
light EG *a few light exercises to warm up*
painless EG *Finding somewhere to stay was pretty painless in the end.*
simple EG *All you have to do is answer a few simple questions.*
smooth EG *a smooth changeover to the new system*
straightforward EG *The route is fairly straightforward so you shouldn't need a map.*

a
b
c
d
e
f
g
h
i
j
k
l
m
n
o
p
q
r
s
t
u
v
w
x
y
z

WORD POWER

▶ **Antonym**
hard

2 easy ADJECTIVE
comfortable and without worries
EG *He has not had an easy life.*
carefree EG *a carefree summer spent on the beach*
comfortable EG *a comfortable teaching job at a small private school*
leisurely EG *a leisurely weekend spent with a few close friends*
quiet EG *a quiet weekend in the sun*
relaxed EG *It's very relaxed here, you can do what you like.*

1 eat VERB
to chew and swallow food
EG *For lunch he ate a cheese sandwich.*
→ see Word Study **eat**

2 eat VERB
to have a meal
EG *We like to eat early.*
breakfast FORMAL EG *The ladies like to breakfast in their rooms.*
dine EG *We usually dine at about six.*
feed EG *Leopards only feed when they are hungry.*
have a meal EG *We could have a meal at Pizza Palace after the film.*
lunch FORMAL EG *We lunched at El Greco's.*
picnic EG *After our walk, we picnicked by the river.*

eat away VERB
to destroy something slowly
EG *The front of the car had been eaten away by rust.*
corrode EG *buildings corroded by acid rain*
destroy EG *Areas of the coast are being destroyed by the sea.*
dissolve EG *Chemicals in the water are dissolving the bridge.*
erode EG *the floods that erode the dry, loose soil*
rot EG *Too many sweets will rot your teeth.*
wear away EG *The weather soon wears away the paintwork.*

1 eccentric ADJECTIVE
regarded as odd or peculiar
EG *His maths teacher was considered a bit eccentric.*
bizarre EG *He's quite a bizarre character.*
outlandish EG *his outlandish behaviour sometimes put people off*
quirky EG *a quirky, delightful film that is full of surprises*
strange EG *his strange views about UFOs*
weird EG *His taste in music is a bit weird.*
whimsical EG *a whimsical old gentleman*

2 eccentric NOUN
someone who is regarded as odd or peculiar
EG *He's always been regarded as a bit of an eccentric.*
character INFORMAL EG *a well-known character who lived in Johnson Street*
crank EG *People regarded vegetarians as cranks in those days.*

1 economic ADJECTIVE
concerning the way money is managed
EG *the need for economic reforms*
budgetary EG *a summit meeting to discuss various budgetary matters*
commercial EG *a purely commercial decision*
financial EG *The financial pressures on the government are mounting.*

WORD POWER

▷ **Synonyms**
fiscal
monetary

2 economic ADJECTIVE
making a profit
EG *goods that happen to be economic to produce*

productive EG *the need to make these industries more productive*
profitable EG *a new venture that has proved highly profitable*
viable EG *businesses that are no longer viable*

WORD POWER

▷ **Synonyms**
money-making
profit-making
remunerative

1 economical ADJECTIVE
cheap to use and saving you money
EG *Our car may not be fast, but it's very economical.*
cheap EG *This isn't a very cheap way of buying stationery.*
cost-effective EG *the most cost-effective way of shopping*
economic EG *the most economic way to see the museum*
inexpensive EG *There are several good inexpensive restaurants in town.*

2 economical ADJECTIVE
careful and sensible with money or materials
EG *He's never been very economical about housekeeping.*
careful EG *She's very careful with her pocket money.*
frugal EG *his frugal lifestyle*
prudent EG *the prudent use of precious natural resources*
thrifty EG *My mother was very thrifty because she had so little spare cash.*

economy NOUN
the careful use of things to save money
EG *improvements in the fuel economy of new cars*
frugality FORMAL EG *We must live with strict frugality if we are to survive.*
prudence EG *A lack of prudence could seriously affect his finances.*
restraint EG *We need to exercise some restraint in our spending.*

thrift EG *He was widely praised for his thrift and imagination.*

ecstasy NOUN
extreme happiness
EG *his feeling of ecstasy after winning the medal*
bliss EG *husband and wife living together in bliss and harmony*
delight EG *He squealed with delight when we told him.*
elation EG *His supporters reacted to the news with elation.*
euphoria EG *There was a sense of euphoria after our election victory.*
exaltation EG *the mood of exaltation that affected everyone*
joy EG *her joy at finding him after so long*
rapture EG *His speech was received with rapture by a huge crowd.*

1 edge NOUN
the place where something ends or meets something else
EG *on the edge of the forest*
border EG *a pillowcase with a lace border*
boundary EG *The area beyond the western boundary belongs to Denmark.*
brim EG *He kept climbing until he reached the brim of the crater.*
fringe EG *the rundown areas on the fringes of the city*
lip EG *The lip of the jug was badly cracked.*
margin EG *standing on the margin of the land where it met the water*
rim EG *a large round mirror with a gold rim*

WORD POWER

▷ **Synonyms**
perimeter
periphery

▶ **Antonym**
centre

❷ edge VERB

to move somewhere slowly

EG *He edged towards the phone, ready to grab it if it rang.*

creep EG *The car crept forward a few feet, then stopped.*

inch EG *The ambulance inched its way through the crowds.*

sidle EG *A man sidled up to him and tried to sell him a ticket.*

educated ADJECTIVE

having a high standard of learning

EG *He is an educated, tolerant and reasonable man.*

cultivated EG *His mother was an elegant, cultivated woman.*

cultured EG *a cultured man with a wide circle of friends*

intellectual EG *He is the intellectual type.*

learned EG *He was a scholar, a very learned man.*

WORD POWER

▷ **Synonyms**
erudite
well-educated

---

education NOUN

the process of learning or teaching

EG *the importance of a good education*

coaching EG *extra coaching to help him pass his exams*

instruction EG *All instruction is provided by qualified experts.*

schooling EG *He began to wish he'd paid more attention to his schooling.*

training EG *His military training was no use to him here.*

tuition EG *personal tuition in the basics of photography*

effect NOUN

a direct result of something

EG *the effect that divorce has on children*

consequence EG *aware of the consequences of their actions*

end result EG *The end result of this process is still unclear.*

fruit EG *The new software is the fruit of three years' hard work.*

result EG *The result of all this uncertainty is that no-one is happy.*

upshot EG *The upshot is that we have a very unhappy workforce.*

efficient ADJECTIVE

able to work well without wasting time or energy

EG *The new hatchback has a much more efficient engine.*

businesslike EG *a highly businesslike approach that impressed everyone*

competent EG *an extremely competent piece of work*

economic EG *The new system is much more economic, and will save millions.*

effective EG *effective use of the time we have left*

organized EG *Tony seemed very organized, and completely in control of the situation.*

productive EG *the need to make farmers much more productive*

WORD POWER

▶ **Antonym**
inefficient

---

❶ effort NOUN

physical or mental energy

EG *It took a lot of effort, but we managed in the end.*

application EG *His talent, application and energy are a credit to the school.*

energy EG *He decided to devote his energy to writing another book.*

exertion EG *Is it really worth all the exertion?*

trouble EG *It's not worth the trouble.*

work EG *All the work I put in has now been wasted!*

❷ effort NOUN

an attempt or struggle

EG *an unsuccessful effort to ban Sunday shopping*

attempt EG *an attempt to obtain an interview with the President*
bid EG *a last-minute bid to stop the trial going ahead*
stab INFORMAL EG *his latest stab at acting*
struggle EG *his struggle to clear his name*

❶ **elaborate** ADJECTIVE
having many different parts
EG *an elaborate research project*
complex EG *a complex explanation*
complicated EG *a complicated plan of the building's security system*
detailed EG *the detailed plans that have been drawn up*
intricate EG *an intricate system of levers and pulleys*
involved EG *a very involved operation, lasting many hours*

WORD POWER

▶ **Antonym**
simple

❷ **elaborate** ADJECTIVE
highly decorated
EG *elaborate wooden carvings*
fancy EG *the fancy plasterwork on the ceiling*
fussy EG *a rather fussy design*
ornate EG *an ornate wrought-iron staircase*

❸ **elaborate** VERB
to add more information about something
EG *He promised to elaborate on what had been said last night.*
develop EG *Maybe we should develop this idea.*
enlarge EG *He was enlarging on proposals made earlier.*
expand EG *a view that I will expand on later*

❶ **eliminate** VERB
to get rid of someone or something
EG *We've eliminated two of the four options so far.*

cut out EG *His guilty plea cut out the need for a long, costly trial.*
do away with EG *the attempt to do away with nuclear weapons altogether*
eradicate EG *Efforts to eradicate malaria seem to be failing.*
get rid of EG *Why don't we just get rid of the middlemen altogether?*
remove EG *You should try and remove these fatty foods from your diet.*
stamp out EG *We need to stamp out this disgusting practice.*

❷ **eliminate** VERB
to beat someone in a competition
EG *His team was eliminated in the first round.*
knock out EG *We were knocked out by the Dutch champions.*
put out EG *Decker finally put her fellow American out in the quarter final.*

embarrass VERB
to make someone feel ashamed or awkward
EG *You always embarrass me in front of my friends!*
disconcert EG *The way Anderson was smirking disconcerted her.*
fluster EG *Nothing could fluster him.*
humiliate EG *How dare you humiliate me like that!*
shame EG *Her son's behaviour had upset and shamed her.*

WORD POWER

▷ **Synonyms**
discomfit
faze
mortify

embarrassed ADJECTIVE
ashamed and awkward
EG *I'm not embarrassed about taking my clothes off.*
ashamed EG *I felt so ashamed I wanted to die.*

a b c d e f g h i j k l m n o p q r s t u v w x y z

A
B
C
D
E
F
G
H
I
J
K
L
M
N
O
P
Q
R
S
T
U
V
W
X
Y
Z

awkward EG *It was a very awkward occasion.*

humiliated EG *A humiliated Mr Stevens admitted that the concert had been cancelled.*

red-faced EG *Red-faced executives had to explain this fact.*

self-conscious EG *I always feel self-conscious when I'm having my picture taken.*

sheepish EG *He looked very sheepish when he finally appeared.*

WORD POWER

▷ **Synonyms**
abashed
bashful
discomfited
mortified

embarrassment NOUN
shame and awkwardness
EG *I laughed loudly to cover my embarrassment.*

awkwardness EG *the awkwardness of our first meeting*

bashfulness EG *Overcome with bashfulness, he lowered his voice.*

humiliation EG *the humiliation of having to ask for money*

self-consciousness EG *her painful self-consciousness*

shame EG *the shame he felt at having let her down*

WORD POWER

▷ **Synonyms**
chagrin
discomfiture
mortification

emergency NOUN
an unexpected and difficult situation
EG *This is an emergency!*

crisis EG *the economic crisis affecting parts of Africa*

pinch EG *I don't mind working late in a pinch.*

emit VERB
to give out or release something
EG *Polly blinked and emitted a long sigh.*

exude EG *a plant that exudes an extremely unpleasant smell*

give off EG *The fumes it gives off are poisonous, so watch out.*

give out EG *The alarm gave out a series of bleeps, then stopped.*

release EG *The factory is still releasing toxic fumes.*

send out EG *The volcano has been sending out smoke for weeks.*

utter EG *He uttered a loud snort and continued eating.*

WORD POWER

▷ **Synonyms**
produce
radiate
send forth

emphasis NOUN
special or extra importance
EG *too much emphasis on commercialism*

accent EG *In the new government the accent will be on co-operation.*

importance EG *There's not enough importance being given to environmental issues.*

prominence EG *Crime prevention has to be given more prominence.*

weight EG *This adds more weight to the government's case.*

emphasize VERB
to make something seem specially important or obvious
EG *He emphasized the need for everyone to remain calm.*

accent EG *a white dress accented by a coloured scarf*

accentuate EG *His shaven head accentuates his round face.*

highlight EG *This disaster has highlighted the difficulty faced by the government.*

play up EG *He played up his bad-boy image.*
stress EG *I would like to stress that we are in complete agreement.*
underline EG *This underlines how important the new trade deal really is.*

WORD POWER

▷ **Synonyms**
foreground
underscore

---

❶ employ VERB
to pay someone to work for you
EG *Mollison was employed by Mr Darnley as a bodyguard.*
appoint EG *We need to appoint a successor to Mr Stevens.*
commission EG *He has been commissioned to design a new bridge.*
engage FORMAL EG *They have finally engaged a suitable nanny.*
hire EG *I was hired as a gardener on the estate.*
take on EG *the need to take on more workers for the summer*

❷ employ VERB
to use something
EG *the tactics employed by the police*
bring to bear EG *We can bring two very different techniques to bear on this.*
make use of EG *He makes use of several highly offensive terms to describe them.*
use EG *the methods used in the investigation*
utilize EG *Engineers will utilize a range of techniques to improve the signal.*

employee NOUN
someone who is paid to work for someone else
EG *the way they look after their employees*
hand EG *He's been working as a farm hand down south.*
worker EG *Workers at the plant have*

been laid off.
workman EG *A council workman finally arrived to fix the door.*

employer NOUN
someone that other people work for
EG *a meeting with her employer to discuss the issue*
boss EG *My boss has always been very fair.*
gaffer INFORMAL EG *You'll need to speak to the gaffer about that.*

employment NOUN
the fact of employing people
EG *the employment of children to work in shops*
engagement EG *the engagement of suitable staff*
enlistment EG *Enlistment in the armed forces is falling.*
hiring EG *The hiring of new staff is our top priority.*
recruitment EG *new policies on recruitment and training*
taking on EG *Taking on extra staff would make life a lot easier.*

❶ empty ADJECTIVE
having no people or things in it
EG *The roads were empty.*
bare EG *When she got there, the cupboard was bare.*
blank EG *all the blank pages in his diary*
clear EG *The runway must be kept clear at all times.*
deserted EG *By nightfall, the square was deserted.*
unfurnished EG *The flat was unfurnished when we moved in.*
uninhabited EG *The house has remained uninhabited since she moved out.*
vacant EG *two vacant lots on the industrial estate*

WORD POWER

▶ **Antonym**
full

---

a
b
c
d
e
f
g
h
i
j
k
l
m
n
o
p
q
r
s
t
u
v
w
x
y
z

2 empty ADJECTIVE
boring or without value or meaning
EG *My life is empty without him.*
inane EG *a series of inane remarks*
meaningless EG *the feeling that his existence was meaningless*
worthless EG *a worthless film with nothing to say about anything*

3 empty VERB
to remove people or things
EG *He emptied all the cupboards before Tony arrived.*
clear EG *The police cleared the building just in time.*
drain EG *She drained the bottles and washed them out.*
evacuate EG *Fortunately the building had been evacuated.*
unload EG *It only took twenty minutes to unload the van.*

WORD POWER
▶ **Antonym**
fill

enclose VERB
to surround a thing or place completely
EG *The book arrived enclosed in a red plastic bag.*
encircle EG *The area had been encircled by barbed wire.*
fence off EG *We decided to fence off the land.*
hem in EG *We were hemmed in by walls and hedges.*
surround EG *the low wall that surrounded the rose garden*
wrap EG *Wrap the chicken in foil and bake it in a medium oven.*

1 encourage VERB
to give someone confidence
EG *We were very encouraged by the response.*
cheer EG *This news cheered us all and helped us keep going.*
hearten EG *I am heartened to hear that.*

reassure EG *He always reassures me when I'm feeling down.*

WORD POWER
▶ **Antonym**
discourage

2 encourage VERB
to support a person or activity
EG *the need to encourage people to be sensible*
aid EG *I tried to aid his creative efforts.*
boost EG *Efforts to boost investment seem to be succeeding.*
favour EG *conditions which favour growth in the economy*
help EG *policies aimed at helping small businesses*
incite EG *He incited his followers to attack the police station.*
support EG *Rowe will support me in this campaign.*

WORD POWER
▷ **Synonyms**
foster
further
promote
strengthen

1 end NOUN
the last part of a period or event
EG *the end of the 20th century*
→ see Word Study **end**

WORD POWER
▶ **Antonym**
beginning

● **Related Words**
adjectives : final, terminal, ultimate

2 end NOUN
the furthest point of something
EG *the room at the end of the corridor*
→ see Word Study **end**

3 end NOUN
the purpose for which something is

done
EG *The army is being used for political ends.*
→ see Word Study **end**

❹ end VERB
to come or bring to a finish
EG *talks being held to end the fighting*
bring to an end EG *The treaty brought to an end fifty years of conflict.*
cease EG *By one o'clock the storm had ceased.*
conclude EG *The evening concluded with the usual speeches.*
finish EG *waiting for the film to finish*
stop EG *When is it all going to stop?*
terminate EG *the decision to terminate their contract*

WORD POWER

▶ **Antonym**
begin

---

endanger VERB
to put someone or something in danger
EG *a dispute that could endanger the peace talks*
compromise EG *We will not allow safety to be compromised.*
jeopardize EG *a scandal that could jeopardize his government*
put at risk EG *those who were put at risk by her stupidity*
risk EG *He is risking the lives of others.*
threaten EG *A breakdown in this system could threaten the whole project.*

❶ endure VERB
to experience something difficult
EG *He had to endure hours of discomfort.*
cope with EG *We've had a lot to cope with in the last few weeks.*
experience EG *The company has experienced heavy financial losses.*
go through EG *having to go through the public humiliation of a court case*

stand EG *I don't know how he stood it for so long.*
suffer EG *Steven has suffered years of pain from arthritis.*

❷ endure VERB
to continue to exist
EG *Our friendship has endured through everything.*
last EG *a car that is built to last*
live on EG *His name will live on as an inspiration to others.*
remain EG *When all the rest is forgotten, this fact will remain.*
survive EG *the few traces of their civilization that have survived*

enemy NOUN
someone who is against you
EG *She has many enemies in the government.*
adversary EG *face to face with his old adversary*
antagonist EG *He killed his antagonist in a duel.*
foe EG *He plays Dracula's foe, Dr. Van Helsing.*
opponent EG *Her political opponents will be delighted at this news.*

WORD POWER

▶ **Antonym**
friend

---

energetic ADJECTIVE
full of energy
EG *an able, energetic and very determined politician*
animated EG *an animated conversation about politics and sport*
dynamic EG *a dynamic and ambitious businessman*
indefatigable EG *trying to keep up with their indefatigable boss*
spirited EG *a spirited defence of his new tax proposals*
tireless EG *a tireless campaigner for the homeless*
vigorous EG *a vigorous campaign*

a
b
c
d
e
f
g
h
i
j
k
l
m
n
o
p
q
r
s
t
u
v
w
x
y
z

energy NOUN
the ability and strength to do things
EG *I'm saving my energy for tomorrow.*
drive EG *a man with immense drive and enthusiasm*
life EG *At 96, she's still as full of life as ever.*
spirit EG *Despite trailing 6-2, they played with a lot of spirit.*
strength EG *She put all her strength into finding a new job.*
vigour EG *They returned to their work with renewed vigour.*
vitality EG *a woman with considerable charm and endless vitality*

WORD POWER

▷ **Synonyms**
élan
verve
zeal
zest

enjoy VERB
to find pleasure in something
EG *I haven't enjoyed a film as much as that in ages!*
appreciate EG *people who don't appreciate Satie's music*
delight in EG *He delights in playing practical jokes.*
like EG *Kirsty likes shopping.*
love EG *He loves skiing.*
relish EG *She relished the opportunity to get back at him.*
revel in EG *Stevens was revelling in the attention.*
take pleasure from EG *He took no pleasure from the knowledge that he had won.*
take pleasure in EG *She seemed to take pleasure in my discomfort.*

enlarge VERB
to make something larger
EG *plans to enlarge the 30,000 seat stadium*
add to EG *We've decided to add to this house rather than move again.*
expand EG *If we want to stay in business, we need to expand.*
extend EG *They extended the house by adding a conservatory.*
increase EG *They have increased the peace-keeping force to 2000.*
magnify EG *A more powerful lens will magnify the image.*

WORD POWER

▷ **Synonyms**
augment
broaden
distend
elongate
lengthen
widen

enlarge on VERB
to give more information about something
EG *I'd like you to enlarge on that last point.*
develop EG *Maybe I should develop this idea a little bit further.*
elaborate on EG *He refused to elaborate on what he had said earlier.*
expand on EG *an idea that I will expand on later*

enormous ADJECTIVE
very large in size or amount
EG *an enormous dust cloud*
colossal EG *a colossal waste of public money*
gigantic EG *The road is bordered by gigantic rocks.*
huge EG *Several painters were working on a huge piece of canvas.*
immense EG *an immense cloud of smoke*
massive EG *The scale of the problem is massive.*
tremendous EG *I felt a tremendous pressure on my chest.*
vast EG *vast stretches of land*

WORD POWER

▶ **Antonym**
tiny

---

ensure VERB
to make sure about something
EG *We must ensure that this never happens again.*
guarantee EG *Further investment should guarantee that profits will rise.*
make certain EG *to make certain that he'll get there*
make sure EG *I will personally make sure that the job gets done.*

❶ enterprise NOUN
a business or company
EG *a small enterprise with a high turnover*
business EG *a medium-sized business*
company EG *a company that was doing very well*
concern EG *It's not a large concern, but it makes a profit.*
establishment EG *a modest establishment dedicated to sailing*
firm EG *a clothing firm*
operation EG *a one-man operation*

❷ enterprise NOUN
a project or task
EG *a risky enterprise such as horse breeding*
effort EG *her latest fund-raising effort for cancer research*
endeavour EG *an endeavour that was bound to end in failure*
operation EG *He'd set up a small mining operation.*
project EG *a project that will attract a lot of media attention*
undertaking EG *This undertaking will rely on the hard work of our volunteers.*
venture EG *a venture that few were willing to invest in*

entertain VERB
to keep people amused or interested
EG *things that might entertain children in the school holidays*
amuse EG *He amused us all evening, singing and telling jokes.*
charm EG *He charmed Mrs Nisbet with his tales of life on the road.*
delight EG *a routine that will delight audiences*
enthral EG *He enthralled audiences all over Europe.*
please EG *He certainly knows how to please a crowd.*

entertainment NOUN
enjoyable activities
EG *Their main form of entertainment is the TV.*
amusement EG *looking for some amusement on a Saturday night*
enjoyment EG *We need a bit of enjoyment to cheer us up.*
fun EG *It's not really my idea of family fun.*
pleasure EG *Hours of pleasure can be had with a pack of cards.*
recreation EG *a healthy and enjoyable form of recreation*

enthusiasm NOUN
eagerness and enjoyment in something
EG *We were disappointed by their lack of enthusiasm.*
eagerness EG *He could barely contain his eagerness.*
excitement EG *Her excitement got the better of her.*
interest EG *He doesn't show much interest in football.*
keenness EG *I don't doubt his keenness, it's his ability that worries me.*
warmth EG *He greeted us with his usual warmth and affection.*

a
b
c
d
e
f
g
h
i
j
k
l
m
n
o
p
q
r
s
t
u
v
w
x
y
z

WORD POWER

▷ **Synonyms**
ardour
fervour
relish
zeal

enthusiastic ADJECTIVE
showing great excitement and
eagerness for something
EG *He was very enthusiastic about the
new scheme.*
ardent EG *one of the government's
most ardent supporters*
avid EG *an avid reader*
devoted EG *a devoted Star Trek fan*
eager EG *He is eager to learn more
about computers.*
excited EG *We are very excited about
getting a new dog.*
keen EG *Dave is an keen angler.*
passionate EG *a passionate
opponent of the government*

WORD POWER

▷ **Synonyms**
fervent
wholehearted
zealous

▶ **Antonym**
apathetic

❶ **entrance** NOUN
the way into a particular place
EG *I met Barry at the entrance to the
station.*
door EG *She was waiting by the front
door.*
doorway EG *the mass of people
blocking the doorway*
entry EG *Kevin had been hanging
round the back entry for hours.*
gate EG *the security guard at the
main gate*
way in EG *Is this the way in?*

❷ **entrance** NOUN
a person's arrival somewhere
EG *She had failed to notice her father's
entrance.*
appearance EG *She had timed her
appearance at the dinner to
perfection.*
arrival EG *journalists awaiting the
arrival of the team*
entry EG *He was arrested on his entry
into Mexico.*

❸ **entrance** NOUN
the right to enter somewhere
EG *He gained entrance to the hotel
where the band were staying.*
access EG *We were denied access to
the stadium.*
admission EG *no admission without
a ticket*
entry EG *I was unable to gain entry to
the meeting.*

❹ **entrance** VERB
to amaze and delight someone
EG *The audience was entranced by her
voice.*
bewitch EG *Young Gordon's smile
bewitched everyone.*
captivate EG *I was captivated by her
piercing blue eyes.*
charm EG *He charmed Mr Darnley
and made him feel young again.*
delight EG *a CD that will delight her
many fans*
enthral EG *Audiences were
enthralled by his spectacular stage
act.*
fascinate EG *She never failed to
fascinate him.*

WORD POWER

▷ **Synonyms**
enchant
enrapture
spellbind

❶ **entry** NOUN
a person's arrival somewhere
EG *her dramatic entry*
appearance EG *She made her
appearance to tumultuous applause.*

arrival EG *He apologized for his late arrival.*

entrance EG *My entrance was spoiled when I tripped over the carpet.*

2 entry NOUN
the way into a particular place
EG *He was hanging around at the entry to the station.*

door EG *I'll meet you at the front door.*

doorway EG *A bicycle was blocking the doorway.*

entrance EG *The bomb had been left outside the entrance to the building.*

gate EG *Guards were posted at the main gate.*

way in EG *I can't find the way in.*

3 entry NOUN
something that has been written down
EG *the final entry in his journal*

item EG *A number of interesting items appear in his diary.*

note EG *He grunted and made a note in his pocket book.*

record EG *There is no record for 13 October in the log book.*

1 envy NOUN
a feeling of resentment about what someone else has
EG *his feelings of envy towards Kevin*

jealousy EG *the jealousy people felt towards him because of his money*

resentment EG *All the anger, bitterness and resentment suddenly melted away.*

2 envy VERB
to want something that someone else has
EG *I don't envy you one bit.*

be envious EG *people who were envious of her good fortune*

begrudge EG *Surely you don't begrudge me one night out.*

be jealous EG *I couldn't help being jealous when I knew he had won.*

covet EG *She coveted his job.*

resent EG *Anyone with money was resented and ignored.*

1 equal ADJECTIVE
the same in size, amount, or value
EG *equal numbers of men and women*

equivalent EG *A kilogram is equivalent to 2.2 pounds.*

identical EG *glasses containing identical amounts of water*

the same EG *different areas of research that have the same importance*

2 equal equal to ADJECTIVE
having the necessary ability for something
EG *She was equal to any task they gave her.*

capable of EG *I'm no longer capable of this kind of work.*

up to EG *He said he wasn't up to a long walk.*

3 equal VERB
to be as good as something else
EG *a time that equalled the European record*

be equal to EG *The final score is equal to his personal best.*

match EG *able to match her previous time for the 100m*

equip VERB
to supply someone with something
EG *The boat was equipped with an outboard motor.*

arm EG *The children arrived armed with a range of gardening tools.*

endow EG *The male bird is endowed with a vicious-looking beak.*

fit out EG *the amount spent on fitting out their offices*

provide EG *We provided them with waterproofs and sandwiches.*

supply EG *They supplied us with camping gear and a stove.*

equipment NOUN
the things you need for a particular job
EG *a shed full of gardening equipment*

a
b
c
d
e
f
g
h
i
j
k
l
m
n
o
p
q
r
s
t
u
v
w
x
y
z

A
B
C
D
E
F
G
H
I
J
K
L
M
N
O
P
Q
R
S
T
U
V
W
X
Y
Z

apparatus EG *All the firemen were wearing breathing apparatus.*
gear EG *Police in riot gear have sealed off the area.*
paraphernalia EG *ashtrays, lighters and other paraphernalia associated with smoking*
stuff EG *The builders had left all their stuff in the garden.*
tackle EG *Martin kept all his fishing tackle in the spare room.*

WORD POWER

▷ **Synonyms**
accoutrements
appurtenances

erode VERB
to wear something away and destroy it.
EG *The cliffs were being eroded by the constant pounding of the sea.*
corrode EG *buildings corroded by acid rain*
destroy EG *ancient monuments destroyed by pollution*
deteriorate EG *The tapestry had deteriorated badly where the roof was leaking.*
disintegrate EG *Once they were exposed to light the documents rapidly disintegrated.*
eat away EG *The chemicals in the water had eaten away the cables.*
wear away EG *rocks worn away by the action of the wind*
wear down EG *Some of her teeth were worn down with gnawing on the bars.*

err VERB
to make a mistake
EG *The builders had erred considerably in their original estimate.*
blunder EG *Fletcher had obviously blundered.*
go wrong EG *We must have gone wrong somewhere in our calculations.*
make a mistake EG *Okay, I made a*

mistake, I'm only human.
miscalculate EG *They miscalculated, and now they're in deep trouble.*

error NOUN
a mistake
EG *a mathematical error*
blunder EG *He made a tactical blunder by announcing his intentions.*
fault EG *It is a fault to think you can learn how to manage people in business school.*
lapse EG *a serious security lapse*
mistake EG *spelling mistakes*
slip EG *We must be careful - we can't afford any slips.*

❶ escape VERB
to manage to get away
EG *Three prisoners who escaped have given themselves up.*
break free EG *He was handcuffed to his bed, but somehow managed to break free.*
break out EG *two prisoners who broke out of the maximum security wing*
get away EG *She got away from her guards.*
make your escape EG *We made our escape down a drainpipe using knotted sheets.*
run away EG *I called him but he just ran away.*
run off EG *The children ran off when they spotted me.*

WORD POWER

▷ **Synonyms**
abscond
bolt

❷ escape VERB
to manage to avoid something
EG *He was lucky to escape injury.*
avoid EG *She has managed to avoid arrest so far.*
dodge EG *He dodged his military service by pretending to be ill.*
duck EG *a pathetic attempt to duck*

her responsibilities

elude EG *He managed to elude the police for 13 years.*

evade EG *He has now been charged with evading tax.*

❸ escape NOUN

something that distracts you from something unpleasant

EG *Cycling gives me an escape from the routine of work.*

distraction EG *a distraction from his troubles*

diversion EG *a pleasant diversion from my studies*

relief EG *The piano provides relief from all the stress.*

❶ essence NOUN

the most basic and important part of something

EG *The essence of good management is the ability to listen.*

core EG *the need to get to the core of the problem*

heart EG *a problem that reaches to the very heart of the party*

nature EG *the nature of what it is to be European*

soul EG *a song that captures the soul of this proud nation*

spirit EG *the spirit of modern manhood*

WORD POWER

▷ **Synonyms**
crux
kernel
quintessence
substance

---

❷ essence NOUN

a concentrated liquid

EG *vanilla essence*

concentrate EG *orange concentrate*

extract EG *lemon extract*

❶ essential ADJECTIVE

extremely important

EG *Good ventilation is essential in a greenhouse.*

crucial EG *Her speech was a crucial part of the campaign.*

indispensable EG *She has become indispensable to the department.*

vital EG *a vital aspect of the plans that everyone has overlooked*

❷ essential ADJECTIVE

basic and important

EG *an essential part of any child's development*

basic EG *the basic laws of physics*

cardinal EG *He had broken one of the cardinal rules of business.*

fundamental EG *the fundamental principles of democracy*

key EG *Mollison had a key role to play in the negotiations.*

main EG *an attempt to analyse the main points of his theory*

principal EG *the principal idea that underpins their argument*

essentials PLURAL NOUN

the things that are most important

EG *We only had enough food money for the essentials.*

basics EG *We need to get back to basics.*

fundamentals EG *the fundamentals of road safety*

necessities EG *Water, food, and shelter are the necessities of life.*

prerequisites EG *Self-confidence is one of the prerequisites for a happy life.*

rudiments EG *teaching him the rudiments of car maintenance*

esteem NOUN

admiration and respect for another person

EG *He is held in high esteem by his colleagues.*

admiration EG *I have always had the greatest admiration for him.*

estimation EG *He has gone down in my estimation.*

regard EG *I had a very high regard for him and his work.*

A
B
C
D
E
F
G
H
I
J
K
L
M
N
O
P
Q
R
S
T
U
V
W
X
Y
Z

respect EG *I have tremendous respect for Dean.*
reverence EG *He is still spoken of with reverence by those who knew him.*

WORD POWER
▷ **Synonyms**
veneration (FORMAL)

estimate NOUN
a guess at an amount, quantity, or outcome
EG *This figure is five times the original estimate.*
appraisal EG *an appraisal of your financial standing*
assessment EG *assessments of mortgaged property*
estimation EG *The first group were correct in their estimation of the man's height.*
guess EG *He examined her and made a guess at her temperature.*
quote EG *Never agree to a job without getting a quote first.*
reckoning EG *By my reckoning we were seven kilometres from the town.*
valuation EG *The valuations reflect prices at the end of the fiscal year.*

eternal ADJECTIVE
lasting forever
EG *the secret of eternal life*
everlasting EG *everlasting love*
immortal EG *your immortal soul*
unchanging EG *the unchanging laws of the cosmos*

❶ even ADJECTIVE
flat and level
EG *I need an even surface to write on.*
flat EG *a small hut with a flat roof*
horizontal EG *He drew a series of horizontal lines on the paper.*
level EG *checking the floor to make sure it was level*
smooth EG *the smooth marble floor tiles*

WORD POWER
▶ **Antonym**
uneven

❷ even ADJECTIVE
without changing or varying
EG *an even flow of liquid*
constant EG *The temperature remained more or less constant.*
regular EG *her quiet, regular breathing*
smooth EG *He caught the ball and passed it in one smooth motion.*
steady EG *a steady stream of people*
uniform EG *The prices rises are not uniform across the country.*

❸ even ADJECTIVE
the same
EG *At halftime the scores were still even.*
equal EG *The two teams shared equal points into the second round.*
identical EG *At the end of the contest, our scores were identical.*
level EG *The scores were level at halftime.*
neck and neck EG *They're still neck and neck with two minutes to go.*

❶ event NOUN
something that happens
EG *still amazed at the events of last week*
affair EG *He preferred to forget the whole affair.*
business EG *Do you remember that business with Jim?*
circumstance EG *due to circumstances beyond our control*
episode EG *a rather embarrassing episode at Yvonne's wedding*
experience EG *an experience that changed his mind about going to university*
incident EG *the incident in the restaurant*
matter EG *She doesn't seem to be taking this matter seriously.*

2 event NOUN
a competition
EG *The next event is the long jump.*
bout EG *This is his fifth heavyweight bout in three months.*
competition EG *the first competition of the afternoon*
contest EG *She's out of the contest for good.*

everyday ADJECTIVE
usual or ordinary
EG *the drudgery of everyday life*
common EG *a common occurrence*
daily EG *In our daily life we follow predictable patterns of behaviour.*
day-to-day EG *I use a lot of spices in my day-to-day cooking.*
mundane EG *the mundane realities of life*
ordinary EG *ordinary tableware*
routine EG *routine maintenance of the machine.*

WORD POWER
▷ **Synonyms**
unexceptional

evident ADJECTIVE
easily noticed or understood
EG *He spoke with evident emotion about his ordeal.*
apparent EG *He spoke with apparent nonchalance about his experience.*
clear EG *It became clear that I hadn't convinced Mike.*
noticeable EG *a noticeable effect*
obvious EG *It's obvious that he doesn't like me.*
palpable EG *The tension between Jim and Amy is palpable.*
plain EG *It was plain to him that she was having a nervous breakdown.*
visible EG *the most visible sign of her distress*

WORD POWER
▷ **Synonyms**
conspicuous
manifest
patent

1 evil NOUN
the force that causes bad things to happen
EG *the conflict between good and evil*
badness EG *behaving that way out of sheer badness*
immorality EG *the immorality that is typical of the arms trade*
sin EG *The whole town is a den of sin and corruption.*
vice EG *a place long associated with vice and immorality*
wickedness EG *the wickedness of his behaviour*

WORD POWER
▷ **Synonyms**
baseness
depravity
sinfulness

▶ **Antonym**
good

2 evil NOUN
something unpleasant or harmful
EG *a lecture on the evils of alcohol*
affliction EG *Hay fever is an affliction that affects thousands.*
ill EG *Many of the nation's ills are his responsibility.*
misery EG *the misery of drug addiction*
sorrow EG *the joys and sorrows of family life*

3 evil ADJECTIVE
morally wrong or bad
EG *an utterly evil man*
bad EG *He's not a bad man, he's just very unhappy.*
depraved EG *a throughly depraved film*

A B C D E F G H I J K L M N O P Q R S T U V W X Y Z

malevolent EG *a malevolent influence on the whole school*
sinful EG *He is a good person in a sinful world.*
vile EG *vile acts of brutality*
wicked EG *a wicked attack on a helpless child*

WORD POWER

▶ **Antonym**
good

❶ **exact** ADJECTIVE
correct in every detail
EG *It's an exact reproduction of the first steam engine.*
accurate EG *an accurate description of the man*
authentic EG *authentic Elizabethan costumes*
faithful EG *faithful copies of ancient stone tools*
faultless EG *She spoke with a faultless French accent.*
precise EG *It's difficult to give a precise date for the painting.*
true EG *Is this a true picture of life in the Middle Ages?*

WORD POWER

▶ **Antonym**
approximate

❷ **exact** VERB; FORMAL
to demand and obtain something
EG *They are certain to exact a high price for their cooperation.*
command EG *an excellent surgeon who commanded the respect of all his colleagues*
extract EG *to extract the maximum political advantage from this situation*
impose EG *the first council to impose a fine for dropping litter*
insist on EG *She insisted on conducting all the interviews herself.*
insist upon EG *He insists upon good service.*

wring EG *attempts to wring concessions from the government*

❶ **exactly** ADVERB
with complete accuracy and precision
EG *He arrived at exactly five o'clock.*
accurately EG *We cannot accurately predict where the missile will land.*
faithfully EG *I translated the play as faithfully as I could.*
just EG *There are no statistics about just how many people won't vote.*
on the dot EG *At nine o'clock on the dot, they have breakfast.*
precisely EG *No-one knows precisely how many people are in the camp.*
quite EG *That wasn't quite what I meant.*

WORD POWER

▶ **Antonym**
approximately

❷ **exactly** INTERJECTION
an expression implying total agreement
EG *"We'll never know the answer." - "Exactly. So let's stop speculating."*
absolutely EG *"It's worrying, isn't it?" - "Absolutely."*
indeed EG *"That's a topic that's getting a lot of media coverage." - "Indeed."*
precisely EG *"So, you're suggesting we do away with these laws?" - "Precisely."*
quite EG *"It's your choice, isn't it?" - "Quite."*

exaggerate VERB
to make things seem worse than they are
EG *He thinks I'm exaggerating, but I'm not!*
overdo EG *I think he's overdoing it a bit when he complains like that.*
overestimate EG *I think we're overestimating their desire to cooperate.*

overstate EG *It's impossible to overstate the seriousness of this situation.*

exam NOUN
a test to find out how much you know
EG *a maths exam*
examination EG *a three-hour written examination*
oral EG *I got good marks for my French oral.*
test EG *I failed my history test again.*

1 examination NOUN
a careful inspection of something
EG *The Navy is carrying out an examination of the wreck.*
analysis EG *An analysis of the ash revealed traces of lead oxide.*
inspection EG *The police inspection of the vehicle found no fingerprints.*
study EG *A study of the wreckage has thrown new light on the crash.*

2 examination NOUN
a check carried out on someone by a doctor
EG *The doctor suggested an immediate examination of his ear.*
check EG *a quick check just to make sure everything's working properly*
checkup EG *my annual checkup at the clinic*
medical EG *He had a medical before leaving England.*

1 examine VERB
to look at something very carefully
EG *Police scientists are examining the scene of the crash.*
analyse EG *We haven't had time to analyse all the samples yet.*
go over EG *I'll go over your report tomorrow.*
go through EG *We went through his belongings and found a notebook.*
inspect EG *Customs officials inspected the vehicle.*
look over EG *Once we've looked the house over we should know what*

caused the fire.
study EG *Experts are studying the frozen remains of a mammoth.*

WORD POWER

▷ **Synonyms**
peruse
scrutinize
---

2 examine NOUN
to give someone a medical examination
EG *I was examined by several specialists.*
check EG *Dr Mollison checked my nose and throat.*
inspect EG *I was inspected twice by Dr Stevens.*
look at EG *He said he wanted to look at my chest again just to make sure.*
test EG *They tested my eyes but my vision was fine.*

1 example NOUN
something that represents a group of things
EG *some examples of medieval wood carving*
illustration EG *Lo's success is an illustration of how well China is doing.*
sample EG *This drawing is a sample of his early work.*
specimen EG *I had to submit a specimen of my handwriting for analysis.*

2 example NOUN
something that people can imitate
EG *His dedication is an example to us all.*
ideal EG *a woman who was the American ideal of beauty*
model EG *His conduct at the talks was a model of dignity.*
paragon EG *She is a paragon of neatness and efficiency.*
prototype EG *He was the prototype of the English gentleman.*

A
B
C
D
E
F
G
H
I
J
K
L
M
N
O
P
Q
R
S
T
U
V
W
X
Y
Z

WORD POWER

▷ Synonyms
archetype
exemplar
paradigm

excellent ADJECTIVE
extremely good
EG *It's an excellent book, one of my favourites.*
beaut AUSTRALIAN AND NEW ZEALAND; INFORMAL EG *a beaut spot to live*
brilliant EG *What a brilliant film!*
cracking BRITISH, AUSTRALIAN, AND NEW ZEALAND; INFORMAL EG *You've done a cracking job in the garden!*
fine EG *There's a fine view from the bedroom window.*
first-class EG *a first-class effort*
great EG *He's a great player and we'll be sorry to lose him.*
outstanding EG *an outstanding performance*
superb EG *a superb craftsman*

WORD POWER

▶ Antonym
terrible

except PREPOSITION
apart from
EG *I don't drink, except for the occasional glass of wine.*
apart from EG *The room was empty apart from one man seated by the fire.*
but EG *He didn't speak anything but Greek.*
other than EG *She makes no reference to any research other than her own.*
save FORMAL EG *We had almost nothing to eat, save the few berries and nuts we could find.*
with the exception of EG *Yesterday was a day off for everybody, with the exception of Tom.*

❶ exceptional ADJECTIVE
unusually excellent, talented, or

clever
EG *His piano playing is exceptional.*
excellent EG *The recording quality is excellent.*
extraordinary EG *He is an extraordinary musician.*
outstanding EG *an outstanding athlete*
phenomenal EG *The performances have been absolutely phenomenal.*
remarkable EG *a remarkable achievement*
talented EG *He is a talented violinist.*

WORD POWER

▶ Antonym
mediocre

❷ exceptional ADJECTIVE
unusual and likely to happen very rarely
EG *The courts hold that this case is exceptional.*
isolated EG *They said the allegations related to an isolated case.*
out of the ordinary EG *I've noticed nothing out of the ordinary.*
rare EG *those rare occasions when he did eat alone*
special EG *In special cases, an exception to this rule may be made.*
unheard-of EG *buying rum at the unheard-of rate of $2 per bottle*
unusual EG *To be appreciated as a parent is unusual.*

WORD POWER

▷ Synonyms
unprecedented
(FORMAL)

▶ Antonym
common

❶ excess NOUN
behaviour that goes beyond what is acceptable
EG *a life of excess*
extravagance EG *Examples of her*

excess >> exchange

extravagance were everywhere.
indulgence EG *a moment of sheer indulgence*

WORD POWER

▷ **Synonyms**
debauchery
dissipation
intemperance
overindulgence

---

2 excess NOUN
a larger amount than necessary
EG *An excess of houseplants made the room look like a jungle.*
glut EG *the current glut of dairy products in Europe*
overdose EG *An overdose of sun can lead to skin problems later.*
surfeit EG *A surfeit of rich food did not help his digestive problems.*
surplus EG *Germany suffers from a surplus of teachers at the moment.*

WORD POWER

▷ **Synonyms**
overabundance
plethora
superabundance
superfluity

▶ **Antonym**
shortage

---

3 excess ADJECTIVE
more than is needed
EG *problems associated with excess weight*
extra EG *Pour any extra liquid into a bowl and set aside.*
superfluous EG *all our superfluous belongings, things we don't need*
surplus EG *Farmers have to sell off their surplus stock cheap.*

excessive ADJECTIVE
too great
EG *an excessive reliance on government funding*
enormous EG *She spent an*

enormous amount on clothes.
exaggerated EG *the exaggerated claims made by their supporters*
needless EG *a film that is full of needless violence*
undue EG *the need to avoid undue expense*
unreasonable EG *unreasonable increases in the price of petrol*

WORD POWER

▷ **Synonyms**
disproportionate
exorbitant
immoderate
inordinate
profligate

---

1 exchange VERB
to give something in return for something else
EG *We exchanged phone numbers.*
barter EG *Traders came from everywhere to barter in the markets.*
change EG *Can you change pesetas for pounds?*
swap EG *I wouldn't swap places with her for anything!*
switch EG *They switched cars and were away before the alarm was raised.*
trade EG *a secret deal to trade arms for hostages*

2 exchange NOUN
the act of giving something for something else
EG *a ceasefire to allow the exchange of prisoners*
interchange EG *a meeting at which the interchange of ideas was encouraged*
swap EG *They agreed to a swap and made the necessary arrangements.*
switch EG *The switch went ahead as planned.*
trade EG *I am willing to make a trade with you.*

A B C D E F G H I J K L M N O P Q R S T U V W X Y Z

❶ excite VERB

to make someone feel enthusiastic
or nervous
EG *The idea of visiting America really
excited the kids.*
agitate EG *I've no idea what has
agitated him.*
animate EG *There was plenty about
this match to animate the capacity
crowd.*
thrill EG *The reception he got at the
meeting thrilled him.*
titillate EG *a meal that will titillate
the taste buds of every gourmet*

❷ excite VERB

to cause a particular feeling or
reaction
EG *The meeting failed to excite strong
feelings in anyone.*
arouse EG *a move that has aroused
deep public anger*
elicit EG *His proposal elicited a storm
of protest.*
evoke EG *The film has evoked a sense
of nostalgia in many older people.*
incite EG *a crude attempt to incite
racial hatred*
inspire EG *The handling of the new
car quickly inspires confidence.*
provoke EG *The suggestion has
provoked anger.*
stir up EG *He's just trying to stir up
trouble.*

WORD POWER

▷ **Synonyms**
fire
foment
inflame
kindle
rouse

excited ADJECTIVE

happy and unable to relax
EG *We are very excited about getting a
new dog.*
agitated EG *in an excited and
agitated state*

enthusiastic EG *Tom usually seems
very enthusiastic.*
feverish EG *a state of feverish
anticipation*
high INFORMAL EG *I was feeling really
high after Lorraine's party.*
thrilled EG *The children were thrilled
when the snow came.*

WORD POWER

▶ **Antonym**
bored

excitement NOUN

interest and enthusiasm
EG *The release of his latest film has
caused great excitement.*
activity EG *a scene of frenzied activity*
adventure EG *setting off in search of
adventure*
agitation EG *He reacted to the news
with considerable agitation.*
commotion EG *We decided to find
out what all the commotion was
about.*
enthusiasm EG *They greeted our
arrival with enthusiasm.*
thrill EG *the thrill of scuba diving*

WORD POWER

▷ **Synonyms**
animation
elation
furore
tumult

exciting ADJECTIVE

making you feel happy and
enthusiastic
EG *the most exciting race I've ever seen*
dramatic EG *Their arrival was
dramatic and exciting.*
electrifying EG *It was an electrifying
performance.*
exhilarating EG *an exhilarating walk
along the cliff tops*
rousing EG *a rousing speech*
stimulating EG *It's a stimulating*

book, full of ideas.
thrilling EG *a thrilling opportunity to watch the lions as they feed*

WORD POWER

▷ **Synonyms**
intoxicating
sensational
stirring

▶ **Antonym**
boring

❶ exclude VERB
to decide not to include something
EG *We cannot exclude this possibility altogether.*
eliminate EG *We can eliminate Mr Darnley from our list of suspects.*
ignore EG *We cannot afford to ignore this option.*
leave out EG *We can narrow it down by leaving out everywhere that's too expensive.*
omit EG *His name seems to have been omitted from the list.*
rule out EG *The police have already ruled out a retrial.*

WORD POWER

▶ **Antonym**
include

❷ exclude VERB
to stop someone going somewhere or doing something
EG *The university used to exclude women from all lectures.*
ban EG *Tony was banned from driving for three years.*
bar EG *She was barred from the tennis club.*
forbid EG *Carver was forbidden to attend any of the society's meetings.*
keep out EG *We need to keep out troublemakers.*

WORD POWER

▷ **Synonyms**
blackball
debar

exclusive ADJECTIVE
available only to a few rich people
EG *one of Britain's most exclusive golf clubs*
chic EG *a chic nightclub in Monaco*
classy EG *a very classy restaurant*
posh INFORMAL EG *She took me to a posh hotel to celebrate.*
select EG *a very lavish and very select party*
up-market EG *The area is much more up-market than it used to be.*

❶ excuse NOUN
a reason or explanation
EG *Stop making excuses and get on with it!*
explanation EG *You'd better have a good explanation for your conduct.*
justification EG *What possible justification can there be for this?*
pretext EG *His pretext for leaving early was an upset stomach.*
reason EG *This gave me the perfect reason for visiting London.*

❷ excuse VERB
to forgive someone or someone's behaviour
EG *Please excuse my late arrival.*
forgive EG *Forgive me, I'm so sorry.*
overlook EG *the need to overlook each other's failings*
pardon EG *Pardon my ignorance, but who is Cliff Hanley?*
turn a blind eye to EG *We can't be expected to turn a blind eye to this behaviour.*

exempt ADJECTIVE
excused from a duty or rule
EG *Teachers were exempt from military service.*
excused EG *Some MPs will have been officially excused attendance.*

A
B
C
D
E
F
G
H
I
J
K
L
M
N
O
P
Q
R
S
T
U
V
W
X
Y
Z

immune EG *Members of the parliament are immune from prosecution.*
not liable EG *They are not liable to pay income tax.*

exercise NOUN
activity that keeps you fit
EG *I need to get more exercise.*
activity EG *a bit of physical activity to get the heart going*
exertion EG *I'm tired out by all this exertion.*
training EG *He needs to do a bit more training before the match.*
work EG *I'm doing a lot more work at the gym now I'm feeling better.*

❶ exhaust VERB
to make very tired
EG *I mustn't exhaust myself as I did last time.*
drain EG *My emotional turmoil had drained me.*
fatigue EG *He is easily fatigued.*
tire out EG *a great new job that tires me out*
wear out EG *Living out of a suitcase wears you out.*

❷ exhaust VERB
to use something up completely
EG *She has exhausted all my patience.*
consume EG *plans which will consume hours of time*
deplete EG *chemicals that deplete the earth's protective ozone shield*
run through EG *The project ran through its funds in months.*
use up EG *The gas has all been used up.*

expand VERB
to make or become larger
EG *The rails expanded and buckled in the fierce heat.*
develop EG *We need to develop the company's engineering division.*
enlarge EG *Plans to enlarge the stadium have been approved.*
extend EG *We're trying to extend our range of sports wear.*

fill out EG *The balloon had filled out and was already almost airborne.*
grow EG *The Japanese share of the market has grown dramatically.*
increase EG *We will need to increase our overseas operations.*
swell EG *The river had swollen rapidly.*

WORD POWER

▶ **Antonym**
decrease

expand on VERB
to give more information about something
EG *an idea that I will expand on later*
develop EG *You should develop this theme a little bit further.*
elaborate on EG *He refused to elaborate on what he had said earlier.*
enlarge on EG *I'd like you to enlarge on that last point.*

❶ expect VERB
to believe that something is going to happen
EG *The trial is expected to last several weeks.*
anticipate EG *We do not anticipate any problems.*
assume EG *He assumed that they would wait for him.*
believe EG *Experts believe the comet will pass close to the earth.*
imagine EG *The meal cost more than we had imagined.*
presume EG *I presume they'll be along shortly.*
reckon EG *We reckon it'll be a fairly quick journey.*
think EG *I thought the concert would be cancelled.*

WORD POWER

▷ **Synonyms**
envisage
forecast
foresee
predict

❷ expect VERB
to believe that something is your right
EG *I was expecting to have a bit of time to myself.*
demand EG *a job that demands a lot of time and money*
rely on EG *I'm relying on you to help me.*
require EG *They require a lot of her, maybe too much.*

expensive ADJECTIVE
costing a lot of money
EG *a very expensive Italian suit*
costly EG *a costly court case*
dear EG *Those trainers are far too dear.*
pricey EG *Medical insurance can be very pricey.*

> *WORD POWER*
>
> ▷ **Synonyms**
> exorbitant
> overpriced
>
> ▶ **Antonym**
> cheap

❶ experience NOUN
knowledge or skill in a particular activity
EG *We're looking for someone with engineering experience.*
expertise EG *They lack the expertise to deal with such a complex case.*
know-how EG *Her technical know-how was invaluable.*
knowledge EG *We need someone with knowledge of computing.*
training EG *His military training made the difference between life and death.*
understanding EG *someone with considerable understanding of the law*

❷ experience NOUN
something that happens to you
EG *a terrifying experience that she still talks about*

adventure EG *a series of hair-raising adventures during the war*
affair EG *He seemed keen to forget the affair and never discussed it.*
encounter EG *his first encounter with alcohol*
episode EG *The episode has proved deeply embarrassing for her.*
incident EG *an incident he would rather forget*
ordeal EG *a painful ordeal that is now over*

❸ experience VERB
to have something happen to you
EG *We are experiencing a few technical problems.*
encounter EG *The storms were the worst they had ever encountered.*
have EG *We're having a few difficulties with the computer.*
meet EG *The next time you meet a situation like this, be careful.*
undergo EG *The market is now undergoing a severe recession.*

experienced ADJECTIVE
very skilful as a result of practice
EG *an experienced diver*
expert EG *an expert pilot*
knowledgeable EG *He's very knowledgeable in this field.*
practised EG *a practised and accomplished surgeon*
seasoned EG *a seasoned climber*
well-versed EG *He is well-versed in many styles of jazz.*

> *WORD POWER*
>
> ▶ **Antonym**
> inexperienced

❶ expert NOUN
a skilled or knowledgeable person
EG *A team of experts will be on hand to offer advice.*
ace INFORMAL EG *former motor-racing ace Stirling Moss*
authority EG *an authority on ancient Egypt*

A
B
C
D
E
F
G
H
I
J
K
L
M
N
O
P
Q
R
S
T
U
V
W
X
Y
Z

buff INFORMAL EG *Cliff is a bit of a film buff.*
guru EG *fashion gurus who predicted a 70's revival*
master EG *He is a master in the art of office politics.*
professional EG *He's widely respected in the theatre as a true professional.*
specialist EG *a specialist in tropical diseases*
wizard EG *a financial wizard who made millions in the early 80's*

WORD POWER

▶ **Antonym**
beginner

❷ expert ADJECTIVE
skilled and knowledgeable
EG *Mollison's expert approach impressed everyone.*
able EG *an able and dedicated surgeon*
adept EG *He's an adept guitar player.*
experienced EG *He was an experienced traveller and knew the area well.*
knowledgeable EG *He's very knowledgeable about Chinese pottery.*
proficient EG *Jackson is proficient in several European languages.*
skilful EG *the skilful use of light in his early paintings*
skilled EG *Ian is a highly skilled photographer.*

WORD POWER

▷ **Synonyms**
adroit
dexterous
masterly
practised

explain VERB
to give extra information about something
EG *He explained to us how the system worked.*

define EG *Can you define what you mean by 'excessive'?*
describe EG *an attempt to describe the whole process*
illustrate EG *Let me illustrate this point with an example.*

WORD POWER

▷ **Synonyms**
elucidate
expound

explanation NOUN
a helpful or clear description
EG *his lucid explanation of Einstein's theories*
clarification EG *Her clarification has done little to help matters.*
definition EG *a definition of what we actually mean by 'symbolism'*
description EG *a fascinating description of how the pyramids were built*
exposition EG *the fullest available exposition of Coleridge's ideas*

❶ explode VERB
to burst or cause to burst loudly
EG *the sound of a bomb exploding nearby*
blow up EG *Their boat blew up as they slept.*
burst EG *Joey blew up the balloon until it burst.*
detonate EG *Troops managed to detonate the mine safely.*
go off EG *The bomb went off without any warning.*
set off EG *No-one knows who planted the bomb, or how it was set off.*

❷ explode VERB
to become angry suddenly
EG *I asked him if he'd finished and he just exploded.*
blow up EG *When she finally told him, he blew up and walked out.*
go berserk EG *He'll go berserk if he*

ever finds out.
go mad EG *He went mad when I mentioned the kids.*

❸ explode VERB
to increase suddenly and rapidly
EG *Sales of computer games have exploded in recent years.*
rocket EG *Inflation has rocketed in the last few months.*
shoot up EG *Prices shot up and the shelves were soon empty.*
soar EG *Demand for shares in his new company has soared.*

explosion NOUN
a violent burst of energy
EG *The explosion shattered windows all along the street.*
bang EG *A loud bang made me run for cover.*
blast EG *Three people were killed in the blast.*

❶ expose VERB
to make something visible
EG *The wreck was exposed by the action of the tide.*
reveal EG *His shirt was open, revealing his tattooed chest.*
show EG *a short skirt which showed too much of her legs*
uncover EG *She removed her scarf and uncovered her head.*

❷ expose VERB
to tell the truth about someone or something
EG *He has been exposed as a liar and a cheat.*
bring to light EG *The truth will be brought to light eventually.*
reveal EG *an investigation that revealed widespread corruption*
show up EG *She was finally shown up as a hypocrite.*
uncover EG *We uncovered evidence of fraud.*
unearth EG *Investigators have unearthed new evidence.*

❶ express VERB
to say what you think
EG *She expressed interest in the plans for the new dam.*
communicate EG *People must learn to communicate their feelings.*
couch EG *Their demands, though extreme, are couched in moderate language.*
phrase EG *It sounds fine, but I would have phrased it differently.*
put EG *Absolutely - I couldn't have put it better.*
put across EG *the need to put across your message without offending anyone*
voice EG *Local people have voiced their concern over plans for a bypass.*

WORD POWER

▷ **Synonyms**
articulate
enunciate
utter
verbalize

❷ express ADJECTIVE
very fast
EG *a special express delivery service*
direct EG *There's also a direct train.*
fast EG *delays due to an accident in the fast lane*
high-speed EG *the high-speed rail link between London and Paris*
nonstop EG *the new nonstop service to New York*

❶ expression NOUN
the look on your face that shows your feelings
EG *an aggrieved expression*
countenance EG *the beaming countenance of the prime minister*
face EG *Why are you all wearing such long faces?*

WORD POWER

▷ **Synonyms**
aspect
mien

a
b
c
d
e
f
g
h
i
j
k
l
m
n
o
p
q
r
s
t
u
v
w
x
y
z

A
B
C
D
E
F
G
H
I
J
K
L
M
N
O
P
Q
R
S
T
U
V
W
X
Y
Z

❷ expression NOUN
a word or phrase used to communicate
EG *a good old American expression*
idiom EG *talking in the idiom of the Home Counties*
phrase EG *What is the origin of the phrase?*
remark EG *her passing remark to the camera*
term EG *a derogatory term for an Arab*

❶ extend VERB
to have a particular size or position
EG *The region will extend way beyond the capital.*
continue EG *The caves continue for miles beneath the hills.*
hang EG *The branches hang down to the ground.*
reach EG *a long shirt that reached to her knees*
stretch EG *an area of forest stretching as far as the eye could see*

❷ extend VERB
to stick out
EG *a brass peg that extended from the end of the mast*
jut out EG *The tip of the island juts out like a finger into the sea.*
project EG *the ruins of a fort which projected from the mud*
protrude FORMAL EG *a huge rock protruding from the surface of the lake*
stick out EG *pieces of rough metal that stuck out like spikes*

❸ extend VERB
to make something larger
EG *We'd like to extend the house and build a conservatory.*
add to EG *They will be adding to their range of children's wear.*
develop EG *He developed the US arm of the company.*
enlarge EG *plans to enlarge the conference centre*
expand EG *an unsuccessful attempt*

to expand the store's range of footwear
widen EG *the need to widen the appeal of the scheme*

WORD POWER

▷ **Synonyms**
augment
broaden
supplement

❶ extensive ADJECTIVE
covering a large area
EG *a manor house set in extensive grounds*
broad EG *a broad expanse of green lawn*
expansive EG *an expansive grassy play area*
large EG *a large country estate*
spacious EG *a spacious dining area*
sweeping EG *the sweeping curve of the bay*
vast EG *vast stretches of land*
wide EG *Worktops should be wide enough to allow food preparation.*

❷ extensive ADJECTIVE
very great in effect
EG *The blast caused extensive damage.*
comprehensive EG *comprehensive television coverage of last week's events*
considerable EG *He has considerable powers within the party.*
far-reaching EG *a decision with far-reaching consequences*
great EG *great changes in British society*
pervasive EG *the pervasive influence of the army in national life*
untold EG *This might do untold damage to her health.*
widespread EG *There is widespread support for the proposals.*

extent NOUN
the length, area, or size of something
EG *The full extent of the losses was revealed yesterday.*

degree EG *To what degree were you in control of these events?*
level EG *the level of public concern over this issue*
measure EG *The full measure of the government's dilemma has become apparent.*
scale EG *He underestimates the scale of the problem.*
size EG *the size of the task*

WORD POWER

▷ **Synonyms**
magnitude

❶ extra ADJECTIVE
more than is usual or expected
EG *The company is taking on extra staff for the summer.*
added EG *The Tandoori Cottage has the added advantage of being cheap.*
additional EG *the need for additional funding*
excess EG *If there's any excess sauce, you can freeze it.*
further EG *the introduction of further restrictions*
more EG *We need three more places at the table.*
new EG *the burden of new legislation on top of all the recent changes*
spare EG *There are spare blankets in the cupboard.*

WORD POWER

▷ **Synonyms**
ancillary
auxiliary
supplementary

❷ extra NOUN
something that is not included with other things
EG *Air conditioning is an optional extra.*
accessory EG *the accessories you have to buy to make the place look good*
addition EG *the latest addition to the team*
bonus EG *The view from the hotel was an added bonus.*

❶ extract VERB
to take or get something out of somewhere
EG *Citric acid can be extracted from orange juice.*
draw EG *Villagers still have to draw their water from wells.*
mine EG *the finest gems, mined from all corners of the world*
obtain EG *Opium is obtained from poppies.*
pull out EG *I can pull that information out of the database for you.*
remove EG *Three bullets were removed from his wounds.*
take out EG *I got an abscess so he took the tooth out.*

❷ extract VERB
to get information from someone
EG *He tried to extract further information from the witness.*
draw EG *They finally drew a confession from him.*
elicit FORMAL EG *the question of how far police should go to elicit a confession*
get EG *How did you get an admission like that out of her?*
glean EG *We're gleaning information from all sources.*
obtain EG *Police have obtained statements from several witnesses.*

❸ extract NOUN
a small section of music or writing
EG *an extract from his latest novel*
excerpt EG *an excerpt from Tchaikovsky's Nutcracker*
passage EG *He read out a passage from Milton.*
reading EG *The author treated us to a reading from his latest novel.*
section EG *Let's study a section of the text in more detail.*
snatch EG *We played them a snatch*

a
b
c
d
e
f
g
h
i
j
k
l
m
n
o
p
q
r
s
t
u
v
w
x
y
z

A B C D E F G H I J K L M N O P Q R S T U V W X Y Z

of a violin concerto.

snippet EG *snippets of popular classical music*

extraordinary ADJECTIVE
unusual or surprising
EG *He really is an extraordinary man.*

amazing EG *What an amazing coincidence!*

bizarre EG *It's such a bizarre thing to happen.*

odd EG *It's an odd combination of colours.*

singular EG *Cathy gave me a smile of singular sweetness.*

strange EG *It's a strange piece of music.*

surprising EG *A surprising number of women prefer to wear trousers to work.*

unusual EG *It's a most unusual way to spend your holiday.*

WORD POWER
▶ **Antonym**
ordinary

❶ **extreme** ADJECTIVE
very great in degree or intensity
EG *those people living in extreme poverty*

acute EG *a mistake that caused acute embarrassment for everyone concerned*

deep EG *a decision that caused deep resentment*

dire EG *He is in dire need of hospital treatment.*

great EG *a change in the law that could cause many people great hardship*

intense EG *A number of people collapsed in the intense heat that day.*

profound EG *feelings of profound shock and anger*

severe EG *a business with severe financial problems*

❷ **extreme** ADJECTIVE
unusual or unreasonable
EG *I think that's rather an extreme reaction.*

drastic EG *Let's not do anything too drastic.*

exceptional EG *I think this is an exceptional case.*

excessive EG *a newspaper feature about the use of excessive force by the police*

extravagant EG *All that money being spent on hospitality seemed a bit extravagant.*

radical EG *The government is introducing a series of radical economic reforms.*

unreasonable EG *I don't think she's being the least bit unreasonable.*

❸ **extreme** NOUN
the highest or furthest degree or point
EG *We're just going from one extreme to the other.*

boundary EG *the boundaries of artistic freedom*

depth EG *the beauty of the countryside in the depths of winter*

end EG *There are extremist groups at both ends of the political spectrum.*

height EG *His behaviour was the height of bad manners.*

limit EG *The ordeal tested the limits of their endurance.*

ultimate EG *A Rolls-Royce is the ultimate in luxury.*

WORD POWER
▷ **Synonyms**
acme
apex
nadir
pinnacle
zenith

Ff

① face NOUN
the front part of the head
EG *A strong wind was blowing in my face.*
countenance EG *He met each enquiry with an impassive countenance.*
features EG *Her features were strongly defined.*
mug SLANG EG *He managed to get his ugly mug on the telly.*

WORD POWER

▷ **Synonyms**
lineaments
physiognomy

② face NOUN
a surface or side of something
EG *the north face of Everest*
aspect EG *The house had a south-west aspect.*
exterior EG *The exterior of the building was made of brick.*
front EG *There was a large veranda at the front of the house.*
side EG *narrow valleys with steep sides*
surface EG *tiny waves on the surface of the water*

③ face VERB
to look towards something or someone
EG *a room that faces on to the street*
be opposite EG *I was opposite her at the breakfast table.*
look at EG *She turned to look at the person who was speaking.*
overlook EG *The pretty room overlooks a beautiful garden.*

fact NOUN
a piece of information that is true
EG *a statement of verifiable fact*
certainty EG *A general election became a certainty three weeks ago.*
reality EG *Fiction and reality became increasingly blurred.*

truth EG *In the town, very few know the whole truth.*

WORD POWER

▶ **Antonym**
lie

factor NOUN
something that helps to cause a result
EG *Physical activity is an important factor in maintaining fitness.*
aspect EG *Exam results illustrate only one aspect of a school's success.*
cause EG *Smoking is the biggest preventable cause of death and disease.*
consideration EG *Money was also a consideration.*
element EG *Fitness has now become an important element in our lives.*
influence EG *Van Gogh was a major influence on the development of modern painting.*
part EG *Respect is a very important part of any relationship.*

WORD POWER

▷ **Synonyms**
circumstance
determinant

factory NOUN
a building where goods are made
EG *He owned furniture factories in several areas.*
mill EG *a textile mill*
plant EG *The plant produces most of the company's output.*
works EG *the steel works*

fade VERB
to make or become less intense
EG *The fabric had faded in the bright sunlight.*
die away EG *The sound died away gradually.*
dim EG *The house lights dimmed.*

a
b
c
d
e
f
g
h
i
j
k
l
m
n
o
p
q
r
s
t
u
v
w
x
y
z

A B C D E F G H I J K L M N O P Q R S T U V W X Y Z

discolour EG *Exposure to bright light can cause wallpaper to discolour.*
dull EG *Repeated washing had dulled the bright finish.*
wash out EG *This dye won't wash out.*

❶ fail VERB
to be unsuccessful
EG *He failed in his attempt to take over the company.*
be defeated EG *The vote to change the law was defeated.*
be in vain EG *It became clear that his efforts had been in vain.*
be unsuccessful EG *My job application was unsuccessful.*
come to grief EG *Many marriages have come to grief over lack of money.*
fall through EG *Negotiations with business leaders fell through last night.*
flunk INFORMAL EG *He flunked all his exams.*

WORD POWER

▶ **Antonym**
succeed

❷ fail VERB
to omit to do something
EG *They failed to phone her.*
neglect EG *They never neglect their duties.*
omit EG *He had omitted to tell her of the change in his plans.*

❸ fail VERB
to become less effective
EG *His eyesight began to fail.*
cease EG *The secrecy about his condition had ceased to matter.*
decline EG *His power declined as he grew older.*
give out EG *All machines give out eventually.*
sink EG *Her spirits sank lower and lower.*
stop working EG *The boat came to a halt when the engine stopped*

working.
wane EG *her mother's waning strength*

❶ failure NOUN
a lack of success
EG *to end in failure*
breakdown EG *a breakdown of the talks between the parties*
defeat EG *It is important not to admit defeat.*
downfall EG *people wishing to see the downfall of the government*
fiasco EG *The evening was a total fiasco.*
miscarriage EG *a miscarriage of justice*

WORD POWER

▶ **Antonym**
success

❷ failure NOUN
an unsuccessful person or thing
EG *The venture was a complete failure.*
disappointment EG *a disappointment to his family*
flop INFORMAL EG *The play turned out to be a flop.*
loser EG *He had always been a loser.*
no-hoper AUSTRALIAN AND NEW ZEALAND EG *hanging around a group of no-hopers*

WORD POWER

▷ **Synonyms**
incompetent
ne'er-do-well

❸ failure NOUN
a weakness in something
EG *a failure in the insurance system*
deficiency EG *a serious deficiency in their defence system*
shortcoming EG *The book has many shortcomings.*

❶ faint ADJECTIVE
lacking in intensity
EG *a faint smell of tobacco*

dim EG *dim lighting*
faded EG *a faded sign on the side of the building*
indistinct EG *The lettering was worn and indistinct.*
low EG *She spoke in a low voice.*
muted EG *some muted cheers from the gallery*
vague EG *a vague memory*

WORD POWER

▶ **Antonym**
strong

2 faint ADJECTIVE
feeling dizzy and unsteady
EG *Feeling faint is one of the symptoms.*
dizzy EG *suffering from dizzy spells*
giddy EG *He felt giddy after the ride.*
light-headed EG *She felt light-headed because she hadn't eaten.*

WORD POWER

▷ **Synonyms**
enervated
vertiginous

3 faint VERB
to lose consciousness temporarily
EG *to faint from shock*
black out EG *The blood drained from his head and he blacked out.*
collapse EG *I collapsed when I heard the news.*
pass out EG *to pass out with pain*
swoon LITERARY EG *Women in the '20s swooned over Valentino.*

1 fair ADJECTIVE
reasonable and just
EG *a fair trial*
equal EG *the commitment to equal opportunities*
equitable EG *an equitable allocation of resources*
impartial EG *an impartial observer*
legitimate EG *a legitimate claim to the money*
proper EG *It's right and proper that he*

should be here.
upright EG *an upright and trustworthy man*

WORD POWER

▷ **Synonyms**
disinterested
dispassionate
unbiased

▶ **Antonym**
unfair

2 fair ADJECTIVE
having light-coloured hair or pale skin
EG *long fair hair*
blonde *or* **blond** EG *a darker shade of blonde*
light EG *He had a light complexion and blue eyes.*

WORD POWER

▶ **Antonym**
dark

3 fair NOUN
an outdoor entertainment
EG *a country fair*
bazaar EG *a fundraising bazaar*
carnival EG *the annual Antigua Carnival*
exhibition EG *an international trade exhibition*
festival EG *a rock festival*
fete EG *The church fete was a popular attraction.*
show EG *an agricultural show*

1 faith NOUN
trust in a thing or a person
EG *to have great faith in something*
confidence EG *They had no confidence in the police.*
trust EG *His trust in them was misplaced.*

2 faith NOUN
a person's or community's religion
EG *They believed in the old faith.*
belief EG *united by belief*

a
b
c
d
e
f
g
h
i
j
k
l
m
n
o
p
q
r
s
t
u
v
w
x
y
z

creed EG *open to all, regardless of creed*
persuasion EG *people of all religious persuasions*
religion EG *the Christian religion*

❶ faithful ADJECTIVE

loyal to someone or something
EG *a faithful dog*
devoted EG *They are devoted to each other.*
loyal EG *a sign of true and loyal friendship*
staunch EG *a staunch member of the party*
true EG *a true believer*

WORD POWER

▷ **Synonyms**
steadfast
unwavering

▶ **Antonym**
unfaithful

❷ faithful ADJECTIVE

accurate and truthful
EG *The film was faithful to the novel.*
accurate EG *an accurate description of the event*
exact EG *an exact copy of the original*
strict EG *We demand strict adherence to the rules.*
true EG *The film was quite true to life.*

❶ fake NOUN

a deceitful imitation of a thing or person
EG *These paintings are fakes.*
copy EG *It wasn't real, just a copy.*
forgery EG *The signature was a forgery.*
fraud EG *Many psychics are frauds.*
imitation EG *The "antique" chair is in fact a clever imitation.*
reproduction EG *a reproduction of a famous painting*
sham EG *The election was denounced as a sham.*

❷ fake ADJECTIVE

imitation and not genuine
EG *fake fur*
artificial EG *It's made with artificial sweeteners.*
counterfeit EG *a large number of counterfeit documents*
false EG *a false passport*
imitation EG *bound in imitation leather*
phoney *or* **phony** INFORMAL EG *He used a phoney accent.*

WORD POWER

▷ **Synonyms**
assumed
pseudo-

▶ **Antonym**
real

❸ fake VERB

to pretend to experience something
EG *He faked his own death.*
feign EG *to feign illness*
pretend EG *Todd shrugged with pretended indifference.*
simulate EG *writhing around in simulated agony*

❶ fall VERB

to descend towards the ground
EG *The tile fell from the roof.*
collapse EG *The bridge collapsed on to the road.*
drop EG *bombs dropping from the sky*
plunge EG *A bus plunged into the river.*
topple EG *He toppled slowly backwards.*
trip EG *She tripped and broke her leg.*

WORD POWER

▶ **Antonym**
rise

❷ fall VERB

to become lower or less
EG *Output fell by more than half.*
decline EG *a declining birth rate*

fall >> fame

decrease EG *The number of bankruptcies decreased last year.*
diminish EG *Resources are diminishing steadily.*
dwindle EG *his dwindling authority*
plummet EG *plummeting share prices*
subside EG *The flood waters have subsided.*

WORD POWER

▷ **Synonyms**
abate
depreciate
ebb

▶ **Antonym**
increase

❸ fall NOUN
a reduction in amount
EG *a fall in the exchange rate*
decline EG *signs of economic decline*
decrease EG *an overall decrease of 10%*
drop EG *the sharp drop in export sales*
reduction EG *The bank announced a reduction in interest rates.*
slump EG *a slump in property prices*

WORD POWER

▶ **Antonym**
rise

❶ false ADJECTIVE
not true or correct
EG *He gave a false name and address.*
erroneous EG *to arrive at an erroneous conclusion*
fictitious EG *the source of the fictitious rumours*
incorrect EG *a decision based on incorrect information*
mistaken EG *I had a mistaken view of what had happened.*
untrue EG *The remarks were completely untrue.*

WORD POWER

▶ **Antonym**
true

❷ false ADJECTIVE
not genuine but intended to seem so
EG *false hair*
artificial EG *an artificial limb*
bogus EG *their bogus insurance claim*
fake EG *a fake tan*
forged EG *They crossed the frontier using forged documents.*
simulated EG *a simulated display of affection*

WORD POWER

▷ **Synonyms**
ersatz
pseudo-
spurious

▶ **Antonym**
genuine

❸ false ADJECTIVE
unfaithful and deceitful
EG *They turned out to be false friends.*
deceitful EG *deceitful and misleading remarks*
disloyal EG *He was accused of being disloyal to the company.*
insincere EG *A lot of actors are insincere.*
unfaithful EG *left alone by her unfaithful husband*

WORD POWER

▷ **Synonyms**
duplicitous
perfidious

fame NOUN
the state of being very well-known
EG *The film brought him international fame.*
eminence EG *to achieve eminence as a politician*
glory EG *my moment of glory*

a
b
c
d
e
f
g
h
i
j
k
l
m
n
o
p
q
r
s
t
u
v
w
x
y
z

A B C D E F G H I J K L M N O P Q R S T U V W X Y Z

prominence EG *He came to prominence with his bestselling novel.*
renown EG *a singer of great renown*
reputation EG *the city's reputation as a place of romance*

familiar ADJECTIVE
knowing something well
EG *Most children are familiar with stories.*
acquainted with EG *Peter was well acquainted with Wordsworth.*
aware of EG *aware of the dangers of smoking*
knowledgeable about EG *They were very knowledgeable about gardening.*
versed in EG *She was well versed in company law.*

WORD POWER

▶ **Antonym**
unfamiliar

❶ family NOUN
a group of relatives
EG *My family are always supportive of me.*
descendants EG *Their descendants lived there for centuries.*
relations EG *friends and relations*
relatives EG *She had relatives in many countries.*

WORD POWER

● **Related Words**
adjective : familial

❷ family NOUN
a group of related species
EG *Tigers are members of the cat family.*
class EG *several classes of butterflies*
classification EG *The classification includes conifers.*
kind EG *different kinds of roses*

famous ADJECTIVE
very well-known
EG *the most famous woman of her time*
celebrated EG *his most celebrated film*
distinguished EG *a distinguished academic family*
illustrious EG *the most illustrious scientists of the century*
legendary EG *His skills are legendary.*
noted EG *He is noted for his generosity.*
renowned EG *The area is renowned for its cuisine.*

WORD POWER

▷ **Synonyms**
lionized
signal

▶ **Antonym**
unknown

fan NOUN
an enthusiast about something or someone
EG *a fan of the new band*
adherent EG *The movement was gaining adherents everywhere.*
admirer EG *one of her many admirers*
devotee EG *a devotee of chamber music*
lover EG *an art lover*
supporter EG *rival football supporters*
zealot EG *a religious zealot*

WORD POWER

▷ **Synonyms**
aficionado
buff
enthusiast

fanatic NOUN
someone who is extremely enthusiastic about something
EG *a football fanatic*
activist EG *political activists*
devotee EG *a devotee of the movement*
extremist EG *groups of religious*

extremists
militant EG *The militants took over the organization.*
zealot EG *He was a supporter but not a zealot.*

fanatical ADJECTIVE
showing extreme support for something
EG *a fanatical patriot*
fervent EG *a fervent supporter*
obsessive EG *obsessive about motor racing*
passionate EG *a passionate interest*
rabid EG *a rabid racist group*
wild EG *I am wild about this band.*

WORD POWER

▷ **Synonyms**
immoderate
zealous

❶ fancy VERB
to want to have or do something
EG *He fancied a drink.*
be attracted to EG *I am attracted to the idea of emigrating.*
hanker after EG *to hanker after a bigger car*
have a yen for EG *She had a yen for some new clothes.*
would like EG *I would really like some ice cream.*

❷ fancy ADJECTIVE
special and elaborate
EG *dressed up in fancy clothes*
decorated EG *She preferred decorated surfaces to plain ones.*
elaborate EG *his elaborate costume ideas*
extravagant EG *the extravagant frescoes in the upper church*
intricate EG *covered with intricate patterns*
ornate EG *an ornate picture frame*

WORD POWER

▷ **Synonyms**
baroque

embellished
ornamented

▶ **Antonym**
plain

❶ far ADVERB
at a great distance from something
EG *The sea was far below us.*
afar EG *seen from afar*
a great distance EG *They travelled a great distance.*
a long way EG *The guy's lonely and a long way from home.*
deep EG *deep into the jungle*
miles EG *He lived miles away.*

❷ far ADVERB
to a great extent or degree
EG *far better than the others*
considerably EG *The dinners were considerably less formal than before.*
incomparably EG *South Africa seems incomparably richer than the rest of Africa.*
much EG *I feel much better now.*
very much EG *Things got very much worse.*

❸ far ADJECTIVE
very distant
EG *in the far south of the country*
distant EG *the distant horizon*
long EG *a long distance from here*
outlying EG *The outlying areas are accessible only by air.*
remote EG *a cottage in a remote village*

WORD POWER

▶ **Antonym**
near

fascinate VERB
to be of intense interest to someone
EG *He was fascinated by the new discovery.*
absorb EG *totally absorbed by her career*
bewitch EG *Bill was bewitched by her charm.*

A
B
C
D
E
F
G
H
I
J
K
L
M
N
O
P
Q
R
T
U
V
W
X
Y
Z

captivate EG *Her looks captivated the whole world.*
enthral EG *She sat enthralled by the actors.*
intrigue EG *Her story intrigued them.*

WORD POWER

▷ **Synonyms**
beguile
enchant
spellbind
transfix

❶ fashion NOUN
a popular style of dress or behaviour
EG *changing fashions in clothing*
craze EG *the latest health craze*
fad EG *just a passing fad*
style EG *a revival of an old style*
trend EG *the current trend in footwear*
vogue EG *a vogue for fitness training*

❷ fashion NOUN
a manner or way of doing something
EG *It works in a similar fashion.*
manner EG *in a friendly manner*
method EG *He did it by his usual method.*
mode EG *a different mode of life*
way EG *in her usual resourceful way*

❸ fashion VERB
to make and shape something
EG *fashioned from rough wood*
construct EG *an inner frame constructed from timber*
create EG *It was created from odds and ends.*
make EG *a doll made from fabric*
mould EG *They moulded the cups from clay.*
shape EG *Shape the dough into a loaf.*
work EG *a machine for working the stone*

fashionable ADJECTIVE
very popular
EG *a fashionable restaurant*
current EG *the current thinking on the subject*

in INFORMAL EG *Jogging was the in thing.*
latest EG *all the latest hairstyles*
popular EG *the most popular movie*
prevailing EG *contrary to prevailing attitudes*

WORD POWER

▷ **Synonyms**
chic
in vogue
trendsetting

▶ **Antonym**
old-fashioned

❶ fast ADJECTIVE
moving at great speed
EG *a fast train*
accelerated EG *at an accelerated pace*
hurried EG *He ate a hurried breakfast.*
quick EG *a quick learner*
rapid EG *a rapid rise through the company*
speedy EG *best wishes for a speedy recovery*
swift EG *as swift as an arrow*

WORD POWER

▷ **Synonyms**
fleet
mercurial
winged

▶ **Antonym**
slow

❷ fast ADVERB
quickly and without delay
EG *You'll have to move fast.*
hastily EG *sheltering in hastily erected tents*
hurriedly EG *students hurriedly taking notes*
quickly EG *She worked quickly and methodically.*
rapidly EG *moving rapidly across the field*

swiftly EG *They had to act swiftly to save him.*

WORD POWER

► **Antonym**
slowly

❸ **fast** ADVERB
firmly and strongly
EG *She held fast to the rail.*
firmly EG *with windows firmly shut*
securely EG *The door was securely locked and bolted.*
tightly EG *held tightly in his arms*

fasten VERB
to close or attach something
EG *Fasten your seat belts.*
attach EG *He attached a label to the plant.*
fix EG *It was fixed on the wall.*
join EG *joined together by string*
lock EG *a locked door*
secure EG *The chest was secured with a lock and chain.*
tie EG *Tie your shoelaces.*

fat ADJECTIVE
weighing too much
EG *a fat man*
→ see Word Study **fat**

WORD POWER

► **Antonym**
thin

❶ **fatal** ADJECTIVE
causing death
EG *fatal injuries*
deadly EG *a deadly disease*
incurable EG *It was regarded as an incurable illness.*
lethal EG *a lethal dose of sleeping pills*
mortal EG *They were in mortal danger.*
terminal EG *terminal cancer*

❷ **fatal** ADJECTIVE
having an undesirable effect
EG *The mistake was fatal to my plans.*
calamitous EG *a calamitous air crash*

catastrophic EG *The water shortage is potentially catastrophic.*
disastrous EG *This could have disastrous consequences for industry.*
lethal EG *a lethal left hook*

fate NOUN
a power believed to control events
EG *the fickleness of fate*
chance EG *a victim of chance*
destiny EG *We are masters of our own destiny.*
fortune EG *Remember, fortune favours the brave.*
providence EG *His death was an act of providence.*

WORD POWER

▷ **Synonyms**
kismet
nemesis
predestination

❶ **fault** NOUN
something for which someone is responsible
EG *It was all my fault.*
blame EG *They put the blame on her.*
liability EG *The company was forced to admit liability.*
responsibility EG *He accepted full responsibility for the error.*

❷ **fault** NOUN
a defective quality in something
EG *a minor technical fault*
blemish EG *a blemish on an otherwise outstanding career*
defect EG *a manufacturing defect*
deficiency EG *serious deficiencies in the system*
drawback EG *The plan had one major drawback.*
failing EG *the country's many failings*
flaw EG *serious character flaws*
imperfection EG *small imperfections on the surface*
weakness EG *his one weakness*

A
B
C
D
E
F
G
H
I
J
K
L
M
N
O
P
Q
R
T
U
V
W
X
Y
Z

WORD POWER

▶ **Antonym**
strength

❸ **fault** VERB
to find reasons to be critical of
someone
EG *Her conduct cannot be faulted.*
blame EG *I don't blame him.*
censure EG *He was censured by the
committee.*
criticize EG *The minister criticized the
police.*

faulty ADJECTIVE
containing flaws or errors
EG *Faulty goods should be sent back.*
defective EG *a lorry with defective
brakes*
flawed EG *The test results were
seriously flawed.*
imperfect EG *an imperfect specimen*
invalid EG *That's an invalid argument.*
unsound EG *a building that is
structurally unsound*

WORD POWER

▷ **Synonyms**
fallacious
imprecise
malfunctioning

❶ **favour** NOUN
a liking or approval of something
EG *The proposals met with favour.*
approval EG *to gain his father's
approval*
esteem EG *in high esteem*
grace EG *to fall from grace*
support EG *They gave us their full
support.*

WORD POWER

▶ **Antonym**
disapproval

❷ **favour** NOUN
a kind and helpful action
EG *Can you do me a favour?*

courtesy EG *the courtesy of a
personal response*
good turn EG *to do someone a good
turn*
kindness EG *She did me the kindness
of calling.*
service EG *a service to your country*

WORD POWER

▶ **Antonym**
wrong

❸ **favour** VERB
to prefer something or someone
EG *They favoured the eldest child.*
prefer EG *the preferred candidate*
single out EG *He is always being
singled out for special treatment.*

❶ **favourable** ADJECTIVE
of advantage and benefit to
someone
EG *favourable conditions*
advantageous EG *the most
advantageous course of action*
beneficial EG *a beneficial effect on
our health*
good EG *He got a very good deal.*
opportune EG *an opportune
moment to attack*
suitable EG *Conditions were not
suitable for life to flourish.*

WORD POWER

▷ **Synonyms**
auspicious
propitious
timely

▶ **Antonym**
unfavourable

❷ **favourable** ADJECTIVE
positive and expressing approval
EG *a positive response*
affirmative EG *to give an affirmative
answer*
amicable EG *amicable discussions*
approving EG *a warm, approving
glance*

friendly EG *The proposal was given a friendly reception.*
positive EG *a positive effect on the situation*
sympathetic EG *He got a sympathetic hearing.*
welcoming EG *a welcoming atmosphere*

WORD POWER

▶ **Antonym**
unfavourable

❶ **favourite** ADJECTIVE
being someone's best-liked person or thing
EG *my favourite hotel*
best-loved EG *our best-loved music*
dearest EG *Her dearest wish was fulfilled.*
favoured EG *the favoured child of elderly parents*
preferred EG *his preferred method of exercise*

❷ **favourite** NOUN
the thing or person someone likes best
EG *The youngest was always her favourite.*
darling EG *the spoilt darling of the family*
idol EG *the idol of his fans*
pet EG *the teacher's pet*
pick EG *the pick of the bunch*

favouritism NOUN
unfair favour shown to a person or group
EG *There was never a hint of favouritism.*
bias EG *political bias in broadcasting*
one-sidedness EG *The committee must show no one-sidedness.*

WORD POWER

▷ **Synonyms**
nepotism
partiality
partisanship

▶ **Antonym**
impartiality

❶ **fear** NOUN
an unpleasant feeling of danger
EG *shivering with fear*
alarm EG *I looked at him with growing alarm.*
awe EG *in awe of his great powers*
dread EG *She thought with dread of the coming storm.*
fright EG *He jumped with fright at the noise.*
panic EG *a moment of panic*
terror EG *to shake with terror*

WORD POWER

▷ **Synonyms**
apprehensiveness
cravenness
trepidation

❷ **fear** VERB
to feel frightened of something
EG *There is nothing to fear.*
be afraid EG *The dog was afraid of him.*
be frightened EG *I am frightened of thunder.*
be scared EG *Are you scared of snakes?*
dread EG *He dreaded angry scenes.*
take fright EG *The horse took fright at the sudden noise.*

❶ **feature** NOUN
a particular characteristic of something
EG *an unusual feature of the room*
aspect EG *every aspect of our lives*
attribute EG *a normal attribute of human behaviour*
characteristic EG *their physical characteristics*
mark EG *distinguishing marks*
property EG *the magnetic properties of iron*
quality EG *skills and personal qualities*

a
b
c
d
e
f
g
h
i
j
k
l
m
n
o
p
q
r
s
t
u
v
w
x
y
z

② feature NOUN
a special article or programme
EG *a news feature*
article EG *a travel article*
column EG *the advice column*
item EG *an item about chemical waste*
piece EG *a specially-written piece*
report EG *a film report on the scandal*
story EG *front-page news stories*

③ feature VERB
to include and draw attention to something
EG *featuring an interview with the president*
emphasize EG *to emphasize their differences*
give prominence to EG *The Times is alone in giving prominence to the visit.*
spotlight EG *a book spotlighting female singers*
star EG *starring a major Australian actor*

① feel VERB
to experience emotionally
EG *I felt enormous happiness.*
experience EG *They seem to experience more distress than the others.*
suffer EG *suffering from pangs of conscience*
undergo EG *to undergo a change of heart*

② feel VERB
to believe that something is the case
EG *She feels she is in control of her life.*
believe EG *I believe they are right.*
consider EG *We consider them to be our friends.*
deem EG *I deemed it best to cancel the party.*
judge EG *She was judged to be capable of anything.*
think EG *I think I am very lucky.*

③ feel VERB
to touch something physically
EG *Feel this lovely material!*

finger EG *He was fingering the coins in his pocket.*
fondle EG *She fondled the dog's ears.*
stroke EG *I stroked the smooth wooden surface.*
touch EG *He touched my face.*

① feeling NOUN
the experiencing of an emotion
EG *feelings of envy*
emotion EG *trembling with emotion*
fervour EG *religious fervour*
heat EG *He spoke with some heat about his experiences.*
passion EG *She argued with great passion.*
sentiment EG *I'm afraid I don't share your sentiments.*

② feeling NOUN
a physical sensation
EG *a feeling of pain*
sensation EG *a very pleasant sensation*
sense EG *a slight sense of heat at the back of my throat*

③ feeling NOUN
an opinion on something
EG *strong feelings on politics*
inclination EG *neither the time nor the inclination*
opinion EG *a consensus of opinion*
point of view EG *an unusual point of view on the subject*
view EG *Make your views known.*

① fellowship NOUN
a feeling of friendliness within a group
EG *a sense of community and fellowship*
brotherhood EG *a symbolic act of brotherhood*
camaraderie EG *the camaraderie among soldiers*
companionship EG *the companionship between old friends*

② fellowship NOUN
a group of people with a common interest

EG *a fellowship of writers*
association EG *a trade association*
brotherhood EG *a secret international brotherhood*
club EG *a youth club*
league EG *the League of Nations*
society EG *the historical society*

① female NOUN
a person or animal which can have babies
EG *Hay fever affects males more than females.*
girl EG *a girls' school*
lady EG *a nice young lady*
sheila AUSTRALIAN AND NEW ZEALAND; INFORMAL EG *his role as a sheila in his own play*
woman EG *the number of women in the police force*

WORD POWER
▶ **Antonym**
male

② female ADJECTIVE
relating to females
EG *the world's greatest female distance runner*
feminine EG *the traditional feminine role*
girlish EG *She gave a girlish giggle.*
womanly EG *a womanly shape*

WORD POWER
▶ **Antonym**
male

fertile ADJECTIVE
capable of producing plants or offspring
EG *fertile soil*
fruitful EG *The fruitful earth gave forth its treasures.*
productive EG *the most productive vineyards.*
prolific EG *Chinchillas are prolific breeders.*

rich EG *This plant grows in moist rich ground.*

WORD POWER
▷ **Synonyms**
fecund
generative

▶ **Antonym**
barren

fervent ADJECTIVE
showing sincere and enthusiastic feeling
EG *a fervent admirer of her work*
ardent EG *one of the most ardent supporters of the policy*
committed EG *a committed socialist*
devout EG *She was a devout Christian.*
enthusiastic EG *a huge and enthusiastic crowd*
impassioned EG *an impassioned appeal for peace*
passionate EG *I'm a passionate believer in public art.*
zealous EG *He was a recent convert, and very zealous.*

① festival NOUN
an organized series of events
EG *an arts festival*
carnival EG *The carnival lasted for three days.*
entertainment EG *theatrical entertainments*
fair EG *The book fair attracted many visitors.*
fete EG *a church fete*
gala EG *the May Day gala*

② festival NOUN
a day or period of religious celebration
EG *open except on days of religious festivals*
anniversary EG *The anniversary is celebrated each spring.*
holiday EG *the Easter holiday*

a
b
c
d
e
f
g
h
i
j
k
l
m
n
o
p
q
r
s
t
u
v
w
x
y
z

Christian festivals
Advent
Ascension Day
Ash Wednesday
Candlemas
Christmas
Corpus Christi
Easter
Epiphany
Good Friday
Lent
Maundy Thursday
Michaelmas
Palm Sunday
Pentecost
Quadragesima
Shrove Tuesday
Trinity
Whitsun

Jewish festivals
Feast of Tabernacles
Hanukkah, Hanukah or Chanukah
Passover or Pesach
Purim
Rosh Hashanah
Shavuot, Shabuoth or Pentecost
Sukkoth or Succoth
Yom Kippur or Day of Atonement

Hindu festivals
Diwali
Durga-puja
Dussehra
Ganesh Chaturthi
Holi
Janmashtami
Navaratri
Raksha Bandhan
Ramanavami
Sarasvati-puja

Muslim festivals
Al Hijrah
Ashura
Eid-ul-Adha or Id-ul-Adha
Eid-ul-Fitr or Id-ul-Fitr
Lailat-ul-Isra' wa'l Mi'raj
Lailat-ul-Qadr
Mawlid al-Nabi
Ramadan

Sikh festivals
Baisakhi Mela
Diwali Mela
Hola Mohalla Mela
the Gurpurabs

Buddhist festivals
Wesak

few ADJECTIVE
small in number
EG *a few moments ago*
infrequent EG *at infrequent intervals*
meagre EG *a society with meagre resources*
not many EG *Not many people attended the meeting.*
scanty EG *scanty memories of his childhood*
scarce EG *Resources are scarce.*
sparse EG *a bare landscape with sparse trees*

WORD POWER

▶ **Antonym**
many

fidget VERB
to move and change position restlessly
EG *fidgeting in his seat*
fiddle INFORMAL EG *She fiddled with her pencil.*
jiggle EG *He's jiggling his keys.*
squirm EG *He squirmed and wriggled with impatience.*
twitch EG *Everybody twitched in their seats.*

❶ **field** NOUN
an area of farm land
EG *a field full of sheep*
green EG *on the village green*
meadow EG *a grassy meadow*
pasture EG *cows grazing in the pasture*

❷ **field** NOUN
a particular subject or interest
EG *a breakthrough in the field of physics*

area EG *a politically-sensitive area*
department EG *Health care isn't my department.*
domain EG *in the domain of art*
province EG *This is the province of a different section.*
speciality EG *His speciality was mythology.*
territory EG *an expert in his own territory of history*

WORD POWER

▷ **Synonyms**
bailiwick
discipline
metier

❶ **fierce** ADJECTIVE
wild and aggressive
EG *a fierce lion*
aggressive EG *encouraging aggressive behaviour in later life*
dangerous EG *These birds are dangerous.*
ferocious EG *two and a half days of ferocious violence*
murderous EG *a murderous attack*

WORD POWER

▷ **Synonyms**
barbarous
fell
feral

▶ **Antonym**
gentle

❷ **fierce** ADJECTIVE
very intense
EG *a fierce contest*
intense EG *We found ourselves standing in intense heat.*
keen EG *a keen interest in cars*
relentless EG *The pressure was relentless.*
strong EG *a strong dislike*

❶ **fight** VERB
to take part in a battle or contest
EG *He fought the world champion.*

battle EG *The gang battled with the police.*
brawl EG *men brawling drunkenly in the street*
grapple EG *grappling with an alligator*
struggle EG *He was struggling with police outside the club.*

❷ **fight** NOUN
an aggressive struggle
EG *a fight to the death*
action EG *wounded in action*
battle EG *a gun battle*
bout EG *a wrestling bout*
combat EG *the end of a long combat*
duel EG *He was killed in a duel.*
skirmish EG *a minor border skirmish*

❸ **fight** NOUN
an angry disagreement
EG *a fight with my mother*
argument EG *an argument over a boyfriend*
blue AUSTRALIAN; SLANG EG *a bloke I'd had a blue with years ago*
dispute EG *a dispute over ticket allocation*
row EG *Maxine and I had a terrible row.*
squabble EG *a family squabble over Sunday lunch*

fighter NOUN
someone who physically fights another person
EG *a tough street fighter*
soldier EG *well-equipped soldiers*
warrior EG *a brave warrior*

❶ **figure** NOUN
a number, or amount represented by a number
EG *No one really knows the true figures.*
amount EG *Postal money orders are available in amounts up to $700.*
digit EG *a code made up of letters and digits*
number EG *A lot of marriages end in divorce, but we don't know the exact*

number.
numeral EG *the numeral six*
statistic EG *Official statistics show wages declining by 24%.*
total EG *Then he added everything together to arrive at the final total.*

❷ figure NOUN
a shape, or the shape of someone's body
EG *A figure appeared in the doorway.*
body EG *She's got nice hair and a great body.*
build EG *a tall woman with a naturally slim build*
form EG *The shadowy form receded into the darkness.*
physique EG *He has the physique and energy of a man half his age.*
silhouette EG *Tuck the shirt in to give yourself a streamlined silhouette.*
shape EG *tall, dark shapes moving in the mist*

❸ figure NOUN
a person
EG *international political figures*
character EG *What a sad character that Nigel is.*
dignitary EG *a visiting dignitary of great importance*
person EG *My grandfather was a person of some influence.*
personality EG *The event was attended by many showbiz personalities.*
player EG *a key player in the negotiations*

❹ figure VERB; INFORMAL
to guess or conclude something
EG *I figure I'll learn from experience*
expect EG *I expect you're just tired.*
guess EG *I guess he's right.*
reckon INFORMAL EG *Toni reckoned that it must be about three o'clock.*
suppose EG *What do you suppose he's up to?*

fill VERB
to make something full

EG *Fill it up with water.*
cram EG *Mourners crammed the small church.*
gorge EG *gorged with food*
pack EG *a lorry packed with explosives*
stock EG *a lake stocked with carp*
stuff EG *Stuff the pillow with feathers.*

WORD POWER

▶ **Antonym**
empty

❶ final ADJECTIVE
being the last one in a series
EG *the fifth and final day*
closing EG *in the closing stages of the race*
concluding EG *the concluding part of the serial*
eventual EG *the eventual aim of their policies*
last EG *his last chance*
ultimate EG *The ultimate outcome will be different.*

WORD POWER

▶ **Antonym**
first

❷ final ADJECTIVE
unable to be changed or questioned
EG *The judges' decision is final.*
absolute EG *absolute authority*
conclusive EG *conclusive proof*
definite EG *too soon to give a definite answer*
definitive EG *the definitive account of the war*

❶ finally ADVERB
happening after a long time
EG *It finally arrived.*
at last EG *He came at last.*
at the last moment EG *They changed their minds at the last moment.*
eventually EG *The flight eventually left.*
in the end EG *It all turned out right in*

the end.
in the long run EG *a success in the long run*

❷ **finally** ADVERB
in conclusion of something
EG *Finally, I'd like to talk about safety measures.*
in conclusion EG *In conclusion, we have to agree.*
in summary EG *It was, in summary, a satisfactory outcome.*
lastly EG *Lastly, I would like to thank my agent.*

❶ **finance** VERB
to provide the money for something
EG *financed by the government*
back EG *a fund backed by local businesses*
fund EG *The scheme is funded by the banks.*
pay for EG *He paid for his trip out of his savings.*
support EG *She supported herself through university.*

❷ **finance** NOUN
the managing of money and investments
EG *the world of high finance*
banking EG *the international banking system*
budgeting EG *We must exercise caution in our budgeting this year.*
commerce EG *industry and commerce*
economics EG *the economics of the third world*
investment EG *tax incentives to encourage investment*

financial ADJECTIVE
relating to money
EG *financial difficulties*
economic EG *an economic crisis*
fiscal EG *the long-term fiscal policy of this country*
money EG *on the money markets*

WORD POWER
▷ **Synonyms**
budgetary
monetary
pecuniary

❶ **find** VERB
to discover something
EG *I can't find my notes.*
come across EG *He came across the book by chance.*
discover EG *They discovered the body in the bushes.*
locate EG *locating the position of the gene*
track down EG *to track down her parents*
turn up EG *They failed to turn up any evidence.*
unearth EG *to unearth the missing copy*

WORD POWER
▷ **Synonyms**
descry
espy
ferret out

▶ **Antonym**
lose

❷ **find** VERB
to realize or learn something
EG *We found that we got on well.*
become aware EG *I became aware of his work last year.*
detect EG *I detected a note of envy in her voice.*
discover EG *It was discovered that the goods were missing.*
learn EG *I flew from New York on learning of his death.*
realize EG *They realized too late that it was wrong.*

❶ **fine** ADJECTIVE
very good and admirable
EG *fine clothes*
admirable EG *with many admirable*

a b c d e f g h i j k l m n o p q r s t u v w x y z

qualities
beautiful EG *a beautiful view of the river*
excellent EG *inns with excellent cuisine*
magnificent EG *his magnificent country house*
outstanding EG *an area of outstanding natural beauty*
splendid EG *a splendid collection of cartoons*

2 fine ADJECTIVE
small in size or thickness
EG *powder with very fine particles*
delicate EG *delicate curtains to let in the light*
lightweight EG *certain lightweight fabrics*
powdery EG *soft powdery dust*
sheer EG *a sheer chiffon shirt*
small EG *netting with a small mesh*

WORD POWER
▷ Synonyms
diaphanous
gauzy
gossamer

3 fine ADJECTIVE
subtle and precise
EG *the fine details*
fastidious EG *fastidious attention to detail*
keen EG *a keen eye for a bargain*
precise EG *a gauge with precise adjustment*
refined EG *a woman of refined tastes*
sensitive EG *The radio had very sensitive tuning.*
subtle EG *a very subtle distinction*

1 finish VERB
to complete something
EG *to finish a report*
close EG *They have closed the deal.*
complete EG *She completed her first novel.*
conclude EG *He concluded his speech.*

end EG *That ended our discussion.*
finalize EG *to finalize an agreement*

WORD POWER
▶ Antonym
start

2 finish NOUN
the last part of something
EG *to see it through to the finish*
close EG *to bring to a close*
completion EG *The project is nearing completion.*
conclusion EG *at the conclusion of the programme*
end EG *the end of the race*
ending EG *The film had an unexpected ending.*
finale EG *the grand finale of the evening*

WORD POWER
▷ Synonyms
culmination
denouement
termination

▶ Antonym
start

3 finish NOUN
the surface appearance of something
EG *a glossy finish*
grain EG *the smooth grain of the wood*
lustre EG *a similar lustre to silk*
polish EG *The bodywork had a high polish.*
shine EG *It gives a beautiful shine to the hair.*
surface EG *a polished surface*
texture EG *paper with a linen-like texture*

1 fire NOUN
the flames produced when something burns
EG *a ball of fire*
blaze EG *The firemen were hurt in the*

blaze.
combustion EG *Energy is released by combustion.*
flames EG *rescued from the flames*
inferno EG *The building was an inferno.*

2 fire VERB
to shoot or detonate something
EG *to fire a cannon*
detonate EG *to detonate an explosive device*
explode EG *They exploded a bomb.*
launch EG *The protesters launched the missile from a boat.*
set off EG *the largest nuclear explosion ever set off on Earth*
shoot EG *people shooting guns in all directions*

3 fire VERB; INFORMAL
to dismiss someone from a job
EG *She was fired yesterday.*
discharge EG *A trooper has been discharged from the army.*
dismiss EG *He was dismissed by the bank.*
make redundant EG *Many people were made redundant.*
sack INFORMAL EG *Jones was sacked for disciplinary reasons.*

1 firm ADJECTIVE
solid and not soft
EG *Leave the ice cream until it is firm.*
compressed EG *compressed wood pulp made into cardboard*
congealed EG *a bowl of congealed grease*
hard EG *The snow was hard and slippery.*
rigid EG *Pour the mixture into a rigid plastic container.*
set EG *The glue wasn't completely set.*
solid EG *a block of solid wax*
stiff EG *egg whites beaten until stiff*

WORD POWER
▷ **Antonym**
soft

2 firm ADJECTIVE
resolute and determined
EG *The department needs a firm manager.*
adamant EG *He was adamant that he would not resign.*
determined EG *She was determined to finish the game.*
inflexible EG *his inflexible routine*
resolute EG *a willingness to take resolute action*
staunch EG *many staunch supporters*
unshakable EG *an unshakable belief in democracy*

WORD POWER
▷ **Synonyms**
obdurate
steadfast
unwavering

3 firm NOUN
a commercial organization
EG *a firm of builders*
business EG *a stockbroking business*
company EG *his software development company*
corporation EG *one of the leading banking corporations*
enterprise EG *small business enterprises*
organization EG *a multinational organization*

1 first ADJECTIVE
done or in existence before anything else
EG *the first moon landing*
earliest EG *The earliest settlers lived there.*
initial EG *our initial meeting*
opening EG *There was a standing ovation on opening night.*
original EG *She was one of the original cast.*
primeval EG *the primeval forests of Europe*

WORD POWER

▶ **Antonym**
last

2 first ADVERB
done or occurring before anything
else
EG *You must do that first.*
beforehand EG *Bill had prepared
beforehand.*
earlier EG *I did that one earlier.*
firstly EG *Firstly, I'd like to thank you
all for coming.*
initially EG *not as bad as they initially
predicted*
to begin with EG *To begin with, we
must prepare the soil.*

3 first ADJECTIVE
more important than anything else
EG *our first responsibility*
chief EG *the chief pilot*
foremost EG *one of our foremost
thinkers*
leading EG *the team's leading scorer*
prime EG *He was the prime suspect.*
principal EG *the principal reason*

first-rate ADJECTIVE
excellent
EG *They were dealing with a first-rate
professional.*
excellent EG *She does an excellent
job as Fred's personal assistant.*
exceptional EG *His piano playing is
exceptional.*
first-class EG *The food was first-
class.*
marvellous EG *He certainly is a
marvellous actor.*
outstanding EG *an outstanding
athlete*
splendid EG *We had a splendid meal.*
superb EG *a superb 18-hole golf
course*

WORD POWER

▷ **Synonyms**
superlative (FORMAL)

fissure NOUN
a deep crack in rock or the ground
EG *There was a rumbling, and a fissure
opened up.*
cleft EG *a narrow cleft in the rocks*
crack EG *The building developed
large cracks in walls and ceilings.*
crevice EG *a huge boulder with ferns
growing in every crevice*
fault EG *the San Andreas Fault*
rift EG *In the open bog are many rifts
and potholes.*
split EG *The slate has a few small
splits around the edges.*

1 fit VERB
to be the right shape or size
EG *made to fit a child*
belong EG *I just didn't belong there.*
correspond EG *The two angles didn't
correspond exactly.*
dovetail EG *The movement's interests
dovetailed with her own.*
go EG *small enough to go in your
pocket*
match EG *Match the pegs with the
holes.*

2 fit VERB
to place something in position
EG *a fitted carpet*
adapt EG *shelves adapted to suit the
smaller books*
arrange EG *Arrange the pieces to
form a picture.*
place EG *Place the card in the slots.*
position EG *plants which are carefully
positioned in the alcove*

3 fit ADJECTIVE
in good physical condition
EG *a reasonably fit person*
healthy EG *a healthy mind in a
healthy body*
in good condition EG *in good
condition for his age*
robust EG *a strong, robust man*
trim EG *a trim figure*
well EG *Alison was looking well.*

WORD POWER

▶ Antonym
unfit

❶ fitting ADJECTIVE
appropriate and suitable for something
EG *a fitting end*
appropriate EG *an appropriate outfit for the occasion*
correct EG *the correct thing to say*
proper EG *It isn't proper that she should be here.*
right EG *He always said just the right thing.*
suitable EG *some hymns suitable for a wedding*

WORD POWER

▷ Synonyms
apposite
decorous
seemly

❷ fitting NOUN
a part attached to something else
EG *fixtures and fittings*
accessory EG *bathroom accessories*
attachment EG *a wide range of attachments*
component EG *special components*
part EG *Extra parts can be added later.*
unit EG *The unit plugs into any TV set.*

❶ fix VERB
to attach or secure something
EG *fixed to the wall*
attach EG *The label was attached with glue.*
bind EG *sticks bound together with string*
fasten EG *Fasten the two parts securely.*
secure EG *firmly secured by strong nails*
stick EG *She stuck the pictures into the book.*

❷ fix VERB
to repair something broken
EG *The bike is fixed now.*
correct EG *to correct our mistakes*
mend EG *They finally got round to mending the roof.*
patch up EG *Patch up those holes.*
repair EG *I had my shoes repaired.*

❸ fix NOUN; INFORMAL
a difficult situation
EG *in a bit of a fix*
difficulty EG *He was in real difficulties with money.*
mess EG *Their economy was in a mess.*
predicament EG *a tricky predicament*
quandary EG *in a quandary about what to do*

flabby ADJECTIVE
fat and with loose flesh
EG *a flabby stomach*
floppy EG *the floppy bodies in tracksuits*
sagging EG *a sagging double chin*
slack EG *The skin around her eyelids is now slack and baggy.*

WORD POWER

▷ Synonyms
flaccid
pendulous

▶ Antonym
taut

❶ flash NOUN
a sudden short burst of light
EG *a flash of lightning*
burst EG *a burst of fire*
flare EG *the sudden flare of a match*
sparkle EG *sparkles from her sequinned dress*

❷ flash VERB
to shine briefly and often repeatedly
EG *They signalled by flashing a light.*
flare EG *matches flaring in the darkness*

a b c d e f g h i j k l m n o p q r s t u v w x y z

A B C D E F G H I J K L M N O P Q R S T U V W X Y Z

glint EG *the low sun glinting off the windscreens*
glitter EG *the glittering crown on his head*
sparkle EG *Diamonds sparkled on her wrists.*
twinkle EG *stars twinkling in the night sky*

flashy ADJECTIVE
showy in a vulgar way
EG *flashy clothes*
flamboyant EG *an unsuitably flamboyant outfit*
garish EG *curtains in garish colours*
showy EG *an expensive and showy watch*
tacky INFORMAL EG *tacky red sunglasses*
tasteless EG *a house with tasteless decor*

WORD POWER
▷ **Synonyms**
meretricious
ostentatious

▶ **Antonym**
modest

① flat NOUN
a set of rooms for living in
EG *a two-bedroomed flat*
apartment EG *a huge apartment overlooking the park*
rooms EG *We shared rooms while we were students.*

② flat ADJECTIVE
level and smooth
EG *a flat surface*
horizontal EG *horizontal with the ground*
level EG *a completely level base*
levelled EG *The floor must be levelled before you start.*
smooth EG *a smooth marble top*
unbroken EG *the unbroken surface of the sea*

WORD POWER
▶ **Antonym**
uneven

③ flat ADJECTIVE
without emotion or interest
EG *a dreadfully flat speech*
boring EG *a boring menu*
dull EG *He told some really dull stories.*
insipid EG *an insipid performance*
monotonous EG *an interesting story expressed in a monotonous voice*
weak EG *A weak ending spoiled the story.*

① flatter VERB
to praise someone insincerely
EG *flattering remarks*
compliment EG *She was often complimented for her looks.*
fawn EG *surrounded by fawning attendants*

② flatter VERB
to make more attractive
EG *clothes that flatter your figure*
enhance EG *an enhancing neckline*
set off EG *Blue sets off the colour of your eyes.*
suit EG *That shade really suits your skin tone.*

flattery NOUN
flattering words and behaviour
EG *susceptible to flattery*
adulation EG *received with adulation by the critics*
fawning EG *the constant fawning of her courtiers*

WORD POWER
▷ **Synonyms**
blandishment
obsequiousness
sycophancy

flaw NOUN
an imperfection in something
EG *The program contained serious flaws.*

blemish EG *A small blemish spoiled the surface.*
defect EG *a manufacturing defect*
fault EG *a fault in the engine*
imperfection EG *slight imperfections in the weave*

flee VERB
to run away from something
EG *to flee the country*
bolt EG *He bolted for the exit.*
escape EG *They escaped across the frontier.*
fly EG *to fly from war*
leave EG *to leave the scene of the crime*
run away EG *to run away from the police*
take flight EG *250,000 took flight from the floods.*

❶ flexible ADJECTIVE
able to bend or be bent easily
EG *long flexible bristles*
elastic EG *an elastic rope*
lithe EG *lithe and graceful movements*
pliable EG *baskets made from pliable cane*
supple EG *exercises to keep you supple*

WORD POWER
▷ **Synonyms**
ductile
lissom *or* lissome
pliant

❷ flexible ADJECTIVE
able to adapt or change
EG *flexible working hours*
adaptable EG *an adaptable attitude to work*
discretionary EG *the discretionary powers of the courts*
open EG *an open mind*

flinch VERB
to move suddenly with fear or pain
EG *The sharp pain made her flinch.*
cringe EG *to cringe in terror*

shrink EG *She shrank from the flames.*
start EG *They started at the sudden noise.*
wince EG *I could see him wincing with pain.*

❶ float VERB
to be supported by water
EG *leaves floating on the river*
be on the surface EG *The oil is on the surface of the sea.*
bob EG *toys bobbing in the bath*
drift EG *to drift in on the tide*
lie on the surface EG *The boat lay on the surface of the lake.*
stay afloat EG *They could stay afloat without swimming.*

WORD POWER
▶ **Antonym**
sink

❷ float VERB
to be carried on the air
EG *floating on the breeze*
drift EG *The music drifted in through the window.*
glide EG *eagles gliding above us*
hang EG *A haze of perfume hung in the room.*
hover EG *Butterflies hovered above the flowers.*

❶ flood NOUN
a large amount of water coming suddenly
EG *Many people were drowned in the floods.*
deluge EG *houses overwhelmed by the deluge*
downpour EG *a downpour of torrential rain*
spate EG *The river was in spate.*
torrent EG *Torrents of water gushed into the reservoir.*

❷ flood NOUN
a sudden large amount of something
EG *a flood of angry letters*
rush EG *a sudden rush of panic*

stream EG *a stream of bad language*
torrent EG *He replied with a torrent of abuse.*

❸ flood VERB
to overflow with water
EG *The river flooded its banks.*
deluge EG *Heavy rain deluged the capital.*
drown EG *a drowned village*
overflow EG *an overflowing bath*
submerge EG *to prevent water submerging the cobbled streets*
swamp EG *His small boat was swamped by the waves.*

❶ flourish VERB
to develop or function successfully or healthily
EG *Business was flourishing.*
bloom EG *Not many economies bloomed during that period.*
boom EG *Sales are booming.*
come on EG *He is coming on very well at his new school.*
do well EG *Out-of-town superstores are doing well.*
prosper EG *The high street banks continue to prosper.*
succeed EG *the qualities needed to succeed in small businesses*
thrive EG *Today the company continues to thrive.*

> *WORD POWER*
>
> ▶ **Antonym**
> fail

❷ flourish VERB
to wave or display something
EG *He flourished his glass.*
brandish LITERARY EG *He appeared brandishing a sword.*
display EG *She proudly displayed the letter and began to read.*
hold aloft EG *He held the cup aloft.*
wave EG *Crowds were waving flags and applauding.*

❸ flourish NOUN
a bold sweeping or waving movement
EG *with a flourish of his hand*
flick EG *a flick of the whip*
sweep EG *With one sweep of her hand she threw back the sheets.*
wave EG *Steve stopped him with a wave of the hand.*

❶ flow VERB
to move or happen in a continuous stream
EG *a river flowing gently down into the valley*
circulate EG *to circulate round the entire house*
glide EG *models gliding down the catwalk*
roll EG *rolling gently to the sea*
run EG *A stream ran beside the road.*
slide EG *Tears slid down her cheeks.*

❷ flow NOUN
a continuous movement of something
EG *traffic flow*
current EG *currents of air*
drift EG *the drift towards the cities*
flood EG *a flood of complaints*
stream EG *a constant stream of visitors*
tide EG *to slow the tide of change*

fluent ADJECTIVE
expressing yourself easily and without hesitation
EG *a fluent speaker of French*
articulate EG *an articulate young woman*
easy EG *the easy flow of his argument*
effortless EG *He spoke with effortless ease.*
flowing EG *a smooth, flowing presentation*
ready EG *a ready answer*

> *WORD POWER*
>
> ▶ **Antonym**
> hesitant

❶ fly VERB
to move through the air

EG *to fly to Paris*
flit EG *butterflies flitting among the flowers*
flutter EG *The birds fluttered on to the feeder.*
sail EG *a kite sailing above the trees*
soar EG *eagles soaring in the sky*

2 fly VERB
to move very quickly
EG *She flew down the stairs.*
dart EG *She darted to the window.*
dash EG *We had to dash.*
hurry EG *They hurried to catch the train.*
race EG *I had to race round the shops.*
rush EG *rushing off to work*
speed EG *The car sped off.*
tear EG *He tore off down the road.*

1 foam NOUN
a mass of tiny bubbles
EG *waves tipped with foam*
bubbles EG *She liked to have bubbles in the bath.*
froth EG *Yeast swells up to form a froth.*
head EG *the foamy head on beer*
lather EG *It took a lot of shampoo to get a good lather.*

2 foam VERB
to swell and form bubbles
EG *a foaming river*
bubble EG *The boiling liquid bubbled up.*
fizz EG *a drink fizzing in the glass*
froth EG *It frothed up over the top.*

1 focus VERB
to concentrate your vision on something
EG *His eyes began to focus.*
aim EG *Astronomers aimed optical telescopes in their direction.*
concentrate EG *concentrating his gaze on a line of ants*
direct EG *He directed the light on to the roof.*
fix EG *Their radar was fixed on the enemy ship.*

2 focus NOUN
the centre of attention
EG *the focus of the conversation*
centre EG *She was the centre of an admiring crowd.*
focal point EG *the focal point of the whole room*
hub EG *the hub of the financial world*
target EG *a target group*

1 foil VERB
to prevent something from happening
EG *The police foiled an armed robbery.*
check EG *to check the rise in crime*
counter EG *countering the threat of strike action*
defeat EG *an important role in defeating the rebellion*
frustrate EG *a frustrated attempt*
thwart EG *to thwart someone's plans*

WORD POWER

▷ **Synonyms**
circumvent
nullify

---

2 foil NOUN
a contrast to something
EG *a perfect foil for his temperament*
antithesis EG *the antithesis of his crooked brother*
background EG *a fitting background for her beauty*
complement EG *the perfect complement to the antique furniture*
contrast EG *The green woodwork is a stunning contrast to the black walls.*

1 fold VERB
to bend something
EG *He folded the paper carefully.*
bend EG *Bend the top towards you.*
crease EG *Crease along the dotted line.*
crumple EG *He crumpled the note and put it in his pocket.*
tuck EG *Tuck in the top and bottom.*
turn under EG *The bottom was turned under.*

a b c d e f g h i j k l m n o p q r s t u v w x y z

❷ fold NOUN
a crease in something
EG *hanging in folds*
bend EG *There was a bend in the photograph.*
crease EG *sharp creases in his shirt*
pleat EG *a skirt with pleats*
wrinkle EG *all the little wrinkles on Paul's face*

❶ follow VERB
to pursue someone
EG *We were being followed.*
hound EG *constantly hounded by photographers*
pursue EG *He was pursued across several countries.*
stalk EG *Her former husband was stalking her.*
track EG *They tracked him to his home.*

❷ follow VERB
to come after someone or something
EG *Night follows day.*
come after EG *Summer comes after spring.*
succeed EG *He was succeeded by his son.*
supersede EG *Horses were superseded by cars.*

WORD POWER

▶ **Antonym**
precede

❸ follow VERB
to act in accordance with something
EG *Follow the instructions carefully.*
comply EG *in order to comply with EC regulations*
conform EG *conforming to the new safety requirements*
obey EG *You must obey the law.*
observe EG *The army was observing a ceasefire.*

follower NOUN
a supporter of a person or belief
EG *a loyal follower of the movement*

believer EG *many devout believers in the faith*
disciple EG *one of his disciples*
fan EG *football fans*
henchman EG *always surrounded by his henchmen*
supporter EG *He was a major supporter of the plan.*

WORD POWER

▷ **Synonyms**
adherent
protagonist

▶ **Antonym**
leader

❶ fond ADJECTIVE
feeling affection or liking
EG *a fond father*
adoring EG *an adoring husband*
affectionate EG *an affectionate smile*
devoted EG *a devoted couple*
doting EG *doting grandparents*
having a liking for EG *She had a great liking for chocolate.*
loving EG *a loving son*

❷ fond ADJECTIVE
unlikely to happen or be fulfilled
EG *fond wishes for a better life*
deluded EG *a deluded belief in future improvement*
empty EG *empty promises of full employment*
foolish EG *What foolish dreams we have!*
naive EG *her naive belief in others' goodness*
vain EG *the vain hope that he might lose weight*

WORD POWER

▷ **Synonyms**
delusory
overoptimistic

food NOUN
things eaten to provide

nourishment
EG *our favourite food*
diet EG *a healthy balanced diet*
fare EG *traditional regional fare*
foodstuffs EG *basic foodstuffs*
kai AUSTRALIAN AND NEW ZEALAND;
INFORMAL EG *There's no kai in the house.*
nourishment EG *unable to take
nourishment*
provisions EG *provisions for two
weeks*
refreshment EG *Refreshments will
be provided.*
tucker AUSTRALIAN AND NEW ZEALAND;
INFORMAL EG *some of the cheapest pub
tucker in town*

WORD POWER

▷ **Synonyms**
provender
subsistence
victuals

● **Related Words**
adjective : alimentary
noun : gastronomy

❶ fool NOUN
an unintelligent person
EG *What a stupid fool he is!*
dope INFORMAL EG *He felt such a dope.*
dunce EG *I was a complete dunce at
chemistry.*
idiot EG *acting like an idiot*
ignoramus EG *the ignoramus of the
group*
moron EG *They treated him like a
moron.*

❷ fool VERB
to trick someone
EG *Don't let him fool you.*
con INFORMAL EG *conned out of all his
money*
deceive EG *deceiving the audience*
dupe EG *in order to dupe the medical
staff*
mislead EG *a deliberately misleading
statement*

trick EG *They tricked him into
believing it.*

WORD POWER

▷ **Synonyms**
bamboozle
hoodwink

foolish ADJECTIVE
silly and unwise
EG *feeling foolish*
inane EG *an inane remark*
nonsensical EG *a nonsensical thing
to say*
senseless EG *It would be senseless to
stop her.*
silly EG *a silly thing to say*
unintelligent EG *a weak and
unintelligent man*
unwise EG *He had made some unwise
investments.*

WORD POWER

▶ **Antonym**
wise

forbid VERB
to order someone not to do
something
EG *forbidden to go out*
ban EG *banned from driving*
exclude EG *Women were excluded
from the classes.*
outlaw EG *the outlawed political
parties*
prohibit EG *Fishing is prohibited.*
veto EG *Their application was vetoed.*

WORD POWER

▶ **Antonym**
allow

❶ force VERB
to compel someone to do
something
EG *We were forced to turn right.*
compel EG *I felt compelled to act.*
drive EG *They are driving the
company into bankruptcy.*

a b c d e f g h i j k l m n o p q r s t u v w x y z

A
B
C
D
E
F
G
H
I
J
K
L
M
N
O
P
Q
R
T
U
V
W
X
Y
Z

make EG *They made me do it.*
oblige EG *We were obliged to abandon the car.*
pressurize EG *trying to pressurize them*

WORD POWER

▷ **Synonyms**
coerce
obligate

② **force** NOUN
a pressure to do something
EG *They made him agree by force.*
compulsion EG *a compulsion to write*
duress EG *carried out under duress*
pressure EG *under pressure to resign*

③ **force** NOUN
the strength of something
EG *the force of the explosion*
impact EG *the impact of the blast*
might EG *the full might of the army*
power EG *massive computing power*
pressure EG *the pressure of work*
strength EG *The storm was gaining strength.*

foreign ADJECTIVE
relating to other countries
EG *foreign travel*
distant EG *in that distant land*
exotic EG *filmed in an exotic location*
overseas EG *a long overseas trip*

foremost ADJECTIVE
most important or best
EG *one of the world's foremost scholars*
best EG *He was the best player in the world throughout the 1950s.*
chief EG *my chief reason for objecting to the plan*
first EG *The first priority is to defeat inflation.*
greatest EG *one of the West Indies' greatest cricketers*
leading EG *the leading researchers in this area*
most important EG *the country's most important politicians and philosophers*

prime EG *I regard this as my prime duty.*
principal EG *one of the country's principal publishing houses*
top EG *The President met with his top military advisers.*

forest NOUN

Types of forest
bush
coppice
copse
grove
jungle
spinney
thicket
wood
woodland

forget VERB
to fail to remember something
EG *I forgot to lock the door.*
fail to remember EG *He failed to remember my name.*
omit EG *omitting to mention the details*
overlook EG *to overlook an important fact*

WORD POWER

▶ **Antonym**
remember

forgive VERB
to stop blaming someone for something
EG *Can you ever forgive me?*
absolve EG *The verdict absolved him from blame.*
condone EG *We cannot condone violence.*
excuse EG *Please excuse our bad behaviour.*
pardon EG *Relatives had begged authorities to pardon him.*

WORD POWER

▶ **Antonym**
blame

forgiveness NOUN
the act of forgiving
EG *I ask for your forgiveness.*
acquittal EG *The jury voted for acquittal.*
mercy EG *to beg for mercy*
pardon EG *a presidential pardon*
remission EG *with remission for good behaviour*

> WORD POWER
>
> ▷ **Synonyms**
> absolution
> exoneration

❶ form NOUN
a type or kind
EG *He contracted a rare form of cancer.*
class EG *a new class of nuclear-powered submarine*
kind EG *a new kind of leadership*
sort EG *Try to do some sort of exercise every day.*
type EG *There are various types of this disease.*
variant EG *The quagga was a beautiful variant of the zebra.*
variety EG *an unusual variety of this common garden flower*

❷ form NOUN
the shape or pattern of something
EG *Valleys often take the form of deep canyons.*
contours EG *the contours of the body*
layout EG *He tried to recall the layout of the farmhouse.*
outline EG *I could just see the outline of a building in the mist.*
shape EG *little pens in the shape of baseball bats*
structure EG *the chemical structure of this molecule*

❸ form VERB
to be the elements that something consists of
EG *the articles that formed the basis of his book*
compose EG *The force would be composed of troops from NATO countries.*
constitute EG *The country's ethnic minorities constitute about 7% of its total population.*
make up EG *Women officers make up 13 per cent of the police force.*
serve as EG *an arrangement of bricks and planks that served as a bookshelf*

❹ form VERB
to organize, create, or come into existence
EG *The bowl was formed out of clay.*
assemble EG *a model assembled entirely from matchsticks*
create EG *These patterns were created by the action of water.*
develop EG *We must develop closer ties with Germany.*
draw up EG *We've drawn up a plan of action.*
establish EG *The school was established in 1989 by an Italian professor.*
fashion EG *Stone Age settlers fashioned necklaces from animals' teeth.*
make EG *The organic waste decomposes to make compost.*

❶ formal ADJECTIVE
in accordance with convention
EG *a formal dinner*
conventional EG *a conventional style of dress*
correct EG *polite and correct behaviour*
precise EG *They spoke very precise English.*
stiff EG *his stiff manner and lack of humour*

> WORD POWER
>
> ▶ **Antonym**
> informal

❷ formal ADJECTIVE
official and publicly recognized

a b c d e f g h i j k l m n o p q r s t u v w x y z

EG *No formal announcement has been made.*
approved EG *a legally approved method of dealing with these*
legal EG *They have a legal responsibility.*
official EG *according to the official figures*
prescribed EG *There is a prescribed procedure for situations like this.*
regular EG *through the regular channels*

former ADJECTIVE
existing in the past
EG *a former tennis champion*
ancient EG *the ancient civilizations*
bygone EG *memories of a bygone age*
old EG *our old school*
past EG *a long list of past winners*

formidable ADJECTIVE
difficult to overcome
EG *They faced formidable obstacles.*
challenging EG *a more challenging job*
daunting EG *a daunting prospect*
difficult EG *A difficult task lay ahead.*
intimidating EG *She was an intimidating opponent.*
mammoth EG *a mammoth undertaking*
onerous EG *onerous responsibilities*

fort NOUN
a building for defence and shelter
EG *They had to abandon the fort.*
castle EG *a heavily-guarded castle*
citadel EG *The citadel towered above the river.*
fortification EG *fortifications along the border*
fortress EG *an ancient fortress*

fossick VERB; AUSTRALIAN AND NEW ZEALAND
to search for something
EG *If you fossick around in some specialist music stores, you may find a copy.*
forage EG *They were forced to forage*

for clothing and fuel.
hunt EG *A forensic team was hunting for clues.*
look EG *I've looked through all my drawers and I can't find it anywhere.*
rummage EG *He rummaged around the post room and found the document.*
search EG *We've searched through the whole house for the keys.*

fragile ADJECTIVE
easily broken or damaged
EG *fragile china*
breakable EG *Anything breakable or sharp had to be removed.*
dainty EG *a dainty Japanese tea service*
delicate EG *a delicate instrument*
flimsy EG *packed in a flimsy box*
frail EG *a frail shell*

WORD POWER

▷ **Synonyms**
frangible
infirm

▶ **Antonym**
tough

---

fragrance NOUN
a pleasant smell
EG *the fragrance of the roses*
aroma EG *the aroma of fresh bread*
bouquet EG *a wine with a lively fruit bouquet*
perfume EG *enjoying the perfume of the lemon trees*
scent EG *flowers chosen for their scent*
smell EG *a sweet smell of pine*

fragrant ADJECTIVE
having a pleasant smell
EG *fragrant oils*
aromatic EG *a plant with aromatic leaves*
perfumed EG *perfumed body cream*

A B C D E F G H I J K L M N O P Q R T U V W X Y Z

sweet-smelling EG *posies of sweet-smelling flowers*

WORD POWER

▶ **Antonym**
smelly

---

frank ADJECTIVE
open and straightforward
EG *a frank discussion*
blunt EG *his blunt approach*
candid EG *She was completely candid with me.*
honest EG *my honest opinion*
open EG *an open, trusting nature*
plain EG *plain talking*
straightforward EG *spoken in a straightforward manner*

❶ fraud NOUN
the act of deceiving someone
EG *electoral fraud*
deceit EG *deliberate deceit*
deception EG *obtaining money by deception*
guile EG *children's lack of guile*
hoax EG *a bomb hoax*
trickery EG *They had to resort to trickery.*

WORD POWER

▷ **Synonyms**
chicanery
duplicity
spuriousness

---

❷ fraud NOUN
someone or something that deceives you
EG *Many psychics are frauds.*
charlatan EG *exposed as a charlatan*
cheat EG *Cheats will be disqualified.*
fake EG *The painting was a fake.*
forgery EG *just a clever forgery*
imposter EG *an imposter with false documents*
quack EG *He tried all sorts of quacks.*

❶ free ADJECTIVE
not being held prisoner

EG *a free man*
at large EG *Three prisoners are at large.*
at liberty EG *the last top Nazi still at liberty*
liberated EG *newly liberated slaves*
loose EG *He broke loose from his bonds.*

WORD POWER

▶ **Antonym**
captive

---

❷ free ADJECTIVE
available without payment
EG *a free brochure*
complimentary EG *complimentary tickets*
gratis EG *The meal was gratis.*
unpaid EG *unpaid voluntary work*
without charge EG *They mended it without charge.*

❸ free VERB
to release from captivity
EG *to free the slaves*
discharge EG *discharged from prison*
liberate EG *liberated under the terms of the amnesty*
release EG *The hostages were soon released.*
set at liberty EG *He was set at liberty after ten years.*
set loose EG *The animals were set loose after treatment.*

WORD POWER

▷ **Synonyms**
emancipate
unfetter

▶ **Antonym**
imprison

---

❶ freedom NOUN
the ability to choose
EG *freedom of action*
discretion EG *Use your own discretion.*
latitude EG *There is more latitude for*

a
b
c
d
e
f
g
h
i
j
k
l
m
n
o
p
q
r
s
t
u
v
w
x
y
z

personal opinions.
leeway EG *granted more leeway to pass reforms*
licence EG *a licence to kill*
scope EG *plenty of scope for improvement*

❷ freedom NOUN
the state of being free or being set free
EG *gaining their freedom after months of captivity*
emancipation EG *the emancipation of the slaves*
liberty EG *three months' loss of liberty*
release EG *the immediate release of the captives*

WORD POWER
▷ **Synonyms**
deliverance
manumission

▶ **Antonym**
captivity

❸ freedom NOUN
the absence of something unpleasant
EG *freedom from pain*
exemption EG *granted exemption from all taxes*
immunity EG *information in exchange for immunity from prosecution*

frenzy NOUN
wild and uncontrolled behaviour
EG *gripped by a frenzy of nationalism*
agitation EG *in a state of intense agitation*
fury EG *She stalked out in a fury.*
hysteria EG *mass hysteria*
madness EG *a moment of madness*
rage EG *She flew into a rage.*

WORD POWER
▷ **Synonyms**
delirium
paroxysm

❶ frequent ADJECTIVE
happening often
EG *his frequent visits*
common EG *a common occurrence*
continual EG *continual demands for money*
everyday EG *an everyday event*
habitual EG *a habitual daydreamer*
recurrent EG *a recurrent theme in her work*
repeated EG *His parents made repeated attempts to visit.*

WORD POWER
▶ **Antonym**
rare

❷ frequent VERB
to go somewhere often
EG *a restaurant which he frequents*
attend EG *He often attends their meetings.*
haunt EG *She haunted their house.*
patronize EG *to patronize a hotel*
visit EG *a place we often visit*

WORD POWER
▶ **Antonym**
avoid

friend NOUN
a person you know and like
EG *lifelong friends*
china SOUTH AFRICAN; INFORMAL EG *a drinking session with his chinas*
companion EG *my constant companion*
confidant *or* **confidante** EG *her only confidant*
crony EG *surrounded by her cronies*
mate INFORMAL EG *going out with his mates*
pal EG *We are great pals.*

WORD POWER
▷ **Synonyms**
alter ego
soul mate

friendly ADJECTIVE
kind and pleasant
EG *a very friendly crowd*
affectionate EG *on affectionate terms*
amiable EG *He was very amiable company.*
close EG *The two were very close.*
cordial EG *a most cordial welcome*
genial EG *a genial host*
welcoming EG *a welcoming house*

WORD POWER

▷ **Synonyms**
companionable
comradely
convivial

▶ **Antonym**
unfriendly

friendship NOUN
a state of being friendly with someone
EG *I value our friendship.*
affection EG *to win their affection*
attachment EG *the deep attachment between them*
closeness EG *her closeness to her sister*
goodwill EG *as a gesture of goodwill*

WORD POWER

▶ **Antonym**
hostility

frighten VERB
to make someone afraid
EG *trying to frighten us*
alarm EG *alarmed by the noise*
intimidate EG *She is intimidated by her boss.*
scare EG *You aren't scared of mice, are you?*
startle EG *I didn't mean to startle you.*
terrify EG *Heights terrified her.*

terrorize EG *The gunmen terrorized the villagers.*
unnerve EG *an unnerving silence*

frightened ADJECTIVE
having feelings of fear about something
EG *frightened of thunder*
afraid EG *Jane was afraid of the other children.*
alarmed EG *Don't be alarmed.*
petrified EG *petrified of wasps*
scared EG *scared of being alone in the house*
startled EG *a startled animal*
terrified EG *a terrified look*

WORD POWER

▷ **Synonyms**
cowed
panicky
terror-stricken

frightening ADJECTIVE
causing someone to feel fear
EG *a frightening experience*
alarming EG *an alarming increase*
hair-raising EG *at hair-raising speed*
intimidating EG *threatening and intimidating behaviour*
menacing EG *a menacing glance*
terrifying EG *one of the most terrifying diseases*

frivolous ADJECTIVE
not serious or sensible
EG *a frivolous new dress*
flippant EG *a flippant comment*
foolish EG *saying foolish and inappropriate things*
juvenile EG *juvenile behaviour*
puerile EG *your puerile schoolboy humour*
silly EG *making silly jokes*

WORD POWER

▶ **Antonym**
serious

▶ **Antonym**
enemy

1 front NOUN

the part that faces forward

EG *the front wall of the house*

face EG *the face of the building*

frontage EG *a restaurant with a river frontage*

WORD POWER

▶ **Antonym**
back

2 front NOUN

the outward appearance of something

EG *a respectable front*

appearance EG *the appearance of fair treatment*

exterior EG *his tough exterior*

face EG *a brave face*

show EG *a convincing show of affection*

3 front in front PREPOSITION

further forward

EG *too close to the car in front*

ahead EG *ahead of the rest of the field*

before EG *I'm before you.*

leading EG *the leading rider*

frown VERB

to draw the eyebrows together

EG *She frowned in concentration.*

glare EG *The woman glared angrily at him.*

glower EG *She glowered but said nothing.*

knit your brows EG *He knitted his brows in concentration.*

scowl EG *He scowled at the waiter.*

frozen ADJECTIVE

extremely cold

EG *frozen to the bone*

arctic EG *arctic weather conditions*

chilled EG *chilled to the marrow*

frigid EG *frigid temperatures*

icy EG *an icy wind*

numb EG *numb with cold*

frustrate VERB

to prevent something from happening

EG *His efforts were frustrated.*

block EG *They are blocking the peace process.*

check EG *to check the spread of the virus*

foil EG *They foiled all my plans.*

thwart EG *his way to thwart your club's ambitions*

WORD POWER

▷ **Synonyms**
forestall
nullify

fulfil VERB

to carry out or achieve something

EG *He decided to fulfil his dream and go to college.*

accomplish EG *If they all work together they can accomplish their goal.*

achieve EG *We will strive to achieve these goals.*

carry out EG *They seem to have very little intention of carrying out their commitments.*

perform EG *Each component performs a different function.*

realize EG *The question is, will our hopes ever be realized?*

satisfy EG *The procedures should satisfy certain basic requirements.*

1 full ADJECTIVE

filled with something

EG *full of books*

filled EG *filled up to the top*

loaded EG *The van was loaded with furniture.*

packed EG *The train was packed.*

saturated EG *completely saturated with liquid*

WORD POWER

▶ **Antonym**
empty

2 full ADJECTIVE

missing nothing out

EG *I want a full account of what happened.*
comprehensive EG *a comprehensive guide to the area*
detailed EG *a detailed descriptions*
exhaustive EG *an exhaustive treatment of the subject*
extensive EG *extensive coverage of the earthquake*
maximum EG *the way to take maximum advantage of pay TV*
thorough EG *a thorough search*

❸ full ADJECTIVE
loose-fitting
EG *a full skirt*
baggy EG *a baggy sweater*
loose EG *hidden under his loose shirt*
voluminous EG *voluminous sleeves*

❶ fun NOUN
an enjoyable activity
EG *It was great fun.*
amusement EG *There is no amusement for teenagers in this village.*
enjoyment EG *It gave us much enjoyment.*
entertainment EG *little opportunity for entertainment*
pleasure EG *to mix business and pleasure*
recreation EG *time for recreation*

❷ fun make fun of VERB
to tease someone
EG *Don't make fun of him.*
deride EG *This theory is widely derided.*
laugh at EG *They laughed at his hat.*
mock EG *He was often mocked by his classmates.*
ridicule EG *She allowed them to ridicule her.*
taunt EG *a fellow pupil who had taunted him about his height*

WORD POWER
▷ **Synonyms**
lampoon

rib
satirize

❶ function NOUN
the useful thing that something or someone does
EG *The main function of merchant banks is to raise capital.*
duty EG *My duty is to look after the animals.*
job EG *Their main job is to keep us healthy.*
purpose EG *The purpose of the occasion was to raise money for charity.*
remit EG *The centre's remit is to advise businesses.*
responsibility EG *He handled his responsibilities as a counsellor in an intelligent fashion.*
role EG *information about the drug's role in preventing infection*

❷ function NOUN
a large formal dinner, reception, or party
EG *We were going down to a function in London.*
dinner EG *a series of official dinners*
gathering EG *I'm always shy at formal gatherings like that.*
party EG *They met at a party.*
reception EG *At the reception they served smoked salmon.*

❸ function VERB
to operate or work
EG *The heater was not functioning properly.*
go EG *My car won't go in fog.*
operate EG *Ceiling and wall lights can operate independently.*
perform EG *When there's snow, how is this car going to perform?*
run EG *The system is now running smoothly.*
work EG *Is the telephone working today?*

❶ fund NOUN
an amount of money

A B C D E F G H I J K L M N O P Q R S T U V W X Y Z

EG *the pension fund*
capital EG *difficulty in raising capital*
foundation EG *money from a research foundation*
pool EG *a reserve pool of cash*
reserve EG *a drain on the cash reserves*
supply EG *to curb money supply and inflation*

❷ fund NOUN
a large amount of something
EG *an extraordinary fund of energy*
hoard EG *his hoard of supplies*
mine EG *a mine of information*
reserve EG *oil reserves*
reservoir EG *the body's short-term reservoir of energy*
store EG *a store of fuel*

❸ fund VERB
to provide the money for something
EG *to raise money to fund research into breast cancer*
finance EG *big projects financed by foreign aid*
pay for EG *His parents paid for his holiday.*
subsidize EG *heavily subsidized by the government*
support EG *He is supporting himself through college.*

fundi NOUN; SOUTH AFRICAN
an expert
EG *The local fundis are wonderfully adept and have created a car for hunting.*
expert EG *our team of experts*
guru EG *Fashion gurus dictate some crazy ideas.*
master EG *a master of the English language*
specialist EG *a specialist in diseases of the nervous system*
virtuoso EG *He was gaining a reputation as a piano virtuoso.*

❶ funny ADJECTIVE
being strange or odd
EG *They heard a funny noise.*

mysterious EG *in mysterious circumstances*
odd EG *There was something odd about her.*
peculiar EG *It tasted very peculiar.*
puzzling EG *a puzzling development*
strange EG *A strange thing happened.*
unusual EG *a most unusual man*

❷ funny ADJECTIVE
causing amusement
EG *a funny story*
amusing EG *a most amusing lecturer*
comic EG *comic moments*
comical EG *the comical expression on his face*
hilarious EG *We thought it was hilarious.*
humorous EG *a humorous magazine*
witty EG *a very witty speech*

WORD POWER

▷ **Synonyms**
droll
jocular
risible

▶ **Antonym**
serious

❶ furious ADJECTIVE
extremely angry
EG *He is furious at the way his wife has been treated.*
enraged EG *I got more and more enraged at my father.*
fuming EG *He was still fuming over the remark.*
infuriated EG *He knew how infuriated the conversation had made me.*
livid EG *She was absolutely livid about it.*
mad EG *I'm pretty mad about this, I can tell you.*
raging EG *Inside, Sally was raging.*

WORD POWER

▷ **Synonyms**
incensed

2 furious ADJECTIVE
involving great energy, effort, or
speed
EG *a furious gunbattle*
breakneck EG *Jack drove to Mayfair
at breakneck speed.*
fierce EG *Competition has been fierce
between the rival groups.*
frantic EG *There was frantic activity
behind the scenes.*
frenzied EG *the frenzied activity of
the general election*
intense EG *The military on both sides
are involved in intense activity.*
manic EG *Preparations continued at a
manic pace.*

WORD POWER

▷ **Synonyms**
frenetic

1 fuss NOUN
anxious or excited behaviour
EG *What's all the fuss about?*
agitation EG *in a state of intense
agitation*
bother EG *I don't want any bother.*
commotion EG *a commotion in the
market*
confusion EG *in the confusion after
an ammunition dump blew up*
stir EG *The play caused a stir here.*
to-do EG *a big to-do*

WORD POWER

▷ **Synonyms**
ado
fluster
palaver

2 fuss VERB
to behave in a nervous or restless
way
EG *Waiters fussed around the table.*
bustle EG *shoppers bustling around*
the store
fidget EG *He was fidgeting with his
tie.*
fret EG *Stop fretting about the details.*

fussy ADJECTIVE
difficult to please
EG *fussy about his food*
choosy INFORMAL EG *Cats can be
choosy about what they eat.*
discriminating EG *a discriminating
visitor*
exacting EG *She failed to meet his
exacting standards.*
fastidious EG *Disney was also
fastidious about cleanliness.*
particular EG *very particular about
the colours he used*

WORD POWER

▷ **Synonyms**
faddish
finicky
pernickety

futile ADJECTIVE
having no chance of success
EG *a futile effort to run away*
abortive EG *the abortive coup
attempt*
forlorn EG *forlorn hopes of future
improvement*
unsuccessful EG *an unsuccessful bid
for independence*
useless EG *It was useless to even try.*
vain EG *in the vain hope of success*

WORD POWER

▶ **Antonym**
successful

future ADJECTIVE
relating to a time after the present
EG *to predict future growth*
approaching EG *concerned about
the approaching winter*
coming EG *in the coming months*
forthcoming EG *candidates for the
forthcoming elections*
impending EG *her impending*

A
B
C
D
E
F
G
H
I
J
K
L
M
N
O
P
Q
R
T
U
V
W
X
Y
Z

marriage
later EG *We'll discuss it at a later date.*
prospective EG *my prospective employers*

<u>WORD POWER</u>

▶ **Antonym**
past

Gg

gadget NOUN
a small machine or tool
EG *kitchen gadgets such as toasters and kettles*
appliance EG *Switch off all electrical appliances when they're not in use.*
device EG *a device that warns you when the batteries need changing*
machine EG *a machine for slicing vegetables*
tool EG *a tool for cutting wood, metal or plastic*

WORD POWER

▷ **Synonyms**
implement
instrument
utensil

❶ gain VERB
to get something gradually
EG *Students can gain valuable experience by working.*
achieve EG *Achieving our goals makes us feel good.*
acquire EG *Companies should reward workers for acquiring more skills.*
earn EG *She has earned the respect of the world's top women cyclists.*
obtain EG *You would need to obtain permission to copy the design.*
secure EG *He failed to secure enough votes for outright victory.*
win EG *The long-term aim is to win promotion.*

WORD POWER

▷ **Synonyms**
attain
capture
reap

❷ gain VERB
to get an advantage
EG *Areas of the world would actually gain from global warming.*
benefit EG *Both sides have benefited from the talks.*
profit EG *Frankie is now profiting from his crimes.*

❸ gain NOUN
an increase or improvement in something
EG *The Party has made substantial gains in local elections.*
advance EG *advances in computer technology*
growth EG *The area has seen a rapid population growth.*
improvement EG *a major improvement in standards*
increase EG *an increase of 7% in visitors to the UK*
rise EG *a 3% rise in electricity prices*

❶ gamble VERB
to bet money on something
EG *John gambled heavily on the horses.*
back EG *I backed Germany to win 1-0.*
bet EG *He bet them 500 pounds they would lose.*

❷ gamble VERB
to take a risk
EG *Few firms will be willing to gamble on new products.*
chance EG *Armstrong chanced a gallop to the water.*
risk EG *One of his daughters risked everything to join him in exile.*
stake EG *He has staked his reputation on the outcome.*

WORD POWER

▷ **Synonyms**
hazard
take a chance
venture

❸ gamble NOUN
a risk that someone takes
EG *We are taking a gamble on a young player.*
chance EG *You take a chance on the*

a
b
c
d
e
f
g
h
i
j
k
l
m
n
o
p
q
r
s
t
u
v
w
x
y
z

weather when you holiday in the UK.
lottery EG *Robinson described the final as a bit of a lottery.*
risk EG *How much risk are you prepared to take?*

game NOUN
an occasion on which people compete
EG *South Africa's first game of the season*
clash EG *the clash between Australia and the West Indies*
contest EG *The rain spoiled a good contest.*
match EG *a football match*

❶ gap NOUN
a space or a hole in something
EG *They squeezed through a gap in the fence.*
break EG *stars twinkling between the breaks in the clouds*
chink EG *All the walls have wide chinks in them.*
crack EG *a crack in the curtains*
hole EG *a hole in the wall*
opening EG *an opening in the trees*
space EG *the space between their car and the one in front*

WORD POWER

▷ **Synonyms**
cleft
cranny
crevice

---

❷ gap NOUN
a period of time
EG *After a gap of nearly a decade, Manley was back.*
hiatus FORMAL EG *The shop is open again after a two year hiatus.*
interlude EG *a happy interlude in the Kents' life*
interval EG *There was a long interval of silence.*
lull EG *a lull in the conversation*
pause EG *Then, after a pause, he goes on.*

❸ gap NOUN
a difference between people or things
EG *the gap between rich and poor*
difference EG *He denied there were any major differences between them.*
disparity FORMAL EG *disparities between poor and wealthy school districts*
inconsistency EG *There were major inconsistencies in his evidence.*

❶ garbage NOUN
things that people do not want
EG *piles of garbage*
debris EG *screws, bolts and other debris from a scrapyard*
junk INFORMAL EG *What are you going to do with all that junk?*
litter EG *If you see litter in the corridor, pick it up.*
refuse FORMAL EG *refuse collection and street cleaning*
rubbish EG *household rubbish*
trash EG *I forgot to take out the trash.*
waste EG *industrial waste*

❷ garbage NOUN; INFORMAL
ideas and opinions that are untrue or unimportant
EG *I personally think this is complete garbage.*
drivel EG *What absolute drivel!*
gibberish EG *a politician talking gibberish*
nonsense EG *all that poetic nonsense about love*
rubbish EG *He's talking rubbish.*

garbled ADJECTIVE
confused or incorrect
EG *A garbled message awaited us at the desk.*
confused EG *the latest twist in a murky and confused story*
distorted EG *a distorted version of what was said*
incomprehensible EG *Her speech was incomprehensible.*
jumbled EG *his jumbled account of*

how Jack had been hired
unintelligible EG *He muttered something unintelligible.*

1 gasp VERB
to breathe in quickly through your mouth
EG *She gasped for air.*
choke EG *People began to choke as smoke filled the air.*
gulp EG *She gulped air into her lungs.*
pant EG *Amy climbed rapidly until she was panting with the effort.*
puff EG *I could see he was unfit because he was puffing.*

> ### WORD POWER
> ▷ **Synonyms**
> catch your breath
> fight for breath

2 gasp NOUN
a short quick breath of air
EG *An audible gasp went round the court.*
gulp EG *I took in a large gulp of air.*
pant EG *Her breath came in pants.*
puff EG *He blew out a little puff of air.*

1 gather VERB
to come together in a group
EG *We gathered around the fireplace.*
assemble EG *a place for students to assemble between classes*
congregate EG *Youngsters love to congregate here in the evenings.*
flock EG *The criticisms will not stop people flocking to see the film.*
mass EG *The General was massing his troops for a counterattack.*
round up EG *The police rounded up a number of suspects.*

> ### WORD POWER
> ▷ **Synonyms**
> convene
> marshal
> muster
>
> ▶ **Antonym**
> scatter

2 gather VERB
to bring things together
EG *I suggest we gather enough firewood to last the night.*
accumulate EG *In five years it has accumulated a huge debt.*
amass EG *She has amassed a personal fortune of $38 million.*
collect EG *1.5 million signatures have been collected.*
hoard EG *They've begun to hoard food and gasoline.*
stockpile EG *People are stockpiling food for the coming winter.*

3 gather VERB
to learn or believe something
EG *"He speaks English." "I gathered that."*
assume EG *I assume the eggs are fresh.*
conclude EG *He concluded that Oswald was somewhat abnormal.*
hear EG *I heard that he was forced to resign.*
learn EG *She wasn't surprised to learn that he was involved.*
understand EG *I understand that he's just taken early retirement.*

gathering NOUN
a meeting with a purpose
EG *polite social gatherings*
assembly EG *an assembly of party members*
congregation EG *The congregation sang hymns and said prayers.*
get-together INFORMAL EG *family get-togethers*
meeting EG *Can we have a meeting to discuss that?*
rally EG *a pre-election rally*

> ### WORD POWER
> ▷ **Synonyms**
> conference
> congress
> convention

a
b
c
d
e
f
g
h
i
j
k
l
m
n
o
p
q
r
s
t
u
v
w
x
y
z

gaudy ADJECTIVE
colourful in a vulgar way
EG *gaudy fake jewellery*
bright EG *fake fur, dyed in bright colours*
flashy EG *women in flashy satin suits*
garish EG *They climbed the garish purple-carpeted stairs.*
loud EG *a loud checked shirt*
showy EG *He favoured large showy flowers.*
tacky INFORMAL EG *tacky red sunglasses*
vulgar EG *I think it's a very vulgar house.*

WORD POWER

▷ **Synonyms**
jazzy
ostentatious
tasteless
tawdry

1 general ADJECTIVE
relating to the whole of something
EG *a general decline in employment*
broad EG *a broad outline of the Society's development*
comprehensive EG *a comprehensive guide to the region*
overall EG *The overall quality of pupils' work had shown a marked improvement.*

WORD POWER

▷ **Synonyms**
generic
indiscriminate
panoramic
sweeping

▶ **Antonym**
specific

2 general ADJECTIVE
widely true, suitable or relevant
EG *The project should raise general awareness about bullying.*
accepted EG *the accepted version of events*
broad EG *a film with broad appeal*
common EG *Such behaviour is common to all young people.*
universal EG *Music and sports programmes have a universal appeal.*
widespread EG *The proposals have attracted widespread support.*

WORD POWER

▶ **Antonym**
special

generosity NOUN
willingness to give money, time or help
EG *She is well known for her generosity.*
benevolence EG *Banks are not known for their benevolence.*
charity EG *private acts of charity*
kindness EG *We have been treated with such kindness by everybody.*

WORD POWER

▷ **Synonyms**
bounty
liberality
munificence
open-handedness

▶ **Antonym**
meanness

1 generous ADJECTIVE
willing to give money, time or help
EG *The gift is generous by any standards.*
charitable EG *Individuals can be charitable and help their neighbours.*
hospitable EG *He was very hospitable to me when I came to New York.*
kind EG *She is warm-hearted and kind to everyone.*
lavish EG *The Princess received a number of lavish gifts from her hosts.*
liberal EG *Don't be too liberal with your spending.*

WORD POWER

▷ **Synonyms**
munificent
open-handed
prodigal
unstinting

▶ **Antonym**
mean

2 generous ADJECTIVE
very large
EG *a generous portion of spaghetti*
abundant EG *an abundant supply of hot food*
ample EG *There is ample space for a good-sized kitchen.*
plentiful EG *a plentiful supply of beer*

WORD POWER

▶ **Antonym**
meagre

1 genius NOUN
a very clever or talented person
EG *a mathematical genius*
brain EG *the financial brain behind the company*
master EG *Spiro Rosakis is a master of his craft.*
mastermind EG *the mastermind of the plot to kill the ex-prime minister*
virtuoso EG *The man is a virtuoso of pop music.*

2 genius NOUN
extraordinary ability or talent
EG *a poet of genius*
brains EG *She has brains as well as beauty.*
brilliance EG *his brilliance as a director*
intellect EG *people of great intellect*

gentle ADJECTIVE
not violent or rough
EG *a quiet and gentle man*
benign EG *a good-looking chap with a benign expression*
kind EG *I fell in love with him because*
of his kind nature.
kindly EG *a kindly old gentleman*
meek EG *He was a meek, mild-mannered fellow.*
mild EG *Alexis was quiet, mild and happy-go-lucky.*
placid EG *a look of impatience on her normally placid face*
soft EG *She had a very soft heart.*
tender EG *Her voice was tender.*

WORD POWER

▷ **Synonyms**
compassionate
humane
lenient
sweet-tempered

▶ **Antonym**
cruel

genuine ADJECTIVE
not false or pretend
EG *They're convinced the picture is genuine.*
authentic EG *an authentic French recipe*
bona fide EG *We are happy to donate to bona fide charities.*
dinkum AUSTRALIAN AND NEW ZEALAND; INFORMAL EG *They are all dinkum stolen bank notes.*
real EG *a real Rembrandt*

WORD POWER

▶ **Antonym**
fake

1 get VERB
to fetch or receive something
EG *I'll get us all a cup of coffee.*
acquire EG *I have recently acquired a new camera.*
fetch EG *Sylvia fetched a towel from the bathroom.*
obtain EG *Evans was trying to obtain a false passport.*
procure FORMAL EG *It remained very difficult to procure food.*

receive EG *I received your letter of November 7.*

secure FORMAL EG *He failed to secure enough votes for outright victory.*

❷ get VERB
to change from one state to another
EG *People draw the curtains once it gets dark.*

become EG *The wind became stronger.*

grow EG *He grew to love his work.*

turn EG *The leaves have turned golden-brown.*

get on VERB
to enjoy someone's company
EG *I get on very well with his wife.*

be compatible EG *Mary and I are very compatible.*

hit it off INFORMAL EG *They hit it off straight away.*

ghost NOUN
the spirit of a dead person
EG *the ghost of the drowned girl*

apparition EG *She felt as if she were seeing a ghostly apparition.*

phantom EG *She was relentlessly pursued by a grossly disfigured phantom.*

spectre EG *The Tower is said to be haunted by the spectre of Anne Boleyn.*

spirit EG *the spirits of our dead ancestors*

WORD POWER

● Related Words
adjective : spectral

---

gidday INTERJECTION; AUSTRALIAN AND NEW ZEALAND
hello
EG *Gidday, mate!*

hello EG *Hello, Trish. Glad you could make it.*

hi INFORMAL EG *Hi, how are you doing?*

good morning FORMAL EG *Good morning, class.*

good afternoon FORMAL EG *Good afternoon, Miss Bates.*

good evening FORMAL EG *Good evening, ladies and gentlemen!*

❶ gift NOUN
something you give someone
EG *He showered her with gifts.*

bequest FORMAL EG *They received a bequest of $310,000.*

bonsela SOUTH AFRICAN EG *a generous bonsela*

contribution EG *companies that make charitable contributions*

donation EG *donations of food and clothing for victims of the hurricane*

legacy EG *What about the legacy from your uncle?*

present EG *This book would make a great Christmas present.*

❷ gift NOUN
a natural skill or ability
EG *a gift for comedy*

ability EG *It's obvious he has an exceptional ability.*

aptitude EG *She realised she had an aptitude for writing.*

flair EG *Tony found he had a real flair for design.*

talent EG *Both her children have a talent for music.*

❶ give VERB
to provide someone with something
EG *I gave her a CD.*

award EG *The Mayor awarded him a medal.*

deliver EG *The Canadians plan to deliver more food to southern Somalia.*

donate EG *Others donated second-hand clothes.*

grant EG *Permission was granted a few weeks ago.*

hand EG *Isabel handed me a glass of orange juice.*

present EG *The Queen presented the prizes.*

provide EG *The government was not in a position to provide them with*

A B C D E F G H I J K L M N O P Q R S T U V W X Y Z

food.
supply EG *a contract to supply radar equipment to the Philippines*

WORD POWER

▷ **Synonyms**
accord
administer
bestow
confer

▶ **Antonym**
take

---

❷ **give** VERB
to collapse or break under pressure
EG *My knees gave under me.*
buckle EG *His left wrist buckled under the strain.*
cave in EG *Half the ceiling caved in.*
collapse EG *The roof supports had collapsed.*
give way EG *He fell when a ledge gave way beneath him.*
yield EG *The handle yielded to her grasp.*

give in VERB
to admit that you are defeated
EG *Juppe should not give in to the strikers.*
capitulate EG *Cohen capitulated to virtually every demand.*
concede EG *Mr Pyke is not prepared to concede defeat.*
submit EG *Mrs Jones submitted to an operation on her right knee.*
succumb EG *The Minister said his country would never succumb to pressure.*
surrender EG *He surrendered to American troops.*
yield EG *an enemy who had shown no desire to yield*

glad ADJECTIVE
happy about something
EG *They'll be glad to get away from it all.*
delighted EG *Frank will be delighted to see you.*

happy EG *Jacques is very happy that you are here.*
joyful EG *a joyful reunion with his mother*
overjoyed EG *Shelley was overjoyed to see me.*
pleased EG *They're pleased to be going home.*

WORD POWER

▶ **Antonym**
sorry

---

❶ **glance** NOUN
a brief look at something
EG *The boys exchanged glances.*
glimpse EG *They caught a glimpse of their hero.*
look EG *Lucille took a last look in the mirror.*
peek EG *Could I just have another quick peek at the bedroom?*
peep EG *Would you take a peep out of the window?*

❷ **glance** VERB
to look at something quickly
EG *He glanced at his watch.*
glimpse EG *I soon glimpsed the doctor in his garden.*
look EG *Bethan looked quickly at the elegant people around her.*
peek EG *She had peeked at him through a crack in the wall.*
peep EG *Now and then she peeped to see if he was noticing her.*
scan EG *She scanned the advertisement pages of the newspaper.*

❸ **glance** VERB
to hit something quickly and bounce away
EG *My fist glanced off his jaw.*
bounce EG *The ball bounced off the opposite post.*
brush EG *She brushed her lips across Michael's cheek.*

a b c d e f g h i j k l m n o p q r s t u v w x y z

skim EG *pebbles skimming across the water*

WORD POWER

▷ **Synonyms**
rebound
ricochet

❶ glare VERB
to look angrily at someone
EG *Joe glared at his brother.*
frown EG *She looked up to see Vic frowning at her.*
glower EG *He glowered at me but said nothing.*
scowl EG *Robert scowled, and slammed the door behind him.*

❷ glare NOUN
an angry look
EG *The waiter lowered his eyes to avoid Harold's furious glare.*
frown EG *There was a deep frown on the boy's face.*
scowl EG *Chris met the remark with a scowl.*

❸ glare NOUN
very bright light
EG *the glare of the headlights*
blaze EG *There was a sudden blaze of light.*
glow EG *the glow of the fire*

❶ gloomy ADJECTIVE
feeling very sad
EG *They are gloomy about their chances of success.*
dejected EG *Everyone has days when they feel dejected.*
down EG *The old man sounded really down.*
glum EG *What on earth are you looking so glum about?*
miserable EG *She went to bed, miserable and depressed.*
sad EG *You must feel sad about what's happened.*

WORD POWER

▷ **Synonyms**
blue
despondent
downhearted

▶ **Antonym**
cheerful

❷ gloomy ADJECTIVE
dark and depressing
EG *a gloomy house on the edge of Phoenix Park*
dark EG *The house looked dark and gloomy.*
dismal EG *damp and dismal weather*
dreary EG *the dreary, industrial city of Ludwigshafen*
dull EG *It's always dull and raining.*

WORD POWER

▶ **Antonym**
sunny

❶ glory NOUN
fame and admiration that someone gets
EG *It was her moment of glory.*
fame EG *The film earned him international fame.*
honour EG *the honour of captaining one's country*
immortality EG *Some people want to achieve immortality through their work.*
praise EG *Holbrooke deserves full praise for his efforts.*
prestige EG *I'm not in this job for the prestige.*

WORD POWER

▷ **Synonyms**
acclaim
renown

▶ **Antonym**
disgrace

❷ glory NOUN
something impressive or beautiful

EG *Spring arrived in all its glory.*
grandeur EG *the grandeur of the country mansion*
magnificence EG *the magnificence of the sunset*
majesty EG *the majesty of Niagara Falls*
splendour EG *the splendour of the palace of Versailles*

❸ **glory** VERB
to enjoy something very much
EG *The workers were glorying in their new-found freedom.*
gloat EG *Their rivals were gloating over their triumph.*
relish EG *He relished the idea of getting some cash.*
revel EG *a ruthless killer who revels in his job*

gloss NOUN
a bright shine on a surface
EG *aluminium foil with a high gloss surface*
brilliance EG *ceramic tiles of great brilliance*
gleam EG *the gleam of brass*
polish EG *His boots had a high polish.*
sheen EG *The carpet had a silvery sheen to it.*
shine EG *This gel gives a beautiful shine to the hair.*

glossy ADJECTIVE
smooth and shiny
EG *The leaves were dark and glossy.*
bright EG *Her eyes were bright with excitement.*
brilliant EG *The woman had brilliant green eyes.*
polished EG *a highly polished floor*
shiny EG *a shiny new sports car*
sleek EG *sleek black hair*

❶ **glow** NOUN
a dull steady light
EG *the glow of the fire*
gleam EG *the first gleam of dawn*
glimmer EG *In the east there was the slightest glimmer of light.*
light EG *the light of the evening sun*

❷ **glow** VERB
to shine with a dull steady light
EG *A light glowed behind the curtains.*
gleam EG *Lights gleamed in the deepening mist.*
glimmer EG *A few stars still glimmered.*
shine EG *Scattered lights shone on the horizon.*
smoulder EG *A very small fire was smouldering in the grate.*

glue VERB
to stick things together
EG *Glue the two halves together.*
fix EG *Fix the fabric to the roller.*
paste EG *The children were busy pasting gold stars on a chart.*
seal EG *He sealed the envelope and put on a stamp.*
stick EG *I stuck the notice on the board.*

❶ **go** VERB
to move or travel somewhere
EG *I went home at the weekend.*
advance EG *Rebel forces are advancing on the capital.*
drive EG *My husband and I drove to Liverpool to see my mum.*
fly EG *He flew to Los Angeles.*
journey FORMAL EG *They intended to journey up the Amazon.*
leave EG *What time are you leaving?*
proceed FORMAL EG *The taxi proceeded along a lonely road.*
set off EG *He set off for the station.*
travel EG *Students often travel hundreds of miles to get here.*

❷ **go** VERB
to work properly
EG *stuck on the motorway with a car that won't go*
function EG *All the instruments functioned properly.*
work EG *The pump doesn't work and we have no running water.*

a b c d e f g h i j k l m n o p q r s t u v w x y z

❸ go NOUN
an attempt to do something
EG *I always wanted to have a go at waterskiing.*

attempt EG *one of his rare attempts at humour*

shot INFORMAL EG *a shot at winning a brand new car*

stab INFORMAL EG *Several sports stars have had a stab at acting and singing.*

try EG *After a few tries, Patrick had given up.*

goal NOUN
something that a person hopes to achieve
EG *The goal is to make as much money as possible.*

aim EG *The aim of the festival is to raise awareness of this issue.*

end EG *This is another policy designed to achieve the same end.*

intention EG *He announced his intention of standing for parliament.*

object EG *The object of the exercise is to raise money for charity.*

objective EG *His objective was to play golf and win.*

purpose EG *His purpose was to make a profit.*

target EG *She failed to achieve her target of losing 20 pounds.*

gobble VERB
to eat food very quickly
EG *Pete gobbled all the beef stew.*

bolt EG *Being under stress can cause you to bolt your food.*

devour EG *She devoured two bars of chocolate.*

wolf EG *Pitt wolfed down a peanut butter sandwich.*

❶ good ADJECTIVE
pleasant, acceptable or satisfactory
EG *We had a really good time.*
→ see Word Study **good**

WORD POWER

▶ **Antonym**
bad

❷ good ADJECTIVE
skilful or successful
EG *I'm not very good at art.*
→ see Word Study **good**

WORD POWER

▶ **Antonym**
incompetent

❸ good ADJECTIVE
kind, thoughtful and loving
EG *You are so good to me.*
→ see Word Study **good**

WORD POWER

▶ **Antonym**
unkind

goodwill NOUN
kindness and helpfulness towards other people
EG *I invited them to dinner as a gesture of goodwill.*

benevolence EG *He chuckles often and radiates benevolence.*

favour EG *in order to gain the favour of whoever is in power*

friendliness EG *Visitors remarked on the friendliness of the people.*

friendship EG *The two countries signed treaties of friendship.*

gossip NOUN
informal conversation about other people
EG *Don't you like a good gossip?*

dirt EG *the latest dirt on the other candidates*

hearsay EG *They have had only hearsay and rumour to go on.*

WORD POWER

▷ **Synonyms**
chitchat
prattle
scandal
tittle-tattle

go through VERB
to experience an unpleasant event

EG *I was going through a very difficult time.*

endure EG *He'd endured years of pain and sleepless nights.*

experience EG *British business was experiencing a severe recession.*

undergo EG *Magee underwent emergency surgery.*

grab VERB
to take hold of something roughly
EG *I grabbed him by the neck.*

clutch EG *Michelle clutched my arm.*

grasp EG *He grasped both my hands.*

seize EG *She seized a carving fork and advanced in my direction.*

snatch EG *Mick snatched the cards from Archie's hand.*

grace NOUN
an elegant way of moving
EG *He moved with the grace of a trained boxer.*

elegance EG *She is elegance personified.*

poise EG *Ballet classes are important for poise and grace.*

> ### WORD POWER
> ▶ **Antonym**
> clumsiness

grade VERB
to arrange things according to quality
EG *The oil is tasted and graded according to quality.*

class EG *They are officially classed as visitors.*

classify EG *Rocks can be classified according to their origin.*

group EG *The fact sheets are grouped into seven sections.*

rate EG *He was rated as one of the country's top young players.*

sort EG *The students are sorted into three ability groups.*

> ### WORD POWER
> ▷ **Synonyms**
> evaluate
> sequence

gradual ADJECTIVE
happening or changing slowly
EG *the gradual improvement in communications*

continuous EG *Our policy is one of continuous improvement.*

progressive EG *One symptom of the disease is progressive loss of memory.*

slow EG *The distribution of passports has been a slow process.*

steady EG *a steady rise in sales*

> ### WORD POWER
> ▶ **Antonym**
> sudden

grammar NOUN

Grammar words
active
aspect
comparative
passive
person
plural
possessive
singular
superlative
tense
voice

❶ grand ADJECTIVE
very impressive in size or appearance
EG *a grand building in the centre of town*

imposing EG *the imposing gates at the entrance to the estate*

impressive EG *The old boat presented an impressive sight.*

magnificent EG *magnificent views over the San Fernando valley*

majestic EG *a stupendous vista of majestic peaks*

monumental EG *a monumental sculpture of a human face*

splendid EG *a splendid Victorian mansion*

WORD POWER

▷ **Synonyms**
glorious
grandiose
palatial

2 grand ADJECTIVE; INFORMAL
pleasant or enjoyable
EG *It was a grand day.*

brilliant INFORMAL EG *I've had a brilliant time.*

great INFORMAL EG *I had a great time at university.*

marvellous INFORMAL EG *It was a marvellous day and we were all so happy.*

terrific INFORMAL EG *Everybody there was having a terrific time.*

wonderful EG *It was a wonderful experience.*

1 grant NOUN
a money award given for a particular purpose
EG *My application for a grant has been accepted.*

allocation EG *The aid allocation for that country is under review.*

allowance EG *She gets an allowance for looking after Lillian.*

award EG *a study award worth £2,000*

handout EG *a cash handout of six thousand rupees*

subsidy EG *state subsidies to public transport companies*

2 grant VERB
to allow someone to have something
EG *France has agreed to grant him political asylum.*

allocate EG *The budget allocated $7 billion for development programmes.*

allow EG *Children should be allowed*

the occasional treat.

award EG *A High Court judge awarded him £6 million damages.*

give EG *We have been given permission to attend the meeting.*

permit EG *The doorman said he could not permit them entry to the film.*

WORD POWER

▷ **Synonyms**
accord
bestow

▶ **Antonym**
deny

3 grant VERB
to admit that something is true
EG *I grant that you had some justification for your actions.*

accept EG *I do not accept that there is a crisis in British science.*

acknowledge EG *He acknowledged that he had been partly to blame.*

admit EG *I admit that I do make mistakes.*

allow EG *He allows that capitalist development may result in social inequality.*

concede EG *Bess finally conceded that Nancy was right.*

WORD POWER

▶ **Antonym**
deny

1 grasp VERB
to hold something firmly
EG *He grasped both my hands.*

clutch EG *I staggered and had to clutch at a chair for support.*

grab EG *I grabbed him by the neck.*

grip EG *She gripped the rope.*

hold EG *He held the pistol tightly in his right hand.*

seize EG *He seized my arm to hold me back.*

snatch EG *I snatched at a hanging branch and pulled myself up.*

grasp >> grave

②grasp VERB
to understand an idea
EG *The Government has not yet grasped the seriousness of the crisis.*
absorb EG *He only absorbed about half the information we gave him.*
appreciate EG *She never really appreciated the bitterness of the conflict.*
assimilate EG *My mind could only assimilate one concept at a time.*
realize EG *People don't realize how serious this recession has been.*
take in EG *She listens to the explanation, but you can see she's not taking it in.*
understand EG *They are too young to understand what is going on.*

③grasp NOUN
a firm hold
EG *She slipped her hand from his grasp.*
clasp EG *He gripped my hand in a strong clasp.*
embrace EG *He held her in a passionate embrace.*
grip EG *His strong hand eased the bag from her grip.*
hold EG *He released his hold on the camera.*

④grasp NOUN
a person's understanding of something
EG *They have a good grasp of foreign languages.*
awareness EG *The children demonstrated their awareness of green issues.*
comprehension FORMAL EG *This was utterly beyond her comprehension.*
grip EG *He has lost his grip on reality.*
knowledge EG *She has a good knowledge of these processes.*
understanding EG *a basic understanding of computers*

grateful ADJECTIVE
pleased and wanting to thank someone
EG *I am grateful to you for your help.*
appreciative EG *We have been very appreciative of their support.*
indebted EG *I am deeply indebted to him for his help.*
thankful EG *I'm just thankful that I've got a job.*

WORD POWER

▶ **Antonym**
ungrateful

---

gratitude NOUN
the feeling of being grateful
EG *I wish to express my gratitude to Kathy Davis for her help.*
appreciation EG *their appreciation of his efforts*
recognition EG *an honour given in recognition of his help to the college*
thanks EG *They accepted their certificates with words of thanks.*

WORD POWER

▶ **Antonym**
ingratitude

---

①grave NOUN
a place where a corpse is buried
EG *They visited her grave twice a year.*
mausoleum EG *the great mausoleum at the top of the hill*
pit EG *The bodies were buried in a shallow pit.*
sepulchre EG *Death holds him in his sepulchre.*
tomb EG *the tomb of the Unknown Soldier*

WORD POWER

● **Related Words**
adjective : sepulchral

---

②grave ADJECTIVE; FORMAL
very serious
EG *The situation in his country is very grave.*

a b c d e f g h i j k l m n o p q r s t u v w x y z

acute EG *The report has caused acute embarrassment to the government.*
critical EG *Its finances are in a critical state.*
heavy EG *Things were just starting to get heavy when the police arrived.*
serious EG *The government faces very serious difficulties.*
sober EG *a room filled with sad, sober faces*
solemn EG *His solemn little face broke into smiles.*
sombre EG *His expression became increasingly sombre.*

1 graze VERB
to slightly injure your skin
EG *He fell heavily and grazed his left arm.*
scrape EG *She stumbled and fell, scraping her palms and knees.*
scratch EG *The branches scratched my hands and face.*
skin EG *He fell and skinned both his knees.*

2 graze NOUN
a slight injury to your skin
EG *He just has a slight graze.*
abrasion FORMAL EG *He had severe abrasions to his right cheek.*
scratch EG *She had scratches to her face.*

1 great ADJECTIVE
very large in size
EG *great columns of ice*
→ see Word Study **great**

WORD POWER

▶ **Antonym**
small

2 great ADJECTIVE
important or famous
EG *the great novels of the nineteenth century*
→ see Word Study **great**

3 great ADJECTIVE; INFORMAL
very good
EG *I thought it was a great idea.*
→ see Word Study **great**

WORD POWER

▶ **Antonym**
terrible

greedy ADJECTIVE
wanting more than you need
EG *greedy bosses who award themselves huge pay rises*
materialistic EG *During the 1980s Britain became a very materialistic society.*
snoep SOUTH AFRICAN; INFORMAL EG *a bunch of snoep businessmen*

WORD POWER

▷ **Synonyms**
acquisitive
avaricious
grasping
voracious

green ADJECTIVE
concerned with environmental issues
EG *Children and adolescents are now aware of green issues.*
conservationist EG *a chorus of protest from conservationist groups*
ecological EG *shared interest in ecological issues*

WORD POWER

▷ **Synonyms**
eco-friendly
environmentally friendly
non-polluting
ozone-friendly

● **Related Words**
adjective : verdant

Shades of green
apple green
avocado
bottle-green
chartreuse
eau de nil
emerald
grass-green
jade
khaki
lime
Lincoln green
olive
pea green
pistachio
sage
sea green
turquoise

greet VERB
to say hello to someone when they arrive
EG *The president was greeted by local political leaders.*
meet EG *A nurse met me at the entrance.*
receive FORMAL EG *250 guests were received by the bride and bridegroom.*
welcome EG *She was there to welcome him home.*

WORD POWER

▷ **Synonyms**
hail
salute

grey NOUN OR ADJECTIVE

Shades of grey
ash
charcoal
gunmetal
hoary
leaden
pewter
platinum
silver
silvery
slate
steel grey
stone
taupe
whitish

grief NOUN
a feeling of extreme sadness
EG *a huge outpouring of national grief*
distress EG *the intense distress they were causing my family*
heartache EG *She has suffered more heartache than anyone deserves.*
misery EG *All that money brought nothing but misery.*
sadness EG *It is with a mixture of sadness and joy that I say farewell.*
sorrow EG *a time of great sorrow*
unhappiness EG *There was a lot of unhappiness in my adolescence.*

WORD POWER

▷ **Synonyms**
anguish
dejection
heartbreak
woe

▶ **Antonym**
happiness

❶ **grieve** VERB
to feel extremely sad
EG *He still grieves for his wife.*
lament EG *All who knew Spender will lament his death.*
mourn EG *The whole nation mourns the death of their great leader.*

❷ **grieve** VERB
to make someone feel extremely sad
EG *It grieved Elaine to be separated from her son.*
distress EG *It distresses me that the President has not tackled crime.*
pain EG *It pains me to think of you struggling all alone.*
sadden EG *The cruelty in the world saddens me.*
upset EG *The news upset me.*

a
b
c
d
e
f
g
h
i
j
k
l
m
n
o
p
q
r
s
t
u
v
w
x
y
z

A
B
C
D
E
F
G
H
I
J
K
L
M
N
O
P
Q
R
S
T
U
V
W
X
Y
Z

WORD POWER

▶ **Antonym**
cheer

grim ADJECTIVE
looking very serious
EG *Her face was grim.*
grave EG *Mrs Williams was looking very grave.*
severe EG *He leaned towards me, a severe expression on his face.*
solemn EG *What a solemn-faced kid he had been.*
stern EG *Michael gave the dog a stern look.*

❶ grip NOUN
a firm hold on something
EG *His strong hand eased the bag from her grip.*
clasp EG *With one last clasp of his hand, she left him.*
grasp EG *The spade slipped from her grasp and fell to the ground.*
hold EG *He released his hold on the camera.*

❷ grip NOUN
someone's control over something
EG *The president maintains an iron grip on his country.*
clutches EG *She fell into the clutches of the wrong sort of person.*
control EG *The port area is under the control of rebel forces.*
influence EG *Alexandra fell under the influence of Grigori Rasputin.*
power EG *I was really in the power of my mother.*

❸ grip VERB
to hold something firmly
EG *Alison gripped the steering wheel and stared straight ahead.*
clutch EG *Michelle clutched my arm.*
grasp EG *He grasped both my hands.*
hold EG *He was struggling to hold on to the rope.*

ground NOUN
the surface of the earth

EG *We slid down the roof and dropped to the ground.*
dirt EG *They sat on the dirt in the shade of a tree.*
earth EG *The road winds for miles through parched earth.*
land EG *800 acres of agricultural land*
soil EG *In Southern India the soil is fertile.*
terrain EG *Farms give way to hilly terrain.*

❶ grounds PLURAL NOUN
the land surrounding a building
EG *the grounds of the university*
estate EG *Lord Wyville's estate in Yorkshire*
gardens EG *an elegant Regency house set in beautiful gardens*
land EG *Their home is on his father's land.*

❷ grounds PLURAL NOUN
the reason for doing or thinking something
EG *Owen was against it on the grounds of expense.*
basis EG *Could you tell me on what basis the fee is calculated?*
cause EG *No one had cause to get angry or unpleasant.*
excuse EG *There's no excuse for behaviour like that.*
justification EG *There was no justification for what I was doing.*
reason EG *Who would have a reason to want to kill her?*

WORD POWER

▷ **Synonyms**
foundation
pretext
rationale

❶ group NOUN
a number of people or things
EG *a group of football supporters*
band EG *a band of rebels*
bunch EG *They're a nice bunch of lads.*
collection EG *a collection of essays*

from foreign affairs experts
crowd EG *A small crowd of onlookers has gathered.*
gang EG *Gangs of teenagers hang out in shop doorways.*
pack EG *a pack of journalists eager to question him*
party EG *a party of sightseers*
set EG *Different sets of people often use the same buildings.*

WORD POWER

▷ **Synonyms**
aggregation
assemblage
coterie

❷ **group** VERB
to link people or things together
EG *Their responses are grouped into 11 categories.*
arrange EG *He started to arrange the books in piles.*
class EG *They are officially classed as visitors.*
classify EG *Rocks can be classified according to their origin.*
organize EG *I was organizing the vast array of junk we had collected.*
sort EG *The students are sorted into three ability groups.*

WORD POWER

▷ **Synonyms**
assort
marshal

❶ **grow** VERB
to increase in size or amount
EG *Bacteria grow more quickly once food is contaminated.*
develop EG *These clashes could develop into open warfare.*
expand EG *Will the universe continue to expand forever?*
increase EG *Industrial output increased by 2%.*

multiply EG *Her husband multiplied his demands on her time.*

WORD POWER

▶ **Antonym**
shrink

❷ **grow** VERB
to be alive or exist
EG *Trees and bushes grew down to the water's edge.*
flourish EG *The plant flourishes in slightly harsher climates.*
germinate EG *Heat will encourage seeds to germinate.*
sprout EG *It only takes a few days for beans to sprout.*

WORD POWER

▷ **Synonyms**
shoot
spring up

❸ **grow** VERB
to change gradually
EG *I grew a little afraid of the guy next door.*
become EG *The wind became stronger.*
get EG *The boys were getting bored.*
turn EG *In October it turned cold.*

growth NOUN
the act of getting bigger
EG *the growth of the fishing industry*
development EG *What are your plans for the development of your company?*
enlargement EG *the enlargement of the European Union*
expansion EG *a new period of economic expansion*
increase EG *a sharp increase in the number of homeless people*

❶ **grumble** VERB
to complain in a bad-tempered way
EG *"This is very inconvenient," he grumbled.*
carp EG *the man whom other actors*

a
b
c
d
e
f
g
h
i
j
k
l
m
n
o
p
q
r
s
t
u
v
w
x
y
z

A B C D E F G H I J K L M N O P Q R S T U V W X Y Z

love to carp about
complain EG *They complained about the high cost of visiting Europe.*
groan EG *parents groaning about the price of college tuition*
moan EG *Sometimes it helps to have a good old moan.*
mutter EG *She could hear the old woman muttering about young people.*
whine EG *children who whine that they are bored*
whinge EG *All she ever does is whinge.*

② grumble NOUN
a bad-tempered complaint
EG *I didn't hear any grumbles from anyone at the time.*
complaint EG *I get nothing but complaints about my cooking.*
moan EG *Sometimes it helps to have a good old moan.*
murmur EG *She paid without a murmur.*
objection EG *If you have any objections, please raise them now.*
protest EG *Despite our protests, they went ahead with the plan.*
whinge EG *It's depressing listening to everybody's whinges.*

grumpy ADJECTIVE
bad-tempered and annoyed
EG *a grumpy old man*
irritable EG *He had missed his dinner and grew irritable.*
sulky EG *She still looked like a sulky teenager.*
sullen EG *Several leading players have maintained a sullen silence.*
surly EG *They were surly, sometimes downright rude to me.*

WORD POWER
▷ **Synonyms**
bad-tempered
cantankerous
ill-tempered

① guarantee NOUN
something that makes another thing

certain
EG *The package offered a guarantee of job security.*
assurance EG *a written assurance that he would start work at once*
pledge EG *a pledge of support from the Ministry of Culture*
promise EG *I'd made him a promise that I'd write a book for him.*
undertaking EG *She gave an undertaking not to repeat the allegations.*
word EG *He simply cannot be trusted to keep his word.*

② guarantee VERB
to make it certain that something will happen
EG *Reports of this kind are guaranteed to cause anxiety.*
ensure EG *We need to ensure that every student has basic literacy skills.*
pledge EG *Both sides pledged that a nuclear war would never be fought.*
promise EG *He promised that the rich would not get preferential treatment.*

① guard VERB
to protect someone
EG *Police were guarding his home yesterday.*
defend EG *He and his friends defended themselves against racist thugs.*
protect EG *What can women do to protect themselves from heart disease?*
safeguard EG *measures to safeguard their forces from chemical weapons*
shelter EG *A neighbour sheltered the boy for seven days.*
shield EG *She had shielded him from the terrible truth.*
watch over EG *two policewomen to watch over him*

② guard VERB
to stop someone making trouble or escaping
EG *The soldiers had been guarding*

paramilitary prisoners.
patrol EG *Prison officers continued to patrol the grounds.*
police EG *It is extremely difficult to police the border.*
supervise EG *Only two staff were supervising over 100 prisoners.*

❸ guard NOUN
someone who guards people or places
EG *The prisoners overpowered their guards and locked them in a cell.*
sentry EG *We can sneak past the sentries.*
warden EG *The siege began when the prisoners seized three wardens.*

WORD POWER

▷ **Synonyms**
sentinel
warder
watchman

❶ guess VERB
to form an idea or opinion about something
EG *Wood guessed that he was a very successful banker.*
estimate EG *It's difficult to estimate how much money is involved.*
imagine EG `Was he meeting someone?' `I imagine so.'*
reckon EG *Toni reckoned that it must be about three o'clock.*
speculate EG *The reader can speculate what will happen next.*
suppose EG *I supposed you would have a meal somewhere.*
suspect EG *I suspect they were right.*
think EG *Nora thought he was seventeen years old.*

WORD POWER

▷ **Synonyms**
conjecture
hazard
surmise

❷ guess NOUN
an attempt to give the right answer
EG *My guess is that the answer will be negative.*
feeling EG *My feeling is that everything will come right for us.*
reckoning EG *By my reckoning, 50% of the team will be available.*
speculation EG *speculations about the future of the universe*

WORD POWER

▷ **Synonyms**
conjecture
hypothesis

❶ guide VERB
to lead someone somewhere
EG *He took Elliott by the arm and guided him out.*
accompany EG *We accompanied Joe to the magazine's midtown offices.*
direct EG *Officials directed him to the wrong airport.*
escort EG *I escorted him to the door.*
lead EG *The nurse led me to a large room.*

WORD POWER

▷ **Synonyms**
conduct
convoy
shepherd
usher

❷ guide VERB
to influence someone
EG *He should have let his instinct guide him.*
counsel FORMAL EG *Green was counselled not to talk to reporters.*
govern EG *Our thinking is as much governed by habit as by behaviour.*
influence EG *My dad influenced me to do electronics.*

❶ guilty ADJECTIVE
having done something wrong
EG *They were found guilty of murder.*
convicted EG *a convicted drug dealer*

a
b
c
d
e
f
g
h
i
j
k
l
m
n
o
p
q
r
s
t
u
v
w
x
y
z

criminal EG *He had a criminal record for petty theft.*

WORD POWER

▷ **Synonyms**
blameworthy
culpable
felonious

▶ **Antonym**
innocent

2 guilty ADJECTIVE
unhappy because you have done something bad
EG *When she saw me she looked guilty.*
ashamed EG *Zumel said he was not ashamed of what he had done.*
regretful EG *Surprisingly, she didn't feel regretful about her actions.*
remorseful FORMAL EG *He felt remorseful for what he had done.*
sorry EG *She was very sorry about all the trouble she'd caused.*

WORD POWER

▷ **Synonyms**
conscience-stricken
contrite
shamefaced

gullible ADJECTIVE
easily tricked

EG *I'm so gullible I would have believed him.*
naive EG *It would be naive to believe Mr Gonzalez's statement.*
trusting EG *She has an open, trusting nature.*

WORD POWER

▷ **Synonyms**
credulous
unsuspecting

▶ **Antonym**
suspicious

gush VERB
to flow in large quantities
EG *Piping-hot water gushed out.*
flow EG *Tears flowed down his cheeks.*
pour EG *Blood was pouring from his broken nose.*
spurt EG *a fountain that spurts water nine stories high*
stream EG *water streaming from the pipes*

WORD POWER

▷ **Synonyms**
cascade
issue
jet

Hh

❶ habit NOUN
something that is done regularly
EG *his habit of smiling at everyone he saw*
convention EG *It's just a social convention that men don't wear skirts.*
custom EG *an ancient Japanese custom*
practice EG *the practice of clocking in at work*
routine EG *my daily routine*
tradition EG *a family tradition at Christmas*

❷ habit NOUN
an addiction to something
EG *her cocaine habit*
addiction EG *his addiction to gambling*
dependence EG *the effects of drug dependence*

habitat NOUN
the natural home of a plant or animal
EG *the habitat of the spotted owl*
environment EG *a safe environment for marine mammals*
territory EG *a bird's territory*

hackneyed ADJECTIVE
used too often to be meaningful
EG *hackneyed postcard snaps of lochs and glens*
banal EG *banal lyrics*
clichéd EG *clichéd slogans*
stale EG *Her relationship with Mark has become stale.*
tired EG *a tired excuse*
trite EG *The film is teeming with trite ideas.*

WORD POWER

▷ **Synonyms**
run-of-the-mill
threadbare
timeworn

▶ **Antonym**
original

❶ hail NOUN
a lot of things falling together
EG *a hail of bullets*
barrage EG *a barrage of angry questions*
bombardment EG *the sound of heavy aerial bombardment*
shower EG *a shower of rose petals*
storm EG *The announcement provoked a storm of protest.*
volley EG *A volley of shots rang out.*

❷ hail VERB
to attract someone's attention
EG *He hailed me from across the street.*
call EG *He called me over the Tannoy.*
signal to EG *The lollipop lady signalled to me to stop.*
wave down EG *I ran on to the road and waved down a taxi.*

❶ halt VERB
to come or bring to a stop
EG *She held her hand out to halt him.*
draw up EG *The car drew up outside the house.*
pull up EG *The cab pulled up, and the driver jumped out.*
stop EG *The event literally stopped the traffic.*

❷ halt VERB
to bring something to an end
EG *Production was halted.*
cease EG *A small number of firms have ceased trading.*
check EG *We have managed to check the spread of terrorism.*
curb EG *efforts to curb the spread of nuclear weapons*
cut short EG *They had to cut short a holiday abroad.*
end EG *They decided to end the ceasefire.*
terminate EG *His contract has been terminated.*

A
B
C
D
E
F
G
H
I
J
K
L
M
N
O
P
Q
R
S
T
U
V
W
X
Y
Z

WORD POWER

▶ **Antonym**
begin

❸ **halt** NOUN
an interruption or end to something
EG *He brought the car to a halt.*
close EG *Their 18-month marriage was brought to a close.*
end EG *The war came to an end.*
pause EG *There was a pause before he replied.*
standstill EG *The country was brought to a standstill by strikes.*
stop EG *He slowed the car almost to a stop.*
stoppage EG *Air and ground crew are staging a 24-hour stoppage today.*

WORD POWER

▷ **Synonyms**
impasse
termination

hamper VERB
to make movement or progress difficult for someone
EG *I was hampered by a lack of information.*
frustrate EG *His attempt was frustrated by the weather.*
hinder EG *A thigh injury hindered her mobility.*
impede EG *Their work was being impeded by shortages of supplies.*
obstruct EG *charged with obstructing the course of justice*
restrict EG *Her life is restricted by asthma.*

WORD POWER

▷ **Synonyms**
encumber
fetter

hand down VERB
to pass from one generation to another
EG *Recipes are handed down from*
mother to daughter.
bequeath EG *He bequeathed all his silver to his children.*
give EG *a typewriter given to me by my father*
pass down EG *an heirloom passed down from generation to generation*
pass on EG *My parents passed on their love of classical music to me.*

WORD POWER

▷ **Synonyms**
bestow
will

❶ **handicap** NOUN
a physical or mental disability
EG *He learnt to overcome his handicap.*
defect EG *a rare birth defect*
disability EG *children with learning disabilities*

❷ **handicap** NOUN
something that makes progress difficult
EG *Being a foreigner was not a handicap.*
barrier EG *Taxes are the most obvious barrier to free trade.*
disadvantage EG *the disadvantage of unemployment*
drawback EG *The flat's only drawback was that it was too small.*
hindrance EG *She was a help rather than a hindrance to my work.*
impediment EG *an impediment to economic development*
obstacle EG *the main obstacle to the deal*

❸ **handicap** VERB
to make something difficult for someone
EG *Greater levels of stress may seriously handicap some students.*
burden EG *We decided not to burden him with the news.*
hamper EG *I was hampered by a lack of information.*

handle >> handy

a b c d e f g h i j k l m n o p q r s t u v w x y z

hinder EG *A thigh injury hindered her mobility.*
impede EG *Fallen rocks impeded the progress of the rescue workers.*
restrict EG *laws to restrict foreign imports*

1 handle NOUN
the part of an object by which it is held
EG *a broom handle*
grip EG *He fitted new grips to his golf clubs.*
hilt EG *the hilt of the small, sharp knife*

2 handle VERB
to hold or move with the hands
EG *Wear rubber gloves when handling cat litter.*
feel EG *The doctor felt his arm.*
finger EG *He fingered the few coins in his pocket.*
grasp EG *Grasp the end firmly.*
hold EG *Hold it by the edge.*
touch EG *She touched his hand reassuringly.*

3 handle VERB
to deal or control with something
EG *She handled the travel arrangements.*
administer EG *The project is administered by the World Bank.*
conduct EG *This is no way to conduct a business.*
deal with EG *The matter has been dealt with by the school.*
manage EG *Within two years he was managing the store.*
supervise EG *I supervise the packing of all mail orders.*
take care of EG *He took care of the catering arrangements.*

1 handsome ADJECTIVE
very attractive in appearance
EG *a handsome man*
attractive EG *an attractive young woman*

good-looking EG *good-looking actors*

WORD POWER
▶ **Antonym**
ugly

2 handsome ADJECTIVE
large and generous
EG *a handsome profit*
ample EG *ample space for a good-sized kitchen*
considerable EG *his considerable wealth*
generous EG *a generous gift*
liberal EG *a liberal donation*
plentiful EG *a plentiful supply of vegetables*
sizable or **sizeable** EG *He inherited the house and a sizeable chunk of land.*

WORD POWER
▶ **Antonym**
small

1 handy ADJECTIVE
conveniently near
EG *Keep a pencil and paper handy.*
at hand EG *Having the right equipment at hand will be enormously useful.*
at your fingertips EG *Firms need information at their fingertips.*
close EG *a secluded area close to her home*
convenient EG *Martin drove along until he found a convenient parking space.*
nearby EG *He tossed the match into a nearby wastepaper bin.*
on hand EG *Experts are on hand to offer advice.*

2 handy ADJECTIVE
easy to handle or use
EG *handy hints on looking after indoor plants*
convenient EG *a convenient way of paying*

A
B
C
D
E
F
G
H
I
J
K
L
M
N
O
P
Q
R
S
T
U
V
W
X
Y
Z

easy to use EG *This ice cream maker is cheap and easy to use.*
helpful EG *helpful instructions*
neat EG *It had been such a neat, clever plan.*
practical EG *the most practical way of preventing crime*
useful EG *useful information*

❶ hang VERB
to be attached at the top with the lower part free
EG *His jacket hung from a hook behind the door.*
dangle EG *A gold bracelet dangled from his left wrist.*
droop EG *Pale wilting roses drooped from a vase.*

❷ hang VERB
to fasten something to another thing by its top
EG *She came out of the house to hang clothes on the line.*
attach EG *He attached the picture to the wall with a nail.*
drape EG *He draped the coat round his shoulders.*
fasten EG *stirrups fastened to the saddle*
fix EG *He fixed a pirate flag to the mast.*
suspend EG *The TV is suspended from the ceiling on brackets.*

happen VERB
to take place
EG *The accident happened on Wednesday.*
come about EG *It came about almost by accident.*
follow EG *He was arrested in the confusion which followed.*
occur EG *The crash occurred on a sharp bend.*
result EG *Ignore the early warnings and illness could result.*
take place EG *The festival took place last September.*

WORD POWER

▷ **Synonyms**
ensue
materialize

---

happiness NOUN
a feeling of great pleasure
EG *Money can't buy happiness.*
delight EG *To my delight, it worked perfectly.*
ecstasy EG *a state of almost religious ecstasy*
elation EG *His supporters reacted to the news with elation.*
joy EG *tears of joy*
pleasure EG *Everybody takes pleasure in eating.*
satisfaction EG *job satisfaction*

WORD POWER

▷ **Synonyms**
exuberance
felicity
merriment

▶ **Antonym**
sadness

---

❶ happy ADJECTIVE
feeling or causing joy
EG *a happy atmosphere*
→ see Word Study **happy**

WORD POWER

▶ **Antonym**
sad

---

❷ happy ADJECTIVE
fortunate or lucky
EG *a happy coincidence*
→ see Word Study **happy**

WORD POWER

▶ **Antonym**
unlucky

---

❶ hard ADJECTIVE
firm, solid, or rigid
EG *a hard piece of cheese*

firm EG *a firm mattress*
rigid EG *rigid plastic containers*
solid EG *solid rock*
stiff EG *stiff metal wires*
strong EG *It has a strong casing which won't crack or chip.*
tough EG *dark brown beans with a rather tough outer skin*

WORD POWER

▶ **Antonym**
soft

❷ **hard** ADJECTIVE
requiring a lot of effort
EG *hard work*
arduous EG *a long, arduous journey*
exhausting EG *It's a pretty exhausting job.*
laborious EG *Keeping the garden tidy can be a laborious task.*
rigorous EG *rigorous military training*
strenuous EG *Avoid strenuous exercise in the evening.*
tough EG *Change is often tough to deal with.*

WORD POWER

▶ **Antonym**
easy

❸ **hard** ADJECTIVE
difficult to understand
EG *That's a very hard question.*
baffling EG *a baffling remark*
complex EG *a complex problem*
complicated EG *a complicated system of voting*
difficult EG *It was a very difficult decision to make.*
puzzling EG *Some of this book is rather puzzling.*

WORD POWER

▶ **Antonym**
simple

harden VERB
to make or become stiff or firm
EG *Give the cardboard two coats of varnish to harden it.*
bake EG *The soil had been baked solid by the heatwave.*
cake EG *The blood had begun to cake and turn brown.*
freeze EG *The lake freezes in winter.*
set EG *Lower the heat and allow the omelette to set.*
stiffen EG *paper that had been stiffened with paste*

WORD POWER

▷ **Synonyms**
anneal
solidify

▶ **Antonym**
soften

hardly ADVERB
almost not or not quite
EG *I could hardly believe what I was seeing.*
barely EG *His voice was barely audible.*
just EG *Her hand was just visible under her coat.*
only just EG *For centuries farmers there have only just managed to survive.*
scarcely EG *He could scarcely breathe.*

hardship NOUN
difficult circumstances
EG *Many people are suffering economic hardship.*
adversity EG *They manage to enjoy life despite adversity.*
destitution EG *a life of poverty and destitution*
difficulty EG *Many new golf clubs are in serious financial difficulty.*
misfortune EG *She seemed to enjoy the misfortunes of others.*
want EG *They were fighting for*

a
b
c
d
e
f
g
h
i
j
k
l
m
n
o
p
q
r
s
t
u
v
w
x
y
z

freedom of speech and freedom from
want.

WORD POWER

▷ **Synonyms**
privation
tribulation

❶ harm VERB
to injure someone or damage
something
EG *The hijackers seemed anxious not
to harm anyone.*
abuse EG *Animals are still being
exploited and abused.*
damage EG *He damaged his knee
during training.*
hurt EG *He fell and hurt his back.*
ill-treat EG *They thought he had been
ill-treating is wife.*
ruin EG *My wife was ruining her
health through worry.*
wound EG *The bomb killed six people
and wounded another five.*

❷ harm NOUN
injury or damage
EG *All dogs are capable of doing harm
to human beings.*
abuse EG *The abuse of animals is
inexcusable.*
damage EG *The bomb caused
extensive damage.*
hurt EG *an evil desire to cause hurt
and damage*
injury EG *The two other passengers
escaped serious injury.*

harmful ADJECTIVE
having a bad effect on something
EG *Whilst most stress is harmful, some
is beneficial.*
damaging EG *damaging allegations
about his personal life*
destructive EG *the awesome
destructive power of nuclear weapons*
detrimental EG *levels of
radioactivity which are detrimental to
public health*
hurtful EG *Her comments can only be*

hurtful to the family.
pernicious EG *The pernicious
influence of secret societies.*

WORD POWER

▷ **Synonyms**
baleful
baneful
deleterious
injurious

▶ **Antonym**
harmless

harmless ADJECTIVE
safe to use or be near
EG *This experiment was harmless to
the animals.*
innocuous EG *Both mushrooms look
innocuous but are in fact deadly.*
nontoxic EG *a cheap and nontoxic
method of cleaning up our water*
not dangerous EG *The tests are not
dangerous to the environment.*
safe EG *The doll is safe for children.*

WORD POWER

▶ **Antonym**
harmful

harsh ADJECTIVE
severe, difficult, and unpleasant
EG *harsh weather conditions*
austere EG *The life of the troops was
still comparatively austere.*
cruel EG *an unusually cruel winter*
hard EG *He had a hard life.*
ruthless EG *the ruthless treatment of
staff*
severe EG *My boss gave me a severe
reprimand.*
stern EG *a stern warning*

WORD POWER

▷ **Synonyms**
Draconian
Spartan

▶ **Antonym**
mild

❶ hassle NOUN; INFORMAL
something that is difficult or causes
trouble
EG *It's not worth the hassle.*
bother EG *I buy sliced bread - it's less
bother.*
effort EG *This chore is well worth the
effort.*
inconvenience EG *the expense and
inconvenience of having central
heating installed*
trouble EG *You've caused us a lot of
trouble.*
upheaval EG *Moving house is always
a big upheaval.*

❷ hassle VERB; INFORMAL
to annoy someone by nagging or
making demands
EG *My husband started hassling me.*
badger EG *They kept badgering me to
go back.*
bother EG *Go away and don't bother
me about all that just now.*
go on at EG *She's always going on at
me to have a baby.*
harass EG *We are routinely harassed
by the police.*
nag EG *She had stopped nagging him
about his drinking.*
pester EG *the creep who's been
pestering you to go out with him*

hasty ADJECTIVE
done or happening suddenly and
quickly
EG *The signs of their hasty departure
could be seen everywhere.*
brisk EG *a brisk walk*
hurried EG *a hurried breakfast*
prompt EG *It is not too late, but
prompt action is needed.*
rapid EG *a rapid retreat*
swift EG *my swift departure*

❶ hate VERB
to have a strong dislike for
something or someone
EG *Most people hate him, but they
don't care to say so.*

abhor EG *He abhorred violence.*
be sick of EG *We're sick of being
ripped off.*
despise EG *A lot of people despise
and loathe what I do.*
detest EG *Jean detested being
photographed.*
dislike EG *those who dislike change*
loathe EG *a play universally loathed
by the critics*

WORD POWER

▶ **Antonym**
love

❷ hate NOUN
a strong dislike
EG *a violent bully, destructive and full
of hate*
animosity EG *The animosity between
the two men grew.*
aversion EG *I've always had an
aversion to being part of a group.*
dislike EG *Consider what your likes
and dislikes are about your job.*
hatred EG *her hatred of authority*
hostility EG *He looked at her with
open hostility.*
loathing EG *Critics are united in their
unmitigated loathing of the band.*

WORD POWER

▷ **Synonyms**
animus
detestation
enmity
odium

▶ **Antonym**
love

hateful ADJECTIVE
extremely unpleasant
EG *It was a hateful thing to say.*
abhorrent EG *Discrimination is
abhorrent to my council and our staff.*
despicable EG *a despicable crime*
horrible EG *a horrible little boy*
loathsome EG *the loathsome*

A B C D E F G H I J K L M N O P Q R S T U V W X Y Z

spectacle we were obliged to witness

obnoxious EG *He was a most obnoxious character. No-one liked him.*

offensive EG *an offensive remark*

hatred NOUN

an extremely strong feeling of dislike
EG *He has been accused of inciting racial hatred.*

animosity EG *The animosity between the two men grew.*

antipathy EG *public antipathy towards scientists*

aversion EG *my aversion to housework*

dislike EG *his dislike of modern buildings*

hate EG *These people are so full of hate.*

revulsion EG *They expressed their revulsion at his violent death.*

WORD POWER

▶ **Antonym**
love

haughty ADJECTIVE

showing excessive pride
EG *He spoke in a haughty tone.*

arrogant EG *an air of arrogant indifference*

conceited EG *They had grown too conceited and pleased with themselves.*

disdainful EG *She cast a disdainful glance at me.*

proud EG *She was said to be proud and arrogant.*

snobbish EG *They had a snobbish dislike for their intellectual inferiors.*

stuck-up INFORMAL EG *She was a famous actress, but she wasn't a bit stuck-up.*

WORD POWER

▶ **Antonym**
humble

❶ have VERB

to own something
EG *We have two tickets for the concert.*

hold EG *He does not hold a firearm certificate.*

keep EG *We keep chickens.*

own EG *His father owns a local pub.*

possess EG *He is said to possess a fortune.*

❷ have VERB

to experience something
EG *He had a marvellous time.*

endure EG *The company endured heavy losses.*

enjoy EG *The average German will enjoy 40 days' paid holiday this year.*

experience EG *Widows seem to experience more distress than do widowers.*

feel EG *I felt a sharp pain in my shoulder.*

sustain EG *He had sustained a cut on his left eyebrow.*

undergo EG *He recently underwent brain surgery.*

❶ head NOUN

a person's mind and mental abilities
EG *I don't have a head for business.*

aptitude EG *an aptitude for accountancy*

brain EG *If you stop using your brain you'll go stale.*

common sense EG *Use your common sense.*

intelligence EG *Try to use your intelligence to solve the puzzle - don't just guess.*

mind EG *I'm trying to clear my mind of all this.*

wits EG *She has used her wits to get where she is today.*

WORD POWER

▷ **Synonyms**
intellect
rationality

❷ head NOUN
the top, front, or start of something
EG *the head of the queue*
beginning EG *the beginning of this chapter*
front EG *Stand at the front of the line.*
source EG *the source of this great river*
start EG *Go back to the start of this section.*
top EG *the top of the stairs*

> *WORD POWER*
> ► **Antonym**
> tail

❸ head NOUN
the person in charge of something
EG *heads of government*
boss EG *the boss of the new company*
chief EG *the President's chief of security*
director EG *the director of the intensive care unit*
leader EG *the leader of the Conservative Party*
manager EG *the manager of our division*
president EG *the president of the medical commission*
principal EG *the principal of the school*

❹ head VERB
to be in charge of something
EG *He heads the department.*
be in charge of EG *She's in charge of the overseas division.*
control EG *He controls the largest fast food empire in the world.*
direct EG *Christopher will direct day-to-day operations.*
lead EG *leading a campaign to save the rainforest*
manage EG *Within two years he was managing the store.*
run EG *Each teacher will run a different workshop.*

❶ health NOUN
the condition of your body
EG *Smoking is bad for your health.*
condition EG *He remains in a critical condition in hospital.*
constitution EG *He must have an extremely strong constitution.*
shape EG *He was still in better shape than many younger men.*

❷ health NOUN
a state in which a person is feeling well.
EG *In hospital they nursed me back to health.*
fitness EG *He has fitness problems.*
good condition EG *He is in great condition for a man of 56.*
wellbeing EG *Singing can create a sense of wellbeing.*

> *WORD POWER*
> ► **Antonym**
> illness

❶ healthy ADJECTIVE
having good health
EG *She was a very healthy child.*
active EG *an active lifestyle*
fit EG *A short, physically fit man of 61.*
in good shape INFORMAL EG *I kept myself in good shape by swimming.*
robust EG *a robust and vibrant young man*
strong EG *a strong constitution*
well EG *I'm not very well today.*

> *WORD POWER*
> ► **Antonym**
> ill

❷ healthy ADJECTIVE
producing good health
EG *a healthy diet*
beneficial EG *Wine in moderation is beneficial to health.*
bracing EG *a bracing walk*
good for you EG *Regular, moderate exercise is good for you.*
nourishing EG *sensible, nourishing*

a b c d e f g h i j k l m n o p q r s t u v w x y z

food
nutritious EG *a hot, nutritious meal*
wholesome EG *fresh, wholesome ingredients*

WORD POWER

▷ **Synonyms**
invigorating
salubrious
salutary

▶ **Antonym**
unhealthy

❶ heap NOUN
a pile of things
EG *a heap of rubble*
hoard EG *a hoard of silver and jewels*
mass EG *a mass of flowers*
mound EG *The bulldozers piled up huge mounds of dirt.*
pile EG *a pile of betting slips*
stack EG *stacks of books on the bedside table*

❷ heap VERB
to pile things up
EG *She heaped vegetables onto his plate.*
pile EG *He was piling clothes into the suitcase.*
stack EG *They stacked up pillows behind his back.*

heaps PLURAL NOUN; INFORMAL
plenty of something
EG *heaps of cash*
loads INFORMAL EG *I've got loads of money.*
lots INFORMAL EG *lots of fun*
plenty EG *We've got plenty of time for a drink.*
stacks EG *stacks of magazines*
tons INFORMAL EG *I've got tons of work to do.*

❶ hear VERB
to listen to something
EG *I heard the sound of gunfire.*
catch EG *I don't believe I caught your name.*

eavesdrop EG *The government illegally eavesdropped on his phone conversations.*
heed EG *Few at the conference heeded his warning.*
listen in EG *Secret agents listened in on his phone calls.*
listen to EG *He spent his time listening to the radio.*
overhear EG *I overheard two doctors discussing my case.*

❷ hear VERB
to learn about something
EG *I heard that he was forced to resign.*
ascertain EG *They had ascertained that he was not a spy.*
discover EG *She discovered that they'd escaped.*
find out EG *As soon as we found this out, we closed the ward.*
gather EG *I gather the report is critical of the judge.*
learn EG *She wasn't surprised to learn that he was involved.*
understand EG *I understand that she's just taken early retirement.*

❶ heat NOUN
the quality of being warm or hot
EG *the heat of the sun*
high temperature EG *The suffering caused by the high temperature has been great.*
warmth EG *the warmth of the sand between her toes*

WORD POWER

▶ **Antonym**
cold

● **Related Words**
adjective : thermal

❷ heat NOUN
a state of strong emotion
EG *in the heat of the election campaign*
excitement EG *in a state of great excitement*
fervour EG *religious fervour*

intensity EG *the intensity of feeling about this issue*
passion EG *He spoke with great passion.*
vehemence EG *I was surprised by the vehemence of his criticism.*

❸ heat VERB
to raise the temperature of something
EG *Heat the oil in a frying pan.*
reheat EG *Reheat the soup to a gentle simmer.*
warm up EG *Just before serving, warm up the tomato sauce.*

WORD POWER
▶ Antonym
cool

heathen NOUN; OLD-FASHIONED
someone who does not believe in an established religion
EG *She called us all heathens and hypocrites.*
pagan EG *the sky-god of the ancient pagans*
unbeliever EG *punishing unbelievers and traitors*

WORD POWER
▷ Synonyms
idolater
infidel

▶ Antonym
believer

❶ heaven NOUN
the place where good people are believed to go when they die
EG *She told them their mother was now in heaven.*
next world EG *He said, "We will see each other again in the next world."*
paradise EG *They believed they would go to paradise if they died in battle.*

WORD POWER
▷ Synonyms
Elysium
happy hunting ground
nirvana
Valhalla
Zion

▶ Antonym
hell

❷ heaven NOUN
a place or situation liked very much
EG *I was in cinematic heaven.*
bliss EG *a scene of domestic bliss*
ecstasy EG *the ecstasy of being in love*
paradise EG *The Algarve is a golfer's paradise.*
rapture EG *the sheer rapture of listening to Bach's music*

❶ heavy ADJECTIVE
great in weight or force
EG *a heavy frying pan*
bulky EG *a bulky grey sweater*
massive EG *a massive blue whale*

WORD POWER
▶ Antonym
light

❷ heavy ADJECTIVE
serious or important
EG *a heavy speech*
deep EG *a period of deep personal crisis*
grave EG *the grave crisis facing the country*
profound EG *Anna's patriotism was profound.*
serious EG *It was a question which deserved serious consideration.*
solemn EG *a simple, solemn ceremony*
weighty EG *Surely such weighty matters merit a higher level of debate.*

a b c d e f g h i j k l m n o p q r s t u v w x y z

A
B
C
D
E
F
G
H
I
J
K
L
M
N
O
P
Q
R
S
T
U
V
W
X
Y
Z

❶ heed VERB
to pay attention to someone's advice
EG *Few at the conference heeded his warning.*
follow EG *If you are not going to follow my advice, we are both wasting our time.*
listen to EG *They won't listen to my advice.*
pay attention to EG *The food industry is now paying attention to young consumers.*
take notice of EG *We want the government to take notice of what we think.*

❷ heed NOUN
careful attention
EG *He pays too much heed to her.*
attention EG *He never paid much attention to his audience.*
notice EG *So do they take any notice of public opinion?*

❶ hell NOUN
the place where souls of evil people are believed to go after death
EG *Milton's Satan would rather "reign in Hell, than serve in Heaven".*
abyss EG *Satan rules over the dark abyss.*
inferno EG *an inferno described in loving detail by Dante*

❷ hell NOUN; INFORMAL
an unpleasant situation or place
EG *Bullies can make your life hell.*
agony EG *the agony of divorce*
anguish EG *the anguish of families unable to trace relatives who've disappeared*
misery EG *All that money brought nothing but sadness and misery.*
nightmare EG *The years in prison were a nightmare.*
ordeal EG *the painful ordeal of the last year*

hello INTERJECTION
a greeting
EG *I popped my head in to say hello.*
gidday AUSTRALIAN AND NEW ZEALAND
eg *Gidday, mate! How you doing?*
hi INFORMAL EG *She smiled and said, "Hi".*
how do you do? FORMAL EG *"How do you do, Mrs Brown?" Sam said, holding out his hand.*
good morning FORMAL EG *Good morning, everyone.*
good afternoon FORMAL EG *Good afternoon. Won't you sit down?*
good evening FORMAL EG *Good evening, and welcome!*

❶ help VERB
to make something easier or better for someone
EG *He began to help with the chores.*
aid EG *a software system to aid managers*
assist EG *information to assist you*
lend a hand EG *I'd be glad to lend a hand.*
support EG *He thanked everyone who had supported the strike.*

❷ help NOUN
assistance or support
EG *The books were not much help.*

advice EG *He has given me lots of good advice in my time here.*
aid EG *millions of dollars of aid*
assistance EG *I would be grateful for any assistance.*
guidance EG *the reports which were produced under his guidance*
helping hand EG *Most mums would be grateful for a helping hand.*
support EG *Only 60 clubs pledged their support for the scheme.*

helper NOUN
a person who gives assistance
EG *There is an adult helper for every two children.*
aide EG *a presidential aide*
assistant EG *a research assistant*
deputy EG *I can't make it so I'll send my deputy.*
henchman EG *Adolf Eichmann, Hitler's notorious henchman*
right-hand man EG *He was the perfect right-hand man for the president.*
supporter EG *He is a strong supporter of the plan.*

❶ **helpful** ADJECTIVE
giving assistance or advice
EG *The staff in the office are very helpful.*
accommodating EG *Lindi seemed a nice, accomodating girl.*
cooperative EG *I made every effort to be cooperative.*
kind EG *I must thank you for being so kind to me.*
supportive EG *Her boss was very supportive.*

WORD POWER
▶ **Antonym**
unhelpful

❷ **helpful** ADJECTIVE
making a situation better
EG *Having the right equipment will be enormously helpful.*
advantageous EG *an advantageous arrangement*
beneficial EG *beneficial changes in the tax system*
constructive EG *constructive criticism*
profitable EG *a profitable exchange of ideas*
useful EG *useful information*

helpless ADJECTIVE
weak or unable to cope
EG *a helpless baby*
defenceless EG *a savage attack on a defenceless girl*
powerless EG *He was powerless to help.*
unprotected EG *She felt unprotected and defenseless.*
vulnerable EG *the most vulnerable members of society*
weak EG *taking ruthless advantage of a weak old man*

hesitant ADJECTIVE
uncertain about something
EG *At first he was hesitant to accept the role.*
diffident EG *John was as outgoing as Helen was diffident.*
doubtful EG *I was very doubtful about the chances for success.*
reluctant EG *She was reluctant to get involved.*
unsure EG *He made her feel awkward and unsure of herself.*
wavering EG *wavering voters*

WORD POWER
▷ **Synonyms**
irresolute
vacillating

hesitate VERB
to pause or show uncertainty
EG *She hesitated before replying.*
dither EG *We're still dithering over whether to marry.*
pause EG *The crowd paused for a minute, wondering what to do next.*

a b c d e f g h i j k l m n o p q r s t u v w x y z

A
B
C
D
E
F
G
H
I
J
K
L
M
N
O
P
Q
R
S
T
U
V
W
X
Y
Z

waver EG *Louise never wavered in her determination to take up the post.*

❶ **hide** VERB
to put something where it cannot be seen
EG *She hid her face in her hands.*
cache EG *He has £289 million cached away.*
conceal EG *The hat concealed her hair.*
secrete EG *She secreted the gun in the kitchen cabinet.*
stash INFORMAL EG *He had stashed money away in a secret offshore account.*

❷ **hide** NOUN
the skin of a large animal
EG *the process of tanning hides*
pelt EG *a bed covered with beaver pelts*
skin EG *a leopard skin coat*

❶ **high** ADJECTIVE
tall or a long way above the ground
EG *a high tower*
→ see Word Study **high**

WORD POWER
▶ **Antonym**
low

❷ **high** ADJECTIVE
great in degree, quantity, or intensity
EG *There is a high risk of heart disease.*
→ see Word Study **high**

WORD POWER
▶ **Antonym**
low

hill NOUN

Types of hill
brae (*Scottish*)
down
dune
elevation
fell

foothill
height
hillock
hummock
knoll
kopje (*South African*)
mound
prominence
tor

hinder VERB
to get in the way of someone or something
EG *A thigh injury hindered her mobility.*
block EG *The President is blocking the release of the two men.*
check EG *We have managed to check the spread of terrorism.*
delay EG *Various problems have delayed producton.*
frustrate EG *They have frustrated his efforts to gain a work permit.*
hamper EG *I was hampered by a lack of information.*
impede EG *Fallen rocks are impeding the progress of rescue workers.*

WORD POWER
▷ **Synonyms**
encumber
stymie

❶ **hint** NOUN
an indirect suggestion
EG *He gave a strong hint that there would be a referendum sooner rather than later.*
clue EG *How a man shaves may be a telling clue to his age.*
indication EG *He gave no indication that he was ready to compromise.*
intimation EG *I did not have any intimation that he was going to resign.*
suggestion EG *We reject any suggestion that the law needs amending.*

❷ **hint** NOUN
a helpful piece of advice

EG *I hope to get some fashion hints.*
advice EG *Don't be afraid to ask for advice.*
pointer EG *Here are a few pointers to help you make your choice.*
suggestion EG *Can I give you a few suggestions?*
tip EG *tips for busy managers*

❸ hint VERB
to suggest something indirectly
EG *Criticism is hinted at but never made explicit.*
imply EG *The report implied that his death was inevitable.*
indicate EG *She has indicated that she may resign.*
insinuate EG *an article which insinuated that he was lying*
intimate EG *He intimated that he was contemplating a shake-up of the company.*
suggest EG *Are you suggesting that I need to lose some weight?*

❶ hire VERB
to pay money to use something
EG *She hired the car for three days.*
charter EG *They chartered a jet to fly her home.*
lease EG *He went to Toronto, where he leased an apartment.*
rent EG *She rents a house with three other girls.*

❷ hire VERB
to employ the services of someone
EG *The staff have been hired on short-term contracts.*
appoint EG *The Prime Minister has appointed a civilian as defence minister.*
commission EG *You can commission her to paint something especially for you.*
employ EG *They employed me as a nanny.*
engage EG *We engaged the services of a recognized engineer.*

sign up EG *He persuaded the company to sign her up.*

❶ hit VERB
to strike someone or something forcefully
EG *Both men had been hit with baseball bats.*
→ see Word Study **hit**

❷ hit VERB
to collide with something
EG *The car had apparently hit a traffic sign.*
bang into EG *She fell after another skier banged into her.*
bump EG *The boat bumped against something.*
collide with EG *He almost collided with Daisy.*
meet head-on EG *Their cars met head-on down a narrow alleyway.*
run into EG *The mail train ran into a derailed goods train at 75mph.*
smash into EG *The car plunged down a cliff and smashed into a tree.*

❸ hit NOUN
the action of hitting something
EG *Give it a good hard hit with the hammer.*
blow EG *He went to hospital after a blow to the face.*
knock EG *a painful knock on the knee*
rap EG *There was a rap on the door.*
slap EG *She reached forward and gave him a slap.*
smack EG *A smack with a ruler*
stroke EG *six strokes of the cane*

❶ hoard VERB
to store for future use
EG *People have begun to hoard food and petrol.*
save EG *Save some fuel in case of emergencies.*
stockpile EG *People are stockpiling food for the coming winter.*
store EG *It's perfect for storing eggs or vegetables.*

a b c d e f g h i j k l m n o p q r s t u v w x y z

❷ hoard NOUN
a store of things
EG *a hoard of silver and jewels*
cache EG *a cache of weapons and explosives*
fund EG *a scholarship fund for engineering students*
reserve EG *the world's oil reserves*
stockpile EG *stockpiles of nuclear warheads*
store EG *I have a store of food and water here.*
supply EG *food supplies*

hoarse ADJECTIVE
rough and unclear
EG *Nick's voice was hoarse with screaming.*
croaky EG *He sounds a bit croaky today.*
gruff EG *his gruff Scottish growl*
husky EG *Her deep husky voice was her trademark.*
rasping EG *Both men sang in a deep rasping tone.*

WORD POWER
▶ **Antonym**
clear

hobby NOUN
an enjoyable activity pursued in your spare time
EG *My hobbies are music and photography.*
diversion EG *Finger painting is very messy but an excellent diversion.*
leisure activity EG *America's top leisure activity is watching television.*
leisure pursuit EG *His main leisure pursuit is hill walking.*
pastime EG *His favourite pastime is golf.*

❶ hold VERB
to carry or support something
EG *Hold the baby while I load the car.*
carry EG *He was carrying a briefcase.*
clasp EG *She clasped the children to her.*

clutch EG *He was clutching a photograph.*
embrace EG *The couple in the corridor were embracing each other.*
grasp EG *He grasped both my hands.*
grip EG *They gripped the rope tightly.*

❷ hold NOUN
power or control over someone or something
EG *The party has a considerable hold over its own leader.*
control EG *He will have to give up his control of the company.*
dominance EG *the gang's dominance of the London underworld*
sway EG *ideas that held sway for centuries*

❸ hold NOUN
the act or a way of holding something
EG *He grabbed the rope and got a hold on it.*
grasp EG *His hand was taken in a warm, firm grasp.*
grip EG *His strong hand eased the bag from her grip.*

❶ hole NOUN
an opening or hollow in something
EG *The builders had cut holes into the stone.*
gap EG *The wind was tearing through gaps in the window frames.*
hollow EG *Water gathers in a hollow and forms a pond.*
opening EG *He squeezed through a narrow opening in the fence.*
pit EG *He lost his footing and began to slide into the pit.*
split EG *The seat has a few small splits around the corners.*
tear EG *I peered through a tear in the van's curtains.*

❷ hole NOUN
a weakness in a theory or argument
EG *There are some holes in that theory.*
defect EG *A defect in the aircraft caused the crash.*

error EG *NASA discovered an error in its calculations.*
fault EG *There is a fault in the computer program.*
flaw EG *Almost all of these studies have serious flaws.*
loophole EG *They exploited a loophole in the law.*

❸ hole NOUN; INFORMAL
a difficult situation
EG *He admitted that the government was in a hole.*
fix INFORMAL EG *This will put homeowners in a fix.*
hot water INFORMAL EG *They have already been in hot water over high prices this year.*
mess EG *the many reasons why the economy is in such a mess*
predicament EG *the once great club's current predicament*
tight spot EG *This was one tight spot he couldn't get out of.*

holiday NOUN
time spent away from home for enjoyment
EG *I'm exhausted - I really need a holiday.*
break EG *They are currently taking a short break in Spain.*
leave EG *Why don't you take a few days' leave?*
recess EG *Parliament returns today after its summer recess.*
time off EG *He took time off to go sailing with wife.*
vacation EG *We went on vacation to Puerto Rico.*

❶ holy ADJECTIVE
relating to God or a particular religion
EG *All Christian holy places were closed for a day in protest.*
blessed EG *Blessed are the peacemakers, for they shall be called the children of God.*
consecrated EG *the consecrated*

bread from the Eucharist
hallowed EG *hallowed ground*
sacred EG *sacred music*
sacrosanct EG *For him the Sabbath was sacrosanct.*
venerated EG *Jerusalem is Christianity's most venerated place.*

❷ holy ADJECTIVE
religious and leading a good life
EG *In the East, holy men have always had long hair.*
devout EG *She is a devout Catholic.*
pious EG *He was brought up by pious female relatives.*
religious EG *They are both very religious.*
saintly EG *his saintly mother*
virtuous EG *a virtuous family man*

WORD POWER

▷ **Synonyms**
god-fearing
godly

▶ **Antonym**
wicked

---

❶ home NOUN
the building in which someone lives
EG *They stayed at home and watched TV.*
abode EG *a luxurious abode*
dwelling EG *One thousand new dwellings are planned for the area.*
house EG *our new house*
residence EG *the Royal Family's private residence*

❷ home ADJECTIVE
involving your own country
EG *the home news pages of this newspaper*
domestic EG *over 100 domestic flights a day to 15 UK destinations*
internal EG *The government stepped up internal security.*
national EG *major national and international issues*

a b c d e f g h i j k l m n o p q r s t u v w x y z

native EG *He was glad to be back on his native soil.*

WORD POWER

▶ **Antonym**
foreign

homely ADJECTIVE
simple, ordinary and comfortable
EG *The room was small and homely.*
comfortable EG *A home should be warm and comfortable.*
cosy EG *Guests can relax in the cosy bar.*
modest EG *the modest home of a family who lived off the land*
simple EG *They celebrated mass in a simple chapel.*
welcoming EG *The restaurant is small and very welcoming.*

WORD POWER

▶ **Antonym**
grand

honest ADJECTIVE
truthful and trustworthy
EG *He is a very honest, decent man.*
law-abiding EG *law-abiding citizens*
reputable EG *a reputable car dealer*
trustworthy EG *He is a trustworthy and level-headed leader.*
truthful EG *She could not give him a truthful answer.*
virtuous EG *a virtuous family man*

WORD POWER

▶ **Antonym**
dishonest

❶ honour NOUN
personal integrity
EG *I can no longer serve with honour in your government.*
decency EG *No-one had the decency to tell me to my face.*
goodness EG *He retains a faith in human goodness.*
honesty EG *His reputation for honesty and integrity is second to none.*
integrity EG *He was praised for his fairness and high integrity.*

WORD POWER

▶ **Antonym**
dishonour

❷ honour NOUN
an award or mark of respect
EG *He was showered with honours - among them an Oscar.*
accolade EG *the ultimate international accolade, the Nobel Peace prize*
commendation EG *The officer received a commendation for brave conduct.*
homage EG *films that pay homage to our literary heritage*
praise EG *He had won consistently high praise for his theatre work.*
recognition EG *At last, her father's work has received popular recognition.*
tribute EG *He paid tribute to the organizing committee.*

WORD POWER

▷ **Synonyms**
acclaim
kudos

❸ honour VERB
to give someone special praise
EG *He was honoured by the French government with the Legion d'Honneur.*
commemorate EG *a plaque commemorating the servicemen who died*
commend EG *I commended her for that action.*
decorate EG *He was decorated for his gallantry by the General.*
glorify EG *My philosophy of life is to glorify God in all I do.*

praise EG *He praised their excellent work.*

hooligan NOUN
a destructive and violent young person
EG *English football hooligans*
delinquent EG *a nine-year-old delinquent*
hoon AUSTRALIAN AND NEW ZEALAND; INFORMAL EG *the rocks hurled by hoons*
lout EG *He was attacked by stone-throwing louts.*
tough EG *Residents may be too terrified of local toughs to protest.*
vandal EG *The Scout hut was burnt down by vandals.*
yob BRITISH AND AUSTRALIAN; SLANG eg *drunken yobs chanting football songs*

hope NOUN
a wish or feeling of desire and expectation
EG *There was little hope of recovery.*
ambition EG *His ambition is to sail around the world.*
dream EG *his dream of becoming a pilot*
expectation EG *The hotel was being renovated in expectation of a tourist boom.*

❶ **hopeless** ADJECTIVE
certain to fail or be unsuccessful
EG *Our situation is hopeless.*
forlorn EG *the forlorn hope of finding a better life*
futile EG *their futile attempts to avoid publicity*
impossible EG *The tax is impossible to administer.*
pointless EG *a pointless exercise that would only waste more time*
useless EG *She knew it was useless to protest.*
vain EG *a vain attempt to sign a goalkeeper*

❷ **hopeless** ADJECTIVE
bad or inadequate

EG *I don't drive and the buses are hopeless.*
inadequate EG *The problem lies with inadequate staffing.*
pathetic EG *the pathetic state of the rail network*
poor EG *The flat was in a poor state of repair.*
useless INFORMAL EG *My husband is useless around the house.*

❶ **horrible** ADJECTIVE
disagreeable or unpleasant
EG *a horrible little boy*
awful EG *I had an awful time.*
disagreeable EG *a disagreeable odour*
horrid EG *My parents are horrid to each other.*
mean EG *Why are you always so mean to me?*
nasty EG *This divorce could turn nasty.*
unpleasant EG *He's a very unpleasant little man.*

❷ **horrible** ADJECTIVE
causing shock, fear, or disgust
EG *horrible crimes*
appalling EG *They have been living under the most appalling conditions.*
dreadful EG *She told me the dreadful news.*
grim EG *a grim discovery*
gruesome EG *gruesome murders*
terrifying EG *a terrifying experience*

horrify VERB
to cause to feel horror or shock
EG *a crime trend that will horrify parents*
appal EG *I was appalled by her behaviour.*
disgust EG *He disgusted everyone with his boorish behaviour.*
dismay EG *He was deeply dismayed by the decision.*
outrage EG *Human rights campaigners were outraged by the execution.*

a b c d e f g h i j k l m n o p q r s t u v w x y z

A
B
C
D
E
F
G
H
I
J
K
L
M
N
O
P
Q
R
S
T
U
V
W
X
Y
Z

shock EG *Pictures of emaciated prisoners shocked the world.*
sicken EG *What he saw at the accident sickened him.*

❶ **horror** NOUN
a strong feeling of alarm or disgust
EG *He gazed in horror at the knife.*
alarm EG *She sat up in alarm.*
dread EG *She thought with dread of the cold winter to come.*
fear EG *I stood there crying and shaking with fear.*
fright EG *He uttered a shriek and jumped with fright.*
panic EG *He felt a sudden rush of panic at the thought.*
terror EG *She shook with terror.*

❷ **horror** NOUN
a strong fear of something
EG *his horror of death*
abhorrence EG *their abhorrence of racism*
aversion EG *Many people have a natural aversion to insects.*
disgust EG *I threw the book aside in disgust.*
hatred EG *My hatred for him is intense.*
loathing EG *She looked at him with loathing.*
revulsion EG *They expressed their revulsion at his violent death.*

WORD POWER

▷ **Synonyms**
abomination
odium
repugnance

horse NOUN
an animal kept for riding
EG *a fall from a horse*
brumby AUSTRALIAN AND NEW ZEALAND
eg *There's a mob of about 30 brumbies up there.*
equine EG *the history and uses of equines*
moke AUSTRALIAN AND NEW ZEALAND;

SLANG EG *a tired old moke*
nag INFORMAL EG *He unhitched his sorry-looking nag from a nearby post.*
pony EG *Peter trotted about on the fat pony he had been given.*

WORD POWER

▷ **Synonyms**
mount
steed

● **Related Words**
adjectives : equestrian, equine, horsey
noun : equitation
male : stallion
female : mare
young : foal, colt, filly

hostile ADJECTIVE
unfriendly, aggressive, and unpleasant
EG *The Governor faced hostile crowds.*
antagonistic EG *They were nearly all antagonistic to the idea.*
belligerent EG *a belligerent war of words between India and Pakistan*
malevolent EG *He fixed our photographer with a malevolent stare.*
unkind EG *All last summer he'd been unkind to her.*

WORD POWER

▶ **Antonym**
friendly

hostility NOUN
aggressive or unfriendly behaviour towards someone or something
EG *hostility to Black and ethnic groups*
animosity EG *The animosity between the two men grew.*
antagonism EG *a history of antagonism between the two sides*
hatred EG *her lifelong hatred of authority*
ill will EG *He didn't bear anyone any ill will.*

malice EG *There was no malice in her voice.*

resentment EG *There is growing resentment against newcomers.*

WORD POWER

▷ **Synonyms**
animus
detestation
enmity

▶ **Antonym**
friendship

❶ **hot** ADJECTIVE
having a high temperature
EG *a hot climate*
boiling EG *It's boiling in here.*
heated EG *a heated swimming pool*
scalding EG *Her son was burned by scalding tea.*
scorching EG *It was a scorching hot day.*
warm EG *a warm, dry summer*

WORD POWER

▶ **Antonym**
cold

❷ **hot** ADJECTIVE
very spicy
EG *a hot, aromatic Thai red curry*
peppery EG *a rich, peppery extra virgin olive oil*
spicy EG *a spicy Cajun sauce*

WORD POWER

▶ **Antonym**
bland

house NOUN
a building where a person or family lives
EG *They live in a large house with eight rooms.*
abode EG *I went round the streets and found his new abode.*
building EG *Their flat was on the first floor of the building.*
dwelling EG *One thousand new*

dwellings are planned for the area.
home EG *One in four people are without adequate homes.*
residence EG *the Royal Family's private residence*

❶ **hug** VERB
to hold someone close to you
EG *Lynn and I hugged each other.*
clasp EG *She clasped the children to her.*
cuddle EG *They used to kiss and cuddle in front of everyone.*
embrace EG *The couple in the corridor were embracing each other.*
squeeze EG *He kissed her on the cheek and squeezed her tight.*

❷ **hug** NOUN
the act of holding someone close to you
EG *She gave him a hug.*
clinch SLANG EG *They were caught in a clinch when her parents returned home.*
embrace EG *a young couple locked in an embrace*

huge ADJECTIVE
extremely large in amount, size, or degree
EG *a huge crowd*
colossal EG *a colossal waste of money*
enormous EG *The main bedroom is enormous.*
giant EG *a giant statue*
immense EG *He wielded immense power.*
massive EG *a massive surge in popularity*
vast EG *this vast area of northern Canada*

WORD POWER

▷ **Synonyms**
gargantuan
prodigious

▶ **Antonym**
tiny

a
b
c
d
e
f
g
h
i
j
k
l
m
n
o
p
q
r
s
t
u
v
w
x
y
z

A
B
C
D
E
F
G
H
I
J
K
L
M
N
O
P
Q
R
S
T
U
V
W
X
Y
Z

hui NOUN; NEW ZEALAND
a meeting
EG *He arranged a hui which called together a broad span of Maori tribes.*
assembly EG *an assembly of prizewinning journalists*
conference EG *a conference attended by 280 delegates*
congress EG *a congress of coal miners*
convention EG *the annual convention of the Society of Professional Journalists*
gathering EG *the annual gathering of the South Pacific Forum*
meeting EG *Can we have a meeting to discuss that?*
rally EG *They held a rally to mark International Human Rights Day.*

humane ADJECTIVE
showing kindness and sympathy towards others
EG *a more just and humane society*
benevolent EG *a most benevolent employer*
caring EG *a very caring boy*
charitable EG *charitable work*
compassionate EG *a deeply compassionate man*
kind EG *She is warmhearted and kind.*
merciful EG *a merciful God*
thoughtful EG *a very thoughtful gesture*

WORD POWER

▷ **Synonyms**
humanitarian

❶ **humble** ADJECTIVE
not vain or boastful
EG *He gave a great performance, but he was very humble.*
meek EG *He was a meek, mild-mannered fellow.*
modest EG *He's modest, as well as being a great player.*

unassuming EG *She has a gentle, unassuming manner.*

WORD POWER

▶ **Antonym**
haughty

❷ **humble** ADJECTIVE
ordinary or unimportant
EG *A splash of wine will transform a humble casserole.*
lowly EG *He was irked by his lowly status.*
modest EG *his modest beginnings*
ordinary EG *It was just an ordinary weekend.*
simple EG *a simple dinner of rice and beans*

❸ **humble** VERB
to make someone feel humiliated
EG *the little car company that humbled the industry giants*
disgrace EG *I have disgraced the family's name.*
humiliate EG *His teacher continually humiliates him in maths lessons.*

humid ADJECTIVE
damp and hot
EG *a hot, humid Italian summer*
clammy EG *My shirt was clammy with sweat.*
muggy EG *The weather was muggy and overcast.*
steamy EG *The air was hot and steamy from the heat of a hundred bodies.*
sticky EG *four hot, sticky days in the middle of August*

humiliate VERB
to hurt someone's pride
EG *He enjoyed humiliating me.*
disgrace EG *I have disgraced my family.*
embarrass EG *It embarrassed him that he had no idea of what was going on.*
humble EG *The champion was humbled by the unseeded qualifier.*

put down EG *I know that I do put people down occasionally.*
shame EG *Her son's affair had shamed her.*

❶ humour NOUN
something which is thought to be funny
EG *The film's humour contains a serious message.*
comedy EG *his career in comedy*
wit EG *She was known for her biting wit.*

WORD POWER

▷ **Synonyms**
drollery
jocularity

❷ humour NOUN
the mood someone is in
EG *He hasn't been in a good humour lately.*
frame of mind EG *Clearly, she was not in the right frame of mind to continue.*
mood EG *Lily was in one of her aggressive moods.*
spirits EG *He was in very low spirits.*
temper EG *Lee stormed off the field in a furious temper.*

❸ humour VERB
to please someone so that they will not become upset
EG *I nodded, partly to humour him.*
flatter EG *I knew she was just flattering me.*
indulge EG *He did not agree with indulging children.*
mollify EG *The investigation was undertaken primarily to mollify pressure groups.*
pander to EG *politicians who pander to big business*

hungry ADJECTIVE
wanting to eat
EG *I didn't have any lunch, so I'm really hungry.*
famished EG *Isn't dinner ready? I'm*

famished.
ravenous EG *a pack of ravenous animals*
starving EG *starving refugees*

❶ hurry VERB
to move or do something as quickly as possible
EG *She hurried through the empty streets.*
dash EG *He dashed upstairs.*
fly EG *I must fly or I'll miss my train.*
get a move on INFORMAL EG *Get a move on because my car's on a double yellow line.*
rush EG *I've got to rush. I've got a meeting in a few minutes.*
scurry EG *Reporters scurried to find telephones.*

❷ hurry VERB
to make something happen more quickly
EG *his attempt to hurry the process of independence*
accelerate EG *They must now accelerate the development of their new car.*
hasten EG *This will hasten the closure of small pubs.*
quicken EG *He quickened his pace a little.*
speed up EG *an effort to speed up the negotiations*

WORD POWER

▶ **Antonym**
slow down

❶ hurt VERB
to cause someone to feel pain
EG *I didn't mean to hurt her.*
harm EG *The hijackers seemed anxious not to harm anyone.*
injure EG *motorists who kill, maim, and injure*
wound EG *The bomb killed six people and wounded another five.*

❷ hurt VERB
to upset someone or something

a
b
c
d
e
f
g
h
i
j
k
l
m
n
o
p
q
r
s
t
u
v
w
x
y
z

A
B
C
D
E
F
G
H
I
J
K
L
M
N
O
P
Q
R
S
T
U
V
W
X
Y
Z

EG *What you said really hurt me.*
distress EG *I did not want to frighten or distress the horse.*
sadden EG *He is saddened that they did not win anything.*
upset EG *I'm sorry if I've upset you.*
wound EG *My relatives have wounded me in the past.*

❸ **hurt** ADJECTIVE
upset or offended
EG *He felt hurt by all the lies.*
aggrieved EG *He is still aggrieved at the size of the fine.*
offended EG *He was offended at being left out.*
upset EG *I'm upset by your attitude.*
wounded EG *I think she feels desperately wounded and unloved.*

WORD POWER

▷ **Synonyms**
piqued
rueful

hygiene NOUN
the principles and practice of health and cleanliness
EG *Be extra careful about personal hygiene.*
cleanliness EG *Many of the beaches fail to meet minimum standards of cleanliness.*
sanitation EG *the hazards of contaminated water and poor sanitation*

hypnotize VERB
to put someone into a state in which they seem to be asleep but can respond to suggestions
EG *She will hypnotize you and will stop you from smoking.*
put in a trance EG *A stage hypnotist put her in a trance.*
put to sleep EG *First the hypnotist will put you to sleep.*

WORD POWER

▷ **Synonyms**
entrance
mesmerize

❶ **hysterical** ADJECTIVE
in a state of uncontrolled excitement or panic
EG *Calm down. Don't get hysterical.*
frantic EG *A bird had been locked in and was by now quite frantic.*
frenzied EG *her frenzied attempts to get free*
overwrought EG *One overwrought man had to be restrained by friends.*
raving EG *He looked at her as if she were a raving lunatic.*

❷ **hysterical** ADJECTIVE; INFORMAL
extremely funny
EG *His stand-up routine was hysterical.*
comical EG *Her expression is almost comical.*
hilarious EG *He had a fund of hilarious jokes on the subject.*

Ii

❶ idea NOUN
a plan or suggestion for something
EG *She said she'd had a brilliant idea.*
plan EG *I have a cunning plan.*
recommendation EG *a range of recommendations for change*
scheme EG *a proposed scheme*
solution EG *He came up with a solution to the problem.*
suggestion EG *Do you have a better suggestion?*

WORD POWER

▷ **Synonyms**
hypothesis
theory

❷ idea NOUN
an opinion or belief about something
EG *old-fashioned ideas about women*
belief EG *my religious beliefs*
conviction EG *a firm conviction that things have improved*
impression EG *your first impressions of college*
notion EG *I have a notion of what he is like.*
opinion EG *a favourable opinion of our neighbours*
view EG *Make your views known to local politicians.*

❸ idea NOUN
what you know about something
EG *They had no idea where they were.*
clue EG *I don't have a clue what you mean.*
guess EG *My guess is he went east.*
hint EG *He gave no hint about where he was.*
inkling EG *We had an inkling that something was happening.*
notion EG *I have a notion how it is done.*
suspicion EG *I have a strong suspicion they are lying.*

❶ ideal NOUN
a principle or idea you try to achieve
EG *I don't live up to my ideal of myself.*
principle EG *acts that go against your principles*
standard EG *My father has high moral standards.*
value EG *the values of liberty and equality*

❷ ideal NOUN
the best example of something
EG *She remains his feminine ideal.*
epitome EG *The hotel was the epitome of luxury.*
example EG *He was held up as an example of courage.*
model EG *a model of good manners*
paragon EG *You are not a paragon of virtue.*
prototype EG *He was the prototype of a strong leader.*
standard EG *the standard by which we are compared*

WORD POWER

▷ **Synonyms**
archetype
criterion
paradigm

❸ ideal ADJECTIVE
being the best example of something
EG *the ideal person for the job*
classic EG *a classic example of hypocrisy*
complete EG *She is the complete athlete.*
consummate EG *a consummate politician*
model EG *She is a model pupil.*
perfect EG *He is the perfect husband for her.*
supreme EG *a supreme method of cooking vegetables*

❶ identify VERB
to recognize or name someone or

A B C D E F G H I J K L M N O P Q R S T U V W X Y Z

something
EG *I tried to identify her perfume.*
diagnose EG *This illness is easily diagnosed.*
label EG *Poisonous substances should be labelled as such.*
name EG *The victims of the fire have been named.*
pinpoint EG *They could not pinpoint the cause of death.*
place EG *The man was familiar, but I couldn't place him.*
recognize EG *a man I recognized as Luke's father*

❷ identify identify with VERB
to understand someone's feelings
EG *I can't identify with the characters.*
associate with EG *I associate myself with the green movement.*
empathize with EG *I empathize with the people who live here.*
feel for EG *I pitied and felt for him.*
relate to EG *We have difficulty relating to each other.*
respond to EG *She responded to his pain.*

idiot NOUN
a stupid person
EG *You're an idiot!*
fool EG *He'd been a fool to get involved.*
galah AUSTRALIAN; INFORMAL
eg *sounding like an illiterate galah*
imbecile EG *I don't want to deal with these imbeciles.*
moron EG *I think that Gordon is a moron.*
oaf EG *You clumsy oaf!*
twit INFORMAL EG *I feel such a twit.*

idiotic ADJECTIVE
extremely foolish or silly
EG *an idiotic thing to do*
crazy EG *You were crazy to leave then.*
daft INFORMAL EG *He's not so daft as to listen to them.*
dumb INFORMAL EG *I've met a lot of dumb people.*

foolish EG *It is foolish to risk injury.*
senseless EG *acts of senseless violence*
stupid EG *stupid ideas*

WORD POWER

▷ **Synonyms**
foolhardy
insane
moronic

idle ADJECTIVE
doing nothing
EG *a popular occupation for idle, wealthy young women*
jobless EG *One in four people are now jobless.*
redundant EG *redundant workers*
unemployed EG *jobs for the unemployed*

WORD POWER

▷ **Synonyms**
inactive
stationary

▶ **Antonym**
busy

❶ ignorant ADJECTIVE
not knowing about something
EG *He was completely ignorant of the rules.*
inexperienced EG *I am inexperienced at decorating.*
innocent EG *He is innocent about the harm he is doing.*
oblivious EG *John appeared oblivious to his surroundings.*
unaware EG *She was unaware that she was being filmed.*
unconscious EG *He was unconscious of his failure.*

❷ ignorant ADJECTIVE
not knowledgeable about things
EG *People are afraid to appear ignorant.*
green EG *The new boy is very green and immature.*

naive EG *a shy, naive man*
unaware EG *Young children are fairly unaware.*

WORD POWER

▷ **Synonyms**
uneducated
unlearned
untutored

ignore VERB
to take no notice of someone or something
EG *Her husband ignored her.*
blank SLANG EG *The crowd blanked her for the first four numbers.*
discount EG *They simply discounted his feelings.*
disregard EG *He disregarded his father's advice.*
neglect EG *They never neglect their duties.*
overlook EG *a fact that we all tend to overlook*

ill ADJECTIVE
unhealthy or sick
EG *Payne was seriously ill with pneumonia.*
ailing EG *The President is said to be ailing.*
poorly BRITISH; INFORMAL EG *Julie is still poorly.*
queasy EG *I feel queasy on boats.*
sick EG *He's very sick and he needs treatment.*
unhealthy EG *an unhealthy-looking fellow*
unwell EG *She felt unwell back at the office.*

WORD POWER

▷ **Synonyms**
indisposed
infirm
under the weather

▶ **Antonym**
healthy

illegal ADJECTIVE
forbidden by the law
EG *an illegal organization*
banned EG *banned substances*
criminal EG *a criminal offence*
illicit EG *illicit drugs*
outlawed EG *a place where hunting is outlawed*
prohibited EG *a country where alcohol is prohibited*
unlawful EG *unlawful acts*

WORD POWER

▷ **Synonyms**
proscribed
unauthorized
wrongful

▶ **Antonym**
legal

illness NOUN
a particular disease
EG *a mystery illness*
affliction EG *a severe mental affliction*
ailment EG *common ailments*
complaint EG *a skin complaint*
disease EG *He has been cured of the disease.*
disorder EG *a rare nervous disorder*
lurgy BRITISH, AUSTRALIAN, AND NEW ZEALAND; INFORMAL EG *It's only a matter of days before Joan gets the lurgy as well.*
sickness EG *radiation sickness*

❶ **illusion** NOUN
a thing that you think you can see
EG *Painters create the illusion of space.*
hallucination EG *Perhaps the footprint was a hallucination.*
mirage EG *I began to see mirages.*
semblance EG *A semblance of normality has been restored.*

WORD POWER

▷ **Synonyms**
chimera
phantasm

a
b
c
d
e
f
g
h
i
j
k
l
m
n
o
p
q
r
s
t
u
v
w
x
y
z

A
B
C
D
E
F
G
H
I
J
K
L
M
N
O
P
Q
R
S
T
U
V
W
X
Y
Z

❷ illusion NOUN
a false belief
EG *Their hopes proved to be an illusion.*
delusion EG *I was under the delusion that I could win.*
fallacy EG *It's a fallacy that the rich are generous.*
fancy EG *childhood fancies*
misconception EG *There are many misconceptions about school.*

imaginary ADJECTIVE
existing in your mind but not in real life
EG *an imaginary friend*
fictional EG *a fictional character*
fictitious EG *a fictitious illness*
hypothetical EG *a hypothetical situation*
ideal EG *in an ideal world*
illusory EG *Freedom is illusory.*
invented EG *distorted or invented stories*
mythological EG *mythological creatures*

WORD POWER

▶ **Antonym**
real

imagination NOUN
the ability to form new ideas
EG *a girl who lacks imagination*
creativity EG *She paints with great creativity.*
ingenuity EG *the ingenuity of engineers*
inventiveness EG *the artistic inventiveness of Mozart*
originality EG *a composer of great originality*
vision EG *a leader with vision*

❶ imagine VERB
to have an idea of something
EG *He could not imagine a more peaceful scene.*
conceive EG *I can't even conceive that much money.*
envisage EG *I envisage them staying*

together.
fantasize EG *I fantasized about writing music.*
picture EG *I tried to picture the place.*
visualize EG *He could not visualize her as old.*

❷ imagine VERB
to believe that something is the case
EG *I imagine you're talking about my brother.*
assume EG *Don't assume we are similar.*
believe EG *I believe you have my pen.*
gather EG *I gather that his mother was Scottish.*
guess INFORMAL EG *I guess he's right.*
suppose EG *He supposed I would be back at school.*
suspect EG *Susan suspected that things would get worse.*

WORD POWER

▷ **Synonyms**
fancy
surmise

imitate VERB
to copy someone or something
EG *She imitated her parents.*
ape EG *She is aping her sister's style.*
copy EG *I used to copy everything my big brother did.*
emulate EG *Sons are expected to emulate their fathers.*
impersonate EG *He could impersonate all the other students.*
mimic EG *He mimicked her accent.*
simulate EG *a machine which simulates natural sounds*

WORD POWER

▷ **Synonyms**
mirror
mock
parody

❶ immediate ADJECTIVE
happening or done without delay
EG *My immediate reaction was fear.*

instant EG *He took an instant dislike to Mark.*
instantaneous EG *The applause was instantaneous.*

❷ immediate ADJECTIVE
most closely connected to you
EG *my immediate family*
close EG *I have a few close friends.*
direct EG *your direct descendants*
near EG *near relatives*

❶ immediately ADVERB
right away
EG *Ingrid answered Peter's letter immediately.*
at once EG *You must come at once.*
directly EG *He will be there directly.*
instantly EG *She'd been knocked down in the street and died almost instantly.*
now EG *Get out, now!*
promptly EG *The telephone was answered promptly.*
right away EG *You'd better tell them right away.*
straightaway EG *I'd like to see you straightaway.*

WORD POWER

▷ **Synonyms**
forthwith
posthaste

❷ immediately ADVERB
very near in time or position
EG *immediately behind the house*
closely EG *He rushed out, closely followed by Kemp.*
directly EG *James stopped directly under the window.*
right EG *He stood right behind me.*

immense ADJECTIVE
very large or huge
EG *an immense cloud of smoke*
colossal EG *a colossal waste of money*
enormous EG *The main bedroom is enormous.*
giant EG *a giant oak table*

gigantic EG *a gigantic task*
huge EG *Several painters were working on a huge piece of canvas.*
massive EG *a massive cruise liner*
vast EG *a vast expanse of water*

WORD POWER

▶ **Antonym**
tiny

imminent ADJECTIVE
going to happen very soon
EG *my sister's imminent arrival*
close EG *My birthday is quite close.*
coming EG *the coming dawn*
forthcoming EG *their forthcoming marriage*
impending EG *impending doom*
looming EG *My exams are looming.*
near EG *in the near future*

immune ADJECTIVE
not subject to or affected by something
EG *He seems immune to pressure.*
exempt EG *She is exempt from blame.*
free EG *He was not completely free of guilt.*
protected EG *He is protected from the law.*
resistant EG *crops that are resistant to disease*
safe EG *I was safe from punishment.*
unaffected EG *She is unaffected by the sight of blood.*

WORD POWER

▷ **Synonyms**
insusceptible
invulnerable

❶ impatient ADJECTIVE
easily annoyed
EG *You are too impatient with others.*
brusque EG *a brusque manner*
curt EG *He had spoken in a very curt tone of voice.*

a b c d e f g h i j k l m n o p q r s t u v w x y z

A B C D E F G H I J K L M N O P Q R S T U V W X Y Z

irritable EG *Brian was nervous and irritable with her.*

WORD POWER

▷ **Synonyms**
intolerant
snappy

▶ **Antonym**
patient

❷ impatient ADJECTIVE
eager to do something
EG *He was impatient to leave.*
eager EG *Children are eager to learn.*
restless EG *The kids were bored and restless.*

impede VERB
to make someone's or something's progress difficult
EG *Fallen rocks are impeding the progress of rescue workers.*
block EG *The country has been trying to block these imports.*
delay EG *Various set-backs delayed production.*
disrupt EG *The drought has severely disrupted agricultural production.*
get in the way EG *She had a job which never got in the way of her hobbies.*
hamper EG *The bad weather hampered rescue operations.*
hinder EG *The investigation was hindered by the loss of vital documents.*
obstruct EG *The authorities are obstructing the inquiry.*

imperfect ADJECTIVE
having faults or problems
EG *We live in an imperfect world.*
broken EG *broken toys*
damaged EG *damaged goods*
defective EG *defective eyesight*
faulty EG *a car with faulty brakes*
flawed EG *a flawed character*

WORD POWER

▷ **Synonyms**
deficient
impaired

▶ **Antonym**
perfect

impersonal ADJECTIVE
not concerned with people and their feelings
EG *I found him strangely distant and impersonal.*
aloof EG *His manner was aloof.*
cold EG *Sharon was very cold with me.*
detached EG *He felt emotionally detached from the victims.*
formal EG *Business relationships are usually formal.*
neutral EG *He told me the news in a neutral manner.*
remote EG *She was beautiful but remote.*

WORD POWER

▷ **Synonyms**
bureaucratic
businesslike
dispassionate

implore VERB
to beg someone to do something
EG *"Tell me what to do!" she implored him.*
beg EG *I begged him to come with me.*
beseech LITERARY EG *I beseech you to show him mercy.*
plead with EG *The lady pleaded with her daughter to come home.*

❶ important ADJECTIVE
necessary or significant
EG *Her sons are the most important thing to her.*
momentous EG *the momentous decision to go to war*
serious EG *a serious matter*
significant EG *a significant discovery*

weighty EG *We discussed weighty matters.*

WORD POWER

▷ **Synonyms**
salient
seminal

▶ **Antonym**
unimportant

❷ important ADJECTIVE
having great influence or power
EG *the most important person in the country*
eminent EG *an eminent scientist*
foremost EG *a foremost expert in American history*
influential EG *one of the most influential books ever written*
leading EG *a leading nation in world politics*
notable EG *notable celebrities*
powerful EG *large, powerful countries*

WORD POWER

▷ **Synonyms**
pre-eminent
prominent

❶ impose VERB
to force something on someone
EG *Fines were imposed on the culprits.*
dictate EG *The policy is dictated from the top.*
enforce EG *It is a difficult law to enforce.*
inflict EG *Inflicting punishment to stop crime is not the answer.*
levy EG *a tax levied on imported goods*
ordain EG *the task of trying to ordain parliamentary behaviour*

❷ impose impose on VERB
to take advantage of someone
EG *I should stop imposing on your hospitality.*
abuse EG *They abused my hospitality*

by eating everything.
take advantage of EG *He took advantage of her generosity.*
use EG *She's just using you.*

impossible ADJECTIVE
unable to happen or be believed
EG *You shouldn't promise impossible things.*
absurd EG *absurd claims to have met big stars*
hopeless EG *a hopeless task*
inconceivable EG *It's inconceivable that people can still be living in those conditions.*
ludicrous EG *his ludicrous plan to build a house*
out of the question EG *Is a pay increase out of the question?*
unthinkable EG *The idea of splitting up is unthinkable.*

WORD POWER

▷ **Synonyms**
outrageous
unattainable
unworkable

▶ **Antonym**
possible

❶ impression NOUN
the way someone or something seems to you
EG *your first impressions of college*
feeling EG *the feeling that she was wasting her life*
hunch EG *Was your hunch right or wrong?*
idea EG *I had my own ideas about what had happened.*
notion EG *I have a notion of what he is like.*
sense EG *She has the sense that she was in trouble.*

❷ impression make an impression VERB
to have a strong effect on people
EG *He certainly made an impression on his teachers.*

a
b
c
d
e
f
g
h
i
j
k
l
m
n
o
p
q
r
s
t
u
v
w
x
y
z

cause a stir EG *News of her death caused a stir.*
influence EG *You can't do anything to influence him.*
make an impact EG *Events can make an impact on our lives.*

impressionable ADJECTIVE
easy to influence
EG *impressionable teenagers*
gullible EG *I'm so gullible I'd have believed him.*
open EG *an open, trusting nature*
receptive EG *moulding their young, receptive minds*
sensitive EG *Ouija boards can be dangerous, especially to sensitive people.*
susceptible EG *Children can be susceptible to advertisements.*
vulnerable EG *vulnerable old people*

WORD POWER
▷ **Synonyms**
ingenuous
suggestible

impressive ADJECTIVE
tending to impress
EG *an impressive achievement*
awesome EG *awesome mountains, deserts and lakes*
exciting EG *He tells the most exciting stories.*
grand EG *a grand old building*
powerful EG *a powerful image*
stirring EG *stirring music*
striking EG *her striking personality*

WORD POWER
▷ **Synonyms**
dramatic
moving

imprison VERB
to lock someone up
EG *He was imprisoned for murder.*
confine EG *Keep your dog confined to the house.*
detain EG *They'll be detained and*

charged.
incarcerate EG *Prisoners were incarcerated in terrible conditions.*
jail EG *An innocent man was jailed.*
lock up EG *You people should be locked up!*
send to prison EG *The judge sent him to prison for life.*

WORD POWER
▷ **Synonyms**
constrain
immure
intern

▶ **Antonym**
free

improbable ADJECTIVE
unlikely or unbelievable
EG *improbable stories*
doubtful EG *It was doubtful if they would arrive on time.*
dubious EG *dubious evidence*
far-fetched EG *This all sounds a bit far-fetched.*
implausible EG *a film with an implausible ending*
unbelievable EG *an unbelievable storyline*
unlikely EG *It is unlikely that he is alive.*

WORD POWER
▶ **Antonym**
probable

improve VERB
to get or make better
EG *He improved their house.*
advance EG *Medical technology has advanced.*
better EG *They tried to better their working conditions.*
enhance EG *Good jewellery enhances your outfits.*
look up INFORMAL EG *Things are looking up for me now.*
progress EG *Jack's condition is*

progressing well.
upgrade EG *You'll have to upgrade your image.*

WORD POWER

▷ **Synonyms**
ameliorate
develop
reform

▶ **Antonym**
worsen

improvement NOUN
the fact or process of getting better
EG *dramatic improvements in conditions*
advance EG *the advances in air safety since the 1970s*
development EG *monitoring her language development*
enhancement EG *the enhancement of the human condition*
progress EG *The doctors are pleased with her progress.*
upturn EG *an upturn in the economy*

impudence NOUN
disrespectful talk or behaviour towards someone
EG *Have you ever heard such impudence?*
audacity EG *He had the audacity to speak up.*
boldness EG *I was amazed at her boldness towards him.*
cheek INFORMAL EG *I can't believe he had the cheek to complain.*
chutzpah AMERICAN; INFORMAL EG *He had the chutzpah to ask us to leave.*
gall EG *the most presumptuous question any interviewer has ever had the gall to ask*
impertinence EG *His words sounded like impertinence.*
insolence EG *I got punished for insolence.*
nerve EG *You've got a nerve coming round here after what you've done.*

inability NOUN
a lack of ability to do something
EG *an inability to concentrate*
impotence EG *a sense of impotence in the situation*
inadequacy EG *my inadequacy as a gardener*
incompetence EG *the incompetence of government officials*
ineptitude EG *political ineptitude*

WORD POWER

▶ **Antonym**
ability

❶ **inadequate** ADJECTIVE
not enough in quantity
EG *Supplies of medicine are inadequate.*
insufficient EG *insufficient evidence to justify criminal proceedings*
lacking EG *Why was military intelligence so lacking?*
poor EG *poor wages*
scarce EG *the region's scarce supplies of water*
short EG *Deliveries are unreliable and food is short.*

WORD POWER

▶ **Antonym**
adequate

❷ **inadequate** ADJECTIVE
not good enough
EG *She felt painfully inadequate in the crisis.*
deficient EG *He made me feel deficient as a mother.*
incapable EG *He lost his job for being incapable.*
incompetent EG *the power to sack incompetent teachers*
inept EG *He was inept and lacked the intelligence to govern.*
pathetic EG *She made some pathetic excuse.*
useless EG *I'm useless around the house.*

a
b
c
d
e
f
g
h
i
j
k
l
m
n
o
p
q
r
s
t
u
v
w
x
y
z

A B C D E F G H I J K L M N O P Q R S T U V W X Y Z

inappropriate NOUN
not suitable for a purpose or occasion
EG *This behaviour is inappropriate.*
improper EG *the improper use of resources*
incongruous EG *an incongruous assortment of clothes*
unfit EG *houses that are unfit for living in*
unseemly EG *He thought crying was unseemly.*
unsuitable EG *food that is unsuitable for children*
untimely EG *their unjustified and untimely interference*

WORD POWER

▶ **Antonym**
appropriate

incentive NOUN
something that encourages you to do something
EG *the incentive to work*
bait EG *He added some bait to make the agreement sweeter.*
encouragement EG *She didn't get much encouragement to do anything.*
inducement EG *Are gangster films an inducement to crime?*
motivation EG *Money is my motivation.*
stimulus EG *He needed all the stimulus he could get.*

WORD POWER

▷ **Synonyms**
lure
motive
spur

incident NOUN
an event
EG *Little incidents can shape our lives.*
circumstance EG *This is a fortunate circumstance.*
episode EG *I'm glad this episode is over.*

event EG *recent events in Europe*
happening EG *the latest happenings in sport*
occasion EG *I remember that occasion fondly.*
occurrence EG *Nancy wondered about the strange occurrence.*

incite VERB
to excite someone into doing something
EG *The campaigners incited a riot.*
agitate EG *Workers agitated for better conditions.*
goad EG *He tried to goad me into a response.*
instigate EG *The violence was instigated by a few people.*
provoke EG *I provoked him into doing something stupid.*
whip up EG *an attempt to whip up public hostility to the president*

include VERB
to have as a part
EG *A British breakfast always includes sausages.*
contain EG *This sheet contains a list of names.*
cover EG *The books covers many topics.*
embrace EG *a small county embracing two cities*
encompass EG *classes which encompass a wide range of activities*
incorporate EG *The new cars incorporate many improvements.*
involve EG *a high-energy workout which involves nearly every muscle*

WORD POWER

▶ **Antonym**
exclude

income NOUN
the money someone or something earns
EG *families on low incomes*
earnings EG *his earnings as an accountant*

pay EG *We complained about our pay.*
profits EG *The bank made profits of millions of dollars.*
salary EG *The lawyer was paid a good salary.*
takings EG *The shop had huge takings that week.*
wages EG *His wages have gone up.*

WORD POWER

▷ **Synonyms**
proceeds
receipts
revenue

incomparable ADJECTIVE
too good to be compared with anything else
EG *an area of incomparable beauty*
inimitable EG *his inimitable style*
peerless LITERARY EG *He gave a peerless performance.*
superlative EG *The hotel has superlative views.*
supreme EG *the supreme piece of writing about the war*
unparalleled EG *unparalleled happiness*
unrivalled EG *an unrivalled knowledge of music*

WORD POWER

▷ **Synonyms**
matchless
unequalled

incompetent ADJECTIVE
lacking the ability to do something properly
EG *You are incompetent, and you know it.*
bungling EG *a bungling amateur*
cowboy BRITISH; INFORMAL EG *cowboy builders*
incapable EG *an incapable leader*
inept EG *an inept performance*
unable EG *He felt unable to handle*

the situation.
useless EG *I felt useless and a failure.*

WORD POWER

▷ **Synonyms**
ineffectual
inexpert
unskilful

▶ **Antonym**
competent

incomplete ADJECTIVE
not finished or whole
EG *an incomplete book*
deficient EG *a deficient diet*
half-pie NEW ZEALAND; INFORMAL EG *His report was half-pie.*
insufficient EG *insufficient information*
partial EG *The concert was a partial success.*

WORD POWER

▷ **Synonyms**
imperfect
undeveloped
unfinished

▶ **Antonym**
complete

❶ **increase** VERB
to make or become larger in amount
EG *The population continues to increase.*
enlarge EG *They are trying to enlarge their customer base.*
expand EG *We will expand the size of the picture.*
extend EG *She plans to extend her stay.*
grow EG *The sound grew in volume.*
multiply EG *viruses which can multiply rapidly in the human body*
swell EG *His anger swelled within him.*

a b c d e f g h i j k l m n o p q r s t u v w x y z

A
B
C
D
E
F
G
H
I
J
K
L
M
N
O
P
Q
R
S
T
U
V
W
X
Y
Z

WORD POWER

▷ **Synonyms**
augment
escalate

▶ **Antonym**
decrease

❷ **increase** NOUN
a rise in the amount of something
EG *a pay increase*
gain EG *a gain in speed*
growth EG *the growth of unemployment*
increment EG *tiny increments of movement*
rise EG *a rise in prices*
upsurge EG *an upsurge of interest in books*

WORD POWER

▶ **Antonym**
decrease

❶ **incredible** ADJECTIVE
totally amazing
EG *a champion with incredible skill*
amazing EG *an amazing success*
astonishing EG *an astonishing piece of good luck*
astounding EG *an astounding discovery*
extraordinary EG *extraordinary beauty*
marvellous EG *a marvellous thing to do*
sensational INFORMAL EG *a sensational performance*

❷ **incredible** ADJECTIVE
impossible to believe
EG *the incredible stories of some children*
absurd EG *absurd ideas*
far-fetched EG *This all sounds very far-fetched to me.*
improbable EG *highly improbable claims*
unbelievable EG *The film has an*

unbelievable plot.
unimaginable EG *unimaginable wealth*
unthinkable EG *It's unthinkable that Tom forgot your birthday.*

WORD POWER

▷ **Synonyms**
implausible
inconceivable
preposterous

indecent ADJECTIVE
shocking or rude
EG *indecent lyrics*
crude EG *crude pictures*
dirty EG *dirty jokes*
improper EG *improper behaviour*
lewd EG *lewd comments*
rude EG *a rude gesture*
vulgar EG *vulgar language*

❶ **independent** ADJECTIVE
separate from other people or things
EG *an independent political party*
autonomous EG *an autonomous country*
free EG *Do we have a free press?*
liberated EG *liberated countries*
separate EG *We live separate lives.*
unrelated EG *two unrelated incidents*

❷ **independent** ADJECTIVE
not needing other people's help
EG *a fiercely independent woman*
individualistic EG *individualistic behaviour*
liberated EG *a genuinely liberated woman*
self-sufficient EG *I am quite self-sufficient.*
unaided EG *She raised her children unaided.*

indicate VERB
to show that something is true
EG *a gesture which indicates his relief*
denote EG *Messy writing denotes a messy mind.*
reveal EG *His diary revealed his*

disturbed state of mind.
show EG *I would like to show my appreciation.*
signal EG *Ted signalled that everything was all right.*
signify EG *A white flag signifies surrender.*

WORD POWER
▷ **Synonyms**
imply
manifest
point to

indication NOUN
a sign of something
EG *He gave no indication that he had heard me.*
clue EG *Did she give any clue as to how she was feeling?*
hint EG *The Minister gave a strong hint that he intended to resign.*
sign EG *Your blood will be checked for any sign of kidney failure.*
signal EG *They saw the visit as an important signal of support.*
suggestion EG *There is no suggestion that the two sides are any closer to agreeing.*
warning EG *a warning of impending doom*

WORD POWER
▷ **Synonyms**
intimation

indirect ADJECTIVE
not done or going directly but by another way
EG *the indirect effects of smoking*
meandering EG *the meandering course of the river*
oblique EG *oblique threats*
rambling EG *In a rambling answer, he denied the charge.*
roundabout EG *a roundabout way of getting information*
tortuous EG *a tortuous path*

wandering EG *a wandering route through the woods*

WORD POWER
▶ **Antonym**
direct

❶ individual ADJECTIVE
relating to separate people or things
EG *individual dishes of trifle*
discrete FORMAL EG *breaking down the job into discrete steps*
independent EG *two independent studies*
separate EG *Use separate chopping boards for different foods.*
single EG *every single house in the street*

❷ individual ADJECTIVE
different and unusual
EG *Develop your own individual writing style.*
characteristic EG *a characteristic feature*
distinctive EG *His voice was very distinctive.*
idiosyncratic EG *a highly idiosyncratic personality*
original EG *a chef with an original touch*
personal EG *his own personal method of playing*
special EG *her own special way of doing things*
unique EG *Each person's signature is unique.*

❸ individual NOUN
a person, different from any other person
EG *the rights of the individual*
character EG *a remarkable character*
human being EG *a fellow human being*
party EG *Who is the guilty party?*
person EG *One person died and*

several others were injured.
soul EG *He's a jolly soul.*

WORD POWER

▷ **Synonyms**
mortal

industrious ADJECTIVE
tending to work hard
EG *industrious groups of students*
busy EG *an exceptionally busy man*
conscientious EG *Sherry was slow
but conscientious.*
diligent EG *Williams was diligent in
the writing of letters.*
hard-working EG *an exceptionally
disciplined and hard-working young
man*
tireless EG *a tireless and willing
worker*

WORD POWER

▶ **Antonym**
lazy

inefficient ADJECTIVE
badly organized and slow
EG *an inefficient government*
disorganized EG *My boss is
completely disorganized.*
incapable EG *If he fails he will be
considered incapable.*
incompetent EG *an incompetent
officer*
inept EG *an inept use of power*
sloppy EG *sloppy management*

WORD POWER

▷ **Synonyms**
ineffectual
inexpert
slipshod

▶ **Antonym**
efficient

inexperienced ADJECTIVE
lacking experience of a situation or
activity
EG *inexperienced drivers*

green INFORMAL EG *He was a young
lad, and very green.*
new EG *a new mother*
raw EG *raw talent*
unaccustomed EG *Kate is
unaccustomed to being on TV.*

WORD POWER

▶ **Antonym**
experienced

infect VERB
to cause disease in something
EG *One mosquito can infect many
people.*
affect EG *Neil has been affected by
the virus.*
blight EG *trees blighted by pollution*
contaminate EG *These substances
can contaminate fish.*
taint EG *blood that had been tainted
with HIV*

infectious ADJECTIVE
spreading from one person to
another
EG *infectious diseases*
catching EG *There is no suggestion
that multiple sclerosis is catching.*
contagious EG *a highly contagious
disease of the lungs*
spreading EG *The spreading virus is
threatening the population.*

WORD POWER

▷ **Synonyms**
communicable
virulent

❶ **inferior** ADJECTIVE
having a lower position than
something or someone else
EG *Women were given inferior status.*
lesser EG *the work of lesser writers*
lower EG *lower animals*
minor EG *a minor celebrity*
secondary EG *He was relegated to a
secondary position.*
second-class EG *second-class
citizens*

subordinate EG *His subordinate officers followed his example.*

WORD POWER

▶ **Antonym**
superior

❷ **inferior** ADJECTIVE
of low quality
EG *inferior quality cassette tapes*
mediocre EG *mediocre music*
poor EG *a poor standard of service*
second-class EG *a second-class education*
second-rate EG *second-rate restaurants*
shoddy EG *Customers no longer tolerate shoddy goods.*

WORD POWER

▶ **Antonym**
superior

❸ **inferior** NOUN
a person in a lower position than another
EG *You must still be polite to your inferiors.*
junior EG *the office junior*
menial EG *menials in poorly paid jobs*
subordinate EG *All her subordinates adored her.*
underling EG *Every underling feared him.*

WORD POWER

▶ **Antonym**
superior

infinite ADJECTIVE
without any limit or end
EG *an infinite number of possibilities*
boundless EG *boundless energy*
eternal EG *the secret of eternal youth*
everlasting EG *our everlasting friendship*
inexhaustible EG *an inexhaustible supply of ideas*
perpetual EG *a perpetual source of*

worry
untold EG *untold wealth*

WORD POWER

▷ **Synonyms**
bottomless
interminable
limitless

❶ **influence** NOUN
power over other people
EG *He has quite a lot of influence.*
authority EG *You have no authority over me.*
control EG *Teachers have a lot of control over students.*
importance EG *a politician of great importance*
power EG *a position of power*
sway EG *My mother holds sway at home.*

WORD POWER

▷ **Synonyms**
ascendancy
domination

❷ **influence** NOUN
an effect that someone or something has
EG *under the influence of alcohol*
effect EG *Your age has an effect on your views.*
hold EG *He is losing his hold on the public.*
magnetism EG *a man of great personal magnetism*
spell EG *under the spell of one of his teachers*
weight EG *the weight of the law*

❸ **influence** VERB
to have an effect on someone or something
EG *I never try to influence my children.*
affect EG *He will not let personal preference affect his choice.*
control EG *I can't control him.*
direct EG *I don't need you directing my life.*

a
b
c
d
e
f
g
h
i
j
k
l
m
n
o
p
q
r
s
t
u
v
w
x
y
z

A
B
C
D
E
F
G
H
I
J
K
L
M
N
O
P
Q
R
S
T
U
V
W
X
Y
Z

guide EG *Let your instinct guide you.*
manipulate EG *I hate the way he manipulates people.*
sway EG *efforts to sway voters*

inform VERB
to tell someone about something
EG *Please inform me of your progress.*
advise FORMAL EG *I can advise you of his whereabouts.*
enlighten EG *a history lesson which enlightens you*
notify EG *Ann was notified of her sister's illness.*
tell EG *Tell me what is going on.*

WORD POWER
▷ **Synonyms**
apprise
communicate

inform on VERB
to tell the police about someone who has committed a crime
EG *Somebody must have informed on the thieves.*
betray EG *They betrayed their associates to the police.*
denounce EG *He was denounced as a dangerous rebel.*
grass on BRITISH; SLANG EG *He grassed on the members of his own gang.*
tell on INFORMAL EG *It's all right, I won't tell on you.*

informal ADJECTIVE
relaxed and casual
EG *His manner was informal and relaxed.*
casual EG *a casual attitude towards money*
colloquial EG *colloquial language*
easy EG *easy conversation*
familiar EG *John was too familiar towards his teacher.*
natural EG *Beth was friendly and natural with us.*
relaxed EG *a relaxed atmosphere in class*

WORD POWER
▶ **Antonym**
formal

information NOUN
the details you know about something
EG *Pat would not give any information about Sarah.*
data EG *The survey provided valuable data.*
drum AUSTRALIAN; INFORMAL EG *I don't have the drum on this yet.*
facts EG *Pass on all the facts to the police.*
material EG *highly secret material*
news EG *We have news of your brother.*
notice EG *advance notice of the event*
word EG *I received word that the guests had arrived.*

ingredient NOUN
a thing that something is made from
EG *Place all the ingredients in a pan.*
component EG *the components of hamburgers*
constituent EG *the main constituent of fish oil*
element EG *the various elements in a picture*

inhabit VERB
to live in a place
EG *the people who inhabit these islands*
dwell EG *the people who dwell in the forest*
live EG *She has lived here for ten years.*
lodge EG *Some people lodged permanently in the hallway.*
occupy EG *Forty tenants occupy the block.*
populate EG *a swamp populated by huge birds*
reside FORMAL EG *He resides in the country.*

inhabitant NOUN
someone who lives in a place

EG *an inhabitant of Norway*
citizen EG *American citizens*
inmate EG *prison inmates*
native EG *Dr Brown is a native of New Zealand.*
occupant EG *the previous occupant of the house*
resident EG *the residents of the retirement home*

inheritance NOUN
something that is passed on
EG *The house would be his son's inheritance.*
bequest EG *His aunt left a bequest for him in her will.*
heritage EG *This building is part of our heritage.*
legacy EG *His politeness was the legacy of his upbringing.*

injure VERB
to damage part of someone's body
EG *A bomb exploded, injuring five people.*
harm EG *The hijackers did not harm anyone.*
hurt EG *He hurt his back in an accident.*
maim EG *Mines in rice paddies maim and kill civilians.*
wound EG *wounded by shrapnel*

injury NOUN
damage to part of the body
EG *He sustained serious injuries in the accident.*
damage EG *brain damage*
harm EG *Dogs can do harm to human beings.*
wound EG *a head wound*

injustice NOUN
unfairness and lack of justice
EG *the injustice of the system*
bias EG *He shows bias against women.*
discrimination EG *racial discrimination*
inequality EG *people concerned about social inequality*

prejudice EG *prejudice against workers over 45*
unfairness EG *the unfairness of the decision*
wrong EG *I intend to right past wrongs.*

WORD POWER

▶ **Antonym**
  justice

innocence NOUN
inexperience of evil or unpleasant things
EG *the innocence of babies*
gullibility EG *I'm paying for my gullibility back then.*
inexperience EG *their inexperience of the real world*
naivety EG *There was a youthful naivety to his honesty.*
simplicity EG *She prayed with childlike simplicity.*

WORD POWER

▷ **Synonyms**
  artlessness
  ingenuousness
  unworldliness

❶ **innocent** ADJECTIVE
not guilty of a crime
EG *the arrest of innocent suspects*
blameless EG *I have led a blameless life.*
clear EG *He was clear of blame for the accident.*
not guilty EG *Both men were found not guilty.*

WORD POWER

▶ **Antonym**
  guilty

❷ **innocent** ADJECTIVE
without experience of evil or unpleasant things
EG *They seem so young and innocent.*
childlike EG *childlike trust*

a b c d e f g h i j k l m n o p q r s t u v w x y z

A
B
C
D
E
F
G
H
I
J
K
L
M
N
O
P
Q
R
S
T
U
V
W
X
Y
Z

guileless EG *Her eyes were as guileless as a doll's.*
naive EG *I was young and naive when I left home.*
pure EG *She had led a pure life.*
spotless EG *a spotless, pure child*
virginal EG *a shy, virginal princess*

WORD POWER

▷ **Synonyms**
artless
ingenuous
unworldly

insane ADJECTIVE
mad
EG *Some people can't take the pressure and go insane.*
crazy EG *If I sat home and worried, I'd go crazy.*
deranged EG *a deranged man who shot 14 people in the main square*
mad EG *She was afraid of going mad.*
mentally ill EG *a patient who is mentally ill*
out of your mind EG *I wonder if I'm going out of my mind.*
unhinged EG *an experience which left her completely unhinged*

insert VERB
to put something into something else
EG *He inserted the key into the lock.*
enter EG *Enter your name in the box.*
implant EG *a device implanted in the arm*
introduce EG *Scientists introduced new genes into mice.*
place EG *Cover the casserole tightly and place in the oven.*
put EG *She put a coin in the slot.*
set EG *diamonds set in gold*

inside ADJECTIVE
surrounded by the main part and often hidden
EG *We booked an inside cabin.*
inner EG *the inner ear*
innermost EG *the innermost parts of*

the galaxy
interior EG *a car with plenty of interior space*
internal EG *your internal organs*

WORD POWER

▶ **Antonym**
outside

insides PLURAL NOUN; INFORMAL
the parts inside your body
EG *My insides ached from eating too much.*
entrails EG *chicken entrails*
guts EG *fish guts*
innards EG *the innards of a human body*
internal organs EG *damage to internal organs*

WORD POWER

▷ **Synonyms**
viscera
vitals

insignificant ADJECTIVE
small and unimportant
EG *a small, insignificant village*
irrelevant EG *irrelevant details*
little EG *It seems such a little thing to get upset over.*
minor EG *Western officials say the problem is minor.*
petty EG *Rows can start over petty things.*
trifling EG *These difficulties may seem trifling to you.*
trivial EG *He tried to wave aside these issues as trivial matters.*
unimportant EG *The age difference seemed unimportant.*

WORD POWER

▷ **Synonyms**
inconsequential

▶ **Antonym**
significant

insincere ADJECTIVE
saying things you do not mean
EG *A lot of actors are insincere.*
deceitful EG *deceitful and misleading remarks*
dishonest EG *dishonest salespeople*
false EG *a false confession*
two-faced EG *the most two-faced politicians in the world*

WORD POWER

▶ **Antonym**
sincere

insist VERB
to demand something forcefully
EG *My family insisted I should not give in.*
demand EG *The teacher demanded an explanation.*
press EG *She is pressing for improvements to education.*
urge EG *We urge vigorous action be taken immediately.*

inspect VERB
to examine something carefully
EG *the right to inspect company files*
check EG *Check each item for obvious flaws.*
examine EG *He examined her passport and stamped it.*
eye EG *We eyed each other thoughtfully.*
investigate EG *Police are investigating the scene of the crime.*
scan EG *The officer scanned the room.*
survey EG *He surveyed the ruins of the building.*

WORD POWER

▷ **Synonyms**
audit
scrutinize
vet

① instant NOUN
a short period of time
EG *The pain disappeared in an instant.*
flash EG *It was all over in a flash.*
minute EG *I'll see you in a minute.*
moment EG *In a moment he was gone.*
second EG *Seconds later, firemen reached his door.*
split second EG *Her gaze met Michael's for a split second.*
trice EG *She was back in a trice.*

② instant ADJECTIVE
immediate and without delay
EG *He had taken an instant dislike to her.*
immediate EG *We need an immediate reply.*
instantaneous EG *an explosion resulting in the instantaneous deaths of all crew members*
prompt EG *Prompt action is needed.*

instinct NOUN
a natural tendency to do something
EG *My first instinct was to protect myself.*
feeling EG *You seem to have a feeling for drawing.*
impulse EG *Peter resisted an impulse to smile.*
intuition EG *You should trust your intuition.*
sixth sense EG *Some sixth sense told him to keep going.*
urge EG *He fought the urge to panic.*

① instruct VERB
to tell someone to do something
EG *They have instructed solicitors to sue.*
command EG *He commanded his troops to attack.*
direct EG *They have been directed to give attention to this problem.*
order EG *Williams ordered him to leave.*
tell EG *A passer-by told him to move his car.*

WORD POWER

▶ **Antonym**
forbid

a b c d e f g h i j k l m n o p q r s t u v w x y z

A
B
C
D
E
F
G
H
I
J
K
L
M
N
O
P
Q
R
S
T
U
V
W
X
Y
Z

❷ instruct VERB
to teach someone about a subject or
skill
EG *He instructs therapists in relaxation
techniques.*
coach EG *He coached me in French.*
educate EG *We need to educate
people about the destructive effects of
alcohol.*
school EG *She's been schooling her
kids herself.*
teach EG *She taught children French.*
train EG *We train them in a range of
building techniques.*
tutor EG *He was tutoring her in the
stringed instruments.*

insufficient ADJECTIVE
not enough for a particular purpose
EG *insufficient information*
deficient EG *a deficient diet*
inadequate EG *The problem lies with
inadequate staffing.*
lacking EG *My confidence is lacking.*
scant EG *Gareth paid scant attention
to what was going on.*
short EG *She was short of breath.*

> ## WORD POWER
>
> ▶ **Antonym**
> sufficient

❶ insult VERB
to offend someone by being rude to
them
EG *I did not mean to insult you.*
abuse EG *footballers abusing referees*
affront EG *He pretended to be
affronted by what I said.*
offend EG *I had no intention of
offending the community.*
put down EG *They seemed to delight
in putting me down.*
slag BRITISH; INFORMAL EG *He's always
slagging me in front of his mates.*
slight EG *They felt slighted by not
being consulted.*

snub EG *He snubbed her in public and
made her feel foolish.*

> ## WORD POWER
>
> ▶ **Antonym**
> compliment

❷ insult NOUN
a rude remark that offends someone
EG *The two men exchanged insults.*
abuse EG *Raft hurled verbal abuse at
his co-star.*
affront EG *She took my words as a
personal affront.*
offence EG *I meant no offence to Mr
Hardy.*
slight EG *She is very sensitive to
slights.*
snub EG *This was a deliberate snub to
me.*

> ## WORD POWER
>
> ▶ **Antonym**
> compliment

intelligence NOUN
the ability to understand and learn
things
EG *students of high intelligence*
cleverness EG *Her cleverness gets in
the way of her emotions.*
comprehension EG *an idea beyond
human comprehension*
intellect EG *Lucy's lack of intellect
disappointed her father.*
perception EG *You have brilliant
perception and insight.*
sense EG *They have the sense to seek
help.*
understanding EG *I've got no sense,
no understanding.*
wit EG *He had the wit to see this was a
good idea.*

> ## WORD POWER
>
> ▷ **Synonyms**
> acumen
> nous

intelligent ADJECTIVE
able to understand and learn things
EG *Dolphins are an intelligent species.*
acute EG *His relaxed exterior hides a very acute mind.*
brainy INFORMAL EG *I don't consider myself brainy.*
bright EG *an exceptionally bright child*
clever EG *a clever girl*
quick EG *His quick mind soon grasped the situation.*
sharp EG *a very sharp intellect*
smart EG *He thinks he's as smart as Sarah.*

WORD POWER

▶ **Antonym**
stupid

---

❶ intend VERB
to decide or plan to do something
EG *She intended to move back to Cape Town.*
aim EG *We aim to raise funds for charity.*
be determined EG *Kate was determined to enjoy the day.*
mean EG *I didn't mean any harm.*
plan EG *He planned to leave Adelaide on Monday.*
propose EG *Where do you propose building such a huge thing?*
resolve EG *She resolved to report the matter.*

❷ intend VERB
to mean for a certain use
EG *a book intended for serious students*
aim EG *children's games aimed at developing quickness*
design EG *The house had been designed for a large family.*
earmark EG *That money was earmarked for house repairs.*
mean EG *I was not meant for domestic life.*

❶ intense ADJECTIVE
very great in strength or amount
EG *intense heat*
acute EG *an acute shortage of accommodation*
deep EG *He felt a deep sense of relief.*
extreme EG *Proceed with extreme caution.*
fierce EG *There was fierce competition for the job.*
great EG *Dawes felt a great pain and weakness.*
powerful EG *I had a powerful urge to scream at him.*
profound EG *The book had a profound effect in the USA.*
severe EG *I had severe problems.*

❷ intense ADJECTIVE
tending to have strong feelings
EG *He was dark-haired and intense.*
ardent EG *one of his most ardent supporters*
earnest EG *Ella was a pious, earnest woman.*
fervent EG *a fervent admirer of Beethoven's music*
fierce EG *fierce loyalty to his friends*
impassioned EG *He made an impassioned appeal for peace.*
passionate EG *He is very passionate about the project.*
vehement EG *a vehement critic of the plan*

intention NOUN
a plan to do something
EG *He announced his intention of retiring.*
aim EG *The aim of this book is to inform you.*
goal EG *The goal is to raise a lot of money.*
idea EG *I bought books with the idea of reading them.*
object EG *It was his object in life to find the island.*
objective EG *His objective was to play golf and win.*

A B C D E F G H I J K L M N O P Q R S T U V W X Y Z

purpose EG *He did not know the purpose of Vincent's visit.*

❶ interest NOUN
a feeling of wanting to know about something
EG *I have a great interest in that period of history.*
attention EG *The book attracted considerable attention.*
fascination EG *a lifelong fascination with the sea*
concern EG *How it happened is of little concern to me.*
curiosity EG *His reply satisfied our curiosity.*

❷ interest NOUN
a hobby
EG *He has a wide range of sporting interests.*
activity EG *I enjoy outdoor activities like canoeing and climbing.*
hobby EG *My hobbies are football, photography and tennis.*
pastime EG *His favourite pastime is golf.*
pursuit EG *his favourite childhood pursuits*

❸ interest VERB
to attract someone's attention and curiosity
EG *This part of the book interests me most.*
appeal EG *The bright colours seem to appeal to children.*
captivate EG *this author's ability to captivate young minds*
fascinate EG *Politics fascinated my father.*
intrigue EG *The situation intrigued him.*
stimulate EG *Bill was stimulated by the challenge.*

WORD POWER

▶ **Antonym**
bore

interesting ADJECTIVE
making you want to know, learn or hear more
EG *an interesting hobby*
absorbing EG *an absorbing conversation*
compelling EG *compelling drama*
entertaining EG *a cheerful and entertaining companion*
gripping EG *a gripping story*
intriguing EG *the intriguing character of the author*
stimulating EG *My trip to India had been stimulating.*

WORD POWER

▶ **Antonym**
boring

❶ interfere VERB
to try to influence a situation
EG *Stop interfering and leave me alone.*
butt in EG *I butted in where I didn't belong.*
intervene EG *Soldiers don't like civilians intervening in their affairs.*
intrude EG *I don't want to intrude on your meeting.*
meddle EG *Scientists should not meddle in such matters.*
tamper EG *the price we pay for tampering with the environment*

❷ interfere VERB
to have a damaging effect on a situation
EG *His problems interfered with his work.*
conflict EG *an evening that conflicted with my work schedule*
disrupt EG *Strikes disrupted air traffic in Italy.*
hinder EG *A thigh injury hindered her movement.*
impede EG *Fallen rocks impeded the progress of the rescue workers.*
inhibit EG *factors which inhibit growth*

obstruct EG *Lack of funds obstructed our progress.*

interrogate VERB
to question someone thoroughly
EG *I interrogated everyone even slightly involved.*
examine EG *Lawyers examined the witnesses.*
grill INFORMAL EG *Jenkins kept telling police who grilled him: "I didn't kill her."*
question EG *He was questioned by police.*
quiz EG *She quizzed me quite closely for a while.*

WORD POWER
▷ **Synonyms**
cross-examine
cross-question

❶ interrupt VERB
to start talking when someone else is talking
EG *He tried to speak, but she interrupted him.*
butt in EG *Mirella butted in without a greeting.*
heckle EG *It is easy to heckle from the safety of the audience.*

❷ interrupt VERB
to stop a process or activity for a time
EG *The match was interrupted by rain.*
break EG *allowing passengers to break their journey with a stay in Fiji*
discontinue EG *Do not discontinue the treatment without seeing your doctor.*
suspend EG *Relief convoys will be suspended until the fighting stops.*

interval NOUN
a period of time between two moments or dates
EG *There was a long interval of silence.*
break EG *a short break from work*
gap EG *the gap between school terms*
hiatus EG *There was a momentary hiatus in the sounds.*

interlude EG *It was a happy interlude in the Kents' life.*
intermission EG *There will be a short intermission between acts.*
pause EG *a pause between two periods of intense activity*

intervene VERB
to step in to prevent conflict
EG *I relied on them to intervene if anything happened.*
arbitrate EG *A committee was set up to arbitrate in the dispute.*
mediate EG *efforts to mediate between the two communities*

❶ introduction NOUN
the act of presenting someone or something new
EG *the introduction of a single European currency*
establishment EG *the establishment of a democratic system*
inauguration EG *the inauguration of the President*
initiation EG *your initiation into adulthood*
institution EG *the institution of new laws*
launch EG *the launch of this popular author's new book*

❷ introduction NOUN
a piece of writing at the beginning of a book
EG *The book contains a new introduction by the author.*
foreword EG *I am happy to write the foreword to this collection.*
preface EG *I read through the preface quickly.*
prologue EG *the General Prologue to The Canterbury Tales*

intrude VERB
to disturb someone or something
EG *I don't want to intrude on your parents.*
butt in EG *I butted in where I didn't belong.*
encroach EG *Does your work*

a
b
c
d
e
f
g
h
i
j
k
l
m
n
o
p
q
r
s
t
u
v
w
x
y
z

encroach on your private life?
infringe EG *She promised not to infringe on his space.*
interrupt EG *Georgina interrupted his thoughts.*
trespass EG *I don't like to trespass on your time.*
violate EG *These men were violating her family's privacy.*

invade VERB
to enter a country by force
EG *The allies invaded the Italian mainland at Anzio.*
attack EG *Government planes attacked the town.*
enter EG *The Taleban entered western Kabul.*
occupy EG *Soldiers occupied the town within a few minutes.*
violate EG *A helicopter violated Greek territory yesterday.*

❶ invent VERB
to be the first person to think of a device
EG *He invented the first electric clock.*
coin EG *Lanier coined the term `virtual reality'.*
come up with INFORMAL EG *He came up with a gadget to relieve hayfever.*
conceive EG *He conceived the first portable computer.*
create EG *The company decided to create a new perfume.*
formulate EG *He formulated his plan for escape.*
originate EG *the designer who originated platform shoes*

WORD POWER

▷ **Synonyms**
design
devise
improvise

❷ invent VERB
to make up a story or excuse
EG *I tried to invent a plausible excuse.*
concoct EG *A newspaper concocted*

an imaginary interview.
fabricate EG *The evidence against them was fabricated.*
make up EG *Donna was known for making up stories about herself.*
manufacture EG *The children manufactured an elaborate tale.*

investigate VERB
to find out all the facts about something
EG *Police are still investigating the incidents.*
examine EG *I have examined all the possible alternatives.*
explore EG *a book which explores the history of technology*
probe EG *He probed into her private life.*
research EG *I'm researching for an article on New England.*
sift EG *I sifted the evidence for conclusions.*
study EG *Experts are studying the security in the building.*

invincible ADJECTIVE
unable to be defeated
EG *When Woods is on form he is invincible.*
impregnable EG *an impregnable fortress*
indomitable EG *the indomitable spirit of the Polish people*
unbeatable EG *a performance record that is unbeatable*

WORD POWER

▷ **Synonyms**
indestructible
insurmountable
unassailable

invisible ADJECTIVE
unable to be seen
EG *His face was invisible beneath his hat.*
concealed EG *a concealed weapon*
disguised EG *a disguised panel in the wall*

hidden EG *a hidden camera*
inconspicuous EG *She tried to make herself inconspicuous.*
unseen EG *His work was guided by an unseen hand.*

WORD POWER

▷ **Synonyms**
imperceptible
indiscernible

▶ **Antonym**
visible

---

involve VERB
to have as a necessary part
EG *Running a kitchen involves a great deal of discipline.*
incorporate EG *The program incorporates a range of activities.*
require EG *Caring for a baby requires special skills.*
take in EG *This study takes in a number of areas.*

WORD POWER

▷ **Synonyms**
entail
necessitate

---

irrational ADJECTIVE
not based on logical reasons
EG *irrational fears*
absurd EG *It was an absurd over-reaction.*
crazy EG *crazy ideas*
illogical EG *his completely illogical arguments*
nonsensical EG *Such an idea sounds paradoxical, if not downright nonsensical.*
unsound EG *The thinking is good-hearted, but muddled and unsound.*

WORD POWER

▷ **Synonyms**
injudicious
silly
unreasoning

---

❶ irregular ADJECTIVE
not smooth or even
EG *an irregular surface*
asymmetrical EG *She has asymmetrical features.*
bumpy EG *bumpy roads*
jagged EG *jagged fragments of stained glass*
lopsided EG *his lopsided smile*
ragged EG *the ragged edges of a tear*
uneven EG *uneven teeth*

WORD POWER

▶ **Antonym**
regular

---

❷ irregular ADJECTIVE
not forming a regular pattern
EG *He worked irregular hours.*
erratic EG *a planet with an erratic orbit*
haphazard EG *a haphazard system*
occasional EG *occasional rain showers*
patchy EG *Her career has been patchy.*
random EG *The stock market is random and unpredictable.*
variable EG *a variable rate of interest*

WORD POWER

▷ **Synonyms**
fitful
sporadic

▶ **Antonym**
regular

---

irresponsible ADJECTIVE
not concerned with the consequences of your actions
EG *an irresponsible attitude*
careless EG *a careless driver*
reckless EG *reckless spending*
thoughtless EG *a thoughtless remark*
wild EG *a night of wild abandon*

A B C D E F G H I J K L M N O P Q R S T U V W X Y Z

WORD POWER

▶ **Antonym**
responsible

irritable ADJECTIVE
easily annoyed
EG *Nicol was unusually tense and irritable.*
bad-tempered EG *You're very bad-tempered today.*
cantankerous EG *a cantankerous old man*
petulant EG *He was like a petulant child.*
ratty BRITISH AND NEW ZEALAND;
INFORMAL EG *There's no need to get ratty.*

WORD POWER

▷ **Synonyms**
irascible
tetchy

irritate VERB
to annoy someone
EG *Their attitude irritates me.*
anger EG *This article angered me.*
annoy EG *It just annoyed me to hear him going on.*
bother EG *Nothing bothers me.*
exasperate EG *Bertha was exasperated by the delay.*
needle INFORMAL EG *If her remark needled him, he didn't show it.*
ruffle EG *He doesn't get ruffled by anything.*

WORD POWER

▷ **Synonyms**
gall
provoke

❶ issue NOUN
a subject that people are talking about
EG *important issues of the day*
concern EG *Political concerns continue to dominate the news.*

matter EG *He touched on many matters in his speech.*
problem EG *the energy problem*
question EG *The whole question of aid is a tricky one.*
subject EG *the president's views on the subject*
topic EG *the main topic for discussion*

❷ issue NOUN
a particular edition of a newspaper or magazine
EG *the latest issue of the Lancet*
copy EG *a copy of "USA Today"*
edition EG *There's an article about the film in next month's edition.*
instalment EG *a magazine published in monthly instalments*

❸ issue VERB
to make a formal statement
EG *They have issued a statement denying the allegations.*
deliver EG *He delivered a speech to his fellow union members.*
give EG *The minister gave a warning that war should be avoided at all costs.*
make EG *He says he was depressed when he made the statement.*
pronounce EG *The authorities took time to pronounce their verdicts.*
read out EG *She read out an announcement outside the court.*
release EG *The police are not releasing any more details about the attack.*

WORD POWER

▶ **Antonym**
withdraw

❹ issue VERB
to give something officially
EG *Staff will be issued with badges.*
equip EG *plans to equip the reserve army with guns*
furnish FORMAL EG *They will furnish you with the necessary items.*
give out EG *The prizes were given out*

by a local dignitary.
provide EG *The government was unable to provide them with food.*
supply EG *an agreement not to supply these countries with chemical weapons*

❶ item NOUN
one of a collection or list of things
EG *an item on the agenda*
article EG *articles of clothing*
matter EG *He dealt with a variety of matters.*
point EG *Many of the points in the report are correct.*

thing EG *Big things are paid for by the government.*

❷ item NOUN
a newspaper or magazine article
EG *There was an item in the paper about him.*
article EG *a short article in one of the papers*
feature EG *The magazine contained a special feature on the project.*
notice EG *notices in today's national newspapers*
piece EG *I disagree with your recent piece about Australia.*
report EG *a film report on the scandal*

a
b
c
d
e
f
g
h
i
j
k
l
m
n
o
p
q
r
s
t
u
v
w
x
y
z

Jj

jagged ADJECTIVE
sharp and spiky
EG *jagged black cliffs*
barbed EG *barbed wire*
craggy EG *craggy mountains*
rough EG *the rough surface of the rock*
serrated EG *a serrated knife*

WORD POWER

▶ **Antonym**
smooth

1 jail NOUN
a place where prisoners are held
EG *sentenced to 18 months in jail*
nick BRITISH, AUSTRALIAN, AND NEW ZEALAND; SLANG EG *He spent seven years in the nick.*
prison EG *his release from prison*

WORD POWER

▷ **Synonyms**
lockup
penitentiary

2 jail VERB
to put in prison
EG *He was jailed for twenty years.*
detain EG *Police can detain a suspect for 48 hours.*
imprison EG *imprisoned for 18 months on charges of theft*
incarcerate EG *They have been incarcerated as political prisoners.*

1 jam NOUN
a crowded mass of people or things
EG *stuck in a jam on the motorway*
crowd EG *elbowing his way through the crowd*
crush EG *We got separated in the crush.*
mass EG *a mass of excited fans*
mob EG *a growing mob of demonstrators*
multitude EG *surrounded by a noisy multitude*

throng EG *An official pushed through the throng.*

2 jam NOUN
a difficult situation
EG *We're in a real jam now.*
dilemma EG *faced with a dilemma*
fix INFORMAL EG *a difficult economic fix*
hole SLANG EG *He admitted that the government was in a hole.*
plight EG *the plight of the Third World countries*
predicament EG *a way out of our predicament*
quandary EG *We're in a quandary over our holiday plans.*
trouble EG *You are in serious trouble.*

3 jam VERB
to push something somewhere roughly
EG *He jammed his hat on to his head.*
cram EG *He crammed the bank notes into his pocket.*
force EG *I forced the key into the ignition.*
ram EG *He rammed the muzzle of the gun against my forehead.*
stuff EG *She stuffed the newspaper into a litter bin.*

4 jam VERB
to become stuck
EG *The second time he fired, his gun jammed.*
stall EG *The engine stalled.*
stick EG *She tried to open the window but it was stuck.*

jealous ADJECTIVE
wanting to have something which someone else has
EG *She was jealous of his success.*
envious EG *envious of the attention his brother was getting*
resentful EG *resentful of her husband's hobby*

WORD POWER

▷ **Synonyms**
covetous
emulous

---

1 job NOUN
the work someone does to earn money
EG *I'm still looking for a job.*
employment EG *unable to find employment*
occupation EG *his occupation as a carpenter*
position EG *He's leaving to take up a position abroad.*
post EG *She has resigned her post as his assistant.*
profession EG *She chose nursing as her profession.*
trade EG *her trade as a jeweller*

2 job NOUN
a duty or responsibility
EG *It's your job to find out what's going on.*
concern EG *The technical aspects are the concern of the engineers.*
duty EG *I consider it my duty to write and thank you.*
function EG *an important function to fill*
responsibility EG *It's not my responsibility to look after my mother.*
role EG *Our role is to keep the peace.*
task EG *She had the task of breaking the bad news.*

1 join VERB
to become a member of something
EG *He joined the Army five years ago.*
enlist EG *He was 18 when he enlisted in the US Navy.*
enrol EG *She has enrolled in an acting class.*
sign up EG *I've signed up as a member.*

WORD POWER

▶ **Antonym**
resign

---

2 join VERB
to fasten two things together
EG *two sticks joined together by a chain*
attach EG *The gadget can be attached to any surface.*
connect EG *two rooms connected by a passage*
couple EG *an engine coupled to a gearbox*
fasten EG *a wooden bench fastened to the floor*
link EG *tree houses linked by ropes*
tie EG *He tied the dog to a post by its leash.*

WORD POWER

▷ **Synonyms**
append
knit
splice

▶ **Antonym**
separate

---

1 joke NOUN
something that makes people laugh
EG *I heard a great joke today.*
gag INFORMAL EG *a gag about unscrupulous lawyers*
jest EG *It was only intended as a jest.*
lark EG *They just did it for a lark.*
prank EG *an end-of-term prank*
quip EG *a famous quip by Groucho Marx*
wisecrack INFORMAL EG *She was tempted to make a wisecrack.*
witticism EG *laughing at each other's witticisms*

WORD POWER

▷ **Synonyms**
jape
sally

❷ joke VERB
to say something funny
EG *She was always joking about her appearance.*
banter EG *He played trick shots and bantered with the crowd.*
chaff EG *They chaffed us about our chances of winning.*
jest EG *drinking and jesting with his cronies*
kid INFORMAL EG *Don't worry, I'm only kidding.*
quip EG *"You'll have to go on a diet," he quipped.*
tease EG *"You must be in love," she teased.*

❶ journey NOUN
the act of travelling from one place to another
EG *the journey from Paris to Bordeaux*
excursion EG *The trip includes an excursion to Zermatt.*
expedition EG *an expedition to the South Pole*
passage EG *a 10-hour passage from Swansea*
tour EG *a two-month tour of Europe*
trek EG *a trek through the Gobi desert*
trip EG *a business trip*
voyage EG *the first space shuttle voyage*

❷ journey VERB
to travel from one place to another
EG *In 1935, she journeyed through Turkey and Africa.*
go EG *We went from Glasgow to London in six hours.*
proceed EG *proceeding along the road in the wrong direction*
tour EG *He toured China in 1993.*
travel EG *Gran travelled down by train.*
trek EG *trekking through the jungle*
voyage EG *They voyaged as far as Spain.*

joy NOUN
great happiness
EG *Her face shone with joy.*
bliss EG *an expression of pure bliss*
delight EG *He let out a yell of delight.*
ecstasy EG *Her eyes closed in ecstasy.*
elation EG *He felt a surge of elation at the news.*
rapture EG *His speech was received with rapture.*

WORD POWER

▷ **Synonyms**
exaltation
exultation
felicity

▶ **Antonym**
misery

joyful ADJECTIVE
extremely happy
EG *a joyful smile*
delighted EG *I'm delighted to be here.*
elated EG *the elated faces of the freed hostages*
jubilant EG *the jubilant crowds*
over the moon INFORMAL EG *I was over the moon to hear about your promotion.*

WORD POWER

▷ **Synonyms**
cock-a-hoop
enraptured

❶ judge NOUN
the person in charge of a law court
EG *The judge awarded him £2000 in damages.*
beak BRITISH; SLANG EG *a third appearance before the beak*
justice EG *his appointment as a Justice of the High Court*
magistrate EG *defendants appearing before a magistrate*

WORD POWER

● **Related Words**
adjective : judicial

❷ judge NOUN

someone who picks the winner or keeps control of a competition
EG *A panel of judges are selecting the finalists.*

referee EG *The referee awarded a free kick against Rourke.*

umpire EG *The umpire's decision is final.*

❸ judge VERB

to form an opinion about someone or something
EG *Don't judge people by their looks.*

appraise EG *The teachers are appraised by an official.*

assess EG *It is too early to assess the impact of the change.*

consider EG *We consider him to be dangerous.*

estimate EG *The cost of the damage is estimated at over a million dollars.*

evaluate EG *a test to evaluate a candidate's potential*

rate EG *The film was rated a hit.*

❹ judge VERB

to pick the winner or keep control in a competition
EG *Entrants will be judged in two age categories.*

referee EG *He has refereed in two World Cups.*

umpire EG *He umpired baseball games.*

WORD POWER

▷ **Synonyms**
adjudge
adjudicate

judgment NOUN

an opinion or decision based on evidence
EG *It's hard to form a judgment without all the facts.*

appraisal EG *a calm appraisal of the situation*

assessment EG *my own personal assessment of our position*

conclusion EG *I've come to the conclusion that she knows what she's talking about.*

opinion EG *Seek a medical opinion before you travel.*

ruling EG *a High Court ruling*

verdict EG *The doctor's verdict was that he was entirely healthy.*

view EG *In my view, things aren't going to get any better.*

❶ jump VERB

to leap up or over something
EG *I jumped over the fence.*

bound EG *He bounded up the steps.*

clear EG *The horse cleared the gate by inches.*

hurdle EG *He crossed the lawn and hurdled the fence.*

leap EG *He had leapt from a window and escaped.*

spring EG *The lion roared once and sprang.*

vault EG *Ned vaulted over a fallen tree.*

❷ jump VERB

to increase suddenly
EG *Sales jumped by 25% last year.*

escalate EG *Costs escalated dramatically.*

increase EG *Trading has increased by 20% this month.*

rise EG *Unemployment is rising rapidly.*

surge EG *The party's share of the vote surged from 10% to 17%.*

❸ jump NOUN

a leap into the air
EG *the longest ever jump by a man*

bound EG *With one bound Jack was free.*

leap EG *Smith took the gold medal with a leap of 2.37 metres.*

vault EG *She regained the record with a vault of 3.80 metres.*

junior ADJECTIVE

having a relatively low position compared to others

EG *a junior minister*

inferior EG *inferior status*

lesser EG *He resigned to take a lesser position and a cut in wages.*

lower EG *the lower ranks of council officers*

subordinate EG *sixty of his subordinate officers*

WORD POWER

▶ **Antonym**
senior

junk NOUN

old articles that people usually throw away

EG *What are you going to do with all that junk?*

clutter EG *She likes her worktops to be clear of clutter.*

odds and ends EG *My handbag's full of useless odds and ends.*

refuse EG *a weekly collection of refuse*

rubbish EG *They piled most of their rubbish into skips.*

scrap EG *a small yard containing a heap of scrap*

trash EG *cluttered with trash*

❶ justice NOUN

fairness in the way that people are treated

EG *He wants freedom, justice and equality.*

equity EG *Income should be distributed with some sense of equity.*

fairness EG *concern about the fairness of the election campaign*

impartiality EG *a system lacking impartiality*

WORD POWER

▶ **Antonym**
injustice

❷ justice NOUN

the person in charge of a law court

EG *his appointment as a Justice of the High Court*

judge EG *The judge awarded him £2000 in damages.*

magistrate EG *defendants appearing before a magistrate*

justify VERB

to show that something is reasonable or necessary

EG *How can you justify what you've done?*

defend EG *Her conduct is hard to defend.*

excuse EG *That still doesn't excuse his behaviour.*

explain EG *She left a note explaining her actions.*

vindicate EG *Ministers are confident their decision will be vindicated.*

warrant EG *These allegations warrant an investigation.*

Kk

kai NOUN; NEW ZEALAND; INFORMAL
food
EG *I'm starving - let's have some kai.*
food EG *Enjoy your food.*
grub INFORMAL EG *Get yourself some grub.*
provisions EG *enough provisions for two weeks*
rations EG *The soldiers sampled the officers' rations.*
tucker AUSTRALIAN AND NEW ZEALAND; INFORMAL EG *I haven't had any decent tucker for days.*

WORD POWER

▷ **Synonyms**
sustenance (FORMAL)

❶ keen ADJECTIVE
showing eagerness and enthusiasm for something
EG *a keen amateur photographer*
ardent EG *one of his most ardent supporters*
avid EG *an avid reader*
eager EG *We're eager to have another baby.*
enthusiastic EG *Tom was very enthusiastic about the place.*
fond of EG *Are you fond of Chinese cuisine?*
into INFORMAL EG *I'm really into football.*

❷ keen ADJECTIVE
quick to notice or understand things
EG *a keen intellect*
astute EG *an astute judge of character*
brilliant EG *She had a brilliant mind.*
perceptive EG *a perceptive gaze*
quick EG *His quick mind soon grasped the situation.*
shrewd EG *Her questions showed a shrewd perception.*

❶ keep VERB
to have and look after something
EG *His father keeps a small shop.*

care for EG *vintage cars lovingly cared for by their owners*
maintain EG *The house costs a fortune to maintain.*
preserve EG *the need to preserve the rainforests*

❷ keep VERB
to store something
EG *She kept her money under the mattress.*
deposit EG *You are advised to deposit your valuables in the hotel safe.*
hold EG *Our stock is held in a warehouse.*
store EG *Store the cookies in an airtight tin.*

❸ keep VERB
to do what you said you would do
EG *I always keep my promises.*
carry out EG *He carried out his threat.*
fulfil EG *He fulfilled all his responsibilities.*
honour EG *The two sides have agreed to honour a new ceasefire.*

kidnap VERB
to take someone away by force
EG *Four tourists have been kidnapped by rebels.*
abduct EG *people claiming to have been abducted by aliens*
capture EG *The guerrillas shot down one plane and captured the pilot.*
seize EG *hostages seized by terrorists*

kill VERB
to make someone or something die
EG *The earthquake killed 62 people.*
assassinate EG *the plot to assassinate Martin Luther King*
butcher EG *The guards butchered hundreds of prisoners.*
destroy EG *The jockey was unhurt but his horse had to be destroyed.*
execute EG *He was executed for treason.*
exterminate EG *an effort to*

A
B
C
D
E
F
G
H
I
J
K
L
M
N
O
P
Q
R
S
T
U
V
W
X
Y
Z

exterminate all the rats
massacre EG *300 civilians have been massacred by the rebels.*
murder EG *the widow of the murdered leader*
slaughter EG *Whales are being slaughtered for commercial gain.*
slay EG *a painting of Saint George slaying the dragon*

> ### WORD POWER
>
> ▷ **Synonyms**
> annihilate
> dispatch

kin NOUN
the people who are related to you
EG *She has gone to live with her husband's kin.*
family EG *There's a history of heart disease in our family.*
kindred EG *his loyalty to his friends and kindred*
people EG *She was reunited with her people.*
relations EG *I was staying with relations in Atlanta.*
relatives EG *On Sundays his relatives come to visit.*

❶ kind NOUN
a particular type of person or thing
EG *I don't like that kind of film.*
brand EG *his favourite brand of whisky*
breed EG *a rare breed of cattle*
category EG *Cereal bars are the fastest-growing category of breakfast products.*
class EG *a better class of restaurant*
classification EG *the cost of coverage for different classifications of motorcycle*
genre EG *a writer who does not confine himself to one particular genre*
grade EG *an improved grade of fertilizer*
sort EG *a dozen trees of various sorts*

species EG *a rare species of moth*
type EG *What type of guns were they?*
variety EG *a new variety of rose*

❷ kind ADJECTIVE
considerate towards other people
EG *Thank you for being so kind to me.*
benevolent EG *a very benevolent employer*
benign EG *a benign ruler*
charitable EG *a charitable nature*
compassionate EG *My father was a deeply compassionate man.*
considerate EG *a caring and considerate husband*
good EG *a good man driven to a desperate act*
humane EG *the humane treatment of prisoners*
kind-hearted EG *Mark was kind-hearted, generous, and loved life.*
kindly EG *a kindly old man*
thoughtful EG *a thoughtful gesture*
unselfish EG *his generous and unselfish attitude towards others*

> ### WORD POWER
>
> ▷ **Synonyms**
> lenient
> philanthropic
>
> ▶ **Antonym**
> cruel

kindness NOUN
the quality of being considerate towards other people
EG *Everyone has treated me with great kindness.*
benevolence EG *an act of selfless benevolence*
charity EG *Ms Rubens writes with warmth and charity.*
compassion EG *He showed no compassion to his victim.*
gentleness EG *the gentleness with which she treated her mother*
humanity EG *Her speech showed great maturity and humanity.*

WORD POWER

▷ **Synonyms**
kindliness
magnanimity
philanthropy
tenderness

▶ **Antonym**
cruelty

king NOUN
a man who is the head of a royal
family
EG *the king and queen of Spain*
monarch EG *the coronation of the
new monarch*
sovereign EG *the first British
sovereign to visit the country*

WORD POWER

● **Related Words**
adjectives : royal,
regal, monarchical

❶ **know** VERB
to understand or be aware of
something
EG *I don't know anything about cars.*
apprehend EG *It is impossible to
apprehend the whole painting at
once.*
be aware of EG *Smokers are aware*
of the risks they run.
comprehend EG *They do not
comprehend the nature of the
problem.*
perceive EG *the world as we perceive
it*
see EG *Don't you see what he's up to?*
understand EG *too young to
understand what was happening*

❷ **know** VERB
to be familiar with a person or thing
EG *I believe you two already know each
other.*
be acquainted with EG *Are you
acquainted with my husband?*
be familiar with EG *I am familiar
with his work.*
recognize EG *She recognized him at
once.*

knowledge NOUN
all you know about something
EG *She had no knowledge of French.*
education EG *a man with little
education*
learning EG *people of great learning*
scholarship EG *a lifetime of
scholarship*
wisdom EG *a source of wisdom and
knowledge*

LL

❶ label NOUN

a piece of paper or plastic attached to something for information
EG *He peered at the label on the bottle.*
sticker EG *She's got a disabled sticker on her car.*
tag EG *a name tag*
ticket EG *a price ticket*

❷ label VERB

to put a label on something
EG *The produce was labelled "Made in China".*
flag EG *Flag the pages which need corrections.*
sticker EG *products stickered at a special price*
tag EG *The pigeon was tagged with a numbered band.*

❶ labour NOUN

very hard work
EG *the labour of weeding and digging*
effort EG *legs aching with the effort of the climb*
exertion EG *She felt dizzy with the exertion of walking.*
industry EG *At last his industry was rewarded.*
toil EG *their day's toil in the fields*
work EG *All our work is starting to pay off.*

❷ labour NOUN

the workforce of a country or industry
EG *unskilled labour*
employees EG *Only a third of all employees are union members.*
workers EG *Thousands of workers have been laid off.*
workforce EG *a country where half the workforce is unemployed*

❸ labour VERB

to work very hard
EG *peasants labouring in the fields*
slave EG *We've been slaving half the night to finish this.*
toil EG *workers toiling in wretched conditions*
work EG *He works twelve hours a day.*

WORD POWER

▶ **Antonym**
relax

❶ lack NOUN

the shortage or absence of something which is needed
EG *a lack of funds*
absence EG *an absence of evidence*
deficiency EG *tests for vitamin deficiency*
scarcity EG *a scarcity of water*
shortage EG *a food shortage*
want EG *becoming weak from want of rest*

WORD POWER

▷ **Synonyms**
dearth
insufficiency
scantiness

▶ **Antonym**
abundance

❷ lack VERB

to be without something that is needed
EG *She lacks confidence.*
be deficient in EG *Your diet is deficient in vitamins.*
be short of EG *I'm short of cash.*
miss EG *Your jacket is missing a button.*

lag VERB

to make slower progress than other people or things
EG *He is now lagging 10 points behind the champion.*
fall behind EG *The city is falling behind in attracting tourists.*
trail EG *The Communist party is trailing badly in the opinion polls.*

lake NOUN

> **Types of lake**
> lagoon
> loch (*Scottish*)
> lough (*Irish*)
> mere
> reservoir
> tarn

1 lame ADJECTIVE
unable to walk properly because of
an injured leg
EG *She was lame in one leg.*
crippled EG *a woman crippled by
arthritis*
hobbling EG *a hobbling old man*
limping EG *limping from a hamstring
injury*

2 lame ADJECTIVE
weak or unconvincing
EG *a lame excuse*
feeble EG *his feeble attempt at
humour*
flimsy EG *MPs condemned his
evidence as flimsy.*
pathetic EG *a pathetic attempt at
humour*
poor EG *a poor effort*
unconvincing EG *an unconvincing
argument*
weak EG *a weak performance*

1 lament VERB
to express sorrow or regret over
something
EG *She lamented the death of her
brother.*
grieve EG *grieving over his dead wife
and son*
mourn EG *We mourned the loss of our
home.*
wail EG *a mother wailing for her lost
child*
weep EG *She wept for her lost love.*

WORD POWER

▷ **Synonyms**
bemoan
bewail

2 lament NOUN
something you say to express
sorrow or regret
EG *a lament for a vanished age*
moan EG *a moan of sorrow*
wail EG *wails of grief*

WORD POWER

▷ **Synonyms**
lamentation
plaint

1 land NOUN
an area of ground which someone
owns
EG *a dispute over land*
estate EG *a shooting party on his
estate in Yorkshire*
grounds EG *the palace grounds*
property EG *travellers who camped
on his property*

2 land NOUN
a region or country
EG *America is the land of opportunity.*
country EG *the boundary between
the two countries*
nation EG *the nation's financial crisis*
province EG *The Algarve is Portugal's
southernmost province.*
region EG *the region of Tuscany*
territory EG *the disputed territory of
Kashmir*

3 land VERB
to arrive on the ground after flying or
sailing
EG *We landed in New York around
noon.*
alight EG *A thrush alighted on a
nearby branch.*
dock EG *The ship docked in Le Havre.*
touch down EG *The plane touched
down in Barbados.*

1 language NOUN
the system of words people use to
communicate
EG *She speaks four languages.*
dialect EG *the Cantonese dialect*
idiom EG *the Gaelic folk idiom*

a b c d e f g h i j k l m n o p q r s t u v w x y z

jargon EG *scientific jargon*
lingo INFORMAL EG *I don't speak the lingo.*
tongue EG *The French feel passionately about their native tongue.*
vernacular EG *an Indian vernacular derived from Sanskrit*
vocabulary EG *a new word in the German vocabulary*

WORD POWER

▷ **Synonyms**
argot
cant
lingua franca
patois

❷ **language** NOUN
the style in which you speak or write
EG *He explained the process in plain language.*
phrasing EG *The phrasing of this report is confusing.*
style EG *a simple writing style*
wording EG *The wording of the contract was ambiguous.*

WORD POWER

▷ **Synonyms**
phraseology
terminology

large ADJECTIVE
of a greater size or amount than usual
EG *a large room*
big EG *Her husband was a big man.*
colossal EG *a colossal task*
enormous EG *an enormous house*
giant EG *a giant bird*
gigantic EG *a gigantic spider*
great EG *a great hall as long as a church*
huge EG *huge profits*
immense EG *an immense chamber*
massive EG *a massive ship*
vast EG *a vast desert*

WORD POWER

▷ **Synonyms**
gargantuan
sizable or sizeable

▶ **Antonym**
small

❶ **last** ADJECTIVE
the most recent
EG *last year*
latest EG *his latest thriller*
most recent EG *her most recent film*
preceding EG *The bank's turnover had risen during the preceding year.*
previous EG *his previous marriage*

WORD POWER

▶ **Antonym**
first

❷ **last** ADJECTIVE
happening or remaining after all the others of its kind
EG *the last three chapters of the book*
closing EG *the closing years of this century*
concluding EG *the concluding scene of the film*
final EG *This is your final chance.*
ultimate EG *the ultimate result of the move*

WORD POWER

▶ **Antonym**
first

❸ **last** VERB
to continue to exist or happen
EG *The film lasted for two and a half hours.*
carry on EG *Our marriage can't carry on like this.*
continue EG *The exhibition continues till 25 November.*
endure EG *Somehow their friendship endures.*
persist EG *The problem persists.*
remain EG *The building remains to*

this day.
survive EG *companies which survived after the recession*

❶ late ADJECTIVE
after the expected time
EG *The train was late.*
behind EG *I've got behind with my payments.*
behind time EG *Hurry up. We're behind time already.*
belated EG *a belated birthday card*
delayed EG *The kick-off was delayed by 10 minutes.*
last-minute EG *buying some last-minute Christmas presents*
overdue EG *The birth is two weeks overdue.*

WORD POWER

▷ **Synonyms**
behindhand
tardy
unpunctual

▶ **Antonym**
early

---

❷ late ADJECTIVE
dead, especially recently
EG *my late husband*
dead EG *He has been dead for a year now.*
deceased EG *his recently deceased mother*
departed EG *memories of departed friends*

WORD POWER

▷ **Synonyms**
defunct

---

❶ laugh VERB
to make a noise which shows you are amused or happy
EG *You never laugh at my jokes.*
chortle EG *He began chortling to himself.*
chuckle EG *He chuckled with pleasure.*

giggle EG *Both girls began to giggle.*
guffaw EG *Everyone guffawed loudly.*
snigger EG *People were sniggering behind my back.*
titter EG *The audience tittered nervously.*

❷ laugh NOUN
the noise you make when amused or happy
EG *She has a very infectious laugh.*
chortle EG *"That's what you think," he said with a chortle.*
chuckle EG *We had a quiet chuckle at his mistake.*
giggle EG *She gave a nervous giggle.*
guffaw EG *He let out a huge guffaw of amusement.*
snigger EG *barely able to stifle a snigger*
titter EG *A titter went round the room.*

❶ law NOUN
a country's system of rules
EG *The use of this drug is against the law.*
charter EG *a citizen's charter for France*
code EG *a code of conduct*
constitution EG *proposed changes to the constitution*

WORD POWER

● **Related Words**
adjectives : legal,
judicial

---

❷ law NOUN
one of the rules of a country
EG *The anti-stalking law was introduced in 1990.*
act EG *A new act has been passed by Parliament.*
code EG *a code designed to protect the rights of children*
decree EG *a decree lifting sanctions against China*
regulation EG *regulations outlawing child labour*

a b c d e f g h i j k l m n o p q r s t u v w x y z

A B C D E F G H I J K L M N O P Q R S T U V W X Y Z

rule EG *a rule that was imposed in 1962*

statute EG *a practice regulated by statute*

WORD POWER

▷ **Synonyms**
edict
ordinance

lawyer NOUN
someone who advises people about the law
EG *I'm discussing the matter with my lawyers.*

advocate EG *A public advocate will be appointed to represent you.*

attorney EG *a prosecuting attorney*

barrister EG *The author is a practising barrister.*

counsel EG *His counsel advised him to appeal against the verdict.*

solicitor EG *She took advice from a solicitor.*

❶ lay VERB
to put something somewhere
EG *Lay a sheet of newspaper on the floor.*

place EG *She placed a mug of coffee in front of him.*

put EG *He put the photograph on the desk.*

set EG *He set his briefcase on the floor.*

set down EG *I set the glasses down on the table.*

settle EG *He settled his coat over my shoulders.*

spread EG *She spread a towel over the sand and lay down.*

❷ lay VERB
to arrange or set something out
EG *A man came to lay the carpet.*

arrange EG *He started to arrange the books in piles.*

set out EG *The flower garden was set out with large beds of roses.*

layer NOUN
something that covers a surface or

comes between two other things
EG *A fresh layer of snow covered the street.*

blanket EG *a blanket of fog*

coat EG *a coat of paint*

coating EG *a crisp chocolate coating*

covering EG *a thin covering of dust*

film EG *a film of plastic*

sheet EG *a sheet of ice*

stratum EG *the correct geological stratum*

layout NOUN
the way in which something is arranged
EG *the layout of the garden*

arrangement EG *the arrangement of a room*

design EG *the design of the museum*

format EG *the format of the book*

plan EG *a detailed plan of the house*

laze VERB
to relax and do no work
EG *We spent a few days lazing around by the pool.*

idle EG *We spent hours idling in one of the cafés.*

loaf EG *loafing around the house all day*

lounge EG *They lounged in the shade.*

WORD POWER

▶ **Antonym**
work

lazy ADJECTIVE
not willing to work
EG *a lazy and incompetent employee*

idle EG *an idle young layabout*

slack EG *Many workers have simply become too slack.*

WORD POWER

▷ **Synonyms**
good-for-nothing
indolent
shiftless
slothful
workshy

▶ **Antonym**
industrious

❶ lead VERB
to guide or take someone somewhere
EG *She led him into the house.*
conduct EG *He asked if he might conduct us to the ball.*
escort EG *They were escorted by police to their plane.*
guide EG *He took me by the arm and guided me out.*
steer EG *Nick steered them towards the door.*
usher EG *I ushered him into the office.*

❷ lead VERB
to be in charge of
EG *He led the country between 1949 and 1984.*
command EG *the general who commanded the troops*
direct EG *He will direct day-to-day operations.*
govern EG *his ability to govern the country*
head EG *Who heads the firm?*
manage EG *I manage a small team of workers.*
supervise EG *He supervised more than 400 volunteers.*

❸ lead NOUN
a clue which may help solve a crime
EG *The police are following up several leads.*
clue EG *a vital clue to the killer's identity*
indication EG *All the indications suggest that he is the murderer.*
trace EG *No traces of violence were found on the body.*

leader NOUN
the person in charge of something
EG *the leader of the Republican Party*
boss INFORMAL EG *Who's the boss around here?*
captain EG *the captain of the team*

chief EG *the chief of police*
commander EG *a commander in the Royal Navy*
director EG *the director of the film*
head EG *Heads of government met in New York.*
principal EG *the principal of the school*
ringleader EG *the ringleader of the gang*

WORD POWER

▶ **Antonym**
follower

leading ADJECTIVE
particularly important, respected, or advanced
EG *a leading industrial nation*
chief EG *one of his chief rivals*
eminent EG *an eminent surgeon*
key EG *the key witness at the trial*
major EG *Exercise has a major part to play in preventing disease.*
main EG *one of the main tourist areas of Amsterdam*
principal EG *one of the principal figures in politics today*
prominent EG *a prominent member of the Law Society*
top EG *a top model*

WORD POWER

▷ **Synonyms**
pre-eminent

lead to VERB
to cause something to happen
EG *Smoking leads to heart disease and cancer.*
cause EG *Knocks can cause damage to the spine.*
contribute to EG *injuries which contributed to his death*
produce EG *The drug produces side effects.*

A B C D E F G H I J K L M N O P Q R S T U V W X Y Z

WORD POWER

▷ **Synonyms**
bring on
conduce to
result in

---

leaflet NOUN
a piece of paper with information
about a subject
EG *Protesters were handing out leaflets
in the street.*
booklet EG *a booklet about
mortgage rates*
brochure EG *a travel brochure*
circular EG *A circular was sent out to
shareholders.*
pamphlet EG *an anti-vivisection
pamphlet*

WORD POWER

▷ **Synonyms**
handbill
mailshot

---

❶ leak VERB
to escape from a container or other
object
EG *The gas had leaked from a cylinder.*
escape EG *A vent was opened to let
some air escape.*
ooze EG *Blood was oozing from the
wound.*
seep EG *Radioactive water has
seeped into underground reservoirs.*
spill EG *70,000 tonnes of oil spilled
from the tanker.*

❷ leak NOUN
a hole which lets gas or liquid escape
EG *Have you plugged the leaks?*
chink EG *A mist rose from the chinks in
the pavement.*
crack EG *The lava oozed through
cracks in the rock.*
fissure EG *Water trickled out of
fissures in the limestone.*
hole EG *The sea was flowing in
through the hole in the ship's hull.*

puncture EG *My tyre has a slow
puncture.*

❶ leap VERB
to jump a great distance or height
EG *The deer leapt into the air.*
bounce EG *She bounced up and down
on the spot, looking for attention.*
bound EG *The dog came bounding up
the stairs.*
jump EG *I jumped over the fence.*
spring EG *He sprang to his feet.*
vault EG *He could easily vault the
wall.*

❷ leap NOUN
a jump of great distance or height
EG *a leap of 2.37 metres*
jump EG *the longest jumps by a man
and a woman*
bound EG *With one bound, Jack was
free.*
spring EG *The cheetah gave a great
spring into the air.*

❶ learn VERB
to gain knowledge by studying or
training
EG *I am trying to learn French.*
grasp EG *The basics of the language
are easy to grasp.*
master EG *He's having trouble
mastering the piano.*
pick up EG *You'll soon pick up enough
German to get by.*

❷ learn VERB
to find out about something
EG *On learning who she was, I asked to
meet her.*
ascertain EG *They had ascertained
that he was not a spy.*
determine EG *calculations to
determine the rate of tax*
discover EG *She discovered that
they'd escaped.*
find out EG *As soon as we found this
out, we closed the ward.*
gather EG *I gather the report is critical
of the judge.*
hear EG *I heard he had moved away.*

understand EG *I understand that she's just taken early retirement.*

learned ADJECTIVE
having gained a lot of knowledge by studying
EG *a very learned man*
academic EG *I feel intimidated by academic people.*
erudite EG *a witty and erudite leader*
intellectual EG *an artistic and intellectual couple*
literate EG *a literate and educated readership*
scholarly EG *a scholarly researcher*

WORD POWER

▷ **Synonyms**
lettered
well-read

least ADJECTIVE
as small or few as possible
EG *Stick to foods with the least fat.*
fewest EG *Which product has the fewest calories?*
lowest EG *the lowest temperatures on record for this time of year*
minimum EG *the minimum height for a policeman*
slightest EG *He showed only the slightest hint of emotion.*
smallest EG *the smallest measurable unit of light*

WORD POWER

▶ **Antonym**
most

❶ leave VERB
to go away from a person or place
EG *He is not allowed to leave the country.*
abandon EG *He claimed that his parents had abandoned him.*
depart EG *A number of staff departed during his time as director.*
desert EG *Medical staff have deserted the city's main hospital.*
forsake EG *I would never forsake my*

children.
go EG *Let me know when you're ready to go.*
quit EG *He quit his job as an office boy.*
withdraw EG *Troops withdrew from the country last month.*

WORD POWER

▷ **Synonyms**
abscond
decamp

❷ leave NOUN
a period of time off work
EG *Why don't you take a few days' leave?*
holiday EG *I still have several days' holiday to take.*
time off EG *He took time off to go sailing with his wife.*
vacation EG *We went on vacation to Puerto Rico.*

WORD POWER

▷ **Synonyms**
furlough
sabbatical

❶ lecture NOUN
a formal talk about a particular subject
EG *In his lecture he covered several topics.*
address EG *an address to the American people*
discourse EG *a lengthy discourse on market strategy*
presentation EG *a business presentation*
sermon EG *his first sermon as a bishop*
speech EG *He delivered his speech in French.*
talk EG *a brief talk on the history of the site*

WORD POWER

▷ **Synonyms**
exposition

a
b
c
d
e
f
g
h
i
j
k
l
m
n
o
p
q
r
s
t
u
v
w
x
y
z

② lecture NOUN
a talk intended to tell someone off
EG *The police gave us a stern lecture on safety.*
reprimand EG *He has been given a severe reprimand.*
scolding EG *given a scolding for offending his opponents*
ticking-off INFORMAL EG *We were given a ticking-off for running in the corridors.*
warning EG *He was given a severe warning from the referee.*

③ lecture VERB
to teach by giving formal talks to audiences
EG *She has lectured all over the world.*
give a talk EG *He set about campaigning, giving talks and fund-raising.*
speak EG *He's been invited to speak at the Democratic Convention.*
talk EG *Today, I plan to talk about the issues of education and nursery care.*
teach EG *She has taught at the university for 34 years.*

left-wing ADJECTIVE
believing in socialist policies
EG *a left-wing demonstration*
leftist EG *three leftist guerrilla groups*
liberal EG *a politician with liberal views*
radical EG *a radical feminist*
socialist EG *Europe's last socialist state*

legacy NOUN
property someone leaves you when they die
EG *He left his sons a generous legacy.*
bequest EG *He made a bequest to his favourite charity.*
estate EG *documents concerning the estate*
heirloom EG *a family heirloom*
inheritance EG *She was worried she'd lose her inheritance to her stepmother.*

① legal ADJECTIVE
relating to the law
EG *the Dutch legal system*
forensic EG *the forensic skill of a good barrister*
judicial EG *a judicial review*
judiciary EG *various levels of the judiciary system*

② legal ADJECTIVE
allowed by the law
EG *The strike was perfectly legal.*
authorized EG *an authorized procedure*
lawful EG *What I did was lawful and proper.*
legitimate EG *a legitimate business*
permissible EG *the current permissible levels of pesticide in food*
rightful EG *the rightful owner of the property*
valid EG *a valid passport*

WORD POWER

▷ **Synonyms**
constitutional
licit
sanctioned

▶ **Antonym**
illegal

leisure NOUN
time when you can relax
EG *There wasn't a lot of time for leisure.*
free time EG *He played piano in his free time.*
recreation EG *Saturday afternoons are for recreation.*
relaxation EG *Make time for a bit of relaxation.*
time off EG *I haven't had any time off all day.*

WORD POWER

▶ **Antonym**
work

leisurely ADJECTIVE
unhurried or calm

EG *a leisurely walk along the beach*
comfortable EG *going at a comfortable speed*
easy EG *an easy pace*
gentle EG *His movements were gentle and deliberate.*
relaxed EG *a relaxed meal*
unhurried EG *an unhurried way of life*

WORD POWER

▶ **Antonym**
hasty

lekker ADJECTIVE; SOUTH AFRICAN; SLANG
pleasant or tasty
EG *We had a really lekker meal.*
delectable EG *delectable chocolates*
delicious EG *a wide selection of delicious desserts*
luscious EG *luscious fruit*
pleasant EG *a pleasant dinner*
tasty EG *Try this tasty dish for supper.*

❶ **length** NOUN
the distance from one end of something to the other
EG *The fish was about a metre in length.*
distance EG *Work out the distance of the journey.*
extent EG *the extent of the rain forest*
span EG *a butterfly with a two-inch wing span*

❷ **length** NOUN
the amount of time something lasts for
EG *The film is over two hours in length.*
duration EG *The duration of the course is one year.*
period EG *for a limited period only*
space EG *A dramatic change takes place in the space of a few minutes.*
span EG *The batteries have a life span of six hours.*
term EG *a 12-month term of service*

lengthen VERB
to make something longer
EG *The runway had to be lengthened.*

extend EG *They have extended the deadline.*
make longer EG *You can make your hair longer by using extensions.*
prolong EG *a move which will prolong the strike*
stretch EG *Take care not to stretch the fabric.*

WORD POWER

▷ **Synonyms**
elongate
protract

▶ **Antonym**
shorten

lessen VERB
to decrease in size or amount
EG *changes to their diet that would lessen the risk of disease*
abate EG *The storm gradually abated.*
decrease EG *Population growth is decreasing by 1.4% each year.*
diminish EG *The threat of war has diminished.*
dwindle EG *his dwindling authority*
lower EG *The Central Bank has lowered interest rates.*
minimize EG *attempts to minimize the risk of developing cancer*
reduce EG *Gradually reduce the dosage.*
shrink EG *The forests have shrunk to half their size.*

WORD POWER

▷ **Synonyms**
de-escalate
downsize

▶ **Antonym**
increase

lesson NOUN
a period of time for being taught
EG *Johanna took piano lessons.*
class EG *I go to dance classes.*
coaching EG *He needs extra coaching in maths.*

a
b
c
d
e
f
g
h
i
j
k
l
m
n
o
p
q
r
s
t
u
v
w
x
y
z

A
B
C
D
E
F
G
H
I
J
K
L
M
N
O
P
Q
R
S
T
U
V
W
X
Y
Z

lecture EG *a series of lectures on art*

period EG *We get six periods of French a week.*

tutoring EG *a growing demand for private tutoring*

❶ let VERB

to allow someone to do something
EG *The authorities won't let her leave the country.*

allow EG *I pleaded to be allowed to go.*

give permission EG *Who gave you permission to come here?*

permit EG *Permit me to express my opinion.*

sanction EG *He may now be ready to sanction the use of force.*

WORD POWER

▶ **Antonym**
forbid

❷ let VERB

to let someone use your property for money
EG *She always lets her house for the summer.*

hire out EG *The machines are hired out to farmers.*

lease EG *She plans to lease the building to students.*

rent EG *He rents rooms to backpackers.*

❶ level ADJECTIVE

completely flat
EG *a plateau of level ground*

flat EG *Cricket should be played on a totally flat field.*

horizontal EG *Every horizontal surface was covered with plants.*

WORD POWER

▶ **Antonym**
uneven

❷ level VERB

to make something flat
EG *We levelled the ground.*

flatten EG *Flatten the dough and cut it into four pieces.*

plane EG *planing the surface of the wood*

smooth EG *He smoothed his hair.*

❸ level NOUN

a point on a scale which measures something
EG *Crime levels have started to decline.*

grade EG *the lowest grade of staff*

rank EG *He rose to the rank of captain.*

stage EG *an early stage of development*

standard EG *a decent standard of living*

status EG *We were reduced to the status of animals.*

❶ lie VERB

to rest somewhere horizontally
EG *The injured man was lying on his back.*

loll EG *He was lolling on the sofa.*

lounge EG *We lounged on the beach all day.*

recline EG *She reclined on the couch.*

sprawl EG *They sprawled in a lawn chair, snoozing.*

WORD POWER

▷ **Synonyms**
be prostrate
be recumbent
be supine
repose

❷ lie VERB

to say something that is not true
EG *She always lies about her age.*

fib EG *He fibbed when she asked him where he'd been.*

perjure oneself EG *All of the witnesses perjured themselves.*

tell a lie EG *He could never tell a lie or do anything devious.*

WORD POWER

▷ **Synonyms**
dissimulate
equivocate
forswear oneself
prevaricate

❸ lie NOUN

something you say which is not true
EG *His whole story was a lie.*
deceit EG *the deceits of political leaders*
fabrication EG *She described the magazine interview as "a complete fabrication".*
falsehood EG *He accused them of spreading falsehoods about him.*
fib EG *I caught him out in another fib.*
fiction EG *His account of events is a complete fiction.*

life NOUN

the time during which you are alive
EG *a long and active life*
existence EG *a very miserable existence*
life span EG *This species of snake has a life span of up to 25 years.*
lifetime EG *a lifetime devoted to service for others*
time EG *If I had my time again, I would do things differently.*

WORD POWER

● **Related Words**
adjectives : animate, vital

❶ lift VERB

to move something to a higher position
EG *straining to lift heavy weights*
elevate EG *a mechanism to elevate the platform*
hoist EG *I hoisted my rucksack on to my shoulder.*
pick up EG *Anthony picked up his*

case from the floor.
raise EG *He raised his hand to wave.*

WORD POWER

▶ **Antonym**
lower

❷ lift VERB

to remove something such as a ban or law
EG *the decision to lift sanctions against Iran*
cancel EG *The government has cancelled the state of emergency.*
end EG *pressure to end the embargo*
relax EG *an attempt to persuade the US Congress to relax the law*
remove EG *an amendment to remove the ban on divorce*

WORD POWER

▷ **Synonyms**
rescind
revoke

❶ light NOUN

brightness that enables you to see things
EG *Cracks of light filtered through the shutters.*
brightness EG *the brightness of the full moon*
brilliance EG *the brilliance of the noonday sun*
glare EG *shading his eyes from the glare*
glow EG *the red glow of the dying fire*
illumination EG *The only illumination came from a small window.*
radiance EG *The bedside lamp cast a soft radiance over her face.*

WORD POWER

▷ **Synonyms**
incandescence
luminescence
luminosity
phosphorescence

A
B
C
D
E
F
G
H
I
J
K
L
M
N
O
P
Q
R
S
T
U
V
W
X
Y
Z

▶ **Antonym**
dark

● **Related Words**
prefix : photo-

② light ADJECTIVE
pale in colour
EG *a light blue shirt*
bleached EG *bleached pine tables*
blonde *or* **blond** EG *blonde hair*
fair EG *to protect my fair skin*
pale EG *dressed in pale pink*
pastel EG *delicate pastel shades*

WORD POWER

▶ **Antonym**
dark

③ light ADJECTIVE
not weighing much
EG *working out with light weights*
flimsy EG *a flimsy cardboard box*
lightweight EG *They will carry lightweight skis on their backs.*
portable EG *a portable television*
slight EG *She is small and slight.*

WORD POWER

▶ **Antonym**
heavy

④ light VERB
to make a place bright
EG *The room was lit by a single candle.*
brighten EG *The late afternoon sun brightened the room.*
illuminate EG *No streetlights illuminated the road.*
light up EG *Fireworks lit up the sky.*

WORD POWER

▶ **Antonym**
darken

⑤ light VERB
to make a fire start burning
EG *It's time to light the barbecue.*
ignite EG *A stray spark ignited the*

fireworks.
kindle EG *I kindled a fire in the stove.*

WORD POWER

▶ **Antonym**
extinguish

① like ADJECTIVE
similar to another thing
EG *He looks just like my father.*
akin EG *She looked at me with something akin to hatred.*
alike EG *They are very alike in temperament.*
analogous EG *a process analogous to the curing of tobacco*
identical EG *Nearly all the houses were identical.*
parallel EG *Our situation is parallel to yours.*
same EG *His uniform was exactly the same colour as the car.*
similar EG *a taste similar to that of celery*

WORD POWER

▶ **Antonym**
unlike

② like VERB
to find someone or something pleasant
EG *I really like this music.*
adore INFORMAL EG *All her employees adored her.*
appreciate EG *I know you appreciate good food.*
be fond of EG *Are you fond of Chinese cuisine?*
be keen on EG *I'm not very keen on sport.*
be partial to EG *I'm partial to men with dark hair.*
enjoy EG *Most children enjoy cartoons.*
go for EG *What kind of man do you go for?*
have a soft spot for EG *I've always had a soft spot for him.*

have a weakness for EG *I have a weakness for slushy romantic novels.*
love EG *She loves reading.*
relish EG *He relished the idea of proving me wrong.*
revel in EG *She appears to revel in being unpopular.*

WORD POWER

▶ **Antonym**
dislike

likely ADJECTIVE
having a good chance of happening
EG *It seems likely that he will come back.*

anticipated EG *the anticipated result*
expected EG *the expected response*
liable EG *He is liable to be a nuisance.*
possible EG *It's quite possible that I'm wrong.*
probable EG *the probable outcome*

WORD POWER

▶ **Antonym**
unlikely

❶ limit NOUN
a point beyond which something cannot go
EG *the speed limit*

bounds EG *the bounds of good taste*
deadline EG *We finished the job within the deadline.*
maximum EG *He was given two years in prison, the maximum allowed for the charges.*
ultimate EG *This hotel is the ultimate in luxury.*
utmost EG *His skills were tested to the utmost.*

❷ limit VERB
to prevent something from going any further
EG *Limit yourself to six units of alcohol a week.*

confine EG *Damage was confined to a small portion of the building.*
curb EG *measures to curb inflation*

fix EG *The mortgage rate is fixed at 8.5%.*
ration EG *I'm rationing myself to ten cigarettes a day.*
restrict EG *The patient was restricted to a meagre diet.*

WORD POWER

▷ **Synonyms**
circumscribe
delimit
demarcate
straiten

limp ADJECTIVE
not stiff or firm
EG *a limp lettuce leaf*

drooping EG *the drooping branches of a birch*
flabby EG *a flabby stomach*
floppy EG *She fondled the dog's floppy ears.*
slack EG *his slack belly*
soft EG *a soft dough*

WORD POWER

▷ **Synonyms**
flaccid
pliable

▶ **Antonym**
stiff

❶ line NOUN
a long thin mark on something
EG *Draw a line down the centre of the page.*

rule EG *He drew a rule under the last name.*
score EG *There was a long score on the car's bonnet.*
streak EG *dark streaks on the surface of the moon*
stripe EG *a green jogging suit with white stripes down the sides*

❷ line NOUN
a row of people or things
EG *a line of spectators*

column EG *a column of figures*

a
b
c
d
e
f
g
h
i
j
k
l
m
n
o
p
q
r
s
t
u
v
w
x
y
z

file EG *A file of mourners walked behind the coffin.*
queue EG *a long queue of angry motorists*
rank EG *ranks of police in riot gear*
row EG *a row of pretty little cottages*

❸ line NOUN
the route along which something moves
EG *the line of flight*
course EG *the course of the river*
path EG *The lava annihilates everything in its path.*
route EG *the most direct route*
track EG *a railway track*
trajectory EG *the trajectory of the missile*

❶ link NOUN
a connection between two things
EG *the link between sunbathing and skin cancer*
affiliation EG *He has no affiliation with any political party.*
association EG *the association between the two companies*
attachment EG *Mother and child form a close attachment.*
bond EG *The experience created a bond between us.*
connection EG *He has denied any connection to the bombing.*
relationship EG *the relationship between humans and their environment*
tie EG *She has ties with this town.*

WORD POWER
▷ **Synonyms**
affinity
liaison

❷ link VERB
to connect two things
EG *tree houses linked by ropes*
attach EG *Attach the curtains to the rods with hooks.*
connect EG *two rooms connected by a passage*

couple EG *The engine is coupled to a gearbox.*
fasten EG *a wooden bench fastened to the floor*
join EG *the skin which joins the eye to the eyelid*
tie EG *He tied the dog to the tree by its lead.*

WORD POWER
▶ **Antonym**
separate

❶ liquid NOUN
a substance which is not solid and can be poured
EG *Drink plenty of liquids for the next few days.*
fluid EG *The fluid can be removed with a syringe.*
liquor EG *Pour the liquor off into the pan.*
solution EG *a solution of honey and vinegar*

❷ liquid ADJECTIVE
in the form of a liquid
EG *wash in warm water with liquid detergent*
fluid EG *a fluid fertiliser*
molten EG *molten metal*
runny EG *a dessertspoon of runny honey*

❶ list NOUN
a set of things written down one below the other
EG *There were six names on the list.*
catalogue EG *a chronological catalogue of the Beatles' songs*
directory EG *a telephone directory*
index EG *The book includes a comprehensive subject index.*
inventory EG *an inventory of stolen goods*
listing EG *a listing of all the schools in the area*
record EG *Keep a record of everything you eat and drink.*

register EG *a register of births, deaths and marriages*

2 list VERB
to set things down in a list
EG *All the ingredients are listed on the label.*
catalogue EG *I was cataloguing my video collection.*
index EG *Most of the archive has been indexed.*
record EG *400 species of fungi have been recorded.*
register EG *a registered charity*

WORD POWER

▷ **Synonyms**
enumerate
itemize
tabulate

listen VERB
to hear and pay attention to something
EG *I'll repeat that for those of you who weren't listening.*
attend EG *Close your books and attend to me.*
hark EG *Hark! I hear the sound of footsteps.*
hear EG *Will you hear me saying my lines?*
pay attention EG *Pay attention or you won't know what to do.*

1 little ADJECTIVE
small in size or amount
EG *a little old lady*
→ see Word Study **little**

WORD POWER

▶ **Antonym**
large

2 little NOUN
a small amount or degree
EG *Would you like a little fruit juice?*
→ see Word Study **little**

1 live VERB
to have your home somewhere

EG *She has lived here for 20 years.*
dwell EG *the people who dwell in the forest*
inhabit EG *the fish that inhabit the coral reefs*
reside EG *He used to reside in England.*
stay SCOTTISH AND SOUTH AFRICAN eg *We've stayed in this house since we got married.*

2 live VERB
to be alive
EG *He will not live much longer.*
be alive EG *You are lucky to be alive.*
exist EG *the chances of finding life existing on Mars*

3 live ADJECTIVE
not dead or artificial
EG *a live spider*
alive EG *It is unlikely that he is still alive.*
animate EG *an animate object*
living EG *living tissue*

lively ADJECTIVE
full of life and enthusiasm
EG *a lively personality*
active EG *an active youngster*
animated EG *an animated discussion*
energetic EG *She gave an energetic performance.*
perky EG *He wasn't quite as perky as usual.*
sparkling EG *I was enjoying a sparkling conversation.*
sprightly EG *a sprightly old man*
vivacious EG *She is vivacious and charming.*

WORD POWER

▶ **Antonym**
dull

1 load NOUN
something being carried
EG *This truck can carry a load of up to 10 tons.*
cargo EG *The boat was carrying its usual cargo of bananas.*

a
b
c
d
e
f
g
h
i
j
k
l
m
n
o
p
q
r
s
t
u
v
w
x
y
z

consignment EG *The first consignment of food has been sent.*
freight EG *Most of the freight was carried by rail.*
shipment EG *a shipment of weapons*

❷ load VERB
to put a lot of things on or into
EG *The trucks were loaded with blankets and supplies.*
fill EG *The van was filled with crates.*
pack EG *helicopters packed with medical supplies*
pile EG *Her trolley was piled with groceries.*
stack EG *stalls stacked with wares*

❶ loan NOUN
a sum of money that you borrow
EG *a small business loan*
advance EG *She was paid a $100,000 advance on her next novel.*
credit EG *He can't get credit to buy the equipment.*
mortgage EG *I took out a second mortgage on the house.*

❷ loan VERB
to lend something to someone
EG *He loaned us the painting for our exhibition.*
advance EG *I advanced him some money till we got home.*
lend EG *Will you lend me your jacket?*

❶ local ADJECTIVE
belonging to the area where you live
EG *This is a local shop for local people.*
community EG *the revival of family and community life*
district EG *the district council*
neighbourhood EG *a neighbourhood watch scheme*
parish EG *the parish priest*
regional EG *the regional elections*

❷ local NOUN
a person who lives in a particular area
EG *That's what the locals call the place.*
inhabitant EG *the inhabitants of Glasgow*

native EG *She is proud to be a native of Sydney.*
resident EG *a protest by residents of the village*

locate VERB
to find out where someone or something is
EG *We have been unable to locate him.*
find EG *They can't find it on the map.*
pinpoint EG *Computers pinpointed where the shells came from.*
track down EG *She has spent years trying to track down her parents.*

located ADJECTIVE
existing or standing in a particular place
EG *The restaurant is located near the cathedral.*
placed EG *The hotel is wonderfully placed right in the city centre.*
sited EG *a castle romantically sited on a river estuary*
situated EG *His hotel is situated in a lovely place.*

location NOUN
a place or position
EG *a house with a beautiful location*
place EG *the place where the temple used to stand*
point EG *a popular meeting point for tourists*
position EG *The ship radioed its position to the coastguard.*
site EG *the site of the murder*
situation EG *The hotel has a superb isolated location.*
spot EG *Can you show me the spot where it happened?*
whereabouts EG *His exact whereabouts are still not known.*

WORD POWER

▷ **Synonyms**
locale
locus

❶ lock VERB
to close and fasten something with a

key
EG *Are you sure you locked the door?*
latch EG *He latched the gate.*
padlock EG *The box has been padlocked shut.*

> ### WORD POWER
>
> ▶ **Antonym**
> unlock

❷ lock NOUN
a device used to fasten something
EG *The lock had been burst open.*
latch EG *A key clicked in the latch of the front door.*
padlock EG *He put a padlock on the door of his flat.*

❶ logical ADJECTIVE
using logic to work something out
EG *a logical argument*
consistent EG *a consistent and well-presented theory*
rational EG *a rational analysis*
reasoned EG *a reasoned discussion*
sound EG *His reasoning is sound, but he has missed the point.*
valid EG *Both sides put forward valid points.*

> ### WORD POWER
>
> ▷ **Synonyms**
> cogent
> coherent
>
> ▶ **Antonym**
> illogical

❷ logical ADJECTIVE
sensible in the circumstances
EG *a logical deduction*
judicious EG *the judicious use of military force*
obvious EG *I jumped to the obvious conclusion.*
plausible EG *a plausible explanation*
reasonable EG *a reasonable course of action*

sensible EG *the sensible thing to do*
wise EG *a wise decision*

> ### WORD POWER
>
> ▶ **Antonym**
> illogical

❶ lonely ADJECTIVE
unhappy because of being alone
EG *She's lonely and just wants to talk.*
alone EG *scared of being alone in the house*
forlorn EG *He looked a forlorn figure as he left the pitch.*
forsaken EG *a forsaken and bitter man*
lonesome EG *I'm lonesome without you.*

❷ lonely ADJECTIVE
isolated and not visited by many people
EG *a lonely hillside*
deserted EG *a deserted farmhouse*
desolate EG *a desolate place*
isolated EG *Many of the villages are in isolated areas.*
remote EG *a remote outpost*
secluded EG *a secluded area close to her home*
uninhabited EG *an uninhabited island*

> ### WORD POWER
>
> ▷ **Synonyms**
> godforsaken
> out-of-the-way
> unfrequented

❶ long ADJECTIVE
continuing for a great amount of time
EG *a long interval when no-one spoke*
→ see Word Study **long**

> ### WORD POWER
>
> ▶ **Antonym**
> short

A B C D E F G H I J K L M N O P Q R S T U V W X Y Z

❷ long ADJECTIVE
great in length or distance
EG *a long line of people*
→ see Word Study **long**

WORD POWER

▶ **Antonym**
short

❸ long VERB
to want something very much
EG *He longed for a cigarette.*
ache EG *She still ached for her dead husband.*
covet EG *She coveted his job.*
crave EG *I crave her approval.*
hunger EG *Jules hungered for adventure.*
lust EG *She lusted after a designer kitchen.*
pine EG *I pine for the countryside.*
yearn EG *He yearned for freedom.*

longing NOUN
a strong wish for something
EG *her longing to return home*
craving EG *a craving for sugar*
desire EG *her desire for a child of her own*
hankering EG *a hankering to be an actress*
hunger EG *a hunger for success*
thirst EG *a thirst for adventure*
yearning EG *a yearning to be part of a normal family*

❶ look VERB
to turn your eyes towards something and see it
EG *She looked at me with something like hatred.*
→ see Word Study **look**

❷ look VERB
to appear or seem to be
EG *the desire to look attractive*
appear EG *He appeared intoxicated.*
look like EG *You look like you need a good night's sleep.*
seem EG *She seemed tense.*

seem to be EG *They seem to be lacking in enthusiasm.*

❸ look NOUN
the action of turning your eyes towards something
EG *Lucy took a last look in the mirror.*
gaze EG *her concentrated gaze*
glance EG *a cursory glance*
glimpse EG *a fleeting glimpse*
peek EG *Give me a peek at his letter.*

❹ look NOUN
the way someone or something appears
EG *He had the look of a desperate man.*
air EG *a nonchalant air*
appearance EG *He was fastidious about his appearance.*
bearing EG *a man of military bearing*
expression EG *I saw his puzzled expression.*
face EG *Why are you all wearing such long faces?*
semblance EG *a semblance of normality*

look after VERB
to take care of someone or something
EG *Will you look after my cats when I go on holiday?*
care for EG *vintage cars lovingly cared for by their owners*
mind EG *Jim will mind the shop while I'm away.*
nurse EG *My mother nursed him while he was ill.*
take care of EG *I'll take care of the house for you.*
tend EG *He tended his flower beds.*
watch EG *My mother will watch the kids while we're out.*

lookalike NOUN
a person who looks like someone else
EG *an Elvis lookalike*
dead ringer INFORMAL EG *a dead ringer for his brother*
double EG *He's the exact double of his*

father at that age.
spitting image INFORMAL EG *She is the spitting image of me.*

look for VERB
to try to find a person or thing
EG *I'm looking for my son.*
forage EG *foraging for food*
hunt EG *Police are hunting for clues.*
search EG *Rescue teams are searching for the missing crew members.*
seek EG *They have had to seek work as labourers.*

❶ loose ADJECTIVE
not firmly held or fixed
EG *a loose tooth*
free EG *She broke her fall with her free hand.*
unsecured EG *corridors blocked by unsecured objects*
wobbly EG *a wobbly bridge*

> ### WORD POWER
> ▶ **Antonym**
> secure

❷ loose ADJECTIVE
not fitting closely
EG *Wear loose clothes for comfort.*
baggy EG *a baggy black jumper*
slack EG *Those trousers are very slack on you.*
sloppy EG *wearing a sloppy t-shirt, jeans and trainers*

> ### WORD POWER
> ▶ **Antonym**
> tight

loosen VERB
to make something looser
EG *He loosened his tie.*
slacken EG *We slackened the guy-ropes.*
undo EG *She began to undo the tiny buttons.*

untie EG *He untied his shoes and slipped them off.*

> ### WORD POWER
> ▶ **Antonym**
> tighten

❶ loot VERB
to steal from a place during a riot or battle
EG *Gangs began breaking windows and looting shops.*
pillage EG *The bandits pillaged the church.*
plunder EG *They plundered and burned the town.*
raid EG *Rustlers have raided a village in the region.*
ransack EG *The three raiders ransacked the house.*

❷ loot NOUN
stolen or illegal money or goods
EG *The loot was never recovered.*
booty EG *They divided the booty between them.*
haul EG *the biggest haul of cannabis ever seized*
plunder EG *pirates in search of easy plunder*
spoils EG *the spoils of war*
swag SLANG EG *The thieves carried the swag off in a stolen car.*

❶ lose VERB
to be unable to find
EG *I've lost my keys.*
drop EG *She's dropped a contact lens.*
mislay EG *I seem to have mislaid my glasses.*
misplace EG *Somehow my suitcase was misplaced.*

> ### WORD POWER
> ▶ **Antonym**
> find

❷ lose VERB
to be beaten
EG *We lost the match.*

be beaten EG *He was soundly beaten in the election.*
be defeated EG *They were defeated in the final.*

WORD POWER

▶ **Antonym**
win

① lost ADJECTIVE
not knowing where you are
EG *I think we're lost.*
adrift EG *two men adrift on a raft in the middle of the sea*
astray EG *Our baggage went astray in transit.*
off-course EG *After a while I realized I was completely off-course.*

② lost ADJECTIVE
unable to be found
EG *a mother wailing for her lost child*
mislaid EG *searching for his mislaid keys*
misplaced EG *I've found your misplaced glasses.*
missing EG *a missing person*
vanished EG *unable to contact the vanished convoy*

① lot a lot or **lots** NOUN
a large amount of something
EG *Remember to drink lots of water.*
abundance EG *an abundance of food*
a great deal EG *I've spent a great deal of time on this project.*
masses INFORMAL EG *There were masses of flowers at her funeral.*
piles INFORMAL EG *He's got piles of money.*
plenty EG *We've got plenty of time.*
quantities EG *She drank quantities of hot, sweet tea.*
scores EG *There were scores of witnesses.*

② lot NOUN
an amount or number
EG *We've just sacked one lot of builders.*
batch EG *a batch of cookies*

bunch INFORMAL EG *My neighbours are a noisy bunch.*
crowd EG *They're a real crowd of villains.*
group EG *a small group of football supporters*
quantity EG *a small quantity of water*
set EG *a set of photographs*

① loud ADJECTIVE
having a high level of sound
EG *a loud explosion*
blaring EG *a blaring television*
deafening EG *a deafening roar*
noisy EG *a noisy old car*
resounding EG *a resounding slap*
strident EG *her strident voice*
thunderous EG *thunderous applause from the crowd*

WORD POWER

▷ **Synonyms**
clamorous
sonorous
stentorian

▶ **Antonym**
quiet

② loud ADJECTIVE
too brightly coloured
EG *a loud tie*
flamboyant EG *a flamboyant outfit*
flashy EG *flashy clothes*
garish EG *a garish three-piece suite*
gaudy EG *a gaudy purple-and-orange hat*
lurid EG *She painted her toenails a lurid pink.*

WORD POWER

▶ **Antonym**
dull

lovable ADJECTIVE
easy to love
EG *His vulnerability makes him very lovable.*
adorable EG *an adorable black kitten*
charming EG *a charming young*

A
B
C
D
E
F
G
H
I
J
K
L
M
N
O
P
Q
R
S
T
U
V
W
X
Y
Z

Frenchman
enchanting EG *He was an enchanting baby.*
endearing EG *one of his most endearing qualities*
sweet EG *a sweet little girl*

WORD POWER

▷ **Synonyms**
engaging
winsome

▶ **Antonym**
hateful

1 love VERB
to feel strong affection for someone
EG *I loved my husband very much.*
adore EG *She adored her parents.*
cherish EG *He genuinely loved and cherished her.*
worship EG *She had worshipped him from afar for years.*

WORD POWER

▷ **Synonyms**
be in love with
dote on
hold dear
idolize

▶ **Antonym**
hate

2 love VERB
to like something very much
EG *We both love fishing.*
appreciate EG *I know you appreciate good food.*
enjoy EG *Do you enjoy opera?*
like EG *I've always liked horror films.*
relish EG *I relish the challenge of dangerous sports.*

WORD POWER

▷ **Synonyms**
delight in
have a weakness for
take pleasure in

▶ **Antonym**
hate

3 love NOUN
a strong feeling of affection
EG *a mother's love for her children*
adoration EG *He had been used to female adoration all his life.*
affection EG *She thought of him with great affection.*
ardour EG *an attempt to rekindle their lost ardour*
devotion EG *At first she was flattered by his devotion.*
infatuation EG *consumed with infatuation for her*
passion EG *the object of her passion*

WORD POWER

▶ **Antonym**
hatred

4 love NOUN
a strong liking for something
EG *her love of animals*
devotion EG *his devotion to literature*
fondness EG *a fondness for good wine*
liking EG *my liking for classical music*
weakness EG *He had a weakness for cats.*

WORD POWER

▷ **Synonyms**
partiality
penchant

▶ **Antonym**
hatred

lovely ADJECTIVE
very attractive and pleasant
EG *You look lovely.*
attractive EG *Polperro is an attractive harbour village.*
beautiful EG *She's a very beautiful woman.*
delightful EG *a delightful garden*
enjoyable EG *I've had a very enjoyable time.*

a
b
c
d
e
f
g
h
i
j
k
l
m
n
o
p
q
r
s
t
u
v
w
x
y
z

pleasant EG *a pleasant little apartment*
pretty EG *a pretty room overlooking a beautiful garden*

WORD POWER

▶ **Antonym**
horrible

loving ADJECTIVE
feeling or showing love
EG *a loving husband and father*
affectionate EG *openly affectionate with each other*
devoted EG *a devoted couple*
doting EG *a doting father*
fond EG *She gave him a fond smile.*
tender EG *Her voice was tender.*
warm EG *a warm and loving mother*

WORD POWER

▷ **Synonyms**
demonstrative
solicitous
warm-hearted

▶ **Antonym**
cold

❶ low ADJECTIVE
short or not far above the ground
EG *The sun was low in the sky.*
little EG *a little table*
short EG *a short flight of steps*
small EG *a small stool*
squat EG *squat stone houses*
stunted EG *stunted trees*
sunken EG *a sunken garden*

WORD POWER

▶ **Antonym**
high

❷ low ADJECTIVE
small in degree or quantity
EG *low prices*
minimal EG *minimal expenditure*
modest EG *a modest rate of unemployment*
poor EG *working for poor wages*

reduced EG *reduced customer demand*
scant EG *scant stocks of fish*
small EG *produced in small numbers*

WORD POWER

▶ **Antonym**
high

❸ low ADJECTIVE
not considered respectable
EG *a man of low birth*
common EG *She might be a little common, but at least she wasn't boring.*
contemptible EG *He mixes with the most contemptible people in society.*
despicable EG *a despicable wretch*
disreputable EG *the company of disreputable women*
lowly EG *his lowly status*
vulgar EG *She considers herself to be above the vulgar rabble.*

❶ lower VERB
to move something downwards
EG *They lowered the coffin into the grave.*
drop EG *He dropped his plate into the sink.*
let down EG *They let the barrier down.*
take down EG *The pilot took the helicopter down.*

WORD POWER

▶ **Antonym**
raise

❷ lower VERB
to make something less in amount
EG *a commitment to lower taxes*
cut EG *The first priority is to cut costs.*
decrease EG *The government plans to decrease interest rates.*
diminish EG *to diminish the prestige of the monarchy*
lessen EG *a diet that would lessen the risk of disease*
minimize EG *attempts to minimize*

A
B
C
D
E
F
G
H
I
J
K
L
M
N
O
P
Q
R
S
T
U
V
W
X
Y
Z

loyal >> lump

the risk of cancer
reduce EG *Gradually reduce the dosage.*
slash EG *We're slashing our prices.*

WORD POWER

▶ **Antonym**
increase

---

loyal ADJECTIVE
firm in your friendship or support
EG *a loyal friend*
constant EG *I've lost my best friend and constant companion.*
dependable EG *a cheerful, dependable mate*
faithful EG *She remained faithful to her husband.*
staunch EG *a staunch supporter*
true EG *a true friend*
trusty EG *a trusty ally*

WORD POWER

▷ **Synonyms**
steadfast
true-hearted
unswerving
unwavering

▶ **Antonym**
treacherous

---

luck NOUN
something that happens by chance
EG *It was just luck that we happened to meet.*
accident EG *It came about almost by accident.*
chance EG *We only met by chance.*
destiny EG *Is it destiny that brings people together?*
fate EG *a simple twist of fate*
fortune EG *smiled on by fortune*

WORD POWER

▷ **Synonyms**
fortuity
predestination

---

① lucky ADJECTIVE
having a lot of good luck
EG *He had always been lucky at cards.*
blessed EG *being blessed with good looks*
charmed EG *She seems to have a charmed life.*
fortunate EG *He was extremely fortunate to survive.*

WORD POWER

▶ **Antonym**
unlucky

---

② lucky ADJECTIVE
happening by chance with good consequences
EG *a lucky break*
fortuitous EG *a fortuitous combination of circumstances*
fortunate EG *a fortunate accident*
opportune EG *I had arrived at an opportune moment.*
timely EG *his timely intervention*

WORD POWER

▷ **Synonyms**
adventitious
propitious
providential

▶ **Antonym**
unlucky

---

① lump NOUN
a solid piece of something
EG *a big lump of dough*
ball EG *a ball of clay*
cake EG *a cake of soap*
chunk EG *a chunk of bread*
hunk EG *a hunk of beef*
piece EG *a piece of cake*
wedge EG *a wedge of cheese*

---

② lump NOUN
a bump on the surface of something
EG *I've got a big lump on my head.*
bulge EG *My purse made a bulge in my pocket.*
bump EG *a bump in the road*

A
B
C
D
E
F
G
H
I
J
K
L
M
N
O
P
Q
R
S
T
U
V
W
X
Y
Z

hump EG *a hump on his back*
swelling EG *a swelling over one eye*

WORD POWER

▷ **Synonyms**
protrusion
protuberance
tumescence

❶ lure VERB
to attract someone somewhere or
into doing something
EG *We are being lured into a trap.*
attract EG *Warm weather attracts
the fish close to the shore.*
beckon EG *The mermaids beckoned
the sailors towards the rocks.*
draw EG *What drew him to the area
was its proximity to London.*
entice EG *Retailers will do anything to
entice shoppers through their doors.*
tempt EG *trying to tempt American
tourists back to Britain*

❷ lure NOUN
something that you find very
attractive
EG *the lure of rural life*
attraction EG *the attraction of living
on the waterfront*
bait EG *using cheap bread and milk as
a bait to get people into the shop*
magnet EG *The park is a magnet for
health freaks.*
pull EG *feel the pull of the past*
temptation EG *the many
temptations to which they will be
exposed*

lustful ADJECTIVE
feeling or showing strong sexual
desire
EG *lustful thoughts*
carnal EG *carnal desires*
lecherous EG *a lecherous old man*
lewd EG *his arrest for lewd behaviour*

WORD POWER

▷ **Synonyms**
lascivious

libidinous
wanton

luxurious ADJECTIVE
expensive and full of luxury
EG *a luxurious lifestyle*
de luxe EG *de luxe cars*
lavish EG *a lavish party*
opulent EG *an opulent office*
plush INFORMAL EG *a plush hotel*
sumptuous EG *a sumptuous feast*

WORD POWER

▶ **Antonym**
plain

❶ luxury NOUN
comfort in expensive surroundings
EG *a life of luxury*
affluence EG *the trappings of
affluence*
opulence EG *the sheer opulence of
her new life*
sumptuousness EG *The hotel lobby
was sumptuousness itself.*

❷ luxury NOUN
something enjoyable which you do
not have often
EG *Telephones are still a luxury in poor
countries.*
extra EG *The car is a basic model with
no extras.*
extravagance EG *Eating out is an
extravagance.*
indulgence EG *This car is one of my
few indulgences.*
treat EG *I only eat cakes as a treat.*

❶ lying NOUN
the action of telling lies
EG *I've had enough of your lying.*
deceit EG *the deceits of political
leaders*
dishonesty EG *deliberate dishonesty*
fabrication EG *His story is pure
fabrication.*
fibbing EG *Her fibbing eventually got
her into trouble.*

perjury EG *This witness has committed perjury.*

WORD POWER

▷ **Synonyms**
dissimulation
duplicity
mendacity

❷ lying ADJECTIVE
telling lies
EG *The man is just a lying cheat.*
deceitful EG *deceitful and misleading remarks*

dishonest EG *a dishonest account of events*
false EG *a false confession*
untruthful EG *She unwittingly gave untruthful answers.*

WORD POWER

▷ **Synonyms**
dissembling
mendacious

▶ **Antonym**
honest

a
b
c
d
e
f
g
h
i
j
k
l
m
n
o
p
q
r
s
t
u
v
w
x
y
z

Mm

machine NOUN
a piece of equipment
EG *a machine to pump water out of mines*
apparatus EG *an apparatus for use in fires*
appliance EG *electrical appliances*
contraption EG *a strange contraption called the General Gordon Gas Bath*
device EG *a timer device for a bomb*
instrument EG *navigation instruments*
mechanism EG *the locking mechanism*

❶ mad ADJECTIVE
mentally ill
EG *She was afraid of going mad.*
barmy SLANG EG *Bill used to say I was barmy.*
batty SLANG EG *some batty uncle of theirs*
crazy INFORMAL EG *If I worried about all this stuff, I'd go crazy.*
deranged EG *after a deranged man shot 14 people*
insane EG *Some people can't take it and go insane.*
loony SLANG EG *She's as loony as her brother!*

WORD POWER

▶ **Antonym**
sane

❷ mad ADJECTIVE
very foolish or unwise
EG *He'd be mad to refuse.*
barmy SLANG EG *a barmy idea*
crazy INFORMAL EG *People thought they were crazy to try it.*
daft INFORMAL EG *That's a daft question.*
foolhardy EG *Some described the act as foolhardy.*
foolish EG *It would be foolish to raise hopes unnecessarily.*

stupid EG *It would be stupid to pretend otherwise.*

❸ mad ADJECTIVE; INFORMAL
angry about something
EG *They both got mad at me for interfering.*
angry EG *She was angry at her husband.*
crazy INFORMAL EG *This sitting around is driving me crazy.*
enraged EG *I got more and more enraged at my father.*
fuming EG *Mrs Vine was still fuming.*
furious EG *He is furious at the way his wife has been treated.*
incensed EG *Mum was incensed at his lack of compassion.*
infuriated EG *He knew how infuriated this would make me.*
irate EG *Bob was very irate, shouting and screaming about the flight delay.*
livid INFORMAL EG *I am absolutely livid about it.*

magic NOUN
a special power
EG *They believe in magic.*
sorcery EG *the use of sorcery to combat evil influences*
witchcraft EG *people who practise witchcraft*

WORD POWER

▷ **Synonyms**
necromancy
occultism

magical ADJECTIVE
wonderful and exciting
EG *Paris is a magical city.*
bewitching EG *bewitching brown eyes*
enchanting EG *an enchanting child*

WORD POWER

▷ **Synonyms**
entrancing
spellbinding

main ADJECTIVE
most important
EG *the main reason*
cardinal EG *one of the cardinal rules of movie reviewing*
chief EG *one of his chief rivals*
foremost EG *one of the foremost scholars on ancient Indian culture*
leading EG *a leading industrial nation*
major EG *one of the major causes of cancer*
predominant EG *Her predominant emotion was confusion.*
primary EG *the primary source of water in the region*
prime EG *the prime suspect*
principal EG *the principal source of sodium in our diets*

mainly ADVERB
true in most cases
EG *The staff were mainly Russian.*
chiefly EG *He painted chiefly portraits.*
generally EG *It is generally true that the darker the fruit the higher its iron content.*
largely EG *The early studies were done on men, largely by male researchers.*
mostly EG *Cars are mostly metal.*
predominantly EG *Business is conducted predominantly by phone.*
primarily EG *The body is made up primarily of bone, muscle, and fat.*
principally EG *This is principally because the market is weak.*

WORD POWER

▷ **Synonyms**
for the most part
in general
on the whole

major ADJECTIVE
very important or serious
EG *a major problem*
critical EG *a critical factor*
crucial EG *He took the crucial*

decisions himself.
leading EG *a leading industrial nation*
outstanding EG *an outstanding contribution*
significant EG *Her upbringing had a significant effect on her relationships.*

WORD POWER

▶ **Antonym**
minor

majority NOUN
more than half
EG *The majority of our cheeses are made with pasteurized milk.*
best part EG *for the best part of 24 hours*
better part EG *I spent the better part of £100 on her.*
bulk EG *the bulk of the world's great poetry*
mass EG *the mass of the population*
most EG *Most of the book is completely true.*

WORD POWER

▷ **Synonyms**
lion's share
preponderance

❶ **make** VERB
to construct something
EG *Sheila makes all her own clothes.*
assemble EG *Workers were assembling planes.*
build EG *Workers at the site build the F-16 jet fighter.*
construct EG *the campaign to construct a temple on the site*
create EG *It's great for a radio producer to create a show like this.*
fabricate EG *All the tools are fabricated from high quality steel.*
fashion EG *Stone Age settlers fashioned necklaces from sheep's teeth.*
form EG *a figure formed from clay*
manufacture EG *They manufacture plastics.*

a b c d e f g h i j k l m n o p q r s t u v w x y z

A
B
C
D
E
F
G
H
I
J
K
L
M
N
O
P
Q
R
S
T
U
V
W
X
Y
Z

produce EG *We try to produce items that are the basics of a stylish wardrobe.*

❷ make VERB
to force someone to do something
EG *Mary made him clean up the plate.*
compel EG *legislation to compel cyclists to wear a helmet*
drive EG *Jealousy drives people to murder.*
force EG *A back injury forced her to withdraw from the competition.*
oblige EG *Finally I was obliged to abandon the car.*

WORD POWER

▷ **Synonyms**
coerce
impel

❸ make NOUN
a particular type
EG *a certain make of wristwatch*
brand EG *a brand of cigarette*
model EG *To keep the cost down, opt for a basic model.*

❶ make up VERB
to form the parts of something
EG *Women police officers make up 13% of the police force.*
compose EG *The force would be composed of troops from NATO countries.*
comprise EG *a crowd comprised of the wives and children of scientists*
constitute EG *Hindus constitute 83% of India's population.*
form EG *Cereals form the staple diet.*

❷ make up VERB
to invent a story
EG *It's very unkind of you to make up stories about him.*
concoct EG *The prisoner concocted the story to get a lighter sentence.*
fabricate EG *Officers fabricated evidence against them.*

invent EG *I must invent something I can tell my mother.*

WORD POWER

▷ **Synonyms**
formulate
manufacture

❶ making NOUN
the act of creating something
EG *the making of this movie*
assembly EG *the assembly of an explosive device*
building EG *The building of the airport continues.*
construction EG *boat construction*
creation EG *the creation of large parks and forests*
fabrication EG *the design and fabrication of the space shuttle*
manufacture EG *the manufacture of nuclear weapons*
production EG *These proteins stimulate the production of blood cells.*

❷ making in the making ADJECTIVE
about to become something
EG *a captain in the making*
budding EG *a budding author*
emergent EG *an emergent state*
potential EG *a potential champion*
up-and-coming EG *an up-and-coming golfer*

male ADJECTIVE
relating to men
EG *a deep male voice*
manly EG *He was the ideal of manly beauty.*
masculine EG *masculine characteristics like facial hair*

WORD POWER

▶ **Antonym**
female

malicious ADJECTIVE
having the intention of hurting someone

EG *She described the charges as malicious.*

cruel EG *Children can be so cruel.*

malevolent FORMAL EG *She gave me a malevolent stare.*

mean EG *Someone's played a mean trick on you.*

spiteful EG *spiteful telephone calls*

vicious EG *a vicious attack on an innocent man's character*

WORD POWER

▷ **Synonyms**
rancorous (FORMAL)

---

❶ man NOUN
an adult male human being
EG *a young man*

bloke BRITISH, AUSTRALIAN, AND NEW ZEALAND; INFORMAL EG *a really nice bloke*

chap INFORMAL EG *I am a very lucky chap.*

gentleman EG *It seems this gentleman was waiting for the doctor.*

guy INFORMAL EG *a guy from Manchester*

male EG *A high proportion of crime is perpetrated by young males.*

WORD POWER

▶ **Antonym**
woman

---

❷ man NOUN
people in general
EG *All men are equal.*

humanity EG *He has rendered a great service to humanity.*

human race EG *Can the human race carry on expanding?*

mankind EG *the evolution of mankind*

WORD POWER

▷ **Synonyms**
Homo sapiens
humankind

---

mana NOUN; NEW ZEALAND
the authority and influence of an important person
EG *a leader of great mana*

authority EG *figures of authority*

influence EG *He denies using any political influence.*

power EG *positions of great power*

standing EG *The Prime Minister's standing was high in the US.*

stature EG *his stature as the world's greatest cellist*

status EG *the status of a national hero*

WORD POWER

▷ **Synonyms**
sway (LITERARY)

---

❶ manage VERB
to succeed in doing something
EG *We managed to find somewhere to sit.*

cope with EG *how my mother coped with bringing up three children*

succeed in EG *We have succeeded in persuading cinemas to show the video.*

❷ manage VERB
to be in charge of something
EG *Within two years he was managing the store.*

be in charge of EG *Who's in charge of the canteen?*

command EG *Who would command the troops in the event of war?*

control EG *He now controls the largest retail development empire in southern California.*

direct EG *Christopher will direct day-to-day operations.*

run EG *Is this any way to run a country?*

❶ management NOUN
the act of running an organization
EG *The zoo needed better management.*

control EG *The restructuring involves*

a
b
c
d
e
f
g
h
i
j
k
l
m
n
o
p
q
r
s
t
u
v
w
x
y
z

Mr Ronson giving up control of the company.

direction EG *Organizations need clear direction.*

running EG *the day-to-day running of the clinic*

❷ management NOUN
the people who run an organization
EG *The management is doing its best.*

administration EG *They would like the college administration to exert more control.*

board EG *a recommendation which he wants to put before the board*

bosses INFORMAL EG *a dispute between workers and bosses*

directors EG *the board of directors of a local bank*

employers EG *Employers are said to be considering the demand.*

manager NOUN
a person in charge of running an organization
EG *the manager of Daiwa's New York branch*

boss INFORMAL EG *He cannot stand his boss.*

director EG *the financial director of Braun UK*

executive EG *an advertising executive*

manifest ADJECTIVE; FORMAL
obvious or easily seen
EG *the manifest failure of the policy*

blatant EG *a blatant attempt to spread the blame*

clear EG *a clear case of homicide*

conspicuous EG *Politics has changed in a conspicuous way.*

glaring EG *a glaring example of fraud*

obvious EG *an obvious injustice*

patent EG *This was patent nonsense.*

plain EG *He's made it plain that he wants to be involved.*

❶ manner NOUN
the way that you do something
EG *She smiled again in a friendly*

manner.

fashion EG *another drug that works in a similar fashion*

mode EG *He switched automatically into interview mode.*

style EG *Kenny's writing style*

way EG *He had a strange way of talking.*

❷ manner NOUN
the way that someone behaves
EG *his kind manner*

bearing EG *his military bearing*

behaviour EG *her anti-social behaviour*

conduct EG *principles of civilized conduct*

demeanour EG *a cheerful demeanour*

WORD POWER

▷ **Synonyms**
comportment
deportment

---

❶ manoeuvre VERB
to move something skilfully
EG *It took expertise to manoeuvre the boat so close to the shore.*

guide EG *He took Elliott by the arm and guided him out.*

navigate EG *He attempted to navigate his way through the crowds.*

negotiate EG *I negotiated my way out of the airport.*

steer EG *I steered him towards the door.*

❷ manoeuvre NOUN
a clever action
EG *manoeuvres to block the electoral process*

dodge EG *a tax dodge*

ploy EG *a cynical marketing ploy*

ruse EG *This was a ruse to divide them.*

tactic EG *The tactic paid off.*

WORD POWER

▷ **Synonyms**
machination
stratagem

1 manufacture VERB
to make goods in a factory
EG *Several models are being manufactured here.*
assemble EG *a factory where they assemble tractors*
fabricate EG *a plant which fabricates aeroplane components*
make EG *making cars at two plants in Europe*
mass-produce EG *the invention of machinery to mass-produce footwear*
produce EG *The company produced computer parts.*
process EG *The material will be processed into plastic pellets.*

2 manufacture NOUN
the making of goods in a factory
EG *the manufacture of nuclear weapons*
assembly EG *the assembly of cars by robots*
fabrication EG *the design and fabrication of the shuttle*
making EG *the steps that go into the making of a book*
mass production EG *the mass production of baby food*
production EG *We need to maintain the production of cars at last year's level.*

1 many ADJECTIVE
a large number
EG *Among his many hobbies was the breeding of fine horses.*
countless EG *She brought joy to countless people.*
innumerable EG *He has invented innumerable excuses.*
myriad EG *the myriad other tasks we are trying to perform*
numerous EG *Sex crimes were just as*

numerous as they are today.
umpteen INFORMAL EG *He has produced umpteen books.*

WORD POWER

▷ **Synonyms**
multifarious
multitudinous

▶ **Antonym**
few

2 many NOUN
a large number of people or things
EG *in many of these neighbourhoods*
a lot EG *A lot of people would agree with you.*
a mass EG *a mass of books and papers*
a multitude EG *for a multitude of reasons*
large numbers EG *Large numbers of people stayed away.*
lots INFORMAL EG *lots of strange new animals*
plenty EG *plenty of vegetables*
scores EG *Scores of people were injured.*

WORD POWER

▶ **Antonym**
few

1 mark NOUN
a small stain
EG *I can't get this mark off the curtain.*
→ see Word Study **mark**

2 mark VERB
to stain something
EG *to stop the horses' hooves from marking the turf*
smudge EG *Her face was smudged with dirt.*
stain EG *His clothing was stained with mud.*
streak EG *Rain had begun to streak the window-panes.*

market NOUN
a place to buy or sell things

a b c d e f g h i j k l m n o p q r s t u v w x y z

EG *the fish market at Billingsgate*
bazaar EG *an Eastern bazaar*
fair EG *a craft fair*

marriage NOUN
the relationship between a husband
and wife
EG *six years of marriage*
matrimony FORMAL EG *the bonds of
matrimony*
wedlock FORMAL EG *a child conceived
out of wedlock*

WORD POWER

● Related Words
adjectives : conjugal,
connubial, marital,
nuptial

marsh NOUN

Types of marsh
bog
fen
mire
morass
mudflats
quagmire
quicksands
saltmarsh
slough
swamp
wetland

marvellous ADJECTIVE
wonderful or excellent
EG *a marvellous actor*
brilliant EG *a brilliant performance*
excellent EG *She does an excellent
job as Bill's secretary.*
first-rate EG *The meal was
absolutely first-rate.*
magnificent EG *She was magnificent
as Lady Macbeth.*
remarkable EG *a remarkable
achievement*
splendid EG *splendid photographs*
superb EG *a superb novel*
wonderful EG *It's wonderful to see
you.*

WORD POWER

▶ Antonym
terrible

❶ **mass** NOUN
a large number or amount
EG *a mass of papers*
crowd EG *A huge crowd of people
gathered in the square.*
heap EG *a heap of bricks*
load EG *a load of kids*
throng EG *A shout went up from the
throng of spectators.*
lump EG *a lump of clay*
mob EG *a growing mob of
demonstrators*
pile EG *a pile of sand*

❷ **mass** ADJECTIVE
involving a large number of people
EG *mass unemployment*
general EG *We are trying to raise
general awareness about this issue.*
popular EG *popular anger at the
decision*
universal EG *universal health care*
widespread EG *widespread support
for the proposals*

❸ **mass** VERB
to gather together in a large group
EG *Police began to mass at the
shipyard.*
assemble EG *Thousands of people
assembled in the stadium.*
congregate EG *Youngsters
congregate here in the evenings.*
gather EG *In the evenings, we
gathered round the fireplace.*
group EG *The children grouped
together under the trees.*

❶ **master** NOUN
a male schoolteacher
EG *a retired maths master*
instructor EG *a college instructor*
teacher EG *her chemistry teacher*
tutor EG *an adult education tutor in
German*

❷ master VERB
to learn how to do something
EG *She found it easy to master the typewriter.*
become proficient in EG *He quickly became proficient in the language.*
get the hang of INFORMAL EG *It's a bit tricky till you get the hang of it.*
grasp EG *It took him a while to grasp the basics of the process.*
learn EG *He enjoyed learning new skills.*

❶ match NOUN
an organized game
EG *a football match*
competition EG *a surfing competition*
contest EG *one of the best contests in recent boxing history*
game EG *England's first game of the new season*

❷ match VERB
to be similar to
EG *The shoes matched her dress.*
agree EG *Their statements do not agree.*
correspond EG *The two maps correspond closely.*
fit EG *The punishment must always fit the crime.*
go with EG *The curtains didn't go with the carpet.*
suit EG *the best package to suit your needs*
tally EG *The figures didn't seem to tally.*

WORD POWER

▷ **Synonyms**
accord
harmonize

❶ material NOUN
any type of cloth
EG *the thick material of her skirt*
cloth EG *a piece of cloth*
fabric EG *silk and other delicate fabrics*

❷ material NOUN
a solid substance
EG *the materials to make red dye*
matter EG *waste matter from industries*
stuff EG *the stuff from which the universe is made*
substance EG *a crumbly black substance*

❶ matter NOUN
something that you have to deal with
EG *business matters*
affair EG *The funeral was a sad affair.*
business EG *This whole business has upset me.*
issue EG *a major political issue*
question EG *the difficult question of unemployment*
situation EG *The situation is now under control.*
subject EG *a difficult subject on which to reach a compromise*

❷ matter NOUN
any substance
EG *The atom is the smallest divisible particle of matter.*
material EG *a conducting material such as metal*
stuff EG *a dress made from some flimsy stuff*
substance EG *a poisonous substance*

❸ matter VERB
to be important
EG *It does not matter how long their hair is.*
be of consequence EG *Their choice of partner is of no consequence to anyone but themselves.*
count EG *It's as if my opinions just don't count.*
make a difference EG *Exercise makes all the difference.*

❶ mature VERB
to become fully developed
EG *Children mature earlier these days.*

a
b
c
d
e
f
g
h
i
j
k
l
m
n
o
p
q
r
s
t
u
v
w
x
y
z

A
B
C
D
E
F
G
H
I
J
K
L
M
N
O
P
Q
R
S
T
U
V
W
X
Y
Z

come of age EG *The money was held in trust until he came of age.*
grow up EG *She grew up in Tokyo.*
reach adulthood EG *She died before reaching adulthood.*

2 mature ADJECTIVE
fully developed
EG *He's very mature for his age.*
adult EG *a pair of adult birds*
full-grown EG *a full-grown male orang-utan*
fully-fledged EG *He has developed into a fully-fledged adult.*
grown EG *a grown man*
grown-up EG *They have two grown-up children.*

1 maximum NOUN
the most that is possible
EG *a maximum of fifty men*
ceiling EG *an agreement to put a ceiling on salaries*
height EG *when emigration was at its height*
most EG *The most he'll make is a hundred pounds.*
upper limit EG *the need to put an upper limit on spending*
utmost EG *He did his utmost to make her agree.*

> _WORD POWER_
>
> ▶ **Antonym**
>   minimum

2 maximum ADJECTIVE
being the most that is possible
EG *the maximum recommended intake*
top EG *a top speed of 200 mph*
utmost EG *a question of the utmost importance*

> _WORD POWER_
>
> ▶ **Antonym**
>   minimum

maybe ADVERB
it is possible that

EG *Maybe I should have done a bit more.*
conceivably EG *The mission could conceivably be accomplished within a week.*
it could be EG *It could be that's why he refused.*
perhaps EG *Perhaps, in time, she'll understand.*
possibly EG *Television is possibly to blame for this.*

> _WORD POWER_
>
> ▷ **Synonyms**
>   mayhap
>   peradventure
>   perchance

meagre ADJECTIVE
very small and inadequate
EG *his meagre pension*
inadequate EG *inadequate portions*
measly INFORMAL EG *The average British bathroom measures a measly 3.5 square metres.*
paltry EG *a paltry fine of £150*
scant EG *She berated the police for paying scant attention to the theft.*
sparse EG *sparse vegetation*

> _WORD POWER_
>
> ▷ **Synonyms**
>   exiguous
>   insubstantial
>   scanty
>   skimpy

meal NOUN
an occasion when people eat
EG *She sat next to him throughout the meal.*
banquet EG *a state banquet at Buckingham Palace*
dinner EG *a series of official dinners*
feast EG *the wedding feast*
kai AUSTRALIAN AND NEW ZEALAND; INFORMAL EG *a cheap kai in a local restaurant*

WORD POWER

▷ **Synonyms**
repast
spread

❶ mean VERB
to convey a message
EG *The red signal means that you can shoot.*
denote EG *Red eyes denote strain and fatigue.*
indicate EG *Today's vote indicates a change in policy.*
signify EG *Becoming a father signified that he was now an adult.*

❷ mean VERB
to intend to do something
EG *I meant to phone you, but didn't have time.*
aim EG *I aim to arrive early.*
intend EG *She intended to move back to France.*
plan EG *They plan to marry in the summer.*

❸ mean ADJECTIVE
unwilling to spend money
EG *Don't be mean with the tip.*
miserly EG *He is miserly with both his time and his money.*
snoep SOUTH AFRICAN; INFORMAL
eg *Have you ever met anyone as snoep as him?*
tight INFORMAL EG *He was so tight that he wouldn't even spend three roubles.*

WORD POWER

▷ **Synonyms**
parsimonious
penny-pinching
stingy
tight-fisted

▶ **Antonym**
generous

meaning NOUN
the idea expressed by something
EG *the meaning of this dream*

drift EG *Grace was beginning to get his drift.*
gist EG *I could not get the gist of their conversation.*
message EG *the message of the film*
sense EG *The word has two main senses.*
significance EG *The President's visit is loaded with symbolic significance.*

WORD POWER

▷ **Synonyms**
connotation
import

❶ measure VERB
to check the size of something
EG *We measured how tall he was.*
gauge EG *He gauged the wind at over 30 knots.*
survey EG *geological experts who surveyed the cliffs*

WORD POWER

▷ **Synonyms**
calibrate
quantify

❷ measure NOUN
an amount of something
EG *There has been a measure of agreement.*
amount EG *a certain amount of disappointment*
degree EG *a degree of success*
portion EG *I have spent a considerable portion of my life here.*
proportion EG *A large proportion of my time was spent abroad.*

❸ measure NOUN
an action in order to achieve something
EG *Tough measures are needed to maintain order.*
expedient EG *I reduced my spending by the simple expedient of destroying my credit card.*
manoeuvre EG *manoeuvres to block the electoral process*

a
b
c
d
e
f
g
h
i
j
k
l
m
n
o
p
q
r
s
t
u
v
w
x
y
z

A
B
C
D
E
F
G
H
I
J
K
L
M
N
O
P
Q
R
S
T
U
V
W
X
Y
Z

means EG *The move is a means to fight crime.*
procedure EG *safety procedures*
step EG *steps to discourage drink-driving*

medicine NOUN
something you take to make you better
EG *They prevent the food and medicine from reaching Iraq.*
drug EG *Three new drugs recently became available.*
medication EG *some medication for her ulcers*
muti SOUTH AFRICAN; INFORMAL EG *muti for treating a fever*
remedy EG *At the moment we are trying a herbal remedy.*

❶ medium ADJECTIVE
average in size
EG *He was of medium height.*
average EG *a ginger tomcat of average size*
medium-sized EG *a medium-sized saucepan*
middling EG *Small and middling flats have increased in price much more than luxury ones.*

❷ medium NOUN
a means of communication
EG *the medium of television*
channel EG *through diplomatic channels*
vehicle EG *The play seemed an ideal vehicle for his music.*

WORD POWER
▷ **Synonyms**
agency
instrument

meek ADJECTIVE
quiet and timid
EG *a meek, mild-mannered fellow*
deferential EG *the traditional requirement for Asian women to be deferential to men*
docile EG *docile, obedient children*

mild EG *a mild man*
submissive EG *Most doctors want their patients to be submissive.*
timid EG *a timid child*
unassuming EG *He's very polite and unassuming.*

WORD POWER
▷ **Synonyms**
acquiescent
compliant
mild-mannered

▶ **Antonym**
bold

❶ meet VERB
to be in the same place as someone
EG *I met her quite by chance.*
bump into INFORMAL EG *I bumped into a friend of yours today.*
come across EG *where I came across a group of noisy children*
come upon EG *We turned the corner and came upon a group of hikers.*
encounter EG *the most gifted child he had ever encountered*
run across EG *We ran across some old friends.*
run into EG *You'll never guess who I ran into the other day.*

❷ meet VERB
to gather in a group
EG *We meet for lunch once a week.*
assemble EG *a convenient place for students to assemble between classes*
congregate EG *Youngsters love to congregate here in the evening.*
convene EG *Senior officials convened in October.*
gather EG *We all gathered in the boardroom.*
get together EG *the last time we all got together*

❸ meet VERB
to fulfil a need
EG *services intended to meet the needs of the elderly*
answer EG *Would communism*

answer their needs?
fulfil EG *All the requirements were fulfilled.*
satisfy EG *Candidates must satisfy the general conditions for admission.*

1 meeting NOUN
an event at which people come together for a purpose
EG *a business meeting*
audience EG *an audience with the Pope*
conference EG *a conference on education*
congress EG *a medical congress*
convention EG *the annual convention of the World Boxing Council*
gathering EG *a social gathering*
get-together INFORMAL EG *a get-together I had at my home*
reunion EG *a family reunion*

WORD POWER

▷ **Synonyms**
conclave
convocation

2 meeting NOUN
an occasion when you meet someone
EG *a chance meeting*
assignation LITERARY EG *She had an assignation with her boyfriend.*
encounter EG *a remarkable encounter with a group of soldiers*
rendezvous EG *Baxter arranged a six o'clock rendezvous.*
tryst EG *a lovers' tryst*

melodramatic ADJECTIVE
behaving in an exaggerated way
EG *Don't you think you're being rather melodramatic?*
histrionic EG *She let out a histrionic groan.*
sensational EG *sensational tabloid newspaper reports*
theatrical EG *In a theatrical gesture Glass clamped his hand over his eyes.*

1 melt VERB
to become liquid
EG *The snow had melted.*
dissolve EG *Heat gently until the sugar dissolves.*
thaw EG *It's so cold the snow doesn't get a chance to thaw.*

WORD POWER

▷ **Synonyms**
deliquesce
liquefy

2 melt VERB
to disappear
EG *Her inhibitions melted.*
disappear EG *The immediate threat has disappeared.*
disperse EG *The crowd dispersed peacefully.*
dissolve EG *His new-found optimism dissolved.*
evaporate EG *My anger evaporated.*
vanish EG *All her fears suddenly vanished.*

memorable ADJECTIVE
likely to be remembered
EG *a memorable victory*
catchy EG *a catchy tune*
historic EG *a historic meeting*
notable EG *with a few notable exceptions*
striking EG *the most striking feature of those statistics*
unforgettable EG *an unforgettable experience*

memory NOUN
the ability to remember
EG *Every detail is fresh in my memory.*
recall EG *a man blessed with total recall*
remembrance FORMAL EG *My remembrance of the incident is somewhat hazy.*

A
B
C
D
E
F
G
H
I
J
K
L
M
N
O
P
Q
R
S
T
U
V
W
X
Y
Z

WORD POWER

▷ **Synonyms**
recollection
retention

mend VERB
to repair something broken
EG *I should have had the catch mended.*
darn EG *a woman darning socks*
fix EG *If something is broken, we get it fixed.*
patch EG *They patched the barn roof.*
renovate EG *The couple spent thousands renovating the house.*
repair EG *to get her car repaired*
restore EG *experts who specialize in restoring ancient parchments*

❶ **mention** VERB
to talk about something briefly
EG *I may not have mentioned it to her.*
allude to EG *She alluded to his absence in vague terms.*
bring up EG *Why are you bringing it up now?*
broach EG *I broached the subject of her early life.*
hint EG *The President hinted that he might make some changes.*
intimate EG *He did intimate that he is seeking legal action.*
refer to EG *In his speech, he referred to a recent trip to Canada.*
touch on EG *The film touches on these issues, but only superficially.*
touch upon EG *I'd like to touch upon a more serious question now.*

❷ **mention** NOUN
a brief comment about something
EG *There was no mention of elections.*
allusion EG *She made an allusion to the events in Los Angeles.*
reference EG *He made no reference to any agreement.*

❶ **merciful** ADJECTIVE
showing kindness
EG *He is merciful and sympathetic to others.*
compassionate EG *a deeply compassionate man*
humane EG *the desire for a more humane society*
kind EG *She is warm-hearted and kind to everyone.*

WORD POWER

▶ **Antonym**
merciless

❷ **merciful** ADJECTIVE
showing forgiveness
EG *We can only hope the court is merciful.*
forgiving EG *I don't think people are in a very forgiving mood.*
lenient EG *He believes the government is already lenient with drug traffickers.*

WORD POWER

▶ **Antonym**
merciless

merciless ADJECTIVE
showing no kindness or forgiveness
EG *the merciless efficiency of a modern police state*
callous EG *his callous disregard for human life*
cruel EG *Children can be so cruel.*
heartless EG *I couldn't believe they were so heartless.*
implacable EG *a powerful and implacable enemy*
ruthless EG *his ruthless treatment of employees*

WORD POWER

▷ **Synonyms**
hard-hearted
pitiless
unforgiving

▶ **Antonym**
merciful

❶ mercy NOUN
the quality of kindness
EG *He showed no mercy.*
compassion EG *his compassion for a helpless woman*
kindness EG *He was treated with kindness by numerous officials.*
pity EG *She saw no pity in their faces.*

> **WORD POWER**
> ▷ **Synonyms**
> benevolence
> charity

❷ mercy NOUN
the quality of forgiveness
EG *He threw himself upon the mercy of the court.*
forgiveness EG *He fell to his knees begging for forgiveness.*
leniency EG *He said he would show no leniency towards them.*

> **WORD POWER**
> ▷ **Synonyms**
> clemency
> forbearance

❶ merit NOUN
worth or value
EG *Box-office success mattered more than artistic merit.*
excellence EG *the top US award for excellence in journalism*
value EG *The value of this work experience should not be underestimated.*
virtue EG *There is little virtue in such an approach.*
worth EG *people who had already proved their worth to their companies*

❷ merit NOUN
a good quality that something has
EG *Whatever its merits, their work would never be used.*
advantage EG *The great advantage of home-grown oranges is their flavour.*
asset EG *Her leadership qualities*
were her greatest asset.
strength EG *The book's strength lay in its depiction of modern-day Tokyo.*
strong point EG *Science was never my strong point at school.*
virtue EG *Its other great virtue is its hard-wearing quality.*

❸ merit VERB
to deserve something
EG *Such ideas merit careful consideration.*
be entitled to EG *She is entitled to feel proud.*
be worthy of EG *The bank might think you're worthy of a loan.*
deserve EG *He deserves a rest.*
earn EG *Companies must earn a reputation for honesty.*
warrant EG *no evidence to warrant a murder investigation*

❶ mess NOUN
a state of untidiness
EG *I'll clear up the mess later.*
chaos EG *Their concerts often ended in chaos.*
disarray EG *He found the room in disarray.*
disorder EG *Inside all was disorder.*

❷ mess NOUN
a situation that is full of problems
EG *the reasons why the economy is in such a mess*
fix INFORMAL EG *The government has really got itself into a fix.*
jam INFORMAL EG *They were in a real jam.*
muddle EG *Our finances are in a muddle.*
turmoil EG *Her marriage was in turmoil.*

❸ mess VERB
to spoil something
EG *He had messed up his career.*
botch up EG *I hate having builders botch up repairs on my house.*
bungle EG *Two prisoners bungled an escape bid.*

make a hash of INFORMAL EG *The government made a total hash of things.*

muck up SLANG EG *He always seemed to muck everything up.*

❶ message NOUN
a piece of information for someone
EG *He left a message on her answerphone.*

bulletin EG *a news bulletin*

communication EG *The ambassador brought a communication from the President.*

despatch *or* **dispatch** EG *this despatch from our West Africa correspondent*

memo EG *office memos*

memorandum EG *a memorandum from the Ministry of Defence*

note EG *I'll have to leave a note for Karen.*

word EG *There is no word from the authorities on the reported attack.*

WORD POWER
▷ **Synonyms**
communiqué
missive

❷ message NOUN
the idea conveyed by something
EG *the story's anti-drugs message*

meaning EG *while we discussed the meaning of the play*

moral EG *the moral of the story*

point EG *My point is that I'm not going to change.*

theme EG *The book's central theme is power.*

messenger NOUN
someone who carries a message
EG *There will be a messenger at the airport to collect the photographs.*

courier EG *a motorcycle courier*

envoy EG *an envoy to the King*

runner EG *a bookie's runner*

WORD POWER
▷ **Synonyms**
emissary
go-between
herald

method NOUN
a way of doing something
EG *the traditional method of making wine*

approach EG *different approaches to gathering information*

mode EG *the capitalist mode of production*

procedure EG *He did not follow the correct procedure.*

technique EG *the techniques of modern agriculture*

way EG *a way of making new friends*

❶ middle NOUN
the part furthest from the edges
EG *in the middle of the room*

centre EG *the centre of the table*

halfway point EG *Postle was third fastest at the halfway point.*

midst EG *a house in the midst of huge trees*

WORD POWER
▷ **Synonyms**
midpoint
midsection

❷ middle ADJECTIVE
furthest from the edges
EG *the middle house*

central EG *central London*

halfway EG *a point halfway between the two posts*

❶ mild ADJECTIVE
not strong or powerful
EG *a mild shampoo*

insipid EG *It tasted bland and insipid.*

weak EG *weak beer*

WORD POWER
▶ **Antonym**
strong

A
B
C
D
E
F
G
H
I
J
K
L
M
N
O
P
Q
R
S
T
U
V
W
X
Y
Z

2 mild ADJECTIVE
gentle and good-tempered
EG *a mild man*
gentle EG *her gentle nature*
meek EG *a meek, mild-mannered fellow*
placid EG *a placid child who rarely cried*

> *WORD POWER*
>
> ▷ **Synonyms**
> easy-going
> equable
> pacific
> peaceable

3 mild ADJECTIVE
warmer than usual
EG *The area is famous for its mild winter climate.*
balmy EG *balmy summer evenings*
temperate EG *a temperate climate*

1 mind NOUN
your ability to think
EG *You have a very suspicious mind.*
brain EG *Once you stop using your brain you soon go stale.*
head EG *I can't get that song out of my head.*
imagination EG *Africa was alive in my imagination.*
intellect EG *good health and a lively intellect*
psyche EG *disturbing elements of the human psyche*

> *WORD POWER*
>
> ● **Related Words**
> *adjective* : mental

2 mind VERB
to be annoyed by something
EG *I don't mind what you do.*
be bothered EG *I'm not bothered if he has another child.*
care EG *young men who did not care whether they lived or died*
object EG *I don't object to his smoking.*

3 mind VERB
to look after something
EG *My mother is minding the shop.*
keep an eye on EG *She asked me to keep an eye on the children.*
look after EG *I looked after the dogs while she was away.*
take care of EG *There was no one else to take care of the children.*
watch EG *She bought the tickets while I watched the cases.*

minimum ADJECTIVE
being the least possible
EG *the minimum height for a policeman*
least possible EG *I try to cause the least amount of trouble possible.*
minimal EG *The aim is to incur minimal expense.*

> *WORD POWER*
>
> ▶ **Antonym**
> maximum

minor ADJECTIVE
less important
EG *a minor injury*
lesser EG *They pleaded guilty to lesser charges.*
petty EG *petty crime*
secondary EG *matters of secondary importance*
slight EG *We have a slight problem.*
trifling EG *Outside California these difficulties may seem trifling.*
trivial EG *trivial details*

> *WORD POWER*
>
> ▶ **Antonym**
> major

1 minute NOUN
a short period of time
EG *I'll be with you in just a minute.*
flash EG *It was all over in a flash.*
instant EG *For an instant, Catherine was tempted to flee.*
moment EG *Stop for one moment and think about what you're doing!*

a
b
c
d
e
f
g
h
i
j
k
l
m
n
o
p
q
r
s
t
u
v
w
x
y
z

A B C D E F G H I J K L M N O P Q R S T U V W X Y Z

second EG *Just a second. I'm coming.*
trice EG *I'll be back in a trice.*

2 minute ADJECTIVE
extremely small
EG *Only a minute amount is needed.*
microscopic EG *microscopic fibres*
negligible EG *They are convinced the strike will have a negligible impact.*
slender EG *We won the vote by a slender majority.*
small EG *small particles of dust*
tiny EG *a tiny fraction of US production*

WORD POWER

▷ **Synonyms**
minuscule

▶ **Antonym**
vast

miracle NOUN
a surprising and fortunate event
EG *the Italian economic miracle*
marvel EG *a marvel of high technology*
wonder EG *the wonders of science*

1 miserable ADJECTIVE
very unhappy
EG *a job which made me miserable*
dejected EG *Everyone has days when they feel dejected.*
depressed EG *He seemed somewhat depressed.*
down EG *Try to support each other when one of you is feeling down.*
downcast EG *After his defeat Mr Rabin looked downcast.*
low EG *"I didn't ask for this job," he tells friends when he is low.*
melancholy EG *It was in these hours that he felt most melancholy.*
mournful EG *He looked mournful, even near to tears.*
sad EG *It left me feeling sad and empty.*
unhappy EG *She is desperately unhappy.*

wretched EG *I feel really confused and wretched.*

WORD POWER

▷ **Synonyms**
disconsolate
sorrowful

▶ **Antonym**
cheerful

2 miserable ADJECTIVE
causing unhappiness
EG *a miserable little flat*
gloomy EG *Officials say the outlook for next year is gloomy.*
pathetic EG *a pathetic sight*
sorry EG *The fires have left the industry in a sorry state.*
wretched EG *He died in wretched poverty.*

misery NOUN
great unhappiness
EG *All that money brought nothing but misery.*
depression EG *He's been suffering from depression.*
despair EG *feelings of despair*
grief EG *her grief at her husband's suicide*
melancholy EG *with an air of melancholy*
sadness EG *with a mixture of sadness and joy*
sorrow EG *a time of great sorrow*
unhappiness EG *There was a lot of unhappiness in my adolescence.*
woe EG *a tale of woe*

WORD POWER

▶ **Antonym**
joy

misfortune NOUN
an unfortunate event
EG *I had the misfortune to fall off my bike.*
adversity EG *times of adversity*

bad luck EG *He has had his share of bad luck.*

misrepresent VERB
to give a false account of something
EG *Keynes deliberately misrepresented the views of his opponents.*
distort EG *The minister said his remarks had been distorted by the press.*
falsify EG *falsifying personal details on his CV*
twist EG *You're twisting my words.*

1 miss VERB
to fail to notice
EG *It's on the second floor. You can't miss it.*
fail to notice EG *He failed to notice that the lights had turned red.*
mistake EG *There's no mistaking her sincerity.*
overlook EG *a fact that we all tend to overlook*

2 miss VERB
to feel the loss of
EG *The boys miss their father.*
long for EG *Steve longed for the good old days.*
pine for EG *Make sure your pet won't pine for you while you're away.*
yearn for EG *He yearned for his freedom.*

1 mistake NOUN
something that is wrong
EG *spelling mistakes*
blunder EG *It had been a monumental blunder to give him the assignment.*
error EG *a mathematical error*
gaffe EG *a social gaffe*
oversight EG *By an unfortunate oversight, full instructions do not come with the product.*
slip EG *There must be no slips.*

> **WORD POWER**
> ▷ **Synonyms**
> inaccuracy
> miscalculation

2 mistake VERB
to think one thing is another thing
EG *I mistook him for the owner of the house.*
confuse with EG *I can't see how anyone could confuse you with your brother!*
misinterpret as EG *She misinterpreted his remarks as a threat.*
mix up with EG *People often mix me up with other actors.*
take for EG *She had taken him for a journalist.*

mistreat VERB
to treat someone badly
EG *She had been mistreated by men in the past.*
abuse EG *parents who abuse their children*
ill-treat EG *They thought Mr Smith had been ill-treating his wife.*

mix VERB
to combine things
EG *Mix the ingredients together slowly.*
amalgamate EG *a need to amalgamate the two companies*
blend EG *Blend the butter with the sugar.*
combine EG *Combine the flour with 3 tablespoons of water.*
merge EG *how to merge the graphic with text*
mingle EG *the mingled smell of flowers and cigar smoke*

> **WORD POWER**
> ▷ **Synonyms**
> intermingle
> interweave

mixture NOUN
a combination of things
EG *a sticky mixture of flour and water*

a b c d e f g h i j k l m n o p q r s t u v w x y z

A
B
C
D
E
F
G
H
I
J
K
L
M
N
O
P
Q
R
S
T
U
V
W
X
Y
Z

alloy EG *an alloy of copper and tin*
amalgamation EG *an amalgamation of two organizations*
blend EG *a blend of wine and sparkling water*
combination EG *a fantastic combination of colours*
compound EG *a compound of water, sugar, vitamins and enzymes*
fusion EG *fusions of jazz and pop*
medley EG *We communicated in a medley of foreign words and gestures.*

WORD POWER
▷ **Synonyms**
amalgam
composite
conglomeration
mix

mix up VERB
to confuse two things
EG *People often mix us up.*
confuse EG *Great care is taken to avoid confusing the two projects.*
muddle EG *Critics have begun to muddle the two names.*

mix-up NOUN
a mistake in something planned
EG *a mix-up with the bookings*
mistake EG *There must be some mistake.*
misunderstanding EG *Ensure that there is no misunderstanding about the instructions.*
muddle EG *There's been a muddle about whose responsibility it is.*

❶ moan VERB
to make a low sound
EG *Laura moaned in her sleep.*
groan EG *He began to groan with pain.*
grunt EG *The driver grunted, convinced that Michael was crazy.*

❷ moan VERB
to complain about something
EG *Carol is always moaning about her husband.*

complain EG *People always complain that the big banks are unfriendly.*
groan EG *His parents were beginning to groan about the price of college tuition.*
grumble EG *A tourist grumbled that the waiter spoke too much Spanish.*
whine EG *They come to me to whine about their troubles.*
whinge INFORMAL EG *Stop whingeing and get on with it.*

WORD POWER
▷ **Synonyms**
bleat
carp

❸ moan NOUN
a low sound
EG *She let out a faint moan.*
groan EG *a groan of disappointment*
grunt EG *grunts of disapproval*

❶ mock VERB
to make fun of someone
EG *Don't mock me.*
deride FORMAL EG *Other countries are derided for selling arms to the enemy.*
laugh at EG *I thought they were laughing at me because I was ugly.*
make fun of EG *Don't make fun of me.*
poke fun at EG *She poked fun at people's shortcomings.*
ridicule EG *Mr Goss ridiculed that suggestion.*
scoff at EG *Some people may scoff at the idea that animals communicate.*

❷ mock ADJECTIVE
not genuine
EG *mock surprise*
artificial EG *artificial limbs*
bogus EG *their bogus insurance claim*
counterfeit EG *counterfeit money*
dummy EG *dummy weapons*
fake EG *a fake fur*
false EG *false teeth*
feigned EG *with feigned indifference*
imitation EG *imitation leather*

phoney or **phony** INFORMAL EG *a phoney excuse*
pretended EG *with pretended zeal*
sham EG *sham marriages*

WORD POWER

▷ **Synonyms**
ersatz
pseudo

---

mockery NOUN
the act of mocking someone
EG *Was there a glint of mockery in his eyes?*
derision EG *shouts of derision*
jeering EG *there was a chorus of jeering, whistles and laughter*
ridicule EG *Davis was subjected to public ridicule.*

❶ model NOUN
a copy of something
EG *an architect's model of a wooden house*
dummy EG *a tailor's dummy*
replica EG *a replica of the Statue of Liberty*
representation EG *a representation of a human figure*

WORD POWER

▷ **Synonyms**
facsimile
mock-up

---

❷ model NOUN
a perfect example of something
EG *The essay is a model of clarity.*
epitome EG *the epitome of good taste*
example EG *He is an example to the younger lads.*
ideal EG *the Japanese ideal of beauty*
paragon EG *a paragon of virtue*

WORD POWER

▷ **Synonyms**
archetype
exemplar

---

❸ model VERB
to make something into a shape
EG *clay modelled into the shape of a bear*
carve EG *One of the prisoners had carved a wooden chess set.*
fashion EG *Stone Age settlers fashioned necklaces from sheep's teeth.*
form EG *figures formed from modelling clay*
mould EG *We moulded a chair out of mud.*
sculpt EG *An artist sculpted a full-size replica of her head.*
shape EG *Shape each half into a loaf.*

❶ moderate ADJECTIVE
neither too much nor too little
EG *moderate exercise*
average EG *I was only average academically.*
fair EG *Reimar had a fair command of English.*
medium EG *a medium size*
middling EG *The Beatles enjoyed only middling success until 1963.*
reasonable EG *reasonable force*

❷ moderate VERB
to become or make less extreme
EG *They are hoping he can be persuaded to moderate his views.*
abate EG *The storm had abated.*
curb EG *You must curb your extravagant tastes.*
ease EG *Tensions had eased.*
relax EG *Rules have been relaxed recently.*
soften EG *to soften the blow of steep price rises*
temper EG *He had to learn to temper his enthusiasm.*
tone down EG *He toned down his statements after the meeting.*

❶ modern ADJECTIVE
relating to the present time
EG *modern society*
contemporary EG *contemporary*

a
b
c
d
e
f
g
h
i
j
k
l
m
n
o
p
q
r
s
t
u
v
w
x
y
z

A B C D E F G H I J K L **M** N O P Q R S T U V W X Y Z

music
current EG *the current situation*
present EG *the government's present economic difficulties*
present-day EG *Even by present-day standards these were large aircraft.*
recent EG *in recent years*

2 modern ADJECTIVE
new and involving the latest ideas
EG *modern technology*
latest EG *the latest fashions*
new EG *new methods of treating cancer*
up-to-date EG *Germany's most up-to-date electric power station*
up-to-the-minute EG *up-to-the-minute information*

WORD POWER

▶ **Antonym**
old-fashioned

1 modest ADJECTIVE
small in size or amount
EG *a modest improvement*
limited EG *They may only have a limited amount of time.*
middling EG *The Beatles enjoyed only middling success until 1963.*
moderate EG *moderate exercise*
small EG *a relatively small problem*

2 modest ADJECTIVE
not boastful
EG *Lord Carrington is modest about his achievements.*
humble EG *He gave a great performance, but he was very humble.*
unassuming EG *She has a gentle, unassuming manner.*

WORD POWER

▷ **Synonyms**
self-effacing
unpretentious

▶ **Antonym**
conceited

1 moment NOUN
a short period of time
EG *He paused for a moment.*
instant EG *The pain disappeared in an instant.*
minute EG *See you in a minute.*
second EG *Seconds later, firemen reached the door.*
split second EG *Her gaze met Michael's for a split second.*

WORD POWER

▷ **Synonyms**
flash
trice

2 moment NOUN
a point in time
EG *At that moment, the doorbell rang.*
instant EG *At that instant the museum was plunged into darkness.*
point EG *At this point Diana arrived.*
time EG *It seemed like a good time to tell her.*

money NOUN
coins or banknotes
EG *I needed to earn some money.*
capital EG *Companies are having difficulty in raising capital.*
cash EG *We were desperately short of cash.*
dosh BRITISH, AUSTRALIAN, AND NEW ZEALAND EG *They'll have the dosh to pay for a new sign.*
dough INFORMAL EG *He worked hard for his dough.*
funds EG *The concert will raise funds for research into AIDS.*

WORD POWER

● **Related Words**
adjective : pecuniary

mood NOUN
a state of mind
EG *She was in a really cheerful mood.*
frame of mind EG *Lewis was not in the right frame of mind to continue.*
humour EG *Could that have been the*

source of his good humour?
spirits EG *A bit of exercise will help lift his spirits.*
state of mind EG *I want you to get into a whole new state of mind.*
temper EG *I was in a bad temper last night.*

❶ moody ADJECTIVE
depressed or unhappy
EG *Tony, despite his charm, could sulk and be moody.*
irritable EG *He had missed his dinner, and grew irritable.*
morose EG *She was morose and reticent.*
sulky EG *a sulky adolescent*
sullen EG *a sullen and resentful workforce*

WORD POWER

▷ **Synonyms**
huffy
ill-tempered
testy
tetchy

❷ moody ADJECTIVE
liable to change your mood
EG *David's mother was unstable and moody.*
temperamental EG *He is very temperamental.*
volatile EG *He has a volatile temper.*

WORD POWER

▷ **Synonyms**
capricious
mercurial

more ADJECTIVE
greater than something else
EG *I've got more chips than you.*
added EG *For added protection choose lipsticks with a sun screen.*
additional EG *The US is sending additional troops to the region.*
extra EG *Extra staff have been taken on.*

further EG *There are likely to be further delays.*

WORD POWER

▶ **Antonym**
less

motivate VERB
to cause a particular behaviour
EG *What motivates athletes to take drugs?*
drive EG *Jealousy drives people to murder.*
inspire EG *What inspired you to change your name?*
lead EG *His abhorrence of racism led him to write the book.*
move EG *It was punk that first moved him to join a band.*
prompt EG *Japan's recession has prompted consumers to cut back on buying cars.*
provoke EG *The destruction of the mosque has provoked much anger.*

mountain NOUN

Types of mountain
alp
ben (*Scottish*)
elevation
height
mount
peak
precipice
range
ridge

❶ move VERB
to change position
EG *The train began to move.*
→ see Word Study **move**

❷ move VERB
to change residence
EG *She had often considered moving to London.*
migrate EG *Peasants have migrated to the cities.*
move house EG *They move house fairly frequently.*

a
b
c
d
e
f
g
h
i
j
k
l
m
n
o
p
q
r
s
t
u
v
w
x
y
z

A
B
C
D
E
F
G
H
I
J
K
L
M
N
O
P
Q
R
S
T
U
V
W
X
Y
Z

relocate EG *if the company was to relocate*

❸ move VERB
to cause a deep emotion
EG *Her story moved us to tears.*
affect EG *Her loss still clearly affects him.*
touch EG *Her enthusiasm touched me.*

❶ movement NOUN
a change of position
EG *They monitor the movement of the fish going up river.*
flow EG *the frantic flow of cars and buses along the street*
motion EG *the wind from the car's motion*

❷ movement NOUN
a group of people with similar aims
EG *the peace movement*
campaign EG *the campaign against public smoking*
faction EG *the leaders of the country's warring factions*
group EG *members of an environmental group*
organization EG *the International Labour Organization*

moving ADJECTIVE
causing deep emotion
EG *It was a moving moment.*
affecting EG *one of the most affecting scenes in the film*
emotional EG *an emotional reunion*
poignant EG *a poignant love story*
stirring EG *a stirring speech*
touching EG *the touching tale of a wife who stood by husband she loved*

❶ muddle NOUN
a state of disorder
EG *Our finances are in a muddle.*
chaos EG *Their concerts often ended in chaos.*
confusion EG *There was confusion when a man fired shots.*
disarray EG *He found the room in disarray.*

disorder EG *Inside all was disorder.*
disorganization EG *a state of complete disorganization*
jumble EG *a meaningless jumble of words*
mess EG *the reasons why the economy is in such a mess*
tangle EG *a tangle of wires*

❷ muddle VERB
to mix things up
EG *One or two critics have begun to muddle the two names.*
confuse EG *Great care is taken to avoid confusing the two projects.*
jumble EG *a number of animals whose remains were jumbled together*
mix up EG *People often mix us up.*

multiply VERB
to increase in number
EG *The trip wore on and the hazards multiplied.*
increase EG *The population continues to increase.*
proliferate EG *Computerized databases are proliferating fast.*
spread EG *Cholera is not spreading as quickly as it did in the past.*

mumble VERB
to speak quietly
EG *He mumbled a few words.*
murmur EG *He murmured something to the professor.*
mutter EG *He sat there muttering to himself.*

❶ murder NOUN
the act of killing someone
EG *after being found guilty of murder*
assassination EG *the assassination of John F. Kennedy*
homicide EG *the scene of the homicide*
killing EG *a brutal killing*
manslaughter EG *She was found guilty of manslaughter.*
slaughter EG *the imperial army's slaughter of Chinese civilians*

slaying LITERARY EG *a trail of motiveless slayings*

2 murder VERB
to kill someone
EG *a thriller about two men who murder a third*
assassinate EG *Robert Kennedy was assassinated in 1968.*
kill EG *a man who killed his wife*
slaughter EG *Thirty four people were slaughtered while queueing up to cast their votes.*
slay LITERARY EG *the field where Saint George is reputed to have slain the dragon*
take the life of EG *He admitted to taking the lives of at least 35 more women.*

1 mysterious ADJECTIVE
strange and not well understood
EG *He died in mysterious circumstances.*
arcane FORMAL EG *the arcane world of high finance*
baffling EG *a baffling array of wires*
cryptic EG *My father's notes are more cryptic here.*
enigmatic EG *one of Orson Welles's most enigmatic films*
mystifying EG *I find your attitude rather mystifying.*

WORD POWER

▷ **Synonyms**
abstruse
recondite

---

2 mysterious ADJECTIVE
secretive about something
EG *Stop being so mysterious.*
furtive EG *with a furtive glance over her shoulder*
secretive EG *the secretive world of spying*

mystery NOUN
something that is not understood
EG *the mystery surrounding his death*
conundrum EG *this theological conundrum*
enigma EG *Iran remains an enigma for the outside world.*
puzzle EG *"Women are a puzzle," he said.*
riddle EG *the answer to the riddle of why it was never finished*

a
b
c
d
e
f
g
h
i
j
k
l
m
n
o
p
q
r
s
t
u
v
w
x
y
z

Nn

1 naked ADJECTIVE
not wearing any clothes
EG *a naked man diving into the sea*
bare EG *her bare feet*
nude EG *nude bathing*
stark-naked EG *She didn't seem to notice I was stark-naked.*
unclothed EG *an unclothed male body*
undressed EG *She couldn't remember getting undressed.*

WORD POWER

▶ **Antonym**
clothed

2 naked ADJECTIVE
openly displayed or shown
EG *naked aggression*
blatant EG *evidence of blatant discrimination*
evident EG *the party's evident dislike of the president*
manifest EG *his manifest enthusiasm*
open EG *open opposition to the government*
unmistakable EG *with unmistakable amusement in his eyes*

WORD POWER

▷ **Synonyms**
overt
patent
stark

▶ **Antonym**
secret

1 name NOUN
a word that identifies a person or thing
EG *My name is Joe.*
designation EG *a level four alert, a designation reserved for very serious incidents*
epithet EG *the common epithet for the Buddha*
nickname EG *He's heard your nickname is Codfish.*
term EG *I don't know the medical term for it.*
title EG *Your actual title would be business manager.*

WORD POWER

▷ **Synonyms**
appellation
denomination
sobriquet

● **Related Words**
adjective : nominal

2 name NOUN
the opinion people have about someone
EG *to protect Janet's good name*
character EG *a series of personal attacks on my character*
reputation EG *I know Chris has a bad reputation.*

3 name VERB
to give a name to someone or something
EG *a little girl named Betsy*
baptize EG *She could be baptized Margaret.*
call EG *in a town called Fishingport*
christen EG *He wanted to christen his son Arthur Albert.*
dub EG *a girl cruelly dubbed "the Worm"*
style EG *a character who styled himself the Memory Man*
term EG *He had been termed a temporary employee.*

narrow ADJECTIVE
having a small distance from side to side
EG *a narrow stream*
fine EG *the fine hairs on her arms*
slender EG *long slender legs*
slim EG *a slim volume of Auden's*

poems
thin EG *a thin layer of clay*

WORD POWER

▶ **Antonym**
wide

---

narrow-minded ADJECTIVE
unwilling to consider new ideas or
other people's opinions
EG *their own narrow-minded view of
the world*
biased EG *a biased view*
bigoted EG *bigoted opinions*
insular EG *those insular British
travellers*
opinionated EG *the most
opinionated rubbish I have read*
prejudiced EG *a whole host of
prejudiced and xenophobic ideas*

WORD POWER

▷ **Synonyms**
parochial
reactionary

▶ **Antonym**
tolerant

---

nasty ADJECTIVE
very unpleasant
EG *a nasty taste*
disagreeable EG *a disagreeable
experience*
disgusting EG *the most disgusting
behaviour*
foul EG *They produce a foul smell of
rotten eggs.*
horrible EG *I've got a horrible feeling
about this one.*
repellent EG *the most repellent
human being I have ever met*
unpleasant EG *some unpleasant
surprises*
vile EG *All the food is vile.*

WORD POWER

▶ **Antonym**
pleasant

---

❶ natural ADJECTIVE
normal and to be expected
EG *the natural reaction to a failed
marriage*
common EG *It is a common response.*
everyday EG *the everyday drudgery
of work*
normal EG *Biting is normal for
puppies when they are teething.*
ordinary EG *The cottage looks quite
ordinary from the road.*
typical EG *typical symptoms of stress*
usual EG *It was not usual for the
women to accompany them.*

WORD POWER

▶ **Antonym**
unnatural

---

❷ natural ADJECTIVE
not trying to pretend
EG *He was so natural with the children.*
candid EG *rather candid about her
marriage*
frank EG *an unusually frank interview*
genuine EG *He always seems so
genuine.*
real EG *She came across as a real
person.*
unaffected EG *She sang with
unaffected simplicity.*

WORD POWER

▷ **Synonyms**
artless
ingenuous

▶ **Antonym**
false

---

❸ natural ADJECTIVE
existing from birth and not learned
EG *I never had much natural rhythm.*
inborn EG *an inborn sense of
optimism*
inherent EG *the inherent goodness of
people*
innate EG *the innate conservatism of
his predecessor*

a
b
c
d
e
f
g
h
i
j
k
l
m
n
o
p
q
r
s
t
u
v
w
x
y
z

instinctive EG *an instinctive distrust of authority*
intuitive EG *an intuitive understanding of the market*
native EG *He relies on his native wit to get him through.*

WORD POWER

▷ **Synonyms**
immanent
indigenous

nature NOUN
someone's character
EG *It's not in my nature to sit still.*
character EG *the funny side of his character*
make-up EG *Compromise was never part of his make-up.*
personality EG *his dominating personality*

❶ naughty ADJECTIVE
tending to behave badly
EG *a naughty little boy*
bad EG *the bad behaviour of their teenage children*
disobedient EG *Lucy was similarly disobedient.*
impish EG *an impish sense of humour*
mischievous EG *a mischievous child*
wayward EG *He tried to control his wayward son.*

WORD POWER

▶ **Antonym**
well-behaved

❷ naughty ADJECTIVE
rude or indecent
EG *a programme all about naughty words*
bawdy EG *a series of bawdy jokes*
lewd EG *his arrest for lewd behaviour*
obscene EG *making obscene gestures to the crowd*
vulgar EG *The lyrics were vulgar.*

WORD POWER

▷ **Synonyms**
ribald
risqué
smutty

❶ near ADJECTIVE
not far away in distance
EG *A beautiful woman is near.*
adjacent EG *an adjacent room*
adjoining EG *A phone rang in an adjoining office.*
close EG *a close neighbour*
nearby EG *the nearby village*

WORD POWER

▶ **Antonym**
far

❷ near ADJECTIVE
not far away in time
EG *The time of judgment is near.*
approaching EG *The deadline was approaching.*
forthcoming EG *the forthcoming football season*
imminent EG *The day of our departure was imminent.*
looming EG *Exams are looming and the students are panicking.*
near at hand EG *His death is near at hand.*
nigh EG *The end of the world is nigh.*
upcoming EG *the upcoming elections*

❸ near PREPOSITION
not far from
EG *He drew his chair nearer the fire.*
adjacent to EG *a garden and maze adjacent to the castle*
alongside EG *the huts set up alongside the river*
close to EG *We parked close to the pavement.*
next to EG *I realised someone was standing next to me.*
not far from EG *a car park not far from the entrance*

nearly ADVERB
not completely but almost
EG *The beach was nearly empty.*
almost EG *Over the past decade their wages have almost doubled.*
as good as EG *The World Championship is as good as over.*
just about EG *We are just about finished with this section.*
practically EG *The house was practically a wreck.*
virtually EG *Their country is virtually bankrupt.*

❶ **neat** ADJECTIVE
having everything arranged in a tidy way
EG *The house was clean and neat.*
orderly EG *an orderly office*
smart EG *a smart navy blue suit*
spruce EG *Mundo was looking spruce in a suit.*
tidy EG *He always kept his bedroom tidy.*
trim EG *a street of trim little villas*

WORD POWER

▶ **Antonym**
untidy

❷ **neat** ADJECTIVE
not mixed with anything else
EG *a small glass of neat vodka*
pure EG *a carton of pure orange juice*
straight EG *calling for a straight whisky*

WORD POWER

▷ **Synonyms**
undiluted
unmixed

❶ **necessary** ADJECTIVE
needed so that something can happen
EG *Make the necessary arrangements.*
essential EG *It is essential that you visit a dentist.*
imperative EG *It is imperative we end up with a win.*

indispensable EG *Jordan is an indispensable part of the peace process.*
required EG *That book is required reading.*
vital EG *Bone marrow is vital for producing blood cells.*

WORD POWER

▷ **Synonyms**
de rigueur
requisite

▶ **Antonym**
unnecessary

❷ **necessary** ADJECTIVE; FORMAL
certain to happen or exist
EG *a necessary consequence of war*
certain EG *one certain outcome of the conference*
inevitable EG *She now accepts that a divorce is inevitable.*
inexorable EG *The growth in travel has been inexorable.*
unavoidable EG *The union knows that job losses are unavoidable.*

need VERB
to believe you must have or do something
EG *You need some fresh air.*
demand EG *The children demand her attention.*
require EG *If you require further information, please telephone.*
want EG *I want a drink.*

❶ **neglect** VERB
to fail to look after someone or something
EG *unhappy and neglected children*
ignore EG *They see the government ignoring poor people.*
overlook EG *Pensioners feel they are being overlooked.*
turn your back on EG *Do not turn your back on the unemployed.*

❷ **neglect** VERB; FORMAL
to fail to do something

a b c d e f g h i j k l m n o p q r s t u v w x y z

EG *He had neglected to give her his address.*
fail EG *I was shattered and I failed to tell her about the good bits.*
forget EG *She forgot to lock her door.*
omit EG *He omitted to mention his connection with the company.*

❸ neglect NOUN
lack of care
EG *Most of her plants died from neglect.*
disregard EG *a callous disregard for his victims*
indifference EG *Indifference to patients is rare in America.*
unconcern EG *the government's unconcern for the environment*

nervous ADJECTIVE
worried about something
EG *She had been nervous before the match.*
anxious EG *I was very anxious about her safety.*
apprehensive EG *Their families are apprehensive about the trip.*
edgy EG *I was edgy and tired.*
jittery INFORMAL EG *She still feels jittery when she visits her sister.*
jumpy EG *The Italians are getting jumpy after drawing against the Swiss.*
tense EG *too tense to sleep*
toey AUSTRALIAN; SLANG EG *Dad's getting a bit toey.*
uptight INFORMAL EG *an uptight British couple*
worried EG *You had me worried for a moment.*

WORD POWER
▶ **Antonym**
calm

neutral ADJECTIVE
not supporting either side
EG *We stayed neutral during the war.*
disinterested EG *a disinterested observer*

dispassionate EG *a full and dispassionate account*
impartial EG *How can he give impartial advice?*
nonaligned EG *the Arab and nonaligned countries*

WORD POWER
▷ **Synonyms**
nonpartisan
unbiased
unprejudiced

▶ **Antonym**
biased

never ADVERB
at no time at all
EG *I never said I was leaving.*
at no time EG *At no time did he see the helicopter.*
not ever EG *The problem won't ever go away.*

new ADJECTIVE
recently created or discovered
EG *a new hotel*
→ see Word Study **new**

WORD POWER
▶ **Antonym**
old

news NOUN
information about things that have happened
EG *news about the civil war*
bulletin EG *the main evening bulletin*
disclosure EG *disclosures about his private life*
dispatch EG *the latest dispatches from the war zone*
information EG *up-to-date information on weather*
intelligence EG *military intelligence from behind Iraqi lines*
latest INFORMAL EG *the latest on the bomb explosion*
tidings FORMAL EG *the bearer of bad tidings*

word EG *There is no word about casualties.*

1 **next** ADJECTIVE
coming immediately after something else
EG *Their next child was a girl.*
ensuing EG *the ensuing years of violence*
following EG *The following day I went to work as usual.*
subsequent EG *As subsequent events showed, he was wrong.*
succeeding EG *succeeding generations of students*

2 **next** ADVERB
coming immediately after something else
EG *Steve arrived next.*
afterwards EG *I felt dizzy afterwards and had to sit down.*
subsequently EG *She was subsequently married to his cousin.*

3 **next** ADJECTIVE
in a position nearest to something
EG *in the next room*
adjacent EG *I pulled into the adjacent driveway.*
adjoining EG *in adjoining streets*
closest EG *Britain's closest neighbours*
nearest EG *the nearest Italian restaurant*
neighbouring EG *Liberians fleeing to neighbouring countries*

nice ADJECTIVE
attractive or enjoyable
EG *Did you have a nice time, dear?*
→ see Word Study **nice**

no INTERJECTION
not at all
EG *"Any problems?" - "No, everything's fine."*
absolutely not EG *"Did they consult you?" - "Absolutely not."*
certainly not EG *"Perhaps it would be better if I withdrew." - "Certainly not!"*

definitely not EG *"Are you going to the party?" - "Definitely not."*
not at all EG *"You're not upset, are you?" - "Not at all."*
of course not EG *"I'd like to talk to the lads, if you don't mind." - "Of course not, Chief."*

<u>WORD POWER</u>

▶ **Antonym**
yes

1 **noble** ADJECTIVE
deserving admiration because of honesty, bravery and unselfishness
EG *a good and noble thing to do*
generous EG *It reflects his generous nature.*
honourable EG *His colleagues were honourable people.*
magnanimous EG *Miss Balding is magnanimous in victory.*
upright EG *a very upright, trustworthy man*
virtuous EG *the virtuous Mrs Friendall*
worthy EG *less worthy members of our profession*

<u>WORD POWER</u>

▶ **Antonym**
ignoble

2 **noble** NOUN
someone from the highest social rank
EG *The Scottish nobles were united.*
aristocrat EG *All his sisters had married German aristocrats.*
lord EG *They assumed that Amy was a snob because her father was a lord.*
nobleman EG *a Spanish nobleman*
peer EG *He was made a life peer in 1981.*

<u>WORD POWER</u>

▶ **Antonym**
peasant

a b c d e f g h i j k l m n o p q r s t u v w x y z

noise NOUN
a loud or unpleasant sound
EG *He is making an awful noise.*
commotion EG *There was a commotion in the corridor.*
din EG *He'd never heard a din like it.*
hubbub EG *the hubbub of Paris in the 1880s*
pandemonium EG *There was pandemonium in the classroom.*
racket EG *There was a terrible racket going on.*
row EG *Whatever is that row?*
uproar EG *The courtroom was in an uproar.*

WORD POWER

▷ **Synonyms**
clamour
rumpus
tumult

▶ **Antonym**
silence

noisy ADJECTIVE
making a lot of noise
EG *a noisy audience of schoolchildren*
deafening EG *a deafening roar*
loud EG *The disco music was a little too loud.*
piercing EG *her piercing laugh*
strident EG *the strident vocals of Joy Malcolm*
tumultuous EG *He took the field to tumultuous applause.*
vociferous EG *vociferous support from the Scottish fans*

WORD POWER

▷ **Synonyms**
clamorous
riotous
uproarious

▶ **Antonym**
quiet

nominate VERB
to suggest someone for a position

EG *The party refused to nominate him as its candidate.*
name EG *He'll be naming a new captain.*
propose EG *Cliff was proposed as chairman.*
recommend EG *He recommended him as his successor at Boston.*
select EG *no prospect of being selected to stand for Parliament*
submit EG *Mr Heath submitted a list of 200 names.*
suggest EG *Some commentators have suggested Clark for the job.*

nonsense NOUN
foolish words or behaviour
EG *I say the allegations are complete nonsense.*
bull SLANG EG *They're teaching our kids a load of bull.*
drivel EG *mindless drivel aimed at Middle America*
garbage INFORMAL EG *One source claimed the rumours were complete garbage.*
inanity EG *the burbling inanities of the tabloids*
rot EG *She is talking complete rot.*
rubbish EG *complete and utter rubbish*
waffle BRITISH; INFORMAL EG *He writes smug, sanctimonious waffle.*

normal ADJECTIVE
usual and ordinary
EG *my normal routine*
average EG *What's your average day like?*
conventional EG *conventional tastes*
habitual EG *their country of habitual residence*
ordinary EG *It was just an ordinary weekend.*
regular EG *It looks like a regular cigarette.*
routine EG *a routine medical check*
standard EG *standard practice*
typical EG *A typical day begins at 8.30.*

A B C D E F G H I J K L M N O P Q R S T U V W X Y Z

usual EG *She did not collect him at the usual time.*

WORD POWER

▶ **Antonym**
unusual

nosy ADJECTIVE
trying to find out about other people's business
EG *nosy neighbours watching us through the curtains*
curious EG *surrounded by a group of curious villagers*
eavesdropping EG *We don't want to be overheard by eavesdropping servants.*
inquisitive EG *Bears are naturally inquisitive creatures.*
prying EG *I hid it away, safe from prying eyes.*

❶ note NOUN
a short letter
EG *I wrote him a note asking him to come round.*
communication FORMAL EG *a communication from the President*
letter EG *I have received a letter from a friend.*
memo EG *a leaked memo to managers*
memorandum EG *A memorandum has been sent to the members of the board.*
message EG *He sent his mate round with a message for me.*
reminder EG *We keep getting reminders from the garage to pay our bill.*

WORD POWER

▷ **Synonyms**
missive (OLD-FASHIONED)

❷ note NOUN
a written record that helps you remember something
EG *I made a note of his address.*
account EG *Keep an account of all your outgoings.*
jotting EG *Carry a notebook with you for your jottings.*
record EG *Keep a record of all payments.*
register EG *She kept a register of each child's progress.*

❸ note NOUN
an atmosphere, feeling, or quality
EG *I detected a note of bitterness in his voice.*
hint EG *Was there was a hint of irony in that remark?*
tone EG *He laughed again, this time with a cold, sharp tone.*
touch EG *There is an unmistakable touch of pathos in his last film.*
trace EG *He wrote on the subject without a trace of sensationalism.*

❹ note VERB
to become aware of or mention a fact
EG *I noted that the rain had stopped.*
mention EG *I mentioned in passing that I liked her dress.*
notice EG *Contact the police if you notice anything suspicious.*
observe FORMAL EG *Hooke observed a reddish spot on the surface of the planet.*
perceive EG *He perceived a certain tension between them.*
register EG *The sound was so familiar that she didn't register it.*
remark EG *Everyone has remarked what a lovely lady she is.*
see EG *A lot of people saw what was happening but did nothing.*

❶ notice VERB
to become aware of something
EG *Then I noticed Billy wasn't laughing.*
detect EG *He detects signs of growing support for his plan.*
discern EG *I did not discern any change in attitudes.*
note EG *I noted that the rain had stopped.*

A B C D E F G H I J K L M N O P Q R S T U V W X Y Z

observe EG *I've observed how hard he had to work.*
perceive EG *gradually perceiving the possibilities*
see EG *I saw that the lobby was swarming with police.*
spot EG *Allen spotted me on the other side of the dance floor.*

② notice NOUN
a written announcement
EG *a handwritten notice in the window*
advertisement EG *one advertisement in a local paper*
bill EG *students posting bills near the campus for a demo*
poster EG *a poster advertising a charity concert*
sign EG *a hand-written cardboard sign hung round his neck*

③ notice NOUN
warning that something is going to happen
EG *She was transferred without notice.*
advance warning EG *advance warning of the attack*
intimation EG *He has given no intimation of an intention to resign.*
notification EG *Official notification is expected to arrive today.*
warning EG *I was sacked without warning.*

noticeable ADJECTIVE
obvious and easy to see
EG *a noticeable improvement*
conspicuous EG *a conspicuous lack of sympathy*
evident EG *He ate with evident enjoyment.*
obvious EG *There are obvious dangers.*
perceptible EG *Germany is showing a perceptible improvement.*
unmistakable EG *a growing but unmistakable impatience*

WORD POWER

▷ **Synonyms**
manifest
salient

---

notify VERB
to officially inform someone of something
EG *The skipper notified the coastguard of the tragedy.*
advise FORMAL EG *I think it best that I advise you of my decision first.*
inform EG *They would inform him of any progress they made.*
tell EG *He told me I was on a final warning.*
warn EG *They warned him of the dangers.*

notorious ADJECTIVE
well-known for something bad
EG *The district was notorious for violent crime.*
disreputable EG *a low and disreputable character*
infamous EG *an industry infamous for late payment of debts*
scandalous EG *her scandalous affair with the president*

now ADVERB
at the present time or moment
EG *I need to talk to him now.*
at once EG *I really must go at once.*
currently EG *The vaccines are currently being tested.*
immediately EG *Please come immediately.*
nowadays EG *I don't see much of Tony nowadays.*
right now EG *Stop that noise right now!*
straightaway EG *I think you should see a doctor straightaway.*
without delay EG *We'll come round without delay.*

nuisance NOUN
someone or something that is annoying

EG *Sorry to be a nuisance.*
annoyance EG *Snoring can be an annoyance.*
bother EG *Most men hate the bother of shaving.*
hassle INFORMAL EG *Writing out a cheque is a hassle.*
inconvenience EG *the inconvenience of a rail strike*
irritation EG *He describes the tourists as "an irritation".*
pain INFORMAL EG *She found dressing up for the occasion a real pain.*
pest EG *I didn't want to be a cry baby or a pest.*

WORD POWER
▷ **Synonyms**
plague
vexation

❶ numb ADJECTIVE
unable to feel anything
EG *Your right arm goes numb.*
dead EG *Hillier suffered a dead leg playing for the reserves.*
frozen EG *a frozen shoulder*
insensitive EG *The brain itself is insensitive to pain.*
paralysed EG *He has been left with a paralysed arm.*

WORD POWER
▷ **Synonyms**
benumbed
insensible

❷ numb VERB
to make you unable to feel anything
EG *The cold numbed my fingers.*
dull EG *morphine to dull the pain*
freeze EG *an epidural to freeze the hip area*
paralyse EG *people paralysed by illness or injury*

stun EG *the gun used to stun the animals*

WORD POWER
▷ **Synonyms**
benumb
deaden
immobilize

❶ number NOUN
a word or symbol used for counting
EG *Pick a number between one and ten.*
digit EG *a six-digit password*
figure EG *a figure between a hundred and a thousand*
numeral EG *Roman numerals*

WORD POWER
▷ **Synonyms**
character
integer

❷ number NOUN
a quantity of things or people
EG *Adrian has introduced me to a large number of people.*
collection EG *a huge collection of books about Keats*
crowd EG *a huge crowd of supporters*
horde EG *a horde of drunken villagers*
multitude EG *Bands can play to multitudes of fans.*

numerous ADJECTIVE
existing or happening in large numbers
EG *on numerous occasions*
lots EG *I've got lots of photos of the kids.*
many EG *I have met Imran many times.*
several EG *He is fluent in several languages.*

a
b
c
d
e
f
g
h
i
j
k
l
m
n
o
p
q
r
s
t
u
v
w
x
y
z

Oo

oaf NOUN
a clumsy or aggressive person
EG *You drunken oaf!*
brute EG *Custer was an idiot and a brute.*
lout EG *a drunken lout*

oath NOUN
a formal promise
EG *He took an oath of loyalty to the government.*
pledge EG *The meeting ended with a pledge to step up cooperation.*
promise EG *If you make a promise, you should keep it.*
vow EG *I made a silent vow to be more careful.*

obedient ADJECTIVE
tending to do what you are told
EG *He was always very obedient to his parents.*
law-abiding EG *law-abiding citizens*
submissive EG *Most doctors want their patients to be submissive.*
subservient EG *her willingness to be subservient to her children*

WORD POWER

▷ **Synonyms**
biddable
compliant

▶ **Antonym**
disobedient

obey VERB
to do what you are told
EG *Most people obey the law.*
abide by EG *They have got to abide by the rules.*
adhere to EG *All members adhere to a strict code of practice.*
comply with EG *The army will comply with the ceasefire.*
follow EG *Take care to follow the instructions carefully.*
observe EG *forcing motorists to observe speed restrictions*

WORD POWER

▶ **Antonym**
disobey

① object NOUN
anything solid and non-living
EG *everyday objects such as wooden spoons*
article EG *household articles*
thing EG *What's that thing in the middle of the fountain?*

② object NOUN
an aim or purpose
EG *The object of the exercise is to raise money for the charity.*
aim EG *The aim of the festival is to increase awareness of Hindu culture.*
goal EG *The goal is to raise as much money as possible.*
idea EG *The idea is to give children the freedom to explore.*
intention EG *It is my intention to remain in my position.*
objective EG *His objective was to win.*
purpose EG *What is the purpose of your visit?*

③ object VERB
to express disapproval
EG *A lot of people will object to the book.*
oppose EG *Many parents oppose bilingual education in schools.*
protest EG *He picked up the cat before Rosa could protest.*

WORD POWER

▷ **Synonyms**
demur
expostulate

▶ **Antonym**
approve

objection NOUN
disapproval of something
EG *despite objections by the White House*
opposition EG *Opposition to this plan has come from the media.*
protest EG *protests against the government*

WORD POWER

▶ **Antonym**
support

obscene ADJECTIVE
indecent and likely to upset people
EG *obscene pictures*
bawdy EG *a bawdy song*
blue EG *a blue movie*
dirty EG *a dirty book*
filthy EG *a filthy joke*
indecent EG *an indecent suggestion*
lewd EG *lewd comments*
pornographic EG *a pornographic magazine*

WORD POWER

▷ **Synonyms**
ribald
salacious
smutty

❶ **obscure** ADJECTIVE
known by only a few people
EG *an obscure Mongolian dialect*
little-known EG *a little-known Austrian composer*
unknown EG *an unknown writer*

WORD POWER

▶ **Antonym**
famous

❷ **obscure** ADJECTIVE
difficult to understand
EG *The news was shrouded in obscure language.*
arcane EG *the arcane world of contemporary classical music*
cryptic EG *cryptic comments*

opaque EG *the opaque language of the inspector's reports*

WORD POWER

▷ **Synonyms**
abstruse
esoteric
recondite

▶ **Antonym**
simple

❸ **obscure** VERB
to make something difficult to see
EG *His view was obscured by trees.*
cloak EG *a land permanently cloaked in mist*
cloud EG *Perhaps anger had clouded his vision.*
conceal EG *The hat concealed her hair.*
hide EG *The compound was hidden by trees and shrubs.*
mask EG *A thick grey cloud masked the sun.*
screen EG *Most of the road was screened by a block of flats.*
shroud EG *Mist shrouded the outline of Buckingham Palace.*

WORD POWER

▶ **Antonym**
expose

observant ADJECTIVE
good at noticing things
EG *Painting makes you really observant of things.*
attentive EG *the attentive audience*
perceptive EG *a perceptive remark*
vigilant EG *He warned the public to be vigilant.*
watchful EG *Keep a watchful eye on babies and toddlers.*

WORD POWER

▷ **Synonyms**
eagle-eyed
sharp-eyed

a
b
c
d
e
f
g
h
i
j
k
l
m
n
o
p
q
r
s
t
u
v
w
x
y
z

A B C D E F G H I J K L M N O P Q R S T U V W X Y Z

❶ observe VERB
to watch something carefully
EG *He has spent years observing their behaviour.*
monitor EG *I have been monitoring his progress carefully.*
scrutinize EG *She scrutinized his features to see if he was telling the truth.*
study EG *Debbie studied her friend's face for a moment.*
survey EG *He surveys American politics from an interesting standpoint.*
view EG *You can view the lesson from the gallery.*
watch EG *A man was watching him from across the square.*

❷ observe VERB
to notice something
EG *I observed a number of strange phenomena.*
discover EG *They discovered that they were being watched.*
note EG *People noted how much care she took over her work.*
notice EG *Contact the police if you notice anything unusual.*
see EG *I saw a man coming towards me.*
spot EG *Moments later, smoke was spotted coming out of the kitchen.*
witness EG *Anyone who witnessed the attack should call the police.*

❸ observe VERB
to make a comment about something
EG *"You've had your hair cut," he observed.*
comment EG *Stuart commented that this was true.*
mention EG *I mentioned that I didn't like contemporary music.*
remark EG *"Some people have more money than sense," he remarked.*
say EG *She said that I looked tired.*
state EG *He stated that this was, indeed, the case.*

obsession NOUN
a compulsion to think about something
EG *her obsession with Christopher*
complex EG *I have never had a complex about my height.*
fixation EG *the country's fixation on the war*
mania EG *a mania for horror films*
preoccupation EG *today's preoccupation with royal misdeeds*
thing INFORMAL EG *He's got this thing about ties.*

obstacle NOUN
something which makes it difficult to go forward
EG *a large obstacle to improving housing conditions*
barrier EG *Taxes are the most obvious barrier to free trade.*
difficulty EG *the difficulties ahead*
hindrance EG *The higher rates have been a hindrance to economic recovery.*
hurdle EG *the first hurdle for many women returning to work*
impediment EG *There was no legal impediment to the marriage.*
obstruction EG *an obstruction in the road*

WORD POWER

▷ **Synonyms**
bar
stumbling block

---

obstinate ADJECTIVE
unwilling to change your mind
EG *He is obstinate and will not give up.*
dogged EG *his dogged insistence on their rights*
headstrong EG *He's young and very headstrong.*
inflexible EG *His opponents viewed him as dogmatic and inflexible.*
intractable EG *He protested but Wright was intractable.*
stubborn EG *a stubborn character*

who is used to getting his own way
wilful EG *a wilful child*

WORD POWER

▷ **Synonyms**
intransigent
recalcitrant
refractory

▶ **Antonym**
flexible

---

obstruct VERB
to block a road or path
EG *Lorries obstructed the road.*
bar EG *He stood there, barring her way.*
block EG *Some students blocked the highway.*
choke EG *The roads are choked with cars.*
clog EG *The traffic clogged the Thames bridges.*

obtain VERB
to get something
EG *He tried to obtain a false passport*
acquire EG *I recently acquired a beautiful old lamp.*
get EG *trying to get enough food to live*
get hold of EG *It's hard to get hold of guns.*
get your hands on INFORMAL
eg *reading everything she could get her hands on*
procure FORMAL EG *It became hard to procure fuel.*
secure FORMAL EG *continuing their efforts to secure a ceasefire*

obvious ADJECTIVE
easy to see or understand
EG *an obvious injustice*
apparent EG *It was apparent that he had lost interest.*
blatant EG *a blatant foul*
clear EG *a clear breach of the rules*
evident EG *His love of nature is evident in his paintings.*
overt EG *parents who showed us no*

overt affection
palpable EG *The tension between them is palpable.*
plain EG *It was plain to him that I was having a nervous breakdown.*
self-evident EG *The implications for this country are self-evident.*

WORD POWER

▷ **Synonyms**
conspicuous
manifest
patent

---

❶ occasion NOUN
an important event
EG *The launch of a ship was a big occasion.*
affair EG *The visit was to be a purely private affair.*
event EG *A new book by Grass is always an event.*

❷ occasion NOUN
an opportunity to do something
EG *an important occasion for setting out government policy*
chance EG *the chance to practise medicine in British hospitals*
opportunity EG *I had an opportunity to go to New York.*
time EG *This was no time to make a speech.*

❸ occasion VERB; FORMAL
to cause something
EG *damage occasioned by fire*
bring about EG *the only way to bring about peace*
give rise to EG *The judge's decision gave rise to practical problems.*
induce EG *an economic crisis induced by high oil prices*
produce EG *The drug is known to produce side-effects in women.*
prompt EG *The demonstration prompted fears of more violence.*
provoke EG *The incident has provoked outrage in Okinawa.*

occasional ADJECTIVE
happening sometimes
EG *an occasional outing*
intermittent EG *after three hours of intermittent rain*
odd EG *at odd moments*
periodic EG *periodic bouts of illness*
sporadic EG *a year of sporadic fighting*

WORD POWER
▶ **Antonym**
frequent

❶ occur VERB
to happen or exist
EG *The disease occurs throughout Africa.*
appear EG *a test to reveal infection before symptoms appear*
arise EG *A problem may arise later in pregnancy.*
be present EG *This vitamin is present in breast milk.*
exist EG *A conflict of interest may exist in such situations.*
happen EG *The accident happened close to Martha's Vineyard.*
take place EG *Elections will take place on the second of November.*

❷ occur VERB
to come into your mind
EG *It didn't occur to me to check.*
cross your mind EG *The possibility of failure did cross my mind.*
dawn on EG *It dawned on me that I shouldn't give up without a fight.*
strike EG *A thought struck her.*

odd ADJECTIVE
strange or unusual
EG *an odd coincidence*
bizarre EG *his bizarre behaviour*
curious EG *a curious mixture of the ancient and modern*
funny EG *There's something funny about him.*
peculiar EG *Rachel thought it tasted peculiar.*

queer OLD-FASHIONED EG *There's something a bit queer going on.*
singular FORMAL EG *Where he got that singular notion I just can't think.*
strange EG *Then a strange thing happened.*
weird EG *That first day was weird.*

WORD POWER
▶ **Antonym**
ordinary

offend VERB
to upset or embarrass someone
EG *He says he had no intention of offending the community.*
affront EG *He pretended to be affronted, but inwardly he was pleased.*
insult EG *Buchanan says he was insulted by the judge's remarks.*
outrage EG *Many people have been outraged by what was said.*

WORD POWER
▶ **Antonym**
please

offensive ADJECTIVE
rude and upsetting
EG *offensive behaviour*
abusive EG *abusive language*
insulting EG *an insulting remark*
objectionable EG *I find your tone highly objectionable.*

❶ offer VERB
to ask if someone wants something
EG *Rhys offered him an apple.*
hold out EG *I held out my ticket for him to check.*
tender EG *She has tendered her resignation.*

WORD POWER
▷ **Synonyms**
extend
proffer

2 offer NOUN
something that someone offers you
EG *He had refused several excellent job offers.*
proposition EG *I made her a proposition.*
tender EG *a tender for a public contract*

1 official ADJECTIVE
approved by someone in authority
EG *the official figures*
authorized EG *the authorized biography*
certified EG *a certified accountant*
formal EG *No formal announcement has been made.*
licensed EG *a licensed doctor*

WORD POWER

▶ **Antonym**
unofficial

2 official NOUN
someone in authority
EG *a senior UN official*
executive EG *a senior bank executive*
officer EG *a local authority education officer*
representative EG *trade union representatives*

WORD POWER

▷ **Synonyms**
bureaucrat
functionary

often ADVERB
happening many times
EG *They often spent Christmas at Prescott Hill.*
frequently EG *He was frequently depressed.*
repeatedly EG *Both men have repeatedly denied the allegations.*

okay *or* **OK** ADJECTIVE; INFORMAL
acceptable or satisfactory
EG *Is it okay if I come by myself?*
acceptable EG *It is becoming more*

acceptable for women to drink.
all right EG *if it's all right with you*

1 old ADJECTIVE
having lived for a long time
EG *an old lady*
→ see Word Study **old**

WORD POWER

▶ **Antonym**
young

2 old ADJECTIVE
in the past
EG *my old art teacher*
→ see Word Study **old**

WORD POWER

▶ **Antonym**
new

old-fashioned ADJECTIVE
no longer fashionable
EG *old-fashioned shoes*
antiquated EG *an antiquated system*
archaic EG *archaic practices such as these*
dated EG *Some of the language sounds quite dated.*
obsolete EG *So much equipment becomes obsolete almost as soon as it's made.*
outdated EG *outdated attitudes*
outmoded EG *toiling in outmoded factories*
out of date EG *a make of car that is now out of date*
passé EG *Punk is passé.*

WORD POWER

▷ **Synonyms**
behind the times
obsolescent
old-time

▶ **Antonym**
fashionable

omen NOUN
a sign of what will happen

a
b
c
d
e
f
g
h
i
j
k
l
m
n
o
p
q
r
s
t
u
v
w
x
y
z

A
B
C
D
E
F
G
H
I
J
K
L
M
N
O
P
Q
R
S
T
U
V
W
X
Y
Z

EG *Her appearance at this moment is an omen of disaster.*
sign EG *people who look to the skies for signs*
warning EG *a warning of trouble to come*

WORD POWER

▷ **Synonyms**
augury
portent

ominous ADJECTIVE
suggesting that something bad will happen
EG *an ominous silence*
sinister EG *a sinister message*
threatening EG *a threatening sky*

WORD POWER

▷ **Synonyms**
inauspicious
portentous
unpropitious

omit VERB
to not include something
EG *Omit the salt in this recipe.*
exclude EG *Women felt excluded form the workplace.*
leave out EG *The Spaniard has been left out of the team.*
miss out EG *What about Sally? You've missed her out!*
skip EG *It is all too easy to skip meals.*

❶ only ADVERB
involving one person or thing
EG *Only Keith knows whether he will continue.*
just EG *It's not just a financial matter.*
merely EG *Watson was far from being merely a furniture expert.*
purely EG *a racing machine, designed purely for speed*
simply EG *Most of the damage was simply because of fallen trees.*
solely EG *decisions based solely upon what we see in magazines*

❷ only ADJECTIVE
having no other examples
EG *their only hit single*
one EG *My one aim is to look after the horses well.*
sole EG *Our sole intention is to reunite her with her baby.*

❶ open VERB
to cause something not to be closed
EG *She opened the door.*
uncover EG *When the seedlings sprout, uncover the tray.*
undo EG *I managed secretly to undo a corner of the parcel.*
unlock EG *She unlocked the case.*

WORD POWER

▷ **Synonyms**
unfasten
unseal

▶ **Antonym**
shut

❷ open ADJECTIVE
not closed
EG *an open box of chocolates*
ajar EG *He left the door ajar.*
uncovered EG *The uncovered bucket in the corner stank.*
undone EG *pictures of him with his shirt undone*
unlocked EG *an unlocked room*

WORD POWER

▷ **Synonyms**
unfastened
unsealed

▶ **Antonym**
shut

❸ open ADJECTIVE
not trying to deceive someone
EG *He had always been open with her.*
candid EG *I haven't been completely candid with him.*
frank EG *My client has been less than frank with me.*
honest EG *He had been honest with her and she had tricked him!*

❶ opening ADJECTIVE
coming first
EG *the opening day of the season*
first EG *the first night of the play*
inaugural EG *his inaugural address*
initial EG *the aim of this initial meeting*
introductory EG *an introductory offer*

❷ opening NOUN
the first part of something
EG *the opening of the film*
beginning EG *the beginning of the book*
commencement FORMAL EG *at the commencement of the course*
start EG *four years after the start of the Great War*

WORD POWER

▶ **Antonym**
conclusion

❸ opening NOUN
a hole or gap
EG *a narrow opening in the fence*
chink EG *a chink in the wall*
cleft EG *a narrow cleft in the rocks*
crack EG *Kathryn had seen him through a crack in the curtains.*
gap EG *the wind tearing through gaps in the window frames*
hole EG *a hole in the wall*
slot EG *a slot in which to insert a coin*
space EG *a half-inch space between the curtains*
vent EG *Steam escaped from the vent at the front of the machine.*

WORD POWER

▷ **Synonyms**
aperture
fissure

opinion NOUN
a belief or view
EG *I wasn't asking for your opinion.*
assessment EG *What is your assessment of the situation?*

belief EG *his religious beliefs*
estimation EG *He has gone down considerably in my estimation.*
judgment EG *In your judgment, what has changed?*
point of view EG *Thanks for your point of view, John.*
view EG *Make your views known to your local MP.*
viewpoint EG *to include as many viewpoints as possible*

oppose VERB
to disagree with something
EG *protesters opposing planned nuclear tests*
fight against EG *a lifetime fighting against racism*
resist EG *They resisted our attempts to modernize.*
speak out against EG *He spoke out strongly against some of the radical ideas.*

WORD POWER

▷ **Synonyms**
take a stand against
take issue with

▶ **Antonym**
support

❶ opposite ADJECTIVE
completely different to something
EG *I take the opposite view to you.*
conflicting EG *three powers with conflicting interests*
contrary EG *He has a contrary opinion to mine.*
contrasting EG *two men with completely contrasting backgrounds*
opposed EG *This was a straight conflict of directly opposed aims.*
reverse EG *The wrong attitude will have exactly the reverse effect.*

WORD POWER

▷ **Synonyms**
antithetical
diametrically opposed

a b c d e f g h i j k l m n o p q r s t u v w x y z

A
B
C
D
E
F
G
H
I
J
K
L
M
N
O
P
Q
R
S
T
U
V
W
X
Y
Z

❷ opposite NOUN
a completely different person or
thing
EG *He was the complete opposite of
Raymond.*
antithesis FORMAL EG *The antithesis
of the Middle Eastern buyer is the
Japanese.*
contrary EG *I'm not a feminist, quite
the contrary.*
converse EG *Don't you think that the
converse might also be possible?*
reverse EG *This didn't upset him at
all, in fact quite the reverse.*

WORD POWER
▷ **Synonyms**
inverse
obverse

opposition NOUN
disagreement about something
EG *Much of the opposition to this plan
has come from the media.*
disapproval EG *His action had been
greeted with almost universal
disapproval.*
hostility EG *There is hostility to this
method among traditionalists.*
resistance EG *Initially I met
resistance from my own family.*

WORD POWER
▶ **Antonym**
support

oppressed ADJECTIVE
treated cruelly or unfairly
EG *a member of an oppressed minority*
abused EG *those who work with
abused children*
downtrodden EG *the downtrodden,
bored housewife*

WORD POWER
▷ **Synonyms**
enslaved
tyrannized

oppression NOUN
cruel or unfair treatment
EG *the oppression of black people
throughout history*
persecution EG *the persecution of
minorities*
tyranny EG *The 1930s was a decade
of tyranny in Europe.*

WORD POWER
▷ **Synonyms**
subjection
subjugation

optimistic ADJECTIVE
hopeful about the future
EG *an optimistic mood*
buoyant EG *She was in a buoyant
mood.*
confident EG *I am confident that
everything will come out right in time.*
hopeful EG *I am hopeful this
misunderstanding will be rectified.*
positive EG *a positive frame of mind*
sanguine EG *They have begun to take
a more sanguine view.*

WORD POWER
▶ **Antonym**
pessimistic

oral ADJECTIVE
spoken rather than written
EG *oral history*
spoken EG *the spoken word*
verbal EG *a verbal agreement*

orange NOUN OR ADJECTIVE

Shades of orange
amber
apricot
carrot
ochre
peach
tangerine

ordeal NOUN
a difficult and unpleasant
experience

EG *the ordeal of being arrested*
hardship EG *One of the worst hardships is having so little time.*
nightmare EG *Taking my son Peter to a restaurant was a nightmare.*
torture EG *Waiting for the result was torture.*
trial EG *the trials of adolescence*
tribulation FORMAL EG *the trials and tribulations of everyday life*

❶ order NOUN
a command by someone in authority
EG *I don't take orders from him any more.*
command EG *The tanker failed to respond to a command to stop.*
decree EG *He issued a decree ordering all armed groups to disband.*
dictate EG *to ensure that the dictates of the Party are followed*
directive EG *a new EU directive*
instruction EG *MPs defied a party instruction to vote against the Bill.*

❷ order NOUN
a well-organized situation
EG *the wish to impose order upon confusion*
harmony EG *the ordered harmony of the universe*
regularity EG *the chessboard regularity of their fields*
symmetry EG *the beauty and symmetry of a snowflake*

WORD POWER

▶ **Antonym**
disorder

❸ order VERB
to tell someone to do something
EG *He ordered his men to stop firing.*
command EG *He commanded his troops to attack.*
decree EG *the rule that decreed no alcohol on the premises*
direct EG *a court order directing the group to leave the land*
instruct EG *The family has instructed*

solicitors to sue Thomson.
ordain EG *Nehru ordained that socialism should rule.*

WORD POWER

▶ **Antonym**
forbid

orderly ADJECTIVE
well-organized or well-arranged
EG *Their vehicles were parked in orderly rows.*
neat EG *She put her wet clothes in a neat pile in the corner.*
regular EG *regular rows of wooden huts*
tidy EG *a tidy desk*

WORD POWER

▶ **Antonym**
disorderly

ordinary ADJECTIVE
not special or different
EG *an ordinary day*
conventional EG *a respectable married woman with conventional opinions*
normal EG *He lives a normal life.*
regular EG *the regular barman*
routine EG *a routine procedure*
standard EG *It was standard practice.*
usual EG *all the usual inner-city problems*

WORD POWER

▷ **Synonyms**
run-of-the-mill
unexceptional
unremarkable

▶ **Antonym**
special

❶ organization NOUN
a group or business
EG *charitable organizations*
association EG *research associations*
body EG *the Chairman of the*

policemen's representative body

company EG *the Ford Motor Company*

confederation EG *the Confederation of Indian Industry*

group EG *an environmental group*

institution EG *financial institutions*

outfit INFORMAL EG *We are a professional outfit.*

❷ organization NOUN
the planning and arranging of something
EG *He was involved in the organization of conferences and seminars.*

organizing EG *His duties involved the organizing of transport.*

planning EG *The trip needs careful planning.*

structuring EG *improvements in the structuring of courses*

organize VERB
to plan and arrange something
EG *Organizing a wedding takes time.*

arrange EG *The bank can arrange a loan for students.*

establish EG *How do you establish a workable system?*

jack up NEW ZEALAND; INFORMAL EG *to jack up a demonstration*

plan EG *A team meeting was planned for last night.*

set up EG *This tribunal was set up by the government.*

❶ origin NOUN
the beginning or cause of something
EG *the origins of the custom*

derivation EG *The derivation of its name is obscure.*

root EG *His sense of guilt had its roots in his childhood.*

source EG *the source of the problem*

WORD POWER

▷ **Synonyms**
genesis
provenance

❷ origin NOUN
someone's family background
EG *She was of Swedish origin.*

ancestry EG *Noel can trace her ancestry to the 11th century.*

descent EG *All the contributors were of African descent.*

extraction EG *a Malaysian citizen of Australian extraction*

lineage EG *a respectable family of ancient lineage*

stock EG *people of Mediterranean stock*

❶ original ADJECTIVE
being the first example of something
EG *the original owner of the cottage*

first EG *Her first reaction was disgust.*

initial EG *His initial response was to disbelieve her.*

❷ original ADJECTIVE
imaginative and clever
EG *a stunningly original idea*

fresh EG *These designers are full of fresh ideas.*

new EG *These proposals aren't new.*

novel EG *a novel way of losing weight*

WORD POWER

▷ **Synonyms**
innovative
innovatory

▶ **Antonym**
unoriginal

ornament NOUN
an object that you display
EG *a shelf containing ornaments*

adornment EG *a building without any adornments*

bauble EG *a Christmas tree decorated with coloured baubles*

decoration EG *The only wall decorations are candles.*

knick-knack EG *Her flat is spilling over with knick-knacks.*

trinket EG *She sold trinkets to tourists.*

ostentatious ADJECTIVE
intended to impress people with
appearances
EG *an ostentatious lifestyle*
extravagant EG *They make
extravagant shows of generosity.*
flamboyant EG *flamboyant clothes*
flashy EG *a flashy sports car*
grandiose EG *the grandiose building
which housed the mayor's offices*
pretentious EG *This pub was smaller
and less pretentious.*
showy EG *large, showy flowers*

outbreak NOUN
a sudden occurrence of something
EG *the outbreak of war*
eruption EG *this sudden eruption of
violence*
explosion EG *the global explosion of
interest in rugby*

outdo VERB
to do something better than another
person
EG *She would love to outdo her sister
Manuela.*
go one better than EG *You always
have to go one better than anyone
else.*
outshine EG *Jesse has begun to
outshine me in sports.*
surpass EG *determined to surpass
the achievements of his older brothers*
top EG *How are you going to top that?*

WORD POWER

▷ **Synonyms**
best
eclipse

① **outline** VERB
to describe something in a general
way
EG *The mayor outlined his plan to
clean up the town's image.*
sketch EG *Tudjman sketched his
vision of a future Bosnia.*

summarize EG *The article can be
summarized in three sentences.*

WORD POWER

▷ **Synonyms**
adumbrate
delineate

② **outline** NOUN
a general description of something
EG *an outline of the survey's findings*
rundown INFORMAL EG *Here's a
rundown of the options.*
summary EG *a summary of the report*
synopsis EG *a brief synopsis of the
book*

WORD POWER

▷ **Synonyms**
résumé
thumbnail sketch

③ **outline** NOUN
the shape of something
EG *the hazy outline of the goalposts*
contours EG *the contours of her body*
figure EG *Alistair saw the dim figure
of Rose in the chair.*
form EG *She'd never been so glad to
see his bulky form.*
shape EG *dark shapes of herons
silhouetted against the moon*
silhouette EG *the dark silhouette of
the castle ruins*

① **outlook** NOUN
your general attitude towards life
EG *I adopted a positive outlook on life.*
attitude EG *Being unemployed
produces negative attitudes to work.*
perspective EG *It gave him a new
perspective on life.*
view EG *an optimistic view of the
future*

② **outlook** NOUN
the future prospects of something
EG *The economic outlook is one of
rising unemployment.*
future EG *a conference on the*

a
b
c
d
e
f
g
h
i
j
k
l
m
n
o
p
q
r
s
t
u
v
w
x
y
z

A
B
C
D
E
F
G
H
I
J
K
L
M
N
O
P
Q
R
S
T
U
V
W
X
Y
Z

country's political future
prospects EG *a detailed review of the company's prospects*

out of date ADJECTIVE
no longer useful
EG *The information is already out of date.*
antiquated EG *an antiquated system*
archaic EG *archaic practices such as these*
obsolete EG *So much equipment becomes obsolete almost as soon as it's made.*
old-fashioned EG *old-fashioned shoes*
outdated EG *outdated attitudes*
outmoded EG *toiling in outmoded factories*

WORD POWER

▶ **Antonym**
modern

❶ outside NOUN
the outer part of something
EG *The moth was on the outside of the glass.*
exterior EG *the exterior of the building*
facade EG *the refurbishing of the cathedral's facade*
face EG *the face of the watch*
surface EG *the surface of the road*

WORD POWER

▶ **Antonym**
inside

❷ outside ADJECTIVE
not inside
EG *an outside toilet*
exterior EG *the oven's exterior surfaces*
external EG *the external walls*
outdoor EG *outdoor activities*
outer EG *the outer suburbs of the city*
outward EG *with no outward sign of injury*

surface EG *Its total surface area was seven thousand square feet.*

WORD POWER

▶ **Antonym**
inside

outskirts PLURAL NOUN
the edges of an area
EG *the outskirts of New York*
edge EG *We were on a hill, right on the edge of town.*
perimeter EG *the perimeter of the airport*
periphery EG *countries on the periphery of Europe*

WORD POWER

▷ **Synonyms**
environs
purlieus

outspan VERB; SOUTH AFRICAN
to relax
EG *Let's take a break and just outspan for a while.*
laze EG *Fred lazed in an easy chair.*
relax EG *I ought to relax and stop worrying.*
rest EG *He rested for a while before starting work again.*
take it easy EG *Try to take it easy for a week or two.*

❶ outstanding ADJECTIVE
extremely good
EG *an outstanding tennis player*
brilliant EG *a brilliant performance*
excellent EG *the recording quality is excellent.*
exceptional EG *children with exceptional ability*
first-class EG *first-class service*
first-rate EG *The show was first-rate.*
great EG *great cultural achievements*
superb EG *a superb 18-hole golf course*

❷ outstanding ADJECTIVE
still owed

EG *The total debt outstanding is $70 billion.*
due EG *They sent me £100 and advised me that no further payment was due.*
overdue EG *pay overdue salaries*
owing EG *There is still some money owing for the rent.*
payable EG *The amount payable is £175.*
unpaid EG *The bills remained unpaid.*

1 over PREPOSITION
more than a particular amount
EG *It cost over a million dollars.*
above EG *speeds above 50 mph*
exceeding EG *a budget exceeding $700 million a year*
in excess of EG *a fortune in excess of 150 million pounds*
more than EG *The airport had been closed for more than a year.*

WORD POWER

● **Related Words**
prefixes : hyper-,
super-, supra-, sur-

2 over ADJECTIVE
completely finished
EG *I am glad it's all over.*
at an end EG *The matter is now at an end.*
complete EG *The work of restoring the farmhouse is complete.*
done EG *When her deal is done, the client emerges with her purchase.*
finished EG *once the season's finished*
gone EG *Any chance of winning was now gone.*
past EG *The time for loyalty is past.*
up EG *when the six weeks were up*

overcome VERB
to manage to deal with something
EG *Molly had overcome her fear of flying.*
conquer EG *He has never conquered his addiction to smoking.*
get the better of EG *She didn't*

allow her emotions to get the better of her.
master EG *His genius alone has mastered every crisis.*
surmount EG *I realized I had to surmount the language barrier.*
triumph over EG *a symbol of good triumphing over evil*
vanquish LITERARY EG *the man who helped vanquish Napoleon*

overlook VERB
to ignore or fail to notice something
EG *We tend to overlook warning signals about our health.*
disregard EG *The police must not be allowed to disregard human rights.*
forget EG *She never forgets his birthday.*
ignore EG *For years her talents were ignored by the film industry.*
miss EG *His searching eye never missed a detail.*
neglect EG *She never neglects her duties.*
turn a blind eye to EG *Are teachers turning a blind eye to these issues?*

overrule VERB
to reject a decision officially
EG *The Court of Appeal overruled this decision.*
overturn EG *when the Russian parliament overturned his decision*
reverse EG *They will not reverse the decision to increase prices.*

WORD POWER

▷ **Synonyms**
countermand
override

oversee VERB
to make sure a job is done properly
EG *Get a supervisor to oversee the work.*
be in charge of EG *She is in charge of day-to-day operations.*
coordinate EG *Government officials have been sent to coordinate the relief*

a
b
c
d
e
f
g
h
i
j
k
l
m
n
o
p
q
r
s
t
u
v
w
x
y
z

effort.

direct EG *his coolness in directing the rescue of the hostages*

manage EG *Within two years, he was managing the project.*

preside EG *Mr Brown will be presiding over the day's events.*

supervise EG *He supervises the vineyards.*

overthrow VERB
to remove someone from power by force
EG *The government was overthrown in a military coup.*

bring down EG *They brought down the government by withdrawing their support.*

depose EG *He fled to Hawaii after being deposed as president.*

oust EG *His opponents tried to oust him with a vote of no confidence.*

topple EG *the revolution which toppled the regime*

❶ overturn VERB
to knock something over
EG *Alex jumped up so violently that he overturned his glass.*

capsize EG *I didn't count on his capsizing the raft.*

knock down EG *Isabel rose so abruptly that she knocked down her chair.*

knock over EG *Emma knocked over the box of cornflakes.*

tip over EG *He tipped the table over in front of him.*

topple EG *Winds and rain toppled trees and electricity lines.*

upset EG *Don't upset the piles of sheets under the box.*

WORD POWER

▷ **Synonyms**
upend
upturn

❷ overturn VERB
to reject a decision officially

EG *when the Russian parliament overturned his decision*

overrule EG *The Court of Appeal overruled this decision.*

reverse EG *They will not reverse the decision to increase prices.*

WORD POWER

▷ **Synonyms**
countermand
override

overweight ADJECTIVE
too fat, and therefore unhealthy
EG *Being overweight increases your risk of heart problems.*

fat EG *I could eat what I liked without getting fat.*

hefty EG *She was quite a hefty woman.*

obese EG *Obese people tend to have higher blood pressure than lean people.*

stout EG *a stout man with grey hair*

WORD POWER

▷ **Synonyms**
corpulent

❶ own ADJECTIVE
belonging to a particular person or thing
EG *She stayed in her own house.*

personal EG *That's my personal opinion.*

private EG *76 bedrooms, all with private bathrooms*

❷ own VERB
to have something that belongs to you
EG *His father owns a local pub.*

have EG *They have a house in France.*

keep EG *His father kept a village shop.*

possess EG *I would give her everything I possess.*

❸ own on your own ADVERB
without other people

EG *I work best on my own.*
alone EG *She lives alone.*
by oneself EG *I didn't know if I could raise a child by myself.*
independently EG *several people working independently*
unaided EG *She brought us up completely unaided.*

owner NOUN
the person to whom something belongs
EG *the owner of the store*
possessor EG *the proud possessor of a truly incredible voice*
proprietor EG *the proprietor of a local restaurant*

a
b
c
d
e
f
g
h
i
j
k
l
m
n
o
p
q
r
s
t
u
v
w
x
y
z

Pp

pacify VERB
to calm down someone who is angry
EG *She shrieked again, refusing to be pacified.*
appease EG *The offer has not appeased separatists.*
calm EG *A business lunch helped calm her nerves.*
mollify EG *The investigation was undertaken to mollify pressure groups.*
placate EG *He went aboard to placate the angry passengers.*
soothe EG *She took him in his arms and soothed him.*

WORD POWER

▷ **Synonyms**
assuage
propitiate

---

❶ pain NOUN
an unpleasant feeling of physical hurt
EG *I felt a sharp pain in my lower back.*
ache EG *Poor posture can cause neck aches.*
discomfort EG *Steve had some discomfort but no real pain.*
irritation EG *These oils may cause irritation to sensitive skin.*
soreness EG *The soreness lasted for about six weeks.*
trouble EG *back trouble*
twinge EG *He felt a slight twinge in his hamstring.*

❷ pain NOUN
a feeling of deep unhappiness
EG *the pain of rejection*
agony EG *the agony of divorce*
anguish EG *Mark looked at him in anguish.*
distress EG *Jealousy causes distress and painful emotions.*
grief EG *The grief soon gave way to anger.*
misery EG *All that money brought nothing but sadness and misery.*

❶ painful ADJECTIVE
causing emotional pain
EG *painful memories*
distressing EG *one of the most distressing episodes in his life*
grievous EG *Their loss would be a grievous blow to our industry.*
saddening EG *a saddening experience*
unpleasant EG *an unpleasant truth*

❷ painful ADJECTIVE
causing physical pain
EG *a painful knock on the knee*
aching EG *his aching joints*
excruciating EG *an excruciating headache*
sore EG *a sore throat*
tender EG *My leg is very tender and sore.*

pale ADJECTIVE
rather white or without much colour
EG *Migrating birds filled the pale sky.*
ashen EG *He fell back, shocked, his face ashen.*
colourless EG *a colourless liquid*
faded EG *a girl in faded jeans*
sallow EG *His face was sallow and shiny with sweat.*
wan EG *He looked wan and tired.*
white EG *He turned white and began to stammer.*

❶ panic NOUN
a very strong feeling of fear or anxiety
EG *The earthquake caused panic among the population.*
alarm EG *She sat up in alarm.*
dismay EG *She discovered to her dismay that she was pregnant.*
fear EG *my fear of the dark*
fright EG *To hide my fright I asked a question.*
hysteria EG *mass hysteria*
terror EG *She shook with terror.*

❷ panic VERB
to become afraid or anxious

A B C D E F G H I J K L M N O P Q R S T U V W X Y Z

EG *Guests panicked when the bomb exploded.*
become hysterical EG *Miss Brady became hysterical when he produced the gun.*
go to pieces EG *England went to pieces when they conceded a goal.*
lose your nerve EG *They lost their nerve and pulled out of the deal.*

parade NOUN
a line of people moving as a display
EG *A military parade marched through the streets.*
cavalcade EG *a cavalcade of limousines and police motorcycles*
march EG *Organizers expect 300,000 protesters to join the march.*
pageant EG *a traditional Christmas pageant*
procession EG *religious processions*
tattoo EG *the world-famous Edinburgh military tattoo*

paragraph NOUN

> **Parts of a paragraph**
> clause
> phrase
> sentence
> word

paralyse VERB
to make someone lose feeling and movement
EG *Her sister had been paralysed in a road accident.*
cripple EG *He heaved his crippled leg into an easier position.*
disable EG *He was disabled by polio.*

parent NOUN
your father or your mother
EG *I told my parents I was moving out.*
father EG *Her father was furious.*
mother EG *the mother of two girls*
old AUSTRALIAN AND NEW ZEALAND; INFORMAL EG *a visit to the olds*
patriarch EG *a domineering patriarch*

parody NOUN
an amusing imitation of someone else's style
EG *a parody of an American sitcom*
imitation EG *I can do a pretty good imitation of him.*
satire EG *a sharp satire on the American political process*
spoof INFORMAL EG *a spoof on Hollywood life*
takeoff INFORMAL EG *She did a brilliant takeoff of the Queen.*

WORD POWER

▷ **Synonyms**
lampoon
skit

---

❶ part NOUN
a piece or section of something
EG *I like that part of Edinburgh.*
bit EG *a bit of paper*
fraction EG *a fraction of a second*
fragment EG *fragments of glass*
piece EG *a piece of cheese*
portion EG *Damage was confined to a small portion of the castle.*
section EG *a large orchestra, with a vast percussion section*

❷ part NOUN
a person's involvement in something
EG *He tried to conceal his part in the accident.*
capacity EG *He has served the club in many capacities.*
duty EG *My duty is to look after the animals.*
function EG *Their main function is to raise capital for industry.*
involvement EG *You have no proof of my involvement in anything.*
role EG *the drug's role in preventing infection*

❸ part take part in VERB
to do an activity with other people
EG *Thousands took part in the demonstrations.*

participate >> partly

be instrumental in EG *He was instrumental in tracking down the killers.*

be involved in EG *My grandparents were involved in the Methodist church.*

have a hand in EG *He had a hand in three of the goals.*

join in EG *I hope that everyone will be able to join in the fun.*

participate in EG *They expected him to participate in the ceremony.*

play a part in EG *He continued to play a part in drug operations from prison.*

participate VERB
to take part in an activity
EG *Over half the population participate in sport.*

be involved in EG *HMS Cardiff was also involved in the exercise.*

engage in EG *They have refused to engage in all-party talks.*

enter into EG *We entered into discussions with them weeks ago.*

join in EG *Their rivals refused to join in any price war.*

take part EG *The oldest car taking part was built in 1907.*

❶ particular ADJECTIVE
relating to only one thing or person
EG *That particular place is dangerous.*

distinct EG *The book is divided into two distinct parts.*

exact EG *Do you think I could get the exact thing I want?*

express EG *I bought the camera for the express purpose of taking railway photographs.*

peculiar EG *This is not a problem peculiar to London.*

precise EG *the precise location of the ship*

specific EG *There are several specific problems to be dealt with.*

❷ particular ADJECTIVE
especially great or intense
EG *Pay particular attention to the forehead.*

exceptional EG *children with exceptional ability*

marked EG *a marked increase in crime in the area*

notable EG *Two other notable events took place last week.*

singular EG *It was a goal of singular brilliance.*

special EG *a special occasion*

uncommon EG *Both are blessed with an uncommon ability to fix things.*

WORD POWER

▷ **Synonyms**
especial
noteworthy

❸ particular ADJECTIVE
not easily satisfied
EG *Ted was very particular about the colours he used.*

choosy INFORMAL EG *Skiers should be choosy about the insurance policy they buy.*

exacting EG *exacting standards of craftsmanship*

fastidious EG *He was fastidious about his appearance.*

fussy EG *She is very fussy about her food.*

meticulous EG *meticulous attention to detail*

partly ADVERB
to some extent but not completely
EG *This is partly my fault.*

in part FORMAL EG *The levels of blood glucose depend in part on what you eat.*

in some measure FORMAL EG *Power is in some measure an act of will.*

partially EG *Jo is partially sighted.*

to some degree EG *These statements are, to some degree, correct.*

to some extent EG *Her concern is, to some extent, understandable.*

❶ partner NOUN
either member of a couple in a relationship
EG *My partner moved in with me last year.*
husband *or* **wife** EG *Are husbands and wives included in the invitation?*
mate EG *She has found her ideal mate.*
spouse EG *Anything left to your spouse is free from inheritance tax.*

❷ partner NOUN
the person someone is doing something with
EG *my tennis partner*
companion EG *her travelling companion*
team-mate EG *his team-mate at Ferrari*

part of speech NOUN

Parts of speech
adjective
adverb
conjunction
noun
plural noun
preposition
pronoun
reflexive verb
verb

❶ party NOUN
a social event where people enjoy themselves
EG *Most teenagers like to go to parties.*
celebration EG *a New Year's Eve celebration*
function EG *a charity function at the hotel*
gathering EG *a gathering of friends and relatives*
get-together INFORMAL EG *a family get-together*
hooley *or* **hoolie** NEW ZEALAND EG *a hooley down on the beach*
reception EG *a wedding reception*

❷ party NOUN
an organization for people with the same political beliefs
EG *his resignation as party leader*
alliance EG *The two parties have agreed to form an electoral alliance.*
clique EG *the clique attached to Prime Minister*
coalition EG *a coalition of right-wing and religious factions*
faction EG *the party's small pro-European faction*
grouping EG *two main political groupings pressing for independence*

❸ party NOUN
a group who are doing something together
EG *a research party of scientists*
band EG *a small but dedicated band of supporters*
crew EG *a ship's crew*
gang EG *a gang of criminals*
squad EG *the West Indies squad to tour Australia*
team EG *Each consultant has a team of doctors under him.*
unit EG *the health services research unit*

❶ pass VERB
to exceed or go past something
EG *He gave a triumphant wave as he passed the winning post.*
exceed EG *The demand for places at some schools exceeds the supply.*
go beyond EG *Did your relationship go beyond a close friendship?*
outdo EG *The Colombian fans outdid the home supporters in fervour.*
outstrip EG *Demand continues to outstrip supply.*
overtake EG *Britain's lottery will this year overtake Japan's as the world's biggest.*
surpass EG *He was determined to surpass the achievements of his brothers.*

a
b
c
d
e
f
g
h
i
j
k
l
m
n
o
p
q
r
s
t
u
v
w
x
y
z

2 pass VERB

to be successful in a test

EG *Wendy has just passed her driving test.*

get through EG *I got through my banking exams last year.*

graduate EG *He graduated in engineering.*

qualify EG *I qualified as a doctor.*

succeed EG *the skills and qualities needed to succeed*

WORD POWER

▶ **Antonym**

fail

3 pass NOUN

a document that allows you to go somewhere

EG *Don't let any cars onto the land unless they've got a pass.*

identification EG *Passport control asked me if I had any further identification.*

passport EG *You should take your passport with you when changing money.*

ticket EG *I'm not going to renew my season ticket.*

1 passage NOUN

a space that connects two places

EG *He cleared a passage for himself through the crammed streets.*

channel EG *a drainage channel*

course EG *the river's twisting course*

path EG *A group of reporters blocked the path.*

road EG *the road between Jerusalem and Bethlehem*

route EG *the most direct route to the town centre*

way EG *This is the way in.*

2 passage NOUN

a narrow space that connects one place with another

EG *up some stairs and along a narrow passage towards a door*

aisle EG *the frozen food aisle*

corridor EG *They sat crowded together in the hospital corridor.*

hall EG *The lights were on in the hall and in the bedroom.*

lobby EG *the cramped pitch-dark lobby*

3 passage NOUN

a section of a book or piece of music

EG *a passage from the Bible*

excerpt EG *an excerpt from her speech*

extract EG *an extract from his new book*

quotation EG *a favourite quotation from St Augustine*

section EG *a section from the first movement of Beethoven's Eroica symphony*

1 passion NOUN

a strong feeling of physical attraction

EG *the passion had gone from their relationship*

desire EG *sexual desire*

infatuation EG *Daisy's infatuation for the doctor*

love EG *our love for each other*

lust EG *He is obsessed by his lust for her.*

2 passion NOUN

any strong emotion

EG *He spoke with great passion.*

emotion EG *Her voice trembled with emotion.*

excitement EG *I was in a state of great excitement.*

fire EG *His speeches were full of fire.*

intensity EG *His intensity alarmed me.*

warmth EG *He greeted us both with warmth and affection.*

zeal EG *his zeal for teaching*

passionate ADJECTIVE

expressing very strong feelings about something

EG *I'm a passionate believer in public art.*

ardent EG *ardent supporters of capital punishment*
emotional EG *an emotional farewell*
heartfelt EG *My heartfelt sympathy goes out to all the relatives.*
impassioned EG *He made an impassioned appeal for peace.*
intense EG *intense hatred*
strong EG *Many viewers have strong opinions about violence on TV.*

passive ADJECTIVE
submissive or not playing an active part
EG *His passive attitude made things easier for me.*
docile EG *docile, obedient children*
receptive EG *The voters had seemed receptive to his ideas.*
resigned EG *She was already resigned to losing her home.*
submissive EG *Most doctors want their patients to be submissive.*

WORD POWER
▷ **Synonyms**
acquiescent
compliant
inactive
quiescent

❶ **past** the past NOUN
the period of time before the present
EG *We would like to put the past behind us.*
antiquity EG *famous monuments of classical antiquity*
days gone by EG *This brings back memories of days gone by.*
former times EG *In former times he would have been clapped in irons.*
long ago EG *The old men told stories of long ago.*

❷ **past** ADJECTIVE
happening or existing before the present
EG *details of his past activities*
ancient EG *ancient history*

bygone EG *a bygone era*
former EG *Remember him as he was in his former years.*
olden EG *We were talking about the olden days on his farm.*
previous EG *She has a teenage daughter from a previous marriage.*

WORD POWER
▷ **Synonyms**
erstwhile
quondam

▶ **Antonym**
future

❸ **past** PREPOSITION
situated on the other side of somewhere
EG *It's just past the church there.*
beyond EG *Beyond the garden was a small orchard.*
by EG *She was sitting in a chair by the window.*
over EG *He lived in the house over the road.*

pastime NOUN
a hobby or something done for pleasure
EG *His favourite pastime is snooker.*
activity EG *activities range from canoeing to birdwatching*
diversion EG *Finger painting is very messy but an excellent diversion.*
hobby EG *My hobbies are squash and swimming.*
recreation EG *Saturday afternoon is for recreation and outings.*

❶ **path** NOUN
a strip of ground for people to walk on
EG *We followed the paths along the clifftops.*
footpath EG *It is accessible only by footpath.*
pathway EG *a pathway leading towards the nearby river*
towpath EG *He took a cycle trip along a canal towpath.*

a
b
c
d
e
f
g
h
i
j
k
l
m
n
o
p
q
r
s
t
u
v
w
x
y
z

track EG We set off over a rough mountain track.
trail EG He was following a broad trail through the trees.
way EG the Pennine Way

2 path NOUN
the space ahead of someone as they move along
EG A group of reporters stood in his path.
course EG obstacles blocking our course
direction EG St Andrews was 10 miles in the opposite direction.
passage EG Two men elbowed a passage through the shoppers.
route EG All escape routes were blocked by armed police.
way EG Get out of my way!

1 pathetic ADJECTIVE
causing someone to feel pity
EG She now looked small, shrunken, and pathetic.
heartbreaking EG a heartbreaking succession of miscarriages
sad EG He seemed a rather sad figure.

WORD POWER
▷ **Synonyms**
pitiable
plaintive

2 pathetic ADJECTIVE
very poor or unsuccessful
EG pathetic excuses
feeble EG This is a particularly feeble argument.
lamentable EG a lamentable display by the league leaders
pitiful EG They are paid pitiful wages.
poor EG The flat was in a poor state of repair.
sorry EG Their oil industry is in a sorry state.

patience NOUN
the ability to stay calm in a difficult situation
EG It was exacting work and required all his patience.
calmness EG calmness under pressure
composure EG He regained his composure and went on to win the match.
cool SLANG EG The big Irishman was on the verge of losing his cool.
restraint EG They behaved with more restraint than I'd expected.
tolerance EG a low tolerance of errors

WORD POWER
▷ **Synonyms**
equanimity
forbearance
imperturbability

1 patient ADJECTIVE
staying calm in a difficult situation
EG Please be patient - your cheque will arrive.
calm EG She is usually a calm and diplomatic woman.
composed EG a composed and charming manner
long-suffering EG long-suffering train commuters
philosophical EG He is philosophical about the defeat.
serene EG She looks dreamily into the distance, serene, calm and happy.

WORD POWER
▶ **Antonym**
impatient

2 patient NOUN
a person receiving medical treatment
EG patients who wish to change their doctor
case EG He is a suitable case for treatment.
invalid EG elderly invalids
sick person EG a ward full of very sick people
sufferer EG asthma sufferers

1 pattern NOUN
a decorative design of repeated
shapes
EG *red and purple thread stitched into
a pattern of flames*
design EG *tableware decorated with
a blackberry design*
motif EG *a rose motif*

2 pattern NOUN
a diagram or shape used as a guide
for making something
EG *sewing patterns*
design EG *They drew up the design for
the house in a week.*
diagram EG *Follow the diagram on
page 20.*
plan EG *a plan of the garden*
stencil EG *flower stencils*
template EG *Make a paper template
of the seat of the chair.*

1 pause VERB
to stop doing something for a short
time
EG *On leaving, she paused for a
moment at the door.*
break EG *They broke for lunch.*
delay EG *Various problems delayed
the launch.*
halt EG *Striking workers halted
production at the plant.*
rest EG *He rested briefly before
pressing on.*
take a break EG *He needs to take a
break from work.*
wait EG *I waited to see how she
responded.*

2 pause NOUN
a short period when activity stops
EG *There was a pause while the
barmaid set down two plates.*
break EG *Do you want to have a little
break?*
halt EG *Agricultural production was
brought to a halt.*
interruption EG *The sudden
interruption stopped her in mid-flow.*
interval EG *I had a drink during the
interval.*
rest EG *I think he's due for a rest now.*
stoppage EG *Miners have voted for a
one-day stoppage next month.*

WORD POWER

▷ **Synonyms**
caesura
entr'acte

1 pay VERB
to give money to someone to settle a
debt
EG *You can pay by credit card.*
compensate EG *Farmers could be
compensated for their loss of
subsidies.*
honour EG *The bank refused to
honour the cheque.*
settle EG *I settled the bill for our
drinks.*

WORD POWER

▷ **Synonyms**
recompense
reimburse
remunerate

2 pay VERB
to give someone a benefit
EG *It pays to be honest.*
be advantageous EG *It is easy to
imagine cases where cheating is
advantageous.*
be worthwhile EG *He believed the
operation had been worthwhile.*

3 pay NOUN
money paid to someone for work
done
EG *their complaints about pay and
conditions*
earnings EG *his earnings as an
accountant*
fee EG *solicitors' fees*
income EG *a modest income*
payment EG *a redundancy payment*
salary EG *The lawyer was paid a good*

a
b
c
d
e
f
g
h
i
j
k
l
m
n
o
p
q
r
s
t
u
v
w
x
y
z

A
B
C
D
E
F
G
H
I
J
K
L
M
N
O
P
Q
R
S
T
U
V
W
X
Y
Z

salary.
wages EG *His wages have gone up.*

WORD POWER

▷ **Synonyms**
emolument
recompense
reimbursement
remuneration
stipend

payment NOUN
an amount of money that is paid to someone
EG *mortgage payments*
advance EG *She was paid a £100,000 advance for her next two novels.*
deposit EG *A $50 deposit is required when ordering.*
instalment EG *The first instalment is payable on application.*
premium EG *higher insurance premiums*
remittance EG *Please make your remittance payable in sterling.*

❶ peace NOUN
a state of undisturbed calm and quiet
EG *They left me in peace to recover from the funeral.*
calm EG *the rural calm of Grand Rapids, Michigan*
quiet EG *He wants some peace and quiet before his match.*
silence EG *They stood in silence.*
stillness EG *An explosion shattered the stillness of the night air.*
tranquillity EG *The hotel is a haven of tranquillity.*

WORD POWER

▷ **Synonyms**
quietude
repose

❷ peace NOUN
freedom from war
EG *The people do not believe that the leaders want peace.*

armistice EG *the armistice between North Korea and the United Nations*
cessation of hostilities EG *a resolution calling for an immediate cessation of hostilities*
truce EG *an uneasy truce between the two sides*

WORD POWER

▶ **Antonym**
war

peaceful ADJECTIVE
quiet and calm
EG *a peaceful house in the heart of the countryside*
calm EG *a calm spot amid the bustle of the city*
placid EG *the placid waters of Lake Erie*
quiet EG *The street was unnaturally quiet.*
serene EG *a beautiful, serene park*
still EG *In the room it was very still.*
tranquil EG *the tranquil paradise of his native Antigua*

❶ peak NOUN
the point at which something is at its greatest or best
EG *the peak of the morning rush hour*
climax EG *The tournament is building up to a dramatic climax.*
culmination EG *The marriage was the culmination of an eight-month romance.*
high point EG *The high point of this trip was a day at the races.*
zenith EG *His career is now at its zenith.*

WORD POWER

▷ **Synonyms**
acme
apogee
ne plus ultra

❷ peak NOUN
the pointed top of a mountain
EG *snow-covered peaks*

brow EG *He overtook a car as he approached the brow of a hill.*
crest EG *Burns was clear over the crest of the hill.*
pinnacle EG *He plunged 25 metres from a rocky pinnacle.*
summit EG *the first man to reach the summit of Mount Everest*
top EG *the top of Mount Sinai*

WORD POWER

▷ **Synonyms**
aiguille
apex

❸ **peak** VERB
to reach the highest point or greatest level
EG *His career peaked during the 1970s.*
be at its height EG *when trade union power was at its height*
climax EG *a tour that climaxed with a three-night stint at Wembley Arena*
come to a head EG *The siege came to a head with the death of a marshal.*
culminate EG *The celebration of the centenary will culminate with a dinner.*
reach its highest point EG *The stockmarket reached its highest point since the 1987 crash.*

❶ **peculiar** ADJECTIVE
strange and perhaps unpleasant
EG *a very peculiar sense of humour*
bizarre EG *bizarre behaviour*
curious EG *a curious mixture of the ancient and modern*
funny EG *Children get some funny ideas sometimes.*
odd EG *Something odd began to happen.*
queer EG *There's something queer going on.*
strange EG *There was something strange about the flickering blue light.*
weird EG *It must be weird to be so rich.*

❷ **peculiar** ADJECTIVE
associated with one particular person or thing
EG *He has his own peculiar way of doing things.*
distinctive EG *She has a very distinctive laugh.*
distinguishing EG *Does he have any distinguishing features?*
individual EG *all part of her very individual personality*
personal EG *cultivating their own personal style*
special EG *Everyone has their own special problems or fears.*
unique EG *a feature unique to humans*

WORD POWER

▷ **Synonyms**
idiosyncratic

❶ **peek** VERB
to have a quick look at something
EG *She peeked at him through a crack in the wall.*
glance EG *He glanced at his watch.*
peep EG *Children came to peep at him round the doorway.*
snatch a glimpse EG *Spectators lined the route to snatch a glimpse of the Queen.*
sneak a look EG *We sneaked a look at his diary.*

❷ **peek** NOUN
a quick look at something
EG *He took his first peek at the new course yesterday.*
glance EG *Trevor and I exchanged a glance.*
glimpse EG *Some people had waited all day to catch a glimpse of her.*
look EG *She took a last look in the mirror.*
peep EG *He took a peep at his watch.*

pent-up ADJECTIVE
held back for a long time without release
EG *She had a lot of pent-up anger to release.*

A
B
C
D
E
F
G
H
I
J
K
L
M
N
O
P
Q
R
S
T
U
V
W
X
Y
Z

inhibited EG *inhibited sexuality*
repressed EG *repressed hostility*
suppressed EG *Deep sleep allowed suppressed anxieties to surface.*

❶ people PLURAL NOUN
men, women, and children
EG *Millions of people have lost their homes.*
human beings EG *The disease can be transmitted to human beings.*
humanity EG *crimes against humanity*
humans EG *millions of years before humans appeared on earth*
mankind EG *the evolution of mankind*

❷ people PLURAL NOUN
all the men, women, and children of a particular place
EG *It's a triumph for the American people.*
citizens EG *the citizens of New York City*
inhabitants EG *the inhabitants of Hong Kong*
population EG *Africa's rapidly rising population*
public EG *the British public*

perceptive ADJECTIVE
good at noticing or realizing things
EG *a perceptive account of the poet's life*
acute EG *His relaxed exterior hides an extremely acute mind.*
astute EG *He made a series of astute business decisions.*
aware EG *They are politically very aware.*
penetrating EG *He never stopped asking penetrating questions.*
sharp EG *He has a sharp eye and an excellent memory.*

WORD POWER
▷ **Synonyms**
insightful

percipient
perspicacious

❶ perfect ADJECTIVE
of the highest standard and without fault
EG *His English was perfect.*
expert EG *There is a great deal to learn from his expert approach.*
faultless EG *faultless technique*
flawless EG *her flawless complexion*
masterly EG *a masterly performance*
polished EG *polished promotional skills*
skilled EG *a skilled repair job*

WORD POWER
▶ **Antonym**
imperfect

❷ perfect ADJECTIVE
complete or absolute
EG *They have a perfect right to say so.*
absolute EG *absolute nonsense*
complete EG *The resignation came as a complete surprise.*
consummate EG *He acted the part with consummate skill.*
sheer EG *an act of sheer desperation*
unmitigated EG *Last year's crop was an unmitigated disaster.*
utter EG *utter nonsense*

❸ perfect VERB
to make something as good as it can be
EG *The technique was perfected during the 1960s.*
hone EG *a chance to hone their skills*
improve EG *Their French has improved enormously.*
polish EG *He spent time polishing the script.*
refine EG *Surgical techniques are constantly being refined.*

❶ perform VERB
to carry out a task or action
EG *people who have performed acts of bravery*

carry out EG *Police believe the attacks were carried out by nationalists.*
complete EG *He completed the test in record time.*
do EG *He crashed trying to do a tricky manoeuvre.*
execute EG *The landing was skilfully executed.*
fulfil EG *Fulfil the tasks you have been allocated.*

❷ perform VERB
to act, dance, or play music in public
EG *students performing Shakespeare's Macbeth*
act EG *acting in Tarantino's films*
do EG *I've always wanted to do a one-man show on Broadway.*
play EG *His ambition is to play the part of Dracula.*
present EG *The company is presenting a new production of "Hamlet".*
put on EG *The band are hoping to put on a UK show.*
stage EG *The group staged their first play in the late 1970s.*

perhaps ADVERB
maybe
EG *Perhaps you're right.*
conceivably EG *The mission could conceivably be accomplished in a week.*
it could be EG *It could be he's upset at what you said.*
maybe EG *Maybe she is in love.*
possibly EG *Do you think that he could possibly be right?*

period NOUN
a particular length of time
EG *a period of a few months*
interval EG *a long interval when no-one spoke*
spell EG *a long spell of dry weather*
stretch EG *an 18-month stretch in the army*
term EG *a 5-year prison term*

perform >> permission

time EG *At 15 he left home for a short time.*
while EG *I haven't seen him for a long while.*

permanent ADJECTIVE
lasting for ever or present all the time
EG *a permanent solution to the problem*
abiding EG *one of his abiding interests*
constant EG *Inflation is a constant threat.*
enduring EG *an enduring friendship*
eternal EG *the quest for eternal youth*
lasting EG *We are well on our way to a lasting peace.*
perpetual EG *a perpetual source of worry*

WORD POWER

▷ **Synonyms**
immutable
steadfast

▶ **Antonym**
temporary

permission NOUN
authorization to do something
EG *He asked permission to leave the room.*
approval EG *The plan will require official approval.*
assent EG *He requires the assent of parliament.*
authorization EG *his request for authorization to use military force*
consent EG *Can she be examined without my consent?*
go-ahead EG *The government gave the go-ahead for five major road schemes.*
licence EG *He has given me licence to do the job as I see fit.*

WORD POWER

▶ **Antonym**
ban

A B C D E F G H I J K L M N O P Q R S T U V W X Y Z

❶ permit VERB
to allow something or make it
possible
EG *The guards permitted me to bring
my camera.*
allow EG *Smoking will not be allowed.*
authorize EG *They are expected to
authorize the use of military force.*
enable EG *The test should enable
doctors to detect the disease early.*
give the green light to EG *He has
been given the green light to resume
training.*
grant EG *Permission was granted a
few weeks ago.*
sanction EG *The chairman will not
sanction a big-money signing.*

> *WORD POWER*
> ▶ **Antonym**
> ban

❷ permit NOUN
an official document allowing
someone to do something
EG *a work permit*
authorization EG *We didn't have
authorization to go.*
licence EG *a driving licence*
pass EG *a rail pass*
passport EG *My passport expires
next year.*
permission EG *Permission for the
march has not been granted.*
warrant EG *Police issued a warrant
for his arrest.*

persecute VERB
to treat someone with continual
cruelty and unfairness
EG *The Communists began by brutally
persecuting the Church.*
hound EG *He has been hounded by
the press.*
ill-treat EG *They thought Mr Smith
had been ill-treating his wife.*
oppress EG *Minorities here have
been oppressed for generations.*
pick on EG *She was repeatedly picked*

on by the manager.
torment EG *They were tormented by
other pupils.*
torture EG *He would not torture her
further by trying to argue with her.*

person NOUN
a man, woman, or child
EG *The amount of sleep we need varies
from person to person.*
human EG *the common ancestor of
humans and the great apes*
human being EG *This protein occurs
naturally in human beings.*
individual EG *the rights and
responsibilities of the individual*
living soul EG *The nearest living soul
was 20 miles away.*
soul EG *a tiny village of only 100 souls*

personal ADJECTIVE
belonging to a particular person or
thing
EG *personal belongings*
individual EG *Divide the vegetables
among four individual dishes.*
own EG *My wife decided I should have
my own shop.*
particular EG *his own particular style
of preaching*
peculiar EG *her own peculiar talents*
private EG *my private life*
special EG *Every person will have his
or her own special problems.*

❶ personality NOUN
a person's character and nature
EG *She has such a kind, friendly
personality.*
character EG *a negative side to his
character*
identity EG *our own sense of cultural
identity*
individuality EG *People should be
free to express their individuality.*
make-up EG *There was some
fundamental flaw in his make-up.*
nature EG *She trusted people. That
was her nature.*

psyche EG *disturbing elements of the human psyche*

❷ **personality** NOUN
a famous person in entertainment or sport
EG *television personalities*
big name EG *the big names in French cinema*
celebrity EG *Hollywood celebrities*
famous name EG *a famous name from Inter Milan's past*
household name EG *The TV series that made him a household name.*
star EG *film stars*

persuade VERB
to make someone do something by reason or charm
EG *He persuaded the company to sign her up.*
bring round INFORMAL EG *We will do what we can to bring them round to our point of view.*
coax EG *She coaxed Bobby into talking about himself.*
induce EG *I would do anything to induce them to stay.*
sway EG *Don't ever be swayed by fashion.*
talk into EG *He talked me into marrying him.*
win over EG *By the end of the day he had won over the crowd.*

WORD POWER
▷ **Synonyms**
impel
inveigle

perverted ADJECTIVE
practising abnormal and unacceptable behaviour
EG *She has been a victim of perverted phone calls and letters.*
depraved EG *the work of depraved and evil criminals*
deviant EG *Not all drug abusers produce deviant offspring.*
immoral EG *those who think that*

birth control is immoral
unhealthy EG *His interest developed into an unhealthy obsession.*

WORD POWER
▷ **Synonyms**
debauched
vitiated

pessimistic ADJECTIVE
believing that bad things will happen
EG *a pessimistic view of life*
despondent EG *despondent about their children's future*
gloomy EG *a gloomy view of the future*
glum EG *They are not entirely glum about the car industry's prospects.*
hopeless EG *Even able pupils feel hopeless about job prospects.*

WORD POWER
▶ **Antonym**
optimistic

❶ **pest** NOUN
an insect or animal that damages crops or livestock
EG *10% of the crop was lost to a pest called corn rootworm.*
bane EG *The bane of farmers across the country is the badger.*
blight EG *potato blight*
scourge EG *This parasitic mite is the scourge of honey bees.*

❷ **pest** NOUN
an annoying person
EG *I didn't want to be a cry baby or a pest.*
bane EG *Student journalists were the bane of my life.*
bore EG *I don't enjoy his company. He's a bore and a fool.*
nuisance EG *He could be a bit of a nuisance when he was drunk.*
pain INFORMAL EG *She's been a real pain recently.*
pain in the neck INFORMAL EG *I've*

a
b
c
d
e
f
g
h
i
j
k
l
m
n
o
p
q
r
s
t
u
v
w
x
y
z

always been a pain in the neck to publishers.

pester VERB
to bother someone continually
EG *He gets fed up with people pestering him for money.*
annoy EG *She kept on annoying me.*
badger EG *She badgered her doctor time and again.*
bother EG *We are playing a trick on a man who keeps bothering me.*
bug INFORMAL EG *Stop bugging me.*
drive someone up the wall SLANG
eg *I sang in the bath and drove my sister up the wall.*
get on someone's nerves
INFORMAL EG *I was beginning to get on her nerves.*

WORD POWER

▷ **Synonyms**
bedevil
chivvy

❶ **petty** ADJECTIVE
small and unimportant
EG *endless rules and petty regulations*
insignificant EG *In 1949, Bonn was a small, insignificant city.*
measly INFORMAL EG *The average bathroom measures a measly 3.5 square metres.*
trifling EG *The sums involved are trifling.*
trivial EG *trivial details*
unimportant EG *It was an unimportant job, and paid very little.*

❷ **petty** ADJECTIVE
selfish and small-minded
EG *I think that attitude is a bit petty.*
cheap EG *politicians making cheap political points*
mean EG *I'd feel mean saying no.*
small-minded EG *their small-minded preoccupation with making money*

phoney ADJECTIVE; INFORMAL
false and intended to deceive
EG *a phoney accent*

bogus EG *a bogus insurance claim*
counterfeit EG *counterfeit currency*
fake EG *fake certificates*
false EG *a false name and address*
forged EG *forged documents*
sham EG *a sham marriage*

WORD POWER

▷ **Synonyms**
spurious

▶ **Antonym**
genuine

❶ **pick** VERB
to choose something
EG *He picked ten people to interview for six sales jobs.*
choose EG *There are several options to choose from.*
decide upon EG *He decided upon a career in publishing.*
hand-pick EG *He was hand-picked for his job by the Admiral.*
opt for EG *I think we should opt for a more cautious approach.*
select EG *the party's policy of selecting candidates*
settle on EG *I finally settled on an Audi TT roadster.*

❷ **pick** VERB
to remove a flower or fruit with your fingers
EG *He helps his mother pick fruit.*
gather EG *We spent the afternoon gathering berries.*
harvest EG *Many farmers are refusing to harvest the cane.*
pluck EG *I plucked a lemon from the tree.*

❸ **pick** NOUN
the best
EG *the pick of the country's young athletes*
elite EG *the elite of women's tennis*
flower EG *the flower of Polish manhood*
pride EG *the hovercraft, once the pride of British maritime engineering*

pick on VERB
to criticize someone unfairly or treat them unkindly
EG *Bullies pick on younger children.*
bait EG *He delighted in baiting his mother.*
tease EG *He teased me mercilessly about going to Hollywood.*
torment EG *They were tormented by other pupils.*

❶ picture NOUN
a drawing, painting, or photograph
EG *It's got a picture of me on the cover.*
drawing EG *She did a drawing of me.*
illustration EG *Tolkien's illustrations for The Hobbit*
painting EG *his collection of Impressionist paintings*
photograph EG *He wants to take some photographs of the house.*
portrait EG *Velazquez's portrait of Pope Innocent X*
sketch EG *pencil sketches*

WORD POWER

● Related Words
adjective : pictorial

❷ picture VERB
to imagine something clearly
EG *He pictured her with long black hair.*
conceive of EG *I can't conceive of doing work that doesn't interest me.*
imagine EG *It's difficult to imagine anything coming between them.*
see EG *A good idea, but can you see Taylor trying it?*
visualize EG *He could not visualize her as old.*

WORD POWER

▷ Synonyms
envision
see in the mind's eye

❶ piece NOUN
a portion or part of something
EG *a piece of cheese*

bit EG *a bit of paper*
chunk EG *He was accused of stealing a tin of pineapple chunks.*
fragment EG *There were fragments of cork in the wine.*
part EG *The engine has got only three moving parts.*
portion EG *Damage was confined to a small portion of the castle.*
slice EG *a slice of bread*

❷ piece NOUN
something that has been written, created, or composed
EG *his piece on fox hunting*
article EG *a newspaper article*
composition EG *Schubert's piano compositions*
creation EG *the fashion designer's latest creations*
study EG *Leonardo's studies of horsemen*
work EG *In my opinion, this is Rembrandt's greatest work.*

piece together VERB
to assemble things or parts to make something complete
EG *Doctors painstakingly pieced together the broken bones.*
assemble EG *He is assembling evidence concerning a murder.*
join EG *Join all the sections together.*
mend EG *I should have had it mended, but never got round to it.*
patch together EG *A hasty deal was patched together.*
repair EG *the cost of repairing earthquake damage*
restore EG *The trust is playing a leading part in restoring old cinemas.*

pierce VERB
to make a hole in something with a sharp instrument
EG *Pierce the potato with a fork.*
bore EG *tunnels bored into the foundations of the building*
drill EG *I drilled five holes at equal distance.*

a
b
c
d
e
f
g
h
i
j
k
l
m
n
o
p
q
r
s
t
u
v
w
x
y
z

A B C D E F G H I J K L M N O P Q R S T U V W X Y Z

lance EG *It's a painful experience having the boil lanced.*
penetrate EG *The Earth's atmosphere was penetrated by a meteor.*
puncture EG *The bullet punctured the skull.*

pig NOUN
a farm animal kept for meat
EG *the number of pigs at the trough*
hog EG *He's as fat as a hog.*
piggy INFORMAL EG *These two piggies are going to market!*
porker EG *a 30kg Vietnamese potbellied porker*
swine EG *herds of oxen, sheep and swine*

WORD POWER

● **Related Words**
adjective : porcine
male : boar
female : sow
young : piglet
collective noun : litter
habitation : sty

❶ pile NOUN
a quantity of things lying one on top of another
EG *a pile of books*
heap EG *a compost heap*
hoard EG *a hoard of jewels*
mound EG *The bulldozers piled up hug mounds of dirt.*
mountain EG *They have mountains of coffee to sell.*
stack EG *a stack of magazines on the table*

❷ pile NOUN
the raised fibres of a soft surface
EG *the carpet's thick pile*
down EG *The whole plant is covered with fine down.*
fur EG *This creature's fur is short and dense.*
hair EG *He has black hair.*

nap EG *The cotton is lightly brushed to heighten the nap.*

❸ pile VERB
to put things one on top of another
EG *A few newspapers were piled on the table.*
heap EG *She heaped more carrots onto his plate.*
hoard EG *They've begun to hoard petrol and food.*
stack EG *They are stacked neatly in piles of three.*

pink NOUN OR ADJECTIVE

Shades of pink
coral
flesh
fuchsia
oyster pink
rose
salmon
shell pink
shocking pink

pit NOUN
a large hole in something
EG *He lost his footing and began to slide into the pit.*
chasm EG *The coach plunged down the chasm.*
hole EG *The builders had cut holes into the soft stone.*
pothole EG *She was seriously injured when she fell 90 feet down a pothole.*

❶ pity VERB
to feel sorry for someone
EG *I don't know whether to hate or pity him.*
feel for EG *She cried on the phone and I really felt for her.*
feel sorry for EG *This is my biggest win but I don't feel sorry for the bookies.*
sympathize with EG *I sympathize with you for your loss.*

❷ pity NOUN
sympathy for other people's suffering

EG *She saw no pity in their faces.*
charity EG *They showed a lack of charity and understanding to her.*
compassion EG *his compassion for a helpless woman*
kindness EG *He was treated with kindness by numerous officials.*
mercy EG *Neither side showed any mercy.*
sympathy EG *We expressed our sympathy for her loss.*
understanding EG *We would like to thank them for their patience and understanding.*

WORD POWER

▷ **Synonyms**
clemency
forbearance

---

❸ **pity** NOUN
a regrettable fact
EG *It's a pity they can't all have the same opportunities.*
crime INFORMAL EG *It would be a crime to travel to Australia and not stop in Sydney.*
crying shame EG *It would be a crying shame to split up a winning partnership.*
shame EG *It's a shame it had to close.*

❶ **place** NOUN
any point or area
EG *The pain is always in the same place.*
area EG *a picnic area*
location EG *The first thing he looked at was his office's location.*
point EG *The pain originated from a point in his right thigh.*
position EG *the ship's position*
site EG *a bat sanctuary with special nesting sites*
spot EG *the island's top tourist spots*

❷ **place** take place VERB
to happen
EG *The meeting took place on Thursday.*

come about EG *That came about when we went to Glastonbury last year.*
go on EG *This has been going on for around a year.*
happen EG *We cannot say for sure what will happen.*
occur EG *The crash occurred when the crew shut down the wrong engine.*

❸ **place** VERB
to put something somewhere
EG *Chairs were placed in rows for the parents.*
deposit EG *Imagine if you were suddenly deposited on a desert island.*
locate EG *the best city in which to locate a business*
plant EG *So far no one has admitted to planting the bomb.*
position EG *plants which are carefully positioned in the alcove*
put EG *She put the photograph on her desk.*
situate EG *The hotel is situated next to the railway station.*

❶ **plain** ADJECTIVE
very simple in style with no decoration
EG *It was a plain, grey stone house.*
austere EG *The church was austere and simple.*
bare EG *bare wooden floors*
spartan EG *her spartan home in a tiny village*
stark EG *a stark white, characterless fireplace*

WORD POWER

▶ **Antonym**
fancy

---

❷ **plain** ADJECTIVE
obvious and easy to recognize or understand
EG *It was plain to him that I was having a nervous breakdown.*
clear EG *The book is clear and readable.*

a
b
c
d
e
f
g
h
i
j
k
l
m
n
o
p
q
r
s
t
u
v
w
x
y
z

comprehensible EG *a comprehensible manual*
distinct EG *a distinct smell of burning coal*
evident EG *His footprints were clearly evident in the heavy dust.*
obvious EG *an obvious injustice*
unmistakable EG *His voice was unmistakable.*

❸ plain NOUN

Types of plain
flat
flatland
grassland
llano
lowland
mesa
plateau
prairie
savannah
steppe
tableland

❶ plan NOUN
a way thought out to do something
EG *a plan to amalgamate the two parties*
method EG *He did it by his usual method.*
proposal EG *The proposals need careful study.*
scheme EG *The scheme was an abject failure.*
strategy EG *What should our marketing strategy achieve?*
system EG *the advantages of the new system over the old one*

❷ plan NOUN
a detailed diagram of something that is to be made
EG *a detailed plan of the prison*
blueprint EG *a blueprint for a new bathroom*
diagram EG *a circuit diagram*
layout EG *He tried to recall the layout of the farmhouse.*
scale drawing EG *scale drawings of locomotives*

❸ plan VERB
to decide in detail what is to be done
EG *when we plan road construction*
arrange EG *We arranged a social event once a year.*
design EG *He approached me to design the restaurant.*
devise EG *We devised a plan.*
draft EG *The legislation was drafted by the committee.*
formulate EG *He formulated his plan for escape.*

❶ play VERB
to take part in games or use toys
EG *Polly was playing with her teddy bear.*
amuse oneself EG *He amused himself by rollerskating round the building.*
entertain oneself EG *I used to entertain myself by building model planes.*
frolic EG *Tourists sunbathe and frolic in the ocean.*
have fun EG *having fun with your friends*

❷ play VERB
to take part in a sport or game
EG *Alain was playing cards with his friends.*
compete EG *Eight entrants competed for the prize.*
participate EG *Sixteen teams participated in the tournament.*
take on EG *Scotland take on South Africa at Murrayfield.*
take part EG *The teams taking part are cricket's bitterest enemies.*
vie with EG *Arsenal are vying with Leeds for second spot in the league.*

❸ play NOUN
a piece of drama performed on stage, radio, or television
EG *Chekhov's best play*
comedy EG *a romantic comedy*
drama EG *He also wrote radio dramas and film scripts.*

A B C D E F G H I J K L M N O P Q R S T U V W X Y Z

pantomime EG *He regularly performs in Christmas pantomimes.*
show EG *a one-woman show*
tragedy EG *Shakespeare's tragedies*

plead VERB
to beg someone for something
EG *She pleaded with her daughter to come home.*
appeal EG *The United Nations appealed for aid from the international community.*
ask EG *I've asked you time and again not to do that.*
beg EG *We are not going to beg for help any more.*
beseech LITERARY EG *She beseeched him to show mercy.*
implore EG *Opposition leaders implored the president to break the deadlock.*

❶ pleasant ADJECTIVE
enjoyable or attractive
EG *I've got a pleasant little flat.*
agreeable EG *workers in more agreeable and better paid occupations*
delightful EG *It was the most delightful garden I'd ever seen.*
enjoyable EG *an enjoyable meal*
lekker SOUTH AFRICAN; SLANG EG *a lekker little town*
lovely EG *He had a lovely voice.*
nice EG *It's nice to be here together again.*
pleasurable EG *He found sailing more pleasurable than skiing.*

WORD POWER
▶ Antonym
unpleasant

❷ pleasant ADJECTIVE
friendly or charming
EG *an extremely pleasant and obliging man*
affable EG *He is an affable and approachable man.*
amiable EG *She had been surprised at*

how amiable and polite he had seemed.
charming EG *He can be charming to his friends.*
friendly EG *She has a friendly relationship with her customers.*
likable or **likeable** EG *He's an immensely likable man.*
nice EG *He's a nice fellow, very quiet and courteous.*

WORD POWER
▶ Antonym
unpleasant

please VERB
to give pleasure to
EG *I was tidying my bedroom to please mum.*
amuse EG *The thought seemed to amuse him.*
charm EG *He charmed all of us.*
delight EG *music that has delighted audiences all over the world*
entertain EG *Children's TV not only entertains but also teaches.*

pleased ADJECTIVE
happy or satisfied
EG *I'm pleased with the way things have been going.*
contented EG *She had a contented smile on her face.*
delighted EG *I know he will be delighted to see you.*
glad EG *I'm glad he changed my mind in the end.*
happy EG *She's a confident and happy child.*
satisfied EG *satisfied customers*

pleasure NOUN
a feeling of happiness and satisfaction
EG *Everybody takes pleasure in eating.*
amusement EG *Her impersonations provided great amusement.*
enjoyment EG *her enjoyment of the countryside*
happiness EG *My happiness helped*

a
b
c
d
e
f
g
h
i
j
k
l
m
n
o
p
q
r
s
t
u
v
w
x
y
z

to erase the bad memories.
joy EG *tears of joy*
satisfaction EG *job satisfaction*

plentiful ADJECTIVE
existing in large amounts
EG *a plentiful supply*
abundant EG *Birds are abundant in the tall vegetation.*
ample EG *The design created ample space for a large kitchen.*
bountiful EG *a bountiful harvest of fruits and vegetables*
copious EG *He attended the lectures and took copious notes.*
infinite EG *an infinite variety of landscapes*

WORD POWER

▷ **Synonyms**
profuse

▶ **Antonym**
scarce

plenty NOUN
a lot of something
EG *There's plenty to go round.*
enough EG *Have you had enough?*
great deal EG *I've spent a great deal of time on this project.*
heaps INFORMAL EG *You have heaps of time.*
lots INFORMAL EG *He has made lots of amendments to the script.*
plethora EG *a plethora of new products*

❶ **plot** NOUN
a secret plan made by a group of people
EG *the plot to assassinate Martin Luther King*
conspiracy EG *a conspiracy to steal nuclear missiles*
intrigue EG *political intrigues*
plan EG *a secret government plan to build a nuclear waste dump*

scheme EG *an elaborate scheme to dupe the police*

WORD POWER

▷ **Synonyms**
cabal
machination
stratagem

❷ **plot** NOUN
the story of a novel or play
EG *The film has a ludicrously complicated plot.*
narrative EG *a fast-moving narrative*
scenario EG *The movie's scenario is nonsensical.*
story EG *I doubt the appeal of cinematic sex without a story.*
story line EG *It sounds like a typical story line from a soap opera.*

❸ **plot** VERB
to plan something secretly with others
EG *Prosecutors allege the defendants plotted to overthrow the government.*
conspire EG *The countries had secretly conspired to acquire nuclear weapons.*
hatch EG *He hatched a plot to murder his wife.*
plan EG *I suspect they are secretly planning to raise taxes.*
scheme EG *He claimed that they were scheming against him.*

WORD POWER

▷ **Synonyms**
cabal
collude
machinate

❶ **plug** NOUN
a small, round object for blocking a hole
EG *She put the plug in the sink and filled it with water.*
bung EG *Remove the bung from the barrel.*
cork EG *the sound of popping*

champagne corks
stopper EG *a bottle sealed with a cork stopper*

❷ plug VERB
to block a hole with something
EG *working to plug a major oil leak*
block EG *When the shrimp farm is built it will block the stream.*
fill EG *Fill small holes with wood filler.*
seal EG *She filled the containers and sealed them with a cork.*

plump ADJECTIVE
rather fat
EG *a plump, fresh-faced young woman*
beefy INFORMAL EG *beefy bodyguards*
burly EG *burly shipyard workers*
chubby EG *I was quite chubby as a child.*
fat EG *I could eat what I liked without getting fat.*
stout EG *He was a tall, stout man of sixty.*
tubby EG *He's a bit on the tubby side.*

❶ point NOUN
the purpose or meaning something has
EG *Cutting costs is not the point of the exercise.*
aim EG *The aim of this book is to inform you.*
goal EG *The goal is to raise a lot of money.*
intention EG *It was never my intention to injure anyone.*
object EG *It was his object in life to find the island.*
purpose EG *He did not know the purpose of Vincent's visit.*

❷ point NOUN
a quality or feature
EG *Tact was never her strong point.*
attribute EG *Cruelty is a regrettable attribute of human behaviour.*
characteristic EG *their physical characteristics*
feature EG *They're one of my best features.*

quality EG *mature people with leadership qualities*
side EG *the dark side of his character*
trait EG *Creativity is a human trait.*

❸ point NOUN
the thin sharp end of something
EG *the point of a needle*
nib EG *the nib of my pen*
prong EG *the prongs of a fork*
tip EG *the tip of my scissors*

poison NOUN
a substance that can kill people or animals
EG *Mercury is a known poison.*
toxin EG *the liver's ability to break down toxins*
venom EG *the cobra's deadly venom*

> *WORD POWER*
>
> ● **Related Words**
>   *adjective* : toxic

poisonous ADJECTIVE
containing something that causes death or illness
EG *a large cloud of poisonous gas*
noxious EG *Many household products give off noxious fumes.*
toxic EG *The cost of cleaning up toxic waste.*
venomous EG *The adder is Britain's only venomous snake.*

❶ poke VERB
to jab or prod someone or something
EG *She poked a fork into the turkey skin.*
dig EG *His companions were digging him in the ribs.*
elbow EG *As I tried to get past him he elbowed me in the face.*
jab EG *Somebody jabbed an umbrella into his leg.*
nudge EG *She nudged me awake after I dozed off.*
prod EG *He prodded Murray with the shotgun.*

a b c d e f g h i j k l m n o p q r s t u v w x y z

A B C D E F G H I J K L M N O P Q R S T U V W X Y Z

stab EG *He stabbed at Frank with his forefinger.*

② poke NOUN
a jab or prod
EG *She gave Richard a playful poke.*
dig EG *She silenced him with a sharp dig in the small of the back.*
jab EG *a quick jab of the brakes*
nudge EG *She slipped her arm under his and gave him a nudge.*
prod EG *He gave the donkey a mighty prod in the backside.*

① polish VERB
to make smooth and shiny by rubbing
EG *He polished his shoes every morning.*
buff EG *He was already buffing the car's hubs.*
shine EG *Let him dust and shine the furniture.*
wax EG *a Sunday morning spent washing and waxing the car*

② polish VERB
to improve a skill or technique
EG *Polish up your writing skills.*
brush up EG *She spent the summer brushing up on her driving.*
improve EG *I want to improve my golf game.*
perfect EG *We perfected a hand-signal system.*
refine EG *Surgical techniques are constantly being refined.*

③ polish NOUN
elegance or refinement
EG *The opera lacks the polish of his later work.*
class INFORMAL EG *For sheer class, Mark Waugh is the best batsman of the World Cup.*
elegance EG *The furniture combined practicality with elegance.*
finesse EG *It's good but it lacks the finesse of vintage champagne.*
grace EG *Ballet classes are important for learning poise and grace.*

refinement EG *a girl who possessed both dignity and refinement*
style EG *Paris, you have to admit, has style.*

WORD POWER
▷ **Synonyms**
politesse
suavity
urbanity

① polite ADJECTIVE
having good manners
EG *It's not polite to point at people.*
civil EG *I have to force myself to be civil to him.*
courteous EG *Her reply was courteous but firm.*
respectful EG *Their children are always respectful to their elders.*
well-behaved EG *well-behaved little girls*
well-mannered EG *a very pleasant and well-mannered student*

WORD POWER
▶ **Antonym**
rude

② polite ADJECTIVE
cultivated or refined
EG *Certain words are not acceptable in polite society.*
cultured EG *He is immensely cultured and well-read.*
genteel EG *two ladies with genteel manners and voices*
refined EG *His speech and manner are very refined.*
sophisticated EG *Recently her tastes have become more sophisticated.*
urbane EG *She describes him as charming and urbane.*

politeness NOUN
the quality of being civil to someone
EG *She listened to him but only out of politeness.*
civility EG *Handle customers with tact and civility.*

courtesy EG *He did not even have the courtesy to reply to my fax.*
decency EG *He should have had the decency to inform me.*
etiquette EG *the rules of diplomatic etiquette*

pollute VERB
to contaminate with something harmful
EG *Heavy industry pollutes our rivers with noxious chemicals.*
contaminate EG *Have any fish been contaminated in the Arctic Ocean?*
infect EG *a virus which is spread mainly by infected blood*
poison EG *Drilling operations have poisoned the Nile delta.*
taint EG *blood tainted with the hepatitis viruses*

WORD POWER

▷ **Synonyms**
adulterate
befoul
smirch

---

pompous ADJECTIVE
behaving in a way that is too serious and self-important
EG *a pompous man with a high opinion of his own capabilities*
arrogant EG *an air of arrogant indifference*
grandiose EG *grandiose plans which never got off the ground*
ostentatious EG *an ostentatious wedding reception*
pretentious EG *His response was full of pretentious nonsense.*
puffed up EG *He is puffed up with own importance.*

WORD POWER

▷ **Synonyms**
pontifical
portentous
vainglorious

---

ponder VERB
to think about something deeply
EG *I'm continually pondering how to improve the team.*
brood EG *I guess everyone broods over things once in a while.*
consider EG *You have to consider the feelings of those around you.*
contemplate EG *He lay in bed contemplating his future.*
mull over EG *I'll leave you alone here so you can mull it over.*
reflect EG *I reflected on the child's future.*
think EG *I have often thought about this problem.*

❶ poor ADJECTIVE
having little money
EG *They see the government ignoring poor people.*
broke INFORMAL EG *He was broke when I married him.*
destitute EG *destitute people living on the streets*
hard up INFORMAL EG *Her parents were very hard up.*
impoverished EG *one of the most impoverished suburbs of Rio de Janeiro*
penniless EG *a penniless refugee*
poverty-stricken EG *a teacher of poverty-stricken kids*

WORD POWER

▶ **Antonym**
rich

---

❷ poor ADJECTIVE
of a low quality or standard
EG *He was a poor actor.*
feeble EG *a feeble attempt to save Figo's shot*
inferior EG *The cassettes were of inferior quality.*
mediocre EG *His school record was mediocre.*
second-rate EG *Passengers are fed up using a second-rate service.*

A
B
C
D
E
F
G
H
I
J
K
L
M
N
O
P
Q
R
S
T
U
V
W
X
Y
Z

shoddy EG *shoddy goods*
unsatisfactory EG *questions to which he received unsatisfactory answers*

❶ popular ADJECTIVE
liked or approved of by a lot of people
EG *These delicious pastries will be very popular.*
fashionable EG *fashionable wine bars*
favourite EG *Britain's favourite soap opera*
in demand EG *He was much in demand as a lecturer.*
in favour EG *He is now back in favour with the manager.*
sought-after EG *one of the most sought-after new names in Hollywood*
well-liked EG *She was very sociable and well-liked by the other students.*

WORD POWER
▶ **Antonym**
unpopular

❷ popular ADJECTIVE
involving or intended for ordinary people
EG *the popular press*
common EG *Much of the countryside has fallen out of common ownership and into private hands.*
conventional EG *a respectable married woman with conventional opinions*
general EG *general awareness about bullying*
prevalent EG *Smoking is becoming increasingly prevalent among younger women.*
universal EG *universal health care*

portion NOUN
a part or amount of something
EG *I have spent a considerable portion of my life here.*
bit EG *I missed the first bit of the meeting.*

chunk EG *Cut the melon into chunks.*
helping EG *She gave them extra helpings of ice-cream.*
part EG *A large part of his earnings went on repaying the loan.*
piece EG *Do you want another piece?*
segment EG *the middle segment of his journey*
serving EG *Each serving contains 240 calories.*

❶ pose VERB
to ask a question
EG *When I finally posed the question, `Why?' he merely shrugged.*
ask EG *I wasn't the only one asking questions.*
put EG *Some workers may be afraid to put questions publicly.*
submit EG *Passengers are invited to submit questions.*

WORD POWER
▷ **Synonyms**
posit
propound

❷ pose VERB
to pretend to be someone else
EG *The team posed as drug dealers to trap the ringleaders.*
impersonate EG *He was once jailed for impersonating a policeman.*
masquerade as EG *He masqueraded as a doctor and fooled everyone.*
pass oneself off as EG *He frequently passed himself off as a lawyer.*
pretend to be EG *We spent the afternoon pretending to be foreign tourists.*

❶ posh ADJECTIVE; INFORMAL
smart, fashionable and expensive
EG *a posh hotel*
classy INFORMAL EG *expensive cars with classy brand names*
elegant EG *an elegant society ball*
exclusive EG *a member of Britain's*

most exclusive club
fashionable EG *fashionable restaurants*
smart EG *smart London dinner parties*
stylish EG *stylish décor*
up-market EG *an up-market agency aimed at professional people*

2 posh ADJECTIVE
upper-class
EG *He sounded very posh on the phone.*
aristocratic EG *a wealthy, aristocratic family*
genteel EG *two ladies with genteel manners and voices*
upper-class EG *upper-class speech*

WORD POWER

▷ **Synonyms**
patrician (FORMAL)

▶ **Antonym**
common

---

1 position NOUN
the place where someone or something is
EG *The ship's name and position were reported to the coastguard.*
location EG *She knew the exact location of their headquarters.*
place EG *The pain is always in the same place.*
point EG *The pain originated from a point in his right thigh.*
whereabouts EG *Finding his whereabouts proved surprisingly easy.*

2 position VERB
to put something somewhere
EG *Position trailing plants near the edges.*
arrange EG *Arrange the books in neat piles.*
lay out EG *Grace laid out the knives and forks at the table.*
locate EG *the best city in which to locate a business*
place EG *Chairs were placed in rows*

for the parents.
put EG *She put the photograph on her desk.*

1 positive ADJECTIVE
completely sure about something
EG *I was positive he'd known about that money.*
certain EG *It wasn't a balloon - I'm certain about that.*
confident EG *My Ryan is confident of success.*
convinced EG *He was convinced that I was part of the problem.*
sure EG *It is impossible to be sure about the value of the land.*

2 positive ADJECTIVE
providing definite proof of the truth or identity of something
EG *positive evidence*
clear EG *a clear case of mistaken identity*
clear-cut EG *The issue is not so clear-cut.*
conclusive EG *Research on the matter is far from conclusive.*
concrete EG *He had no concrete evidence.*
firm EG *There is no firm evidence to prove this.*

WORD POWER

▷ **Synonyms**
incontrovertible
indisputable
unequivocal

---

3 positive ADJECTIVE
tending to emphasize what is good
EG *I anticipate a positive response.*
constructive EG *We welcome constructive criticism.*
helpful EG *Camilla's helpful comments*

WORD POWER

▶ **Antonym**
negative

---

a
b
c
d
e
f
g
h
i
j
k
l
m
n
o
p
q
r
s
t
u
v
w
x
y
z

A
B
C
D
E
F
G
H
I
J
K
L
M
N
O
P
Q
R
S
T
U
V
W
X
Y
Z

❶ possess VERB
to have something as a quality
EG *He possesses both stamina and great technique.*
be blessed with EG *She was blessed with a photographic memory.*
be born with EG *Mozart was born with perfect pitch.*
enjoy EG *I have always enjoyed good health.*
have EG *They have talent in abundance.*

❷ possess VERB
to own something
EG *He was said to possess a huge fortune.*
acquire EG *I have acquired a new car.*
control EG *He now controls the entire company.*
hold EG *He does not hold a firearm certificate.*
occupy EG *US forces now occupy part of the country.*
seize EG *Troops have seized the airport and railway terminals.*
take over EG *They plan to take over another airline.*

possession NOUN
ownership of something
EG *How did this picture come into your possession?*
control EG *The restructuring involves his giving up control of the firm.*
custody EG *She will have custody of their two children.*
ownership EG *the growth of home ownership*
tenure EG *his 28-year tenure of the house*

possessions PLURAL NOUN
the things owned by someone
EG *People had lost all their possessions.*
assets EG *The group had assets worth over 10 million dollars.*
belongings EG *He was identified only by his personal belongings.*

effects EG *His daughters were collecting his effects.*
estate EG *She left her entire estate to a charity.*
property EG *the rightful owner of the property*
things EG *She told him to take all his things and not to return.*

possibility NOUN
something that might be true or might happen
EG *the possibility of a ban*
chance EG *There's no chance of that happening.*
hope EG *We had absolutely no hope of raising the money.*
likelihood EG *the likelihood of infection*
odds EG *What are the odds of that happening?*
prospect EG *There is little prospect of peace.*
risk EG *It reduces the risk of heart disease.*

❶ possible ADJECTIVE
likely to happen or able to be done
EG *I am grateful to the staff for making this work possible.*
attainable EG *I always thought promotion was attainable.*
feasible EG *Whether such cooperation is feasible is a matter of doubt.*
practicable EG *It was not reasonably practicable for Mr Tyler to attend.*
viable EG *commercially viable products*
workable EG *This isn't a workable solution in most cases.*

WORD POWER

▶ **Antonym**
impossible

❷ possible ADJECTIVE
likely or capable of being true or correct
EG *It's possible there's an explanation*

for all this.
conceivable EG *It is just conceivable that a survivor might be found.*
imaginable EG *a place of no imaginable strategic value*
likely EG *Experts say a `yes' vote is still the likely outcome.*
potential EG *the channel's potential audience*

postpone VERB
to put off to a later time
EG *The visit has been postponed until tomorrow.*
adjourn EG *The proceedings have been adjourned until next week.*
defer EG *Customers often defer payments for as long as possible.*
delay EG *I wanted to delay my departure until June.*
put back EG *The news conference has been put back a couple of hours.*
put off EG *The Association has put off the event until October.*
shelve EG *Sadly, the project has now been shelved.*

❶ potential ADJECTIVE
possible but not yet actual
EG *potential sources of finance*
likely EG *A draw is the likely outcome.*
possible EG *Her family is discussing a possible move to America.*
probable EG *A bomb was the accident's most probable cause.*

❷ potential NOUN
ability to achieve future success
EG *Denmark recognized the potential of wind energy early.*
ability EG *You have the ability to become a good pianist.*
aptitude EG *more aptitude for academic work than the others*
capability EG *We experience differences in mental capability depending on the time of day.*
capacity EG *people's creative capacities*
power EG *the power of speech*

wherewithal EG *She didn't have the financial wherewithal to do it.*

pour VERB
to flow quickly and in large quantities
EG *Blood was pouring from his broken nose.*
course EG *The tears coursed down her cheeks.*
flow EG *compressor stations that keep that gas flowing*
gush EG *Piping-hot water gushed out.*
run EG *Water was running down the walls.*
spout EG *a fountain that spouts water 40 feet into the air*
stream EG *She came in, rain streaming from her clothes and hair.*

poverty NOUN
the state of being very poor
EG *Garvey died in loneliness and poverty.*
destitution EG *refugees living in destitution*
hardship EG *Many people are suffering economic hardship.*
insolvency EG *Several companies are on the brink of insolvency.*
want EG *We are fighting for freedom from want.*

WORD POWER

▷ **Synonyms**
beggary
indigence
penury
privation

---

❶ power NOUN
control over people and activities
EG *a position of great power and influence*
ascendancy EG *The extremists in the party are gaining ascendancy.*
control EG *He has been forced to give up control over the company.*
dominion EG *They truly believe they have dominion over us.*

A
B
C
D
E
F
G
H
I
J
K
L
M
N
O
P
Q
R
S
T
U
V
W
X
Y
Z

sovereignty EG *the resumption of Chinese sovereignty over Hong Kong in 1997*
supremacy EG *The party has re-established its supremacy.*

❷ power NOUN
authority to do something
EG *The police have the power of arrest.*
authority EG *The judge had no authority to order a second trial.*
authorization EG *I don't have the authorization to make such a decision.*
licence EG *He has given me licence to do the job as I see fit.*
privilege EG *the ancient powers and privileges of parliament*
right EG *the right to vote*

❸ power NOUN
physical strength
EG *Power and bulk are vital to success in rugby.*
brawn EG *He's got plenty of brains as well as brawn.*
might EG *The might of the army could prove a decisive factor.*
strength EG *He threw it forward with all his strength.*
vigour EG *His body lacks the vigour of a normal two-year-old.*

❶ powerful ADJECTIVE
able to control people and events
EG *Russia and India, two large, powerful countries*
commanding EG *We're in a more commanding position than we've been in for ages.*
dominant EG *He was a dominant figure in the Italian film industry.*
influential EG *He had been influential in shaping economic policy.*

❷ powerful ADJECTIVE
physically strong
EG *It's such a big powerful dog.*
mighty EG *a mighty river*
strapping EG *He was a bricklayer - a big, strapping fellow.*

strong EG *I'm not strong enough to carry him.*
sturdy EG *The camera was mounted on a sturdy tripod.*
vigorous EG *He was a vigorous, handsome young man.*

WORD POWER

▶ **Antonym**
weak

❸ powerful ADJECTIVE
having a strong effect
EG *a powerful argument*
compelling EG *a compelling reason to leave*
convincing EG *convincing evidence*
effective EG *Antibiotics are effective against this organism.*
forceful EG *forceful action to stop the suffering*
persuasive EG *Mr. Knight made a persuasive case for removing the tax.*
telling EG *He spoke reasonably, carefully, and with telling effect.*

powerless ADJECTIVE
unable to control or influence events
EG *I was powerless to save her.*
helpless EG *Many people felt helpless against the violence.*
impotent EG *The West is impotent to influence the Balkan war.*
incapable EG *He is incapable as a manager.*

❶ practical ADJECTIVE
involving experience rather than theory
EG *practical suggestions for healthy eating*
applied EG *plans to put more plans into applied research*
pragmatic EG *a pragmatic approach to the problems of Latin America*

❷ practical ADJECTIVE
likely to be effective
EG *The clothes are lightweight and practical for holidays.*
functional EG *The design is*

functional but stylish.
sensible EG *sensible footwear*

WORD POWER

▶ **Antonym**
impractical

---

3 practical ADJECTIVE
able to deal effectively with
problems
EG *the practical common sense
essential in management*
accomplished EG *an accomplished
cook*
experienced EG *a team packed with
experienced professionals*
proficient EG *A great number of
them are proficient in foreign
languages.*
seasoned EG *The author is a
seasoned academic.*
skilled EG *amateur but highly skilled
observers of wildlife*
veteran EG *a veteran broadcaster*

1 practice NOUN
something that people do regularly
EG *a public inquiry into bank practices*
custom EG *I have tried to adapt to
local customs.*
habit EG *a survey on eating habits*
method EG *her usual method of
getting through the traffic*
routine EG *We had to change our
daily routine and lifestyle.*
way EG *a return to the old ways of
doing things*

2 practice NOUN
regular training or exercise
EG *I need more practice.*
drill EG *The teacher ran them through
the drill again.*
exercise EG *Lack of exercise can lead
to feelings of exhaustion.*
preparation EG *Behind any
successful event lie months of
preparation.*
rehearsal EG *rehearsals for a concert
tour*

training EG *her busy training
schedule*

1 practise VERB
to do something repeatedly so as to
gain skill
EG *Lauren practises the piano every
day.*
polish EG *They just need to polish
their technique.*
rehearse EG *She was in her room
rehearsing her lines.*
train EG *He was training for the new
season.*

2 practise VERB
to take part in the activities of a
religion, craft, or custom
EG *Acupuncture has been practised in
China for thousands of years.*
do EG *I used to do karate.*
follow EG *Do you follow any
particular religion?*
observe EG *American forces are
observing Christmas quietly.*

1 praise VERB
to express strong approval of
someone
EG *Many others praised Sanford for
taking a strong stand.*
admire EG *All those who knew him
will admire him for his work.*
applaud EG *He should be applauded
for his courage.*
approve EG *Not everyone approves of
the festival.*
congratulate EG *I must
congratulate the organizers for a well
run event.*
pay tribute to EG *He paid tribute to
his captain.*

WORD POWER

▷ **Synonyms**
acclaim
eulogize
extol
laud

A B C D E F G H I J K L M N O P Q R S T U V W X Y Z

▶ **Antonym**
criticize

❷ **praise** NOUN
something said or written to show approval
EG *She is full of praise for the range of services available.*
accolade EG *the ultimate international accolade, the Nobel Peace Prize*
approval EG *an obsessive drive to gain her mother's approval*
commendation EG *They received a commendation from the Royal Society of Arts.*
congratulation EG *I offered her my congratulations.*
tribute EG *We marched past in tribute to our fallen comrades.*

WORD POWER

▷ **Synonyms**
encomium
eulogy
panegyric

▶ **Antonym**
criticism

precaution NOUN
an action intended to prevent something from happening
EG *It's still worth taking precautions against accidents.*
insurance EG *Farmers grew a mixture of crops as an insurance against crop failure.*
preventative measure EG *a preventative measure against heart disease*
protection EG *protection against damage to buildings*
provision EG *People need to make decent provision for their old age.*
safeguard EG *legislation that offers safeguards against discrimination*

precious ADJECTIVE
of great value and importance

EG *precious jewels*
expensive EG *an expensive new coat*
invaluable EG *I was to gain invaluable experience over that year.*
priceless EG *his priceless collection of Chinese art*
prized EG *These shells were very highly prized by the Indians.*
valuable EG *valuable books*

WORD POWER

▶ **Antonym**
worthless

precise ADJECTIVE
exact and accurate
EG *We may never know the precise details.*
accurate EG *an accurate description of his attackers*
actual EG *The actual number of victims is higher than statistics suggest.*
correct EG *This information was correct at the time of going to press.*
exact EG *The exact number of protest calls has not been revealed.*
particular EG *a very particular account of events*
specific EG *I asked him to be more specific.*
very EG *Those were his very words.*

WORD POWER

▶ **Antonym**
vague

predicament NOUN
a difficult situation
EG *The decision will leave her in a peculiar predicament.*
fix INFORMAL EG *The government has really got itself into a fix.*
hot water INFORMAL EG *His antics keep landing him in hot water with officials.*
jam INFORMAL EG *We are in a real jam now.*
scrape INFORMAL EG *He's had his fair*

share of scrapes with the law.
tight spot EG *This was one tight spot he couldn't get out of.*

predict VERB
to say that something will happen in the future
EG *The opinion polls are predicting a very close contest.*
forecast EG *He forecasts that house prices will rise by 5% this year.*
foresee EG *He did not foresee any problems.*
foretell EG *prophets who have foretold the end of the world*
prophesy EG *She prophesied a bad ending for the expedition.*

WORD POWER

▷ **Synonyms**
forebode
portend
presage
prognosticate
soothsay

prediction NOUN
something that is forecast in advance
EG *He was unwilling to make a prediction for the coming year.*
forecast EG *a forecast of heavy weather to come*
prophecy EG *the interpreters of Biblical prophecy*

prefer VERB
to like one thing more than another thing
EG *Does he prefer a particular sort of music?*
be partial to EG *I'm quite partial to mussels.*
favour EG *Both sides favour a diplomatic solution.*
go for EG *They went for a more up-market approach.*
incline towards EG *The majority are inclined towards a forgiving attitude.*

like better EG *I like the flat shoes better.*

prefix NOUN

Prefixes
ante-
anti-
auto-
bi-
centi-
co-
contra-
de-
demi-
dis-
ex-
extra-
hyper-
in-
inter-
intra-
mega-
micro-
mid-
milli-
mini-
mono-
multi-
neo-
non-
over-
poly-
post-
pre-
pro-
pseudo-
re-
self-
semi-
step-
sub-
super-
tele-
trans-
tri-
ultra-
un-
under-
vice-

❶ prejudice NOUN
an unreasonable or unfair dislike or preference
EG *prejudice against workers over 45*
bias EG *Bias against women permeates every level of the judicial system.*
partiality EG *She is criticized for her one-sidedness and partiality.*
preconception EG *preconceptions about the sort of people who did computing*

❷ prejudice NOUN
intolerance towards certain people or groups
EG *racial prejudice*
bigotry EG *religious bigotry*
chauvinism EG *the growth of Russian chauvinism*
discrimination EG *sex discrimination*
racism EG *the fight to rid sport of racism*
sexism EG *sexism in the workplace*

premonition NOUN
a feeling that something unpleasant is going to happen
EG *He had a premonition that he would die.*
foreboding EG *His triumph was overshadowed by an uneasy sense of foreboding.*
funny feeling INFORMAL EG *I have a funny feeling something unpleasant is about to happen.*
omen EG *Her appearance at this moment is an omen of disaster.*
sign EG *a sign of impending doom*

> ### WORD POWER
>
> ▷ **Synonyms**
> portent
> presage
> presentiment

preoccupied ADJECTIVE
totally involved with something or deep in thought

EG *I am preoccupied with my tennis career.*
absorbed EG *They were completely absorbed in each other.*
engrossed EG *Tom didn't notice because he was too engrossed in his work.*
immersed EG *He's becoming really immersed in his studies.*
oblivious EG *When he was in his car he was totally oblivious to everybody else.*
wrapped up EG *She's wrapped up in her new career.*

❶ present ADJECTIVE
being at a place or event
EG *He had been present at the birth of his son.*
at hand EG *Having the right equipment at hand will be very useful.*
here EG *He was here a minute ago.*
in attendance EG *Police and several fire engines are in attendance.*
there EG *The group of old buildings is still there today.*
to hand EG *I haven't got the instructions to hand.*

> ### WORD POWER
>
> ▶ **Antonym**
> absent

❷ present NOUN
something given to someone
EG *a birthday present*
bonsela SOUTH AFRICAN EG *your kind bonsela to the hospital*
donation EG *Employees make regular donations to charity.*
gift EG *a Christmas gift*
offering EG *Hindus kill turtles ritually as an offering to their gods.*

❸ present VERB
to give something to someone
EG *The Mayor presented the prizes.*
award EG *For his dedication he was awarded a medal of merit.*
bestow EG *The Queen bestowed on*

him a knighthood.
donate EG *He frequently donates large sums to charity.*
give EG *She gave me a pen for my birthday.*
grant EG *France has agreed to grant him political asylum.*
hand out EG *One of my jobs was to hand out the prizes.*

❶ press VERB
to apply force or weight to something
EG *Press the blue button.*
compress EG *Poor posture compresses the body's organs.*
crush EG *Peel and crush the garlic.*
mash EG *Mash the bananas with a fork.*
push EG *She pushed the door open.*
squeeze EG *He squeezed her arm reassuringly.*

❷ press VERB
to try hard to persuade someone to do something
EG *Trade Unions are pressing him to stand firm.*
beg EG *I begged him to come back with me.*
implore EG `Tell me what to do!' she implored him.*
petition EG *All the attempts to petition the government had failed.*
plead EG *I pleaded to be allowed to go.*
pressurize EG *He thought she was trying to pressurize him.*
urge EG *He had urged her to come to Ireland.*

WORD POWER

▷ **Synonyms**
entreat
exhort
importune

pretend VERB
to claim or give the appearance of something untrue

EG *Sometimes the boy pretended to be asleep.*
counterfeit EG *the coins he is alleged to have counterfeited*
fake EG *He faked his own death last year.*
falsify EG *He was charged with falsifying business records.*
feign EG *The striker was accused of feigning injury.*
pass oneself off as EG *She tried to pass herself off as an actress.*

pretentious ADJECTIVE
making unjustified claims to importance
EG *Many critics thought her work and ideas pretentious and empty.*
affected EG *She passed along with an affected air and a disdainful look.*
conceited EG *I thought him conceited and arrogant.*
ostentatious EG *an ostentatious wedding reception*
pompous EG *He's pompous and has a high opinion of his own capabilities.*
snobbish EG *a snobbish dislike for their intellectual inferiors*

WORD POWER

▷ **Synonyms**
bombastic
grandiloquent
magniloquent
vainglorious

❶ pretty ADJECTIVE
attractive in a delicate way
EG *She's a very charming and very pretty girl.*
attractive EG *She has a round attractive face.*
beautiful EG *a beautiful child*
cute EG *a cute little baby*
lovely EG *his lovely wife*

❷ pretty ADVERB; INFORMAL
quite or rather
EG *He spoke pretty good English.*
fairly EG *Both ships are fairly new.*

a
b
c
d
e
f
g
h
i
j
k
l
m
n
o
p
q
r
s
t
u
v
w
x
y
z

kind of INFORMAL EG *I was kind of embarrassed about it.*
quite EG *It was quite hard.*
rather EG *She's rather vain.*

prevent VERB
to stop something from happening
EG *the most practical way of preventing crime*
avert EG *A fresh tragedy was narrowly averted yesterday.*
foil EG *The plot was foiled by policemen.*
hinder EG *Research is hindered by lack of cash.*
impede EG *Fallen rocks are impeding the progress of the rescue workers.*
stop EG *a new diplomatic initiative to try to stop the war*
thwart EG *Her ambition to become an artist was thwarted by failing eyesight.*

previous ADJECTIVE
happening or existing before something else
EG *the previous year*
earlier EG *His earlier works include impressive still lifes.*
former EG *a former president of Mexico*
one-time EG *the country's one-time military rulers*
past EG *a return to the turbulence of past centuries*
preceding EG *This is examined in detail in the preceding chapter.*
prior EG *I can't make it. I have a prior engagement.*

❶ price NOUN
the amount of money paid for something
EG *a sharp increase in the price of petrol*
amount EG *I was asked to pay the full amount.*
charge EG *an annual management charge of 1.25%*
cost EG *the cost of a loaf of bread*

fee EG *the annual membership fee*
figure EG *A figure of £2000 was mentioned.*
value EG *The company's market value rose to 5.5 billion dollars.*

❷ price VERB
to fix the price or value of something
EG *I just can't imagine why it has been priced at this level.*
cost EG *We hope it won't cost too much.*
estimate EG *His personal riches were estimated at $368 million.*
put a price on EG *The company has refused to put a price on its bid.*
value EG *I had my jewellery valued for insurance purposes.*

❶ pride NOUN
a feeling of satisfaction about your achievements
EG *We take pride in offering you the highest standards.*
delight EG *Haig took obvious delight in proving his critics wrong.*
pleasure EG *Our first win gave me great pleasure.*
satisfaction EG *His success was a great source of satisfaction to him.*

❷ pride NOUN
an excessively high opinion of yourself
EG *His pride may still be his downfall.*
arrogance EG *He has a swaggering arrogance.*
conceit EG *He knew, without conceit, that he was considered a genius.*
egotism EG *typical showbiz egotism*
smugness EG *a trace of smugness in his voice*
snobbery EG *intellectual snobbery*
vanity EG *her vanity about her long hair*

WORD POWER
▷ **Synonyms**
haughtiness
hauteur

A B C D E F G H I J K L M N O P Q R S T U V W X Y Z

hubris
superciliousness

▶ **Antonym**
humility

priest NOUN

> **Types of priest**
> guru
> high priest or high priestess
> imam
> lama
> minister
> priest
> rabbi
> shaman or medicine man
> vicar

prim ADJECTIVE
behaving very correctly and easily
shocked by anything rude
EG *We tend to assume the Victorians
were very prim and proper.*
proper EG *He was very pompous and
proper.*
prudish EG *I'm not prudish but I think
those photos are obscene.*
puritanical EG *He has a puritanical
attitude towards sex.*
strait-laced EG *He very strait-laced
and narrow-minded.*

❶ **prime** ADJECTIVE
main or most important
EG *a prime cause of brain damage*
chief EG *The job went to one of his
chief rivals.*
leading EG *a leading industrial nation*
main EG *the city's main tourist area*
principal EG *our principal source of
foreign exchange earnings*

❷ **prime** ADJECTIVE
of the best quality
EG *prime beef*
best EG *He'll have the best care.*
choice EG *our choicest chocolates*
first-rate EG *He's a first-rate officer.*
select EG *With that historic win he
now joins a select band of golfers.*
superior EG *superior coffee beans*

primitive ADJECTIVE
very simple or basic
EG *a very small primitive cottage*
crude EG *crude stone carvings*
rough EG *a rough wooden table*
rude EG *He constructed a rude cabin
for himself.*
rudimentary EG *The bomb was
rudimentary but lethal.*
simple EG *a simple shelter*

principal ADJECTIVE
main or most important
EG *Their principal concern is that of
winning the election.*
chief EG *his chief reason for
withdrawing*
first EG *The first duty of this
government is to tackle poverty.*
foremost EG *one of the world's
foremost scholars of classical poetry*
main EG *What are the main
differences between them?*
major EG *the major factor in her
decision*
primary EG *the primary cause of his
problems*
prime EG *Police will see me as the
prime suspect!*

❶ **principle** NOUN
a set of moral rules guiding personal
conduct
EG *a woman of principle*
conscience EG *the law on freedom of
conscience and religious
organizations*
integrity EG *He has always been a
man of integrity.*
morals EG *public morals*
scruples EG *a man with no moral
scruples*
sense of duty EG *He did it out of a
sense of duty to his men.*

❷ **principle** NOUN
a general rule or scientific law
EG *the basic principles of Marxism*

a
b
c
d
e
f
g
h
i
j
k
l
m
n
o
p
q
r
s
t
u
v
w
x
y
z

axiom EG *the long-held axiom that education leads to higher income*
canon EG *the canons of political economy*
doctrine EG *Christian doctrine*
fundamental EG *the fundamentals of astronomy*
law EG *the laws of motion*

WORD POWER

▷ **Synonyms**
dictum
precept
verity

printing NOUN

> **Printing words**
> bold print
> character
> fount *or* font
> italics
> lower case
> roman
> size
> typeface
> upper case

prison NOUN
a building where criminals are kept in captivity
EG *a high-security prison*
dungeon EG *The castle's dungeons haven't been used for years.*
jail EG *Three prisoners escaped from the jail.*
nick BRITISH, AUSTRALIAN, AND NEW ZEALAND; SLANG EG *I was banged up in the nick for six months.*
penal institution EG *Thirty years in a penal institution is indeed a harsh penalty.*

prisoner NOUN
someone kept in prison or captivity
EG *top-security prisoners*
captive EG *the difficulties of spending four months as a captive*
convict EG *convicts serving life sentences*

hostage EG *negotiations to release the hostages*

❶ private ADJECTIVE
for few people rather than people in general
EG *a private bathroom*
exclusive EG *Many of our cheeses are exclusive to our shops in Britain.*
individual EG *Divide the vegetables among four individual dishes.*
personal EG *It's for my own personal use.*
special EG *her own special problems*

❷ private ADJECTIVE
taking place among a small number of people
EG *He was buried in a private ceremony.*
clandestine EG *He had a clandestine meeting with his lover.*
confidential EG *confidential information about her private life*
secret EG *a secret love affair*

WORD POWER

▶ **Antonym**
public

❶ prize NOUN
a reward given to the winner of something
EG *He won first prize at the Leeds Piano Competition.*
accolade EG *the ultimate international accolade, the Nobel Peace Prize*
award EG *the Booker Prize, Britain's top award for fiction*
honour EG *He was showered with honours - among them an Oscar.*
trophy EG *They haven't won a trophy since 1991.*

❷ prize ADJECTIVE
of the highest quality or standard
EG *a prize bull*
award-winning EG *an award-winning restaurant*
first-rate EG *a first-rate thriller writer*

A B C D E F G H I J K L M N O P Q R S T U V W X Y Z

outstanding EG *an outstanding horse*
top EG *Holland's top striker*

❸ **prize** VERB
to value highly
EG *These ornaments are prized by collectors.*
cherish EG *We cherish our independence.*
esteem EG *one of Europe's most esteemed awards*
treasure EG *She treasures her memories of those joyous days.*
value EG *I value the work he gives me.*

probability NOUN
the likelihood of something happening
EG *the probability of a serious earthquake*
chances EG *The chances of success for the product are good.*
likelihood EG *the likelihood of infection*
odds EG *The odds are that you are going to fail.*
prospect EG *the prospect for peace in Rwanda*

probable ADJECTIVE
likely to be true or to happen
EG *a misunderstanding about the probable cost*
apparent EG *There is no apparent reason for the crime.*
feasible EG *Whether this is feasible is a matter of doubt.*
likely EG *Further delays are likely.*
on the cards EG *A promotion is definitely on the cards for you.*
plausible EG *a plausible explanation*

WORD POWER

▷ **Synonyms**
ostensible
verisimilar

▶ **Antonym**
improbable

---

probably ADVERB
in all likelihood
EG *The wedding's probably going to be in late August.*
doubtless EG *He will doubtless try to change my mind.*
in all probability EG *Victory will, in all probability, earn France the title.*
likely EG *The entire surplus will most likely be handed over.*
presumably EG *The spear is presumably the murder weapon.*

❶ **problem** NOUN
an unsatisfactory situation causing difficulties
EG *the economic problems of the inner city*
difficulty EG *This company is facing great difficulties.*
predicament EG *the once great club's current predicament*
quandary EG *We're in a quandary over our holiday plans.*
trouble EG *I had trouble parking this morning.*

❷ **problem** NOUN
a puzzle that needs to be solved
EG *a mathematical problem*
conundrum EG *an apparently insoluble conundrum*
puzzle EG *The data has presented astronomers with a puzzle.*
riddle EG *the riddle of the birth of the universe*

procedure NOUN
the correct or usual way of doing something
EG *He did not follow the correct procedure in applying for a visa.*
method EG *new teaching methods*
policy EG *It is our policy to prosecute shoplifters.*
practice EG *a public inquiry into bank practices*
process EG *the production process*
strategy EG *a strategy for controlling*

a b c d e f g h i j k l m n o **p** q r s t u v w x y z

A
B
C
D
E
F
G
H
I
J
K
L
M
N
O
P
Q
R
S
T
U
V
W
X
Y
Z

malaria
system EG *an efficient filing system*

❶ proceed VERB
to start doing or continue to do something
EG *I had no idea how to proceed.*
begin EG *He stood up and began to move about the room.*
carry on EG *"Can I start with a couple of questions?" - "Carry on."*
continue EG *I need some advice before I can continue with this task.*
get under way EG *The court case got under way last autumn.*
go on EG *Go on with your work.*
start EG *I started to follow him up the stairs.*

WORD POWER

▶ **Antonym**
cease

❷ proceed VERB; FORMAL
to move in a particular direction
EG *She proceeded along the hallway.*
advance EG *I advanced slowly, one step at a time.*
continue EG *He continued rapidly up the path.*
go on EG *They went on through the forest.*
make your way EG *He made his way to the marketplace.*
progress EG *He progressed slowly along the coast in an easterly direction.*
travel EG *You can travel to Helsinki tomorrow.*

❶ process NOUN
a method of doing or producing something
EG *The building process was spread over three years.*
course of action EG *It is important that we take the right course of action.*
means EG *The move is a means to fight crime.*
method EG *new teaching methods*

procedure EG *the correct procedure for applying for a visa*
system EG *an efficient filing system*

❷ process VERB
to deal with or treat something
EG *Your application is being processed.*
deal with EG *the way that banks deal with complaints*
dispose of EG *They disposed of the problem quickly.*
handle EG *She didn't know how to handle the problem.*
take care of EG *They left it to me to try and take care of the problem.*

❶ produce VERB
to make something
EG *a white wine produced mainly from black grapes*
construct EG *an inner frame constructed from timber*
create EG *It was created from odds and ends.*
invent EG *He invented the first electric clock.*
make EG *One of my jobs was to make the tea.*
manufacture EG *They manufacture plastics.*

❷ produce VERB
to bring out something so it can be seen or discussed
EG *To hire a car you must produce a driving licence.*
advance EG *Many new theories have been advanced recently.*
bring forward EG *We will bring forward new proposals for legislation.*
bring to light EG *new evidence brought to light by the police*
put forward EG *He has put forward new peace proposals.*

product NOUN
something that is made to be sold
EG *Many household products give off noxious fumes.*
commodity EG *basic commodities such as bread and milk*

goods EG *imported goods*
merchandise EG *The club sells a wide range of merchandise.*
produce EG *locally grown produce*

❶ **productive** ADJECTIVE
producing a large number of things
EG *Training makes workers highly productive.*
fertile EG *a product of his fertile imagination*
fruitful EG *a landscape that was fruitful and lush*
prolific EG *She is a prolific writer of novels and short stories.*

WORD POWER

▷ **Synonyms**
fecund
generative

▶ **Antonym**
unproductive

---

❷ **productive** ADJECTIVE
bringing favourable results
EG *I'm hopeful the talks will be productive.*
constructive EG *constructive criticism*
useful EG *We made some progress during a useful exchange.*
valuable EG *The experience was very valuable.*
worthwhile EG *It had been a worthwhile discussion.*

WORD POWER

▶ **Antonym**
unproductive

---

profession NOUN
a job that requires advanced education or training
EG *Harper was a teacher by profession.*
business EG *May I ask you what business you're in?*
career EG *a career in journalism*
occupation EG *her new occupation as an author*

proficient ADJECTIVE
able to do something well
EG *They tend to be proficient in foreign languages.*
able EG *an able young rider*
accomplished EG *an accomplished fundraiser*
adept EG *an adept guitar player*
capable EG *a very capable speaker*
competent EG *a competent civil servant*
efficient EG *a team of efficient workers*
skilful EG *He is skilful at managing people.*
skilled EG *a network of amateur but highly skilled observers of wildlife*

WORD POWER

▶ **Antonym**
incompetent

---

❶ **profit** NOUN
money gained in business or trade
EG *The bank made pre-tax profits of $3.5 million.*
earnings EG *his earnings as an accountant*
proceeds EG *The proceeds from the concert will go to charity.*
revenue EG *tax revenues*
surplus EG *Japan's trade surplus*
takings EG *the pub's weekly takings*

WORD POWER

▶ **Antonym**
loss

---

❷ **profit** VERB
to gain or benefit from something
EG *They profited shamefully at the expense of my family.*
capitalize on EG *The rebels are trying to capitalize on the public's discontent.*
exploit EG *They are trying to exploit the troubles to their advantage.*
make the most of EG *Happiness is the ability to make the most of what*

a
b
c
d
e
f
g
h
i
j
k
l
m
n
o
p
q
r
s
t
u
v
w
x
y
z

A
B
C
D
E
F
G
H
I
J
K
L
M
N
O
P
Q
R
S
T
U
V
W
X
Y
Z

you have.
take advantage of EG *She took advantage of him even after their divorce.*

❶ **programme** NOUN
a planned series of events
EG *a programme of official engagements*
agenda EG *This is sure to be an item on the agenda again next week.*
schedule EG *We both have such hectic schedules.*
timetable EG *We've finally managed to agree on a timetable for formal talks.*

❷ **programme** NOUN
a broadcast on radio or television
EG *local news programmes*
broadcast EG *a broadcast by the President*
show EG *my favourite TV show*

❶ **progress** NOUN
improvement or development
EG *progress in the fight against cancer*
advance EG *dramatic advances in road safety*
breakthrough EG *a breakthrough in their research*
headway EG *The police are making little headway in the investigation.*
improvement EG *considerable room for improvement in facilities for patients*

❷ **progress** VERB
to become more advanced or skilful
EG *His reading is progressing well.*
advance EG *Japan has advanced from a rural society to an industrial power.*
blossom EG *In just a few years it has blossomed into an international event.*
develop EG *workshops designed to develop acting skills*
improve EG *Their French has improved enormously.*

prohibit VERB
to forbid something or make it illegal
EG *a law which prohibited trading on Sundays*
ban EG *The country will ban smoking in all offices this year.*
forbid EG *The country's constitution forbids the military use of nuclear energy.*
outlaw EG *In 1975 gambling was outlawed.*
prevent EG *Residents may be prevented from leaving the islands.*

WORD POWER

▶ **Antonym**
allow

❶ **prominent** ADJECTIVE
important
EG *the children of very prominent or successful parents*
eminent EG *an eminent scientist*
famous EG *England's most famous modern artist*
important EG *an important figure in the media*
notable EG *the notable linguist, Henriette Walter*
noted EG *a noted Hebrew scholar*
renowned EG *Sir William Crookes, the renowned chemist*
well-known EG *He liked to surround himself with well-known people.*

❷ **prominent** ADJECTIVE
very noticeable, or sticking out a long way
EG *a prominent feature of the landscape*
conspicuous EG *a conspicuous landmark*
eye-catching EG *I outlined it in black to make it more eye-catching.*
jutting EG *a jutting chin*
noticeable EG *Squeezing spots only makes them more noticeable.*
obvious EG *His cultural roots are most obvious in his poetry.*

pronounced EG *The exhibition has a pronounced Scottish theme.*
striking EG *a striking aspect of these statistics*

WORD POWER
▷ **Synonyms**
salient

promiscuous ADJECTIVE
having many casual sexual relationships
EG *a promiscuous teenager*
loose EG *If you wear a short skirt in here you're considered a loose woman.*
wanton EG *A woman with many sexual partners is still considered wanton.*

WORD POWER
▷ **Synonyms**
libertine
licentious
of easy virtue

❶ **promise** VERB
to say that you will definitely do or not do something
EG *I promise not to be back too late.*
assure EG *She assured me that she would deal with the problem.*
give your word EG *He had given us his word he would join the club.*
guarantee EG *Most countries guarantee the right to free education.*
pledge EG *They have pledged to support the opposition.*
vow EG *I vowed that someday I would return to live in Europe.*

❷ **promise** VERB
to show signs of
EG *This promised to be a very long night.*
hint at EG *One finding hints at support for this theory.*
indicate EG *His early work indicates talent.*

show signs of EG *Already she shows signs of beauty.*

WORD POWER
▷ **Synonyms**
augur
bespeak
betoken
bid fair

❸ **promise** NOUN
an undertaking to do or not do something
EG *If you make a promise, you should keep it.*
assurance EG *He gave written assurance that he would start work at once.*
guarantee EG *They can give no guarantee that they will fulfil their obligations.*
pledge EG *a pledge to step up cooperation between the two countries*
undertaking EG *an undertaking that he would be a responsible parent*
vow EG *I kept my marriage vows.*

❶ **promote** VERB
to encourage the progress or success of something
EG *All attempts to promote a ceasefire have failed.*
back EG *She backed the new initiative enthusiastically.*
support EG *He thanked everyone who had supported the strike.*

❷ **promote** VERB
to encourage the sale of a product by advertising
EG *She's in Europe promoting her new film.*
advertise EG *She is contracted to advertise their beauty products.*
plug INFORMAL EG *He was on the show to plug his latest film.*
publicize EG *I was publicizing the film in London.*

a b c d e f g h i j k l m n o p q r s t u v w x y z

A B C D E F G H I J K L M N O P Q R S T U V W X Y Z

❸ promote VERB
to raise someone to a higher rank or position
EG *He has been promoted twice in two years.*
elevate EG *He was elevated to the post of Prime Minister.*
upgrade EG *He was upgraded to supervisor.*

❶ prompt VERB
to make someone decide to do something
EG *Falling rates of pay have prompted consumers to stop buying new cars.*
cause EG *What caused you to change your mind?*
induce EG *Many teachers were induced to take early retirement.*
inspire EG *These herbs will inspire you to try out all sorts of dishes.*
motivate EG *How do you motivate people to work hard?*
spur EG *Is it the money that spurs these firefighters to risk their lives?*

❷ prompt VERB
to encourage someone to say something
EG *"What was that you were saying about a guided tour?" he prompted her.*
coax EG *"Tell us what happened next," he coaxed me.*
remind EG *"You stopped in the middle of your story," I reminded mother.*

❸ prompt ADVERB
exactly at the time mentioned
EG *The invitation specifies eight o'clock prompt.*
exactly EG *He arrived at exactly five o'clock.*
on the dot EG *At nine o'clock on the dot, they have breakfast.*
precisely EG *The meeting began at precisely 4.00 pm.*
sharp EG *She planned to get up at 8.00 sharp.*

❹ prompt ADJECTIVE
done without any delay
EG *a serious condition which needs prompt treatment*
immediate EG *These incidents had an immediate effect.*
instant EG *He took an instant dislike to this woman.*
instantaneous EG *This would result in his instantaneous dismissal.*
quick EG *hoping for a quick end to the dispute*
rapid EG *their rapid response to the situation*
swift EG *make a swift decision*

❶ prone ADJECTIVE
having a tendency to be affected by or do something
EG *She is prone to depression.*
disposed EG *I might have been disposed to like him in other circumstances.*
given EG *I am not very given to emotional displays.*
inclined EG *Nobody felt inclined to argue with Smith.*
liable EG *equipment that is liable to break*
susceptible EG *She's very susceptible to colds and flu.*

❷ prone ADJECTIVE
lying flat and face downwards
EG *We were lying prone on the grass.*
face down EG *He was lying face down on his bed.*
prostrate EG *The injured jockey lay prostrate on the ground.*

proof NOUN
evidence that confirms that something is true or exists
EG *You have to have proof of residence in the state of Texas.*
confirmation EG *further confirmation that house prices are no longer falling*
evidence EG *To date there is no evidence to support this theory.*

testimony EG *His testimony was an important element of the prosecution case.*
verification EG *verification of her story*

WORD POWER

▷ **Synonyms**
authentication
certification
corroboration
substantiation

❶ proper ADJECTIVE
correct or most suitable
EG *the proper course of action*
appropriate EG *a smart outfit appropriate to the job*
apt EG *an apt title for the book*
correct EG *the correct way to do things*
fitting EG *His address was a fitting end to a bitter campaign.*
right EG *He's the right man for the job.*
suitable EG *She had no other dress suitable for the occasion.*

WORD POWER

▶ **Antonym**
improper

❷ proper ADJECTIVE
accepted or conventional
EG *She wanted a proper wedding.*
accepted EG *the accepted way of doing things*
conventional EG *conventional surgical methods*
orthodox EG *orthodox police methods*

❶ property NOUN
the things that belong to someone
EG *her personal property*
assets EG *The company has assets of 3.5 billion francs.*
belongings EG *I collected my belongings and left.*
effects EG *After the funeral he sorted his father's personal effects.*

estate EG *His estate was valued at $150,000.*
possessions EG *People had lost their homes and all their possessions.*

❷ property NOUN
a characteristic or quality
EG *Mint has powerful healing properties.*
attribute EG *a normal attribute of human behaviour*
characteristic EG *their physical characteristics*
feature EG *a feature of the local culture*
hallmark EG *The killing had the hallmarks of a professional assassination.*
quality EG *mature people with leadership qualities*
trait EG *Creativity is a human trait.*

proportion NOUN
part of an amount or group
EG *a tiny proportion of the population*
percentage EG *It has a high percentage of protein.*
quota EG *Britain's fishing quota has been cut.*
segment EG *a fast-growing segment of the market*
share EG *I pay a share of the phone and gas bills.*

prospect NOUN
expectation or something anticipated
EG *There was no prospect of going home.*
expectation EG *The hotel was being renovated in expectation of a tourist boom.*
hope EG *There is little hope of improvement now.*
outlook EG *Officials say the outlook for next year is gloomy.*
promise EG *New Year brought the promise of better things to come.*

protect VERB
to prevent someone or something

A
B
C
D
E
F
G
H
I
J
K
L
M
N
O
P
Q
R
S
T
U
V
W
X
Y
Z

from being harmed
EG *Cash dispensers are protected by thick steel and glass.*
defend EG *I had to defend myself against the attack.*
guard EG *Soldiers guarded homes near the airport.*
safeguard EG *action to safeguard the ozone layer*
shelter EG *a wooden house, sheltered by a low pointed roof*
shield EG *He shielded his head from the sun with a newspaper.*

protection NOUN
something that protects
EG *a diet believed to offer protection against some cancers*
barrier EG *a flood barrier*
buffer EG *Keep savings as a buffer against unexpected cash needs.*
cover EG *air cover for ground operations*
safeguard EG *a safeguard against weeds*
shelter EG *an air-raid shelter*

❶ protest VERB
to disagree with someone or object to something
EG *She protested that she was a patriot, not a traitor.*
complain EG *People always complain that the big banks are unhelpful.*
disagree EG *I disagree with the drug laws in general.*
disapprove EG *Her mother disapproved of her working in a pub.*
object EG *We objected strongly but were outvoted.*
oppose EG *Many parents oppose bilingual education in schools.*

WORD POWER
▷ **Synonyms**
demur
expostulate
remonstrate

❷ protest NOUN
a strong objection
EG *The council has ignored their protests by backing the scheme.*
complaint EG *the way that banks deal with complaints*
objection EG *I questioned the logic of his objections.*
outcry EG *The incident caused an international outcry.*

proud ADJECTIVE
feeling pleasure or satisfaction
EG *I was proud of our players today.*
gratified EG *He was gratified by the audience's response.*
honoured EG *I am honoured to work with her.*
pleased EG *I was pleased to call him my friend.*

prove VERB
to provide evidence that something is definitely true
EG *History will prove him to have been right all along.*
ascertain EG *They had ascertained that he was not a spy.*
confirm EG *X-rays confirmed that he had not broken any bones.*
demonstrate EG *You have to demonstrate that you are reliable.*
establish EG *The autopsy established the cause of death.*
verify EG *I can verify that it takes about thirty seconds.*

WORD POWER
▷ **Synonyms**
authenticate
corroborate
evince
substantiate

▶ **Antonym**
disprove

provide VERB
to make something available to someone
EG *I'll be glad to provide a copy of this.*

contribute EG *NATO agreed to contribute troops and equipment.*
equip EG *proposals to equip all officers with body armour*
furnish EG *They'll be able to furnish you with the rest of the details.*
outfit EG *They outfitted him with artificial legs.*
supply EG *the blood vessels supplying oxygen to the brain*

❶ **provoke** VERB
to try to make someone angry
EG *I didn't want to do anything to provoke him.*
anger EG *It's important not to anger her.*
annoy EG *You're just trying to annoy me.*
enrage EG *He enraged the government by going back on the agreement.*
goad EG *My little brother was always goading me.*
insult EG *I didn't mean to insult you.*
irritate EG *If you go on irritating that dog, it'll bite you.*
tease EG *I'm sorry, I shouldn't tease you like that.*

❷ **provoke** VERB
to cause an unpleasant reaction
EG *His comments have provoked a shocked reaction.*
cause EG *These policies are likely to cause problems.*
evoke EG *The programme has evoked a storm of protest.*
produce EG *The decision produced a furious reaction among fans.*
prompt EG *The allegations prompted an indignant response from the accused.*
rouse EG *This roused a feeling of rebellion in him.*
set off EG *The arrival of the supply van set off a minor riot among waiting villagers.*
spark off EG *a political crisis sparked off by religious violence*

pry VERB
to try to find out about someone else's private business
EG *We do not want people prying into our business.*
interfere EG *I wish everyone would stop interfering and just leave me alone.*
intrude EG *The press were intruding into my personal life.*
poke your nose in INFORMAL EG *Who asked you to poke your nose in?*
poke your nose into INFORMAL
eg *strangers who poke their noses into our affairs*
snoop INFORMAL EG *He was snooping around Kim's hotel room.*

pub NOUN
a place where alcoholic drinks are served
EG *He goes to the pub most nights.*
bar BRITISH EG *He works in a bar.*
boozer BRITISH, AUSTRALIAN, AND NEW ZEALAND; INFORMAL EG *the local boozer*
inn EG *a village inn*
lounge EG *the hotel lounge*
public house EG *a robbery at a public house in New Milton*
saloon EG *a Wild West saloon*
tavern EG *an old country tavern*

❶ **public** NOUN
people in general
EG *the public's confidence in the government*
masses EG *a quest to bring the Internet to the masses*
nation EG *The President spoke to the nation.*
people EG *the will of the people*
populace EG *a large proportion of the populace*
society EG *a menace to society*

❷ **public** ADJECTIVE
relating to people in general
EG *public support for the idea*
civic EG *a sense of civic pride*
general EG *The project should raise*

a b c d e f g h i j k l m n o p q r s t u v w x y z

general awareness about bullying.
popular EG *Popular anger has been expressed in demonstrations.*
universal EG *the universal outrage at the deaths*

❸ public ADJECTIVE
provided for everyone to use or open to anyone
EG *public transport*
communal EG *a communal dining room*
community EG *a village community centre*
open to the public EG *Part of the castle is now open to the public.*
universal EG *universal health care*

WORD POWER
▶ **Antonym**
private

publicity NOUN
information or advertisements about an item or event
EG *government publicity campaigns*
advertising EG *tobacco advertising in women's magazines*
plug INFORMAL EG *The whole interview was an unashamed plug for her new book.*
promotion EG *They've spent a lot of money on advertising and promotion.*

publicize VERB
to advertise something or make it widely known
EG *The author appeared on TV to publicize her book.*
advertise EG *The product has been much advertised in specialist magazines.*
plug INFORMAL EG *another celebrity plugging their latest book*
promote EG *a tour to promote his second solo album*

publish VERB
to make a piece of writing available for reading
EG *We publish a range of titles.*

bring out EG *The newspapers all brought out special editions.*
print EG *a letter printed in the Times yesterday*
put out EG *a statement put out by the Iraqi news agency*

puke VERB; INFORMAL
to vomit
EG *They got drunk and puked.*
be sick EG *She got up and was sick in the handbasin.*
chunder AUSTRALIAN AND NEW ZEALAND; SLANG EG *the time you chundered in the taxi*
spew INFORMAL EG *He's really drunk. I hope he doesn't start spewing.*
throw up INFORMAL EG *She threw up after reading reports of the trial.*
vomit EG *Anything containing cow's milk made him vomit.*

❶ pull VERB
to draw an object towards you
EG *a wooden plough pulled by oxen*
drag EG *He dragged his chair towards the table.*
draw EG *He drew his chair nearer the fire.*
haul EG *A crane was used to haul the car out of the stream.*
tow EG *They threatened to tow away my van.*
tug EG *She kicked him, tugging his thick hair.*
yank EG *She yanked open the drawer.*

WORD POWER
▶ **Antonym**
push

❷ pull NOUN
the attraction or influence of something
EG *The pull of Mexico was too strong.*
attraction EG *The attraction of Hollywood began to pall.*
lure EG *The lure of rural life is as strong as ever.*

magnetism EG *the sheer magnetism of his presence*

punctual ADJECTIVE
arriving or leaving at the correct time
EG *The most punctual airline last year was Swissair.*
in good time EG *It is now 5am and we are in good time.*
on time EG *I'm generally early or on time for an appointment.*
prompt EG *We expect you to be prompt for all your classes.*

punctuation NOUN

Punctuation marks
apostrophe
asterisk
bracket
bullet point
colon
comma
dash
exclamation mark
full stop
hyphen
question mark
semicolon
speech marks *or* quotation marks

punish VERB
to make someone suffer a penalty for some misbehaviour
EG *I got punished for insolence.*
discipline EG *He was disciplined by his company but not dismissed.*
penalize EG *Bad teaching is not penalized in a formal way.*
rap someone's knuckles EG *The company got its knuckles rapped for this advertisement.*
sentence EG *He has admitted the charge and will be sentenced later.*
throw the book at EG *The football authorities seem certain to throw the book at him.*

punishment NOUN
a penalty for a crime or offence
EG *The punishment must always fit the crime.*
penalty EG *One of those arrested could face the death penalty.*
retribution EG *He didn't want any further involvement for fear of retribution.*

> *WORD POWER*
>
> ▷ **Synonyms**
> chastening
> chastisement
> just deserts

puny ADJECTIVE
very small and weak
EG *He's always been a puny lad.*
feeble EG *He was old and feeble.*
frail EG *She lay in bed looking frail.*
sickly EG *He has been a sickly child.*
skinny EG *a skinny little boy*
weak EG *His arms and legs were weak.*

pupil NOUN
a student taught at a school
EG *She is a model pupil.*
scholar SOUTH AFRICAN EG *a bunch of rowdy scholars*
schoolboy *or* **schoolgirl** EG *a group of ten-year-old schoolboys*
schoolchild EG *The bus was packed with schoolchildren.*
student EG *The students are sorted into three ability groups.*

➊ pure ADJECTIVE
clean and free from harmful substances
EG *The water is pure enough to drink.*
clean EG *Tiled kitchen floors are easy to keep clean.*
germ-free EG *chlorine gas used to keep water germ-free*
pasteurized EG *The milk is pasteurized to kill bacteria.*
spotless EG *She kept the kitchen spotless.*
sterilized EG *sterilized surgical equipment*

a b c d e f g h i j k l m n o p q r s t u v w x y z

WORD POWER

▷ **Synonyms**
unadulterated
unblemished
uncontaminated
unpolluted
untainted

▶ **Antonym**
impure

---

❷ **pure** ADJECTIVE
complete and total
EG *a matter of pure luck*
absolute EG *You're talking absolute nonsense.*
complete EG *complete and utter rubbish*
outright EG *an outright rejection of the deal*
sheer EG *acts of sheer desperation*
unmitigated EG *Last year's crop was an unmitigated disaster.*
utter EG *This, of course, is utter nonsense.*

purple NOUN OR ADJECTIVE

Shades of purple
amethyst
aubergine
gentian
heather
heliotrope
indigo
lavender
lilac
magenta
mauve
mulberry
plum
puce
royal purple
violet

❶ **purpose** NOUN
the reason for something
EG *What is the purpose of this meeting?*
aim EG *the aim of the policy*

function EG *Their main function is to raise capital for industry.*
intention EG *The intention of the scheme is to encourage faster sales.*
object EG *the object of the exercise*
point EG *I don't see the point of it.*
reason EG *What is the real reason for the delay?*

❷ **purpose** on purpose ADVERB
deliberately
EG *Did you do that on purpose?*
by design EG *The pair met often - at first by chance but later by design.*
deliberately EG *It looks as if the fire was started deliberately.*
intentionally EG *I've never hurt anyone intentionally.*
knowingly EG *He said that he'd never knowingly taken illegal drugs.*
purposely EG *They are purposely withholding information.*

❶ **push** VERB
to apply force to something in order to move it
EG *She pushed the door open.*
press EG *He pressed his back against the door.*
ram EG *He rammed the key into the lock.*
shove EG *He shoved her aside.*
thrust EG *They thrust him into the back of the jeep.*

WORD POWER

▶ **Antonym**
pull

---

❷ **push** VERB
to persuade someone into doing something
EG *His mother pushed him into auditioning for a part.*
encourage EG *She encouraged me to stick to the diet.*
persuade EG *They persuaded him to moderate his views.*
press EG *Trade unions are pressing him to stand firm.*

A B C D E F G H I J K L M N O P Q R S T U V W X Y Z

urge EG *He had urged her to come to Ireland.*

pushy ADJECTIVE; INFORMAL
unpleasantly forceful and determined
EG *a confident and pushy young woman*
aggressive EG *a very aggressive business executive*
ambitious EG *You have to be ambitious to make it in this business.*
assertive EG *Women have become more assertive over the last ten years.*
bossy EG *She remembers being a rather bossy little girl.*
forceful EG *Sarah is notorious for her forceful and quarrelsome nature.*
obtrusive EG *"You are rude and obtrusive, Mr Smith," said Tommy.*

❶ put VERB
to place something somewhere
EG *She put the photograph on the desk.*
deposit EG *On his way out he deposited a glass in front of me.*
lay EG *Lay a sheet of newspaper on the floor.*
place EG *He placed it in the inside pocket of his jacket.*
position EG *Plants were carefully positioned in the alcove.*
rest EG *He rested his arms on the back of the chair.*

❷ put VERB
to express something
EG *I think you put that very well.*
phrase EG *I would have phrased it quite differently.*
word EG *You misinterpreted his letter, or else he worded it poorly.*

❶ put down VERB
to criticize someone and make them appear foolish
EG *Racist jokes come from wanting to put down other people.*
belittle EG *She's always belittling her husband in public.*

criticize EG *She rarely criticized any of her children.*
find fault EG *I wish you wouldn't find fault with me in front of the kids.*
humiliate EG *His teacher continually humiliates him.*

❷ put down VERB
to kill an animal that is ill or dangerous
EG *Magistrates ordered the dog to be put down immediately.*
destroy EG *The horse had to be destroyed.*
kill EG *Animals should be killed humanely.*
put out of its misery EG *The bird was so badly injured I decided to put it out of its misery.*
put to sleep EG *Take the dog to the vet's and have her put to sleep.*

put off VERB
to delay something
EG *Ministers have put off making a decision until next month.*
defer EG *Customers often defer payment for as long as possible.*
delay EG *She wants to delay the wedding.*
postpone EG *The visit has been postponed indefinitely.*
put back EG *The news conference has been put back a couple of hours.*
put on ice EG *The decision has been put on ice until October.*
reschedule EG *Since I'll be away, I'd like to reschedule the meeting.*

put up with VERB
to tolerate something disagreeable
EG *They won't put up with a return to the bad old days.*
abide EG *I can't abide arrogant people.*
bear EG *He can't bear to talk about it.*
stand EG *She cannot stand her boss.*
stand for EG *We won't stand for it any more.*
stomach EG *He could not stomach*

A
B
C
D
E
F
G
H
I
J
K
L
M
N
O
P
Q
R
S
T
U
V
W
X
Y
Z

violence.

tolerate EG *She can no longer tolerate the position she is in.*

WORD POWER

▷ **Synonyms**
brook
countenance

❶ **puzzle** VERB
to perplex and confuse
EG *There was something about her that puzzled me.*

baffle EG *An apple tree producing square fruit is baffling experts.*

bewilder EG *His silence bewildered her.*

confuse EG *German politics surprised and confused him.*

mystify EG *The audience were mystified by the plot.*

stump EG *I was stumped by an unexpected question.*

WORD POWER

▷ **Synonyms**
confound
flummox
nonplus
perplex

❷ **puzzle** NOUN
a game or question that requires a lot of thought to solve
EG *a crossword puzzle*

brain-teaser INFORMAL EG *It took me ages to solve that brain-teaser.*

poser EG *Here is a little poser for you.*

problem EG *a mathematical problem*

riddle EG *See if you can answer this riddle.*

Qq

① qualification NOUN
a skill or achievement
EG *His qualifications are impressive.*
ability EG *a man of considerable abilities*
accomplishment EG *Carl was proud of his son's accomplishments.*
achievement EG *the highest academic achievement*
capability EG *Her capabilities were not fully appreciated.*
quality EG *Colley's leadership qualities*
skill EG *a skill you can use*

> WORD POWER
>
> ▷ Synonyms
> attribute
> endowment

② qualification NOUN
something added to make a statement less strong
EG *The argument is not true without qualification.*
condition EG *You can make any conditions you like.*
exception EG *a major exception to this general argument*
modification EG *to consider modifications to his proposal*
reservation EG *men whose work I admire without reservation*

qualify VERB
to pass the tests necessary for an activity
EG *I qualified as a doctor 30 years ago.*
get certified EG *They wanted to get certified as divers.*
become licensed EG *You can only become licensed by doing an accredited course.*
gain qualifications EG *the opportunity to gain medical qualifications*
graduate EG *She graduated as a physiotherapist in 1960.*

① quality NOUN
the measure of how good something is
EG *The quality of food is very poor.*
calibre EG *a man of your calibre*
distinction EG *a chef of great distinction*
grade EG *high grade meat and poultry*
merit EG *a work of real merit*
value EG *He set a high value upon their friendship.*
worth EG *a person's true worth*

② quality NOUN
a characteristic of something
EG *These qualities are essential for success.*
aspect EG *every aspect of our lives*
characteristic EG *their physical characteristics*
feature EG *the most striking feature of his work*
mark EG *the mark of a great composer*
property EG *the magnetic properties of iron*
trait EG *the young Ms Rankine's personality traits*

> WORD POWER
>
> ▷ Synonyms
> attribute
> peculiarity

① quantity NOUN
an amount you can measure or count
EG *a large quantity of alcohol*
amount EG *a small amount of mayonnaise*
number EG *There are a limited number of seats available.*
part EG *the greater part of his wealth*
sum EG *a large sum of money*

a b c d e f g h i j k l m n o p q r s t u v w x y z

A B C D E F G H I J K L M N O P Q R S T U V W X Y Z

WORD POWER

▷ **Synonyms**
portion
quota

❷ quantity NOUN
the amount of something that there
is
EG *emphasis on quality rather than
quantity*
extent EG *the extent of the damage*
measure EG *The government has
had a fair measure of success.*
size EG *He gauged the size of the
audience.*
volume EG *the sheer volume of traffic
and accidents*

WORD POWER

▷ **Synonyms**
bulk
expanse
magnitude

❶ quarrel NOUN
an angry argument
EG *I had a terrible quarrel with my
brother.*
argument EG *an argument about
money*
disagreement EG *My instructor and I
had a brief disagreement.*
dispute EG *Brand eavesdropped on
the petty dispute.*
feud EG *a two-year feud between
neighbours*
fight EG *It was a silly fight about
where we parked the car.*
row EG *Maxine and I had a terrible
row.*
squabble EG *minor squabbles about
phone bills*

WORD POWER

▷ **Synonyms**
altercation
fracas
fray

❷ quarrel VERB
to have an angry argument
EG *My brother quarrelled with my
father.*
argue EG *They were still arguing later.*
bicker EG *They bickered endlessly
over procedure.*
clash EG *She had clashed with Doyle
in the past.*
fall out INFORMAL EG *Mum and I used
to fall out a lot.*
fight EG *The couple often fought with
their son.*
row EG *He had rowed with his
girlfriend.*
squabble EG *The children were
squabbling over the remote control.*

queasy ADJECTIVE
feeling slightly sick
EG *He already felt queasy.*
ill EG *I was feeling ill.*
nauseous EG *The medication may
make you feel nauseous.*
queer EG *Twenty minutes later, he
began to feel queer.*
sick EG *The very thought of food
made him feel sick.*
unwell EG *He felt unwell this
afternoon.*

❶ query NOUN
a question
EG *If you have any queries, please
contact us.*
inquiry EG *I'll be happy to answer all
your inquiries, if I can.*
question EG *The President refused to
answer further questions on the
subject.*

WORD POWER

▶ **Antonym**
response

❷ query VERB
to question something because it
seems wrong
EG *No one queried my decision.*
challenge EG *The move was*

challenged by two countries.
dispute EG *He disputed the allegations.*
object to EG *A lot of people objected to the plan.*
question EG *It never occurred to me to question the doctor's decisions.*

❶ question NOUN
a problem that needs to be discussed
EG *Can we get back to the question of the car?*
issue EG *What is your view on this issue?*
motion EG *The conference is now debating the motion.*
point EG *There is another point to consider.*
subject EG *He raised the subject of money.*
topic EG *the topic of where to go on holiday*

❷ question VERB
to ask someone questions
EG *A man is being questioned by police.*
examine EG *Lawyers examined the witnesses.*
interrogate EG *I interrogated everyone even slightly involved.*
probe EG *tabloid journalists probing us for details*
quiz EG *She quizzed me quite closely for a while.*

WORD POWER
▷ **Synonyms**
cross-examine
interview
investigate

▶ **Antonym**
answer

❸ question VERB
to express doubts about something
EG *He never stopped questioning his own beliefs.*
challenge EG *Rose convincingly*

challenged the story.
dispute EG *Nobody disputed that Davey was clever.*
distrust EG *I distrusted my ability to keep quiet.*
doubt EG *Nobody doubted his sincerity.*
query EG *No one queried my decision.*
suspect EG *Do we suspect the motives of our friends?*

❶ quick ADJECTIVE
moving with great speed
EG *You'll have to be quick to catch the flight.*
brisk EG *a brisk walk*
fast EG *a very fast driver*
hasty EG *He spoke in a hasty, nervous way.*
rapid EG *a rapid rise through the company*
speedy EG *a speedy recovery*
swift EG *She is as swift as an arrow.*

WORD POWER
▷ **Synonyms**
express
headlong

▶ **Antonym**
slow

❷ quick ADJECTIVE
lasting only a short time
EG *a quick chat*
brief EG *a brief meeting*
cursory EG *a cursory glance inside the van*
hasty EG *a hasty meal of bread and soup*
hurried EG *He ate a hurried breakfast.*
perfunctory EG *With a perfunctory smile, she walked past Jessica.*

WORD POWER
▶ **Antonym**
long

❸ quick ADJECTIVE
happening without any delay

a b c d e f g h i j k l m n o p q r s t u v w x y z

EG *a quick response*
hasty EG *This is no hasty decision.*
prompt EG *Prompt action is needed.*
sudden EG *this week's sudden cold snap*

quickly ADVERB
with great speed
EG *Stop me if I'm speaking too quickly.*
fast EG *How fast were you driving?*
hastily EG *sheltering in hastily erected tents*
hurriedly EG *students hurriedly taking notes*
rapidly EG *moving rapidly across the field*
speedily EG *She speedily recovered herself.*
swiftly EG *They had to act swiftly to save him.*

WORD POWER

▶ **Antonym**
slowly

❶ **quiet** ADJECTIVE
making very little noise
EG *The children were quiet and contented.*
hushed EG *Tales were exchanged in hushed tones.*
inaudible EG *a tiny, almost inaudible squeak*
low EG *I spoke in a low voice to Sullivan.*
silent EG *He could speak no English and was silent.*
soft EG *There was some soft music playing.*

WORD POWER

▷ **Synonyms**
noiseless
soundless

▶ **Antonym**
noisy

❷ **quiet** ADJECTIVE
peaceful and calm

EG *a quiet evening at home*
calm EG *The city seems relatively calm today.*
mild EG *The night was mild.*
peaceful EG *a peaceful old house*
restful EG *a restful scene*
serene EG *the beautiful, serene park*
tranquil EG *a tranquil lake*

WORD POWER

▷ **Synonyms**
motionless
placid
untroubled

❸ **quiet** NOUN
silence or lack of noise
EG *The teacher called for quiet.*
calmness EG *the calmness of this area*
peace EG *I enjoy peace and quiet.*
serenity EG *the peace and serenity of a tropical sunset*
silence EG *There was a silence around the table.*
stillness EG *the stillness of the summer night*
tranquillity EG *the tranquillity of village life*

WORD POWER

▶ **Antonym**
noise

quit VERB
to leave a place or stop doing something
EG *Leigh quit his job as a salesman.*
discontinue EG *Do not discontinue the treatment without seeing your doctor.*
give up EG *She gave up smoking last year.*
leave EG *He left school with no qualifications.*
resign EG *Scott resigned from the firm.*
retire EG *Littlejohn was forced to retire from the race.*

stop EG *I stopped working last year to have a baby.*

WORD POWER

▷ **Synonyms**
abandon
cease

---

❶ **quite** ADVERB
fairly but not very
EG *He is quite old.*
fairly EG *Both ships are fairly new.*
moderately EG *a moderately attractive man*
rather EG *I made some rather bad mistakes.*
reasonably EG *I can dance reasonably well.*
somewhat EG *He's somewhat deaf.*

❷ **quite** ADVERB
completely and totally
EG *Jane lay quite still.*
absolutely EG *I absolutely refuse to get married.*
completely EG *something completely different*

entirely EG *an entirely new approach*
fully EG *He has still not fully recovered.*
perfectly EG *They are perfectly safe to eat.*
totally EG *The fire totally destroyed the house.*

WORD POWER

▷ **Synonyms**
precisely
wholly

---

quote VERB
to repeat the exact words someone has said
EG *She quoted a great line from Shakespeare.*
cite EG *She cites a favourite poem by George Herbert.*
extract EG *This material has been extracted from the handbook.*
recite EG *They recited poetry to one another.*
repeat EG *Could you repeat the whole interview word for word?*

a
b
c
d
e
f
g
h
i
j
k
l
m
n
o
p
q
r
s
t
u
v
w
x
y
z

Rr

❶ race NOUN
a group of human beings with similar physical characteristics
EG *Discrimination on the grounds of race is illegal.*
ethnic group EG *Ethnic group and nationality are often different.*
nation EG *a mature and cultured nation*
people EG *an address to the American people*

❷ race VERB
to move very quickly
EG *Her heart raced uncontrollably.*
dash EG *He dashed upstairs.*
fly EG *I must fly or I'll miss my train.*
hurry EG *They hurried down the street.*
run EG *The gunmen escaped by running into the woods.*
speed EG *speeding along as fast as I could*
tear EG *The door flew open and she tore into the room.*

❶ racket NOUN
a lot of noise
EG *The racket went on past midnight.*
clamour EG *She could hear a clamour in the road.*
commotion EG *He heard a commotion outside.*
din EG *make themselves heard over the din of the crowd*
hubbub EG *His voice was drowned out by the hubbub of the fans.*
noise EG *There was too much noise in the room.*
row EG *"Whatever is that row?" she demanded.*
rumpus EG *There was such a rumpus, she had to shout to make herself heard.*

❷ racket NOUN
an illegal way of making money
EG *a drugs racket*
enterprise EG *a money-laundering enterprise*
fraud EG *tax frauds*
scheme EG *a quick money-making scheme*

❶ rage NOUN
a feeling of very strong anger
EG *trembling with rage*
anger EG *She felt deep anger at what he had said.*
frenzy EG *Their behaviour drove her into a frenzy.*
fury EG *Her face was distorted with fury and pain.*
wrath EG *He incurred the wrath of the referee.*

❷ rage VERB
to be angry or speak angrily about something
EG *He was raging at their lack of response.*
be furious EG *He is furious at the way his wife has been treated.*
fume EG *I was still fuming over her remark.*
lose your temper EG *They had never seen me lose my temper before.*
rave EG *She cried and raved for weeks.*
storm EG *"It's a disaster", he stormed.*

❸ rage VERB
to continue with great force
EG *The fire raged out of control.*
be at its height EG *when the storm was at its height*
rampage EG *a mob rampaging through the town*
storm EG *armies storming across the continent*

surge EG *The flood surged through the village.*

❶ raid VERB
to attack something by force
EG *Soldiers raided the capital.*
assault EG *Their stronghold was assaulted by pirates.*
attack EG *We are being attacked!*
break into EG *No-one saw them break into the warehouse.*
invade EG *The invading army took all their food supplies.*
plunder EG *plundering the homes of the inhabitants*

WORD POWER

▷ **Synonyms**
pillage
rifle
sack

❷ raid NOUN
an attack on something
EG *a bank raid*
attack EG *a surprise attack on the house*
break-in EG *The break-in occurred last night.*
foray EG *Guerillas made forays into the territory.*

WORD POWER

▷ **Synonyms**
incursion
sortie

❶ rain NOUN
water falling from the clouds
EG *A spot of rain fell on her hand.*
deluge EG *homes damaged in the deluge*
downpour EG *A two-day downpour swelled water levels.*
drizzle EG *The drizzle had stopped and the sun was shining.*
rainfall EG *four years of below average rainfall*
showers EG *bright spells followed by scattered showers*

❷ rain VERB
to fall from the sky in drops
EG *It rained the whole weekend.*
drizzle EG *It was starting to drizzle when I left.*
pour EG *We drove all the way in pouring rain.*
teem EG *It teemed the entire day.*

❶ raise VERB
to make something higher
EG *a drive to raise standards of literacy*
elevate EG *Emotional stress can elevate blood pressure.*
heave EG *He heaved his crippled leg into an easier position.*
hoist EG *He climbed on the roof to hoist the flag.*
lift EG *She lifted the last of her drink to her lips.*

WORD POWER

▶ **Antonym**
lower

❷ raise VERB
to look after children until they are grown up
EG *the house where she was raised*
bring up EG *She brought up four children single-handed.*
nurture EG *the best way to nurture a child to adulthood*
rear EG *He reared his sister's family as well as his own.*

❸ raise VERB
to mention or suggest something
EG *He had raised no objections at the time.*
advance EG *Some important ideas were advanced at the conference.*
bring up EG *I hesitate to bring up this matter with you, but I have no choice.*
broach EG *Eventually I broached the subject of her early life.*
introduce EG *always willing to introduce a new topic*
moot EG *The project was first mooted last year.*

a
b
c
d
e
f
g
h
i
j
k
l
m
n
o
p
q
r
s
t
u
v
w
x
y
z

A
B
C
D
E
F
G
H
I
J
K
L
M
N
O
P
Q
R
S
T
U
V
W
X
Y
Z

suggest EG *one possibility that might be suggested*

❶ ramble NOUN
a long walk in the countryside
EG *They went for a ramble through the woods.*
excursion EG *They organized an excursion into the hills.*
hike EG *a long hike along the valley floor*
stroll EG *The next day we took a stroll along the river bank.*
walk EG *We often go for walks in the country.*

❷ ramble VERB
to go for a long walk
EG *freedom to ramble across the moors*
amble EG *ambling along a country lane*
stray EG *You mustn't stray across the border.*
stroll EG *whistling as he strolled along the road*
walk EG *We finished the evening by walking along the beach.*
wander EG *He loved to wander in the woods.*

WORD POWER

▷ **Synonyms**
perambulate
rove

❸ ramble VERB
to talk in a confused way
EG *He started rambling and repeating himself.*
babble EG *She babbled on and on about the visitors.*
chatter EG *I was so nervous that I chattered away like an idiot.*

❶ rampage VERB
to rush about angrily or violently
EG *children rampaging round the garden*
go berserk EG *The crowd went berserk at the sight of him.*

rage EG *His shop was stormed by a raging mob.*
run amok EG *He was arrested after running amok with a gun.*
run riot EG *The prisoners ran riot after the announcement.*

❷ rampage on the rampage
ADJECTIVE
rushing about in a wild and violent way
EG *a bull on the rampage*
amok EG *The gunman ran amok and killed several people.*
berserk EG *The fans went berserk and mobbed the stage.*
wild EG *They just went wild after he left.*

❶ random ADJECTIVE
not based on a definite plan
EG *random violence against innocent victims*
aimless EG *after several hours of aimless searching*
arbitrary EG *Arbitrary arrests and detention without trial were common.*
haphazard EG *He had never seen such a haphazard approach to writing.*
indiscriminate EG *the indiscriminate use of fertilisers*
spot EG *picked up in a spot check*

WORD POWER

▷ **Synonyms**
desultory
fortuitous
unpremeditated

❷ random at random ADVERB
without any definite plan
EG *chosen at random*
aimlessly EG *wandering around aimlessly for hours*
arbitrarily EG *The questions were chosen quite arbitrarily.*
haphazardly EG *The books were stacked haphazardly on the shelves.*
indiscriminately EG *This disease*

strikes indiscriminately.
randomly EG *a randomly selected sample*

WORD POWER

▷ **Synonyms**
adventitiously
unsystematically
willy-nilly

---

❶ **range** NOUN
the maximum limits of something
EG *Tactical nuclear weapons have shorter ranges.*
bounds EG *the bounds of good taste*
extent EG *the full extent of my knowledge*
field EG *The subject covers a very wide field.*
limits EG *outside the city limits*
province EG *This doesn't fall within our province.*
scope EG *He promised to widen the scope of their activities.*

❷ **range** NOUN
a number of different things of the same kind
EG *a wide range of colours*
assortment EG *There was a good assortment to choose from.*
class EG *Cars in this class are expensive.*
gamut EG *I experienced the whole gamut of emotions.*
selection EG *a wide selection of delicious meals*
series EG *a completely new model series*
variety EG *The shop stocks a variety of local craft products.*

❸ **range** VERB
to vary between two extremes
EG *goods ranging between the everyday and the exotic*
extend EG *The reclaimed land extends from here to the river.*
go EG *Their sizes go from very small to enormous.*

run EG *Accommodation runs from log cabins to high-standard hotels.*
stretch EG *with interests that stretched from chemicals to sugar*
vary EG *The cycle of sunspots varies between 8 to 15 years.*

❶ **rank** NOUN
someone's level in a group
EG *He rose to the rank of captain.*
class EG *relationships between social classes*
echelon EG *the upper echelons of society*
grade EG *Staff turnover is high among the junior grades.*
level EG *various levels of the judiciary system*
standing EG *a woman of wealth and social standing*
station EG *a humble station in life*
status EG *promoted to the status of foreman*

❷ **rank** NOUN
a row of people or things
EG *ranks of police in riot gear*
column EG *a column of figures*
file EG *They walked in single file to the top.*
line EG *He waited in a line of slow-moving vehicles.*
row EG *She lived in the middle of a row of pretty cottages.*

❸ **rank** ADJECTIVE
complete and absolute
EG *It was rank stupidity to go there alone.*
absolute EG *not intended for absolute beginners*
complete EG *her complete ignorance*
downright EG *That was just downright rudeness.*
sheer EG *his sheer stupidity*
unmitigated EG *an unmitigated villain*
utter EG *his utter disregard for other people*

A
B
C
D
E
F
G
H
I
J
K
L
M
N
O
P
Q
R
S
T
U
V
W
X
Y
Z

WORD POWER

▷ **Synonyms**
arrant
egregious

rare ADJECTIVE
not common or frequent
EG *a rare species of bird*
exceptional EG *in exceptional circumstances*
few EG *Genuine friends are few.*
scarce EG *Jobs are becoming increasingly scarce.*
sparse EG *Information about the tests is sparse.*
sporadic EG *occurring at only sporadic intervals*
uncommon EG *The disease is uncommon in younger women.*
unusual EG *an unusual variety but a very attractive one*

WORD POWER

▶ **Antonym**
common

❶ **rash** ADJECTIVE
acting in a hasty and foolish way
EG *It would be rash to act on such flimsy evidence.*
foolhardy EG *Some described his behaviour as foolhardy.*
hasty EG *This is no hasty decision.*
impetuous EG *As usual, he reacted in a heated and impetuous way.*
impulsive EG *He is too impulsive to take this responsibility.*
reckless EG *his reckless driving*

WORD POWER

▷ **Synonyms**
heedless
injudicious
unthinking

❷ **rash** NOUN
an irritated area on your skin
EG *I noticed a rash on my leg.*
eruption EG *an unpleasant skin eruption*
outbreak EG *an outbreak of blisters around his mouth*

❸ **rash** NOUN
a large number of events happening together
EG *a rash of strikes*
epidemic EG *A victim of the recent epidemic of shootings.*
flood EG *a flood of complaints about the programme*
plague EG *Last year there was a plague of burglaries.*
spate EG *a spate of attacks on horses*
wave EG *the current wave of violent attacks*

❶ **rate** NOUN
the speed or frequency of something
EG *appearing at the rate of one a week*
frequency EG *She phoned with increasing frequency.*
pace EG *at an accelerated pace*
speed EG *moving at the speed of light*
tempo EG *They wanted to speed up the tempo of change.*
velocity EG *changes in wind velocity*

❷ **rate** NOUN
the cost or charge for something
EG *phone calls at cheap rates*
charge EG *An annual charge will be made for this service.*
cost EG *a low-cost mortgage*
fee EG *The work will be invoiced at the usual fee.*
price EG *falling share prices*
tariff EG *How much you pay depends on your tariff.*

❸ **rate** VERB
to give an opinion of someone's qualities
EG *He was rated as one of the best.*
appraise EG *She gave me an appraising glance.*
class EG *classed as one of the top ten athletes*
consider EG *I considered myself to be*

quite good at maths.
count EG *That would be counted as wrong.*
rank EG *The hotel was ranked as one of the world's best.*
regard EG *a highly regarded member of staff*

WORD POWER

▷ **Synonyms**
adjudge
esteem
evaluate

rather ADVERB
to a certain extent
EG *We got along rather well.*
fairly EG *Both ships are fairly new.*
pretty INFORMAL EG *I'm pretty tired now.*
quite EG *The cottage looks quite ordinary from the road.*
relatively EG *I think I'm relatively easy to get on with.*
slightly EG *slightly startled by his sudden appearance*
somewhat EG *He said, somewhat unconvincingly, that he would pay.*

rational ADJECTIVE
using reason rather than emotion
EG *to arrive at a rational conclusion*
enlightened EG *enlightened companies who take a pragmatic view*
logical EG *There must be a logical explanation for it.*
reasonable EG *a perfectly reasonable decision*
sensible EG *The sensible thing is to leave them alone.*

❶ rave VERB
to talk in an uncontrolled way
EG *He started raving about being treated badly.*
babble EG *She babbled on and on about her plans.*
rage EG *He was raging at their lack of response.*

rant EG *She started ranting about her boss's attitude.*

❷ rave VERB; INFORMAL
to be enthusiastic about something
EG *She raved about the facilities there.*
be wild about INFORMAL EG *He was just wild about the play.*
enthuse EG *She enthused about the local architecture.*
gush EG *"It was brilliant", he gushed.*

❶ reach VERB
to arrive somewhere
EG *He did not stop until he reached the door.*
arrive at EG *to arrive at an erroneous conclusion*
attain EG *She worked hard to attain a state of calm.*
get as far as EG *If we get as far as the coast we will be quite satisfied.*
get to EG *You must get to the end before noon.*
make EG *They didn't think they would make the summit.*

❷ reach VERB
to extend as far as something
EG *Her cloak reached to the ground.*
extend to EG *The boundaries extend to the edge of the lake.*
go as far as EG *Try to make the ball go as far as the trees.*
touch EG *I could touch both walls with my arms extended.*

❸ reach VERB
to arrive at a certain stage or level
EG *Unemployment has reached record levels.*
arrive at EG *They planted a flag when they arrived at the top.*
attain EG *He was close to attaining his personal best.*
climb to EG *Attendance climbed to a record level this year.*
fall to EG *Profits are expected to fall to their lowest level.*
rise to EG *She rose rapidly to the top of her profession.*

❶ reaction NOUN
a person's response to something
EG *Reaction to the visit was mixed.*
acknowledgment EG *She made no acknowledgment of my question.*
answer EG *In answer to speculation in the press, she declared her interest.*
feedback EG *Continue to ask for feedback on your work.*
response EG *in response to a request from the members*

❷ reaction NOUN
a response to something unpopular
EG *a reaction against religious leaders*
backlash EG *the male backlash against feminism*
counterbalance EG *an organization set up as a counterbalance to the official group*

❶ read VERB
to look at something written
EG *I love to read in bed.*
glance at EG *He just glanced briefly at the article.*
look at EG *She was looking at the evening paper.*
pore over EG *poring over a dictionary*
scan EG *There's only time to scan through it quickly.*
study EG *I'll study the text more closely later.*

❷ read VERB
to understand what someone means
EG *as if he could read her thoughts*
comprehend EG *Her expression was difficult to comprehend.*
decipher EG *She was still no closer to deciphering the code.*
interpret EG *You have to interpret their gestures, too.*

❶ ready ADJECTIVE
prepared for action or use
EG *The plums are ready to eat now.*
organized EG *Everything is organized for the party tomorrow.*
prepared EG *He was prepared for a*

tough fight.
primed EG *The other side is primed for battle.*
ripe EG *Are those strawberries ripe yet?*
set EG *We'll be set to go in five minutes.*

❷ ready ADJECTIVE
willing to do something
EG *She was always ready to give interviews.*
agreeable EG *We can go ahead if you are agreeable.*
eager EG *Children are eager to learn.*
happy EG *always happy to help*
keen EG *He wasn't keen to get involved.*
willing EG *questions which they were not willing to answer*

WORD POWER
▷ **Synonyms**
minded
predisposed

❸ ready ADJECTIVE
easily produced or obtained
EG *ready cash*
accessible EG *The system should be accessible to everyone.*
available EG *Food is available round the clock.*
convenient EG *a convenient excuse*
handy EG *Keep a pencil and paper handy.*

❶ real ADJECTIVE
actually existing and not imagined
EG *You're dealing with real life now.*
actual EG *She was the actual basis for the leading character.*
authentic EG *containing authentic details of what happened*
concrete EG *I don't have any concrete evidence.*
factual EG *a factual account*
genuine EG *His worries about the future were genuine ones.*
legitimate EG *These are legitimate*

concerns.

tangible EG *I cannot see any tangible benefits in these changes.*

true EG *the true story of his life*

WORD POWER

▶ **Antonym**
imaginary

---

❷ **real** ADJECTIVE
genuine and not imitation
EG *Is that a real gun?*

authentic EG *an authentic French recipe*

bona fide EG *We are happy to donate to bona fide charities.*

dinkum AUSTRALIAN AND NEW ZEALAND; INFORMAL EG *a place which serves dinkum Aussie tucker*

genuine EG *It's a genuine Rembrandt, all right.*

honest EG *It was an honest attempt to set things right.*

sincere EG *His remorse was completely sincere, not just an act.*

rightful EG *the rightful heir to the throne*

true EG *He is a true believer in human rights.*

unaffected EG *her genuine and unaffected sympathy for the victims*

WORD POWER

▶ **Antonym**
fake

---

❶ **realistic** ADJECTIVE
accepting the true situation
EG *It's only realistic to admit that things will go wrong.*

down-to-earth EG *We welcomed her down-to-earth approach.*

level-headed EG *a sensible, level-headed approach*

matter-of-fact EG *He sounded matter-of-fact and unemotional.*

practical EG *a highly practical attitude to life*

sensible EG *I'm trying to persuade*

---

you to be more sensible.

sober EG *a more sober assessment of the situation*

❷ **realistic** ADJECTIVE
true to real life
EG *His novels are more realistic than his short stories.*

authentic EG *They have to look authentic.*

faithful EG *faithful copies of old household items*

lifelike EG *almost as lifelike as a photograph*

true EG *It gave a true picture of how things were.*

WORD POWER

▷ **Synonyms**
naturalistic
representational
vérité

---

reality NOUN
something that is true and not imagined
EG *Fiction and reality were increasingly blurred.*

authenticity EG *The film's authenticity impressed the critics.*

fact EG *No-one knew how much of what he said was fact.*

realism EG *His stories had an edge of realism.*

truth EG *I must tell you the truth about this situation.*

realize VERB
to become aware of something
EG *People don't realize how serious it is.*

appreciate EG *He appreciates the difficulties we face.*

comprehend EG *They do not comprehend the nature of the problem.*

grasp EG *She still couldn't grasp what had really happened.*

recognize EG *Of course I recognize that evil exists.*

a
b
c
d
e
f
g
h
i
j
k
l
m
n
o
p
q
r
s
t
u
v
w
x
y
z

A
B
C
D
E
F
G
H
I
J
K
L
M
N
O
P
Q
R
S
T
U
V
W
X
Y
Z

understand EG *I didn't understand what he meant until later.*

❶ really ADVERB
very or certainly
EG *I've had a really good time.*
absolutely EG *feeling absolutely exhausted*
certainly EG *I am certainly getting tired of hearing about it.*
extremely EG *My mobile phone is extremely useful.*
remarkably EG *They have been remarkably successful.*
terribly EG *I'm terribly sorry to bother you.*
truly EG *a truly splendid man*
very EG *learning very quickly*

❷ really ADVERB
in actual fact
EG *He didn't really love her.*
actually EG *I pretended I was interested, but I was actually half asleep.*
in fact EG *It sounds simple, but in fact it's very difficult.*
in reality EG *He came across as streetwise, but in reality he was not.*
truly EG *I truly never minded caring for Rusty.*

❶ reason NOUN
the cause of something that happens
EG *for a multitude of reasons*
cause EG *The true cause of the accident may never be known.*
grounds EG *some grounds for optimism*
incentive EG *There is no incentive to adopt these measures.*
motive EG *Police have ruled out robbery as a motive.*
purpose EG *the purpose of their visit*

❷ reason NOUN
the ability to think
EG *a conflict between emotion and reason*
intellect EG *good health and a lively*

intellect
judgment EG *His judgment was impaired.*
rationality EG *We live in an era of rationality.*
reasoning EG *a lack of sound reasoning and logic*
sense EG *He should have had more sense.*

❸ reason VERB
to try to persuade someone of something
EG *It's better to reason with them than to use force.*
bring round INFORMAL EG *We'll try to bring you round to our point of view.*
persuade EG *I had to persuade him of the advantages.*
win over EG *They still hoped to win him over to their way of thinking.*

❶ reasonable ADJECTIVE
fair and sensible
EG *a reasonable sort of chap*
fair EG *You can be sure she will be fair with you.*
moderate EG *an easygoing man of very moderate views*
rational EG *Please try to be rational about this.*
sane EG *No sane person wishes to see a war.*
sensible EG *She was a sensible girl and did not panic.*
sober EG *We are now more sober and realistic.*
steady EG *a politician who was steady almost to the point of being boring*
wise EG *You're a wise old man: tell me what to do.*

> **WORD POWER**
> ▷ **Synonyms**
> judicious

❷ reasonable ADJECTIVE
based on good reasoning
EG *It seems reasonable to expect rapid*

urban growth.
justifiable. EG *Our violence was justifiable on the grounds of political necessity.*
legitimate EG *That's a perfectly legitimate fear.*
logical EG *There was a logical explanation.*
sensible EG *a sensible solution*
sound EG *sound advice*
understandable EG *His unhappiness was understandable.*

❸ **reasonable** ADJECTIVE
not too expensive
EG *His fees were quite reasonable.*
cheap EG *She said she'd share a flat if I could find somewhere cheap enough.*
competitive EG *homes offered for sale at competitive prices*
fair EG *It's a fair price for a car like that.*
inexpensive EG *an inexpensive divorce settlement*
low EG *The low prices and friendly service made for a pleasant evening.*
modest EG *a modest charge*

reassure VERB
to make someone feel less worried
EG *She reassured me that everything was fine.*
bolster EG *measures intended to bolster morale*
cheer up EG *I wrote it just to cheer myself up.*
comfort EG *He tried to comfort her as far as he could.*
encourage EG *Investors were encouraged by the news.*

WORD POWER

▷ **Synonyms**
buoy up
hearten
inspirit

rebel VERB
to fight against authority and accepted values
EG *I rebelled against everything when I*

was young.
defy EG *It was the first time she had defied her mother.*
mutiny EG *Sailors mutinied against their officers.*
resist EG *activists convicted of resisting apartheid*
revolt EG *The islanders revolted against the prince.*

rebellion NOUN
an organized opposition to authority
EG *the ruthless suppression of the rebellion*
insurrection EG *They were plotting to stage an armed insurrection.*
mutiny EG *convicted of mutiny and high treason*
revolt EG *The revolt ended in failure.*
revolution EG *after the French Revolution*
uprising EG *Isolated attacks turned into a full-scale uprising.*

❶ **receive** VERB
to accept something from someone
EG *Did they receive my letter?*
accept EG *They accepted the parcel gratefully.*
be given EG *We were all given presents.*
get EG *She got some lovely things.*
pick up EG *He picked up an award for his performance.*
take EG *Will you take this parcel for your neighbour?*

❷ **receive** VERB
to experience something
EG *We received a very warm welcome.*
encounter EG *He encountered some unexpected opposition.*
suffer EG *He suffered some bangs and bumps.*
sustain EG *She had sustained a cut on her arm.*
undergo EG *You may have to undergo a bit of teasing.*

❸ **receive** VERB
to welcome visitors

a b c d e f g h i j k l m n o p q r s t u v w x y z

EG *You must be there to receive your guests.*
entertain EG *She loved to entertain friends at home.*
greet EG *They greeted the visitors at the door.*
meet EG *I'll come down to meet you.*
take in EG *The country took in many refugees.*
welcome EG *Several people came by to welcome me.*

recent ADJECTIVE
happening a short time ago
EG *his most recent acquisition*
current EG *a sound knowledge of current affairs*
fresh EG *fresh footprints in the snow*
new EG *the subject of a new film*
present-day EG *Even by present-day standards these were large aircraft.*
up-to-date EG *the most up-to-date computers*

WORD POWER

▷ **Synonyms**
contemporary
latter-day

recession NOUN
a decline in economic conditions
EG *companies which survived after the recession*
decline EG *signs of economic decline*
depression EG *the Great Depression of the 1930s*
downturn EG *due to a sharp downturn in the industry*
slump EG *Many jobs were lost during the slump.*

❶ reckon VERB; INFORMAL
to think or believe something is the case
EG *I reckon he's still fond of her.*
assume EG *If mistakes occurred, they were assumed to be my fault.*
believe FORMAL EG *"You've never heard of him?" "I don't believe so."*
consider EG *Barbara considers that*

people who sell these birds are acting illegally.
judge EG *I would judge that my earnings are considerably below those of my sister.*
suppose EG *I suppose I'd better do some homework.*
think EG *I think there should be a ban on tobacco advertising.*

WORD POWER

▷ **Synonyms**
deem (FORMAL)
hold to be
surmise (FORMAL)

❷ reckon VERB
to calculate an amount
EG *The figure is now reckoned to be 15%.*
calculate EG *We calculate that the average size farm in the county is 65 acres.*
count EG *The years before their arrival in prison are not counted as part of their sentence.*
estimate EG *Analysts estimate its current popularity at around ten per cent.*
figure out EG *I roughly figured out the total.*
work out EG *It is proving hard to work out the value of their assets.*

❶ recognize VERB
to know who or what someone or something is
EG *I recognized him at once.*
identify EG *She tried to identify the perfume.*
know EG *You'd know him if you saw him again.*
place EG *He couldn't place my voice immediately.*
spot EG *I spotted the house quite easily.*

❷ recognize VERB
to accept or acknowledge something

EG *He was recognized as an outstanding pilot.*
acknowledge EG *Her great bravery was acknowledged.*
appreciate EG *In time you'll appreciate his good points.*
honour EG *achievements honoured with the Nobel Prize*
salute EG *We salute your great courage.*

① reconstruct VERB
to rebuild something that has been damaged
EG *The city centre has been completely reconstructed.*
rebuild EG *The task of rebuilding would be very expensive.*
recreate EG *They try to recreate the atmosphere of former times.*
regenerate EG *the ability to regenerate damaged tissues*
renovate EG *The hotel was being renovated.*
restore EG *experts who specialize in restoring old furniture*

WORD POWER

▷ **Synonyms**
reassemble
remodel

② reconstruct VERB
to build up from small details
EG *The police reconstructed the scene of the crime.*
build up EG *They built up an image of him from several different descriptions.*
deduce EG *The date can be deduced from other documents.*
piece together EG *It was easy to piece together the shattered fragments.*

① record NOUN
a stored account of something
EG *medical records*
account EG *The company keeps detailed accounts.*

archives EG *Earlier issues are stored in the archives.*
file EG *the right to inspect company files*
journal EG *He kept a journal while he was travelling.*
minute EG *Did you read the minutes of the last meeting?*
register EG *a register of births, deaths and marriages*

② record NOUN
what someone has done in the past
EG *You will be rejected if you have a criminal record.*
background EG *His background was in engineering.*
career EG *His career spoke for itself.*
curriculum vitae EG *I must update my curriculum vitae.*
track record INFORMAL EG *Her track record as a teacher was impeccable.*

③ record VERB
to note and store information
EG *Her diary records her daily life in detail.*
document EG *All these facts have been well documented.*
enter EG *All the names are entered in this book.*
log EG *They log everyone who comes in or out.*
note EG *I must note your birthday.*
register EG *We registered his birth straight away.*
write down EG *If I don't write it down, I'll forget it.*

① recover VERB
to get better again
EG *He has still not fully recovered.*
convalesce EG *those convalescing from illness or surgery*
get better EG *He never really got better again.*
get well EG *Get well soon!*
improve EG *The condition of your hair will soon improve.*
recuperate EG *recuperating from a*

serious injury

revive EG *Business soon revived once he came back.*

2 recover VERB
to get something back again
EG *They took legal action to recover the money.*

get back EG *We got everything back after the burglary.*

recapture EG *trying to recapture the atmosphere of our holiday*

recoup EG *trying to recoup their losses*

regain EG *It took him a while to regain his composure.*

retrieve EG *I retrieved my bag from the back seat.*

1 recovery NOUN
the act of getting better again
EG *He made a remarkable recovery after his illness.*

healing EG *Adams claims that humour is an integral part of healing.*

improvement EG *Germany is showing a perceptible improvement.*

recuperation EG *great powers of recuperation*

revival EG *little chance of a revival of interest*

WORD POWER

▷ **Synonyms**
convalescence
rally

2 recovery NOUN
the act of getting something back
EG *a reward for the recovery of the painting*

recapture EG *An offensive was launched for the recapture of the airbase.*

reclamation EG *the reclamation of dry land from the marshes*

restoration EG *She owed the restoration of her sight to this remarkable technique.*

retrieval EG *electronic storage and retrieval systems*

1 recruit VERB
to persuade people to join a group
EG *He helped to recruit volunteers.*

draft EG *drafted into the armed forces*

enlist EG *I had to enlist the help of six people to move it.*

enrol EG *She enrolled me on her evening course.*

muster EG *trying to muster support for the movement*

2 recruit NOUN
someone who has recently joined a group
EG *the latest batch of recruits*

beginner EG *The course is suitable for beginners.*

convert EG *a recent convert to their religion*

novice EG *I'm a novice at these things.*

trainee EG *My first job was as a graduate trainee with a bank.*

WORD POWER

▷ **Synonyms**
neophyte
proselyte
tyro

red NOUN OR ADJECTIVE

WORD POWER

● **Related Words**
adjectives : rubicund, ruddy

Shades of red
burgundy
cardinal
carmine
cerise
cherry
claret
crimson
cyclamen
flame
fuchsia

magenta
maroon
poppy
raspberry
ruby
scarlet
strawberry
vermilion

❶ reduce VERB
to make something smaller in size or amount
EG *Gradually reduce the dosage.*
curtail EG *His powers will be severely curtailed.*
cut EG *The first priority is to cut costs.*
cut down EG *Try to cut down your coffee consumption.*
decrease EG *The government plans to decrease interest rates.*
diminish EG *to diminish the prestige of the monarchy*
lessen EG *a diet that would lessen the risk of disease*
lower EG *a commitment to lower taxes*
shorten EG *taking steps to shorten queues*

WORD POWER
▶ **Antonym**
increase

❷ reduce VERB
to bring to a weaker or inferior state
EG *The village was reduced to rubble.*
degrade EG *I wouldn't degrade myself by going out with him.*
demote EG *The Soviet team have been demoted to second place.*
downgrade EG *The female role has been downgraded in the drive for equality.*
drive EG *an old woman driven to shoplifting to survive*
force EG *The men were so hungry they were forced to eat grass.*

❶ refer VERB
to mention something

EG *In his speech, he referred to a recent trip to Canada.*
allude EG *She alluded to his absence in vague terms.*
bring up EG *Why are you bringing that up now?*
cite EG *She cites a favourite poem by George Herbert.*
mention EG *She did not mention her mother's illness.*

❷ refer VERB
to look at to find something out
EG *I had to refer to the manual.*
consult EG *He had to consult a dictionary.*
look up EG *I looked up your file to get your address.*

❶ refined ADJECTIVE
polite and well-mannered
EG *His speech and manner are very refined.*
civilized EG *the demands of civilized behaviour*
genteel EG *two ladies with genteel manners and voices*
gentlemanly EG *Sopwith behaved in his usual gentlemanly manner.*
ladylike EG *They are models of ladylike decorum.*
polite EG *polite and correct behaviour*

WORD POWER
▶ **Antonym**
common

❷ refined ADJECTIVE
processed to remove impurities
EG *refined sugar*
distilled EG *distilled water*
filtered EG *two pints of spring or filtered water*
processed EG *a diet high in processed foods*
pure EG *crisp pure air*
purified EG *freshly purified drinking water*

❶ reform NOUN
a major change or improvement

EG *radical economic reforms*

amendment EG *an amendment to remove the ban on divorce*

correction EG *a correction of social injustice*

improvement EG *She is pressing for improvements to education.*

rehabilitation EG *the rehabilitation of young offenders*

WORD POWER

▷ **Synonyms**
amelioration
betterment
rectification

❷ reform VERB
to make major changes or improvements to something
EG *his plans to reform the economy*

amend EG *They want to amend the current system.*

better EG *industrial action to better their working conditions*

correct EG *keen to correct injustices*

rectify EG *measures suggested to rectify the financial situation*

rehabilitate EG *a loan for Bulgaria to rehabilitate its railway system*

WORD POWER

▷ **Synonyms**
ameliorate
emend
revolutionize

refresh VERB
to make you feel more energetic
EG *A glass of fruit juice will refresh you.*

brace EG *a bracing walk*

enliven EG *Music can enliven the spirit.*

rejuvenate EG *He was told that the Italian climate would rejuvenate him.*

revive EG *The cold water revived me a bit.*

stimulate EG *a toner to stimulate the skin*

WORD POWER

▷ **Synonyms**
freshen
invigorate
revitalize
revivify

refuge NOUN
a place where you go for safety
EG *a mountain refuge*

asylum EG *political asylum*

harbour EG *Patches of gorse were a great harbour for foxes.*

haven EG *The island is a haven for international criminals.*

sanctuary EG *a sanctuary from the outside world*

shelter EG *an underground shelter*

❶ refuse VERB
to say you will not do something
EG *He refused to speculate about the contents of the letter.*

abstain EG *people who abstain from eating meat*

decline EG *He declined to comment on the story.*

withhold EG *Financial aid for Britain has been withheld.*

❷ refuse VERB
to say you will not allow or accept something
EG *He offered me a drink, which I refused.*

decline EG *He declined their invitation.*

reject EG *The court rejected their petition.*

spurn EG *You spurned his last offer.*

turn down EG *He has turned down the job.*

WORD POWER

▶ **Antonym**
accept

❸ refuse NOUN
rubbish or waste
EG *a weekly collection of refuse*

garbage EG *rotting piles of garbage*

junk INFORMAL EG *What are you going to do with all that junk?*

litter EG *If you see litter in the corridor, pick it up.*

rubbish EG *They had piled most of their rubbish into yellow skips.*

trash EG *I forgot to take out the trash.*

waste EG *a law that regulates the disposal of waste*

❶ regard VERB
to have particular views about someone or something
EG *I regard creativity as a gift.*

consider EG *I consider activities such as jogging a waste of time.*

judge EG *This may or may not be judged as reasonable.*

look on EG *A lot of people looked on him as a healer.*

see EG *I don't see it as my duty to take sides.*

think of EG *We all thought of him as a father.*

view EG *They view the United States as a land of opportunity.*

❷ regard VERB; LITERARY
to look at someone in a particular way
EG *She regarded him curiously for a moment.*

contemplate EG *He contemplated her in silence.*

eye EG *We eyed each other thoughtfully.*

gaze EG *gazing at herself in the mirror*

look EG *She looked at him earnestly.*

scrutinize EG *She scrutinized his features to see if he was to be trusted.*

watch EG *Chris watched him sipping his brandy.*

region NOUN
a large area of land
EG *a remote mountainous region of Afghanistan*

area EG *The area is renowned for its cuisine.*

district EG *I drove around the business district.*

land EG *a land permanently cloaked in mist*

locality EG *All other factories in the locality went on strike.*

quarter EG *We wandered through the Chinese quarter.*

sector EG *the northeast sector of Bosnia*

territory EG *the disputed territory of Kashmir*

tract EG *They cleared large tracts of forest.*

zone EG *a different time zone*

❶ regret VERB
to be sorry something has happened
EG *I gave in to him, and I have regretted it ever since.*

be sorry EG *I'm sorry you feel that way about it.*

grieve EG *grieving over the death of his wife*

lament EG *We lament the loss of a fine novelist.*

mourn EG *to mourn the loss of a loved one*

repent EG *He repents his past sins.*

WORD POWER

▷ **Synonyms**
bemoan
bewail
rue

❷ regret NOUN
the feeling of being sorry about something
EG *He expressed regret that he had caused any offence.*

grief EG *his guilt and grief over the failed relationship*

pang of conscience EG *He need not feel any pangs of conscience over his decision.*

penitence EG *an abject display of penitence*

remorse EG *He expressed remorse*

a b c d e f g h i j k l m n o p q r s t u v w x y z

over his own foolishness.
repentance EG *an apparent lack of genuine repentance*
sorrow EG *I feel real sorrow that my dad did this.*

WORD POWER

▷ **Synonyms**
compunction
contrition
ruefulness
self-reproach

❶ regular ADJECTIVE
even or equally spaced
EG *soft music with a regular beat*
consistent EG *a consistent heart-rate*
constant EG *a constant temperature*
even EG *an even level of sound*
periodic EG *Periodic checks are carried out.*
rhythmic EG *the rhythmic beating of the drum*
steady EG *a steady pace*
uniform EG *The Earth rotates on its axis at a uniform rate.*

WORD POWER

▶ **Antonym**
irregular

❷ regular ADJECTIVE
usual or normal
EG *I was filling in for the regular bartender.*
customary EG *her customary place at the table*
everyday EG *part of everyday life*
habitual EG *habitual practices*
normal EG *a normal day*
ordinary EG *It was just an ordinary weekend.*
routine EG *a routine knee operation*
typical EG *My typical day begins at 8.30.*
usual EG *In a usual week I watch about 15 hours of television.*

reject VERB
to refuse to accept or agree to something
EG *We reject any suggestion that the law needs amending.*
decline EG *They declined his proposal.*
deny EG *He denied our offer of assistance.*
rebuff EG *She rebuffed his advances.*
refuse EG *He offered me a drink, which I refused.*
renounce EG *She renounced her parents' religion.*
say no to EG *Just say no to drugs.*
spurn EG *He spurned the advice of management consultants.*
turn down EG *She turned down his offer of marriage.*

WORD POWER

▷ **Synonyms**
disallow
repudiate

▶ **Antonym**
accept

rejoice VERB
to be very happy about something
EG *Today we can rejoice in our success.*
be overjoyed EG *I was overjoyed to see him.*
celebrate EG *We should celebrate our victory.*
delight EG *He delighted in her success.*
glory EG *glorying in the achievement of his troops*

WORD POWER

▷ **Synonyms**
exult
revel

❶ relation NOUN
a connection between two things
EG *This theory bears no relation to reality.*

bearing EG *Diet has an important bearing on your general health.*
bond EG *the bond between a mother and child*
connection EG *a possible connection between BSE and human disease*
correlation EG *the correlation between unemployment and crime*
link EG *a link between obesity and heart problems*
relationship EG *the relationship between success and effort*

❷ **relation** NOUN
a member of your family
EG *I was staying with relations in Atlanta.*
kin EG *She has gone to live with her husband's kin.*
kinsman *or* **kinswoman** EG *the prince who murdered his father and kinsmen*
relative EG *Get a relative to look after the children.*

❶ **relationship** NOUN
the way people act towards each other
EG *He has a friendly relationship with his customers.*
affinity EG *the natural affinity between the female members of the community*
association EG *the association between the two countries*
bond EG *The experience created a bond between us.*
connection EG *He felt a personal connection with her.*
rapport EG *He has a terrific rapport with kids.*

❷ **relationship** NOUN
a close friendship, especially a sexual one
EG *I found myself in a relationship I couldn't handle.*
affair EG *an affair with a married man*
liaison EG *Nobody knew of their brief liaison.*

❸ **relationship** NOUN
the connection between two things
EG *the relationship between humans and their environment*
connection EG *the connection between age and ill-health*
correlation EG *the correlation between unemployment and crime*
link EG *the link between smoking and lung cancer*
parallel EG *the parallel between painting and music*

relax VERB
to be calm and become less worried
EG *I never have any time to relax.*
laze EG *I'm just going to laze around and do nothing.*
rest EG *Try to rest as much as you can.*
take it easy EG *the chance to just take it easy for a week or two*
unwind EG *It helps them to unwind after a busy day at work.*

❶ **relaxed** ADJECTIVE
calm and not worried or tense
EG *As soon as I made the decision, I felt more relaxed.*
at ease EG *It is essential to feel at ease with your therapist.*
calm EG *Diane felt calm and unafraid as she entered the courtroom.*
comfortable EG *He liked me and I felt comfortable with him.*
cool EG *He was marvellously cool, smiling as if nothing had happened.*
easy EG *By then I was feeling a little easier about the situation.*
serene EG *that serene smile of his*
unflustered EG *He has a calm, unflustered temperament.*

WORD POWER

▶ **Antonym**
tense

---

❷ **relaxed** ADJECTIVE
calm and peaceful
EG *The atmosphere at lunch was relaxed.*

a b c d e f g h i j k l m n o p q r s t u v w x y z

A
B
C
D
E
F
G
H
I
J
K
L
M
N
O
P
Q
R
S
T
U
V
W
X
Y
Z

calm EG *The city appears relatively calm today.*
casual EG *We have a very casual relationhsip.*
comfortable EG *a comfortable silence*
informal EG *an informal occasion*
peaceful EG *Sundays are usually quiet and peaceful in our house.*

WORD POWER

▶ **Antonym**
tense

❶ release VERB
to set someone or something free
EG *negotiations to release the hostages*
deliver EG *I thank God for delivering me from that pain.*
discharge EG *He may be discharged from hospital today.*
extricate EG *They managed to extricate the survivors from the wreckage.*
free EG *Israeli is set to free more Lebanese prisoners.*
let go EG *They held him for three hours and then let him go.*
liberate EG *liberated under the terms of the amnesty*
set free EG *birds set free into the wild*

WORD POWER

▷ **Synonyms**
emancipate
manumit

❷ release VERB
to make something available
EG *The new album is released next week.*
issue EG *He has issued a press statement.*
launch EG *The company has just launched a new range of products.*
publish EG *His latest book will be published in May.*

put out EG *putting out a series of novels by Nobel prize winners*

❸ release NOUN
the setting free of someone or something
EG *his release from prison*
discharge EG *a discharge from the army*
emancipation EG *the emancipation of slaves in the 19th century*
freedom EG *Hinckley campaigned for his freedom.*
liberation EG *their liberation from a Nazi concentration camp*
liberty EG *her television appearances pleading for his liberty*

WORD POWER

▷ **Synonyms**
deliverance
manumission

relentless ADJECTIVE
never stopping or becoming less intense
EG *The pressure was relentless.*
incessant EG *incessant rain*
nonstop EG *nonstop background music*
persistent EG *in the face of persistent criticism*
sustained EG *a sustained attack*
unrelenting EG *unrelenting protests*
unremitting EG *the unremitting demands of duty*

relevant ADJECTIVE
connected with what is being discussed
EG *We have passed on all relevant information.*
applicable EG *These fees are not applicable to mortgages in Scotland.*
apposite EG *He could not think of anything apposite to say.*
appropriate EG *The name seemed very appropriate.*
apt EG *an apt comment*

pertinent EG *She had asked some pertinent questions.*

WORD POWER

▷ **Synonyms**
appurtenant
germane
material

▶ **Antonym**
irrelevant

reliable ADJECTIVE
able to be trusted
EG *You have to demonstrate that you are reliable.*
dependable EG *dependable information*
faithful EG *a faithful friend*
safe EG *It's all right, you're in safe hands.*
sound EG *sound advice*
staunch EG *a staunch supporter*
sure EG *a sure sign of rain*
true EG *a true account*
trustworthy EG *a trustworthy and level-headed leader*

WORD POWER

▶ **Antonym**
unreliable

religion NOUN

Religions
animism
Baha'ism
Buddhism
Christianity
Confucianism
Hinduism
Islam
Jainism
Judaism
Rastafarianism
shamanism
Shinto
Sikhism
Taoism

Zen
Zoroastrianism *or* Zoroastrism

❶ religious ADJECTIVE
connected with religion
EG *religious worship*
devotional EG *an altar covered with devotional pictures*
divine EG *a request for divine guidance*
doctrinal EG *their doctrinal differences*
holy EG *To Tibetans, this is a holy place.*
sacred EG *Bach's sacred music*
scriptural EG *scriptural and theological references*
spiritual EG *We've got no spiritual values.*
theological EG *theological studies*

❷ religious ADJECTIVE
having a strong belief in a god or gods
EG *They are both very religious.*
devout EG *She is a devout Catholic.*
God-fearing EG *They brought up their children to be God-fearing Christians.*
godly EG *a learned and godly preacher*
pious EG *He was brought up by pious female relatives.*
righteous EG *struggling to be righteous and chaste*

reluctant ADJECTIVE
unwilling to do something
EG *He was reluctant to ask for help.*
averse EG *I'm not averse to going along with the idea.*
disinclined EG *He was disinclined to talk about himself.*
hesitant EG *His advisers are hesitant to let the United States enter the conflict.*
loath EG *The finance minister is loath to cut income tax.*
slow EG *The world community has been slow to respond to the crisis.*

a b c d e f g h i j k l m n o p q r s t u v w x y z

A
B
C
D
E
F
G
H
I
J
K
L
M
N
O
P
Q
R
S
T
U
V
W
X
Y
Z

unwilling EG *For months I had been unwilling to go through with it.*

<u>WORD POWER</u>

▶ **Antonym**
eager

❶ remain VERB
to stay somewhere
EG *You'll have to remain in hospital for the time being.*
be left EG *He was left in the car.*
linger EG *I lingered for a few days until he arrived.*
stay behind EG *I was told to stay behind after the class.*
wait EG *Wait here until I come back.*

❷ remain VERB
to stay the same
EG *The men remained silent.*
continue EG *This state of affairs cannot continue.*
endure EG *Somehow their friendship endures.*
go on EG *The debate goes on.*
last EG *Nothing lasts forever.*
stay EG *They could stay afloat without swimming.*
survive EG *companies which survived after the recession*

remainder NOUN
the part that is left of something
EG *He gulped down the remainder of his coffee.*
balance EG *pay the balance on delivery*
last EG *He finished off the last of the wine.*
others EG *She took one and put the others back.*
remnants EG *The remnants of the force were fleeing.*
remains EG *tidying up the remains of their picnic*
rest EG *I'm going to throw a party, then invest the rest of the money.*

remains PLURAL NOUN
the parts of something left over

EG *the remains of an ancient mosque*
debris EG *screws, bolts and other debris from a scrapyard*
dregs EG *Colum drained the dregs from his cup.*
leftovers EG *Refrigerate any leftovers.*
relics EG *a museum of war relics*
remnants EG *Beneath the present church were remnants of Roman flooring.*
residue EG *Discard the milky residue left behind.*
scraps EG *the scraps from the dinner table*
vestiges EG *an attempt to destroy the last vestiges of evidence*

<u>WORD POWER</u>

▷ **Synonyms**
detritus
leavings

❶ remark VERB
to mention or comment on something
EG *She had remarked on the boy's improvement.*
comment EG *So far, he has not commented on these reports.*
mention EG *I mentioned that I didn't like jazz.*
observe EG *"You're very pale," he observed.*
say EG *"Well done," he said.*
state EG *We stated that he had resigned.*

❷ remark NOUN
something you say
EG *a vulgar remark*
comment EG *his abrasive wit and caustic comments*
observation EG *a few general observations*
statement EG *That statement puzzled me.*
utterance EG *admirers who hung on her every utterance*

word EG *No-one had an unkind word to say about him.*

remember VERB
to bring to mind something from the past
EG *I do not remember the exact words.*
call to mind EG *He invited the congregation to call to mind their sins.*
recall EG *He tried to recall the layout of the farmhouse.*
recognize EG *I don't recognize that name.*
retain EG *information which can be retained in the memory*

> ### WORD POWER
>
> ▷ **Synonyms**
> recollect
> reminisce
>
> ▶ **Antonym**
> forget

remind VERB
to make someone remember something
EG *He reminds me of myself at that age.*
bring back to EG *Talking about the accident brought it all back to me.*
jog someone's memory EG *See if this picture helps jog your memory.*
make someone remember
EG *Your article made me remember my own traumas.*
put in mind EG *His eagerness to please put her in mind of a puppy.*
refresh someone's memory EG *I read through the list to refresh my memory.*

❶ remote ADJECTIVE
far off in distance or in the past
EG *a remote farm in the hills*
distant EG *in that distant land*
far-off EG *She has entirely forgotten those far-off days.*
inaccessible EG *people living in inaccessible parts of the country*
isolated EG *Many of the refugee villages are in isolated areas.*
lonely EG *It felt like the loneliest place in the world.*
outlying EG *Tourists can visit outlying areas by jeep.*

❷ remote ADJECTIVE
not wanting to be friendly
EG *She looked beautiful, but at the same time so remote.*
aloof EG *He seemed aloof, standing watching the others.*
cold EG *What a cold, unfeeling woman she was.*
detached EG *He tries to remain emotionally detached from the prisoners.*
distant EG *He is courteous but distant.*
reserved EG *She's quite a reserved person.*
withdrawn EG *Her husband had become withdrawn and moody.*

❸ remote ADJECTIVE
not very great
EG *The chances of his surviving are pretty remote.*
poor EG *The odds of it happening again are very poor.*
slender EG *There is a slender possibility that the plan might work.*
slight EG *Is there even a slight hope that she might change her mind?*
slim EG *There's still a slim chance that he may become Prime Minister.*
small EG *There was still a small possibility that he might phone.*

remove VERB
to take something off or away
EG *I removed the splinter from her finger.*
delete EG *He deleted files from the computer system.*
detach EG *Detach and keep the bottom part of the form.*
eject EG *He was ejected from the restaurant.*
eliminate EG *Eliminate dairy*

a b c d e f g h i j k l m n o p q r s t u v w x y z

A B C D E F G H I J K L M N O P Q R S T U V W X Y Z

products from your diet.
erase EG *She had erased the message.*
extract EG *She is having a tooth extracted today.*
get rid of EG *to get rid of raw sewage by pumping it out to sea*
take away EG *She took away the tray.*
take off EG *I won't take my coat off, I'm not staying.*
take out EG *Take that dog out of here.*
withdraw EG *She withdrew her hand from Roger's.*

> ### WORD POWER
> ▷ **Synonyms**
> efface
> excise
> expunge

renew VERB
to begin something again
EG *Syria renewed diplomatic relations with Egypt.*
begin again EG *The audience began the slow handclap again.*
recommence EG *He recommenced work on his novel.*
re-establish EG *He had re-established his close friendship with Anthony.*
reopen EG *It is feared that this issue could re-open the controversy.*
resume EG *Rebels have refused to resume peace talks.*

renounce VERB; FORMAL
to reject something or give it up
EG *She renounced terrorism.*
disown EG *The comments were later disowned by an official spokesman.*
give up EG *He did not want to give up his right to the title.*
reject EG *children who reject their parents' political and religious beliefs*

relinquish EG *He does not intend to relinquish power.*

> ### WORD POWER
> ▷ **Synonyms**
> eschew (FORMAL)

renovate VERB
to repair an old building or machine
EG *They spent thousands renovating the house.*
do up EG *his father's obsession with doing up old cars*
modernize EG *plans to modernize the refinery*
recondition EG *The company specializes in reconditioning photocopiers.*
refurbish EG *This hotel has been completely refurbished.*
repair EG *He has repaired the roof to make the house more windproof.*
restore EG *The old town square has been beautifully restored.*
revamp EG *plans to revamp the airport*

❶ repair NOUN
something you do to mend something that is damaged
EG *The landlord carried out the repairs himself.*
darn EG *a sock with a big darn in it*
mend EG *Spray the area with paint to make the mend invisible.*
patch EG *jackets with patches on the elbows*
restoration EG *the restoration of a war-damaged building*

❷ repair VERB
to mend something that is damaged
EG *The money will be used to repair faulty equipment.*
fix EG *If something is broken, get it fixed.*
mend EG *They mended it without charge.*
patch EG *They patched the barn roof.*
patch up EG *Patch up those holes.*

renovate EG *They spent thousands renovating the house.*
restore EG *experts who specialize in restoring ancient parchments*

repay VERB
to give back money which is owed
EG *It will take me years to repay the loan.*
pay back EG *I'll pay you back that money tomorrow.*
refund EG *Any extra that you have paid will be refunded to you.*
settle up EG *If we owe you anything we can settle up when you come.*

WORD POWER
▷ Synonyms
make restitution
recompense
reimburse
remunerate
square

repeat VERB
to say or write something again
EG *Since you didn't listen, I'll repeat that.*
echo EG *"Are you frightened?" "Frightened?" she echoed. "Of what?"*
reiterate EG *The lawyer could only reiterate what he had said before.*
say again EG *"I'm sorry," she said again.*

WORD POWER
▷ Synonyms
iterate
recapitulate
restate

❶ repel VERB
to horrify and disgust
EG *The thought of spiders repels me.*
disgust EG *He disgusted everyone with his boorish behaviour.*
offend EG *viewers who are easily offended*
revolt EG *The smell revolted him.*

sicken EG *What he saw there sickened him.*

WORD POWER
▶ Antonym
attract

❷ repel VERB
to fight and drive back enemy forces
EG *troops along the border ready to repel an enemy attack*
drive off EG *They drove the guerrillas off with infantry and air strikes.*
repulse EG *Cavalry and artillery were sent to repulse the enemy forces.*
resist EG *The tribe resisted the Spanish invaders.*

replace VERB
to take the place of something else
EG *the man who replaced him as England skipper*
succeed EG *He was succeeded by his son.*
supersede EG *Horses were superseded by cars.*
supplant EG *Anger supplanted all other feelings.*
take over from EG *the man taking over from Mr Berry as chairman*
take the place of EG *Debit cards are taking the place of cash and cheques.*

replacement NOUN
a person or thing that takes the place of another
EG *He has nominated Adams as his replacement.*
proxy EG *They must nominate a proxy to vote on their behalf.*
stand-in EG *He was a stand-in for my regular doctor.*
substitute EG *an artificial substitute for silk*
successor EG *He recommended him as his successor.*
surrogate EG *They had expected me to be a surrogate for my sister.*

❶ reply VERB
to give someone an answer

a b c d e f g h i j k l m n o p q r s t u v w x y z

EG *He did not even have the courtesy to reply to my fax.*
answer EG *He avoided answering the question.*
counter EG *"It's not that simple," he countered in a firm voice.*
respond EG *`Mind your manners, lady!' I responded.*
retort EG *"Nobody asked you," he retorted.*
return EG *"I can manage," she returned coldly.*

WORD POWER

▷ **Synonyms**
reciprocate
rejoin
riposte

❷ reply NOUN
an answer given to someone
EG *There was a trace of irony in his reply.*
answer EG *She could not give him a truthful answer.*
response EG *His response was brusque.*
retort EG *His sharp retort clearly made an impact.*

WORD POWER

▷ **Synonyms**
rejoinder
riposte

❶ report VERB
to tell about or give an official account of something
EG *He reported the theft to the police.*
cover EG *The US news media will cover the trial closely.*
describe EG *His condition was described as "improving".*
inform of EG *Inform the police of any suspicious activity.*
notify EG *The skipper notified the coastguard of the tragedy.*
state EG *The police stated that he had been arrested.*

❷ report NOUN
an account of an event or situation
EG *reports of serious human rights violations*
account EG *a dishonest account of events*
description EG *a detailed description of the match*
statement EG *a deliberately misleading statement*

❶ represent VERB
to stand for something else
EG *This rune represents wealth and plenty.*
mean EG *This tarot card means the death of your present situation.*
stand for EG *The olive branch stands for peace.*
symbolize EG *a scene which symbolizes the movie's message*

WORD POWER

▷ **Synonyms**
betoken
equate with

❷ represent VERB
to describe something in a particular way
EG *The popular press tends to represent him as a hero.*
depict EG *Children's books usually depict farm animals as lovable.*
describe EG *She was always described as an intellectual.*
picture EG *In the American press she was pictured as a heroine.*
portray EG *She was portrayed as a heartless, terrible woman.*
show EG *He was shown as an intelligent and courageous man.*

❶ representative NOUN
a person who acts on behalf of another or others
EG *Employees from each department elect a representative.*
agent EG *You are buying direct, rather than through an agent.*

A
B
C
D
E
F
G
H
I
J
K
L
M
N
O
P
Q
R
S
T
U
V
W
X
Y
Z

delegate EG *a union delegate*
deputy EG *I can't make it so I'll send my deputy.*
proxy EG *They must nominate a proxy to vote on their behalf.*
spokesman or **spokeswoman** EG *the party's education spokesman*

❷ representative ADJECTIVE
typical of the group to which it belongs
EG *fairly representative groups of adults*
characteristic EG *a characteristic feature*
illustrative EG *an illustrative example*
typical EG *a typical Italian menu*

WORD POWER

▷ **Synonyms**
archetypal
emblematic

reputation NOUN
the opinion that people have of a person or thing
EG *The college has a good reputation.*
character EG *a man of good character*
name EG *I have disgraced the family's name.*
renown EG *a singer of great renown*
repute EG *a writer and scholar of some repute*
standing EG *This has done nothing to improve his standing.*
stature EG *his stature as the world's greatest cellist*

❶ request VERB
to ask for something politely or formally
EG *She requested that the door be left open.*
ask EG *The government is being asked to consider the plan.*
beg EG *May I beg a favour of you?*

seek EG *You should seek a medical opinion.*

WORD POWER

▷ **Synonyms**
entreat
solicit

❷ request NOUN
the action of asking for something politely or formally
EG *France had agreed to his request for political asylum.*
appeal EG *an appeal for witnesses to come forward*
application EG *Their application was vetoed.*
call EG *calls to decrease income tax*
plea EG *his plea for help in solving the killing*

WORD POWER

▷ **Synonyms**
entreaty
petition

❶ require VERB
to need something
EG *A baby requires warmth and security.*
demand EG *The task of reconstruction would demand patience and hard work.*
depend on EG *I depend on this money to survive.*
be in need of EG *The house was in need of modernization.*
need EG *He desperately needed money.*
want INFORMAL EG *The windows wanted cleaning.*

❷ require VERB
to say that someone must do something
EG *The rules require employers to provide safety training.*
compel EG *legislation that would compel cyclists to wear a helmet*
demand EG *This letter demands an*

a
b
c
d
e
f
g
h
i
j
k
l
m
n
o
p
q
r
s
t
u
v
w
x
y
z

A
B
C
D
E
F
G
H
I
J
K
L
M
N
O
P
Q
R
S
T
U
V
W
X
Y
Z

immediate reply.
direct EG *a court order directing the group to leave the area*
instruct EG *They have instructed their solicitor to sue for compensation.*
oblige EG *This decree obliges unions to delay strikes.*
order EG *The court ordered him to pay the sum in full.*

requirement NOUN
something that you must have or do
EG *The products met all legal requirements.*
demand EG *the demands and challenges of his new job*
essential EG *the basic essentials for bachelor life*
necessity EG *food and other daily necessities*
need EG *special nutritional needs*
specification EG *These companies will have to meet new European specifications.*

WORD POWER
▷ **Synonyms**
prerequisite (FORMAL)
stipulation (FORMAL)

❶ **research** NOUN
the act of studying and finding out about something
EG *funds for research into AIDS*
analysis EG *They collected blood samples for laboratory analysis.*
examination EG *a framework for the examination of these topics*
exploration EG *an exploration of classical myths*
investigation EG *Further investigation was hindered by the loss of all documentation.*
study EG *The study demonstrated a link between obesity and heart problems.*

❷ **research** VERB
to study and find out about something

EG *I'm researching for an article on New England.*
analyse EG *We haven't had time to analyse those samples yet.*
examine EG *The spacecraft will examine how solar wind affects Earth's magnetic field.*
explore EG *I would probably be wise to explore the matter further.*
investigate EG *Gas officials are investigating the cause of the explosion.*
study EG *She's been studying chimpanzees for thirty years.*

resemblance NOUN
a similarity between two things
EG *I can see a resemblance between you.*
analogy EG *the analogy between racism and homophobia*
correspondence EG *There's little correspondence between our lifestyles.*
likeness EG *These myths have a startling likeness to one another.*
parallel EG *There were parallels between the two murders.*
similarity EG *similarities between mother and son*

WORD POWER
▷ **Synonyms**
comparability
parity
semblance
similitude

resemble VERB
to be similar to something else
EG *Venison resembles beef in flavour.*
bear a resemblance to EG *She bears a resemblance to Marilyn Monroe.*
be like EG *The ground is like concrete.*
be similar to EG *The gun was similar to an air pistol.*
look like EG *He looks like his father.*
parallel EG *His fate paralleled that of*

his predecessor.
take after EG *You take after your grandmother.*

resent VERB
to feel bitter and angry about something
EG *I resent the slur on my integrity.*
be angry about EG *I was angry at the way he spoke to me.*
be offended by EG *She was offended by his comments.*
dislike EG *I dislike his patronizing attitude.*
object to EG *I object to being treated like an idiot.*
take offence at EG *She took offence at the implied criticism.*

resentful ADJECTIVE
bitter about something that has happened
EG *a sullen and resentful workforce*
aggrieved EG *He is still aggrieved at the size of the fine.*
angry EG *I was angry that I wasn't consulted.*
bitter EG *a forsaken and bitter man*
embittered EG *He had grown into an embittered, hardened adult.*
huffy EG *He's so huffy if he doesn't get his own way.*
indignant EG *They were indignant that they had not been consulted.*
offended EG *He was offended at being left out.*

> ### WORD POWER
> ▷ **Synonyms**
> in high dudgeon
> peeved
> piqued

resentment NOUN
a feeling of anger and bitterness
EG *There is growing resentment against newcomers.*
anger EG *Perhaps anger had clouded his vision.*
animosity EG *The animosity between*

the two men grew.
bitterness EG *I feel bitterness towards the person who knocked me down.*
grudge EG *It was an accident and I bear no grudges.*
huff EG *She went off in a huff.*
indignation EG *He could hardly contain his indignation.*
rancour EG *There was no trace of envy or rancour in her face.*

> ### WORD POWER
> ▷ **Synonyms**
> pique
> umbrage

❶ reserve VERB
to keep for a particular person or purpose
EG *Hotel rooms have been reserved for us.*
hoard EG *They've begun to hoard food and petrol.*
hold EG *The information is held in a database.*
keep EG *Grate the lemon zest and keep it for later.*
put by EG *She had enough put by for her fare.*
save EG *Save me a seat.*
set aside EG *funds set aside for education*
stockpile EG *People are stockpiling food for the coming winter.*
store EG *potatoes stored for sale out of season*

❷ reserve NOUN
a supply kept for future use
EG *a drain on the cash reserves*
cache EG *a cache of weapons and explosives*
fund EG *a pension fund*
hoard EG *a hoard of food and petrol*
stock EG *stocks of paper and ink*
stockpile EG *stockpiles of chemical weapons*

store EG *a secret store of sweets*
supply EG *food supplies*

❶ resign VERB
to leave a job
EG *Scott resigned from the firm.*
abdicate EG *The King abdicated to marry an American divorcee.*
hand in your notice EG *I handed in my notice on Friday.*
leave EG *I am leaving to become a teacher.*
quit EG *He quit his job as an office boy.*
step down INFORMAL EG *He headed the government until he stepped down in 1990.*

❷ resign **resign oneself** VERB
to accept an unpleasant situation
EG *She had resigned herself to losing her home.*
accept EG *You've got to accept the fact that he's left you.*
bow EG *He bowed to the inevitable and allowed her to go.*
reconcile oneself EG *She had reconciled herself to never seeing him again.*

resist VERB
to refuse to accept something and try to prevent it
EG *They resisted our attempts to modernize.*
defy EG *arrested for defying the ban on street trading*
fight EG *He vigorously fought the proposal.*
oppose EG *Many parents oppose bilingual education in schools.*
refuse EG *The patient has the right to refuse treatment.*
struggle against EG *nations struggling against Communist takeovers*

WORD POWER

▶ **Antonym**
accept

❶ resolve VERB
to decide firmly to do something
EG *She resolved to report the matter.*
decide EG *She decided to quit smoking.*
determine EG *He determined to rescue his two countrymen.*
intend EG *I intended to teach him a lesson he wouldn't forget.*
make up your mind EG *Once he made up his mind to do it, there was no stopping him.*

❷ resolve VERB
to find a solution to a problem
EG *We must find a way to resolve these problems.*
clear up EG *The confusion was soon cleared up.*
find a solution to EG *the ability to find an effective solution to the crisis*
overcome EG *Find a way to overcome your difficulties.*
solve EG *These reforms did not solve the problem of unemployment.*
sort out EG *The two countries have sorted out their trade dispute.*
work out EG *It seems like a nightmare, but I'm sure we can work it out.*

❸ resolve NOUN
absolute determination
EG *He doesn't weaken in his resolve.*
determination EG *the expression of fierce determination on her face*
resolution EG *"I'm going on a diet," she said with sudden resolution.*
tenacity EG *Hard work and sheer tenacity are crucial to career success.*

WORD POWER

▷ **Synonyms**
doggedness
single-mindedness
willpower

❶ respect VERB
to have a good opinion of someone
EG *I want him to respect me as a career*

woman.
admire EG *I admire him for his honesty.*
have a good opinion of EG *Nobody seems to have a good opinion of him.*
have a high opinion of EG *He had a very high opinion of Neil.*
honour EG *the Scout's promise to honour God and the Queen*
look up to EG *He looks up to his dad.*
think highly of EG *His boss thinks very highly of him.*
venerate EG *My father venerated General Eisenhower.*

WORD POWER

▷ **Synonyms**
esteem
revere
reverence
set store by

▶ **Antonym**
disrespect

2 respect NOUN
a good opinion of someone
EG *We have no respect for him at all.*
admiration EG *I have always had the greatest admiration for him.*
esteem EG *We have to win the trust and esteem of our clients.*
regard EG *I hold him in high regard.*
reverence EG *We did it out of reverence for the dead.*

WORD POWER

▶ **Antonym**
disrespect

1 respectable ADJECTIVE
considered to be acceptable and correct
EG *respectable families*
decent EG *They married after a decent interval.*
good EG *He comes from a good family.*
honourable EG *His colleagues were*

honourable people.
proper EG *It was not proper for women to go on the stage.*
reputable EG *a reputable firm*
upright EG *an upright and trustworthy man*
worthy EG *worthy citizens*

2 respectable ADJECTIVE
adequate or reasonable
EG *a respectable rate of economic growth*
appreciable EG *making appreciable progress*
considerable EG *a considerable amount*
decent EG *a decent standard of living*
fair EG *She had a fair command of English.*
reasonable EG *He couldn't make a reasonable living from his writing.*

1 responsibility NOUN
the duty to deal with or take care of something
EG *The garden is your responsibility.*
duty EG *My duty is to look after the animals.*
obligation EG *You have an obligation to help him.*
onus EG *The onus was on him to make sure he didn't fail.*

2 responsibility NOUN
the blame for something which has happened
EG *We must all accept responsibility for our mistakes.*
blame EG *I'm not going to take the blame for this.*
fault EG *This is all your fault.*
guilt EG *He was not completely free of guilt.*
liability EG *He admitted liability for the crash.*

WORD POWER

▷ **Synonyms**
accountability
culpability

a
b
c
d
e
f
g
h
i
j
k
l
m
n
o
p
q
r
s
t
u
v
w
x
y
z

A
B
C
D
E
F
G
H
I
J
K
L
M
N
O
P
Q
R
S
T
U
V
W
X
Y
Z

❶ responsible ADJECTIVE
being the person in charge of
something
EG *The Cabinet is collectively
responsible for policy.*
in charge EG *I wish someone else was
in charge of this inquiry.*
in control EG *Who is in control of the
operation?*

❷ responsible ADJECTIVE
being to blame for something
EG *I hold you responsible for this mess.*
at fault EG *I was not at fault as my
vehicle was stationary.*
guilty EG *I still maintain that I am not
guilty.*
to blame EG *Television is possibly to
blame for this.*

❸ responsible ADJECTIVE
sensible and dependable
EG *He had to show that he would be a
responsible parent.*
dependable EG *a dependable,
trustworthy teacher*
level-headed EG *a sensible, level-
headed approach*
reliable EG *You have to demonstrate
that you are reliable.*
sensible EG *She's a sensible girl, if a
bit headstrong.*
sound EG *sound advice*
trustworthy EG *He is a trustworthy
leader.*

WORD POWER

▶ **Antonym**
irresponsible

❶ rest NOUN
the remaining parts of something
EG *Take what you want and leave the
rest.*
balance EG *You pay half now and the
balance on delivery.*
others EG *She took one and put the
others back.*
remainder EG *He gulped down the
remainder of his coffee.*

surplus EG *Coat with seasoned flour,
shaking off the surplus.*

❷ rest NOUN
a period when you relax and do
nothing
EG *I'll start again after a rest.*
break EG *He needs to take a break
from work.*
holiday EG *I could really do with a
holiday.*
leisure EG *We get no leisure, no time
off, no overtime pay.*
relaxation EG *Make time for a bit of
relaxation.*
respite EG *a respite from the rush of
everyday life*

❸ rest VERB
to relax and do nothing for a while
EG *He rested briefly before going on.*
have a break EG *Paul felt he had to
have a break.*
idle EG *He sat idling in his room.*
laze EG *lazing on the beach*
put your feet up EG *Nobody's
home, so I can put my feet up for a
while.*
relax EG *Guests can relax in the cosy
bar.*
sit down EG *I'll have to sit down for a
minute.*
take it easy EG *the chance to just
take it easy for a couple of weeks*

restless ADJECTIVE
unable to sit still or relax
EG *She had been restless and irritable
all day.*
edgy EG *She was nervous and edgy,
still chain-smoking.*
fidgety EG *bored, fidgety youngsters*
fretful EG *The whole family was
fretful and argumentative.*
jumpy EG *If she can't smoke she gets
jumpy and irritable.*
on edge EG *She's been on edge for
weeks.*
unsettled EG *The staff were unsettled
and demoralized.*

❶ restore VERB
to cause something to return to its previous state
EG *He was anxious to restore his reputation.*
re-establish EG *an attempt to re-establish diplomatic relations*
reinstate EG *the failure to reinstate the ceasefire*
reintroduce EG *the plan to reintroduce wolves to the Highlands*
return EG *their attempts to return the country to an agrarian economy*

❷ restore VERB
to clean and repair something
EG *experts who specialize in restoring ancient parchments*
fix up EG *It took us months to fix this house up.*
mend EG *They finally got round to mending the roof.*
rebuild EG *plans to rebuild the opera house*
reconstruct EG *reconstructing paintings by old masters*
refurbish EG *The city is refurbishing the cathedral's facade.*
renovate EG *The hotel was being renovated in expectation of a tourist boom.*
repair EG *The money will be used to repair faulty equipment.*

WORD POWER

▷ **Synonyms**
recondition
retouch

restrain VERB
to hold someone or something back
EG *He had to be restrained by his friends.*
contain EG *He could hardly contain his rage.*
control EG *She tried to control her excitement.*
curb EG *You must curb your extravagant tastes.*

hamper EG *I was hampered by a lack of information.*
hinder EG *Research is hindered by lack of cash.*
hold back EG *He could no longer hold back his laughter.*
inhibit EG *factors which inhibit growth*

WORD POWER

▷ **Synonyms**
constrain
rein
straiten

restrict VERB
to limit the movement or actions of someone or something
EG *laws to restrict foreign imports*
confine EG *Keep your dog confined to the house.*
contain EG *The curfew had contained the violence.*
hamper EG *I was hampered by a lack of information.*
handicap EG *handicapped by the terms of the contract*
impede EG *Their work was being impeded by shortages of supplies.*
inhibit EG *factors which inhibit growth*
limit EG *He limited payments on the country's foreign debt.*
restrain EG *the need to restrain wage rises*

WORD POWER

▷ **Synonyms**
circumscribe
demarcate
straiten

restriction NOUN
a rule or situation that limits what you can do
EG *a speed restriction*
constraint EG *financial constraints*
control EG *a call for stricter gun control*

a
b
c
d
e
f
g
h
i
j
k
l
m
n
o
p
q
r
s
t
u
v
w
x
y
z

A
B
C
D
E
F
G
H
I
J
K
L
M
N
O
P
Q
R
S
T
U
V
W
X
Y
Z

curb EG *support for a curb on migration from neighbouring countries*
limitation EG *A slipped disc causes severe limitation of movement.*
regulation EG *regulations outlawing child labour*
restraint EG *new restraints on trade unions*
stipulation EG *The only dress stipulation was "no jeans".*

❶ result NOUN
the situation that is caused by something
EG *the result of lengthy deliberation*
consequence EG *This could have disastrous consequences for industry.*
effect EG *the intended effect of the revised guidelines*
outcome EG *The ultimate outcome will be different.*
product EG *the product of five years' work*
upshot EG *The upshot is that our employees are all unhappy.*

❷ result VERB
to be caused by something
EG *The crash resulted from a defect in the aircraft.*
arise EG *the publicity that arises from incidents of this kind*
derive EG *Poor health often derives from poverty.*
develop EG *a determination which has developed from his new-found confidence*
ensue EG *If the system collapses, chaos will ensue.*
follow EG *the consequences which followed his release from prison*
happen EG *What will happen if the test proves positive?*
stem EG *Her hatred of cars stems from her mother's death in a crash.*

result in VERB
to cause something to happen
EG *50% of road accidents result in*

head injuries.
bring about EG *The Suez crisis brought about petrol rationing.*
cause EG *The play caused a stir here.*
lead to EG *brain damage which leads to paralysis*

retaliate VERB
to do something to someone in return for what they did
EG *The militia said it would retaliate against any attacks.*
get back at EG *a desire to get back at our enemies*
get even with INFORMAL EG *He wanted to get even with his former employers.*
get your own back INFORMAL EG *the opportunity to get your own back on your husband*
hit back EG *In this article he hits back at his critics.*
pay someone back EG *I'll pay him back for what he's done.*
take revenge EG *taking revenge for his father's murder*

❶ retreat VERB
to move away from someone or something
EG *damage inflicted by the rebels as they retreated from the town*
back away EG *He put up his hands in protest and began to back away.*
back off EG *I stood up for myself and they backed off.*
draw back EG *They drew back in fear.*
pull back EG *Their forces have pulled back in all areas.*
withdraw EG *Troops withdrew from the country last month.*

WORD POWER

▶ **Antonym**
advance

❷ retreat NOUN
the action of moving away from someone or something
EG *the long retreat from Moscow*

departure EG *the departure of all foreign forces from the country*
evacuation EG *the evacuation of British troops from Dunkirk*
flight EG *my panicked flight from London*
withdrawal EG *French withdrawal from Algeria*

WORD POWER
▶ **Antonym**
advance

❸ **retreat** NOUN
a quiet place you can go to
EG *He spent the day hidden away in his country retreat.*
haven EG *The hotel is a haven of tranquillity.*
refuge EG *a refuge from the harsh realities of the world*
sanctuary EG *a sanctuary located on an island*

❶ **return** VERB
to go back to a place
EG *The plane failed to return at the scheduled time.*
come back EG *He said he'd come back later.*
go back EG *I love going back home.*
reappear EG *He reappeared two nights later.*
turn back EG *We've come too far now to turn back.*

❷ **return** VERB
to give something back
EG *They guarantee to return your original investment.*
give back EG *He is refusing to give the dog back.*
pay back EG *You have to pay back the loan, plus an arrangement fee.*
refund EG *The company will refund the full cost.*
repay EG *I can afford to repay the loan.*

WORD POWER
▷ **Synonyms**
recompense
reimburse

❶ **reveal** VERB
to tell people about something
EG *They were not ready to reveal any of the details.*
announce EG *She was planning to announce her engagement.*
disclose EG *He will not disclose the name of his patient.*
divulge EG *I do not want to divulge where the village is.*
get off your chest INFORMAL EG *I feel it's done me good to get it off my chest.*
let on EG *She never let on that anything was wrong.*

❷ **reveal** VERB
to uncover something that is hidden
EG *The carpet was removed to reveal the original pine floor.*
bring to light EG *The truth is unlikely to be brought to light.*
lay bare EG *His real motives were laid bare.*
uncover EG *Auditors said they had uncovered evidence of fraud.*
unearth EG *Quarry workers have unearthed the skeleton of a mammoth.*
unveil EG *The statue will be unveiled next week.*

❶ **revenge** NOUN
vengeance for wrongs or injury received
EG *acts of revenge*
reprisal EG *Witnesses are unwilling to testify through fear of reprisals.*
retaliation EG *The attack was in retaliation for his murder.*
retribution EG *They did not want their names used for fear of retribution.*
vengeance EG *He swore vengeance on everyone involved in the murder.*

a b c d e f g h i j k l m n o p q r s t u v w x y z

A B C D E F G H I J K L M N O P Q R S T U V W X Y Z

❷ revenge VERB
to take vengeance on someone
EG *to revenge himself on the press*
avenge EG *He was trying to avenge the death of his friend.*
get even EG *I'm going to get even with you for this.*
get your own back INFORMAL EG *I simply want to get my own back on him.*
hit back EG *He hit back at those who criticized him.*
pay someone back EG *Some day I'll pay you back for this.*
retaliate EG *I was sorely tempted to retaliate.*

❶ reverse VERB
to change into something different or contrary
EG *They won't reverse the decision to increase prices.*
change EG *They should change the law to make this practice illegal.*
invalidate EG *A contract signed now might be invalidated at a future date.*
overrule EG *In 1998 the Court of Appeal overruled the decision.*
overturn EG *When the parliament overturned his decision, he backed down.*
retract EG *He was asked to retract his comments but refused.*

> *WORD POWER*
>
> ▷ **Synonyms**
> countermand
> negate
> rescind
> revoke

❷ reverse NOUN
the opposite of what has just been said or done
EG *The reverse seldom applies.*
contrary EG *I'm not a feminist, quite the contrary.*
converse EG *In fact, the converse is true.*

opposite EG *When I told him to do something he always did the opposite.*

❶ review NOUN
a critical assessment of a book or performance
EG *We've never had a good review in the music press.*
commentary EG *He'll be writing a weekly commentary on American culture.*
criticism EG *literary criticism*
notice EG *Richards's solo work received good notices.*

❷ review NOUN
a general survey or report
EG *a review of safety procedures*
analysis EG *an analysis of American trade policy*
examination EG *an examination of the top 250 companies*
report EG *the committee's annual report*
study EG *a recent study of treatments for back pain*
survey EG *a survey of 250 businessmen*

revise VERB
to alter or correct something
EG *The second edition was completely revised.*
amend EG *They voted unanimously to amend the constitution.*
correct EG *time spent correcting his students' work*
edit EG *We have the right to edit this book once it's finished.*
revamp EG *It is time to revamp the system.*
update EG *He was back in the office, updating the work schedule.*

revive VERB
to make or become lively or active again
EG *an attempt to revive the Russian economy*
rally EG *Markets began to rally worldwide.*

resuscitate EG *a bid to resuscitate the weekly magazine*

WORD POWER

▷ **Synonyms**
invigorate
reanimate
rekindle
revitalize

reward NOUN
something given in return for a service
EG *As a reward for good behaviour, treat your child to a new toy.*
bonus EG *We don't get a Christmas bonus any more.*
bounty EG *They paid bounties to people to give up their weapons.*
payment EG *Players now expect payment for interviews.*
prize EG *He won first prize.*

rhythm NOUN
a regular movement or beat
EG *His body twists and sways to the rhythm.*
beat EG *the thumping beat of rock music*
pulse EG *the repetitive pulse of the drum beat*
tempo EG *Elgar supplied his works with precise indications of tempo.*
time EG *A reel is in four-four time.*

❶ **rich** ADJECTIVE
having a lot of money and possessions
EG *You're going to be a very rich man.*
affluent EG *an affluent neighbourhood*
loaded SLANG EG *Of course he can afford it. He's loaded.*
opulent EG *his opulent lifestyle*
prosperous EG *the youngest son of a relatively prosperous family*
wealthy EG *a wealthy international businessman*

well off EG *My grandparents were quite well off.*

WORD POWER

▶ **Antonym**
poor

❷ **rich** ADJECTIVE
abundant in something
EG *Bananas are rich in vitamin A.*
abundant EG *the Earth's most abundant natural resources*
fertile EG *a fertile imagination*
plentiful EG *a plentiful supply of vegetables*

WORD POWER

▷ **Synonyms**
fecund
plenteous

rid get rid of VERB
to remove or destroy something
EG *a senior manager who wanted to get rid of him*
dispose of EG *He disposed of the murder weapon.*
dump EG *We dumped our bags at the hotel.*
eject EG *Officials used guard dogs to eject the protestors.*
jettison EG *The crew jettisoned excess fuel.*
remove EG *Most of her fears had been removed.*
weed out EG *We must weed these people out as soon as possible.*

ridiculous ADJECTIVE
very foolish
EG *It is ridiculous to suggest we are having a romance.*
absurd EG *absurd claims to have met big stars*
laughable EG *He claims the allegations are "laughable".*
ludicrous EG *It's a completely ludicrous idea.*
preposterous EG *their preposterous claim that they had unearthed a plot*

a b c d e f g h i j k l m n o p q r s t u v w x y z

❶ right ADJECTIVE

in accordance with the facts

EG *That clock never tells the right time.*

accurate EG *an accurate record of events*

correct EG *The correct answers can be found at the bottom of the page.*

exact EG *That clock never tells the exact time.*

factual EG *His version of events is not strictly factual.*

genuine EG *a genuine eyewitness account*

precise EG *Officials did not give precise figures.*

strict EG *He has never been a playboy in the strict sense of the word.*

true EG *The true cost often differs from that.*

valid EG *Your point is a valid one.*

WORD POWER

▷ **Synonyms**
unerring
veracious

▶ **Antonym**
wrong

---

❷ right ADJECTIVE

most suitable

EG *The time is right for our escape.*

acceptable EG *This was beyond the bounds of acceptable behaviour.*

appropriate EG *an appropriate outfit for the occasion.*

desirable EG *This goal is neither achievable nor desirable.*

done EG *It just isn't done to behave like that in public.*

fit EG *a subject which is not fit for discussion*

fitting EG *a fitting end to an exciting match*

okay *or* **ok** INFORMAL EG *Is it okay if I bring a friend with me?*

proper EG *It was not thought proper for a woman to appear on the stage.*

seemly EG *the rules of civility and seemly conduct*

suitable EG *the most suitable man for the job*

❸ right NOUN

what is just and fair

EG *At least he knew right from wrong.*

fairness EG *a decision based not on fairness but on expediency*

equity EG *Income should be distributed with some sense of equity.*

honour EG *His whole life was domintaed by his sense of honour.*

integrity EG *They always strove to maintain a high level of integrity.*

justice EG *He has no sense of justice or fair play.*

legality EG *They are expected to observe the principles of legality.*

morality EG *standards of morality and justice in society*

virtue EG *Virtue is not confined to the Christian world.*

WORD POWER

▷ **Synonyms**
lawfulness
rectitude
righteousness
uprightness

---

right-wing ADJECTIVE

believing in capitalist policies

EG *some right-wing politicians*

conservative EG *the conservative manifesto*

reactionary EG *reactionary army people*

Tory BRITISH EG *a senior Tory peer*

❶ rigid ADJECTIVE

unchangeable and often considered severe

EG *Hospital routines for nurses are very rigid.*

fixed EG *fixed laws*

inflexible EG *Workers said the system was too inflexible.*

set EG *They have very set ideas about how to achieve this.*

strict EG *a strict diet*
stringent EG *stringent rules*

2 rigid ADJECTIVE
not easy to bend
EG *rigid plastic containers*
firm EG *a firm platform*
hard EG *Something cold and hard pressed into his back.*
solid EG *The concrete will stay as solid as a rock.*
stiff EG *Her fingers were stiff with cold.*

WORD POWER
▶ Antonym
flexible

1 ring VERB
to make a loud clear sound
EG *He heard the school bell ring.*
chime EG *The clock chimed three o'clock.*
clang EG *A little later the church bell clanged.*
peal EG *Church bells pealed at the stroke of midnight.*
resonate EG *a strap hung with bells and resonating gongs*
toll EG *The pilgrims tolled the bell.*

2 ring NOUN
an object or group of things in the shape of a circle
EG *a ring of blue smoke*
band EG *a black arm-band*
circle EG *Cut out four circles of pastry.*
hoop EG *a steel hoop*
loop EG *a loop of garden hose*
round EG *small fresh rounds of goats' cheese*

3 ring NOUN
a group of people involved in an illegal activity
EG *a drug-trafficking ring*
band EG *a small band of plotters*
cell EG *a cell of neo-Nazis*
clique EG *A small clique of people is trying to take over the party.*

syndicate EG *a major crime syndicate*

1 riot NOUN
a disturbance made by an unruly mob
EG *a prison riot*
anarchy EG *a decade of civil war and anarchy*
disorder EG *mass public disorder*
disturbance EG *Three fans were injured in a violent disturbance outside a pub.*
mob violence EG *last week's mob violence in Bucharest*
strife EG *communal strife in Los Angeles*

2 riot VERB
to take part in a riot
EG *They rioted in protest against the Government.*
go on the rampage EG *Rock fans went on the rampage after a concert.*
rampage EG *A curfew was imposed as gangs rampaged through the streets.*
run riot EG *hooligans running riot in the streets*
take to the streets EG *Workers and students took to the streets in protest.*

1 rise VERB
to move upwards
EG *Wilson watched the smoke rise from his cigar.*
ascend EG *He held her hand as they ascended the steps.*
climb EG *We climbed up the steps on to the bridge.*
go up EG *He went up the ladder quickly.*
move up EG *They moved up to second place after their win.*

2 rise VERB
to increase
EG *House prices are expected to rise this year.*
go up EG *Life expectancy has gone up*

a
b
c
d
e
f
g
h
i
j
k
l
m
n
o
p
q
r
s
t
u
v
w
x
y
z

from 50 to 58.

grow EG *The Chinese economy continues to grow.*

increase EG *the decision to increase prices*

intensify EG *The conflict is bound to intensify.*

mount EG *For several hours the tension mounted.*

WORD POWER

▶ **Antonym**
fall

---

❸ rise NOUN
an increase in something
EG *a rise in prices*

improvement EG *a major improvement in standards*

increase EG *a substantial increase in workload*

upsurge EG *an upsurge of interest in books*

WORD POWER

▶ **Antonym**
fall

---

❶ risk NOUN
a chance that something unpleasant might happen
EG *That's a risk I'm happy to take.*

danger EG *the dangers of smoking*

gamble EG *Booking a holiday can be a gamble.*

peril EG *the perils of starring in a TV commercial*

pitfall EG *the pitfalls of working abroad*

❷ risk VERB
to do something knowing that something unpleasant might happen
EG *If he doesn't play, he risks losing his place in the team.*

chance EG *No assassin would chance a shot from amongst that crowd.*

dare EG *Few people dared go anywhere on foot.*

gamble EG *gambling his life savings on the stock market*

jeopardize EG *The talks may still be jeopardized by disputes.*

put in jeopardy EG *A series of setbacks have put the whole project in jeopardy.*

❶ rival NOUN
the person someone is competing with
EG *He is well ahead of his nearest rival.*

adversary EG *political adversaries*

antagonist EG *Greece's key rival and chief antagonist, Turkey*

challenger EG *his only challenger for the presidency*

opponent EG *He's a tough opponent but I'm too good for him.*

❷ rival VERB
to be the equal or near equal of
EG *As a holiday destination, South Africa rivals Kenya for weather.*

be a match for EG *On our day we are a match for anyone.*

equal EG *The victory equalled Portugal's best in history.*

match EG *I think we matched them in every department.*

river NOUN

Types of river
beck
brook
burn (*Scottish*)
creek
estuary
rivulet
stream
tributary
watercourse
waterway

road NOUN
a route used by travellers and vehicles
EG *There was very little traffic on the roads.*

motorway EG *Britain's first*

motorway, the M1
route EG *the most direct route to the town centre*
street EG *He walked briskly down the street.*
track EG *a rough mountain track*

rob VERB
to take something from a person illegally
EG *He was beaten senseless and robbed of all his money.*
burgle EG *He admitted that he was trying to burgle the surgery.*
con INFORMAL EG *The businessman had conned him of $10,000.*
defraud EG *charges of conspiracy to defraud the government*
loot EG *thugs who have looted shops*
steal from EG *trying to steal from a woman in the street*
swindle EG *two executives who swindled their employer*

romantic ADJECTIVE
connected with sexual love
EG *a romantic relationship*
amorous EG *The object of his amorous intentions is Wendy.*
loving EG *a loving husband*
passionate EG *a passionate love affair*
tender EG *They embraced and kissed. It was a tender moment.*

1 room NOUN
a separate section in a building
EG *You can stay in my spare room.*
chamber EG *the council chamber*
office EG *I'm in the office at the end of the corridor.*

2 room NOUN
unoccupied space
EG *There wasn't enough room for his gear.*
capacity EG *a seating capacity of 17,000*
elbow room EG *There wasn't too much elbow room in the cockpit.*
space EG *the high cost of office space*

1 rot VERB
to become rotten
EG *The grain started rotting in the silos.*
decay EG *The bodies buried in the fine ash slowly decayed.*
decompose EG *The debris slowly decomposes into compost.*
fester EG *The wound is festering and gangrene has set in.*
spoil EG *Fats spoil by becoming rancid.*

WORD POWER

● **Related Words**
adjective : putrid

2 rot NOUN
the condition that affects things when they rot
EG *The timber frame was not protected against rot.*
decay EG *tooth decay*
deterioration EG *gum deterioration*
mould EG *He scraped the mould off the cheese.*

WORD POWER

▷ **Synonyms**
putrefaction
putrescence

1 rotten ADJECTIVE
decayed and no longer of use
EG *The front bay window is rotten.*
bad EG *That milk in the fridge is bad.*
decayed EG *teeth so decayed they need to be pulled*
decomposed EG *The body was too badly decomposed to be identified at once.*
mouldy EG *mouldy bread*
sour EG *sour milk*

2 rotten ADJECTIVE; INFORMAL
of very poor quality
EG *It's a rotten idea.*
inferior EG *overpriced and inferior products*
lousy SLANG EG *The menu is limited and the food is lousy.*

A B C D E F G H I J K L M N O P Q **R** S T U V W X Y Z

poor EG *The wine was very poor.*
unsatisfactory EG *if you have obtained unsatisfactory goods or services*

❶ rough ADJECTIVE
uneven and not smooth
EG *My bicycle bumped along the rough ground.*
bumpy EG *bumpy cobbled streets*
craggy EG *craggy mountains*
rocky EG *a bleak and rocky shore*
rugged EG *a remote and rugged plateau*
uneven EG *The ball bobbled awkwardly on the uneven surface.*

WORD POWER
▶ Antonym
smooth

❷ rough ADJECTIVE
difficult or unpleasant
EG *Teachers have been given a rough time.*
difficult EG *It's been a difficult month for us.*
hard EG *I've had a hard life.*
tough EG *She had a pretty tough childhood.*
unpleasant EG *The last few weeks here have been very unpleasant.*

❸ rough ADJECTIVE
only approximately correct
EG *At a rough guess it is five times more profitable.*
approximate EG *The times are approximate only.*
estimated EG *There are an estimated 90,000 gangsters in the country.*
sketchy EG *a sketchy account of the incident*
vague EG *She could only give a vague description of the intruder.*

WORD POWER
▷ Synonyms
imprecise
inexact

❶ round ADJECTIVE
shaped like a ball or a circle
EG *She has a round attractive face.*
circular EG *a circular hole twelve feet wide*
cylindrical EG *a cylindrical container*
rounded EG *a low rounded hill*
spherical EG *gold spherical earrings*

❷ round NOUN
one of a series of events
EG *After round three, two Americans shared the lead.*
lap EG *the last lap of the race*
period EG *the second period of extra time*
session EG *The World Champion was ahead after the first two sessions.*
stage EG *the second stage of the Tour de France*

route NOUN
a way from one place to another
EG *the direct route to the town centre*
channel EG *a safe channel avoiding the reefs*
course EG *The ship was on a course that followed the coastline.*
itinerary EG *The next place on our itinerary was Silistra.*
path EG *We followed the path along the clifftops.*
road EG *The coastal road is longer, but more scenic.*
way EG *I'm afraid I can't remember the way.*

❶ routine ADJECTIVE
ordinary, and done regularly
EG *a series of routine medical tests*
everyday EG *an everyday occurrence*
normal EG *The hospital claimed they were following their normal procedure.*
ordinary EG *It was just an ordinary weekend for us.*
regular EG *one of the regular checks we carry out*
standard EG *It was standard practice for untrained clerks to do this work.*

typical EG *This was a fairly typical morning scene in our house.*
usual EG *The usual methods were not effective.*

2 routine NOUN
the usual way or order someone does things
EG *The players had to change their daily routine.*
order EG *Babies respond well to order in their daily lives.*
pattern EG *All three attacks followed the same pattern.*
practice EG *a public inquiry into bank practices*
procedure EG *The White House said there would be no change in procedure.*
programme EG *It is best to follow some sort of structured programme.*
schedule EG *He has been forced to adjust his schedule.*
system EG *an efficient filing system*

1 row NOUN
several things arranged in a line
EG *He was greeted by a row of glum faces.*
bank EG *a bank of video screens*
column EG *a column of figures*
line EG *a sparse line of spectators*
queue EG *a queue of shoppers*
rank EG *a rank of taxis*

2 row NOUN
a serious disagreement
EG *This could provoke a major diplomatic row with France.*
altercation EG *He had an altercation with the umpire.*
argument EG *an argument about money*
quarrel EG *I had a terrible quarrel with my brother.*
squabble EG *There have been minor squabbles about phone bills.*

rowdy ADJECTIVE
rough and noisy
EG *He complained to the police about rowdy neighbours.*
boisterous EG *Most of the children were noisy and boisterous.*
noisy EG *My neighbours are a noisy bunch.*
unruly EG *a mother accompanied by her ghastly unruly child*
wild EG *They loved fast cars and wild parties.*

WORD POWER

▷ **Synonyms**
obstreperous
uproarious

---

royal ADJECTIVE
concerning a king or a queen or their family
EG *the royal yacht*
imperial EG *the Imperial palace in Tokyo*
regal EG *Never has she looked more regal.*
sovereign EG *the Queen's sovereign authority*

1 rubbish NOUN
unwanted things or waste material
EG *tons of rubbish waiting to be dumped*
garbage EG *I found all kinds of garbage left behind by the tide.*
litter EG *fines for dropping litter*
refuse EG *The Council made a weekly collection of refuse.*
trash EG *The yards are overgrown and covered with trash.*
waste EG *the safe disposal of toxic waste*

2 rubbish NOUN
foolish words or speech
EG *Don't talk rubbish!*
drivel EG *mindless drivel*
garbage EG *I personally think this is complete garbage.*
hot air INFORMAL EG *His justification was just hot air.*
nonsense EG *all that poetic nonsense*

A B C D E F G H I J K L M N O P Q R S T U V W X Y Z

about love
rot EG *What a load of pompous rot!*

❶ rude ADJECTIVE
not polite
EG *He is rude to her friends.*
disrespectful EG *They shouldn't treat their mother in this disrespectful way.*
impertinent EG *I don't like being asked impertinent questions.*
impudent EG *his rude and impudent behaviour*
insolent EG *a defiant, almost insolent look*

WORD POWER

▷ **Synonyms**
churlish
discourteous
peremptory

▶ **Antonym**
polite

❷ rude ADJECTIVE
unexpected and unpleasant
EG *a rude awakening*
abrupt EG *The recession brought an abrupt end to his happiness.*
unpleasant EG *an unpleasant surprise*
violent EG *violent mood swings*

❶ ruin VERB
to destroy or spoil something
EG *The crops have been ruined.*
break EG *He's broken all his toys.*
damage EG *This could damage our chances of winning.*
destroy EG *a recipe for destroying the economy*
devastate EG *A fire had devastated large parts of the castle.*
impair EG *The flavour is impaired by overcooking.*
mar EG *The celebrations were marred by violence.*
mess up EG *He's messed up his whole career.*
spoil EG *Don't let a stupid mistake*

spoil your life.
undo EG *He intends to undo everything I have fought for.*
wreck EG *He wrecked the garden.*

❷ ruin NOUN
the state of being destroyed or spoiled
EG *The vineyards were falling into ruin.*
decay EG *The house fell into a state of decay.*
destruction EG *the destruction caused by the rioters*
devastation EG *A bomb brought chaos and devastation to the city centre yesterday.*
disrepair EG *Many of the buildings had fallen into disrepair.*
downfall EG *His lack of experience led to his downfall.*
fall EG *the fall of the Roman empire*

❸ ruin NOUN
the remaining parts of a severely damaged thing
EG *the burnt-out ruins of houses*
remains EG *the remains of an ancient mosque*
shell EG *the shells of burned buildings*
wreck EG *We thought of buying the house as a wreck and doing it up.*

❶ rule NOUN
a statement of what is allowed
EG *This was against the rules.*
decree EG *a decree lifting sanctions against China*
guideline EG *Are there strict guidelines for animal experimentation?*
law EG *inflexible moral laws*
order EG *He was sacked for disobeying orders.*
regulation EG *new safety regulations*

WORD POWER

▷ **Synonyms**
dictum
ordinance
precept

❷ rule as a rule ADVERB

usually or generally

EG *As a rule, I eat my meals in front of the TV.*

generally EG *It is generally true that the darker the fruit the higher its iron content.*

mainly EG *Mainly I work alone.*

normally EG *Normally, the transport system carries 50,000 passengers a day.*

on the whole EG *Their wines are, on the whole, of a very high standard.*

usually EG *She is usually a calm and diplomatic woman.*

❸ rule VERB

to govern people

EG *For four centuries, he says, foreigners have ruled Angola.*

administer EG *calls for the UN to administer the country until the election*

be in power EG *They were in power for eighteen years.*

govern EG *The citizens are thankful they are not governed by a dictator.*

lead EG *He led the country between 1949 and 1984.*

reign EG *Henry II reigned from 1154 to 1189.*

ruler NOUN

a person who rules or commands

EG *He was a weak-willed and indecisive ruler.*

commander EG *He is commander of the US Fifth Fleet.*

governor EG *He was governor of the province in the late 1970s.*

head of state EG *the heads of state of all the countries in the European Union*

leader EG *the leader of the German Social Democratic Party*

monarch EG *the coronation of the new monarch*

sovereign EG *the first British sovereign to set foot on Spanish soil*

rumour NOUN

a story which may or may not be true

EG *persistent rumours of quarrels within the movement*

gossip EG *We spent the first hour exchanging gossip.*

hearsay EG *Much of what was reported to them was hearsay.*

whisper EG *I've heard a whisper that the Bishop intends to leave.*

word EG *What's the latest word from Washington?*

❶ run VERB

to move on foot at a rapid pace

EG *I excused myself and ran back to the telephone.*

bolt EG *The pig rose, squealing, and bolted.*

gallop EG *The horses galloped away.*

jog EG *He could scarcely jog around the block that first day.*

sprint EG *She sprinted to the car.*

❷ run VERB

to manage

EG *He ran a small hotel.*

administer EG *the authorities who administer the island*

be in charge of EG *He is in charge of public safety.*

control EG *He now controls a large retail development empire.*

direct EG *Christopher will direct day-to-day operations.*

look after EG *I look after his finances for him.*

manage EG *Within two years he was managing the store.*

❶ rush VERB

to move fast or do something quickly

EG *Someone rushed out of the building.*

dash EG *She dashed in from the garden.*

fly EG *I must fly or I'll miss my train.*

gush EG *Piping-hot water gushed out.*

hasten EG *One of them hastened*

A
B
C
D
E
F
G
H
I
J
K
L
M
N
O
P
Q
R
S
T
U
V
W
X
Y
Z

towards me.

hurry EG *She had to hurry home to look after her son.*

race EG *He raced across town to her house.*

run EG *I excused myself and ran to the door.*

scurry EG *Reporters scurried to get to the phones.*

shoot EG *The car shot out of a junction and smashed into them.*

❷ rush VERB

to force into immediate action without sufficient preparation

EG *Ministers won't be rushed into a response.*

hurrry EG *I don't want to hurry you.*

hustle EG *You won't hustle me into making a commitment.*

press EG *attempting to press me into making a statement*

pressurize EG *Do not be pressurized into making your decision immediately*

push EG *Don't be pushed into signing anything.*

❸ rush NOUN

a state of hurrying

EG *the rush not to be late for school*

bustle EG *the bustle of modern life*

dash EG *a 160-mile dash to the hospital*

hurry EG *Eric left the house in a hurry.*

race EG *a race to get the work finished before the deadline*

scramble EG *the scramble to get a seat on the early morning flight*

stampede EG *There was a stampede for the exit.*

Ss

❶ sack VERB; INFORMAL
to dismiss from a job
EG *sacked for punching his boss*
discharge EG *discharged from the army*
dismiss EG *the power to dismiss employees*
fire INFORMAL EG *He was fired for poor timekeeping.*

❷ sack the sack NOUN; INFORMAL
dismissal from a job
EG *He got the sack after three months.*
discharge EG *He plans to appeal his discharge.*
dismissal EG *the case for his dismissal*
termination of employment
EG *wrongful termination of employment*

❶ sacrifice VERB
to give something up
EG *She sacrificed her family life for her career.*
forego EG *If we forego our summer holiday we can afford a car.*
forfeit EG *The company is forfeiting safety for the sake of profit.*
give up EG *I gave up my job to be with you.*
surrender EG *We have surrendered our political authority for economic gain.*

❷ sacrifice NOUN
the action of giving something up
EG *He was willing to make any sacrifice for peace.*
renunciation EG *religious principles of renunciation and dedication*
self-denial EG *an unprecedented act of self-denial*

❶ sad ADJECTIVE
feeling unhappy about something
EG *The loss of our friendship makes me sad.*
blue EG *I don't know why I'm feeling so blue today.*

dejected EG *Everyone has days when they feel dejected.*
depressed EG *She's depressed about this whole situation.*
dismal EG *What are you all looking so dismal about?*
down EG *The old man sounded really down.*
downcast EG *a downcast expression*
glum EG *a row of glum faces*
gloomy EG *Don't look so gloomy, Mr Todd. I'll do my best for you.*
grief-stricken EG *comforting the grief-stricken relatives*
low EG *He used to listen when I was feeling low.*
melancholy EG *melancholy thoughts*
mournful EG *the mournful expression on his face*
unhappy EG *I hate to see you so unhappy.*
wistful EG *I found myself feeling wistful at the memory of him.*

WORD POWER

▷ **Synonyms**
disconsolate
doleful
heavy-hearted
low-spirited
lugubrious
woebegone

▶ **Antonym**
happy

---

❷ sad ADJECTIVE
making you feel unhappy
EG *a sad song*
depressing EG *a depressing film*
dismal EG *a dark, dismal day*
gloomy EG *a gloomy tale of a poor orphan*
harrowing EG *a harrowing documentary about drug addicts*
heart-rending EG *heart-rending pictures of the victims*
melancholy EG *the melancholy*

A
B
C
D
E
F
G
H
I
J
K
L
M
N
O
P
Q
R
S
T
U
V
W
X
Y
Z

music used throughout the film
mournful EG *a mournful ballad*
moving EG *a deeply moving account of her life*
pathetic EG *the pathetic sight of oil-covered sea birds*
poignant EG *a poignant love story*
tragic EG *his tragic death*
upsetting EG *I'm afraid I have some upsetting news for you.*

sadness NOUN
the feeling of being unhappy
EG *I said goodbye with a mixture of sadness and joy.*
dejection EG *a feeling of dejection and despair*
depression EG *plunged into the deepest depression*
despondency EG *Deep despondency set in again.*
melancholy EG *Dean had shaken off his melancholy.*
unhappiness EG *His unhappiness shows in his face.*

WORD POWER

▷ **Synonyms**
cheerlessness
dolefulness

▶ **Antonym**
happiness

❶ **safe** ADJECTIVE
not causing harm or danger
EG *This is not a safe place for a woman on her own.*
harmless EG *harmless substances*
innocuous EG *Both mushrooms look innocuous but are in fact deadly.*
wholesome EG *fresh, wholesome ingredients*

WORD POWER

▶ **Antonym**
dangerous

❷ **safe** ADJECTIVE
not in any danger

EG *I felt warm and safe with him.*
all right EG *I'll be all right on my own.*
in safe hands EG *It's all right, you're in safe hands.*
okay or **OK** INFORMAL EG *Could you check that the baby's okay?*
out of danger EG *We were not out of danger yet.*
out of harm's way EG *I'm keeping him well out of harm's way.*
protected EG *Keep the plants dry and protected from frost.*
safe and sound EG *I'm hoping he will come home safe and sound.*
secure EG *I would like to feel financially secure.*

❶ **safeguard** VERB
to protect something
EG *international action to safeguard the ozone layer*
defend EG *his courage in defending religious and civil rights*
guard EG *He closely guarded her identity.*
look after EG *People tend to look after their own property.*
preserve EG *We need to preserve the forest.*
protect EG *What can we do to protect ourselves against heart disease?*
save EG *This machine could help save babies from cot death.*
shield EG *They moved to shield their children from adverse publicity.*

❷ **safeguard** NOUN
something that protects people or things
EG *adequate safeguards for civil liberties*
barrier EG *a barrier against the outside world*
cover EG *Airlines are required to provide cover against such incidents.*
defence EG *The immune system is our main defence against disease.*
protection EG *Innocence is no protection from the evils in our society.*

safety NOUN

the state of being safe from harm or danger

EG *I was very anxious about her safety.*

immunity EG *natural immunity to the disease*

protection EG *protection from harmful rays*

security EG *a false sense of security*

WORD POWER

▶ **Antonym**
danger

---

salty ADJECTIVE

tasting of or containing salt

EG *a good rasher of salty bacon*

brak SOUTH AFRICAN EG *the brak shallow water near the dam wall*

briny EG *the flow of the briny water*

salted EG *8 ounces of slightly salted butter*

same ADJECTIVE

exactly like one another

EG *The two words sound the same but have different spellings.*

alike EG *No two families are alike.*

equal EG *Mix equal quantities of soy sauce and rice vinegar.*

equivalent EG *One unit is roughly equivalent to a glass of wine.*

identical EG *Nearly all the houses were identical.*

indistinguishable EG *symptoms indistinguishable from those of AIDS*

WORD POWER

▶ **Antonym**
different

---

① sanction VERB

to officially approve of or allow something

EG *He is ready to sanction the use of force.*

allow EG *I cannot be seen to allow violence on school premises.*

approve EG *The parliament has approved a programme of economic reforms.*

authorize EG *We are willing to authorize a police raid.*

back EG *persuading the government to back the plan*

endorse EG *policies endorsed by the voting public*

permit EG *Will he let the court's decision stand and permit the execution?*

support EG *The party is under pressure to support the ban.*

WORD POWER

▶ **Antonym**
veto

---

② sanction NOUN

official approval of something

EG *The king could not enact the law without the sanction of parliament.*

approval EG *The chairman has given his approval.*

authorization EG *You will need the authorization of a parent or guardian.*

backing EG *He said the president had the backing of his government.*

blessing EG *With the blessing of the White House, the group is meeting to identify more budget cuts.*

permission EG *Finally she gave permission for him to marry.*

support EG *The prime minister gave his support to the reforms.*

WORD POWER

▷ **Synonyms**
assent
mandate
ratification (FORMAL)

---

sanctions NOUN

penalties for countries which break the law

EG *The United States is considering imposing sanctions against the regime.*

ban EG *After four years, he lifted the ban.*

a b c d e f g h i j k l m n o p q r s t u v w x y z

boycott EG *the lifting of the economic boycott against the country*
embargo EG *They called on the government to lift its embargo on trade with the country.*
penalties EG *legally binding penalties against treaty violators*

1 sane ADJECTIVE
having a normal healthy mind
EG *This was not the act of a sane person.*
lucid EG *She was lucid right up until her death.*
normal EG *the question of what constitutes normal behaviour*
rational EG *He seemed perfectly rational to me.*

WORD POWER

▷ Synonyms
compos mentis
in your right mind
of sound mind

▶ Antonym
mad

2 sane ADJECTIVE
showing good sense
EG *a sane and practical policy*
judicious EG *the judicious use of military force*
level-headed EG *a sensible, level-headed approach*
rational EG *a rational analysis*
reasonable EG *a reasonable course of action*
sensible EG *the sensible thing to do*
sound EG *sound advice*

sarcastic ADJECTIVE
saying the opposite of what you mean to make fun of someone
EG *A sarcastic remark was on the tip of her tongue.*
caustic EG *his abrasive wit and caustic comments*
ironic EG *an ironic remark*
sardonic EG *a sardonic sense of humour*
satirical EG *a satirical TV show*

WORD POWER

▷ Synonyms
derisive
mordacious
mordant

satisfactory ADJECTIVE
acceptable or adequate
EG *a satisfactory explanation*
acceptable EG *The air pollution exceeds acceptable levels.*
adequate EG *One in four people are without adequate homes.*
all right EG *The meal was all right, but nothing special.*
good enough EG *He's not good enough for you.*
passable EG *She speaks passable French.*
sufficient EG *One teaspoon of sugar should be sufficient.*

WORD POWER

▶ Antonym
unsatisfactory

satisfied ADJECTIVE
happy because you have got what you want
EG *We are not satisfied with these results.*
content EG *I'm perfectly content where I am.*
contented EG *She led a quiet, contented life.*
happy EG *I'm not happy with the situation.*
pleased EG *He seemed pleased with the arrangement.*

WORD POWER

▶ Antonym
disappointed

1 satisfy VERB
to give someone as much of

satisfy >> save

something as they want
EG *a solution which I hope will satisfy everyone*

gratify EG *He was gratified by the audience's response.*

indulge EG *I don't believe in indulging children.*

please EG *Our prime objective is to please our customers.*

WORD POWER

▷ **Synonyms**
assuage
pander to
sate
satiate
slake

❷ satisfy VERB
to convince someone of something
EG *He had to satisfy the doctors that he was fit to play.*

convince EG *trying to convince the public that its product is safe*

persuade EG *I had to persuade him of the advantages.*

put someone's mind at rest
EG *He has done his best to put my mind at rest.*

reassure EG *I tried to reassure them, but they knew I was lying.*

❸ satisfy VERB
to fulfil a requirement
EG *Candidates must satisfy the conditions for admission.*

fulfil EG *All the minimum requirements were fulfilled.*

meet EG *The current arrangements are inadequate to meet their needs.*

❶ savage ADJECTIVE
cruel and violent
EG *a savage attack*

barbarous EG *the barbarous customs of earlier times*

barbaric EG *a particularly barbaric act of violence*

brutal EG *a very brutal murder*

cruel EG *the cruel practice of*

bullfighting

ferocious EG *the most ferocious violence ever seen on the streets of London*

inhuman EG *the inhuman slaughter of these beautiful creatures*

vicious EG *a vicious blow to the head*

violent EG *violent crimes*

❷ savage NOUN
a violent and uncivilized person
EG *They really are a bunch of savages.*

barbarian EG *Our maths teacher was a complete barbarian.*

beast EG *You beast! Let me go!*

brute EG *He was a brute and he deserved his fate.*

lout EG *a drunken lout*

monster EG *These men were total monsters.*

❸ savage VERB
to attack and bite someone
EG *He was savaged to death by the animal.*

attack EG *A lion attacked him when he was a child.*

bite EG *Every year thousands of children are bitten by dogs.*

maul EG *The dog went berserk and mauled one of the girls.*

❶ save VERB
to rescue someone or something
EG *He saved my life.*

come to someone's rescue EG *His uncle came to his rescue.*

deliver EG *I thanked God for delivering me from the pain.*

redeem EG *to redeem souls from purgatory*

rescue EG *rescued from the flames*

salvage EG *salvaging equipment from the wreckage*

❷ save VERB
to keep someone or something safe
EG *a new machine which could save babies from cot death*

keep safe EG *to keep my home safe from germs*

a b c d e f g h i j k l m n o p q r s t u v w x y z

preserve EG *preserving old buildings*
protect EG *What can we do to protect ourselves from heart disease?*
safeguard EG *measures to safeguard the ozone layer*

❸ save VERB
to keep something for later use
EG *They are saving for a house.*
hoard EG *They've begun to hoard food and petrol.*
keep EG *Grate the lemon zest and keep it for later.*
put by EG *He's putting his money by in a deposit account.*
reserve EG *Drain the fruit and reserve the juice.*
set aside EG *£130 million would be set aside for repairs to schools.*

WORD POWER
▷ **Synonyms**
economize
husband
retrench

▶ **Antonym**
waste

❶ say VERB
to speak words
EG *She said they were very impressed.*
→ see Word Study **say**

❷ say NOUN
a chance to express your opinion
EG *voters who want a say in the matter*
voice EG *parents are given a voice in decision-making*
vote EG *Every employee felt he had a vote in the company's future.*

saying NOUN
a well-known sentence or phrase
EG *the saying, "charity begins at home"*
adage EG *the old adage, "the show must go on"*
axiom EG *the long-held axiom that education leads to higher income*
maxim EG *I believe in the maxim, "If it*

ain't broke, don't fix it".
proverb EG *an old Chinese proverb*

WORD POWER
▷ **Synonyms**
aphorism
apophthegm
dictum
saw

scarce ADJECTIVE
rare or uncommon
EG *Jobs are becoming increasingly scarce.*
few EG *Our options are few.*
rare EG *Puffins are now rare in this country.*
uncommon EG *an extreme but by no means uncommon case*
unusual EG *To be appreciated as a parent is quite unusual.*

WORD POWER
▶ **Antonym**
common

❶ scare VERB
to frighten someone
EG *You're scaring me.*
alarm EG *We could not see what had alarmed him.*
frighten EG *He knew that Soli was trying to frighten him.*
give someone a fright EG *The snake moved and gave everyone a fright.*
intimidate EG *Jones had set out to intimidate and dominate Paul.*
startle EG *Sorry, I didn't mean to startle you.*
terrify EG *Flying terrifies him.*
terrorize EG *pensioners terrorized by anonymous phone calls*
unnerve EG *We were unnerved by the total silence.*

❷ scare NOUN
a short period of feeling very frightened
EG *We got a bit of a scare.*

fright EG *the last time I had a real fright*

shock EG *It gave me quite a shock to see his face on the screen.*

start EG *The sudden noise gave me quite a start.*

❸ **scare** NOUN
a situation where people worry about something
EG *Despite the health scare there are no plans to withdraw the drug.*

alert EG *a security alert*

hysteria EG *Everyone was getting carried away by the hysteria.*

panic EG *the panic over GM foods*

scary ADJECTIVE; INFORMAL
frightening
EG *Prison is going to be a scary thing for him.*

alarming EG *an alarming report on the rise of street crime*

chilling EG *a chilling account of the accident*

creepy INFORMAL EG *places that are really creepy at night*

eerie EG *the eerie dark path*

frightening EG *a very frightening experience*

hair-raising EG *a hair-raising encounter with a wild boar*

spooky EG *The whole place has a slightly spooky atmosphere.*

terrifying EG *I find it terrifying to be surrounded by a crowd of people.*

unnerving EG *It is very unnerving to find out that someone you know is carrying the virus.*

scatter VERB
to throw or drop things all over an area
EG *She scattered the petals over the grave.*

shower EG *The bomb exploded, showering shrapnel over a wide area.*

sow EG *Sow the seeds in a warm place.*

sprinkle EG *Sprinkle a tablespoon of sugar over the fruit.*

throw about EG *They started throwing food about.*

WORD POWER

▷ **Synonyms**
broadcast
disseminate
strew

▶ **Antonym**
gather

---

❶ **scene** NOUN
a picture or view of something
EG *a village scene*

landscape EG *Arizona's desert landscape*

panorama EG *a panorama of fertile valleys*

view EG *a view of the lake*

WORD POWER

▷ **Synonyms**
outlook
vista

---

❷ **scene** NOUN
the place where something happens
EG *the scene of the crime*

location EG *filmed in an exotic location*

place EG *Can you show me the place where the attack happened?*

setting EG *Rome is the perfect setting for romance.*

site EG *the site of the battle*

spot EG *the ideal spot for a picnic*

❸ **scene** NOUN
an area of activity
EG *the music scene*

arena EG *the political arena*

business EG *the potential to revolutionize the publishing business*

environment EG *the Japanese business environment*

world EG *the fashion world*

scenery NOUN
the things you see in the countryside

a b c d e f g h i j k l m n o p q r **s** t u v w x y z

A
B
C
D
E
F
G
H
I
J
K
L
M
N
O
P
Q
R
S
T
U
V
W
X
Y
Z

EG *drive slowly down the lane enjoying the scenery*
landscape EG *Arizona's desert landscape*
panorama EG *admiring the distant mountain panorama*
surroundings EG *a holiday home in beautiful surroundings*
terrain EG *The terrain changed from arable land to desert.*
view EG *The view from our window was spectacular.*

WORD POWER

▷ **Synonyms**
vista

scold VERB
to tell someone off
EG *She scolded her daughter for being cheeky.*
chide EG *Cross chided himself for worrying.*
lecture EG *My mother always used to lecture me about not eating properly.*
rebuke EG *I turned to him and sharply rebuked him.*
reprimand EG *reprimanded for talking in the corridor*
tell off INFORMAL EG *The teacher really told her off.*
tick off INFORMAL EG *ticked off for being late*

WORD POWER

▷ **Synonyms**
berate
castigate
reprove
upbraid

❶ scorn NOUN
great contempt felt for something
EG *The proposal was greeted with scorn.*
contempt EG *I treated this remark with the contempt it deserved.*
derision EG *shouts of derision*
disdain EG *Janet looked at him with*

disdain.
mockery EG *his mockery of all things English*

❷ scorn VERB
to treat with great contempt
EG *Eleanor scorns the work of others.*
despise EG *She secretly despises him.*
disdain EG *He disdained politicians.*
look down on EG *I wasn't successful so they looked down on me.*
slight EG *He felt slighted by this treatment.*

WORD POWER

▷ **Synonyms**
be above
contemn
hold in contempt

scornful ADJECTIVE
showing contempt for something
EG *He is deeply scornful of his rivals.*
contemptuous EG *She gave a contemptuous little laugh.*
disdainful EG *He is disdainful of politicians.*
scathing EG *He made some scathing comments about the design.*
sneering EG *a sneering tone*
supercilious EG *His manner is supercilious and arrogant.*
withering EG *Her mother gave her a withering look.*

❶ scrape VERB
to rub a rough or sharp object against something
EG *We had to scrape the frost from the windscreen.*
graze EG *He had grazed his knees a little.*
scour EG *Scour the pans.*
scratch EG *The branches scratched my face and hands.*
scuff EG *scuffed shoes*
skin EG *I found that I had skinned my knuckles.*

❷ scrape VERB
to make a harsh noise by rubbing

EG *his shoes scraping across the ground*

grate EG *His chair grated as he got to his feet.*

grind EG *Blocks of ice ground against each other.*

rasp EG *The blade rasped over his skin.*

scratch EG *He scraped his knife over the worktop.*

❶ scream VERB
to shout or cry in a high-pitched voice
EG *If he says that again, I shall scream.*

cry EG *a crying baby*

howl EG *He howled like a wounded animal.*

screech EG *"Get me some water!" I screeched.*

shout EG *I shouted at mother to get the police.*

shriek EG *She shrieked and leapt from the bed.*

squeal EG *Jennifer squealed with delight.*

yell EG *I pushed him away, yelling abuse.*

❷ scream NOUN
a loud, high-pitched cry
EG *Hilda let out a scream.*

cry EG *a cry of horror*

howl EG *a howl of rage*

screech EG *The figure gave a screech.*

shriek EG *a shriek of joy*

squeal EG *the squeal of piglets*

yell EG *Something brushed Bob's face and he let out a yell.*

scrounge VERB; INFORMAL
to get something by asking rather than working for it
EG *He's always scrounging lifts.*

beg EG *They managed to beg a lift from a passing fisherman.*

bludge AUSTRALIAN AND NEW ZEALAND; INFORMAL EG *They've come here to bludge food and money.*

cadge EG *Can I cadge a cigarette?*

sponge INFORMAL EG *I got tired of him sponging off me and threw him out.*

scruffy ADJECTIVE
dirty and untidy
EG *four scruffy youths*

ragged EG *a ragged band of men*

seedy EG *his seedy clothes*

shabby EG *a shabby, tall man with dark eyes*

tatty EG *a tatty old cardigan*

unkempt EG *His hair was unkempt and filthy.*

WORD POWER

▷ **Synonyms**
disreputable
slovenly
ungroomed

▶ **Antonym**
smart

---

scrutinize VERB
to examine something very carefully
EG *She scrutinized his features.*

examine EG *He examined her passport.*

inspect EG *Cut the fruit in half and inspect the pips.*

pore over EG *We spent hours poring over the files.*

scan EG *She kept scanning the crowd for Paul.*

search EG *Her eyes searched his face.*

study EG *Debbie studied the document for a moment.*

scungy ADJECTIVE; AUSTRALIAN AND NEW ZEALAND; SLANG
dirty
EG *living in some scungy flat on the outskirts of town*

dirty EG *He was wearing a dirty old mac.*

filthy EG *This flat is so filthy I can't possibly stay here.*

foul EG *foul polluted water*

seedy EG *a seedy hotel*

sleazy EG *sleazy bars*

a b c d e f g h i j k l m n o p q r **s** t u v w x y z

sordid EG *sordid little rooms*
squalid EG *a squalid bedsit*

1 search VERB

to look for something
EG *The security forces are searching for the missing men.*
comb EG *Police combed the woods for the murder weapon.*
forage EG *foraging for food*
fossick AUSTRALIAN AND NEW ZEALAND eg *to help Gaston fossick for food around the hut*
hunt EG *hunting for a job*
look EG *He's looking for a way out of this situation.*
scour EG *They had scoured the intervening miles of moorland.*
seek EG *the man he had been seeking for weeks*
sift EG *sifting through the wreckage for clues*

2 search NOUN

the action of looking for something
EG *Police will resume the search today.*
hunt EG *the hunt for my lost boy*
quest EG *his quest to find true love*

secret ADJECTIVE

known about by only a few people
EG *a secret location*
closet INFORMAL EG *a closet Fascist*
confidential EG *a confidential report*
covert EG *She gave him a covert glance.*
furtive EG *furtive meetings*
hidden EG *a hidden camera*
undercover EG *undercover FBI agents*
underground EG *the underground communist movement*

WORD POWER

▷ **Synonyms**
cloak-and-dagger
conspiratorial
undisclosed

● **Related Words**
adjective : cryptic

secretive ADJECTIVE

hiding your feelings and intentions
EG *Jake was very secretive about his family affairs.*
cagey INFORMAL EG *He is cagey about what he was paid for the business.*
reserved EG *He was unemotional and reserved.*
reticent EG *She is very reticent about her achievements.*

WORD POWER

▷ **Synonyms**
tight-lipped
uncommunicative
unforthcoming

section NOUN

one of the parts into which something is divided
EG *this section of the motorway*
division EG *the company's sales division*
instalment EG *Payment can be made in instalments.*
part EG *the upper part of the body*
piece EG *The equipment was taken down the shaft in pieces.*
portion EG *I had learnt a portion of the Koran.*
segment EG *the third segment of the journey*

1 secure VERB; FORMAL

to manage to get something
EG *His achievements helped him to secure the job.*
acquire EG *General Motors recently acquired a 50% stake in the company.*
gain EG *Hard work may not be enough to gain a place at university.*
get EG *I got a job at the sawmill.*
obtain EG *He tried to obtain a false passport.*
procure FORMAL EG *trying to procure the release of the hostages*

2 secure VERB

to make something safe
EG *We need to secure the building*

against attack.
fortify EG *British soldiers are working to fortify the airbase.*
make impregnable EG *Their intention was to make the old fort impregnable.*
make safe EG *Crime Prevention Officers will suggest ways to make your home safe.*
strengthen EG *In the 14th century they strengthened this wall against raiders.*

❸ **secure** VERB
to fasten or attach something firmly
EG *The frames are secured by rails to the wall.*
attach EG *The gadget can be attached to any vertical surface.*
bind EG *Bind the ends of the cord together with thread.*
fasten EG *Her long hair was fastened by an elastic band.*
fix EG *He fixed a bayonet to the end of his rifle.*
lock EG *Are you sure you locked the front door?*
moor EG *She moored her barge on the river bank.*
tie up EG *They dismounted and tied up their horses.*

WORD POWER
▶ **Antonym**
release

❹ **secure** ADJECTIVE
tightly locked or well protected
EG *Make sure your home is as secure as possible.*
fortified EG *The door is fortified against flooding.*
impregnable EG *The old castle was completely impregnable against raids.*
protected EG *the right of women to be protected from sexual harassment*
safe EG *We want to go to a football match knowing we are safe from*

hooliganism.
shielded EG *The company is shielded from takeover attempts.*

❺ **secure** ADJECTIVE
firmly fixed in place
EG *Shelves are only as secure as their fixings.*
fastened EG *Make sure the safety belt is fastened.*
firm EG *If you have to climb up, use a firm platform.*
fixed EG *Check the holder is fixed in its place on the wall.*
locked EG *Leave doors and windows locked.*
solid EG *I yanked on the bracket to see if it was solid.*
stable EG *The structure must be stable.*
tight EG *He kept a tight hold of her arm.*

❻ **secure** ADJECTIVE
feeling safe and happy
EG *She felt secure when she was with him.*
confident EG *In time he became more confident.*
protected EG *It's good to have a place in which you feel protected and loved.*
reassured EG *I feel much more reassured when I've been for a health check.*
relaxed EG *There are very few people he feels relaxed with.*
safe EG *He kissed me and I felt warm and safe.*

WORD POWER
▶ **Antonym**
insecure

❶ **see** VERB
to look at or notice something
EG *Did you see what happened?*
behold EG *She looked into his eyes and beheld madness.*
discern EG *We could just discern the*

a b c d e f g h i j k l m n o p q r s t u v w x y z

outline of the island.

glimpse EG *She glimpsed the man's face briefly.*

look EG *She turned to look at him.*

notice EG *She noticed a bird sitting on the roof.*

observe EG *He observed a reddish spot on the planet's surface.*

perceive EG *Infants start to perceive objects at a very early age.*

sight EG *A fleet of French ships was sighted.*

spot EG *I think he spotted me but didn't want to be seen.*

WORD POWER

▷ **Synonyms**
catch sight of
descry
espy

❷ see VERB

to realize or understand something
EG *I see what you mean.*

appreciate EG *He appreciates the difficulties.*

comprehend EG *They do not comprehend the nature of the problem.*

follow EG *Do you follow what I'm saying?*

get EG *You don't seem to get the point.*

grasp EG *They have not grasped the seriousness of the crisis.*

realize EG *They realized too late that they were wrong.*

understand EG *I'm not sure I understand.*

❸ see VERB

to find something out
EG *I'll see what's happening outside.*

ascertain EG *Ascertain what services your bank provides.*

determine EG *The investigation will determine what happened.*

discover EG *Try to discover what you are good at.*

find out EG *Watch the next episode to find out what happens.*

❶ seek VERB

to try to find something
EG *The police were still seeking information.*

be after EG *At last I found what I was after.*

hunt EG *Police are hunting for clues.*

look for EG *I'm looking for a lost child.*

search for EG *searching for answers*

❷ seek VERB

to try to do something
EG *De Gaulle sought to reunite the country.*

aim EG *We aim to raise funds for charity.*

aspire to EG *He aspired to work in music journalism.*

attempt EG *He was forever attempting to arrange deals.*

endeavour EG *They are endeavouring to protect trade union rights.*

strive EG *The school strives to treat pupils as individuals.*

try EG *We are trying to bring about a better world.*

seem VERB

to appear to be
EG *He seemed such a quiet man.*

appear EG *She appeared intoxicated.*

give the impression EG *He gave the impression of being the perfect husband.*

look EG *The cottage looks quite ordinary from the road.*

look like EG *You look like a nice guy.*

❶ seize VERB

to grab something firmly
EG *He seized the phone.*

grab EG *I grabbed him by the neck.*

grasp EG *He grasped both my hands.*

snatch EG *Mick snatched the cards from Archie's hand.*

❷ seize VERB

to take control of something

EG *Rebels have seized the airport.*
annex EG *the plan to invade and annex Kuwait*
appropriate EG *The land was appropriated by Communists.*
confiscate EG *The police confiscated weapons and ammunition.*
hijack EG *Almost 250 trucks were hijacked.*
impound EG *The ship was impounded under the terms of the trade embargo.*

WORD POWER

▷ **Synonyms**
commandeer
take possession of

❶ **select** VERB
to choose something
EG *They selected only the brightest pupils.*
choose EG *Houston was chosen as the site for the conference.*
decide on EG *I'm still trying to decide on an outfit for the wedding.*
opt for EG *You may wish to opt for one method straight away.*
pick EG *He had picked ten people to interview for the jobs.*
settle on EG *I finally settled on the estate car because it was so roomy.*
single out EG *His boss has singled him out for a special mission.*
take EG *"I'll take the grilled tuna," she told the waiter.*

❷ **select** ADJECTIVE
of good quality
EG *a select band of top-ranking sportsmen*
choice EG *We use only the choicest ingredients.*
exclusive EG *Britain's most exclusive club*
first-class EG *a first-class hotel*
first-rate EG *The first-rate cast includes many famous names.*
hand-picked EG *a hand-picked series of timeless classics*

prime EG *one of the City's prime sites, with a view of several historic buildings*
special EG *a special group of government officials*
superior EG *a superior range of products*

selfish ADJECTIVE
caring only about yourself
EG *his greedy and selfish behaviour*
egoistic *or* **egoistical** EG *egoistic motives*
egotistic *or* **egotistical** EG *an intensely egotistic streak*
greedy EG *greedy bosses awarding themselves big rises*
self-centred EG *He was self-centred, but he wasn't cruel.*

WORD POWER

▷ **Synonyms**
self-interested
self-seeking
ungenerous

sell VERB
to let someone have something in return for money
EG *a tobacconist that sells stamps*
deal in EG *They deal in antiques.*
hawk EG *vendors hawking trinkets*
peddle EG *arrested for peddling drugs*
stock EG *The shop stocks a variety of local craft products.*
trade in EG *They trade in spices and all kinds of grain.*

WORD POWER

▷ **Synonyms**
market
merchandise
retail
vend

▶ **Antonym**
buy

❶ **send** VERB
to arrange for something to be

a b c d e f g h i j k l m n o p q r s t u v w x y z

delivered
EG *He sent a basket of fruit and a card.*
dispatch EG *He dispatched a telegram of congratulation.*
forward EG *A letter was forwarded from the clinic.*
remit EG *Many immigrants regularly remit money to their families.*

2 send VERB
to transmit a signal or message
EG *The pilot was trying to send a distress signal.*
broadcast EG *to broadcast a message to a whole group of people at once*
transmit EG *the most efficient way to transmit data*

senior ADJECTIVE
the highest and most important in an organization
EG *senior jobs*
best EG *These officers have traditionally taken the best jobs.*
better EG *Well-qualified women are now attaining better positions.*
high-ranking EG *a high-ranking officer in the medical corps*
superior EG *negotiations between crew members and their superior officers*

WORD POWER

▶ **Antonym**
junior

1 sense NOUN
a feeling you have about something
EG *an overwhelming sense of guilt*
consciousness EG *a consciousness of tension*
feeling EG *It gave me a feeling of satisfaction.*
impression EG *The music creates an impression of menace.*

2 sense NOUN
the ability to think and behave sensibly
EG *He had the good sense to call me at*

once.
brains INFORMAL EG *At least I had the brains to keep quiet.*
common sense EG *completely lacking in common sense*
intelligence EG *He didn't have the intelligence to understand what was happening.*
judgment EG *I respect his judgment.*
reason EG *a conflict between emotion and reason*
wisdom EG *the wisdom that comes of old age*

WORD POWER

▶ **Synonyms**
nous
sagacity
wit *or* wits

3 sense VERB
to become aware of something
EG *She sensed he wasn't telling her the whole story.*
be aware of EG *He was aware of her anger.*
feel EG *Suddenly, I felt a presence behind me.*
get the impression EG *I get the impression he's lying.*
have a hunch EG *Lowe had a hunch he was on to something.*
realize EG *We realized something was wrong.*

sensible ADJECTIVE
showing good sense and judgment
EG *a sensible, level-headed approach*
down-to-earth EG *the most down-to-earth person I've ever met*
judicious EG *the judicious use of military force*
practical EG *practical suggestions*
prudent EG *It is prudent to start any exercise programme gradually.*
rational EG *a rational decision*
sound EG *sound advice*
wise EG *a wise move*

WORD POWER

▶ **Antonym**
foolish

sensitive ADJECTIVE
easily upset about something
EG *He was sensitive about his height.*
easily offended EG *I am not a feminist, nor am I easily offended.*
easily upset EG *He remained deeply neurotic and easily upset.*
thin-skinned EG *I'm too thin-skinned - I want everyone to like me.*
touchy EG *She is very touchy about her weight.*

sentimental ADJECTIVE
expressing exaggerated sadness or tenderness
EG *sentimental love stories*
maudlin EG *Jimmy turned maudlin after three drinks.*
mushy INFORMAL EG *I go completely mushy when I see a baby.*
nostalgic EG *nostalgic for the good old days*
sloppy INFORMAL EG *I hate sloppy romantic films.*
slushy INFORMAL EG *slushy ballads*

WORD POWER

▷ **Synonyms**
dewy-eyed
mawkish
overemotional

❶ **separate** ADJECTIVE
not connected to something else
EG *The question muddles up two separate issues.*
detached EG *a detached house*
disconnected EG *sequences of disconnected events*
discrete EG *two discrete sets of nerves*
divorced EG *speculative theories divorced from reality*
isolated EG *He lives as if isolated from the rest of the world.*

unconnected EG *The two murders are unconnected.*

WORD POWER

▶ **Antonym**
connected

❷ **separate** VERB
to end a connection between people or things
EG *Police moved in to separate the two groups.*
detach EG *Three of the carriages on the train became detached.*
disconnect EG *Make sure supply plugs are disconnected from the mains.*
divide EG *This was a ruse to divide them.*

WORD POWER

▷ **Synonyms**
sunder
uncouple

▶ **Antonym**
connect

❸ **separate** VERB
to end a relationship or marriage
EG *Her parents separated when she was very young.*
break up EG *She hadn't used his name since they broke up.*
divorce EG *We divorced ten years ago.*
part EG *He is parting from his Swedish-born wife Eva.*
split up EG *I split up with my boyfriend last year.*

❶ **sequence** NOUN
a number of events coming one after another
EG *an unbroken sequence of victories*
chain EG *the chain of events leading to the assassination*
course EG *a course of injections*
cycle EG *the cycle of birth, growth, decay, and death*

progression EG *The story of American freedom is anything but a linear progression.*
series EG *a series of explosions*
string EG *a string of burglaries*
succession EG *He took a succession of jobs that stood him in good stead.*

❷ sequence NOUN
a particular order in which things are arranged
EG *the colour sequence: yellow, orange, purple, blue*
arrangement EG *a simple arrangement of coloured tiles*
order EG *Music shops should arrange their recordings in alphabetical order.*
pattern EG *a systematic pattern of behaviour*
progression EG *the natural progression of the seasons*
structure EG *The bricks had been arranged in a regular structure.*

series NOUN
a number of things coming one after the other
EG *a series of loud explosions*
chain EG *a bizarre chain of events*
run EG *The England skipper is haunted by a run of low scores.*
sequence EG *a sequence of novels*
string EG *a string of burglaries*
succession EG *He had a succession of jobs.*

❶ serious ADJECTIVE
very bad and worrying
EG *They survived their serious injuries.*
acute EG *an acute attack of appendicitis*
alarming EG *the alarming increase in drug abuse*
bad EG *a bad bout of flu*
critical EG *He remains in a critical condition in hospital.*
dangerous EG *His wound proved more dangerous than it seemed at first.*
extreme EG *the most extreme case*

doctors have ever seen
grave EG *We are all in grave danger.*
grievous EG *grievous wounds*
grim EG *Our situation is grim indeed.*
intense EG *Intense fighting has broken out in the capital.*
precarious EG *He is in a very precarious position.*
severe EG *a severe shortage of drinking water*
worrying EG *It is a worrying situation.*

❷ serious ADJECTIVE
important and deserving careful thought
EG *I regard this as a serious matter.*
crucial EG *Negotiations were at a crucial stage.*
deep EG *This novel raises deep questions about the nature of faith.*
difficult EG *The government faces even more difficult problems.*
far-reaching EG *His actions will have far-reaching consequences.*
grave EG *a grave situation*
important EG *We've got more important things to worry about now.*
momentous EG *the momentous decision to go to war*
pressing EG *a pressing problem*
profound EG *a man who thinks about the more profound issues of life*
significant EG *the most significant question of all*
urgent EG *He is not equipped to deal with an urgent situation like this.*
weighty EG *a weighty problem*

WORD POWER

▶ **Antonym**
funny

❸ serious ADJECTIVE
sincere about something
EG *I was not quite sure whether he was serious.*
earnest EG *It is my earnest hope that we can work things out.*
genuine EG *a genuine offer*

serious >> settle

heartfelt EG *a full and heartfelt apology*
honest EG *He looked at me in honest surprise.*
in earnest EG *I can never tell if he is in earnest or not.*
resolute EG *He was resolute about his ideals.*
resolved EG *They are quite resolved about their decision.*
sincere EG *He's sincere in his views.*

❹ serious ADJECTIVE
quiet and not laughing much
EG *He's quite a serious person.*
earnest EG *She looked up at me with an earnest expression.*
grave EG *He was looking unusually grave.*
humourless EG *a dour, humourless Scotsman*
pensive EG *We're both in a pensive mood today.*
sober EG *sad, sober faces*
solemn EG *His solemn little face broke into a smile.*
staid EG *bored with her marriage to a staid country doctor*
stern EG *a stern headmaster feared by all the pupils*

❶ set NOUN
a group of things that belong together
EG *a set of tools*
batch EG *the latest batch of recruits*
kit EG *I forgot my gym kit.*
outfit EG *She was wearing a brand new outfit.*
series EG *a series of books covering the history of aviation*

WORD POWER

▷ **Synonyms**
assemblage
compendium
ensemble

---

❷ set VERB
to put or place something

somewhere
EG *He set his case down on the floor.*
deposit EG *Imagine if you were suddenly deposited on a desert island.*
lay EG *Lay a sheet of newspaper on the floor.*
locate EG *The restaurant is located near the cathedral.*
place EG *She placed a mug of coffee in front of him.*
position EG *Plants were carefully positioned in the alcove.*
put EG *He put the photograph on the desk.*
rest EG *He rested one of his crutches against the rail.*
stick EG *Just stick your bag down anywhere.*

❸ set ADJECTIVE
fixed and not varying
EG *a set charge*
arranged EG *We arrived at the arranged time.*
established EG *the established order*
firm EG *a firm booking*
fixed EG *a fixed rate of interest*
predetermined EG *His destiny was predetermined from the moment of his birth.*
scheduled EG *The plane failed to return at the scheduled time.*

set on ADJECTIVE
determined to do something
EG *She was set on going to the States.*
bent EG *He's bent on suicide.*
determined EG *His enemies are determined to ruin him.*
intent EG *an actress who was intent on making a comeback*

❶ settle VERB
to put an end to an argument or problem
EG *The dispute has been settled.*
clear up EG *Eventually the confusion was cleared up.*
decide EG *None of the cases had been decided.*

a b c d e f g h i j k l m n o p q r s t u v w x y z

dispose of EG *the way in which you disposed of that problem*

put an end to EG *I just want to put and end to this situation.*

reconcile EG *urging the two parties to reconcile their differences*

resolve EG *They hoped the crisis could be resolved peacefully.*

straighten out EG *doing their best to straighten out this confusion*

❷ settle VERB
to decide or arrange something
EG *Let's settle where we're going tonight.*

agree EG *We haven't agreed a date yet.*

arrange EG *Have you arranged our next appointment?*

decide on EG *They decided on an evening to meet.*

determine EG *The final wording had not yet been determined.*

fix EG *He's going to fix a time when I can see him.*

❸ settle VERB
to make your home in a place
EG *refugees settling in Britain*

make your home EG *those who had made their homes in China*

move to EG *His family moved to New Zealand when he was 12.*

people EG *The plateau was peopled by nomadic tribes.*

populate EG *The island was populated by Native Americans.*

WORD POWER
▷ **Synonyms**
colonize
put down roots
take up residence

set up VERB
to make arrangements for something
EG *setting up a system of communication*

arrange EG *We have arranged a series of interviews.*

establish EG *We have established links with industry and commerce.*

install EG *I'm having cable installed next week.*

institute EG *to institute better levels of quality control*

organize EG *a two-day meeting organized by the UN*

several ADJECTIVE
indicating a small number
EG *several boxes filled with albums*

assorted EG *overnight stops in assorted hotels*

some EG *some cheers from the gallery*

sundry EG *He has won sundry music awards.*

various EG *a dozen trees of various sorts*

❶ severe ADJECTIVE
extremely bad or unpleasant
EG *severe cash flow problems*

acute EG *an acute economic crisis*

critical EG *if the situation becomes critical*

deep EG *We will be in deep trouble if this goes on.*

dire EG *This would have dire consequences for domestic peace.*

extreme EG *people living in extreme poverty*

grave EG *He said the situation was very grave.*

intense EG *A number of people collapsed in the intense heat.*

serious EG *The government faces very serious difficulties.*

terrible EG *terrible injuries*

WORD POWER
▶ **Antonym**
mild

❷ severe ADJECTIVE
stern and harsh
EG *This was a dreadful crime and a severe sentence is necessary.*

disapproving EG *Janet gave him a*

disapproving look.
grim EG *Her expression was grim and unpleasant.*
hard EG *His father was a hard man.*
harsh EG *the cold, harsh cruelty of her husband*
stern EG *He said stern measures would be taken.*
strict EG *My parents were very strict.*

sexy ADJECTIVE
sexually attractive or exciting
EG *a sexy voice*
erotic EG *an erotic film*
seductive EG *I love dressing up to look seductive.*
sensual EG *a wide, sensual mouth*
sensuous EG *his sensuous young mistress*
voluptuous EG *a voluptuous figure*

❶ shabby ADJECTIVE
ragged and worn in appearance
EG *a shabby overcoat*
dilapidated EG *a dilapidated old building*
ragged EG *dressed in a ragged coat*
scruffy EG *a scruffy basement flat in London*
seedy EG *his seedy clothes*
tatty EG *a tatty old cardigan*
threadbare EG *a square of threadbare carpet*
worn EG *a worn corduroy jacket*

> *WORD POWER*
>
> ▷ **Synonyms**
> down at heel
> run-down
> the worse for wear

❷ shabby ADJECTIVE
behaving meanly and unfairly
EG *shabby treatment*
contemptible EG *contemptible behaviour*
despicable EG *a despicable thing to do*
dirty EG *That was a dirty trick.*
mean EG *It was mean of you to hurt*

her like that.
rotten INFORMAL EG *That's a rotten thing to say!*

> *WORD POWER*
>
> ▷ **Synonyms**
> dishonourable
> ignoble
> scurvy

❶ shake VERB
to move something from side to side or up and down
EG *You have to shake the bottle before use.*
agitate EG *Gently agitate the water.*
brandish EG *He appeared brandishing a knife.*
flourish EG *He flourished his glass to make the point.*
wave EG *The crowd were waving flags and cheering.*

❷ shake VERB
to move from side to side or up and down
EG *The whole building shook with the force of the blast.*
jolt EG *The train jolted again.*
quake EG *The whole mountain quaked.*
quiver EG *Her bottom lip began to quiver.*
shiver EG *shivering with fear*
shudder EG *Elaine shuddered with cold.*
tremble EG *The leaves trembled in the breeze.*
vibrate EG *The engine began to vibrate alarmingly.*

> *WORD POWER*
>
> ▷ **Synonyms**
> joggle
> oscillate

❸ shake VERB
to shock and upset someone
EG *The news shook me quite a bit.*
distress EG *Her death had*

profoundly distressed me.
disturb EG *dreams so vivid that they disturb me for days*
rattle INFORMAL EG *He was obviously rattled by events.*
shock EG *Pictures of emaciated prisoners shocked the world.*
unnerve EG *unnerved by the sight*
upset EG *I was too upset to speak.*

WORD POWER

▷ **Synonyms**
discompose
traumatize

shaky ADJECTIVE
weak and unsteady
EG *threatening an already shaky economy*
rickety EG *Mona climbed the rickety wooden stairway.*
tottering EG *the baby's first tottering steps*
trembling EG *She held out one frail, trembling hand.*
unstable EG *an unstable lamp on top of an old tea-chest*
unsteady EG *His voice was unsteady.*
wobbly EG *I'm sorry, this table's a bit wobbly.*

❶ shame NOUN
a feeling of guilt or embarrassment
EG *She felt a deep sense of shame.*
embarrassment EG *He turned red with embarrassment.*
humiliation EG *the humiliation of discussing her husband's affair*
ignominy EG *the ignominy of being made redundant*

WORD POWER

▷ **Synonyms**
abashment
loss of face
mortification

❷ shame NOUN
something that makes people lose respect for you

EG *I don't want to bring shame on the family.*
discredit EG *It was to his discredit that he did nothing.*
disgrace EG *He had to resign in disgrace.*
dishonour EG *his sense of dishonour at his brother's conduct*
scandal EG *They often abandoned their children because of fear of scandal.*

❸ shame VERB
to make someone feel ashamed
EG *Her son's affair had shamed her.*
disgrace EG *I have disgraced my country.*
embarrass EG *It embarrassed him that he had no idea of what was going on.*
humiliate EG *His teacher continually humiliates him in maths lessons.*

WORD POWER

▷ **Synonyms**
abash
mortify

shameless ADJECTIVE
behaving badly without showing any shame
EG *shameless dishonesty*
barefaced EG *a barefaced lie*
brazen EG *a brazen theft*
flagrant EG *a flagrant violation of the law*
unabashed EG *an unabashed egotist*
unashamed EG *blatant, unashamed hypocrisy*
wanton EG *a wanton woman*

❶ shape NOUN
the outline of something
EG *a round shape*
contours EG *the contours of the mountains*
figure EG *a trim figure*
form EG *the form of the human body*
lines EG *The belt spoilt the lines of her long dress.*

outline EG *the dim outline of a small boat*

❷ shape VERB
to make something in a particular form
EG *Shape the dough into a loaf.*
fashion EG *buttons fashioned from bone*
form EG *The polymer is formed into a thin sheet.*
make EG *gold made into wedding rings*
model EG *She began modelling animals from clay.*
mould EG *Mould the cheese into small ovals.*

❶ share VERB
to divide something between two or more people
EG *We shared a bottle of champagne.*
divide EG *The prize money was divided between the two winners.*
split EG *We split the bill between us.*

❷ share NOUN
a portion of something
EG *a share of the profits*
allotment EG *a daily allotment of three ounces of bread*
portion EG *his portion of the inheritance*
quota EG *a quota of four tickets per person*
ration EG *their daily ration of water*

❶ sharp ADJECTIVE
having a fine cutting edge or point
EG *a sharp knife*
jagged EG *jagged rocks*
keen EG *a keen edge*
pointed EG *pointed teeth*
razor-sharp EG *the razor-sharp blade*

WORD POWER
▶ **Antonym**
blunt

❷ sharp ADJECTIVE
quick to notice or understand things
EG *a sharp intellect*
alert EG *She is alert and sprightly despite her 85 years.*
astute EG *He made a series of astute business decisions.*
bright EG *an exceptionally bright child*
observant EG *an observant eye*
perceptive EG *a perceptive gaze*
quick EG *His quick mind soon grasped the situation.*
quick-witted EG *He is very alert and quick-witted.*

❸ sharp ADJECTIVE
sudden and significant
EG *a sharp rise in prices*
abrupt EG *Her idyllic world came to an abrupt end when her parents died.*
marked EG *a marked increase in crimes against property*
sudden EG *a sudden change in course*

❶ sheer ADJECTIVE
complete and total
EG *acts of sheer desperation*
absolute EG *I think it's absolute nonsense.*
complete EG *He shook his head in complete bewilderment.*
pure EG *To have an uninterrupted night's sleep was pure bliss.*
total EG *This is total madness!*
unqualified EG *It has been an unqualified disaster.*
utter EG *a look of utter confusion*

WORD POWER
▷ **Synonyms**
unmitigated (FORMAL)

❷ sheer ADJECTIVE
vertical
EG *There was a sheer drop just outside my window.*
perpendicular EG *the perpendicular wall of sandstone*
steep EG *a narrow valley with steep*

a
b
c
d
e
f
g
h
i
j
k
l
m
n
o
p
q
r
s
t
u
v
w
x
y
z

A B C D E F G H I J K L M N O P Q R S T U V W X Y Z

sides
vertical EG *The climber inched up a vertical wall of rock.*

❸ **sheer** ADJECTIVE
very light and delicate
EG *sheer black tights*
delicate EG *delicate fabric*
fine EG *a fine, pale grey material*
lightweight EG *lightweight materials with Lycra*
thin EG *the thin silk of her blouse*

WORD POWER

▶ **Antonym**
thick

❶ **shelter** NOUN
a place providing protection
EG *a bus shelter*
hostel EG *She spent two years living in a hostel.*
refuge EG *a mountain refuge*
sanctuary EG *His church became a sanctuary for people fleeing the civil war.*

❷ **shelter** NOUN
protection from bad weather or danger
EG *the hut where they were given food and shelter*
asylum EG *refugees who sought political asylum*
cover EG *They ran for cover from the storm.*
harbour EG *Patches of gorse were a great harbour for foxes.*
haven EG *The island is a haven for international criminals.*
protection EG *Riot shields acted as protection against the attack.*
refuge EG *They took refuge in an old barn.*
safety EG *the safety of one's own home*
sanctuary EG *Some of them sought sanctuary in the church.*

❸ **shelter** VERB
to stay somewhere in order to be safe
EG *a man sheltering in a doorway*
hide EG *They hid behind a tree.*
huddle EG *She huddled inside the porch.*
take cover EG *Shoppers took cover behind cars as the shots rang out.*

❹ **shelter** VERB
to hide or protect someone
EG *A neighbour sheltered the boy for seven days.*
harbour EG *He was accused of harbouring terrorist suspects.*
hide EG *They hid me until the coast was clear.*
protect EG *A purple headscarf protected her against the wind.*
shield EG *He shielded his head from the sun with a sack.*

shine VERB
to give out a bright light
EG *The sun is shining.*
beam EG *The spotlight beamed down on the stage.*
gleam EG *The moonlight gleamed on the water.*
glow EG *The lantern glowed softly in the darkness.*
radiate EG *the amount of light radiated by an ordinary light bulb*
shimmer EG *The lake shimmered in the sunlight.*
sparkle EG *Diamonds sparkled on her wrists.*

shining ADJECTIVE
giving out or reflecting light
EG *shining stainless steel tables*
bright EG *a bright star*
brilliant EG *brilliant sunshine*
gleaming EG *gleaming headlights*
luminous EG *the luminous dial on the clock*
radiant EG *He saw a figure surrounded by a radiant light.*
shimmering EG *a shimmering gold fabric*

sparkling EG *elegant cutlery and sparkling crystal*

WORD POWER

▷ **Synonyms**
effulgent
incandescent

❶ shock NOUN
a sudden upsetting experience
EG *The extent of the damage came as a shock.*
blow EG *It was a terrible blow when he was made redundant.*
bombshell EG *His departure was a bombshell for the team.*
distress EG *She wanted to save her mother all the distress she could.*
trauma EG *the trauma of losing a parent*

❷ shock VERB
to make you feel upset
EG *I was shocked by his appearance.*
numb EG *numbed by suffering and terror*
paralyse EG *He stood paralysed with horror.*
shake EG *The news of her death has shaken us all.*
stagger EG *The judge said he was staggered by the defendant's callousness.*
stun EG *Audiences were stunned by the film's violent ending.*
traumatize EG *My wife was traumatized by the experience.*

❸ shock VERB
to offend because of being rude or immoral
EG *She is very easily shocked.*
appal EG *I was appalled by her rudeness.*
disgust EG *He disgusted everyone with his boorish behaviour.*
offend EG *Many people are offended by strong swearwords.*

outrage EG *They were outraged by his racist comments.*

WORD POWER

▷ **Synonyms**
nauseate
scandalize

shop NOUN
a place where things are sold
EG *I had to race round the shops.*
boutique EG *He owns a jewellery boutique.*
market EG *He sold fruit on a small market stall.*
store EG *Within two years he was managing the store.*
supermarket EG *Most of us do our food shopping in the supermarket.*

WORD POWER

▷ **Synonyms**
emporium
hypermarket
mart

shore NOUN

Types of shore
bank
beach
coast
foreshore
front
lakeside
sands
seaboard
seashore
shingle
strand
waterside

❶ short ADJECTIVE
not lasting very long
EG *a short break*
brief EG *a brief meeting*
fleeting EG *a fleeting glimpse*
momentary EG *a momentary lapse of reason*
short-lived EG *a short-lived craze*

a b c d e f g h i j k l m n o p q r s t u v w x y z

2 short ADJECTIVE
small in height
EG *a short, elderly man*
→ see Word Study **short**

WORD POWER

▶ **Antonym**
tall

3 short ADJECTIVE
not using many words
EG *a short speech*
brief EG *a brief description*
concise EG *a concise summary*
succinct EG *a succinct account*
terse EG *a terse comment*

WORD POWER

▷ **Synonyms**
abridged
laconic
pithy

shortage NOUN
a lack of something
EG *a shortage of funds*
dearth EG *the dearth of good fiction by English authors*
deficiency EG *tests for vitamin deficiency*
lack EG *I was hampered by a lack of information.*
scarcity EG *a scarcity of water*
shortfall EG *a shortfall in income*
want EG *a want of manners and charm*

WORD POWER

▷ **Synonyms**
insufficiency
paucity

▶ **Antonym**
abundance

WORD POWER

▶ **Antonym**
long

shorten VERB
to make something shorter
EG *Smoking can shorten your life.*
abbreviate EG *He abbreviated his name to Alec.*
cut EG *The film was cut to two hours.*
trim EG *I need to get my hair trimmed.*

WORD POWER

▷ **Synonyms**
abridge
downsize
truncate

▶ **Antonym**
lengthen

1 shout NOUN
a loud call or cry
EG *I heard a distant shout.*
bellow EG *a bellow of rage*
cry EG *She gave a cry of horror.*
roar EG *a roar of approval*
scream EG *screams of terror*
yell EG *He let out a yell of delight.*

2 shout VERB
to call or cry loudly
EG *He shouted something to his brother.*
bawl EG *Laura and Peter were bawling at each other.*
bellow EG *He bellowed orders down the phone.*
call EG *He could hear them calling his name.*
cry EG *"You're under arrest!" he cried.*
roar EG *"I'll kill you for that!" he roared.*
scream EG *screaming at them to get out of my house*
yell EG *She pushed him away, yelling abuse.*

1 show NOUN
to prove something
EG *Tests show that smoking can cause cancer.*
demonstrate EG *The study demonstrated a link between obesity and heart problems.*

prove EG *History will prove him to be right.*

2 show VERB
to do something in order to teach someone else
EG *I'll show you how to set the video timer.*
demonstrate EG *She demonstrated how to make ice cream.*
instruct EG *He instructed us on how to give first aid.*
teach EG *She taught me how to ride.*

3 show VERB
to display a quality or characteristic
EG *Her sketches showed artistic promise.*
demonstrate EG *He has demonstrated his ability.*
display EG *He displayed remarkable courage.*
indicate EG *Her choice of words indicated her real feelings.*
manifest EG *Fear can manifest itself in many ways.*
reveal EG *His reaction revealed a lack of self-confidence.*

WORD POWER

▷ **Synonyms**
evince
testify to

4 show NOUN
a public exhibition
EG *a fashion show*
display EG *a gymnastics display*
exhibition EG *an art exhibition*
presentation EG *Julie's successful presentation to the board*

5 show NOUN
a display of a feeling or quality
EG *a show of affection*
air EG *an air of indifference*
display EG *a display of remorse*
pose EG *a pose of injured innocence*
pretence EG *They have given up all pretence of neutrality.*

semblance EG *trying to maintain a semblance of order*

shrewd ADJECTIVE
showing intelligence and good judgment
EG *a shrewd businessman*
astute EG *an astute judge of character*
canny EG *He was far too canny to give himself away.*
crafty EG *He is a clever man and a crafty politician.*
perceptive EG *a perceptive analysis of the situation*
sharp EG *He is very sharp, and a quick thinker.*
smart EG *a very smart move*

WORD POWER

▷ **Synonyms**
perspicacious
sagacious

shrill ADJECTIVE
high-pitched and piercing
EG *the shrill whistle of the engine*
penetrating EG *a penetrating voice*
piercing EG *a piercing squawk*
sharp EG *the sharp cry of a vixen*

shrink VERB
to become smaller
EG *All my jumpers have shrunk in the wash.*
contract EG *The ribcage expands and contracts as you breathe.*
diminish EG *The threat of nuclear war has diminished.*
dwindle EG *The factory's workforce has dwindled from 4000 to 200.*
get smaller EG *Electronic systems are getting smaller.*
narrow EG *The gap between the two parties has narrowed.*

WORD POWER

▶ **Antonym**
grow

A
B
C
D
E
F
G
H
I
J
K
L
M
N
O
P
Q
R
S
T
U
V
W
X
Y
Z

❶ shut VERB
to close something
EG *Someone had forgotten to shut the door.*
close EG *If you are cold, close the window.*
fasten EG *He fastened the diamond clasp of the necklace.*
slam EG *He slammed the gate shut behind him.*

WORD POWER

▶ **Antonym**
open

❷ shut ADJECTIVE
closed or fastened
EG *A smell of burning came from behind the shut door.*
closed EG *All the exits were closed.*
fastened EG *The pockets are fastened with buttons.*
sealed EG *a sealed envelope*

WORD POWER

▶ **Antonym**
open

shy ADJECTIVE
nervous in the company of other people
EG *a shy, quiet-spoken girl*
bashful EG *Offstage, he is bashful and awkward.*
retiring EG *He was the quiet, retiring type.*
self-conscious EG *I felt a bit self-conscious in my swimming costume.*
timid EG *a timid little boy*

WORD POWER

▷ **Synonyms**
diffident
self-effacing

▶ **Antonym**
bold

❶ sick ADJECTIVE
unwell or ill
EG *a ward full of very sick people*
ailing EG *She tenderly nursed her ailing mother.*
poorly INFORMAL EG *I called Julie and she's still poorly.*
under par INFORMAL EG *The flu has left me feeling under par.*
under the weather EG *Are you still a bit under the weather?*
unwell EG *She had been unwell for some time.*

WORD POWER

▶ **Antonym**
well

❷ sick ADJECTIVE
feeling as if you are going to vomit
EG *The very thought of food made him sick.*
ill EG *The smell of curry always makes me ill.*
nauseous EG *These drugs may make you feel nauseous.*
queasy EG *The motion of the ship was already making him queasy.*

❸ sick **sick of** ADJECTIVE; INFORMAL
tired of something
EG *I'm sick of your complaints.*
bored EG *I'm getting bored with the whole business.*
fed up EG *He is fed up with this country.*
tired EG *I am tired of this music.*
weary EG *She was weary of being alone.*

❶ side NOUN
the edge of something
EG *Her head hung over the side of the bed.*
edge EG *She fell over the edge of the balcony.*
verge EG *He parked on the verge of the road.*

WORD POWER

● **Related Words**
adjective : lateral

2 side NOUN
one of two groups involved in a dispute or contest
EG *Both sides began to prepare for battle.*
camp EG *Most of his supporters had now defected to the opposite camp.*
faction EG *leaders of the warring factions*
party EG *the candidates for the three main parties*
team EG *Both teams played well.*

side with VERB
to support someone in an argument
EG *Louise always sided with her sister.*
agree with EG *She's bound to agree with her husband.*
stand up for EG *I was the one who always stood up for my mother.*
support EG *a fellow prisoner who supported her*
take the part of EG *Why do you always take his part?*

1 sight NOUN
the ability to see
EG *My sight is so bad now that I can't read any more.*
eyesight EG *He suffered from weak eyesight.*
visibility EG *Visibility was very poor.*
vision EG *It can cause blindness or serious loss of vision.*

WORD POWER

● **Related Words**
adjectives : optical, visual

---

2 sight NOUN
something you see
EG *It was a ghastly sight.*
display EG *These flowers make a colourful display in spring.*
scene EG *a bizarre scene*
spectacle EG *an impressive spectacle*

3 sight VERB
to see something or someone
EG *He had been sighted in Cairo.*

see EG *I saw a deer in the woods today.*
spot EG *I drove round till I spotted her.*

1 sign NOUN
a mark or symbol
EG *The negative number is preceded by a minus sign.*
character EG *the characters used in the hallmarking system*
emblem EG *a small yellow hammer-and-sickle emblem*
logo EG *the company's logo*
mark EG *Put a tick mark against the statements you agree with.*
symbol EG *the chemical symbol for mercury*

2 sign NOUN
a notice put up to give a warning or information
EG *a sign saying that the highway was closed*
board EG *He studied the destination board on the front of the bus.*
notice EG *a notice saying "no entry"*
placard EG *The protesters sang songs and waved placards.*

3 sign NOUN
evidence of something
EG *the first signs of recovery*
clue EG *the only real clue that something was wrong*
evidence EG *there has been no evidence of criminal activity*
hint EG *He showed only the slightest hint of emotion.*
indication EG *All the indications suggest that he is the murderer.*
symptom EG *typical symptoms of stress*
token EG *a token of goodwill*
trace EG *No traces of violence were found on the body.*

1 signal NOUN
something which is intended to give a message
EG *a distress signal*
beacon EG *an emergency beacon*

cue EG *He gave me my cue to speak.*
gesture EG *She made a menacing gesture with her fist.*
sign EG *They gave him the thumbs-up sign.*

2 signal VERB
to make a sign as a message to someone
EG *He was frantically signalling to her to shut up.*
beckon EG *I beckoned her over.*
gesticulate EG *He was gesticulating at a hole in the ground.*
gesture EG *I gestured towards the house, and he went in.*
motion EG *He motioned to her to go behind the screen.*
nod EG *They nodded goodnight to the security man.*
sign EG *She signed to me to come near.*
wave EG *He waved the servants out of the tent.*

significant ADJECTIVE
large or important
EG *This drug seems to have a significant effect on the disease.*
considerable FORMAL EG *Doing it properly makes considerable demands on our time.*
important EG *The strike represents an important challenge to the government.*
impressive EG *an impressive achievement*
marked EG *a marked increase in crimes against property*
notable EG *With a few notable exceptions, doctors are a pretty sensible lot.*
pronounced EG *The exhibition has a pronounced Scottish theme.*
striking EG *The most striking feature of these statistics is the rate of growth.*

WORD POWER
▶ **Antonym**
insignificant

1 silence NOUN
an absence of sound
EG *There was a momentary silence.*
calm EG *He liked the calm of the evening.*
hush EG *A hush fell over the crowd.*
lull EG *a lull in the momentary silence*
peace EG *I love the peace of the countryside.*
quiet EG *The quiet of the flat was very soothing.*
stillness EG *An explosion shattered the stillness of the night air.*

WORD POWER
▶ **Antonym**
noise

2 silence NOUN
an inability or refusal to talk
EG *breaking his silence for the first time about the affair*
dumbness EG *a woman traumatized into dumbness*
muteness EG *He retreated into stubborn muteness.*
reticence EG *Fran didn't seem to notice my reticence.*
speechlessness EG *He was shy to the point of speechlessness.*

WORD POWER
▷ **Synonyms**
taciturnity
uncommunicativeness

3 silence VERB
to make someone or something quiet
EG *The shock silenced her completely.*
deaden EG *We hung up curtains to try and deaden the noise.*
gag EG *I gagged him with a towel.*
muffle EG *You can muffle the sound with absorbent material.*

A B C D E F G H I J K L M N O P Q R S T U V W X Y Z

quiet EG *A look from her husband quieted her at once.*
quieten EG *She tried to quieten her breathing.*
stifle EG *He put his hand to his mouth to stifle a giggle.*
still EG *He raised a hand to still Alex's protest.*
suppress EG *She barely suppressed a gasp.*

❶ silent ADJECTIVE
not saying anything
EG *The class fell silent as the teacher entered.*
dumb EG *We were all struck dumb for a moment.*
mute EG *a mute look of appeal*
speechless EG *speechless with rage*
taciturn EG *a taciturn man with a solemn expression*
wordless EG *They exchanged a wordless look of understanding.*

WORD POWER

▷ **Synonyms**
tongue-tied
uncommunicative

❷ silent ADJECTIVE
making no noise
EG *The room was silent except for the ticking of the clock.*
hushed EG *the vast, hushed space of the cathedral*
quiet EG *a quiet engine*
soundless EG *My bare feet were soundless on the carpet.*
still EG *The room was suddenly still.*

WORD POWER

▶ **Antonym**
noisy

silly ADJECTIVE
foolish or ridiculous
EG *I know it's silly to get so upset.*
absurd EG *He found fashion absurd.*
daft EG *That's a daft question.*
foolish EG *It is foolish to risk injury.*

idiotic EG *What an idiotic thing to say!*
inane EG *He stood there with an inane grin on his face.*
ridiculous EG *a ridiculous suggestion*
stupid EG *a stupid mistake*

WORD POWER

▷ **Synonyms**
asinine
fatuous
puerile
witless

similar ADJECTIVE
like something else
EG *an accident similar to Hakkinen's*
alike EG *You two are very alike.*
analogous EG *a ritual analogous to those of primitive tribal cultures*
comparable EG *paying the same wages for work of comparable value*
like EG *They're as like as two peas in a pod.*
uniform EG *droplets of uniform size*

WORD POWER

▶ **Antonym**
different

similarity NOUN
the quality of being like something else
EG *the similarity of our backgrounds*
analogy EG *the analogy between racism and homophobia*
likeness EG *These myths have a startling likeness to one another.*
resemblance EG *I could see the resemblance to his grandfather.*
sameness EG *He grew bored by the sameness of the speeches.*

WORD POWER

▷ **Synonyms**
comparability
congruence
similitude

a
b
c
d
e
f
g
h
i
j
k
l
m
n
o
p
q
r
s
t
u
v
w
x
y
z

▶ Antonym
difference

❶ **simple** ADJECTIVE
easy to understand or do
EG *a simple task*
easy EG *This ice cream maker is cheap and easy to use.*
elementary EG *elementary computer skills*
straightforward EG *It was a straightforward question.*
uncomplicated EG *an uncomplicated story*
understandable EG *He writes in a clear, understandable style.*

WORD POWER

▶ Antonym
complicated

❷ **simple** ADJECTIVE
plain in style
EG *a simple but stylish outfit*
classic EG *classic designs which will fit in anywhere*
clean EG *the clean lines of Shaker furniture*
plain EG *Her dress was plain but hung well on her.*
severe EG *hair scraped back in a severe style*

WORD POWER

▶ Antonym
elaborate

simplify VERB
to make something easier to do or understand
EG *measures intended to simplify the procedure*
make simpler EG *restructuring the tax system to make it simpler*
streamline EG *an effort to cut costs and streamline operations*

❶ **sin** NOUN
wicked and immoral behaviour
EG *preaching against sin*

crime EG *a life of crime*
evil EG *You can't stop all the evil in the world.*
offence EG *an offence which can carry the death penalty*
wickedness EG *a sign of human wickedness*
wrong EG *I intend to right that wrong.*

WORD POWER

▷ **Synonyms**
iniquity
misdeed
transgression
trespass

❷ **sin** VERB
to do something wicked and immoral
EG *I admit that I have sinned.*
do wrong EG *They have done wrong and they know it.*

sincere ADJECTIVE
saying things that you really mean
EG *my sincere apologies*
genuine EG *a display of genuine emotion*
heartfelt EG *heartfelt sympathy*
real EG *the real affection between them*
wholehearted EG *a wholehearted and genuine response*

WORD POWER

▶ Antonym
insincere

❶ **single** ADJECTIVE
only one and no more
EG *A single shot was fired.*
lone EG *A lone policeman guarded the doors.*
one EG *I just had one drink.*
only EG *My only regret is that I never knew him.*
sole EG *the sole survivor of the accident*
solitary EG *There is not one solitary scrap of evidence.*

A
B
C
D
E
F
G
H
I
J
K
L
M
N
O
P
Q
R
S
T
U
V
W
X
Y
Z

2 single ADJECTIVE
not married
EG *I'm surprised you're still single.*
unattached EG *I only know two or three unattached men.*
unmarried EG *an unmarried mother*

3 single ADJECTIVE
for one person only
EG *a single room*
individual EG *an individual portion*
separate EG *separate beds*

singular ADJECTIVE; FORMAL
unusual and remarkable
EG *a smile of singular sweetness*
exceptional EG *children with exceptional ability*
extraordinary EG *The task requires extraordinary patience and endurance.*
rare EG *a leader of rare strength and instinct*
remarkable EG *a remarkable achievement*
uncommon EG *She read Cecilia's letter with uncommon interest.*
unique EG *a woman of unique talent and determination*
unusual EG *He had an unusual aptitude for mathematics.*

sinister ADJECTIVE
seeming harmful or evil
EG *There was something cold and sinister about him.*
evil EG *an evil smile*
forbidding EG *a huge, forbidding building*
menacing EG *His dark eyebrows gave him a menacing look.*
ominous EG *A dark and ominous figure stood in the doorway.*
threatening EG *his threatening appearance*

WORD POWER
▷ **Synonyms**
baleful

bodeful
disquieting

situation NOUN
what is happening
EG *a serious situation*
case EG *a clear case of mistaken identity*
circumstances EG *I wish we could have met in happier circumstances.*
plight EG *the plight of Third World countries*
scenario EG *a nightmare scenario*
state of affairs EG *This state of affairs cannot continue.*

size NOUN
how big or small something is
EG *the size of the audience*
bulk EG *Despite his bulk, he moved gracefully.*
dimensions EG *He considered the dimensions of the problem.*
extent EG *the extent of the damage*
immensity EG *The immensity of the universe is impossible to grasp.*
proportions EG *In the tropics, plants grow to huge proportions.*

WORD POWER
▷ **Synonyms**
magnitude
vastness

skilful ADJECTIVE
able to do something very well
EG *the country's most skilful politician*
able EG *a very able businessman*
accomplished EG *an accomplished pianist*
adept EG *an adept diplomat*
competent EG *a competent and careful driver*
expert EG *He is expert at handling complex negotiations.*
masterly EG *a masterly performance*
proficient EG *proficient with*

a b c d e f g h i j k l m n o p q r s t u v w x y z

computers
skilled EG *a skilled wine maker*

WORD POWER

▷ **Synonyms**
adroit
dexterous

▶ **Antonym**
incompetent

skill NOUN
the ability to do something well
EG *This task requires great skill.*
ability EG *a man of considerable abilities*
competence EG *his high professional competence*
dexterity EG *Reid's dexterity on the guitar*
expertise EG *the expertise to deal with these problems*
facility EG *a facility for languages*
knack EG *the knack of getting on with people*
proficiency EG *basic proficiency in English*

skilled ADJECTIVE
having the knowledge to do something well
EG *skilled workers, such as plumbers*
able EG *an able craftsman*
accomplished EG *an accomplished pianist*
competent EG *a competent and careful driver*
experienced EG *lawyers who are experienced in these matters*
expert EG *It takes an expert eye to see the symptoms.*
masterly EG *the artist's masterly use of colour*
professional EG *professional people like doctors and engineers*
proficient EG *He is proficient in several foreign languages.*
skilful EG *the artist's skilful use of light and shade*

trained EG *Our workforce is highly trained.*

WORD POWER

▶ **Antonym**
incompetent

skinny ADJECTIVE
extremely thin
EG *a skinny little boy*
bony EG *a long bony finger*
emaciated EG *television pictures of emaciated prisoners*
lean EG *a tall, lean figure*
scrawny EG *the vulture's scrawny neck*
thin EG *He is small and very thin with white skin.*
underfed EG *Kate still looks pale and underfed.*
undernourished EG *undernourished children*

WORD POWER

▶ **Antonym**
plump

❶ slander NOUN
something untrue and malicious said about someone
EG *He is now suing the company for slander.*
libel EG *defendants seeking damages for libel*
scandal EG *She loves spreading scandal.*
slur EG *a vicious slur on his character*
smear EG *He called the allegation "an evil smear".*

WORD POWER

▷ **Synonyms**
aspersion
calumny
defamation
obloquy

❷ slander VERB
to say untrue and malicious things

about someone
EG *He has been charged with slandering the Prime Minister.*
libel EG *The newspaper which libelled him had to pay compensation.*
malign EG *He claims he is being unfairly maligned.*
smear EG *an attempt to smear their manager*

WORD POWER

▷ **Synonyms**
calumniate
defame
traduce
vilify

slang NOUN

Some slang words
babe
bug
celeb
chill
cool
fave
fit
gimp
goss
grass on
gross
hols
hot
jammy
manky
minging
minted
pants
snazzy
tidy
24/7
wicked
yonks

❶ sleep NOUN
the natural state of rest in which you are unconscious
EG *They were exhausted from lack of sleep.*
doze EG *I had a doze after lunch.*

hibernation EG *Many animals go into hibernation during the winter.*
kip BRITISH; SLANG EG *Mason went home for a couple of hours' kip.*
nap EG *I might take a nap for a while.*
slumber EG *He had fallen into exhausted slumber.*
snooze INFORMAL EG *a little snooze after dinner*

WORD POWER

▷ **Synonyms**
dormancy
repose
siesta

❷ sleep VERB
to rest in a natural state of unconsciousness
EG *The baby slept during the car journey.*
doze EG *He dozed in an armchair.*
hibernate EG *Dormice hibernate from October to May.*
kip BRITISH; SLANG EG *He kipped on my sofa last night.*
slumber EG *The girls were slumbering peacefully.*
snooze INFORMAL EG *Mark snoozed in front of the television.*
take a nap EG *Try to take a nap every afternoon.*

❶ sleepy ADJECTIVE
tired and ready to go to sleep
EG *Do you feel sleepy during the day?*
drowsy EG *This medicine may make you feel drowsy.*
lethargic EG *He felt too lethargic to get dressed.*
sluggish EG *I was still feeling sluggish after my nap.*

WORD POWER

▷ **Synonyms**
somnolent
torpid

❷ sleepy ADJECTIVE
not having much activity or

excitement
EG *a sleepy little village*
dull EG *a dull town*
quiet EG *a quiet rural backwater*

1 slender ADJECTIVE
attractively thin
EG *a tall, slender woman*
lean EG *Like most athletes, she was lean and muscular.*
slight EG *She is small and slight.*
slim EG *Jean is pretty, with a slim build.*

WORD POWER
▷ **Synonyms**
svelte
sylphlike
willowy

2 slender ADJECTIVE
small in amount or degree
EG *He won, but only by a slender majority.*
faint EG *They now have only a faint chance of survival.*
remote EG *a remote possibility*
slight EG *There is a slight improvement in his condition.*
slim EG *a slim hope*
small EG *a small chance of success*

WORD POWER
▷ **Synonyms**
inconsiderable
tenuous

slight ADJECTIVE
small in amount or degree
EG *a slight dent*
insignificant EG *an insignificant amount*
minor EG *a minor inconvenience*
negligible EG *The strike will have a negligible impact.*
small EG *It only makes a small difference.*
trivial EG *trivial details*

WORD POWER
▷ **Synonyms**
inconsiderable
paltry
scanty

▶ **Antonym**
large

1 slip VERB
to go somewhere quickly and quietly
EG *Amy slipped downstairs and out of the house.*
creep EG *I crept up to my room.*
sneak EG *Sometimes he would sneak out to see me.*
steal EG *They can steal away at night to join us.*

2 slip NOUN
a small mistake
EG *There must be no slips.*
blunder EG *an embarrassing blunder*
error EG *a tactical error*
mistake EG *Many people are anxious about making mistakes in grammar.*

WORD POWER
▷ **Synonyms**
faux pas
indiscretion

slogan NOUN
a short easily-remembered phrase
EG *a poster with the slogan, "Your country needs you"*
jingle EG *a catchy advertising jingle*
motto EG *"Who Dares Wins" is the motto of the Special Air Service.*

1 slope NOUN
a flat surface with one end higher than the other
EG *The street is on a slope.*
gradient EG *a steep gradient*
incline EG *The car was unable to negotiate the incline.*

ramp EG *There is a ramp allowing access for wheelchairs.*

WORD POWER

▷ **Synonyms**
declination
declivity
inclination

2 slope VERB
to be at an angle
EG *The bank sloped sharply down to the river.*
fall EG *The road fell steeply.*
rise EG *The climb is arduous, rising steeply through thick bush.*
slant EG *His handwriting slanted to the left.*

1 slow ADJECTIVE
moving or happening with little speed
EG *slow, regular breathing*
gradual EG *Losing weight is a gradual process.*
leisurely EG *He walked at a leisurely pace.*
lingering EG *a lingering death*
ponderous EG *His steps were heavy and ponderous.*
sluggish EG *a sluggish stream*
unhurried EG *She rose with unhurried grace.*

WORD POWER

▶ **Antonym**
fast

2 slow ADJECTIVE
not very clever
EG *He got hit in the head and he's been a bit slow ever since.*
dense EG *He's not a bad man, just a bit dense.*
dim EG *He is rather dim.*
dumb INFORMAL EG *too dumb to realise what was going on*
obtuse EG *It should be obvious even to the most obtuse person.*
stupid EG *He can't help being a bit*
stupid.
thick EG *I can't believe I've been so thick.*

slow (down) VERB
to go or cause to go more slowly
EG *The car slowed and then stopped.*
check EG *attempts to check the spread of AIDS*
decelerate EG *He decelerated when he saw the warning sign.*

slowly ADVERB
not quickly or hurriedly
EG *He turned and began to walk away slowly.*
by degrees EG *By degrees, the tension passed out of him.*
gradually EG *Their friendship gradually deepened.*
unhurriedly EG *The islanders drift along unhurriedly from day to day.*

WORD POWER

▶ **Antonym**
quickly

sly ADJECTIVE
cunning and deceptive
EG *She is devious, sly and manipulative.*
crafty EG *a crafty villain*
cunning EG *Some of these kids can be very cunning.*
devious EG *an extremely dangerous, evil and devious man*
scheming EG *You're a scheming little rat, aren't you?*
underhand EG *underhand tactics*
wily EG *a wily politician*

1 small ADJECTIVE
not large in size, number or amount
EG *a small child*
→ see Word Study **small**

WORD POWER

▶ **Antonym**
large

A B C D E F G H I J K L M N O P Q R S T U V W X Y Z

2 small ADJECTIVE
not important or significant
EG *small changes*
→ see Word Study **small**

1 smart ADJECTIVE
clean and neat in appearance
EG *a smart navy blue outfit*
chic EG *chic Parisian women*
elegant EG *Patricia looked beautiful and elegant, as always.*
neat EG *a neat grey flannel suit*
spruce EG *Chris was looking spruce in his uniform.*
stylish EG *stylish white shoes*

WORD POWER

▷ **Synonyms**
modish
natty
snappy

► **Antonym**
scruffy

2 smart ADJECTIVE
clever and intelligent
EG *a smart idea*
astute EG *a series of astute business decisions*
bright EG *She is not very bright.*
canny EG *He was far too canny to give himself away.*
clever EG *Nobody disputed that Davey was clever.*
ingenious EG *an ingenious plan*
intelligent EG *Dolphins are an intelligent species.*
shrewd EG *a shrewd businessman*

WORD POWER

► **Antonym**
dumb

1 smell NOUN
the quality of something which you sense through your nose
EG *a smell of damp wood*
aroma EG *the aroma of fresh bread*
fragrance EG *the fragrance of his cologne*
odour EG *a disagreeable odour*
perfume EG *enjoying the perfume of the lemon trees*
pong BRITISH AND AUSTRALIAN; INFORMAL
eg *What's that horrible pong?*
reek EG *the reek of whisky*
scent EG *flowers chosen for their scent*
stench EG *a foul stench*
stink EG *the stink of stale beer on his breath*

WORD POWER

▷ **Synonyms**
bouquet
fetor
malodour

2 smell VERB
to have an unpleasant smell
EG *Do my feet smell?*
pong BRITISH AND AUSTRALIAN; INFORMAL
eg *She said he ponged a bit.*
reek EG *The whole house reeks of cigar smoke.*
stink EG *His breath stinks of garlic.*

3 smell VERB
to become aware of the smell of something
EG *I could smell liquor on his breath.*
scent EG *The dog had scented something in the bushes.*
sniff EG *He opened his window and sniffed the air.*

smelly ADJECTIVE
having a strong unpleasant smell
EG *smelly socks*
foul EG *His breath was foul.*
reeking EG *poisoning the air with their reeking cigars*
stinking EG *piles of stinking rubbish*

WORD POWER

▷ **Synonyms**
fetid
malodorous
noisome

▶ **Antonym**
fragrant

---

❶ smile VERB
to move the corners of your mouth upwards because you are pleased
EG *When he saw me, he smiled and waved.*
beam EG *She beamed at him in delight.*
grin EG *He grinned broadly.*
smirk EG *The two men looked at me, nudged each other and smirked.*

❷ smile NOUN
the expression you have when you smile
EG *She gave me a big smile.*
beam EG *a strange beam of satisfaction on his face*
grin EG *She looked at me with a sheepish grin.*
smirk EG *a smirk of triumph*

smooth ADJECTIVE
not rough or bumpy
EG *a smooth wooden surface*
glassy EG *glassy green pebbles*
glossy EG *glossy dark fur*
polished EG *He slipped on the polished floor.*
silky EG *The sauce should be silky in texture.*
sleek EG *her sleek, waist-length hair*

WORD POWER

▶ **Antonym**
rough

---

smug ADJECTIVE
pleased with yourself
EG *They looked at each other in smug satisfaction.*
complacent EG *an aggravating, complacent little smile*
conceited EG *They had grown too conceited and pleased with themselves.*
self-satisfied EG *a self-satisfied little snob*

superior EG *He stood there looking superior.*

snag NOUN
a small problem or disadvantage
EG *The snag was that he had no transport.*
catch EG *It sounds too good to be true - what's the catch?*
difficulty EG *The only difficulty may be the price.*
disadvantage EG *The disadvantage is that this plant needs frequent watering.*
drawback EG *The flat's only drawback was its size.*
problem EG *The only problem about living here is the tourists.*

WORD POWER

▷ **Synonyms**
downside
stumbling block

---

❶ sneak VERB
to go somewhere quietly
EG *Sometimes he would sneak out to see me.*
lurk EG *I saw someone lurking outside.*
sidle EG *He sidled into the bar, trying to look inconspicuous.*
slip EG *Amy slipped downstairs and out of the house.*
steal EG *They can steal out and join us later.*

WORD POWER

▷ **Synonyms**
skulk
slink

---

❷ sneak VERB
to put or take something somewhere secretly
EG *I sneaked the books out of the library.*
slip EG *He slipped me a note.*
smuggle EG *We smuggled a camera into the concert.*

a
b
c
d
e
f
g
h
i
j
k
l
m
n
o
p
q
r
s
t
u
v
w
x
y
z

A B C D E F G H I J K L M N O P Q R **S** T U V W X Y Z

spirit EG *treasures spirited away to foreign museums*

sneaky ADJECTIVE
doing things secretly or being done secretly
EG *He only won by using sneaky tactics.*
crafty EG *the crafty methods used by salesmen to get people to sign up*
deceitful EG *They claimed the government had been deceitful.*
devious EG *He was devious, saying one thing to me and another to her.*
dishonest EG *It would be dishonest to mislead people in that way.*
mean EG *That was a mean trick.*
slippery EG *She's a slippery customer, and should be watched.*
sly EG *He's a sly old beggar.*
untrustworthy EG *His opponents say he's untrustworthy.*

snooper NOUN
a person who interferes in other people's business
EG *a tabloid snooper*
meddler EG *a meddler in the affairs of state*
stickybeak AUSTRALIAN AND NEW ZEALAND; INFORMAL EG *She's just an old stickybeak.*

WORD POWER

▷ **Synonyms**
busybody
nosy parker

soak VERB
to make something very wet
EG *The water had soaked his jacket.*
bathe EG *Bathe the infected area in a salt solution.*
permeate EG *The water had permeated the stone.*
steep EG *green beans steeped in olive oil*
wet EG *Wet the hair and work the shampoo through it.*

WORD POWER

▷ **Synonyms**
drench
saturate

sociable ADJECTIVE
enjoying the company of other people
EG *She's usually outgoing and sociable.*
friendly EG *The people here are very friendly.*
gregarious EG *I'm not a gregarious person.*
outgoing EG *He was shy and she was very outgoing.*

WORD POWER

▷ **Synonyms**
companionable
convivial

❶ society NOUN
the people in a particular country or region
EG *a major problem in society*
civilization EG *an ancient civilization*
culture EG *people from different cultures*

❷ society NOUN
an organization for people with the same interest or aim
EG *the school debating society*
association EG *the Football Association*
circle EG *a local painting circle*
club EG *He was at the youth club.*
fellowship EG *the Visual Arts Fellowship*
group EG *an environmental group*
guild EG *the Screen Writers' Guild*
institute EG *the Women's Institute*
league EG *the World Muslim League*
organization EG *student organizations*
union EG *the International Astronomical Union*

❶ soft ADJECTIVE
not hard, stiff or firm
EG *a soft bed*
flexible EG *a flexible material*
pliable EG *a pliable dough*
squashy EG *a squashy tomato*
supple EG *supple leather*
yielding EG *yielding cushions*

WORD POWER

▷ **Synonyms**
bendable
ductile
gelatinous
malleable
tensile

▶ **Antonym**
hard

❷ soft ADJECTIVE
quiet and not harsh
EG *a soft tapping at my door*
gentle EG *a gentle voice*
low EG *She spoke in a low whisper.*
mellow EG *mellow background music*
muted EG *Their loud conversation became muted.*
quiet EG *He always spoke in a quiet tone to which everyone listened.*
subdued EG *His voice was more subdued than usual.*

WORD POWER

▷ **Synonyms**
dulcet
mellifluous

❸ soft ADJECTIVE
not bright
EG *The bedside lamp cast a soft radiance over her face.*
dim EG *The light was dim and eerie.*
faint EG *The stars cast a faint light.*
light EG *The walls were painted a light yellow.*
mellow EG *Their colour schemes tend towards rich, mellow shades.*
pale EG *dressed in pale pink*

pastel EG *delicate pastel hues*
subdued EG *subdued lighting*

WORD POWER

▶ **Antonym**
bright

❶ soil NOUN
the surface of the earth
EG *The soil is reasonably moist after the rain.*
clay EG *a thin layer of clay*
dirt EG *The bulldozers piled up huge mounds of dirt.*
earth EG *a huge pile of earth*
ground EG *a hole in the ground*

❷ soil VERB
to make something dirty
EG *He looked at her as though her words might soil him.*
dirty EG *He was afraid the dog's hairs might dirty the seats.*
foul EG *The cage was fouled with droppings.*
pollute EG *chemicals which pollute rivers*
smear EG *The pillow was smeared with makeup.*
spatter EG *Her dress was spattered with mud.*
stain EG *Some foods can stain the teeth.*

WORD POWER

▷ **Synonyms**
befoul
begrime
besmirch
defile
smirch
sully

▶ **Antonym**
clean

solemn ADJECTIVE
not cheerful or humorous
EG *a taciturn man with a solemn expression*

a
b
c
d
e
f
g
h
i
j
k
l
m
n
o
p
q
r
s
t
u
v
w
x
y
z

A
B
C
D
E
F
G
H
I
J
K
L
M
N
O
P
Q
R
S
T
U
V
W
X
Y
Z

earnest EG *Ella was a pious, earnest woman.*
grave EG *He was looking unusually grave.*
serious EG *She looked at me with big, serious eyes.*
sober EG *sad, sober faces*
staid EG *He is boring, old fashioned and staid.*

❶ solid ADJECTIVE
hard and firm
EG *a block of solid wax*
firm EG *a firm mattress*
hard EG *The snow was hard and slippery.*

❷ solid ADJECTIVE
not likely to fall down
EG *a solid structure*
stable EG *stable foundations*
strong EG *a strong fence*
sturdy EG *The camera was mounted on a sturdy tripod.*
substantial EG *The posts are made of concrete and are fairly substantial.*

solitude NOUN
the state of being alone
EG *He went to the cottage for a few days of solitude.*
isolation EG *the isolation he endured while in captivity*
loneliness EG *I have a fear of loneliness.*
privacy EG *the privacy of my own room*
seclusion EG *She lived in seclusion with her husband.*

solve VERB
to find the answer to a problem or question
EG *attempts to solve the mystery*
clear up EG *During dinner the confusion was cleared up.*
crack EG *He finally managed to crack the code.*
decipher EG *trying to decipher the symbols on the stone tablets*
get to the bottom of EG *The police*

wanted to get to the bottom of the case.
resolve EG *Scientists hope this will finally resolve the mystery.*
work out EG *I've worked out where I'm going wrong.*

sometimes ADVERB
now and then
EG *Her voice was so low she was sometimes mistaken for a man.*
at times EG *She can be a little common at times.*
every now and then EG *He checks up on me every now and then.*
every so often EG *Every so often he does something silly.*
from time to time EG *I go back to see my mum from time to time.*
now and again EG *I enjoy a day out now and again.*
now and then EG *These people like a laugh now and then.*
occasionally EG *I know that I do put people down occasionally.*
once in a while EG *It does you good to get out once in a while.*

soon ADVERB
in a very short time
EG *You'll be hearing from us very soon.*
any minute now EG *Any minute now she's going to start crying.*
before long EG *Interest rates will come down before long.*
in a minute EG *I'll be with you in a minute.*
in the near future EG *The controversy is unlikely to be resolved in the near future.*
presently EG *I'll deal with you presently.*
shortly EG *The trial will begin shortly.*

WORD POWER

▶ **Antonym**
later

---

❶ sophisticated ADJECTIVE
having refined tastes

EG *a charming, sophisticated companion*
cosmopolitan EG *The family are rich and extremely cosmopolitan.*
cultivated EG *an elegant and cultivated woman*
cultured EG *He is immensely cultured and well-read.*
refined EG *a woman of refined tastes*
urbane EG *a polished, urbane manner*

2 sophisticated ADJECTIVE
advanced and complicated
EG *a sophisticated piece of equipment*
advanced EG *the most advanced optical telescope in the world*
complex EG *complex machines*
complicated EG *a complicated voting system*
elaborate EG *an elaborate design*
intricate EG *intricate controls*
refined EG *a more refined engine*

WORD POWER
▶ **Antonym**
simple

sore ADJECTIVE
causing pain and discomfort
EG *a sore throat*
inflamed EG *Her eyes were red and inflamed.*
painful EG *a painful knock on the knee*
raw EG *Her hands were rubbed raw by the rope.*
sensitive EG *the pain of sensitive teeth*
smarting EG *My eyes were smarting from the smoke.*
tender EG *My stomach feels very tender.*

1 sorrow NOUN
deep sadness or regret
EG *a time of great sorrow*
grief EG *Their grief soon gave way to anger.*
heartache EG *suffering the*

---

heartache of a divorce
melancholy EG *She has an air of melancholy.*
misery EG *All his money brought him nothing but misery.*
mourning EG *a day of mourning*
pain EG *My heart is full of pain.*
regret EG *She accepted his resignation with regret.*
sadness EG *It is with a mixture of sadness and joy that I say farewell.*
unhappiness EG *I had a lot of unhappiness in my adolescence.*
woe FORMAL EG *a tale of woe*

WORD POWER
▶ **Antonym**
joy

2 sorrow NOUN
things that cause deep sadness and regret
EG *the joys and sorrows of family life*
heartache EG *all the heartaches of parenthood*
hardship EG *One of the worst hardships is having so little time with my family.*
misfortune EG *She seems to enjoy the misfortunes of others.*
trouble EG *She told me all her troubles.*
woe WRITTEN EG *He did not tell his friends about his woes.*
worry EG *a life with no worries*

WORD POWER
▷ **Synonyms**
tribulation (FORMAL)

▶ **Antonym**
joy

1 sorry ADJECTIVE
feeling sadness or regret
EG *I'm terribly sorry to bother you.*
apologetic EG *"I'm afraid I can't help," she said with an apologetic smile.*
penitent EG *He sat silent and*

A
B
C
D
E
F
G
H
I
J
K
L
M
N
O
P
Q
R
S
T
U
V
W
X
Y
Z

penitent in a corner.
regretful EG *Now I'm totally regretful that I did it.*
remorseful EG *He was genuinely remorseful.*
repentant EG *repentant sinners*

WORD POWER

▷ **Synonyms**
conscience-stricken
contrite
guilt-ridden
shamefaced

2 sorry ADJECTIVE
feeling sympathy for someone
EG *I was sorry to hear about your husband's death.*
moved EG *I'm moved by what you say.*
sympathetic EG *She gave me a sympathetic glance.*

3 sorry ADJECTIVE
in a bad condition
EG *He was in a pretty sorry state when we found him.*
deplorable EG *living in deplorable conditions*
miserable EG *a miserable existence*
pathetic EG *the pathetic sight of oil-covered sea birds*
pitiful EG *a pitiful creature*
poor EG *the poor condition of the pitch*
sad EG *a sad state of affairs*
wretched EG *the wretched victims of war*

WORD POWER

▷ **Synonyms**
piteous
pitiable

1 sort NOUN
one of the different kinds of something
EG *a dozen trees of various sorts*
brand EG *his favourite brand of whisky*
category EG *The topics were divided*

into six categories.
class EG *a better class of restaurant*
group EG *Weathermen classify clouds into several different groups.*
kind EG *different kinds of roses*
make EG *a certain make of car*
species EG *400 species of fungi have been recorded.*
style EG *Several styles of hat were available.*
type EG *What type of dog should we get?*
variety EG *many varieties of birds*

WORD POWER

▷ **Synonyms**
ilk
stamp

2 sort VERB
to arrange things into different kinds
EG *He sorted the material into three folders.*
arrange EG *Arrange the books in neat piles.*
categorize EG *ways to categorize information*
classify EG *Rocks can be classified according to their mode of origin.*
divide EG *The subjects were divided into four groups.*
grade EG *musical pieces graded according to difficulty*
group EG *The fact sheet is grouped into seven sections.*
separate EG *His work can be separated into three main categories.*

1 sound NOUN
something that can be heard
EG *the sound of gunfire*
din EG *make themselves heard over the din of the crowd*
hubbub EG *the hubbub of excited conversation*
noise EG *the noise of bombs and guns*
racket EG *the racket of drills and*

electric saws
tone EG *the clear tone of the bell*

WORD POWER

▶ **Antonym**
silence

● **Related Words**
adjectives : sonic,
acoustic

② sound VERB
to produce or cause to produce a
noise
EG *A young man sounded the bell.*
blow EG *A guard was blowing his
whistle.*
chime EG *He heard the doorbell
chime.*
clang EG *The church bell clanged.*
peal EG *Church bells pealed at the
stroke of midnight.*
ring EG *She heard the school bell
ringing.*
set off EG *Any escape sets off the
alarm.*
toll EG *The pilgrims tolled the bell.*

③ sound ADJECTIVE
healthy, or in good condition
EG *His body was still sound.*
all right EG *Does the roof seem all
right?*
fine EG *She told me her heart was
perfectly fine.*
fit EG *Exercise is the first step to a fit
body.*
healthy EG *His once healthy mind
was deteriorating.*
in good condition EG *The timbers
were all in good condition.*
intact EG *The boat did not appear
damaged and its equipment seemed
intact.*
robust EG *He is in robust health for a
man of his age.*

④ sound ADJECTIVE
reliable and sensible
EG *a sound financial proposition*

down-to-earth EG *Their ideas seem
very down-to-earth.*
good EG *Give me one good reason
why I should tell you.*
reasonable EG *a perfectly
reasonable decision*
reliable EG *It's difficult to give a
reliable estimate.*
sensible EG *sensible advice*
solid EG *good solid information*
valid EG *Both sides made some valid
points.*

① sour ADJECTIVE
having a sharp taste
EG *The stewed apple was sour even
with sugar added.*
acid EG *The wine had an acid taste.*
bitter EG *a bitter drink*
pungent EG *a pungent sauce*
sharp EG *a clean, sharp flavour*
tart EG *the tart qualities of citrus fruit*

WORD POWER

▷ **Synonyms**
acerbic
acetic

▶ **Antonym**
sweet

② sour ADJECTIVE
unpleasant in taste because no
longer fresh
EG *This cream's gone sour.*
curdled EG *curdled milk*
off EG *This meat's gone off.*
rancid EG *rancid butter*

③ sour ADJECTIVE
bad-tempered and unfriendly
EG *a sour expression*
disagreeable EG *a shallow,
disagreeable man*
embittered EG *an embittered old
lady*
jaundiced EG *a jaundiced attitude*
tart EG *a tart reply*

a b c d e f g h i j k l m n o p q r s t u v w x y z

A
B
C
D
E
F
G
H
I
J
K
L
M
N
O
P
Q
R
S
T
U
V
W
X
Y
Z

WORD POWER

▷ **Synonyms**
churlish
peevish
waspish

source NOUN
the place where something comes from
EG *the source of his confidence*
beginning EG *the beginning of all the trouble*
cause EG *the cause of the problem*
derivation EG *The derivation of the name is obscure.*
origin EG *the origin of life*
originator EG *the originator of the theory*

WORD POWER

▷ **Synonyms**
fount
fountainhead
wellspring

souvenir NOUN
something you keep as a reminder
EG *a souvenir of our holiday*
keepsake EG *a cherished keepsake*
memento EG *a memento of the occasion*
relic EG *the threadbare teddy bear, a relic of childhood*
reminder EG *a permanent reminder of this historic event*

❶ space NOUN
an area which is empty or available
EG *a car with plenty of interior space*
accommodation EG *We have accommodation for six people.*
capacity EG *the capacity of the airliner*
room EG *no room to manoeuvre*

WORD POWER

● **Related Words**
adjective : spatial

❷ space NOUN
the gap between two things
EG *the space between the two tables*
blank EG *I've left a blank here for your signature.*
distance EG *the distance between the island and the mainland*
gap EG *The wind was tearing through gaps in the window frames.*
interval EG *the intervals between the trees*

❸ space NOUN
a period of time
EG *two incidents in the space of a week*
interval EG *a long interval of silence*
period EG *for a limited period only*
span EG *The batteries have a life span of six hours.*
time EG *At 15 he left home for a short time.*
while EG *Sit down for a while.*

spacious ADJECTIVE
having or providing a lot of space
EG *a spacious lounge*
ample EG *the city's ample car parks*
broad EG *a broad expanse of green lawn*
expansive EG *an expansive play area*
extensive EG *The palace stands in extensive grounds.*
huge EG *a huge apartment overlooking the park*
large EG *a large detached house*
vast EG *a vast chamber*

WORD POWER

▷ **Synonyms**
capacious
commodious
roomy
sizable *or* sizeable

❶ spare ADJECTIVE
in addition to what is needed
EG *Luckily I had a spare pair of glasses.*
extra EG *Allow yourself some extra time in case of emergencies.*
free EG *I'll do it as soon as I get some*

free time.
superfluous EG *I got rid of all my superfluous belongings.*
surplus EG *They sell their surplus produce.*

WORD POWER

▷ **Synonyms**
leftover
supernumerary

2 spare VERB
to make something available
EG *Can you spare some money for a cup of tea?*
afford EG *It's all I can afford to give you.*
give EG *It's good of you to give me some of your time.*
let someone have EG *I can let you have some milk and sugar.*

3 spare VERB
to save someone from an unpleasant experience
EG *I wanted to spare her that suffering.*
let off INFORMAL EG *I'll let you off this time.*
pardon EG *Relatives had begged authorities to pardon him.*
relieve from EG *a machine which relieves you of the drudgery of housework*
save from EG *I was trying to save you from unnecessary worry.*

sparkle VERB
to shine with small bright points of light
EG *Diamonds sparkled on her wrists.*
gleam EG *sunlight gleaming on the water*
glisten EG *The wall glistened with frost.*
glitter EG *A million stars glittered in the black sky.*
shimmer EG *In the distance the lake shimmered.*

twinkle EG *The old man's eyes twinkled.*

WORD POWER

▷ **Synonyms**
coruscate
scintillate

speak VERB
to use your voice to say words
EG *She turned to look at the person who was speaking.*
→ see Word Study **say**

1 special ADJECTIVE
more important or better than others of its kind
EG *You are very special to me.*
exceptional EG *children with exceptional ability*
important EG *This is an important occasion.*
significant EG *of significant importance*
unique EG *a unique talent*

WORD POWER

▶ **Antonym**
ordinary

2 special ADJECTIVE
relating to one person or group in particular
EG *the special needs of the chronically sick*
characteristic EG *a characteristic feature*
distinctive EG *the distinctive smell of chlorine*
individual EG *Each family needs individual attention.*
particular EG *Fatigue is a particular problem for women.*
peculiar EG *This is not a problem peculiar to London.*
specific EG *the specific needs of the elderly*

a
b
c
d
e
f
g
h
i
j
k
l
m
n
o
p
q
r
s
t
u
v
w
x
y
z

A B C D E F G H I J K L M N O P Q R S T U V W X Y Z

WORD POWER

▶ **Antonym**
general

specify VERB
to state or describe something
precisely
EG *Specify which size and colour you
want.*

be specific about EG *She was never
very specific about her date of birth.*
indicate EG *Please indicate your
preference below.*
name EG *The victims of the fire have
been named.*
spell out EG *He spelled out the
reasons why he was leaving.*
state EG *Please state your name.*
stipulate EG *His duties were
stipulated in the contract.*

spectator NOUN
a person who watches something
EG *Spectators lined the route.*
bystander EG *an innocent bystander*
eyewitness EG *Eyewitnesses say the
police opened fire in the crowd.*
observer EG *a disinterested observer*
onlooker EG *A small crowd of
onlookers was there to greet her.*
witness EG *There were scores of
witnesses.*

speech NOUN
a formal talk given to an audience
EG *He delivered his speech in French.*
address EG *an address to the
American people*
discourse EG *a lengthy discourse on
strategy*
lecture EG *a series of lectures on art*
talk EG *a talk on Celtic mythology*

WORD POWER

▷ **Synonyms**
disquisition
harangue
homily
oration

❶ speed NOUN
the rate at which something moves
or happens
EG *a top speed of 200 mph*
haste EG *the old saying "more haste,
less speed"*
hurry EG *the hurry and excitement of
the city*
momentum EG *This campaign is
gaining momentum.*
pace EG *He walked at a leisurely pace.*
rapidity EG *My moods alternate with
alarming rapidity.*
swiftness EG *Time is passing with
incredible swiftness.*
velocity EG *the velocity of light*

❷ speed VERB
to move quickly
EG *The pair sped off when the police
arrived.*
career EG *His car careered into a
river.*
flash EG *The bus flashed past me.*
gallop EG *galloping along the
corridor*
race EG *He raced across town.*
rush EG *He rushed off, closely
followed by Kemp.*
tear EG *Miranda tore off down the
road.*

spin VERB
to turn quickly around a central
point
EG *as the earth spins on its axis*
pirouette EG *She pirouetted in front
of the mirror.*
revolve EG *The satellite revolves
around the planet.*
rotate EG *rotating propellers*
turn EG *a turning wheel*
whirl EG *The fallen leaves whirled
around.*

❶ spirit NOUN
the part of you that is not physical
EG *His spirit had left his body.*
life force EG *the life force of all
animate things*

soul EG *praying for the soul of her dead husband*

❷ spirit NOUN
a ghost or supernatural being
EG *a protection against evil spirits*
apparition EG *an apparition of her dead son*
ghost EG *the premise that ghosts exist*
phantom EG *People claimed to have seen the phantom.*
spectre EG *a spectre from the other world*
sprite EG *a water sprite*

❸ spirit NOUN
liveliness and energy
EG *They played with spirit.*
animation EG *They both spoke with animation.*
energy EG *At 80 her energy is amazing.*
enthusiasm EG *They seem to be lacking in enthusiasm.*
fire EG *His performance was full of fire.*
force EG *She expressed her feelings with some force.*
vigour EG *We resumed the attack with renewed vigour.*
zest EG *He threw himself into the project with typical zest.*

WORD POWER
▷ **Synonyms**
brio
mettle

❶ spite in spite of PREPOSITION
even though something is the case
EG *In spite of all the gossip, Virginia stayed behind.*
despite EG *They manage to enjoy life despite adversity.*
even though EG *They did it even though I warned them not to.*
notwithstanding
eg *Notwithstanding his age, Sikorski had an important job.*

regardless of EG *He led from the front, regardless of the danger.*
though EG *I enjoy painting, though I am not very good at it.*

❷ spite NOUN
a desire to hurt someone
EG *He just did it out of spite.*
ill will EG *He didn't bear anyone any ill will.*
malevolence EG *a streak of malevolence*
malice EG *There was no malice in her voice.*
spitefulness EG *petty spitefulness*
venom EG *His wit had a touch of venom about it.*

WORD POWER
▷ **Synonyms**
malignity
rancour

spiteful ADJECTIVE
saying or doing nasty things to hurt people
EG *a stream of spiteful telephone calls*
bitchy INFORMAL EG *It's not just women who are bitchy.*
catty INFORMAL EG *She's always making catty remarks.*
cruel EG *They gave him a cruel nickname.*
malevolent EG *a malevolent stare*
malicious EG *spreading malicious gossip*
nasty EG *What nasty little snobs you all are.*
snide EG *He made a snide comment about her weight.*
venomous EG *a venomous attack*
vindictive EG *How can you be so vindictive?*

❶ splendid ADJECTIVE
very good indeed
EG *I've had a splendid time.*
cracking BRITISH, AUSTRALIAN, AND NEW ZEALAND; INFORMAL EG *It's a cracking script.*

A B C D E F G H I J K L M N O P Q R S T U V W X Y Z

excellent EG *The recording quality is excellent.*

fantastic INFORMAL EG *a fantastic combination of colours*

fine EG *a fine little fellow*

glorious EG *a glorious career*

great INFORMAL EG *a great bunch of guys*

marvellous EG *a marvellous thing to do*

wonderful EG *a wonderful movie*

❷ splendid ADJECTIVE

beautiful and impressive
EG *a splendid old mansion*

gorgeous EG *a gorgeous Renaissance building*

grand EG *a grand hotel*

imposing EG *imposing wrought-iron gates*

impressive EG *an impressive spectacle*

magnificent EG *magnificent views across the valley*

superb EG *The hotel has a superb isolated location.*

❶ split VERB

to divide into two or more parts
EG *The ship split in two.*

diverge EG *Their paths began to diverge.*

fork EG *Ahead of us, the road forked.*

part EG *For a moment the clouds parted.*

separate EG *Fluff the rice with a fork to separate the grains.*

WORD POWER

▷ **Synonyms**
bifurcate
cleave
disunite

❷ split VERB

to have a crack or tear
EG *His trousers split.*

burst EG *A water pipe has burst.*

come apart EG *My jacket's coming apart at the seams.*

crack EG *A gas main cracked.*

rip EG *I felt the paper rip as we pulled in opposite directions.*

❸ split NOUN

a crack or tear in something
EG *There's a split in my mattress.*

crack EG *The larvae burrow into cracks in the floor.*

fissure EG *Water trickled out of fissures in the limestone.*

rip EG *the rip in her new dress*

tear EG *the ragged edges of a tear*

❹ split NOUN

a division between two things
EG *the split between rugby league and rugby union*

breach EG *a serious breach in relations between the two countries*

breakup EG *the breakup of the Soviet Union in 1991*

divergence EG *a divergence between France and its allies*

division EG *the conventional division between "art" and "life"*

rift EG *There is a rift between us and the rest of the family.*

schism EG *the schism which divided the Christian world*

❶ spoil VERB

to damage or destroy something
EG *Don't let it spoil your holiday.*

damage EG *This could damage our chances of winning.*

destroy EG *His criticism has destroyed my confidence.*

harm EG *This product harms the environment.*

impair EG *The flavour is impaired by overcooking.*

mar EG *The celebrations were marred by violence.*

mess up EG *He's messed up his life.*

ruin EG *My wife was ruining her health through worry.*

wreck EG *the injuries which nearly wrecked his career*

2 spoil VERB
to give someone everything they
want
EG *Grandparents often spoil their
grandchildren.*
cosset EG *We did not cosset our
children.*
indulge EG *a heavily indulged
youngest daughter*
pamper EG *pampered pets*

WORD POWER

▷ **Synonyms**
coddle
mollycoddle
overindulge

spoilsport NOUN
a person who spoils other people's
fun
EG *They made me feel like a spoilsport
for saying no.*
misery BRITISH; INFORMAL EG *the
miseries in the government*
wowser AUSTRALIAN; SLANG EG *a small
group of wowsers*

spooky ADJECTIVE
eerie and frightening
EG *The whole place had a slightly
spooky atmosphere.*
creepy INFORMAL EG *a place that is
really creepy at night*
eerie EG *The wind made eerie noises
in the trees.*
frightening EG *Whenever I fall
asleep, I see these frightening faces.*
ghostly EG *The moon shed a ghostly
light on the fields.*
haunted EG *a haunted house*
supernatural EG *The blade glowed
with a supernatural light.*
scary EG *a scary ruined castle*
uncanny EG *The strange, uncanny
feeling was creeping all over me.*

1 spot NOUN
a small round mark on something
EG *a navy blue dress with white spots*
blemish EG *A small blemish spoiled*

the surface.
blot EG *an ink blot*
blotch EG *His face was covered in red
blotches.*
mark EG *a little red mark on my neck*
smudge EG *There was a dark smudge
on his forehead.*
speck EG *a speck of dirt*

2 spot NOUN
a location or place
EG *an out-of-the-way spot*
location EG *The hotel is in a superb
isolated location.*
place EG *Jerusalem is Christianity's
most venerated place.*
point EG *the point where the river had
burst its banks*
position EG *She moved the body to a
position where it would not be seen.*
scene EG *He left a note at the scene of
the crime.*
site EG *plans to construct a temple on
the site*

3 spot VERB
to see or notice something
EG *Her drama teacher spotted her
ability.*
catch sight of EG *I caught sight of
an ad in the paper.*
detect EG *The test should enable
doctors to detect the disease early.*
discern EG *I did not discern any
change.*
observe EG *Can you observe any
difference?*
see EG *I can see a resemblance
between you.*
sight EG *A fleet of French ships was
sighted.*

WORD POWER

▷ **Synonyms**
descry
espy

1 spread VERB
to open out or extend over an area
EG *He spread his coat over the bed.*

a
b
c
d
e
f
g
h
i
j
k
l
m
n
o
p
q
r
s
t
u
v
w
x
y
z

extend EG *The new territory would extend over one-fifth of Canada's land mass.*

fan out EG *She spun, and her dress's full skirt fanned out in a circle.*

open EG *She opened her arms and gave me a big hug.*

sprawl EG *The recreation area sprawls over 900 acres.*

unfold EG *When the bird lifts off, its wings unfold to a six-foot span.*

unfurl EG *We began to unfurl the sails.*

unroll EG *I unrolled my sleeping bag.*

❷ spread VERB

to put a thin layer on a surface
EG *Spread the bread with the cream cheese.*

apply EG *Apply the preparation evenly over the wood's surface.*

coat EG *Coat the fish with the paste.*

cover EG *I covered the table with a cloth.*

overlay EG *The floor was overlaid with rugs.*

plaster EG *She plastered herself in sun lotion.*

smear EG *Smear a little oil over the inside of the bowl.*

smother EG *He likes to smother his bread with butter.*

❸ spread VERB

to reach or affect more people gradually
EG *The sense of fear is spreading in the neighbourhood.*

circulate EG *Rumours were circulating that the project was to be abandoned.*

grow EG *Opposition grew and the government agreed to negotiate.*

expand EG *The industry is looking for opportunities to expand into other countries.*

increase EG *The population continues to increase.*

proliferate EG *the free Internet services that are proliferating across the world*

travel EG *News of his work travelled all the way to Asia.*

❹ spread NOUN

the extent or growth of something
EG *the gradual spread of information*

diffusion EG *the development and diffusion of ideas*

expansion EG *the rapid expansion of private health insurance*

extent EG *the growing extent of the problem*

growth EG *the growth of nationalism*

increase EG *an increase of violence along the border*

progression EG *This drug slows the progression of HIV.*

proliferation EG *the proliferation of nuclear weapons*

upsurge EG *the upsurge in interest in these books*

❶ squabble VERB

to quarrel about something trivial
EG *Mum and Dad squabble all the time.*

argue EG *They went on arguing all the way down the road.*

bicker EG *The two women bickered constantly.*

fall out EG *Mum and I used to fall out a lot.*

feud EG *feuding neighbours*

fight EG *Mostly, they fight about paying bills.*

quarrel EG *At one point we quarrelled over something silly.*

row EG *They rowed all the time.*

wrangle EG *The two sides spend their time wrangling over procedural problems.*

❷ squabble NOUN

a quarrel
EG *There have been minor squabbles about phone bills.*

altercation EG *an altercation with the referee*

argument EG *a heated argument*

barney BRITISH, AUSTRALIAN, AND NEW ZEALAND; INFORMAL EG *We had such a barney that we nearly split up.*
disagreement EG *My instructor and I had a brief disagreement.*
dispute EG *a dispute between the two countries over farm subsidies*
fight EG *He had a big fight with his dad that night.*
quarrel EG *I had a terrible quarrel with my brother.*
row EG *A man had been stabbed to death in a family row.*
tiff EG *She was walking home after a tiff with her boyfriend.*

staff NOUN
the people who work for an organization
EG *She made little effort to socialize with other staff.*
employees EG *a temporary employee*
personnel EG *An announcement was made to all personnel.*
team EG *The team worked well under his direction.*
workers EG *weekend and night-shift workers*
workforce EG *a sullen and resentful workforce*

❶ stage NOUN
a part of a process
EG *the closing stages of the race*
lap EG *The first lap was clocked at under a minute.*
period EG *We went through a period of unprecedented change.*
phase EG *a passing phase*
point EG *a critical point in the campaign*
step EG *the next step in the process*

❷ stage VERB
to organize something
EG *Workers have staged a number of one-day strikes.*
arrange EG *We're arranging a surprise party for her.*
engineer EG *He was the one who engineered the merger.*
mount EG *a security operation mounted by the army*
orchestrate EG *a carefully orchestrated campaign*
organize EG *a two-day meeting organized by the UN*

❶ stain NOUN
a mark on something
EG *grass stains*
blot EG *an ink blot*
mark EG *I can't get this mark to come off.*
spot EG *brown spots on the skin caused by the sun*

❷ stain VERB
to make a mark on something
EG *Some foods can stain the teeth.*
dirty EG *Sheets can be reused until they are damaged or dirtied.*
mark EG *the places where Steve's boots had marked the wood*
soil EG *a soiled white apron*
spot EG *her coat was spotted with blood*

WORD POWER

▷ **Synonyms**
discolour
smirch

---

stale ADJECTIVE
no longer fresh
EG *a lump of stale bread*
flat EG *flat beer*
old EG *mouldy old cheese*
sour EG *sour milk*
stagnant EG *stagnant water*

WORD POWER

▷ **Synonyms**
fusty
musty

▶ **Antonym**
fresh

---

❶ standard NOUN
a particular level of quality or

a b c d e f g h i j k l m n o p q r s t u v w x y z

A
B
C
D
E
F
G
H
I
J
K
L
M
N
O
P
Q
R
S
T
U
V
W
X
Y
Z

achievement
EG *There will be new standards of hospital cleanliness.*
calibre EG *the high calibre of these researchers*
criterion EG *The most important criterion for entry is excellence in your chosen field.*
guideline EG *The accord lays down guidelines for the conduct of government agents.*
level EG *The exercises are marked according to their level of difficulty.*
norm EG *the commonly accepted norms of democracy*
quality EG *Everyone can improve their quality of life.*
requirement EG *These products meet all legal requirements.*

❷ standard ADJECTIVE
usual, normal, and correct
EG *It was standard practice for them to consult the parents.*
accepted EG *It is accepted wisdom that the state of your body impacts on your state of mind.*
correct EG *the correct way to produce a crop of tomato plants*
customary EG *It is customary to offer a drink or a snack to guests.*
normal EG *Some shops were closed, but that's quite normal for a Thursday.*
orthodox EG *orthodox police methods*
regular EG *This product looks and tastes like regular lemonade.*
usual EG *It is usual to tip waiters.*

standards PLURAL NOUN
moral principles of behaviour
EG *My father has always had high moral standards.*
ethics EG *the difference between our personal and social ethics*
ideals EG *The party has drifted too far from its socialist ideals.*
morals EG *Western ideas and morals*
principles EG *He refused to do anything that went against his*

principles.
rules EG *They were expected to adhere to the rules of the convent.*
scruples EG *a man with no moral scruples*
values EG *the values of liberty and equality*

star NOUN
a famous person
EG *a film star*
celebrity EG *A host of celebrities attended the premiere.*
idol EG *the city's greatest soccer idol*
luminary LITERARY EG *The event attracted such pop luminaries as Madonna.*

stare VERB
to look at something for a long time
EG *He stared at the floor, lost in meditation.*
gaze EG *gazing at herself in the mirror*
look EG *He looked at her with open hostility.*
ogle EG *ogling the girls as they went past*

WORD POWER

▷ **Synonyms**
gawp
goggle

---

❶ start VERB
to begin to take place
EG *School starts again next week.*
arise EG *A conflict is likely to arise.*
begin EG *A typical day begins at 8.30.*
come into being EG *The festival came into being in 1986.*
come into existence EG *a club that came into existence only 30 years ago*
commence EG *The academic year commences at the beginning of October.*
get under way EG *The game got under way.*
originate EG *The disease originated in Africa.*

WORD POWER

▶ Antonym
finish

② start VERB
to begin to do something
EG *Susie started to cry.*
begin EG *He began to groan with pain.*
commence EG *The hunter commenced to skin the animal.*
embark upon EG *He's embarking on a new career as a writer.*
proceed EG *He proceeded to get drunk.*
set about EG *How do you set about getting a mortgage?*

WORD POWER

▶ Antonym
stop

③ start VERB
to cause something to begin
EG *a good time to start a business*
begin EG *The US is prepared to begin talks immediately.*
create EG *Criticism will only create feelings of failure.*
establish EG *The school was established in 1899.*
found EG *Baden-Powell founded the Boy Scouts in 1908.*
get going EG *I've worked hard to get this business going.*
inaugurate FORMAL EG *the company which inaugurated the first scheduled international flight*
initiate EG *They wanted to initiate a discussion.*
instigate EG *The violence was instigated by a few people.*
institute EG *We have instituted a number of measures.*
introduce EG *The government has introduced other money-saving schemes.*
launch EG *The police have launched*

an investigation into the incident.
open EG *We opened the srvice with a hymn.*
pioneer EG *the man who invented and pioneered DNA testing*
set in motion EG *Several changes have already been set in motion.*
set up EG *A committee was set up to arbitrate in the dispute.*
trigger EG *Nuts can trigger an allergic reaction in some people.*

WORD POWER

▶ Antonym
stop

④ start NOUN
the beginning of something
EG *His career had an auspicious start.*
beginning EG *the beginning of all the trouble*
birth EG *the birth of modern art*
commencement EG *Applicants should be at least 16 before the commencement of the course.*
dawn EG *the dawn of a new age*
foundation EG *the foundation of the National Organization for Women*
inauguration EG *the inauguration of new exam standards*
inception FORMAL EG *Since its inception the company has produced 53 different aircraft designs.*
initiation EG *There was a year between initiation and completion.*
onset EG *the onset of puberty*
opening EG *the opening of the trial*
outset EG *There were lots of problems from the outset.*

WORD POWER

▶ Antonym
finish

① state NOUN
the condition or circumstances of something
EG *the pathetic state of the rail network*

a b c d e f g h i j k l m n o p q r s t u v w x y z

circumstances EG *He's in desperate circumstances.*

condition EG *He remains in a critical condition in hospital.*

plight EG *the plight of Third World countries*

position EG *We are in a privileged position.*

predicament EG *the once great club's current predicament*

shape EG *Her finances were in terrible shape.*

situation EG *a precarious situation*

❷ state NOUN
a country
EG *the state of Denmark*

country EG *a country where alcohol is prohibited*

kingdom EG *The kingdom's power declined.*

land EG *in that distant land*

nation EG *a leading nation in world politics*

republic EG *In 1918, Austria became a republic.*

WORD POWER
▷ **Synonyms**
body politic
commonwealth

❸ state VERB
to say something, especially in a formal way
EG *Please state your occupation.*

affirm EG *a speech in which he affirmed his policies*

articulate EG *an attempt to articulate his feelings*

assert EG *He asserted his innocence.*

declare EG *He declared that he would fight on.*

express EG *He expressed regret that he had caused any offence.*

say EG *The police said he had no connection with the security forces.*

specify EG *Please specify your preferences below.*

WORD POWER
▷ **Synonyms**
aver
expound
propound

statement NOUN
a short written or spoken piece giving information
EG *He was depressed when he made that statement.*

account EG *He gave a detailed account of what happened that night.*

announcement EG *He made his announcement after talks with the President.*

bulletin EG *A bulletin was released announcing the decision.*

declaration EG *a public declaration of support*

explanation EG *They have given no public explanation for his dismissal.*

proclamation EG *The proclamation of independence was broadcast over the radio.*

report EG *A press report said that at least six people had died.*

testimony EG *His testimony was an important part of the prosecution case.*

status NOUN
a person's social position
EG *the status of children in society*

position EG *a privileged position*

prestige EG *to diminish the prestige of the monarchy*

rank EG *He was stripped of his rank.*

standing EG *This has done nothing to improve his standing.*

stay VERB
to remain somewhere
EG *She stayed in bed till noon.*

hang around INFORMAL EG *I can't hang around here all day.*

linger EG *I lingered on for a few days*

until he arrived.
loiter EG *We loitered around looking in shop windows.*
remain EG *You'll have to remain in hospital for the time being.*
tarry EG *The shop's aim is to persuade you to tarry and spend.*
wait EG *I'll wait here till you come back.*

steadfast ADJECTIVE
refusing to change or give up
EG *He remained steadfast in his belief.*
constant EG *He has been her constant companion for the last four months.*
faithful EG *this party's most faithful voters*
firm EG *He held a firm belief in the afterlife.*
immovable EG *On one issue, however, she was immovable.*
resolute EG *a decisive and resolute international leader*
staunch EG *a staunch supporter of these proposals*
steady EG *He was firm and steady, unlike many men she knew.*
unshakeable EG *his unshakeable belief in the project*

❶ steady ADJECTIVE
continuing without interruptions
EG *a steady rise in profits*
consistent EG *consistent support*
constant EG *under constant pressure*
continuous EG *Japanese-style programmes of continuous improvement*
even EG *an even level of sound*
nonstop EG *nonstop background music*
regular EG *a regular beat*
uninterrupted EG *28 years of uninterrupted growth*

❷ steady ADJECTIVE
not shaky or wobbling
EG *O'Brien held out a steady hand.*
firm EG *Make sure the tree is securely*

mounted on a firm base.
secure EG *Check joints are secure and the wood is sound.*
stable EG *stable foundations*

❸ steady VERB
to prevent something from shaking or wobbling
EG *Two men were steadying a ladder.*
brace EG *the old timbers which braced the roof*
secure EG *The frames are secured by horizontal rails.*
stabilize EG *gyros which stabilize the platform*
support EG *Thick wooden posts support the ceiling.*

❶ steal VERB
to take something without permission
EG *He was accused of stealing a tin of pineapple chunks.*
appropriate EG *Several other companies have appropriated the idea.*
nick BRITISH, AUSTRALIAN, AND NEW ZEALAND; SLANG EG *I nicked that money from the till.*
pilfer EG *Staff were pilfering behind the bar.*
pinch INFORMAL EG *Someone's pinched my wallet.*
swipe SLANG EG *Did you just swipe that book?*
take EG *The burglars took anything they could carry.*

WORD POWER

▷ **Synonyms**
embezzle
filch
misappropriate
purloin
thieve

❷ steal VERB
to move somewhere quietly and secretly
EG *They can steal out and join us later.*

a b c d e f g h i j k l m n o p q r s t u v w x y z

A
B
C
D
E
F
G
H
I
J
K
L
M
N
O
P
Q
R
S
T
U
V
W
X
Y
Z

creep EG *We crept away under cover of darkness.*
slip EG *I wanted to duck down and slip past but they saw me.*
sneak EG *Sometimes he would sneak out to see me.*
tiptoe EG *She slipped out of bed and tiptoed to the window.*

❶ steep ADJECTIVE
rising sharply and abruptly
EG *a steep hill*
sheer EG *a sheer drop*
vertical EG *The slope was almost vertical.*

WORD POWER

▶ **Antonym**
gradual

❷ steep ADJECTIVE
larger than is reasonable
EG *steep prices*
excessive EG *excessive charges*
extortionate EG *an extortionate rate of interest*
high EG *high loan rates*
unreasonable EG *unreasonable interest charges*

WORD POWER

▷ **Synonyms**
exorbitant
overpriced

❸ steep VERB
to soak something in a liquid
EG *green beans steeped in olive oil*
immerse EG *Immerse the gammon in cold water to remove the salt.*
marinate EG *Marinate the chicken for at least four hours.*
soak EG *Soak the beans overnight.*

❶ sterile ADJECTIVE
free from germs
EG *Protect the cut with a sterile dressing.*
antiseptic EG *an antiseptic hospital room*

germ-free EG *Keep your working surfaces germ-free.*
sterilized EG *a sterilized laboratory*

❷ sterile ADJECTIVE
unable to produce
EG *He found out he was sterile.*
barren EG *a barren mare*
unproductive EG *70 million acres of unproductive land*

WORD POWER

▷ **Synonyms**
infecund
unfruitful

▶ **Antonym**
fertile

❶ stick NOUN
a long, thin piece of wood
EG *crowds armed with sticks and stones*
bat EG *a baseball bat*
cane EG *He wore a grey suit and leaned heavily on his cane.*
mace EG *a statue of a king holding a golden mace*
pole EG *He reached up with a hooked pole to roll down the shutter.*
rod EG *a witch-doctor's rod*
truncheon EG *a policeman's truncheon*
twig EG *the sound of a twig breaking underfoot*
wand EG *You can't wave a magic wand and make everything okay.*

❷ stick VERB
to thrust something somewhere
EG *They stuck a needle in my back.*
dig EG *She dug her spoon into the moussaka.*
insert EG *He inserted the key into the lock.*
jab EG *A needle was jabbed into my arm.*
poke EG *He poked his finger into the hole.*
push EG *She pushed her thumb into his eye.*

stick >> stiff

put EG *Just put it through my letter-box when you're finished with it.*
ram EG *He rammed the jacket under the seat.*
shove EG *We shoved a copy of the newsletter beneath their door.*
stuff EG *I stuffed my hands in my pockets.*
thrust EG *A small aerial thrust up from the grass verge.*

❸ **stick** VERB
to attach or become attached
EG *Stick down any loose bits of flooring.*
adhere EG *Small particles adhere to the seed.*
attach EG *We attach labels to things before we file them away.*
bond EG *Strips of wood are bonded together.*
cling EG *His sodden trousers were clinging to his shins.*
fix EG *Fix the photo to the card using double-sided tape.*
fuse EG *The flakes fuse together and produce ice crystals.*
glue EG *Glue the fabric around the window.*
paste EG *The children were busy pasting stars on to a chart.*

❹ **stick** VERB
to jam or become jammed
EG *The dagger stuck tightly in the silver scabbard.*
catch EG *His jacket buttons caught in the net.*
jam EG *Every few moments the machinery became jammed.*
lodge EG *The car has a bullet lodged in the passenger door.*
snag EG *The fishermen said their nets kept snagging on underwater objects.*

sticky ADJECTIVE
covered with a substance that sticks to other things
EG *She thrust her hand into the sticky mess.*

adhesive EG *adhesive tape*
tacky EG *covered with a tacky resin*

WORD POWER

▷ **Synonyms**
glutinous
viscid
viscous

❶ **stiff** ADJECTIVE
firm and not easily bent
EG *stiff metal wires*
firm EG *a firm mattress*
hard EG *the hard wooden floor*
rigid EG *a rigid plastic container*
solid EG *a block of solid wax*
taut EG *He lifted the wire until it was taut.*

WORD POWER

▶ **Antonym**
limp

❷ **stiff** ADJECTIVE
not friendly or relaxed
EG *the rather stiff and formal surroundings of the Palace*
cold EG *Sharon was very cold with me.*
forced EG *a forced smile*
formal EG *His voice was grave and formal.*
stilted EG *Our conversation was stilted and polite.*
unnatural EG *a strained and unnatural atmosphere*
wooden EG *a wooden performance*

WORD POWER

▷ **Synonyms**
constrained
prim
standoffish

❸ **stiff** ADJECTIVE
difficult or severe
EG *a stiff exam*
arduous EG *an arduous undertaking*
difficult EG *a difficult job*
exacting EG *exacting standards*

a
b
c
d
e
f
g
h
i
j
k
l
m
n
o
p
q
r
s
t
u
v
w
x
y
z

A
B
C
D
E
F
G
H
I
J
K
L
M
N
O
P
Q
R
S
T
U
V
W
X
Y
Z

formidable EG *a formidable task*
hard EG *a hard day's work*
rigorous EG *rigorous military training*
tough EG *a tough challenge*

still ADJECTIVE
not moving
EG *The air was still.*
calm EG *the calm waters of the harbour*
inert EG *He covered the inert body with a blanket.*
motionless EG *He stood there, motionless.*
stationary EG *The train was stationary for 90 minutes.*
tranquil EG *a tranquil lake*

❶ stink VERB
to smell very bad
EG *His breath stinks of garlic.*
pong BRITISH AND AUSTRALIAN; INFORMAL
eg *She said he ponged a bit.*
reek EG *The whole house reeks of cigar smoke.*

❷ stink NOUN
a very bad smell
EG *the stink of stale beer on his breath*
pong BRITISH AND AUSTRALIAN; INFORMAL
eg *What's that horrible pong?*
stench EG *a foul stench*

WORD POWER

▷ **Synonyms**
fetor
malodour

❶ stock NOUN
shares bought in an investment company
EG *the buying of stocks*
bonds EG *the recent sharp decline in bond prices*
investments EG *Earn a rate of return of 8% on your investments.*
shares EG *He was keen to buy shares in the company.*

❷ stock NOUN
a supply of something
EG *The shop withdrew a quantity of stock from sale.*
goods EG *Are all your goods on display?*
merchandise FORMAL EG *25% off selected merchandise*
reserve EG *65% of the world's oil reserves*
reservoir EG *the body's short-term reservoir of energy*
stockpile EG *treaties to cut stockpiles of chemical weapons*
store EG *my secret store of chocolate biscuits*
supply EG *What happens when food supplies run low?*

❸ stock NOUN
an animal or person's ancestors
EG *We are both from working-class stock.*
ancestry EG *a family who can trace their ancestry back to the sixteenth century*
descent EG *All the contributors were of African descent.*
extraction EG *Her father was of Italian extraction.*
lineage EG *a respectable family of ancient lineage*
parentage EG *She's a Londoner of mixed parentage.*
origin EG *people of Asian origin*

❹ stock VERB
to keep a supply of goods to sell
EG *The shop stocks a wide range of paint.*
deal in EG *They deal in kitchen equipment.*
sell EG *It sells everything from hair ribbons to oriental rugs.*
supply EG *We supply office furniture and accessories.*
trade in EG *He had been trading in antique furniture for 25 years.*

⑤ stock ADJECTIVE
commonly used
EG *National security is the stock excuse for government secrecy.*
hackneyed EG *It may be an old hackneyed phrase, but it's true.*
overused EG *an overused catch phrase*
routine EG *We've tried all the routine methods of persuasion.*
standard EG *the standard ending for a formal letter*
stereotyped EG *stereotyped ideas about women*
typical EG *the typical questions journalists ask celebrities*
usual EG *He came out with all the usual excuses.*

① stockpile VERB
to store large quantities of something
EG *People are stockpiling food for the winter.*
accumulate EG *Some people get rich by accumulating wealth very gradually.*
amass EG *It is best not to enquire how he amassed his fortune.*
collect EG *Two young girls were collecting firewood.*
gather EG *We gathered enough wood to last the night.*
hoard EG *They've begun to hoard food and petrol.*
save EG *Scraps of material were saved for quilts.*
stash INFORMAL EG *He had stashed money in an offshore account.*
store up EG *Investors were storing up cash in anticipation of disaster.*

② stockpile NOUN
a large store of something
EG *stockpiles of fuel*
arsenal EG *a formidable arsenal of guns and landmines*
cache EG *a cache of weapons and explosives*
hoard EG *a hoard of silver and jewels*

worth $40m
reserve EG *The country's reserves of food are running low.*
stash INFORMAL EG *her mother's stash of sleeping pills*
stock EG *Stocks of ammunition were being used up.*
store EG *his secret store of sweets*

stocky ADJECTIVE
short but solid-looking
EG *a stocky, middle-aged man*
chunky EG *the chunky South African tennis player*
solid EG *a solid build*
sturdy EG *a short, sturdy woman in her early sixties*

WORD POWER

▷ **Synonyms**
stubby
thickset

---

stomach NOUN
the front part of the body below the waist
EG *Breathe out and flatten your stomach.*
belly EG *the enormous belly of the Italian foreign minister*
paunch EG *Nicholson surveyed his spreading paunch.*
puku NEW ZEALAND EG *a pain in my puku*
tummy INFORMAL EG *I'd like a flatter tummy, but then who doesn't?*

① stop VERB
to cease doing something
EG *I stopped working last year to have a baby.*
cease EG *A small number of firms have ceased trading.*
cut out INFORMAL EG *Will you cut out that racket?*
desist EG *boycotting Norwegian products until they desist from whaling*
discontinue EG *Do not discontinue the treatment without seeing your*

a b c d e f g h i j k l m n o p q r s t u v w x y z

doctor.
end EG *public pressure to end the embargo*
quit EG *He's trying to quit smoking.*

WORD POWER

▶ **Antonym**
start

② stop VERB
to come to an end
EG *He prayed for the blizzard to stop.*
cease EG *At 1 o'clock the rain ceased.*
come to an end EG *An hour later, the meeting came to an end.*
conclude EG *The evening concluded with dinner and speeches.*
end EG *The talks ended in disagreement.*
finish EG *The teaching day finishes at around 4 pm.*
halt EG *Discussions have halted again.*

WORD POWER

▶ **Antonym**
start

③ stop VERB
to prevent something
EG *measures to stop the trade in ivory*
arrest EG *trying to arrest the bleeding*
check EG *a policy to check fast population growth*
prevent EG *the most practical way of preventing crime*

WORD POWER

▷ **Synonyms**
forestall
nip something in
the bud

① store NOUN
a supply kept for future use
EG *I have a store of food and water here.*
cache EG *a cache of weapons and*

explosives
fund EG *an extraordinary fund of energy*
hoard EG *a hoard of supplies*
reserve EG *the world's oil reserves*
reservoir EG *the body's short-term reservoir of energy*
stock EG *stocks of paper and ink*
stockpile EG *stockpiles of nuclear warheads*
supply EG *food supplies*

② store NOUN
a place where things are kept
EG *a grain store*
depot EG *a government arms depot*
storeroom EG *a storeroom filled with furniture*
warehouse EG *a carpet warehouse*

WORD POWER

▷ **Synonyms**
depository
repository
storehouse

③ store VERB
to keep something for future use
EG *The information can be stored in a computer.*
hoard EG *They've begun to hoard food and petrol.*
keep EG *Grate the lemon zest and keep it for later.*
save EG *His allotment of gas had to be saved for emergencies.*
stash INFORMAL EG *He had stashed money away in a secret offshore account.*
stockpile EG *People are stockpiling food for the coming winter.*

story NOUN
a tale told or written to entertain people
EG *a poignant love story*
account EG *a true account*
anecdote EG *her store of theatrical anecdotes*
legend EG *an old Scottish legend*

narrative EG *a fast-moving narrative*
tale EG *a fairy tale*
yarn EG *a children's yarn about giants*

❶ **straight** ADJECTIVE
upright or level
EG *Keep your arms straight.*
erect EG *The upper back and neck are held in an erect position.*
even EG *to ensure an even hem*
horizontal EG *a horizontal line*
level EG *a completely level base*
perpendicular EG *Position your body perpendicular with the slope.*
upright EG *He sat upright in his chair.*
vertical EG *Keep the spine vertical.*

WORD POWER

▶ **Antonym**
crooked

❷ **straight** ADJECTIVE
honest, frank and direct
EG *They wouldn't give me a straight answer.*
blunt EG *She is blunt about her personal life.*
candid EG *I haven't been completely candid with you.*
forthright EG *a forthright reply*
frank EG *a frank discussion*
honest EG *Please be honest with me.*
outright EG *This was outright rejection.*
plain EG *plain talking*
point-blank EG *a point-blank refusal*

❶ **straightforward** ADJECTIVE
easy and involving no problems
EG *The question seemed straightforward enough.*
basic EG *The film's story is pretty basic.*
easy EG *The shower is easy to install.*
elementary EG *elementary computer skills*
routine EG *a fairly routine procedure*
simple EG *simple advice on filling in your tax form*
uncomplicated EG *good British*

cooking with its uncomplicated,
natural flavours

WORD POWER

▶ **Antonym**
complicated

❷ **straightforward** ADJECTIVE
honest, open, and frank
EG *I liked his straightforward, intelligent manner.*
candid EG *I haven't been completely candid with you.*
direct EG *He avoided giving a direct answer.*
forthright EG *He was known for his forthright manner.*
frank EG *They had a frank discussion about the issue.*
honest EG *I was totally honest about what I was doing.*
open EG *He had always been open with her.*
plain EG *I believe in plain talking.*
straight EG *He never gives a straight answer to a straight question.*

WORD POWER

▶ **Antonym**
devious

❶ **strain** NOUN
worry and nervous tension
EG *the stresses and strains of a busy career*
anxiety EG *Her voice was full of anxiety.*
pressure EG *the pressure of work*
stress EG *the stress of exams*
tension EG *Laughing relieves tension and stress.*

❷ **strain** VERB
to make something do more than it is able to do
EG *You'll strain your eyes reading in this light.*
overwork EG *Too much food will overwork your digestive system.*

a b c d e f g h i j k l m n o p q r s t u v w x y z

A
B
C
D
E
F
G
H
I
J
K
L
M
N
O
P
Q
R
S
T
U
V
W
X
Y
Z

tax EG *He is beginning to tax my patience.*

WORD POWER

▷ **Synonyms**
overexert
overtax
push to the limit

❶ strange ADJECTIVE
unusual or unexpected
EG *A strange thing happened.*
abnormal EG *an abnormal fear of spiders*
bizarre EG *a bizarre scene*
curious EG *a curious mixture of ancient and modern*
extraordinary EG *an extraordinary occurrence*
funny EG *a funny feeling*
odd EG *There was something odd about her.*
peculiar EG *It tasted very peculiar.*
queer EG *I think there's something a bit queer going on.*
uncommon EG *A 15-year lifespan is not uncommon for a dog.*
weird EG *He's a really weird guy.*

WORD POWER

▷ **Synonyms**
out-of-the-way
outré
unaccountable

❷ strange ADJECTIVE
new or unfamiliar
EG *alone in a strange country*
alien EG *transplanted into an alien culture*
exotic EG *filmed in an exotic location*
foreign EG *This was a foreign country, so unlike his own.*
new EG *I'm always open to new experiences.*
novel EG *a novel idea*
unfamiliar EG *visiting an unfamiliar city*

❶ strength NOUN
physical energy and power
EG *an astonishing display of physical strength*
brawn EG *He's got plenty of brains as well as brawn.*
might EG *the full might of the army*
muscle EG *demonstrating both muscle and skill*
stamina EG *The race requires a lot of stamina.*

WORD POWER

▷ **Synonyms**
brawniness
lustiness
sinew

▶ **Antonym**
weakness

❷ strength NOUN
the degree of intensity
EG *an indication of the strength of feeling among parents*
force EG *the force of his argument*
intensity EG *the intensity of their emotions*
potency EG *the extraordinary potency of his personality*
power EG *the overwhelming power of love*
vehemence EG *I was surprised by the vehemence of his criticism.*
vigour EG *We resumed the attack with renewed vigour.*

WORD POWER

▶ **Antonym**
weakness

❶ strengthen VERB
to give something more power
EG *This move will strengthen his political standing.*
consolidate EG *to consolidate an already dominant position*
encourage EG *encouraged by the shouts of their supporters*

harden EG *evidence which hardens suspicions about their involvement*
stiffen EG *This only stiffened his resolve to quit.*
toughen EG *new laws to toughen police powers*

WORD POWER

▷ **Synonyms**
fortify
hearten
invigorate

▶ **Antonym**
weaken

---

2 strengthen VERB
to support the structure of something
EG *The builders had to strengthen the joists with timber.*
bolster EG *steel beams used to bolster the roof*
brace EG *tottering pillars braced by scaffolding*
fortify EG *citadels fortified by high stone walls*
reinforce EG *They had to reinforce the walls with exterior beams.*
support EG *the thick wooden posts that supported the ceiling*

WORD POWER

▶ **Antonym**
weaken

---

1 stress NOUN
worry and nervous tension
EG *the stresses and strains of a busy career*
anxiety EG *Her voice was full of anxiety.*
hassle INFORMAL EG *I don't think it's worth the money or the hassle.*
pressure EG *I felt the pressure of being the first woman in the job.*
strain EG *She was tired and under great strain.*

tension EG *Laughing relieves tension.*
worry EG *It was a time of worry for us.*

2 stress VERB
to emphasize something
EG *The leaders have stressed their commitment to the talks.*
accentuate EG *make-up which accentuates your best features*
emphasize EG *He flourished his glass to emphasize the point.*
repeat EG *We are not, I repeat not, in the negotiating process.*
underline EG *The report underlined his concern about falling standards.*

WORD POWER

▷ **Synonyms**
belabour
dwell on
point up
underscore

---

1 stretch VERB
to extend over an area or time
EG *an artificial reef stretching the length of the coast*
continue EG *The road continued into the distance.*
cover EG *The oil slick covered a total area of seven miles.*
extend EG *The caves extend for some 18 kilometres.*
go on EG *The dispute looks set to go on into the new year.*
hang EG *The branches hang right down to the ground.*
last EG *His difficulties are likely to last well beyond childhood.*
reach EG *a caravan park which reached from one end of the bay to the other*
spread EG *The estuary spreads as far as the eye can see.*

2 stretch VERB
to reach out with part of your body
EG *She arched her back and stretched herself.*
extend EG *Stand straight with your*

a
b
c
d
e
f
g
h
i
j
k
l
m
n
o
p
q
r
s
t
u
v
w
x
y
z

arms extended at your sides.
reach EG *He reached up for an overhanging branch.*
straighten EG *Point your toes and straighten both legs slowly.*

WORD POWER

▶ **Antonym**
bend

❸ stretch NOUN

an area of land or water
EG *It's a very dangerous stretch of road.*
area EG *extensive mountainous areas of Europe and South America*
expanse EG *a huge expanse of grassland*
extent EG *a vast extent of fertile country*
sweep EG *The ground fell away in a broad sweep down the river.*
tract EG *They cleared large tracts of forest for farming.*

❹ stretch NOUN

a period of time
EG *He would study for eight hour stretches.*
period EG *a long period of time*
run EG *The show will transfer to the West End, after a month's run in Birmingham.*
space EG *They've come a long way in a short space of time.*
spell EG *a long spell of dry weather*
stint EG *He is coming home after a five-year stint abroad.*
term EG *She worked the full term of her pregnancy.*
time EG *doing very little exercise for several weeks at a time*

❶ strict ADJECTIVE

very firm in demanding obedience
EG *My parents were very strict.*
authoritarian EG *He has an authoritarian approach to parenthood.*
firm EG *the guiding hand of a firm father figure*

rigid EG *a rigid hospital routine*
rigorous EG *rigorous military training*
stern EG *Her mother was stern and hard to please.*
stringent EG *stringent rules*

❷ strict ADJECTIVE

precise and accurate
EG *He has never been a playboy in the strict sense of the word.*
accurate EG *an accurate record of events*
exact EG *I do not remember the exact words.*
meticulous EG *meticulous attention to detail*
particular EG *very particular dietary requirements*
precise EG *precise instructions*
true EG *a true account*

strive VERB

to make a great effort to achieve something
EG *He strives hard to keep himself fit.*
attempt EG *He attempted to smile, but found it difficult.*
do your best EG *I'll do my best to find out.*
do your utmost EG *She was certain he would do his utmost to help her.*
endeavour FORMAL EG *They are endeavouring to protect trade union rights.*
make an effort EG *He made no effort to hide his disappointment.*
seek EG *We have never sought to impose our views.*
try EG *He tried to block her advancement in the Party.*

❶ strong ADJECTIVE

having powerful muscles
EG *a strong, robust man*
→ see Word Study **strong**

WORD POWER

▶ **Antonym**
weak

2 strong ADJECTIVE
able to withstand rough treatment
EG *a strong casing, which won't crack or chip*
→ see Word Study **strong**

WORD POWER

▶ **Antonym**
fragile

3 strong ADJECTIVE
great in degree or intensity
EG *Despite strong opposition, she was victorious.*
→ see Word Study **strong**

WORD POWER

▶ **Antonym**
faint

1 structure NOUN
the way something is made or organized
EG *the structure of this molecule*
arrangement EG *an intricate arrangement of treadles, rods and cranks*
construction EG *The chairs were light in construction but very strong.*
design EG *The shoes were of good design and good quality.*
make-up EG *the chemical make-up of the oceans and atmosphere*
organization EG *the organization of the economy*

WORD POWER

▷ **Synonyms**
configuration
conformation

2 structure NOUN
something that has been built
EG *The museum is an impressive structure.*
building EG *an ugly modern building*
construction EG *an impressive steel and glass construction*
edifice EG *historic edifices in the area*

1 struggle VERB
to try hard to do something
EG *They had to struggle to make ends meet.*
strain EG *straining to lift heavy weights*
strive EG *He strives hard to keep himself fit.*
toil EG *toiling to make up for lost time*
work EG *I had to work hard for everything I've got.*

2 struggle NOUN
something that is hard to achieve
EG *Life became a struggle for survival.*
effort EG *It was an effort to finish in time.*
labour EG *weary from their labours*
toil EG *another day of toil and strife*
work EG *It's been hard work, but rewarding.*

stubborn ADJECTIVE
determined not to change or give in
EG *a stubborn character who is used to getting his own way*
dogged EG *his dogged insistence on his rights*
inflexible EG *His opponents viewed him as dogmatic and inflexible.*
obstinate EG *a wicked and obstinate child*
tenacious EG *a tenacious and persistent interviewer*
wilful EG *a headstrong and wilful young lady*

WORD POWER

▷ **Synonyms**
intractable
obdurate
recalcitrant
refractory

stuck-up ADJECTIVE; INFORMAL
proud and conceited
EG *She was famous, but she wasn't a bit stuck-up.*
arrogant EG *He was so arrogant, he never even said hello to me.*

a
b
c
d
e
f
g
h
i
j
k
l
m
n
o
p
q
r
s
t
u
v
w
x
y
z

A
B
C
D
E
F
G
H
I
J
K
L
M
N
O
P
Q
R
S
T
U
V
W
X
Y
Z

conceited EG *He's a very conceited young man.*
disdainful EG *She cast a disdainful glance at me.*
haughty EG *She looks haughty, but when you get to know her, she's very friendly.*
proud EG *He's too proud to use public transport.*
snobbish EG *I'd expected her to be snobbish, but she was warm and welcoming.*

❶ study VERB
to spend time learning about something
EG *He is studying History and Economics.*
learn EG *I'm learning French.*
read up EG *She spent a year reading up on farming techniques.*
swot BRITISH, AUSTRALIAN, AND NEW ZEALAND; INFORMAL EG *swotting for their finals*

❷ study VERB
to look at something carefully
EG *He studied the map in silence.*
contemplate EG *He contemplated his hands, frowning.*
examine EG *He examined her passport and stamped it.*
pore over EG *We spent hours poring over travel brochures.*

WORD POWER
▷ **Synonyms**
peruse
scrutinize

❸ study NOUN
the activity of learning about a subject
EG *the serious study of medieval architecture*
lessons EG *He was lagging behind in his lessons.*
research EG *funds for research into AIDS*
school work EG *She buried herself in school work.*

swotting BRITISH, AUSTRALIAN, AND NEW ZEALAND; INFORMAL EG *She put her success down to last-minute swotting.*

❶ stuff NOUN
a substance or group of things
EG *"That's my stuff," he said, pointing to a bag.*
apparatus EG *all the apparatus you'll need for the job*
belongings EG *I collected my belongings and left.*
equipment EG *outdoor playing equipment*
gear EG *fishing gear*
kit EG *I forgot my gym kit.*
material EG *organic material.*
substance EG *The substance that's causing problems comes from barley.*
tackle EG *Martin kept his fishing tackle in his room.*
things EG *Sara told him to take all his things and not to return.*

WORD POWER
▷ **Synonyms**
paraphernalia

❷ stuff VERB
to push something somewhere quickly and roughly
EG *He stuffed the newspapers into a litter bin.*
cram EG *I crammed her hat into a waste-basket.*
force EG *I forced the key into the ignition.*
jam EG *Pete jammed his hands into his pockets.*
push EG *Someone had pushed a tissue into the keyhole.*
ram EG *He rammed his clothes into a drawer.*
shove EG *We shoved a newsletter beneath their door.*
squeeze EG *I squeezed everything into my rucksack.*

thrust EG *She thrust a stack of photos into my hands.*

❸ **stuff** VERB
to fill something with a substance or objects
EG *He stood there, stuffing his mouth with popcorn.*
cram EG *I crammed my bag full of clothes and set off.*
fill EG *I filled the box with polystyrene chips.*
load EG *They loaded all their equipment into backpacks.*
pack EG *a lorry packed with explosives*

❶ **stuffy** ADJECTIVE
formal and old-fashioned
EG *his lack of stuffy formality*
dull EG *They are nice people but rather dull.*
formal EG *an austere and formal family*
old-fashioned EG *She was condemned as an old-fashioned prude.*
staid EG *He is boring, old-fashioned and staid.*
strait-laced EG *She is very strait-laced and narrow-minded.*

WORD POWER
▷ **Synonyms**
fusty
old-fogeyish
priggish
stodgy

❷ **stuffy** ADJECTIVE
not containing enough fresh air
EG *It was hot and stuffy in the classroom.*
close EG *The atmosphere was close.*
heavy EG *The air was heavy, moist and sultry.*
muggy EG *It was muggy and overcast.*
oppressive EG *The little room was windowless and oppressive.*
stale EG *A layer of smoke hung in the stale air.*
stifling EG *the stifling heat of the room*

WORD POWER
▷ **Synonyms**
frowsty
sultry
unventilated

stupid ADJECTIVE
lacking intelligence or good judgment
EG *How could I have been so stupid?*
absurd EG *absurd ideas*
daft INFORMAL EG *That's a daft question.*
dim EG *He is rather dim.*
foolish EG *It is foolish to risk injury.*
idiotic EG *What an idiotic thing to say!*
inane EG *She's always asking inane questions.*
obtuse EG *It should be obvious even to the most obtuse person.*
thick EG *I must have seemed incredibly thick.*

WORD POWER
▷ **Synonyms**
asinine
crass
cretinous
fatuous
imbecilic
moronic

▶ **Antonym**
clever

stupidity NOUN
lack of intelligence or good judgment
EG *I was astonished by his stupidity.*
absurdity EG *the absurdity of the suggestion*
folly EG *the danger and folly of taking drugs*
foolishness EG *He expressed remorse over his own foolishness.*

a b c d e f g h i j k l m n o p q r **s** t u v w x y z

inanity EG *The inanity of the conversation.*

silliness EG *He sounded quite exasperated by my silliness.*

WORD POWER

▷ **Synonyms**
asininity
fatuity
imbecility
obtuseness

sturdy ADJECTIVE
strong and unlikely to be damaged
EG *The camera was mounted on a sturdy tripod.*

durable EG *Fine china is surprisingly durable.*

hardy EG *He looked like a farmer, round-faced and hardy.*

robust EG *very robust, simply-designed machinery*

solid EG *The car feels very solid.*

substantial EG *Jack had put on weight - he seemed more substantial.*

stout EG *a stout oak door*

strong EG *a strong casing which won't crack or chip*

well-built EG *Mitchell is well-built and of medium height.*

WORD POWER

▶ **Antonym**
fragile

❶ **style** NOUN
the way in which something is done
EG *a dictatorial management style*

approach EG *his blunt approach*

manner EG *a satire in the manner of Dickens*

method EG *a new method of education*

mode EG *a cheap and convenient mode of transport*

technique EG *his driving technique*

way EG *He had a strange way of talking.*

❷ **style** NOUN
smartness and elegance
EG *She has not lost her grace and style.*

chic EG *French designer chic*

elegance EG *Princess Grace's understated elegance*

flair EG *dressed with typical Italian flair*

sophistication EG *to add a touch of sophistication to any wardrobe*

taste EG *impeccable taste*

WORD POWER

▷ **Synonyms**
élan
panache
savoir-faire

subdue VERB
to bring people under control by force
EG *The government have not been able to subdue the rebels.*

crush EG *ruthless measures to crush the revolt*

defeat EG *an important role in defeating the rebellion*

overcome EG *working to overcome the enemy forces*

overpower EG *The police eventually overpowered him.*

quell EG *tough new measures to quell the disturbances*

vanquish EG *his vanquished foe*

❶ **subject** NOUN
the thing or person being discussed
EG *They exchanged views on a wide range of subjects.*

issue EG *an issue that had worried him for some time*

matter EG *I don't want to discuss the matter.*

object EG *the object of much heated discussion*

point EG *There is another point to consider.*

question EG *the difficult question of unemployment*

theme EG *The book's central theme is power.*

topic EG *The weather is a constant topic of conversation.*

❷ subject VERB

to make someone experience something

EG *He was subjected to constant interruptions.*

expose EG *people exposed to high levels of radiation*

put through EG *My husband put me through hell.*

submit EG *The old woman was submitted to a terrifying ordeal.*

❶ submit VERB

to accept or agree to something unwillingly

EG *I submitted to their requests.*

agree EG *Management has agreed to the union's conditions.*

bow EG *Some shops are bowing to consumer pressure and stocking the product.*

capitulate EG *He capitulated to their ultimatum.*

comply EG *The commander said his army would comply with the ceasefire.*

give in EG *Officials say they won't give in to the workers' demands.*

surrender EG *We'll never surrender to these terrorists.*

yield EG *She yielded to her mother's nagging and took the child to a specialist.*

WORD POWER

▶ Antonym
resist

❷ submit VERB

to formally present a document or proposal

EG *They submitted their reports to the Chancellor.*

hand in EG *I'm supposed to hand in my dissertation on Friday.*

present EG *The group intends to present this petition to the parliament.*

propose EG *He has proposed a bill to abolish the House of Commons.*

put forward EG *He has put forward new peace proposals.*

send in EG *Applicants are asked to send in a CV and covering letter.*

table EG *They've tabled a motion criticizing the Government for its actions.*

tender EG *She tendered her resignation.*

WORD POWER

▶ Antonym
withdraw

substance NOUN

a solid, powder, liquid or gas

EG *Poisonous substances should be labelled as such.*

element EG *a chart of the chemical elements*

fabric EG *Condensation will rot the fabric of the building.*

material EG *an armchair of some resilient plastic material*

stuff EG *the stuff from which the universe is made*

❶ substitute VERB

to use one thing in place of another

EG *You can substitute honey for the sugar.*

exchange EG *exchanging one set of problems for another*

interchange EG *Meat can be interchanged with pulses as a source of protein.*

replace EG *We dug up the concrete and replaced it with grass.*

swap EG *Some hostages were swapped for convicted prisoners.*

switch EG *They switched the tags on the cables.*

❷ substitute NOUN

something used in place of another thing

EG *an artificial substitute for silk*

a b c d e f g h i j k l m n o p q r **s** t u v w x y z

deputy EG *I can't make it so I'll send my deputy.*

proxy EG *They must nominate a proxy to vote on their behalf.*

replacement EG *He has nominated Adams as his replacement.*

representative EG *Employees from each department elect a representative.*

surrogate EG *They had expected me to be a surrogate for my sister.*

WORD POWER

▷ **Synonyms**
locum
locum tenens
makeshift
stopgap

subtract VERB
to take one number away from another
EG *If you subtract 3 from 5 you get 2.*

deduct EG *Marks will be deducted for spelling mistakes.*

take away EG *Take away the number you first thought of.*

take from EG *Take the 5% discount from the total amount due.*

WORD POWER

▶ **Antonym**
add

❶ **succeed** VERB
to achieve the result you intend
EG *To succeed, you must learn to overcome obstacles.*

be successful EG *We must help our clubs to be successful in Europe.*

do well EG *Their team did well.*

flourish EG *The business flourished.*

make it INFORMAL EG *It is hard for an English actress to make it in Hollywood.*

prosper EG *His team have always prospered in cup competitions.*

thrive EG *The company has thrived by selling cheap, simple products.*

triumph EG *a symbol of good triumphing over evil*

work EG *The plan worked.*

WORD POWER

▶ **Antonym**
fail

❷ **succeed** VERB
to be the next person to have someone's job
EG *David is almost certain to succeed him as chairman.*

replace EG *the man who replaced him as England skipper*

take over from EG *Last year he took over from Bauman as chief executive.*

❶ **success** NOUN
the achievement of a goal, fame, or wealth
EG *Do you believe that work is the key to success?*

celebrity EG *I never expected this kind of celebrity when I was writing my novel.*

eminence EG *a pilot who achieved eminence in the aeronautical world*

fame EG *her rise to fame as a dramatist*

prosperity EG *the country's economic prosperity*

triumph EG *last year's Republican triumph in the elections*

victory EG *Union leaders are heading for victory in their battle over workplace rights.*

wealth EG *His hard work brought him wealth and respect.*

WORD POWER

▷ **Synonyms**
ascendancy (FORMAL)
coup

▶ **Antonym**
failure

❷ **success** NOUN
a person or thing achieving

popularity or greatness
EG *Everyone who knows her says she will be a huge success.*
celebrity EG *At the age of 12, Dan is already a celebrity.*
hit EG *The song became a massive hit.*
sensation EG *the film that turned her into an overnight sensation*
star EG *I always knew she would be a star.*
triumph EG *a triumph of modern surgery*
winner EG *Selling was my game and I intended to be a winner.*

WORD POWER
▶ **Antonym**
failure

successful ADJECTIVE
having achieved what you intended to do
EG *Mr Singh was a highly successful salesman.*
flourishing EG *a flourishing business*
lucrative EG *a lucrative career*
profitable EG *a profitable exchange of ideas*
rewarding EG *a rewarding investment*
thriving EG *a thriving housebuilding industry*
top EG *a top model*

sudden ADJECTIVE
happening quickly and unexpectedly
EG *a sudden cry*
abrupt EG *Her idyllic world came to an abrupt end when her parents died.*
hasty EG *his hasty departure*
quick EG *I had to make a quick decision.*
swift EG *a swift blow to the stomach*
unexpected EG *His death was totally unexpected.*

WORD POWER
▶ **Antonym**
gradual

suffer VERB
to be affected by pain or something unpleasant
EG *I knew he was suffering some discomfort.*
bear EG *He bore his trials with dignity and grace.*
endure EG *The writer endured a harsh life.*
experience EG *Widows seem to experience more distress than do widowers.*
go through EG *I wouldn't like to go through that again.*
sustain EG *He had sustained massive facial injuries.*
undergo EG *He had to undergo a body search.*

sufficient ADJECTIVE
being enough for a purpose
EG *He had sufficient time to prepare his speech.*
adequate EG *an adequate income*
ample EG *an ample supply of petrol*
enough EG *enough cash to live on*

WORD POWER
▶ **Antonym**
insufficient

suffix NOUN

Suffixes
-less
-like
-logy *or* -ology
-ness
-ward *or* -wards

❶ **suggest** VERB
to mention something as a possibility or recommendation
EG *Clive suggested going out for tea.*
advise EG *I advise you to keep quiet.*
advocate EG *Mr Jones advocates*

a b c d e f g h i j k l m n o p q r **s** t u v w x y z

A
B
C
D
E
F
G
H
I
J
K
L
M
N
O
P
Q
R
S
T
U
V
W
X
Y
Z

longer school days.
propose EG *And where do you propose building such a huge thing?*
recommend EG *I have no qualms about recommending this approach.*

2 suggest VERB
to hint that something is the case
EG *Reports suggested the factory would close.*
hint EG *The President hinted that he might make some changes.*
imply EG *The tone of the report implied that his death was inevitable.*
indicate EG *She has indicated that she may resign.*
insinuate EG *an article which insinuated that he was lying*
intimate EG *He did intimate that he is seeking legal action.*

1 suggestion NOUN
an idea mentioned as a possibility
EG *practical suggestions*
plan EG *The government is being asked to consider the plan.*
proposal EG *the proposal to do away with nuclear weapons*
proposition EG *a business proposition*
recommendation EG *a range of recommendations for change*

2 suggestion NOUN
a slight indication of something
EG *a suggestion of dishonesty*
hint EG *He showed only the slightest hint of emotion.*
indication EG *He gave no indication of remorse.*
insinuation EG *The insinuation is that I have something to hide.*
intimation EG *He did not give any intimation that he was going to resign.*
trace EG *No traces of violence were found on the body.*

1 suit VERB
to be acceptable
EG *They will only move if it suits them.*

be acceptable to EG *The name chosen had to be acceptable to everyone.*
do EG *A holiday at home will do me just fine.*
please EG *I'll leave when it pleases me and not before.*
satisfy EG *Nothing you can do will satisfy him.*

2 suit VERB
to match something else
EG *The battery can be shaped to suit any device.*
agree EG *His statement agrees with those of the other witnesses.*
conform to EG *designed to conform to the new safety requirements*
correspond EG *a number which corresponds to a horse running in the race*
go with EG *Do these shoes go with this dress?*
match EG *tan slacks with a safari jacket to match*

WORD POWER

▷ **Synonyms**
become
befit
harmonize

---

suitable ADJECTIVE
right or acceptable for a particular purpose
EG *Conditions were not suitable for life to flourish.*
acceptable EG *a mutually acceptable new contract*
appropriate EG *an appropriate outfit for the occasion*
apt EG *an apt name*
fit EG *the suggestion that she is not a fit mother*
fitting EG *a fitting background for her beauty*
proper EG *It was not thought proper for a woman to be on stage.*
right EG *He always said just the right*

thing.
satisfactory EG *a satisfactory arrangement*

WORD POWER

▷ **Synonyms**
apposite
befitting
pertinent
seemly

▶ **Antonym**
unsuitable

sulky ADJECTIVE
showing annoyance by being silent and moody
EG *a sulky adolescent*
huffy EG *What are you being so huffy about?*
moody EG *Her husband had become withdrawn and moody.*
petulant EG *He's just being childish and petulant.*
resentful EG *a resentful workforce*
sullen EG *He lapsed into a sullen silence.*

summary NOUN
a short account of something's main points
EG *a summary of the report*
outline EG *an outline of the proposal*
review EG *a film review*
rundown EG *Here's a rundown of the options.*
summing-up EG *The judge concluded his summing-up.*
synopsis EG *a brief synopsis of the book*

WORD POWER

▷ **Synonyms**
abridgment
digest
précis
recapitulation
résumé

sum up VERB
to describe briefly
EG *He summed up his weekend in one word: "Disastrous".*
recapitulate EG *Let's just recapitulate the essential points.*
summarize EG *The article can be summarized in three sentences.*

superb ADJECTIVE
very good indeed
EG *With superb skill, he managed to make a perfect landing.*
breathtaking EG *The house has breathtaking views.*
excellent EG *You've done an excellent job.*
exquisite EG *His photography is exquisite.*
magnificent EG *a magnificent country house*
marvellous EG *She is a marvellous cook.*
outstanding EG *an outstanding performance*
splendid EG *a splendid Victorian mansion*
superior EG *a superior blend of the finest coffee beans*
unrivalled EG *He has an unrivalled knowledge of British politics.*
wonderful EG *The sun setting over the mountains was a wonderful sight.*

WORD POWER

▷ **Synonyms**
superlative

❶ **superior** ADJECTIVE
better than other similar things
EG *superior coffee beans*
better EG *I'd like to move to a better area.*
choice EG *the choicest cuts of meat*
de luxe EG *a de luxe model*
exceptional EG *children with exceptional ability*
first-rate EG *a first-rate thriller*
surpassing EG *her surpassing*

a b c d e f g h i j k l m n o p q r s t u v w x y z

A B C D E F G H I J K L M N O P Q R S T U V W X Y Z

achievements
unrivalled EG *colour printing of unrivalled quality*

WORD POWER

▶ **Antonym**
inferior

❷ superior ADJECTIVE
showing pride and self-importance
EG *He stood there looking superior.*
condescending EG *I'm fed up with your condescending attitude.*
disdainful EG *She passed along with a disdainful look.*
haughty EG *He spoke in a haughty tone.*
lofty EG *lofty disdain*
patronizing EG *his patronizing attitude to the homeless*
snobbish EG *a snobbish dislike for their intellectual inferiors*
stuck-up INFORMAL EG *She was a famous actress, but she wasn't a bit stuck-up.*
supercilious EG *His manner is supercilious and arrogant.*

❸ superior NOUN
a person in a higher position than you
EG *his immediate superior*
boss INFORMAL EG *Her boss was very supportive.*
manager EG *His plans found favour with his manager.*
senior EG *He was described by his seniors as a model officer.*
supervisor EG *Each student has a supervisor.*

WORD POWER

▶ **Antonym**
inferior

supervise VERB
to oversee a person or activity
EG *He supervised more than 400 volunteers.*
be in charge of EG *He is in charge of*

the whole project.
direct EG *Christopher will direct day-to-day operations.*
have charge of EG *He has charge of a three-acre estate.*
keep an eye on EG *I told you to keep an eye on the children.*
manage EG *I manage a small team of workers.*
oversee EG *an architect to oversee the work*
run EG *Each teacher will run a different workshop.*

WORD POWER

▷ **Synonyms**
preside over
superintend

❶ supplement VERB
to add to something to improve it
EG *I suggest supplementing your diet with vitamin A.*
add to EG *A good bathroom adds to the value of any house.*
augment EG *a way to augment the family income*
complement EG *an in-work benefit that complements earnings*
reinforce EG *measures which will reinforce their current strengths*
top up EG *compulsory contributions to top up pension schemes*

❷ supplement NOUN
something added to something else
EG *a supplement to their basic pension*
addition EG *an addition to the existing system*
appendix EG *The report includes a six-page appendix.*
complement EG *The photographs are a perfect complement to the text.*
extra EG *an optional extra*

supplies PLURAL NOUN
food or equipment for a particular purpose
EG *I had only two pints of water in my emergency supplies.*

equipment EG *vital medical equipment*
provisions EG *provisions for two weeks*
rations EG *Aid officials said food rations had been distributed.*
stores EG *an important part of a ship's stores*

① supply VERB
to provide someone with something
EG *an agreement not to supply chemical weapons*
equip EG *plans for equipping the island with water*
furnish EG *They'll be able to furnish you with the details.*
give EG *We'll give you all the information you need.*
provide EG *They'll provide all the equipment.*

WORD POWER

▷ **Synonyms**
endow
purvey

② supply NOUN
an amount of something available for use
EG *a plentiful supply of vegetables*
cache EG *a cache of weapons and explosives*
fund EG *an extraordinary fund of energy*
hoard EG *a hoard of food and petrol*
reserve EG *The Gulf has 65% of the world's oil reserves.*
stock EG *stocks of paper and ink*
stockpile EG *stockpiles of chemical weapons*
store EG *I have a store of food and water here.*

① support VERB
to agree with someone's ideas or aims
EG *We supported his political campaign.*
back EG *a new witness to back his*

claim
champion EG *He passionately championed the cause.*
defend EG *He defended all of Clarence's decisions, right or wrong.*
promote EG *He continued to promote the idea of Scottish autonomy.*
second EG *The Prime Minister seconded the call for discipline.*
side with EG *accused of siding with terrorists*
uphold EG *We uphold the capitalist free economy.*

WORD POWER

▶ **Antonym**
oppose

② support VERB
to help someone in difficulties
EG *Try to support each other when one of you is feeling down.*
encourage EG *When things aren't going well, he encourages me.*
help EG *He'd do anything to help a friend.*

③ support VERB
to hold something up from underneath
EG *Thick wooden posts support the ceiling.*
bolster EG *steel beams used to bolster the roof*
brace EG *The roll-over bar braces the car's structure.*
hold up EG *Her legs wouldn't hold her up.*
prop up EG *Use sticks to prop the plants up.*
reinforce EG *They had to reinforce the walls with exterior beams.*

WORD POWER

▷ **Synonyms**
buttress
shore up

❹ support NOUN
an object that holds something up
EG *the metal supports which hold up the canvas*
brace EG *He will have to wear a neck brace for several days.*
foundation EG *the foundation on which the bridge was built*
pillar EG *the pillars supporting the roof*
post EG *The device is fixed to a post.*
prop EG *a structural part such as a beam or prop*

WORD POWER

▷ **Synonyms**
abutment
stanchion

supporter NOUN
a person who agrees with or helps someone
EG *He is a strong supporter of the plan.*
adherent EG *Communism was gaining adherents in Latin America.*
advocate EG *a strong advocate of free market policies*
ally EG *a close political ally*
champion EG *a champion of women's causes*
fan EG *fans of this football club*
follower EG *followers of the Dalai Lama*
sponsor EG *the first sponsor of Buddhism in Japan*

WORD POWER

▷ **Synonyms**
patron
protagonist

suppose VERB
to think that something is probably the case
EG *Where do you suppose he has gone?*
assume EG *I assume you have permission to be here?*
believe EG *We believe them to be*

hidden somewhere in the area.
expect EG *I don't expect you've had much experience in the job yet.*
guess EG *I guess you're right.*
imagine EG *We tend to imagine that the Victorians were prim and proper.*
presume EG *I presume you're here on business.*
think EG *Do you think she was embarrassed?*

WORD POWER

▷ **Synonyms**
conjecture
surmise (FORMAL)

❶ supposed ADJECTIVE
planned, expected, or required to do something
EG *You're not supposed to leave a child on its own.*
expected EG *You were expected to arrive much earlier than this.*
meant EG *Parties are meant to be fun.*
obliged EG *He is legally obliged to declare his interests.*
required EG *Will I be required to come to every meeting?*

❷ supposed ADJECTIVE
generally believed or thought to be the case
EG *What is his son supposed to have said?*
alleged EG *The accused is alleged to have killed a man.*
assumed EG *As usual, the mistakes were assumed to be my fault.*
believed EG *He is believed to have died in 1117.*
meant EG *They are meant to be one of the top teams in the world.*
presumed EG *This area is presumed to be safe.*
reputed EG *The monster is reputed to live in the deep waters of a Scottish loch.*
rumoured EG *They are rumoured to be on the verge of splitting up.*

❶ suppress VERB
to prevent people from doing something
EG *international attempts to suppress drug trafficking*
crush EG *a plan to crush the uprising*
quash EG *It may help to quash these rumours.*
quell EG *The army moved in to quell the uprising.*
stamp out EG *steps to stamp out bullying in schools*
stop EG *measures to stop the trade in ivory*

❷ suppress VERB
to stop yourself from expressing a feeling or reaction
EG *She barely suppressed a gasp.*
conceal EG *Robert could not conceal his relief.*
contain EG *He could hardly contain his rage.*
curb EG *He curbed his temper.*
repress EG *people who repress their emotions*
restrain EG *unable to restrain her anger*
smother EG *I smothered a chuckle.*
stifle EG *Miller stifled a yawn and looked at his watch.*

supreme ADJECTIVE
of the highest degree or rank
EG *They conspired to seize supreme power.*
chief EG *his chief rival*
foremost EG *the world's foremost scientists*
greatest EG *the city's greatest soccer idol*
highest EG *the highest academic achievement*
leading EG *the world's leading basketball players*
paramount EG *a factor of paramount importance*
pre-eminent EG *a pre-eminent political figure*
principal EG *the principal reason*

top EG *the president's top military advisers*
ultimate EG *the ultimate international accolade, the Nobel Prize*

❶ sure ADJECTIVE
having no doubts
EG *She was no longer sure how she felt about him.*
certain EG *certain of getting a place on the team*
clear EG *He is not clear on how he will go about it.*
convinced EG *He is convinced it's your fault.*
definite EG *a definite answer*
positive EG *I'm positive it will happen.*
satisfied EG *We must be satisfied that the treatment is safe.*

WORD POWER
▶ Antonym
unsure

❷ sure ADJECTIVE
reliable or definite
EG *a sure sign that something is wrong*
definite EG *a definite advantage*
dependable EG *dependable information*
foolproof EG *a foolproof system*
infallible EG *an infallible eye for detail*
reliable EG *a reliable source*
trustworthy EG *trustworthy reports*
undeniable EG *a sad but undeniable fact*

❶ surprise NOUN
something unexpected
EG *The resignation came as a complete surprise.*
bombshell EG *His departure was a bombshell for the team.*
jolt EG *Henderson was jolted by the news.*
revelation EG *Degas's work had been a revelation to her.*
shock EG *I got a shock when I saw her.*
start EG *You gave me quite a start.*

2 surprise NOUN
the feeling caused by something
unexpected
EG *an exclamation of surprise*
amazement EG *He stared in baffled
amazement.*
astonishment EG *"What?" Meg
asked in astonishment.*
incredulity EG *The announcement
has been met with incredulity.*
wonder EG *Cross shook his head in
wonder.*

3 surprise VERB
to give someone a feeling of surprise
EG *I was surprised by the vehemence of
his criticism.*
amaze EG *Most of the cast were
amazed by the play's success.*
astonish EG *I was astonished to
discover his true age.*
astound EG *He was astounded at the
result.*
stagger EG *I was staggered by his
reaction.*
stun EG *Audiences were stunned by
the film's tragic end.*
take aback EG *Derek was taken
aback when a man answered the
phone.*

WORD POWER
▷ **Synonyms**
flabbergast
nonplus

1 surrender VERB
to agree that the other side has won
EG *We'll never surrender to the
terrorists.*
capitulate EG *They had no choice but
to capitulate.*
give in EG *She gave in to him on
everything.*
submit EG *I refuse to submit to their
demands.*
succumb EG *The Minister said his
country would never succumb to
pressure.*

yield EG *The government had to yield
to local opinion.*

2 surrender VERB
to give something up to someone
else
EG *We have surrendered our political
authority for economic gain.*
cede EG *After the war, Spain ceded the
island to America.*
give up EG *She is loath to give up her
hard-earned liberty.*
relinquish EG *He does not intend to
relinquish power.*
renounce EG *He renounced his claim
to the throne.*
yield EG *He was obliged to yield
territory to France.*

3 surrender NOUN
a situation in which one side gives in
to the other
EG *unconditional surrender*
capitulation EG *the German
capitulation at the end of the First
World War*
submission EG *The army intends to
starve the city into submission.*

surround VERB
to be all around a person or thing
EG *He was surrounded by bodyguards.*
encircle EG *A forty-foot-high
concrete wall encircles the jail.*
enclose EG *The land was enclosed by
a fence.*
encompass EG *the largest lake in
Canada wholly encompassed by a
town*
envelop EG *The rich smell of the forest
enveloped us.*
hem in EG *a valley hemmed in by
mountains*

surroundings PLURAL NOUN
the area and environment around a
person or place
EG *He felt a longing for familiar
surroundings.*
background EG *a fitting background
for her beauty*

environment EG *a safe environment for marine mammals*
location EG *filmed in an exotic location*
neighbourhood EG *living in an affluent neighbourhood*
setting EG *Rome is the perfect setting for romance.*

WORD POWER

▷ **Synonyms**
environs
milieu

survive VERB
to live or exist in spite of difficulties
EG *companies which survived after the recession*
endure EG *Somehow their friendship endures.*
last EG *Nothing lasts forever.*
live EG *having lived through the 1930s depression*
outlive EG *They have outlived the horror of the war.*
pull through EG *He should pull through okay.*

❶ **suspect** VERB
to think something is likely
EG *I suspect they are secretly planning to raise taxes.*
believe EG *Police believe the attacks were carried out by nationalists.*
feel EG *I somehow feel he was involved.*
guess EG *As you probably guessed, I don't like him much.*
suppose EG *The problem is more complex than he supposes.*

❷ **suspect** VERB
to have doubts about something
EG *He suspected her motives.*
distrust EG *I don't have any particular reason to distrust them.*
doubt EG *Do you doubt my word?*
mistrust EG *He mistrusts all journalists.*

❸ **suspect** ADJECTIVE
not to be trusted
EG *a rather suspect holy man*
dodgy BRITISH, AUSTRALIAN, AND NEW ZEALAND; INFORMAL EG *a dodgy car dealer*
doubtful EG *These details are of doubtful origin.*
dubious EG *dubious practices*
fishy INFORMAL EG *There's something very fishy about it.*
questionable EG *the questionable motives of politicians*

❶ **suspicion** NOUN
a feeling of mistrust
EG *I was always regarded with suspicion because of my background.*
distrust EG *an instinctive distrust of authority*
doubt EG *I have my doubts about his ability to govern.*
misgiving EG *His first words filled us with misgiving.*
mistrust EG *a deep mistrust of banks*
scepticism EG *The report has been greeted with scepticism.*

WORD POWER

▷ **Synonyms**
dubiety
qualm

❷ **suspicion** NOUN
a feeling that something is true
EG *I have a strong suspicion they are lying.*
hunch EG *Lowe had a hunch he was on to something.*
idea EG *I had an idea that he joined the army later.*
impression EG *I get the impression he's hiding something.*

❶ **suspicious** ADJECTIVE
feeling distrustful of someone or something
EG *He was rightly suspicious of their motives.*
apprehensive EG *She was*

a b c d e f g h i j k l m n o p q r s t u v w x y z

apprehensive of strangers.
distrustful EG *Voters are deeply distrustful of all politicians.*
doubtful EG *At first I was doubtful about their authenticity.*
sceptical EG *Other archaeologists are sceptical about his findings.*
wary EG *Many people are wary of lawyers.*

❷ suspicious ADJECTIVE
causing feelings of distrust
EG *suspicious circumstances*
dodgy BRITISH, AUSTRALIAN, AND NEW ZEALAND; INFORMAL EG *He was a bit of a dodgy character.*
doubtful EG *selling something of doubtful quality*
dubious EG *This claim seems to us rather dubious.*
fishy INFORMAL EG *There's something fishy going on here.*
funny EG *There's something funny about him.*
questionable EG *the questionable motives of politicians*
shady INFORMAL EG *shady deals*
suspect EG *The whole affair has been highly suspect.*

swap VERB
to replace one thing for another
EG *Some hostages were swapped for convicted prisoners.*
barter EG *bartering wheat for cotton and timber*
exchange EG *exchanging one set of problems for another*
interchange EG *Meat can be interchanged with pulses as a source of protein.*
switch EG *They switched the tags on the cables.*
trade EG *They traded land for goods and money.*

❶ sweet ADJECTIVE
containing a lot of sugar
EG *a mug of sweet tea*
cloying EG *a cloying apricot chutney*

sugary EG *a sugary meringue pie*
sweetened EG *sweetened shortcrust pastry*

WORD POWER

▶ **Antonym**
sour

❷ sweet ADJECTIVE
having a pleasant smell
EG *the sweet smell of roses*
aromatic EG *a plant with aromatic leaves*
fragrant EG *fragrant clover*
perfumed EG *perfumed soaps*
sweet-smelling EG *cottage gardens filled with sweet-smelling flowers and herbs*

❸ sweet ADJECTIVE
pleasant-sounding and tuneful
EG *the sweet sounds of children's singing*
harmonious EG *harmonious sounds*
mellow EG *mellow background music*
melodious EG *The melodious tones of the organ echoed around the great cathedral.*
musical EG *He had a soft, musical voice.*
tuneful EG *The band were noted for their tuneful backing vocals.*

WORD POWER

▷ **Synonyms**
dulcet
euphonious

❹ sweet NOUN
a sweet-tasting thing such as a toffee
EG *His sack was full of packets of sweets.*
candy AMERICAN EG *We were sick after eating some syrupy candies she had made.*
confectionery EG *The company specializes in selling confectionery from all over the world.*
lolly AUSTRALIAN AND NEW ZEALAND
eg *avoid feeding him too many lollies*

sweetie EG *She presented him with a jar of his favourite sweeties as a thank-you.*

swerve VERB
to change direction suddenly to avoid hitting something
EG *He swerved to avoid a truck.*
swing EG *The car swung off the road.*
turn EG *He turned sharply to the left.*
veer EG *The vehicle veered out of control.*

swift ADJECTIVE
happening or moving very quickly
EG *make a swift decision*
brisk EG *walking at a brisk pace*
express EG *a special express service*
fast EG *The question is how fast the process will be.*
hurried EG *a hurried breakfast*
prompt EG *Prompt action is needed.*
quick EG *The country has been developing at a very quick pace.*
rapid EG *Will the Tunnel provide more rapid transport than ferries?*
speedy EG *We wish Bill a speedy recovery.*

WORD POWER

▶ **Antonym**
slow

---

symbol NOUN
a design or idea used to represent something
EG *the chemical symbol for mercury*
emblem EG *His badge bore a small yellow hammer-and-sickle emblem.*
figure EG *the figure of a five-pointed star*
logo EG *the company's logo*
mark EG *a mark of identification*
representation EG *This rune is a representation of a spearhead.*

sign EG *a multiplication sign*
token EG *He gave her a ring as a token of his love.*

sympathy NOUN
kindness and understanding towards someone in trouble
EG *My heartfelt sympathy goes out to all the relatives.*
compassion EG *I was impressed by the compassion he showed for a helpless old woman.*
empathy EG *They displayed an admirable understanding of the crime and empathy with the victim.*
pity EG *He showed no pity for his victims.*
understanding EG *I'd like to thank you for your patience and understanding.*

system NOUN
an organized way of doing or arranging something
EG *the advantages of the new system over the old one*
arrangement EG *an intricate arrangement of treadles, rods and cranks*
method EG *the methods employed in the study*
procedure EG *This is now the standard procedure.*
routine EG *his daily routine*
structure EG *the structure of local government*
technique EG *a new technique for processing sound*

WORD POWER

▷ **Synonyms**
methodology
modus operandi

---

a
b
c
d
e
f
g
h
i
j
k
l
m
n
o
p
q
r
s
t
u
v
w
x
y
z

Tt

tact NOUN
the ability not to offend people
EG *He has handled the affair with great tact.*
delicacy EG *Both countries are behaving with rare delicacy.*
diplomacy EG *It took all Minnelli's diplomacy to get him to return.*
discretion EG *I appreciate your discretion.*
sensitivity EG *The police treated the victims with great sensitivity.*

tactful ADJECTIVE
showing tact
EG *Sorry, that wasn't a very tactful question.*
diplomatic EG *She is very direct. I tend to be more diplomatic.*
discreet EG *They were gossip and not always discreet.*
sensitive EG *his sensitive handling of the situation*

WORD POWER

▶ **Antonym**
tactless

① take VERB
to require something
EG *He takes three hours to get ready.*
demand EG *The task of rebuilding would demand much patience.*
require EG *The race requires a lot of stamina.*

② take VERB
to carry something
EG *I'll take these papers home and read them.*
bear FORMAL EG *They bore the hardwood box into the kitchen.*
bring EG *He poured a brandy for Dena and brought it to her.*
carry EG *She carried the shopping from the car.*
convey FORMAL EG *The minibus conveyed us to the city centre.*
ferry EG *A plane arrives to ferry guests to the island.*
fetch EG *Sylvia fetched a towel from the bathroom.*
transport EG *They use tankers to transport the oil to Los Angeles.*

③ take VERB
to lead someone somewhere
EG *She took me to a Mexican restaurant.*
bring EG *Come to my party and bring a girl with you.*
conduct FORMAL EG *He asked if he might conduct us to the ball.*
escort EG *I escorted him to the door.*
guide EG *a young Egyptologist who guided us through the tombs*
lead EG *She confessed to the killing and led police to his remains.*
usher EG *I ushered him into the office.*

① take care of VERB
to look after someone or something
EG *There was no-one to take care of the children.*
care for EG *They hired a nurse to care for her.*
look after EG *I love looking after the children.*
mind EG *Jim will mind the shop while I'm away.*
nurse EG *All the years he was sick, my mother had nursed him.*
protect EG *He vowed to protect her all the days of her life.*
tend EG *He tends the flower beds that he has planted.*
watch EG *Are parents expected to watch their children 24 hours a day?*

WORD POWER

▶ **Antonym**
neglect

② take care of VERB
to deal with a problem, task, or situation
EG *"Do you need clean sheets?" "No, Mrs May took care of that."*

attend to EG *We have business to attend to first.*
cope with EG *A new system has been designed to cope with the increased demand.*
deal with EG *the way that building societies deal with complaints*
handle EG *She handled the president's travel arrangements during the campaign.*
manage EG *He expects me to manage all the household expenses on very little.*
see to EG *While Frank saw to the luggage, Sara took the children home.*

❶ take in VERB
to deceive someone
EG *He was a real charmer who totally took me in.*
con INFORMAL EG *The British public has been conned by the government.*
deceive EG *He has deceived us all.*
dupe EG *Some offenders dupe the psychologists who assess them.*
fool EG *Art dealers fool a lot of people.*
mislead EG *It appears we were misled by a professional con artist.*
trick EG *He'll be upset when he finds out how you tricked him.*

❷ take in VERB
to understand something
EG *She seemed to take in all he said.*
absorb EG *It will take time for us to absorb the news.*
appreciate EG *She never really appreciated the bitterness of the conflict.*
assimilate EG *My mind could only assimilate one of these ideas at a time.*
comprehend EG *He failed to comprehend the significance of this remark.*
digest EG *They need time to digest the information they have learned.*
get EG *You just don't get what I'm saying, do you?*
grasp EG *The Government has not yet grasped the seriousness of the crisis.*

understand EG *They are too young to understand what is going on.*

talent NOUN
a natural ability
EG *Both her children have a talent for music.*
ability EG *Her drama teacher spotted her ability.*
aptitude EG *Alan has no aptitude for music.*
capacity EG *people's creative capacities*
flair EG *a dentist with a flair for invention*
genius EG *his genius for chess*
gift EG *a gift for teaching*
knack EG *He's got the knack of getting people to listen.*

❶ talk VERB
to say things
EG *They were talking about American food.*
→ see Word Study **say**

❷ talk NOUN
a conversation
EG *We had a long talk about her father.*
chat EG *I had a chat with him.*
chatter EG *idle chatter*
conversation EG *We had a long conversation.*

❸ talk NOUN
an informal speech
EG *a talk about AIDS*
address EG *an address to the American people*
discourse EG *a lengthy discourse on strategy*
lecture EG *a series of lectures*
sermon EG *a church sermon*
speech EG *He delivered his speech in French.*

WORD POWER

▷ **Synonyms**
disquisition
oration

a
b
c
d
e
f
g
h
i
j
k
l
m
n
o
p
q
r
s
t
u
v
w
x
y
z

A
B
C
D
E
F
G
H
I
J
K
L
M
N
O
P
Q
R
S
T
U
V
W
X
Y
Z

talkative ADJECTIVE
talking a lot
EG *His eyes grew bright and he suddenly became very talkative.*
chatty EG *She's quite a chatty person.*
communicative EG *She has become a lot more communicative.*
long-winded EG *I hope I'm not being too long-winded.*

tall ADJECTIVE
higher than average
EG *tall buildings*
high EG *a high wall*
lanky EG *He was six foot four, all lanky and leggy.*
lofty EG *lofty ceilings*
soaring EG *the soaring spires of churches like St Peter's*
towering EG *towering cliffs of black granite*

WORD POWER
▶ **Antonym**
short

❶ tangle NOUN
a mass of long things knotted together
EG *a tangle of wires*
jumble EG *a jumble of twisted tubes*
knot EG *Her hair was full of knots.*
mass EG *a flailing mass of arms and legs*
mat EG *the thick mat of sandy hair on his chest*
muddle EG *The back of the tapestry was a muddle of threads.*
web EG *a thick web of fibres*

❷ tangle VERB
to twist together or catch someone or something
EG *Dolphins can get tangled in fishing nets and drown.*
catch EG *a fly caught in a spider's web*
jumble EG *The wires were all jumbled together and tied in a knot.*
knot EG *The kite strings had got knotted together.*

twist EG *Her hands began to twist the handles of the bag.*

task NOUN
a job that you have to do
EG *Walker had the task of breaking the bad news.*
assignment EG *written assignments and practical tests*
chore EG *household chores*
duty EG *I carried out my duties conscientiously.*
job EG *He was given the job of tending the fire.*
mission EG *Salisbury sent him on a diplomatic mission to North America.*
undertaking EG *Organizing the show has been a massive undertaking.*

❶ taste NOUN
the flavour of something
EG *I like the taste of wine.*
flavour EG *a crumbly texture with a strong flavour*
tang EG *the tang of lemon*

❷ taste NOUN
a small amount of food or drink
EG *He swirled the brandy around before taking another small taste.*
bite EG *Chew each mouthful fully before the next bite.*
mouthful EG *She gulped down a mouthful of coffee.*
sip EG *a sip of wine*

❸ taste NOUN
a liking for something
EG *a taste for adventure*
appetite EG *his appetite for success*
fondness EG *I've always had a fondness for jewels.*
liking EG *She had a liking for good clothes.*
penchant FORMAL EG *He had a penchant for playing jokes on people.*

WORD POWER
▷ **Synonyms**
partiality
predilection

❶ tasteless ADJECTIVE
having little flavour
EG *The fish was mushy and tasteless.*
bland EG *It tasted bland, like warmed cardboard.*
insipid EG *a rather insipid meal*

WORD POWER

▶ **Antonym**
tasty

---

❷ tasteless ADJECTIVE
vulgar and unattractive
EG *a house crammed with tasteless ornaments*
flashy EG *a flashy sports car*
garish EG *garish bright red boots*
gaudy EG *her gaudy floral hat*
tacky INFORMAL EG *tacky holiday souvenirs*
tawdry EG *a tawdry seaside town*
vulgar EG *a very vulgar house*

WORD POWER

▶ **Antonym**
tasteful

---

tasty ADJECTIVE
having a pleasant flavour
EG *The food was very tasty.*
appetizing EG *a choice of appetizing dishes*
delicious EG *a wide selection of delicious desserts*
lekker SOUTH AFRICAN; SLANG EG *a lekker meal*
luscious EG *luscious fruit*
palatable EG *some very palatable wines*

WORD POWER

▷ **Synonyms**
flavourful
flavoursome

▶ **Antonym**
tasteless

---

❶ tax NOUN
money paid to the government
EG *the tax on new cars*
duty EG *customs duties*
excise EG *These products are excused VAT and excise.*
levy FORMAL EG *an annual motorway levy on all drivers*
tariff EG *America wants to eliminate tariffs on items such as electronics.*

❷ tax VERB
to make heavy demands on someone
EG *They must be told not to tax your patience.*
drain EG *conflicts that drain your energy*
exhaust EG *She has exhausted my sympathy.*
sap EG *The illness sapped his strength.*
strain EG *The volume of flights is straining the air traffic control system.*
stretch EG *The drought there is stretching American resources to their limits.*

teach VERB
to instruct someone how to do something
EG *She taught Julie to read.*
coach EG *He coached the basketball team.*
drill EG *He drills the choir to a high standard.*
educate EG *He was educated at Haslingden Grammar School.*
instruct EG *He instructed family members in nursing techniques.*
school EG *He had been schooled to take over the family business.*
train EG *They train teachers in counselling skills.*
tutor EG *She was tutored at home by her parents.*

teacher NOUN
someone who teaches something
EG *a geography teacher*
coach EG *her drama coach*
don EG *a Cambridge don*
guru EG *a religious guru*
instructor EG *a driving instructor*

a
b
c
d
e
f
g
h
i
j
k
l
m
n
o
p
q
r
s
t
u
v
w
x
y
z

lecturer EG *a lecturer in law*
master *or* **mistress** EG *a retired maths master*
professor EG *a professor of economics*
tutor EG *He surprised his tutors by failing the exam.*

WORD POWER
▷ **Synonyms**
educator
pedagogue

❶ team NOUN
a group of people
EG *the football team*
band EG *a band of rebels*
crew EG *the ship's crew*
gang EG *a gang of workmen*
group EG *The students work in groups.*
side EG *Italy were definitely the better side.*
squad EG *the England under-21 squad*
troupe EG *troupes of travelling actors*

❷ team VERB
to work together
EG *A friend suggested that we team up for a working holiday.*
collaborate EG *The two men met and agreed to collaborate.*
cooperate EG *They would cooperate in raising their child.*
join forces EG *The groups joined forces to fight against the ban.*
link up EG *the first time the two armies have linked up*
pair up EG *Men and teenage girls pair up to dance.*
unite EG *The two parties have been trying to unite.*
work together EG *We have always wanted to work together.*

❶ tear NOUN
a hole in something
EG *I peered through a tear in the curtains.*

hole EG *the hole in my shoe*
ladder EG *There was a ladder in her tights.*
rip EG *the rip in her new dress*
rupture EG *a rupture in the valve*
scratch EG *I pointed to a number of scratches in the tile floor.*
split EG *the split in his trousers*

❷ tear VERB
to make a hole in something
EG *She nearly tore my overcoat.*
ladder EG *after she laddered her tights*
rip EG *I tried not to rip the paper.*
rupture EG *a ruptured appendix*
scratch EG *Knives will scratch the worktop.*
shred EG *They may be shredding documents.*
split EG *I'd split my trousers.*

WORD POWER
▷ **Synonyms**
rend
sunder

❸ tear VERB
to go somewhere in a hurry
EG *He tore through busy streets in a high-speed chase.*
charge EG *He charged through the door.*
dart EG *Ingrid darted across the deserted street.*
dash EG *He dashed upstairs.*
fly EG *She flew to their bedsides when they were ill.*
race EG *He raced across town.*
shoot EG *Another car shot out of a junction.*
speed EG *A low shot sped past Lukic.*
zoom EG *We zoomed through the gallery.*

WORD POWER
▷ **Synonyms**
bolt
career

tease VERB
to make fun of someone
EG *He used to tease me about wanting to act.*
make fun of EG *The kids at school made fun of me and my Cockney accent.*
mock EG *Don't mock me!*
needle INFORMAL EG *He used to enjoy needling people.*
taunt EG *Other youths taunted him about his clothes.*

❶ **tell** VERB
to let someone know something
EG *They told us the dreadful news.*
inform EG *My daughter informed me that she was pregnant.*
notify EG *We have notified the police.*

WORD POWER

▷ **Synonyms**
acquaint
apprise

❷ **tell** VERB
to give someone an order
EG *A passer-by told the driver to move his car.*
command EG *He commanded his troops to attack.*
direct FORMAL EG *They have been directed to give special attention to the problem.*
instruct EG *The family has instructed solicitors to sue the company.*
order EG *He ordered his men to cease firing.*

WORD POWER

▷ **Synonyms**
call upon
enjoin

❸ **tell** VERB
to judge something correctly
EG *I could tell he was scared.*
discern EG *It was hard to discern why this was happening.*
see EG *I could see she was lonely.*

temporary ADJECTIVE
lasting a short time
EG *a temporary loss of memory*
ephemeral EG *a reminder that earthly pleasures are ephemeral*
fleeting EG *a fleeting glimpse*
interim EG *an interim measure*
momentary EG *a momentary lapse*
passing EG *a passing phase*
provisional EG *a provisional coalition government*
transient EG *Modelling is a transient career.*
transitory EG *the transitory nature of political success*

WORD POWER

▷ **Synonyms**
impermanent
short-lived

▶ **Antonym**
permanent

tempt VERB
to persuade someone to do something
EG *Children not attending schools may be tempted into crime.*
entice EG *She resisted attempts to entice her into politics.*
lure EG *The company aims to lure smokers back to cigarettes.*
seduce EG *We are seduced into buying all these items.*

❶ **tend** VERB
to happen usually or often
EG *I tend to forget things.*
be apt EG *She was apt to raise her voice.*
be inclined EG *He was inclined to self-pity.*
be liable EG *equipment that is liable to break*
be prone EG *We know males are more prone to violence.*
have a tendency EG *Shetland jumpers have a tendency to be annoyingly itchy.*

a b c d e f g h i j k l m n o p q r s t u v w x y z

A
B
C
D
E
F
G
H
I
J
K
L
M
N
O
P
Q
R
S
T
U
V
W
X
Y
Z

2 tend VERB
to look after someone or something
EG *the way we tend our cattle*
care for EG *They hired a nurse to care for her.*
look after EG *I love looking after the children.*
nurse EG *In hospital they nursed me back to health.*
take care of EG *There was no one else to take care of the animals.*

tendency NOUN
behaviour that happens very often
EG *a tendency to be critical*
inclination EG *his artistic inclinations*
leaning EG *their socialist leanings*
propensity EG *his propensity for violence*

WORD POWER

▷ **Synonyms**
predisposition
proclivity
proneness

1 tender ADJECTIVE
showing gentle and caring feelings
EG *tender, loving care*
affectionate EG *She gave him an affectionate smile.*
caring EG *He is a lovely boy, and very caring.*
compassionate EG *a deeply compassionate film*
gentle EG *Michael's voice was gentle and consoling.*
kind EG *She is warmhearted and kind to everyone and everything.*
loving EG *He was a most loving husband and father.*
sensitive EG *He was always so sensitive.*
warm EG *She was a very warm person.*

WORD POWER

▶ **Antonym**
tough

2 tender ADJECTIVE
painful and sore
EG *My tummy felt very tender.*
aching EG *The weary holidaymakers soothed their aching feet in the sea.*
bruised EG *bruised legs*
inflamed EG *Her eyes were inflamed.*
painful EG *Her glands were swollen and painful.*
raw EG *the drag of the rope against the raw flesh of my shoulders*
sensitive EG *Ouch! I'm sorry, my lip is still a bit sensitive.*
sore EG *My chest is still sore from the surgery.*

3 tender VERB
to offer something such as an apology or resignation
EG *She tendered her resignation.*
hand in EG *All the opposition members have handed in their resignation.*
offer EG *May I offer my sincere condolences?*

4 tender NOUN
a proposal to provide something at a price
EG *Builders will be asked to submit a tender for the work.*
bid EG *Sydney's successful bid for the 2000 Olympic Games*
estimate EG *The firm is preparing an estimate for the work.*
package EG *We opted for the package submitted by the existing service provider.*
submission EG *A written submission has to be prepared.*

1 tense ADJECTIVE
nervous and unable to relax
EG *Never had she seen him so tense.*
anxious EG *She had become very anxious and alarmed.*
edgy EG *She was nervous and edgy, still chain-smoking.*
jittery INFORMAL EG *Investors have become jittery about the country's*

economy.
jumpy EG *I told myself not to be so jumpy.*
nervous EG *It has made me very nervous about going out.*
uptight INFORMAL EG *Penny never got uptight about exams.*

WORD POWER

▶ **Antonym**
calm

2 tense ADJECTIVE
causing anxiety
EG *the tense atmosphere at the talks*
anxious EG *They had to wait ten anxious days.*
nerve-racking EG *It was more nerve-racking than taking a World Cup penalty.*
stressful EG *a stressful job*

3 tense ADJECTIVE
having tight muscles
EG *She lay, eyes shut, body tense.*
rigid EG *Andrew went rigid whenever he saw a dog.*
strained EG *His shoulders were strained with effort.*
taut EG *when muscles are taut or cold*
tight EG *It is better to stretch the tight muscles first.*

WORD POWER

▶ **Antonym**
relaxed

1 term NOUN
a fixed period of time
EG *a 12 month term of service*
period EG *for a limited period only*
session EG *The parliamentary session ends on October 4th.*
spell EG *a six-month spell of practical experience*
stretch EG *He did an 18-month stretch in prison.*

time EG *He served the time of his contract and then left the company.*

WORD POWER

▷ **Synonyms**
duration

2 term NOUN
a name or word for a particular thing
EG *the medical term for a heart attack*
designation EG *Level Four Alert is a designation reserved for very serious incidents.*
expression EG *She used some remarkably coarse expressions.*
name EG *The correct name for this condition is bovine spongiform encephalopathy.*
word EG *The word ginseng comes from the Chinese "Shen-seng".*

terms PLURAL NOUN
conditions that have been agreed
EG *the terms of the merger agreement*
conditions EG *They may be breaching the conditions of their contract.*
provisions EG *the provisions of the Amsterdam treaty*
proviso EG *He left me the house with the proviso that it had to stay in the family.*
stipulations EG *He left, violating the stipulations of his parole.*

1 terrible ADJECTIVE
serious and unpleasant
EG *a terrible illness*
appalling EG *an appalling headache*
awful EG *an awful crime*
desperate EG *a desperate situation*
dreadful EG *a dreadful mistake*
frightful OLD-FASHIONED EG *He got himself into a frightful muddle.*
horrendous EG *horrendous injuries*
horrible EG *a horrible mess*
horrid OLD-FASHIONED EG *What a horrid smell!*
rotten EG *What rotten luck!*

A
B
C
D
E
F
G
H
I
J
K
L
M
N
O
P
Q
R
S
T
U
V
W
X
Y
Z

❷ terrible ADJECTIVE
of very poor quality
EG *Paddy's terrible haircut*
abysmal EG *The standard of play was abysmal.*
appalling EG *Her singing is appalling.*
awful EG *Jeans look awful on me.*
dire EG *Most of the poems were dire.*
dreadful EG *My financial situation is dreadful.*
horrible EG *a horrible meal*
rotten EG *I think it's a rotten idea.*

> ### WORD POWER
>
> ▶ **Antonym**
> excellent

territory NOUN
the land that a person or country controls
EG *gangs fighting to defend their territories*
area EG *They claim that the entire area belongs to Syria.*
country EG *He is an ambassador to a foreign country.*
district EG *Stick to your own district and stay out of ours.*
domain EG *He surveyed his domain from the roof of the castle.*
dominion EG *men who ruled their dominions with ruthless efficiency*
land EG *New mines were discovered on what had been Apache land.*
province EG *debates about the political future of their province*
state EG *This state remains suspended from the Commonwealth.*

❶ test VERB
to find out what something is like
EG *travelling to Holland to test a British-built boat*
assess EG *The test was to assess aptitude rather than academic achievement.*
check EG *It's worth checking each item for obvious flaws.*
try EG *Howard wanted me to try the*

wine.
try out EG *London Transport hopes to try out the system in September.*

❷ test NOUN
an attempt to test something
EG *the banning of nuclear tests*
assessment EG *He was remanded for assessment by doctors.*
check EG *regular checks on his blood pressure*
trial EG *clinical trials*

texture NOUN
the way that something feels
EG *Her skin is pale, the texture of fine wax.*
consistency EG *Mix the dough to the right consistency.*
feel EG *Linen raincoats have a crisp, papery feel.*

theft NOUN
the crime of stealing
EG *the theft of classified documents*
robbery EG *The man was serving a sentence for robbery.*
stealing EG *She was jailed for six months for stealing.*
thieving EG *an ex-con who says he's given up thieving*

> ### WORD POWER
>
> ▷ **Synonyms**
> larceny
> pilfering

theory NOUN
an idea that explains something
EG *Darwin's theory of evolution*
conjecture EG *That was a conjecture, not a fact.*
hypothesis EG *Different hypotheses have been put forward.*
supposition EG *As with many such suppositions, no one had ever tested it.*
surmise FORMAL EG *His surmise proved correct.*

therefore ADVERB
as a result

EG *Muscles need lots of fuel and therefore burn lots of calories.*
as a result EG *I slept in, and, as a result, I was late for work.*
consequently EG *He's more experienced, and consequently earns a higher salary.*
for that reason EG *I'd never met my in-laws before. For that reason, I was a little nervous.*
hence FORMAL EG *These products are all natural, and hence, better for you.*
so EG *I was worried about her, so I phoned to check how she was.*
thus EG *His men were getting tired, and thus, careless.*

thesaurus NOUN

> **Parts of a dictionary or thesaurus**
> antonym
> definition
> entry
> example
> homonym
> homophone
> pronunciation
> root word
> synonym
> word derivation

❶ thick ADJECTIVE
measuring a large distance from side to side
EG *a thick stone wall*
fat EG *a fat book*
wide EG *a desk that was almost as wide as the room*

> *WORD POWER*
>
> ▶ **Antonym**
> thin

❷ thick ADJECTIVE
containing little water
EG *thick soup*
clotted EG *clotted cream*
concentrated EG *a glass of*

concentrated orange juice
condensed EG *tins of condensed milk*

> *WORD POWER*
>
> ▶ **Antonym**
> watery

❸ thick ADJECTIVE
grouped closely together
EG *thick dark hair*
bristling EG *a bristling moustache*
dense EG *a large dense forest*
lush EG *the lush green meadows*
luxuriant EG *the luxuriant foliage of Young Island*

> *WORD POWER*
>
> ▶ **Antonym**
> sparse

thicken VERB
to become thicker
EG *The clouds thickened.*
clot EG *The patient's blood refused to clot.*
condense EG *Water vapour condenses to form clouds.*
congeal EG *The blood had started to congeal.*
set EG *as the jelly starts to set*

> *WORD POWER*
>
> ▷ **Synonyms**
> coagulate
> jell
>
> ▶ **Antonym**
> thin

thief NOUN
someone who steals something
EG *a car thief*
burglar EG *Burglars broke into their home.*
crook INFORMAL EG *a petty crook*
mugger INFORMAL EG *after being threatened by a mugger*
pickpocket EG *a gang of pickpockets*

a
b
c
d
e
f
g
h
i
j
k
l
m
n
o
p
q
r
s
t
u
v
w
x
y
z

robber EG *armed robbers*
shoplifter EG *a persistent shoplifter*

WORD POWER

▷ Synonyms
housebreaker
pilferer

❶ **thin** ADJECTIVE
measuring a small distance from side to side
EG *The material was too thin.*
fine EG *the fine hairs on her arms*
narrow EG *a narrow strip of land*
slim EG *a slim volume of verse*

WORD POWER

▶ Antonym
thick

❷ **thin** ADJECTIVE
not carrying a lot of fat
EG *a tall, thin man with grey hair*
→ see Word Study **thin**

WORD POWER

▶ Antonym
fat

❸ **thin** ADJECTIVE
containing a lot of water
EG *thin soup*
dilute *or* **diluted** EG *a dilute solution of bleach*
runny EG *a runny soft cheese*
watery EG *watery beer*
weak EG *a cup of weak tea*

WORD POWER

▶ Antonym
thick

thing NOUN
a physical object
EG *What's that thing doing here?*
article EG *household articles*
object EG *everyday objects such as wooden spoons*

things PLURAL NOUN
someone's clothes or belongings
EG *Sara told him to take all his things with him.*
belongings EG *He was identified only by his personal belongings.*
effects EG *His daughters were collecting his effects.*
gear EG *They helped us put our gear back into the van.*
possessions EG *People had lost all their possessions.*
stuff EG *Where have you put all your stuff?*

❶ **think** VERB
to consider something
EG *Let's think what we can do next.*
consider EG *The government is being asked to consider the plan.*
contemplate EG *He cried as he contemplated his future.*
deliberate EG *She deliberated over the decision for a good few years.*
meditate EG *He meditated on the problem.*
mull over EG *I'll leave you alone so you can mull it over.*
muse LITERARY EG *Many of the papers muse on the fate of the President.*
ponder EG *I'm continually pondering how to improve the team.*
reflect EG *I reflected on the child's future.*

WORD POWER

▷ Synonyms
cogitate
ruminate

❷ **think** VERB
to believe something
EG *I think she has a secret boyfriend.*
believe EG *Experts believe that the drought will be extensive.*
consider EG *He considers that this is the worst recession this century.*
deem FORMAL EG *Many people have ideas that their society deems to be*

dangerous.

hold EG *The theory holds that minor events are the trigger for larger events.*

imagine EG *I imagine he was just showing off.*

judge EG *He judged that this was the moment to say what had to be said.*

reckon EG *Toni reckoned that it must be about three o'clock.*

thorough ADJECTIVE
careful and complete
EG *a thorough examination*

complete EG *a complete overhaul of the engine*

comprehensive EG *a comprehensive guide to the region*

exhaustive EG *exhaustive enquiries*

full EG *Mr Primakov gave a full account of his meeting with the President.*

intensive EG *four weeks of intensive study*

meticulous EG *A happy wedding day requires meticulous planning.*

painstaking EG *a painstaking search*

scrupulous EG *Observe scrupulous hygiene when preparing and cooking food.*

___

WORD POWER

▷ **Synonyms**
all-embracing
in-depth

___

❶ thought NOUN
an idea or opinion
EG *his thoughts on love*

idea EG *his ideas about democracy*

notion EG *We each have a notion of what kind of person we'd like to be.*

opinion EG *most of those who expressed an opinion*

view EG *Make your views known to your MP.*

❷ thought NOUN
the activity of thinking
EG *After much thought I decided to end my marriage.*

thorough >> thoughtful

consideration EG *There should be careful consideration of the BBC's future role.*

contemplation EG *He was lost in contemplation of the landscape.*

deliberation EG *the result of lengthy deliberation*

meditation EG *He stared at the floor, lost in meditation.*

reflection EG *after days of reflection*

thinking EG *THis is definitely a time for decisive action and quick thinking.*

___

WORD POWER

▷ **Synonyms**
cogitation
introspection
rumination

___

❶ thoughtful ADJECTIVE
quiet and serious
EG *He was looking very thoughtful.*

contemplative EG *a quiet, contemplative sort of chap*

pensive EG *He looked unusually pensive before the start.*

reflective EG *I walked on in a reflective mood.*

___

WORD POWER

▷ **Synonyms**
introspective
meditative
ruminative

___

❷ thoughtful ADJECTIVE
showing consideration for others
EG *a thoughtful and caring man*

attentive EG *an attentive husband*

caring EG *a caring son*

considerate EG *the most considerate man I've ever known*

kind EG *She is warmhearted and kind to everyone.*

___

WORD POWER

▷ **Synonyms**
solicitous
unselfish

___

A
B
C
D
E
F
G
H
I
J
K
L
M
N
O
P
Q
R
S
T
U
V
W
X
Y
Z

▶ **Antonym**
thoughtless

thoughtless ADJECTIVE
showing a lack of consideration
EG *It was thoughtless of her to mention it.*
insensitive EG *My husband is very insensitive about my problem.*
tactless EG *a tactless remark*

WORD POWER

▷ **Synonyms**
inconsiderate
undiplomatic

▶ **Antonym**
thoughtful

❶ **threat** NOUN
a statement that someone will harm you
EG *death threats*
menace EG *demanding money with menaces*
threatening remark EG *He was overheard making threatening remarks to the couple.*

❷ **threat** NOUN
something that seems likely to harm you
EG *the threat of tropical storms*
hazard EG *a health hazard*
menace EG *a menace to the public*
risk EG *a fire risk*

❶ **threaten** VERB
to promise to do something bad
EG *He threatened her with a knife.*
make threats to EG *despite all the threats he'd made to harm her*
menace EG *She's being menaced by her sister's latest boyfriend.*

❷ **threaten** VERB
to be likely to cause harm
EG *The newcomers threaten the livelihood of the workers.*
endanger EG *Toxic waste could endanger lives.*

jeopardize EG *He has jeopardized the future of his government.*
put at risk EG *If they have the virus, they are putting patients at risk.*
put in jeopardy EG *A series of setbacks have put the whole project in jeopardy.*

thrifty ADJECTIVE
careful not to waste money or resources
EG *Britain become a nation of thrifty consumers and bargain hunters.*
careful EG *He's very careful with his money.*
economical EG *a very economical way to travel*
frugal EG *a frugal lifestyle*
prudent EG *the need for a much more prudent use of energy*

❶ **thrill** NOUN
a feeling of excitement
EG *the thrill of waking up on Christmas morning*
high INFORMAL EG *the high of a win over New Zealand*
kick INFORMAL EG *I got a kick out of seeing my name in print.*

❷ **thrill** VERB
to cause a feeling of excitement
EG *It thrilled me to see her looking so happy.*
excite EG *I only take on work that excites me.*
give a kick INFORMAL EG *It gave me a kick to actually meet her.*

thrive VERB
to be successful
EG *His company continues to thrive.*
do well EG *Connie did well at school.*
flourish EG *Racism and crime still flourish in the ghetto.*
prosper EG *His team have always prospered in cup competitions.*

throw VERB
to make something move through the air
EG *throwing a tennis ball against a*

wall

cast EG *He cast the stone away.*
chuck INFORMAL EG *He chucked the paper in the bin.*
fling EG *Peter flung his shoes into the corner.*
hurl EG *Groups of angry youths hurled stones at police.*
lob EG *Thugs lobbed a grenade into the crowd.*
pitch EG *Simon pitched the empty bottle into the lake.*
sling EG *He took off his anorak and slung it into the back seat.*
toss EG *She tossed her suitcase onto one of the beds.*

thug NOUN
a very violent person
EG *a gang of armed thugs*
bandit EG *terrorist acts carried out by bandits*
hooligan EG *severe measures against soccer hooligans*
tough EG *The neighbourhood toughs beat them both up.*
tsotsi SOUTH AFRICAN EG *Many are too terrified of local tsotsis to protest.*

❶ tidy ADJECTIVE
arranged in an orderly way
EG *a tidy desk*
neat EG *She put her clothes in a neat pile.*
orderly EG *a beautiful, clean and orderly city*

WORD POWER

▷ **Synonyms**
shipshape
spick-and-span

▶ **Antonym**
untidy

❷ tidy VERB
to make something neat
EG *He tidied his garage.*
spruce up EG *Many buildings have been spruced up.*

straighten EG *straightening cushions and organizing magazines*

WORD POWER

▶ **Antonym**
mess up

❶ tie VERB
to fasten something
EG *They tied the ends of the bag securely.*
bind EG *Bind the ends of the cord together with thread.*
fasten EG *instructions on how to fasten the strap to the box*
knot EG *He knotted the laces securely together.*
lash EG *The shelter is built by lashing poles together.*
rope EG *I roped myself to the chimney.*
secure EG *He secured the canvas straps as tight as they would go.*
tether EG *tethering his horse to a tree*
truss EG *She trussed him quickly with stolen bandage.*

WORD POWER

▶ **Antonym**
untie

❷ tie VERB
to have the same score
EG *Rafferty tied with Nobilo.*
be level EG *At the end of 90 minutes the teams were level.*
draw EG *Holland and Ireland drew 1-1.*

❸ tie NOUN
a connection with something
EG *I had very close ties with the family.*
affiliation EG *They asked her what her political affiliations were.*
affinity EG *He has a close affinity with the landscape.*
bond EG *The experience created a special bond between us.*
connection EG *The police say he had no connection with the security forces.*
relationship EG *family relationships*

a
b
c
d
e
f
g
h
i
j
k
l
m
n
o
p
q
r
s
t
u
v
w
x
y
z

1 tight ADJECTIVE
fitting closely
EG *The shoes are too tight.*
constricted EG *His throat began to feel swollen and constricted.*
cramped EG *families living in cramped conditions*
snug EG *a snug black T-shirt*

WORD POWER

▶ **Antonym**
loose

2 tight ADJECTIVE
firmly fastened
EG *a tight knot*
firm EG *He managed to get a firm grip of it.*
secure EG *Check joints are secure and the wood is sound.*

3 tight ADJECTIVE
not slack or relaxed
EG *Pull the elastic tight.*
rigid EG *I went rigid with shock.*
taut EG *The clothes line is pulled taut and secured.*
tense EG *A bath can relax tense muscles.*

WORD POWER

▶ **Antonym**
slack

1 tilt VERB
to raise one end of something
EG *Leonard tilted his chair back on two legs.*
incline EG *Jack inclined his head.*
lean EG *Lean the plants against a wall.*
slant EG *The floor slanted down to the window.*
slope EG *The bank sloped down sharply to the river.*
tip EG *She had to tip her head back to see him.*

WORD POWER

▷ **Synonyms**
cant
list

2 tilt NOUN
a raised position
EG *the tilt of the earth's axis*
angle EG *The boat is now leaning at a 30 degree angle.*
gradient EG *a gradient of 1 in 3*
incline EG *at the edge of a steep incline*
slant EG *The house is on a slant.*
slope EG *The street must have been on a slope.*

WORD POWER

▷ **Synonyms**
camber
list

1 time NOUN
a particular period
EG *I enjoyed my time in Durham.*
interval EG *a long interval of silence*
period EG *a period of calm*
spell EG *a brief spell teaching*
stretch EG *an 18-month stretch in the army*
while EG *They walked on in silence for a while.*

WORD POWER

● **Related Words**
adjective : temporal

2 time VERB
to plan when something will happen
EG *We had timed our visit for March 7.*
schedule EG *The space shuttle had been scheduled to blast off at 04:38.*
set EG *A court hearing has been set for December 16.*

timid ADJECTIVE
lacking courage or confidence
EG *a timid child*
bashful EG *Offstage, he is bashful and*

awkward.
cowardly EG *I was too cowardly to complain.*
diffident EG *Helen was diffident and reserved.*
nervous EG *a very nervous woman*
shy EG *a shy, quiet-spoken girl*

WORD POWER

▷ **Synonyms**
faint-hearted
pusillanimous
timorous

▶ **Antonym**
bold

tiny ADJECTIVE
very small
EG *The living room is tiny.*
diminutive EG *a diminutive figure standing at the entrance*
microscopic EG *a microscopic amount of the substance*
miniature EG *He looked like a miniature version of his brother.*
minute EG *Only a minute amount is needed.*
negligible EG *The pay that the soldiers received was negligible.*
wee SCOTTISH EG *a wee boy*

WORD POWER

▷ **Synonyms**
infinitesimal
Lilliputian

▶ **Antonym**
huge

tire VERB
to use a lot of energy
EG *If driving tires you, take the train.*
drain EG *My emotional turmoil had drained me.*
exhaust EG *Walking in deep snow had totally exhausted him.*
fatigue EG *He is easily fatigued.*

WORD POWER

▷ **Synonyms**
enervate
wear out
weary

tired ADJECTIVE
having little energy
EG *She was too tired to take a shower.*
drained EG *as United stalked off, stunned and drained*
drowsy EG *He felt pleasantly drowsy.*
exhausted EG *She was too exhausted and distressed to talk.*
fatigued EG *Winter weather can leave you feeling fatigued.*
sleepy EG *I was beginning to feel sleepy.*
tuckered out AUSTRALIAN AND NEW ZEALAND; INFORMAL EG *You must be tuckered out after that bus trip.*
weary EG *a weary traveller*
worn out EG *He's just worn out after the drive.*

❶ together ADVERB
with other people
EG *We went on long bicycle rides together.*
collectively EG *The Cabinet is collectively responsible for policy.*
en masse EG *The people marched en masse.*
in unison EG *Michael and the landlady nodded in unison.*
jointly EG *an agency jointly run by New York and New Jersey*
shoulder to shoulder EG *They could fight shoulder to shoulder against a common enemy.*
side by side EG *areas where different nationalities live side by side*

❷ together ADVERB
at the same time
EG *Three horses crossed the finish line together.*
as one EG *The 40,000 crowd rose as one.*

a
b
c
d
e
f
g
h
i
j
k
l
m
n
o
p
q
r
s
t
u
v
w
x
y
z

A
B
C
D
E
F
G
H
I
J
K
L
M
N
O
P
Q
R
S
T
U
V
W
X
Y
Z

at once EG *You can't do two things at once.*
concurrently EG *There were three races running concurrently.*
simultaneously EG *The two guns fired almost simultaneously.*
with one accord EG *With one accord they turned and walked back.*

❶ tolerable ADJECTIVE
able to be tolerated
EG *The pain was tolerable.*
acceptable EG *a mutually acceptable new contract*
bearable EG *A cool breeze made the heat bearable.*

WORD POWER
▶ **Antonym**
unbearable

❷ tolerable ADJECTIVE
fairly satisfactory
EG *a tolerable salary*
acceptable EG *We've made an acceptable start.*
adequate EG *The level of service was adequate.*
okay *or* **OK** INFORMAL EG *For a fashionable restaurant like this the prices are okay.*
passable EG *Ms Campbell speaks passable French.*
reasonable EG *able to make a reasonable living from his writing*
so-so INFORMAL EG *Their lunch was only so-so.*

tolerant ADJECTIVE
accepting of different views and behaviour
EG *more tolerant attitudes to unmarried couples having children*
broad-minded EG *a very fair and broad-minded man*
liberal EG *She is known to have liberal views on divorce.*
open-minded EG *I am very open-minded about that question.*

understanding EG *Fortunately for John, he had an understanding wife.*

WORD POWER
▷ **Synonyms**
forbearing
latitudinarian

▶ **Antonym**
narrow-minded

❶ tolerate VERB
to accept something you disagree with
EG *We will not tolerate such behaviour.*
accept EG *Urban dwellers often accept noise as part of city life.*
put up with EG *You're late again and I won't put up with it.*

❷ tolerate VERB
to accept something unpleasant
EG *She can no longer tolerate the position that she's in.*
bear EG *He can't bear to talk about it.*
endure EG *unable to endure the pain*
stand EG *He can't stand me smoking.*

tomb NOUN
a burial chamber
EG *Carter discovered Tutankhamun's tomb.*
grave EG *They used to visit her grave twice a year.*
mausoleum EG *the elaborate mausoleums of the Paris cemetery*
sarcophagus EG *an Egyptian sarcophagus*
sepulchre LITERARY EG *the ornate lid of the sepulchre*
vault EG *the family vault*

❶ too ADVERB
also or as well
EG *You were there too.*
as well EG *She published historical novels as well.*
besides EG *You get to take lots of samples home as well.*
in addition EG *There are, in addition, other objections to the plan.*

into the bargain EG *The machine can play CDs into the bargain.*
likewise EG *She sat down and he did likewise.*
moreover EG *He didn't know, and moreover, he didn't care.*

2 too ADVERB
more than a desirable or acceptable amount
EG *You've had too many late nights.*
excessively EG *He had an excessively protective mother.*
over- EG *I didn't want to seem over-eager.*
overly EG *Most people consider him to be overly ambitious.*
unduly EG *She's unduly concerned with what people think of her.*
unreasonably EG *These prices seem unreasonably high to me.*

tool NOUN
a hand-held instrument for doing a job
EG *The best tool for the purpose is a pair of shears.*
implement EG *knives and other useful implements*
instrument EG *instruments for cleaning and polishing teeth*
utensil EG *cooking utensils*

1 top NOUN
the highest part of something
EG *I waited at the top of the stairs.*
apex EG *at the very apex of the pyramid*
brow EG *the brow of the hill*
crest EG *the crest of the wave*
crown EG *the crown of the head*
culmination EG *the culmination of his career*
head EG *A different name was placed at the head of the chart.*
height EG *at the height of his success*
high point EG *the high point of his movie career*
peak EG *at the peak of the morning rush hour*

pinnacle EG *the pinnacle of sporting achievement*
ridge EG *He died after falling from a ridge on Mount Snowdon.*
summit EG *the summit of the mountain*
zenith LITERARY EG *His career is now at its zenith.*

WORD POWER

▷ **Synonyms**
acme
apex
apogee

▶ **Antonym**
bottom

---

2 top NOUN
the lid of a container
EG *a bottle top*
cap EG *She unscrewed the cap of her water bottle.*
lid EG *the lid of the jar*
stopper EG *a scent bottle with a stopper in blue frosted glass*

3 top ADJECTIVE
being the best of its kind
EG *He was the top student in physics.*
best EG *the best pupil of his year*
chief EG *one of the world's chief nuclear scientists*
elite EG *the elite troops of the presidential bodyguard*
foremost EG *the foremost urban painter of his age*
head EG *He was head boy when he was at school.*
highest EG *He achieved one of the highest positions in the land.*
lead EG *She has landed the lead role in a major film.*
leading EG *a leading member of the community*
pre-eminent EG *a pre-eminent political figure*
premier EG *the country's premier theatre company*
prime EG *The store will be built in a*

a b c d e f g h i j k l m n o p q r s t u v w x y z

A B C D E F G H I J K L M N O P Q R S T U V W X Y Z

prime location.
principal EG *the principal singer with the Royal Opera House*

4 top VERB
to be greater than something
EG *The temperature topped 90 degrees.*
cap EG *He capped his display with two fine goals.*
exceed EG *Its research budget exceeds $700 million a year.*
go beyond EG *This goes beyond anything I've ever attempted before.*
outstrip EG *Demand is outstripping supply.*
surpass EG *He has surpassed the record of nine wins in one season.*

5 top VERB
to be better than someone or something
EG *You'll never manage to top that story.*
beat EG *Nothing beats a nice, long bath at the end of a day.*
better EG *As an account of adolescence, this novel cannot be bettered.*
eclipse EG *Nothing is going to eclipse winning the Olympic title.*
improve on EG *We need to improve on our performance against France.*
outdo EG *Both sides are trying to outdo each other.*
surpass EG *He was determined to surpass the achievements of his brothers.*

1 total NOUN
several things added together
EG *The companies have a total of 1776 employees.*
aggregate EG *three successive defeats by an aggregate of 12 goals*
sum EG *the sum of all the angles*
whole EG *taken as a percentage of the whole*

2 total ADJECTIVE
complete in all its parts

EG *a total failure*
absolute EG *absolute beginners*
complete EG *a complete mess*
out-and-out EG *an out-and-out lie*
outright EG *an outright rejection of the deal*
unconditional EG *unconditional surrender*
undivided EG *You have my undivided attention.*
unmitigated EG *an unmitigated failure*
unqualified EG *an unqualified success*
utter EG *utter nonsense*

WORD POWER

▷ **Synonyms**
all-out
thoroughgoing

3 total VERB
to reach the sum of
EG *Their debts totalled over 300,000 dollars.*
add up to EG *Profits can add up to millions of dollars.*
amount to EG *Spending on sports-related items amounted to £9.75 billion.*
come to EG *That comes to over a thousand pounds.*

1 touch VERB
to put your hand on something
EG *Don't touch that dial.*
feel EG *The doctor felt his head.*
finger EG *He fingered the few coins in his pocket.*
handle EG *Wear rubber gloves when handling cat litter.*

2 touch VERB
to come into contact with
EG *Annie lowered her legs until her feet touched the floor.*
brush EG *Something brushed against her leg.*
graze EG *A bullet had grazed his arm.*

meet EG *when the wheels meet the ground*

WORD POWER

● **Related Words**
adjective : tactile

❸ **touch** VERB
to emotionally affect someone
EG *I was touched by his kindness.*
affect EG *Jazza was badly affected by his divorce.*
move EG *These stories surprised and moved me.*
stir EG *She stirred something very deep in me.*

touching ADJECTIVE
causing sadness or sympathy
EG *a touching tale*
affecting LITERARY EG *an affecting memorial to Countess Rachel*
moving EG *It was a moving moment for Marianne.*
poignant EG *a poignant love story*

touchy ADJECTIVE
easily upset
EG *She is very touchy about her past.*
easily offended EG *viewers who are easily offended*
sensitive EG *Young people are very sensitive about their appearance.*
toey NEW ZEALAND; SLANG EG *Don't be so toey.*

WORD POWER

▷ **Synonyms**
oversensitive
thin-skinned

❶ **tough** ADJECTIVE
able to put up with hardship
EG *She is tough and ambitious.*
hardened EG *hardened criminals*
hardy EG *a hardy race of pioneers*
resilient EG *a good soldier, calm and resilient*
robust EG *Perhaps men are more robust than women?*

rugged EG *Rugged individualism forged America's frontier society.*
strong EG *Eventually I felt strong enough to look at him.*

❷ **tough** ADJECTIVE
difficult to break or damage
EG *beans with a rather tough outer skin*
durable EG *Fine bone china is both strong and durable.*
hard-wearing EG *hard-wearing cotton shirts*
leathery EG *leathery skin*
resilient EG *an armchair of some resilient plastic material*
robust EG *very robust machinery*
rugged EG *You need a rugged, four-wheel drive vehicle.*
solid EG *The car feels very solid.*
strong EG *a strong casing, which won't crack or chip*
sturdy EG *The camera was mounted on a sturdy tripod.*

WORD POWER

▶ **Antonym**
fragile

❸ **tough** ADJECTIVE
full of hardship
EG *She had a pretty tough childhood.*
arduous EG *an arduous journey*
difficult EG *We're living in difficult times.*
exacting EG *an exacting task*
hard EG *a hard life*

WORD POWER

▶ **Antonym**
easy

❶ **trace** VERB
to look for and find something
EG *Police are trying to trace the owner.*
locate EG *We've simply been unable to locate him.*
track down EG *She had spent years trying to track down her parents.*

a b c d e f g h i j k l m n o p q r s t u v w x y z

2 trace NOUN

a sign of something
EG *No trace of his father had been found.*
evidence EG *He'd seen no evidence of fraud.*
hint EG *I saw no hint of irony on her face.*
indication EG *He gave no indication of remorse.*
record EG *There's no record of any marriage or children.*
sign EG *Sally waited for any sign of illness.*
suggestion EG *a faint suggestion of a tan*
whiff EG *Not a whiff of scandal has ever tainted his private life.*

3 trace NOUN

a small amount of something
EG *to write without a trace of sensationalism*
dash EG *a story with a dash of mystery*
drop EG *a drop of sherry*
remnant EG *Beneath the present church were remnants of Roman flooring.*
suspicion EG *large blooms of white with a suspicion of pale pink*
tinge EG *Could there have been a slight tinge of envy in Eva's voice?*
touch EG *a touch of flu*
vestige EG *the last vestige of a UN force that once numbered 30,000*

WORD POWER

▷ **Synonyms**
iota
jot
soupçon

1 trade NOUN

the buying and selling of goods
EG *foreign trade*
business EG *a career in business*
commerce EG *They have made their fortunes from industry and commerce.*

WORD POWER

● **Related Words**
adjective : mercantile

2 trade NOUN

the kind of work someone does
EG *He learnt his trade as a diver in the North Sea.*
business EG *the music business*
line EG *Are you in the publishing line too?*
line of work EG *In my line of work I often get home too late for dinner.*
occupation EG *her new occupation as an author*
profession EG *Harper was a teacher by profession.*

3 trade VERB

to buy and sell goods
EG *They had years of experience of trading with the West.*
deal EG *They deal in antiques.*
do business EG *the different people who did business with me*
traffic EG *those who traffic in illegal drugs*

trader NOUN

someone who trades in goods
EG *a timber trader*
broker EG *a financial broker*
dealer EG *dealers in commodities*
merchant EG *a wine merchant*

tradition NOUN

a long-standing custom
EG *the rich traditions of Afro-Cuban music*
convention EG *It's just a social convention that men don't wear skirts.*
custom EG *an ancient Japanese custom*

traditional ADJECTIVE

existing for a long time
EG *her traditional Indian dress*
conventional EG *conventional family planning methods*

established EG *the established church*

WORD POWER

▶ **Antonym**
unconventional

---

tragic ADJECTIVE
very sad
EG *a tragic accident*
distressing EG *distressing news*
heartbreaking EG *a heartbreaking succession of miscarriages*
heart-rending EG *heart-rending pictures of refugees*

train VERB
to teach someone how to do something
EG *We train them in bricklaying and other building techniques.*
coach EG *He coached the basketball team.*
drill EG *He drills the choir to a high standard.*
educate EG *I was educated at the local grammar school.*
instruct EG *All their members are instructed in first aid.*
school EG *He has been schooled to take over the family business.*
teach EG *This is something they teach us to do in our first year.*
tutor EG *She decided to tutor her children at home.*

transform VERB
to change something completely
EG *This technology has transformed our society.*
alter EG *New curtains can completely alter the look of a room.*
change EG *alchemists attempting to change base metals into gold*
convert EG *They have converted the church into a restaurant.*
reform EG *He was totally reformed by this experience.*
revolutionize EG *a device which will revolutionize the way you cook*

transparent ADJECTIVE
able to be seen through
EG *a sheet of transparent plastic*
clear EG *a clear glass panel*
crystalline LITERARY EG *crystalline lakes*
sheer EG *a sheer black shirt*
translucent EG *translucent corrugated plastic*

WORD POWER

▷ **Synonyms**
diaphanous
see-through

▶ **Antonym**
opaque

---

❶ transport NOUN
the moving of goods and people
EG *The prices quoted include transport costs.*
removal EG *the furniture removal business*
shipment EG *transported to the docks for shipment overseas*
transportation EG *the transportation of refugees*

❷ transport VERB
to move people or goods somewhere
EG *They use tankers to transport the oil to Los Angeles.*
carry EG *The ship could carry seventy passengers.*
convey FORMAL EG *a branch line to convey fish direct to Billingsgate*
ship EG *the food being shipped to Iraq*
transfer EG *She was transferred to another hospital.*

❶ trap NOUN
a device for catching animals
EG *a rabbit trap*
net EG *a fishing net*
snare EG *a snare for catching birds*

❷ trap VERB
to catch animals
EG *The locals were encouraged to trap*

A
B
C
D
E
F
G
H
I
J
K
L
M
N
O
P
Q
R
S
T
U
V
W
X
Y
Z

and kill the birds.
catch EG *an animal caught in a trap*
corner EG *like a cornered rat*
snare EG *He'd snared a rabbit earlier in the day.*

❸ **trap** VERB
to trick someone
EG *Were you trying to trap her into making some admission?*
dupe EG *a plot to dupe stamp collectors into buying fake rarities*
trick EG *His family tricked him into going to Pakistan.*

WORD POWER

▷ **Synonyms**
ensnare
entrap

❶ **trash** NOUN
waste material
EG *He picks up your trash on Mondays.*
garbage EG *rotting piles of garbage*
refuse EG *a weekly collection of refuse*
rubbish EG *They had piled most of their rubbish into yellow skips.*
waste EG *a law that regulates the disposal of waste*

❷ **trash** NOUN
something of poor quality
EG *Don't read that awful trash.*
garbage INFORMAL EG *He spends his time watching garbage on TV.*
rubbish EG *He described her book as absolute rubbish.*

travel VERB
to make a journey somewhere
EG *You had better travel to Helsinki tomorrow.*
go EG *We went to Rome.*
journey FORMAL EG *He intended to journey up the Amazon.*
make your way EG *He made his way home at last.*

take a trip EG *We intend to take a trip there sometime.*

WORD POWER

▷ **Synonyms**
proceed
voyage

❶ **treacherous** ADJECTIVE
likely to betray someone
EG *He denounced the party's treacherous leaders.*
disloyal EG *disloyal Cabinet colleagues*
faithless EG *an oppressive father and faithless husband*
unfaithful EG *his unfaithful wife*
untrustworthy EG *Jordan has tried to brand his opponents as untrustworthy.*

WORD POWER

▷ **Synonyms**
perfidious
traitorous

▶ **Antonym**
loyal

❷ **treacherous** ADJECTIVE
dangerous or unreliable
EG *treacherous mountain roads*
dangerous EG *a dangerous stretch of road*
hazardous EG *hazardous seas*
perilous LITERARY EG *The roads grew even steeper and more perilous.*

treasure VERB
to consider something very precious
EG *He treasures his friendship with her.*
cherish EG *The previous owners had cherished the house.*
hold dear EG *forced to renounce everything he held most dear*
prize EG *one of the gallery's most prized possessions*
value EG *if you value your health*

WORD POWER

▷ **Synonyms**
revere
venerate

1 treat VERB
to behave towards someone
EG *Artie treated most women with indifference.*
act towards EG *the way you act towards other people*
behave towards EG *He always behaved towards me with great kindness.*
deal with EG *in dealing with suicidal youngsters*

2 treat VERB
to give someone medical care
EG *the doctor who treated her*
care for EG *They hired a nurse to care for her.*
nurse EG *All the years he was sick my mother had nursed him.*

trendy ADJECTIVE; INFORMAL
fashionable
EG *a trendy night club*
fashionable EG *a very fashionable place to go on holiday*
in SLANG EG *what's in and what's not*
in fashion EG *Calf-length skirts are in fashion this season.*
in vogue EG *African art is in vogue at the moment.*
latest EG *the latest thing in camera technology*
stylish EG *This city has got a lot more stylish in recent years.*

tribute NOUN
something that shows admiration
EG *Police paid tribute to her courage.*
accolade FORMAL EG *To play for your country is the ultimate accolade.*
compliment EG *We consider it a compliment to be called "conservative".*
honour EG *Only two writers are granted the honour of a solo display.*

praise EG *That is high praise indeed.*
testimony EG *a testimony to her dedication*

1 trick NOUN
something that deceives someone
EG *We are playing a trick on a man who keeps bothering me.*
con INFORMAL EG *Slimming snacks that offer miraculous weight loss are a con.*
deception EG *the victim of a cruel deception*
hoax EG *a bomb hoax*
ploy EG *a cynical marketing ploy*
ruse EG *This was a ruse to divide them.*

WORD POWER

▷ **Synonyms**
stratagem
subterfuge

2 trick VERB
to deceive someone
EG *They tricked me into giving them all my money.*
con INFORMAL EG *We have been conned for 20 years.*
deceive EG *He deceived me into thinking her money was his.*
dupe EG *I was duped into letting them in.*
fool EG *They tried to fool you into coming after us.*
take in INFORMAL EG *I wasn't taken in for a minute.*

WORD POWER

▷ **Synonyms**
hoax
hoodwink

tricky ADJECTIVE
difficult to do or to deal with
EG *This could be a very tricky problem.*
complex EG *the whole complex issue of crime and punishment*
complicated EG *a complicated operation*
delicate EG *This brings us to the*

a b c d e f g h i j k l m n o p q r s t u v w x y z

delicate question of his future.

difficult EG *It was a difficult decision to make.*

hard EG *That's a hard question to answer.*

problematic EG *It's a very problematic piece to play.*

puzzling EG *a puzzling case to solve*

sensitive EG *The death penalty is a very sensitive issue.*

❶ trip NOUN
a journey to a place
EG *a business trip*

excursion EG *a coach excursion to Trondheim*

jaunt EG *a jaunt in the car*

journey EG *the journey to Bordeaux*

outing EG *a school outing*

voyage EG *Columbus's voyage to the West Indies*

❷ trip VERB
to fall over
EG *I tripped on the stairs.*

fall over EG *Plenty of top skiers fell over.*

lose your footing EG *He lost his footing and slid into the water.*

stumble EG *He stumbled and almost fell.*

❶ triumph NOUN
a great success
EG *The championships proved to be a personal triumph for the coach.*

success EG *The jewellery was a great success.*

victory EG *a victory for common sense*

WORD POWER

▷ **Synonyms**
coup
feather in your cap
tour de force

▶ **Antonym**
failure

❷ triumph VERB
to be successful
EG *a symbol of good triumphing over evil*

come out on top INFORMAL EG *The only way to come out on top is to adopt a different approach.*

prevail EG *I do hope he will prevail over the rebels.*

succeed EG *if they can succeed in America*

win EG *The top four teams all won.*

WORD POWER

▶ **Antonym**
fail

trivial ADJECTIVE
not important
EG *She doesn't concern herself with such trivial details.*

insignificant EG *The dangers are insignificant compared with those of smoking.*

minor EG *a minor inconvenience*

negligible EG *The strike will have a negligible impact.*

paltry EG *They had no interest in paltry domestic concerns.*

petty EG *I wouldn't indulge in such petty schoolboy pranks.*

slight EG *It's only a slight problem.*

trifling EG *The sums involved were trifling.*

unimportant EG *Too much time is spent discussing unimportant matters.*

WORD POWER

▷ **Synonyms**
inconsequential

▶ **Antonym**
important

❶ trouble NOUN
a difficulty or problem
EG *financial troubles*

bother EG *Vince is having a spot of*

bother with the law.
difficulty EG *economic difficulties*
hassle INFORMAL EG *We had loads of hassles trying to find somewhere to rehearse.*
problem EG *The main problem is unemployment.*

❷ trouble VERB
to make someone feel worried
EG *He was troubled by the lifestyle of his son.*
agitate EG *The thought agitates her.*
bother EG *Is something bothering you?*
disturb EG *dreams so vivid that they disturb me for days*
worry EG *I didn't want to worry you.*

❸ trouble VERB
to cause someone inconvenience
EG *Can I trouble you for some milk?*
bother EG *I don't know why he bothers me with this kind of rubbish.*
disturb EG *a room where you won't be disturbed*
impose upon EG *I was afraid you'd feel we were imposing on you.*
inconvenience EG *He promised to be quick so as not to inconvenience them further.*
put out EG *I've always put myself out for others.*

❶ true ADJECTIVE
not invented
EG *The film is based on a true story.*
accurate EG *an accurate assessment of the situation*
correct EG *a correct diagnosis*
factual EG *any comparison that is not strictly factual*

WORD POWER

▶ **Antonym**
inaccurate

❷ true ADJECTIVE
real or genuine
EG *She was a true friend.*
authentic EG *authentic Italian food*

bona fide EG *We are happy to donate to bona fide charities.*
genuine EG *There was a risk of genuine refugees being returned to Vietnam.*
real EG *No, it wasn't a dream. It was real.*

WORD POWER

▶ **Antonym**
false

trust VERB
to believe that someone will do something
EG *The president can't be trusted.*
count on EG *I can always count on you to cheer me up.*
depend on EG *You can depend on me.*
have confidence in EG *We have the utmost confidence in your abilities.*
have faith in EG *I have no faith in him any more.*
place your trust in EG *I would never place my trust in one so young.*
rely upon EG *I know I can rely on you to sort it out.*

trusty ADJECTIVE
considered to be reliable
EG *a trusty member of the crew*
dependable EG *a dependable and steady worker*
faithful EG *his faithful black Labrador*
firm EG *Betty became a firm friend of the family.*
reliable EG *the problem of finding reliable staff*
solid EG *one of my most solid supporters*
staunch EG *He proved himself a staunch ally.*
true EG *a true friend*
trustworthy EG *trying to find a trustworthy adviser*

truth NOUN
the facts about something
EG *Marcel is keen to get to the truth of*

a b c d e f g h i j k l m n o p q r s t u v w x y z

A
B
C
D
E
F
G
H
I
J
K
L
M
N
O
P
Q
R
S
T
U
V
W
X
Y
Z

what happened.
fact EG *How much was fact and how much fancy no one knew.*
reality EG *Fiction and reality were increasingly blurred.*

WORD POWER

● **Related Words**
adjectives : veritable, veracious

---

❶ **try** VERB
to make an effort to do something
EG *I tried hard to persuade him to stay.*
attempt EG *They are accused of attempting to murder British soldiers.*
endeavour FORMAL EG *I will endeavour to arrange it.*
make an attempt EG *He made three attempts to break the record.*
make an effort EG *He made no effort to hide his disappointment.*
seek EG *We have never sought to impose our views.*
strive EG *The school strives to treat pupils as individuals.*

❷ **try** VERB
to test the quality of something
EG *Howard wanted me to try the wine.*
check out EG *We went to the club to check it out.*
sample EG *We sampled a selection of different bottled waters.*
test EG *The drug was tested on rats.*
try out EG *London Transport hopes to try out the system in September.*

❸ **try** NOUN
an attempt to do something
EG *After a few tries he pressed the right button.*
attempt EG *a deliberate attempt to destabilize the defence*
effort EG *his efforts to improve*
endeavour FORMAL EG *His first endeavours in the field were wedding films.*
go INFORMAL EG *She won on her first go.*

shot INFORMAL EG *I have had a shot at professional cricket.*

tubby ADJECTIVE
rather fat
EG *He's a bit on the tubby side.*
chubby EG *She was very chubby as a child.*
fat EG *He was short and fat.*
overweight EG *Being overweight is bad for your health.*
plump EG *a plump, good-natured little woman*
podgy EG *Eddie is a little podgy round the middle.*
portly EG *a portly gentleman*
stout EG *His wife was a small, stout lady.*

❶ **tug** VERB
to give something a quick, hard pull
EG *A little boy tugged at her skirt excitedly.*
drag EG *He grabbed my ankle and dragged me back.*
draw EG *She took his hand and drew him along.*
haul EG *I gripped his wrist and hauled him up.*
heave EG *They heaved the last bag into the van.*
jerk EG *He jerked his hand out of mine angrily.*
pluck EG *The beggar plucked at her sleeve as she passed.*
pull EG *She pulled down the hem of her skirt over her knees.*
wrench EG *The horse wrenched its head free.*
yank EG *He grabbed my arm and yanked me out of the car.*

❷ **tug** NOUN
a quick, hard pull
EG *He felt a tug at his arm.*
heave EG *With a mighty heave, she pulled herself away from him.*
jerk EG *He gave a sudden jerk of the reins.*
pull EG *Give the cord three sharp pulls.*

wrench EG *He lowered the flag with a quick wrench.*
yank EG *He gave the phone a savage yank.*

tune NOUN
a series of musical notes
EG *She was humming a merry little tune.*
melody EG *a beautiful melody*
strains EG *She could hear the tinny strains of a chamber orchestra.*

WORD POWER
▷ **Synonyms**
air
theme

❶ turn VERB
to change the direction or position of something
EG *She had turned the bedside chair to face the door.*
rotate EG *Take each foot in both your hands and rotate it.*
spin EG *He spun the wheel sharply and made a U-turn.*
swivel EG *She swivelled her chair round.*
twirl EG *Bonnie twirled her empty glass in her fingers.*
twist EG *She twisted her head sideways.*

❷ turn VERB
to become or make something different
EG *A hobby can be turned into a career.*
change EG *She has now changed into a happy, self-confident woman.*
convert EG *a table that converts into an ironing board*
mutate EG *Overnight, the gossip begins to mutate into headlines.*
transform EG *the speed at which your body transforms food into energy*

WORD POWER
▷ **Synonyms**
metamorphose
transfigure
transmute

❸ turn NOUN
someone's right or duty to do something
EG *Tonight it's my turn to cook.*
chance EG *All eligible people would get a chance to vote.*
go EG *Whose go is it?*
opportunity EG *Now is your opportunity to say what you've always wanted.*

❶ twist VERB
to turn something round
EG *Her hands began to twist the handles of the bag.*
bend EG *Bend the bar into a horseshoe.*
curl EG *She sat with her legs curled under her.*
twine EG *He had twined his chubby arms around Vincent's neck.*
weave EG *He weaves his way through a crowd.*
wring EG *after wringing the chicken's neck*

WORD POWER
▷ **Synonyms**
entwine
wreathe

❷ twist VERB
to bend into a new shape
EG *The car was left a mess of twisted metal.*
distort EG *A painter may exaggerate or distort shapes and forms.*
mangle EG *the mangled wreckage*
screw up EG *Amy screwed up her face.*

a b c d e f g h i j k l m n o p q r s **t** u v w x y z

WORD POWER

▷ **Synonyms**
contort
warp

❸ **twist** VERB
to injure a part of your body
EG *I've twisted my ankle.*
sprain EG *He fell and sprained his wrist.*
wrench EG *He had wrenched his back badly from the force of the fall.*

WORD POWER

▷ **Synonyms**
rick
turn

two-faced ADJECTIVE
not honest in dealing with other people
EG *a two-faced, manipulative woman*
deceitful EG *a deceitful, conniving liar*
dishonest EG *He's been dishonest in his dealings with us both.*
disloyal EG *I can't stand people who are disloyal.*
false EG *He had been betrayed by his false friends.*
hypocritical EG *a hypocritical and ambitious careerist*
insincere EG *They are still widely seen as insincere and untrustworthy.*
treacherous EG *He has been consistently treacherous to both sides.*

type NOUN
a group of things that have features in common
EG *There are various types of dog suitable as pets.*
brand EG *his favourite brand of whisky*
breed EG *a rare breed of cattle*
class EG *a better class of restaurant*
group EG *Weather forecasters classify clouds into several different groups.*
kind EG *I don't like that kind of film.*
make EG *He'll only drive a certain make of car.*
sort EG *a dozen trees of various sorts*
species EG *a rare species of moth*
style EG *Several styles of hat were available.*
variety EG *Many varieties of birds live here.*

typical ADJECTIVE
having the usual characteristics of something
EG *a typical American child*
average EG *The average adult man burns 1500 to 2000 calories per day.*
characteristic EG *a characteristic feature of the landscape*
normal EG *a normal day*
regular EG *He describes himself as just a regular guy.*
representative EG *fairly representative groups of adults*
standard EG *It was standard practice in cases like this.*
stock EG *He had a stock answer for all problems.*
usual EG *a neighborhood beset by all the usual inner-city problems*

WORD POWER

▷ **Synonyms**
archetypal
archetypical
stereotypical

▶ **Antonym**
uncharacteristic

Uu

ugly ADJECTIVE
having a very unattractive
appearance
EG *She makes me feel dowdy and ugly.*
plain EG *a shy, plain girl with a pale
complexion*
unattractive EG *painted in an
unattractive shade of green*
unsightly EG *The view was spoiled by
some unsightly houses.*

WORD POWER

▷ **Synonyms**
unlovely
unprepossessing

▶ **Antonym**
beautiful

❶ ultimate ADJECTIVE
being the final one of a series
EG *It is not possible to predict the
ultimate outcome.*
eventual EG *Reunification is the
eventual aim.*
final EG *the fifth and final day*
last EG *This is his last chance to do
something useful.*

❷ ultimate ADJECTIVE
the most important or powerful
EG *the ultimate goal of any player*
greatest EG *Our greatest aim was to
take the gold medal.*
paramount EG *His paramount
ambition was to be an actor.*
supreme EG *the supreme test of his
abilities*
utmost EG *This has to be our utmost
priority.*

❸ ultimate NOUN
the finest example of something
EG *This hotel is the ultimate in luxury.*
epitome EG *She was the epitome of
the successful businesswoman.*
extreme EG *This was shyness taken
to the extreme.*
height EG *the height of bad manners*

peak EG *roses at the peak of
perfection*

unaware ADJECTIVE
not knowing about something
EG *Many people are unaware of how
much they eat.*
ignorant EG *They are completely
ignorant of the relevant facts.*
oblivious EG *John appeared oblivious
to his surroundings.*
unconscious EG *totally unconscious
of my presence*
unsuspecting EG *The cars were then
sold to unsuspecting buyers.*

WORD POWER

▶ **Antonym**
aware

unbearable ADJECTIVE
too unpleasant to be tolerated
EG *Life was unbearable for the
remaining citizens.*
intolerable EG *The heat and
humidity were intolerable.*
oppressive EG *An oppressive sadness
weighed upon him.*
unacceptable EG *She left her
husband because of his unacceptable
behaviour.*

WORD POWER

▷ **Synonyms**
insufferable
unendurable

▶ **Antonym**
tolerable

❶ unbelievable ADJECTIVE
extremely great or surprising
EG *He showed unbelievable courage.*
colossal EG *There has been a colossal
waste of public money.*
incredible EG *You're always an
incredible help on these occasions.*
stupendous EG *It cost a stupendous
amount of money.*

2 unbelievable ADJECTIVE
so unlikely it cannot be believed
EG *He came up with some unbelievable story.*
implausible EG *a film with an implausible ending*
improbable EG *highly improbable claims*
inconceivable EG *It was inconceivable that he'd hurt anyone.*
incredible EG *It seems incredible that anyone would want to do that.*
preposterous EG *The whole idea was preposterous.*
unconvincing EG *In response he was given the usual unconvincing excuses.*

WORD POWER

▶ **Antonym**
believable

1 uncertain ADJECTIVE
not knowing what to do
EG *For a moment he looked uncertain as to how to respond.*
doubtful EG *He was a bit doubtful about starting without her.*
dubious EG *We were a bit dubious about it at first.*
unclear EG *I'm unclear about where to go.*
undecided EG *Even then she was still undecided about her future plans.*

WORD POWER

▷ **Synonyms**
irresolute
vacillating

▶ **Antonym**
certain

2 uncertain ADJECTIVE
not definite
EG *facing an uncertain future*
ambiguous EG *The wording of the contract was ambiguous.*
doubtful EG *The outcome of the match is still doubtful.*

indefinite EG *suspended for an indefinite period*
indeterminate EG *a woman of indeterminate age*

WORD POWER

▷ **Synonyms**
conjectural
undetermined

▶ **Antonym**
certain

unclear ADJECTIVE
confusing and not obvious
EG *It is unclear how much popular support they have.*
ambiguous EG *in order to clarify the earlier ambiguous statement*
confused EG *The situation remains confused, as no clear victor has emerged.*
vague EG *The description was pretty vague.*

WORD POWER

▶ **Antonym**
clear

1 uncomfortable ADJECTIVE
feeling or causing discomfort
EG *an uncomfortable bed*
awkward EG *Its shape made it awkward to carry.*
cramped EG *living in very cramped conditions*
disagreeable EG *designed to make flying a less disagreeable experience*
ill-fitting EG *Walking was difficult because of her ill-fitting shoes.*
painful EG *a painful back injury*

WORD POWER

▶ **Antonym**
comfortable

2 uncomfortable ADJECTIVE
not relaxed or confident
EG *Talking about money made her uncomfortable.*

awkward EG *Offstage, he is bashful and awkward.*
embarrassed EG *an embarrassed silence*
ill at ease EG *I always feel ill at ease in their company.*
self-conscious EG *She was always self-conscious about her height.*
uneasy EG *He looked uneasy and refused to answer any more questions.*

WORD POWER

▶ **Antonym**
comfortable

---

❶ **uncommon** ADJECTIVE
not happening or seen often
EG *This type of cancer is uncommon among young women.*
exceptional EG *These are exceptional circumstances.*
extraordinary EG *an act of extraordinary generosity*
few EG *Genuine friends are few.*
infrequent EG *one of the infrequent visitors to the island*
out of the ordinary EG *My story is nothing out of the ordinary.*
scarce EG *places where jobs are scarce*
sparse EG *Traffic is sparse on this stretch of road.*
rare EG *a rare occurrence*
unusual EG *an unusual sight these days*

WORD POWER

▷ **Synonyms**
unprecedented

▶ **Antonym**
common

---

❷ **uncommon** ADJECTIVE
unusually great
EG *She had read Cecilia's last letter with uncommon interest.*
acute EG *He has an acute dislike of children.*

exceptional EG *a woman of exceptional beauty*
extraordinary EG *a young player of extraordinary energy*
extreme EG *regions suffering from extreme poverty*
great EG *They share a great love of Bach's music.*
intense EG *intense heat*
remarkable EG *a musician of remarkable talent*

WORD POWER

▷ **Synonyms**
unparalleled

---

❶ **unconscious** ADJECTIVE
in a state similar to sleep
EG *By the time the ambulance arrived, he was unconscious.*
asleep EG *They were fast asleep in their beds.*
senseless EG *He was beaten senseless and robbed of all his money.*
stunned EG *stunned by a blow to the head*

WORD POWER

▷ **Synonyms**
comatose
insensible

▶ **Antonym**
conscious

---

❷ **unconscious** ADJECTIVE
not aware of what is happening
EG *quite unconscious of their presence*
oblivious EG *He seemed oblivious of his surroundings.*
unaware EG *He was unaware of the chaos he was causing.*
unknowing EG *unknowing accomplices in his crimes*
unsuspecting EG *She was an unsuspecting victim of his deceit.*

A
B
C
D
E
F
G
H
I
J
K
L
M
N
O
P
Q
R
S
T
U
V
W
X
Y
Z

WORD POWER

▶ **Antonym**
aware

❶ uncover VERB

to find something out
EG *Auditors said they had uncovered evidence of fraud.*
bring to light EG *The truth is unlikely to be brought to light.*
expose EG *His lies were exposed in court.*
reveal EG *He will reveal the truth behind the scandal.*
show up EG *His true character has been shown up for what it is.*
unearth EG *a campaign to unearth supposed conspiracies*

❷ uncover VERB

to remove the lid or cover from something
EG *When the seedlings sprout, uncover the tray.*
expose EG *The wreck was exposed by the action of the tide.*
lay bare EG *Layers of paint and flaking plaster were laid bare.*
open EG *I opened a new jar of coffee.*
reveal EG *His shirt was open, revealing a tattooed chest.*
unearth EG *Quarry workers have unearthed the skeleton of a mammoth.*
unveil EG *The statue will be unveiled next week.*
unwrap EG *unwrapping Christmas presents*

under PREPOSITION

at a lower level than something
EG *a labyrinth of tunnels under the ground*
below EG *The sun had already sunk below the horizon.*
beneath EG *the frozen grass crunching beneath his feet*

underneath EG *people trapped underneath the wreckage*

WORD POWER

▶ **Antonym**
above

undergo VERB

to have something happen to you
EG *He had to undergo major surgery.*
be subjected to EG *She was subjected to constant interruptions.*
endure EG *The company endured heavy losses.*
experience EG *They seem to experience more distress than the others.*
go through EG *I wouldn't like to go through that again.*
suffer EG *The peace process had suffered a serious setback.*

undermine VERB

to make something less secure or strong
EG *You're trying to undermine my confidence again.*
impair EG *Their actions will impair France's national interests.*
sap EG *I was afraid the illness had sapped my strength.*
subvert EG *an attempt to subvert their culture from within*
weaken EG *Her authority had been fatally weakened.*

WORD POWER

▶ **Antonym**
strengthen

❶ understand VERB

to know what someone means
EG *Do you understand what I'm saying?*
catch on INFORMAL EG *I didn't catch on immediately to what he meant.*
comprehend EG *Whenever she failed to comprehend, she just laughed.*
follow EG *I don't follow you at all.*
get EG *Did you get that joke?*

grasp EG *He instantly grasped that they were talking about him.*
see EG *"I see", she said at last.*
take in EG *too much to take in at once*

❷ understand VERB
to know why or how something is happening
EG *too young to understand what was going on*
appreciate EG *You must appreciate how important this is.*
comprehend EG *I just cannot comprehend your viewpoint.*
fathom EG *His attitude was hard to fathom.*
grasp EG *We immediately grasped the seriousness of the crisis.*
realize EG *People just don't realize how serious it could be.*

WORD POWER
▷ **Synonyms**
conceive
discern

❸ understand VERB
to hear of something
EG *I understand she hasn't been well.*
believe EG *She's coming back tomorrow, I believe.*
gather EG *We gather the report is critical of the judge.*
hear EG *I hear you've been having some problems.*
learn EG *On learning who he was, I wanted to meet him.*

❶ understanding NOUN
a knowledge of something
EG *a basic understanding of computers*
appreciation EG *some appreciation of the problems of consumers*
comprehension EG *completely beyond our comprehension*
grasp EG *a good grasp of foreign languages*
knowledge EG *I have no knowledge of his business affairs.*

perception EG *Her questions showed a shrewd perception.*

❷ understanding NOUN
an informal agreement
EG *There was an understanding between us.*
accord EG *trying to reach an accord*
agreement EG *A new defence agreement was signed last month.*
pact EG *an electoral pact between the parties*

❸ understanding ADJECTIVE
having a sympathetic nature
EG *Fortunately he had an understanding wife.*
compassionate EG *a deeply compassionate man*
considerate EG *They should be more considerate towards the prisoners.*
sensitive EG *He was always sensitive and caring.*
sympathetic EG *a sympathetic listener*

undertaking NOUN
a task which you have agreed to do
EG *Organizing the show has been a massive undertaking.*
affair EG *It's going to be a tricky affair to arrange.*
business EG *Livestock farming is an arduous and difficult business.*
endeavour EG *an endeavour that was bound to end in failure*
enterprise EG *a risky enterprise such as horse breeding*
job EG *What made you decide to take this job on?*
operation EG *the man in charge of the entire operation*
project EG *I can't take responsibility for such a huge project.*
task EG *a task I do not feel equipped to take on*
venture EG *a venture that few were willing to invest in*

uneasy ADJECTIVE
worried that something may be

a b c d e f g h i j k l m n o p q r s t u v w x y z

A B C D E F G H I J K L M N O P Q R S T U V W X Y Z

wrong
EG *I was very uneasy about these developments.*
agitated EG *She seemed agitated about something.*
anxious EG *He admitted he was still anxious about the situation.*
nervous EG *Consumers say they are nervous about their jobs.*
perturbed EG *I am not too perturbed at this setback.*
worried EG *If you're worried about it, just ask for more details.*

WORD POWER

▷ **Synonyms**
apprehensive
discomposed
restive

▶ **Antonym**
comfortable

unemployed ADJECTIVE
not having a job
EG *an unemployed mechanic*
idle EG *He has been idle for almost a month.*
jobless EG *One in four people are now jobless.*
redundant EG *aid for the 30,000 redundant miners*

WORD POWER

▶ **Antonym**
employed

❶ uneven ADJECTIVE
having an unlevel or rough surface
EG *I tripped and fell on an uneven pavement.*
bumpy EG *bumpy cobbled streets*
not level EG *It was hard to walk because the road was not level.*
not smooth EG *The icing isn't smooth enough.*
rough EG *She picked her way across the rough ground.*

WORD POWER

▶ **Antonym**
level

❷ uneven ADJECTIVE
not the same or consistent
EG *six lines of uneven length*
fluctuating EG *a fluctuating temperature*
inconsistent EG *Their performance was inconsistent over the whole season.*
irregular EG *at irregular intervals*
patchy EG *Her career has been patchy.*
variable EG *The potassium content of food is very variable.*

WORD POWER

▶ **Antonym**
even

unexpected ADJECTIVE
not considered likely to happen
EG *His death was completely unexpected.*
astonishing EG *What an astonishing piece of good luck!*
chance EG *a chance meeting*
surprising EG *a most surprising turn of events*
unforeseen EG *The show was cancelled due to unforeseen circumstances.*

WORD POWER

▷ **Synonyms**
fortuitous
unanticipated

unfair ADJECTIVE
without right or justice
EG *It was unfair that he should suffer so much.*
unjust EG *an unjust decision*
wrong EG *It would be wrong to allow the case to go any further.*

wrongful EG *his claim for wrongful dismissal*

WORD POWER

▷ **Synonyms**
inequitable
iniquitous

▶ **Antonym**
fair

unfaithful ADJECTIVE
not being faithful to your partner
EG *He was unfaithful to her for years.*
adulterous EG *an adulterous relationship*
two-timing INFORMAL EG *She called him a two-timing rat.*

WORD POWER

▶ **Antonym**
faithful

unfamiliar ADJECTIVE
not having been seen or heard of before
EG *She grew many plants which were unfamiliar to me.*
alien EG *transplanted into an alien culture*
exotic EG *filmed in an exotic location*
foreign EG *This was a foreign country, so unlike his own.*
new EG *This was a new experience for me.*
novel EG *having to cope with many novel situations*
strange EG *All these faces were strange to me.*
unknown EG *I'd discovered a writer quite unknown to me.*

unfriendly ADJECTIVE
not showing any warmth or kindness
EG *He can expect an unfriendly welcome.*
aloof EG *His manner was aloof.*
antagonistic EG *They were always antagonistic to newcomers.*
cold EG *She was a cold, unfeeling woman.*
disagreeable EG *He may be clever but he's most disagreeable.*
hostile EG *The prisoner eyed him in hostile silence.*
unkind EG *They're always unkind to newcomers.*

WORD POWER

▷ **Synonyms**
ill-disposed
uncongenial

▶ **Antonym**
friendly

ungrateful ADJECTIVE
not appreciating the things you have
EG *the most miserable and ungrateful people on earth*
unappreciative EG *He was unappreciative of our efforts.*
unthankful EG *mercenary players and unthankful supporters*

WORD POWER

▶ **Antonym**
grateful

unhappy ADJECTIVE
feeling sad or depressed
EG *He was a shy, sometimes unhappy man.*
depressed EG *She's depressed about this whole situation.*
despondent EG *After the interview John was despondent.*
down EG *They felt really down after they spoke to him.*
miserable EG *My job made me really miserable sometimes.*
sad EG *I felt sad to leave our little house.*

A
B
C
D
E
F
G
H
I
J
K
L
M
N
O
P
Q
R
S
T
U
V
W
X
Y
Z

WORD POWER

▷ **Synonyms**
crestfallen
disconsolate
sorrowful

► **Antonym**
happy

❶ unhealthy ADJECTIVE
likely to cause illness
EG *an unhealthy lifestyle*
bad for you EG *the argument that eating meat is bad for you*
harmful EG *Try to avoid harmful habits like smoking.*
insanitary EG *the insanitary conditions of slums*
noxious EG *factories belching out noxious fumes*
unwholesome EG *an epidemic originating from the unwholesome food they ate*

WORD POWER

► **Antonym**
healthy

❷ unhealthy ADJECTIVE
not well
EG *an unhealthy looking man with a bad complexion*
ailing EG *The President is said to be ailing.*
crook AUSTRALIAN AND NEW ZEALAND; INFORMAL EG *I'm sorry to hear you've been crook, mate.*
ill EG *He didn't look at all ill when I last saw him.*
not well EG *When I'm not well, she looks after me.*
poorly BRITISH; INFORMAL EG *She's still poorly after that bout of pneumonia.*
sick EG *He's very sick and he needs treatment.*
unwell EG *an infection which could make you very unwell*

WORD POWER

► **Antonym**
healthy

unimportant ADJECTIVE
having little significance or importance
EG *The difference in their ages seemed unimportant at the time.*
insignificant EG *In 1949, Bonn was a small, insignificant city.*
minor EG *a minor inconvenience*
paltry EG *They had little interest in paltry domestic concerns.*
slight EG *We have a slight problem.*
trivial EG *She waved aside the trivial details.*

WORD POWER

► **Antonym**
important

uninterested ADJECTIVE
not interested in something
EG *I'm completely uninterested in anything you have to say.*
apathetic EG *apathetic about politics*
bored EG *She looked bored with the whole performance.*
impassive EG *He remained impassive while she ranted on.*
indifferent EG *He is totally indifferent to our problems.*
nonchalant EG *"Suit yourself," I said, trying to sound nonchalant.*
passive EG *That passive attitude of his drives me mad.*
unconcerned EG *She is unconcerned about anything except herself.*

WORD POWER

► **Antonym**
interested

❶ union NOUN
an organization of people or groups with mutual interests
EG *a trades union*

association EG *a member of several different associations*
coalition EG *governed by a coalition of three parties*
confederation EG *a confederation of mini-states*
federation EG *a federation of six separate agencies*
league EG *the League of Nations*

❷ **union** NOUN
the joining together of two or more things
EG *The majority voted for union with Russia.*
amalgamation EG *an amalgamation of two organizations*
blend EG *a blend of traditional charm and modern amenities*
combination EG *the combination of science and art*
fusion EG *fusions of jazz and pop*
mixture EG *a mixture of nuts, raisins, and capers*

WORD POWER
▷ **Synonyms**
amalgam
conjunction
synthesis

unite VERB
to join together and act as a group
EG *We must unite to fight our common enemy.*
collaborate EG *They all collaborated on the project.*
combine EG *The companies have combined to form a multinational.*
join EG *People of all kinds joined to make a dignified protest.*
join forces EG *The two parties are joining forces.*
link up EG *the first time the two armies have linked up*
merge EG *The media group hopes to merge with its rival company.*
pull together EG *The staff and management are pulling together to*
save the company.
work together EG *industry and government working together*

WORD POWER
▶ **Antonym**
divide

universal ADJECTIVE
relating to everyone or to the whole universe
EG *These programmes have a universal appeal.*
common EG *The common view is that it is a good thing.*
general EG *This project should raise general awareness about the problem.*
unlimited EG *destruction on an unlimited scale*
widespread EG *Food shortages are widespread.*
worldwide EG *the fear of a worldwide epidemic*

WORD POWER
▷ **Synonyms**
catholic
omnipresent
overarching

unkind ADJECTIVE
lacking in kindness and consideration
EG *It's very unkind to describe her in those terms.*
cruel EG *Children can be so cruel.*
malicious EG *spreading malicious gossip*
mean EG *I'd feel mean saying no.*
nasty EG *What nasty little snobs you are!*
spiteful EG *How can you say such spiteful things about us?*
thoughtless EG *a small minority of thoughtless and inconsiderate people*

a b c d e f g h i j k l m n o p q r s t u v w x y z

A
B
C
D
E
F
G
H
I
J
K
L
M
N
O
P
Q
R
S
T
U
V
W
X
Y
Z

WORD POWER

▶ **Antonym**
kind

unknown ADJECTIVE
not familiar or famous
EG *He was an unknown writer at that time.*
humble EG *He started out as a humble fisherman.*
obscure EG *an obscure Greek composer*
unfamiliar EG *There were several unfamiliar names on the list.*
unsung EG *among the unsung heroes of our time*

WORD POWER

▶ **Antonym**
famous

unlike ADJECTIVE
different from
EG *She was unlike him in every way.*
different from EG *I've always felt different from most people.*
dissimilar to EG *a cultural background not dissimilar to our own*
distinct from EG *Their cuisines are quite distinct from each other.*
divergent from FORMAL EG *That viewpoint is not much divergent from that of his predecessor.*
far from EG *His politics are not all that far from mine.*

WORD POWER

▶ **Antonym**
like

unlikely ADJECTIVE
probably not true or likely to happen
EG *a military coup seems unlikely*
implausible EG *a film with an implausible ending*
incredible EG *an incredible pack of lies*
unbelievable EG *I know it sounds unbelievable, but I wasn't there that*

day.
unconvincing EG *He came up with a very unconvincing excuse.*

WORD POWER

▶ **Antonym**
likely

unlucky ADJECTIVE
having bad luck
EG *He was unlucky not to score during the first half.*
cursed EG *the most cursed family in history*
hapless EG *a hapless victim of chance*
luckless EG *the luckless parents of a difficult child*
unfortunate EG *Some unfortunate person nearby could be injured.*
wretched EG *wretched people who had to sell or starve*

WORD POWER

▶ **Antonym**
lucky

unnecessary ADJECTIVE
completely needless
EG *He frowns upon unnecessary expense.*
needless EG *causing needless panic*
pointless EG *pointless meetings*
uncalled-for EG *uncalled-for rudeness*

WORD POWER

▶ **Antonym**
necessary

❶ **unpleasant** ADJECTIVE
causing feelings of discomfort or dislike
EG *It has a very unpleasant smell.*
bad EG *I have some bad news.*
disagreeable EG *a disagreeable experience*
distasteful EG *I find her gossip distasteful.*

nasty EG *This divorce could turn nasty.*
repulsive EG *repulsive fat white slugs*
unpalatable EG *Only then did I learn the unpalatable truth.*

WORD POWER

▶ **Antonym**
pleasant

❷ **unpleasant** ADJECTIVE
rude or unfriendly
EG *a thoroughly unpleasant person*
disagreeable EG *He may be clever, but he's a very disagreeable man.*
horrid EG *I must have been a horrid little girl.*
objectionable EG *His tone was highly objectionable.*
obnoxious EG *Clarissa's obnoxious brother James*
rude EG *He was frequently rude to waiters and servants.*
unfriendly EG *spoken in a rather unfriendly voice*

WORD POWER

▶ **Antonym**
pleasant

unpopular ADJECTIVE
disliked by most people
EG *an unpopular idea*
detested EG *The rebels toppled the detested dictator.*
disliked EG *one of the most disliked choices on offer*
shunned EG *the shunned former minister*
undesirable EG *all sorts of undesirable effects on health*

WORD POWER

▶ **Antonym**
popular

unpredictable ADJECTIVE
unable to be foreseen
EG *Britain's notoriously unpredictable*
weather
chance EG *A chance meeting can change your life.*
doubtful EG *The outcome remains doubtful.*
hit and miss INFORMAL EG *Farming can be a very hit and miss affair.*
unforeseeable EG *unforeseeable weather conditions*

WORD POWER

▶ **Antonym**
predictable

unsatisfactory ADJECTIVE
not good enough
EG *His work was judged unsatisfactory.*
disappointing EG *The results were disappointing.*
inadequate EG *The problem goes far beyond inadequate staffing.*
mediocre EG *a mediocre string of performances*
poor EG *Her school record was poor at first.*
unacceptable EG *The quality of his work was unacceptable.*

WORD POWER

▶ **Antonym**
satisfactory

unsteady ADJECTIVE
not held or fixed securely and likely to fall over
EG *a slightly unsteady item of furniture*
precarious EG *The beds are precarious-looking hammocks strung from the walls.*
rickety EG *She stood on a rickety old table.*
shaky EG *He climbed up the shaky ladder to the scaffold.*
tottering EG *a tottering pile of bricks*
unsafe EG *That bridge looks decidedly unsafe to me.*
unstable EG *funds used to demolish dangerously unstable buildings*

a
b
c
d
e
f
g
h
i
j
k
l
m
n
o
p
q
r
s
t
u
v
w
x
y
z

wobbly EG *cat-scratched upholstery and wobbly chairs*

WORD POWER

▶ **Antonym**
steady

unsuitable ADJECTIVE
not appropriate for a purpose
EG *Her shoes were unsuitable for walking any distance.*
improper EG *an improper diet*
inappropriate EG *inappropriate use of the Internet*
unacceptable EG *using completely unacceptable language*
unfit EG *unfit for human habitation*

WORD POWER

▷ **Synonyms**
inapposite
unseemly

▶ **Antonym**
suitable

untidy ADJECTIVE
not neatly arranged
EG *The place quickly became untidy.*
bedraggled EG *My hair was a bedraggled mess.*
chaotic EG *the chaotic mess of papers on his desk*
cluttered EG *There was no space on the cluttered worktop.*
jumbled EG *We moved our supplies into a jumbled heap.*
messy EG *She was a good, if messy, cook.*
unkempt EG *the unkempt grass in front of the house*

WORD POWER

▷ **Synonyms**
disordered
shambolic

▶ **Antonym**
tidy

untrue ADJECTIVE
not true
EG *The allegations were completely untrue.*
erroneous EG *an erroneous description*
false EG *He gave a false name and address.*
fictitious EG *the source of the fictitious rumours*
inaccurate EG *the passing on of inaccurate or misleading information*
incorrect EG *an incorrect account of the sequence of events*
misleading EG *It would be misleading to say we were friends.*
mistaken EG *I had a mistaken idea of what had happened.*

WORD POWER

▶ **Antonym**
true

unusual ADJECTIVE
not occurring very often
EG *many rare and unusual plants*
curious EG *a curious mixture of ancient and modern*
exceptional EG *exceptional circumstances*
extraordinary EG *What an extraordinary thing to happen!*
rare EG *one of the rarest species in the world*
uncommon EG *It's a very uncommon surname.*
unconventional EG *produced by an unconventional technique*

WORD POWER

▷ **Synonyms**
atypical
unwonted

▶ **Antonym**
common

unwell ADJECTIVE
ill or sick

EG *He felt unwell and had to go home early.*
ailing EG *The President is said to be ailing.*
crook AUSTRALIAN AND NEW ZEALAND; INFORMAL EG *I'm sorry to hear you've been crook, mate.*
ill EG *Payne was seriously ill with pneumonia.*
poorly BRITISH; INFORMAL EG *Julie is still poorly after her bout of flu.*
queasy EG *I always feel queasy on boats.*
sick EG *He's very sick and he needs treatment.*

WORD POWER

▷ **Synonyms**
indisposed
under the weather

▶ **Antonym**
well

unwilling ADJECTIVE
not wanting to do something
EG *an unwilling participant in school politics*
averse EG *I'm not averse to going along with the suggestion.*
grudging EG *a grudging acceptance of the situation*
loath EG *She is loath to give up her hard-earned liberty.*
reluctant EG *They were reluctant to get involved at first.*

WORD POWER

▶ **Antonym**
willing

unwise ADJECTIVE
foolish or not sensible
EG *It would be unwise to expect too much of her.*
daft EG *You'd be daft to get on the wrong side of him.*
foolish EG *It was foolish to risk injury like that.*

idiotic EG *What an idiotic thing to do!*
irresponsible EG *irresponsible plans for tax cuts*
rash EG *Don't panic or do anything rash.*
senseless EG *It would be senseless to try and stop him now.*
silly EG *You're not going to go and do something silly, are you?*
stupid EG *I've had enough of your stupid suggestions.*

WORD POWER

▷ **Synonyms**
imprudent
injudicious

▶ **Antonym**
wise

upkeep NOUN
the process and cost of maintaining something
EG *The money will be used for the upkeep of the grounds.*
keep EG *He does not contribute towards his keep.*
maintenance EG *the regular maintenance of government buildings*
overheads EG *We must cut our overheads or we shall have to close.*
preservation EG *the preservation of historical sites*
running EG *The running of the house took up all her time.*

❶ upset ADJECTIVE
feeling unhappy about something
EG *She was very upset when she heard the news.*
agitated EG *in an excited and agitated state*
distressed EG *The animals were distressed by the noise.*
frantic EG *frantic with worry*
hurt EG *I was very hurt when they refused.*
troubled EG *He sounded deeply troubled.*

a b c d e f g h i j k l m n o p q r s t u v w x y z

A
B
C
D
E
F
G
H
I
J
K
L
M
N
O
P
Q
R
S
T
U
V
W
X
Y
Z

unhappy EG *The divorce made him very unhappy.*

❷ upset VERB
to make someone worried or unhappy
EG *The whole incident upset me terribly.*
agitate EG *The thought agitates her.*
bother EG *Don't let his manner bother you.*
distress EG *The whole thing really distressed him.*
disturb EG *These dreams disturb me for days afterwards.*
grieve EG *deeply grieved by their suffering*
ruffle EG *She doesn't get ruffled by anything.*

WORD POWER

▷ **Synonyms**
discompose
faze
perturb

❸ upset VERB
to turn something over accidentally
EG *Don't upset that pile of papers.*
capsize EG *He capsized the boat through his carelessness.*
knock over EG *The kitten knocked over the vase.*
overturn EG *She overturned her glass of wine as she stood up.*
spill EG *The waiter spilled the drinks all over the table.*

❶ urge NOUN
a strong wish to do something
EG *stifling the urge to scream*
compulsion EG *a compulsion to write*
desire EG *I had a strong desire to help and care for people.*
drive EG *a demonic drive to succeed*
impulse EG *Peter resisted an impulse to smile.*
longing EG *his longing to return home*
wish EG *She had a genuine wish to make amends.*

❷ urge VERB
to try hard to persuade someone
EG *He urged the government to change the law.*
beg EG *I begged him to leave me alone.*
beseech EG *Her eyes beseeched him to show mercy.*
implore EG *He left early, although they implored him to stay.*
plead EG *kneeling on the floor pleading for mercy*
press EG *The unions are pressing him to stand firm.*

WORD POWER

▷ **Synonyms**
entreat
exhort
solicit

urgent ADJECTIVE
needing to be dealt with quickly
EG *an urgent need for food and water*
compelling EG *There are compelling reasons to act swiftly.*
immediate EG *The immediate problem is transportation.*
imperative EG *It is imperative we end up with a win.*
pressing EG *one of our most pressing problems*

❶ use VERB
to perform a task with something
EG *Use a sharp knife to trim the edges.*
apply EG *The company applies this technology to solve practical problems.*
employ EG *the methods employed in the study*
operate EG *Can you operate a fax machine?*
utilize EG *The body utilizes many different minerals.*

WORD POWER

▷ **Synonyms**
avail oneself of
ply

2 use NOUN
the act of using something
EG *the use of force*
application EG *Her theory was put into practical application.*
employment EG *the employment of completely new methods*
operation EG *the operation of the computer mouse*
usage EG *Parts of the motor wore out because of constant usage.*

3 use NOUN
the purpose for which something is utilized
EG *of no practical use whatsoever*
end EG *The police force was manipulated for political ends.*
object EG *the object of the exercise*
point EG *I don't see the point of a thing like that.*
purpose EG *It is wrong to use it for military purposes.*

useful ADJECTIVE
something which helps or makes things easier
EG *a great deal of useful information*
beneficial EG *It may be beneficial to study the relevant guidelines.*
effective EG *Antibiotics are effective against this organism.*
helpful EG *a number of helpful booklets*
practical EG *practical suggestions for healthy eating*
valuable EG *Here are a few valuable tips to help you to succeed.*
worthwhile EG *a worthwhile source of income*

WORD POWER

▶ **Antonym**
useless

useless ADJECTIVE
not suitable or useful
EG *We realized that our money was useless here.*
futile EG *It would be futile to make any further attempts.*
impractical EG *A tripod is impractical when following animals on the move.*
unproductive EG *increasingly unproductive land*
unsuitable EG *This tool is completely unsuitable for use with metal.*
worthless EG *The old skills are worthless now.*

WORD POWER

▷ **Synonyms**
disadvantageous
ineffectual
unavailing

▶ **Antonym**
useful

usual ADJECTIVE
done or happening most often
EG *sitting at his usual table*
accustomed EG *She acted with her accustomed shrewdness.*
common EG *the commonest cause of death*
customary EG *It's customary to offer guests a drink.*
habitual EG *He soon recovered his habitual geniality.*
normal EG *That's quite normal for a Friday.*
regular EG *samples from one of their regular suppliers*
standard EG *It was standard practice to put them outside.*

utter ADJECTIVE
complete or total

a
b
c
d
e
f
g
h
i
j
k
l
m
n
o
p
q
r
s
t
u
v
w
x
y
z

A
B
C
D
E
F
G
H
I
J
K
L
M
N
O
P
Q
R
S
T
U ▸
V
W
X
Y
Z

EG *scenes of utter chaos*
absolute EG *This is absolute madness!*
complete EG *a complete mess*
consummate EG *a consummate professional*
out-and-out EG *an out-and-out lie*
outright EG *an outright rejection of the deal*
perfect EG *a perfect stranger*

pure EG *She did it out of pure malice.*
sheer EG *an act of sheer stupidity*
thorough EG *She is a thorough snob.*
total EG *a total failure*

WORD POWER

▷ **Synonyms**
unconditional
unmitigated
unqualified

Vv

vague ADJECTIVE
not clearly expressed or clearly visible
EG *vague promises about raising standards*
hazy EG *Many details remain hazy.*
indefinite EG *at some indefinite time in the future*
indistinct EG *The lettering was worn and indistinct.*
loose EG *a loose translation*
uncertain EG *Students are facing an uncertain future.*
unclear EG *The proposals were sketchy and unclear.*

WORD POWER

▷ **Synonyms**
ill-defined
indeterminate
nebulous

▶ **Antonym**
definite

❶ **vain** ADJECTIVE
very proud of your looks or qualities
EG *I think he is shallow and vain.*
conceited EG *They had grown too conceited and pleased with themselves.*
egotistical EG *an egotistical show-off*
ostentatious EG *He was generous with his money without being ostentatious.*
proud EG *She was said to be proud and arrogant.*
stuck-up INFORMAL EG *She was a famous actress, but she wasn't a bit stuck-up.*

WORD POWER

▷ **Synonyms**
narcissistic
swaggering

❷ **vain** ADJECTIVE
not successful in achieving what was intended
EG *He made a vain effort to cheer her up.*
abortive EG *the abortive coup attempt*
fruitless EG *It was a fruitless search.*
futile EG *their futile attempts to avoid publicity*
unproductive EG *an unproductive strategy*
useless EG *a useless punishment which fails to stop crime*

WORD POWER

▶ **Antonym**
successful

❸ **vain** in vain ADJECTIVE
unsuccessful in achieving what was intended
EG *Her complaints were in vain.*
fruitless EG *Four years of negotiation were fruitless.*
to no avail EG *His protests were to no avail.*
unsuccessful EG *Previous attempts have been unsuccessful.*
wasted EG *Their efforts were wasted.*

valley NOUN

Types of valley
canyon
chasm
coomb
cwm (*Welsh*)
dale
defile
dell
depression
dingle
glen
gorge
gulch
gully

A
B
C
D
E
F
G
H
I
J
K
L
M
N
O
P
Q
R
S
T
U
V
W
X
Y
Z

hollow
ravine
strath (*Scottish*)
vale

➊ valuable ADJECTIVE
having great importance or
usefulness
EG *The experience was very valuable.*
beneficial EG *Using computers has a
beneficial effect on learning.*
helpful EG *a number of helpful
booklets*
important EG *Her sons are the most
important thing in her life.*
prized EG *one of the gallery's most
prized possessions*
useful EG *a mine of useful
information*
worthwhile EG *a worthwhile source
of income*

WORD POWER

▷ **Synonyms**
cherished
esteemed
treasured

▶ **Antonym**
useless

➋ valuable ADJECTIVE
worth a lot of money
EG *valuable old books*
costly EG *a small and costly bottle of
scent*
expensive EG *exclusive, expensive
possessions*
precious EG *rings set with precious
jewels*

WORD POWER

▶ **Antonym**
worthless

valuables PLURAL NOUN
the things you own that cost a lot of
money
EG *Leave your valuables in the hotel
safe.*

heirlooms EG *family heirlooms*
treasures EG *The house was full of
art treasures.*

➊ value NOUN
the importance or usefulness of
something
EG *Studies are needed to see if these
therapies have any value.*
advantage EG *the great advantage
of this method*
benefit EG *They see no benefit in
educating these children.*
effectiveness EG *the effectiveness of
the new system*
importance EG *They have always
placed great importance on live
performances.*
merit EG *the artistic merit of their
work*
use EG *This is of no use to anyone.*
usefulness EG *the usefulness of the
Internet in disseminating new ideas*
virtue EG *the great virtue of modern
technology*
worth EG *This system has already
proved its worth.*

➋ value NOUN
the amount of money that
something is worth
EG *The value of his house has risen by
more than 100%.*
cost EG *the cost of a loaf of bread*
market price EG *buying shares at
the current market price*
price EG *a sharp increase in the price
of petrol*
selling price EG *the average selling
price of a new home*
worth EG *He sold the car for less than
half its worth.*

➌ value VERB
to appreciate something and think it
is important
EG *Do you value your friends enough?*
appreciate EG *I would appreciate
your advice.*
cherish EG *Cherish every moment*

you have with your children.
have a high opinion of EG *Your boss seems to have a high opinion of you.*
prize EG *These items are prized by collectors.*
rate highly EG *He is an excellent keeper and I rate him highly.*
respect EG *I respect his talent as a pianist.*
treasure EG *memories I will treasure for the rest of my life*

4 value VERB
to decide how much money something is worth
EG *I have had my jewellery valued for insurance purposes.*
appraise EG *He was called in to appraise and sell the cottage.*
assess EG *Experts are now assessing the cost of the restoration.*
cost EG *an operation costed at around $649m*
estimate EG *a personal fortune estimated at more than $400m*
evaluate EG *The company needs to evaluate the cost of leasing the building.*
price EG *The property was priced at less than £1m.*

1 vanish VERB
to disappear
EG *The moon vanished behind a cloud.*
become invisible EG *The plane became invisible in the clouds.*
be lost to view EG *They watched the ship until it was lost to view.*
disappear EG *The aircraft disappeared off the radar.*
fade EG *We watched the harbour fade into the mist.*
recede EG *Gradually Luke receded into the distance.*

WORD POWER

▶ **Antonym**
appear

---

2 vanish VERB
to cease to exist
EG *Dinosaurs vanished from the earth millions of years ago.*
become extinct EG *Without help, these animals will become extinct.*
cease EG *At one o'clock the rain ceased.*
cease to exist EG *Without trees, the world as we know it would cease to exist.*
die out EG *Britain's bear population died out about 2,000 years ago.*
dissolve EG *The crowds dissolved and we were alone.*
evaporate EG *All my pleasure evaporated when I saw him.*
fade away EG *Her black mood faded away.*
go away EG *All she wanted was for the pain to go away.*
melt away EG *All my cares melted away.*
pass EG *Breathe deeply and the panic attack will pass.*

vanquish VERB
to defeat someone completely
EG *a happy ending in which the hero vanquishes the monsters*
beat EG *the team that beat us in the finals*
conquer EG *a great warrior who conquers the enemies of his people*
crush EG *their bid to crush the rebels*
defeat EG *His guerrillas defeated the colonial army in 1954.*
overcome EG *They overcame the opposition to win the cup.*
rout EG *the battle at which the Norman army routed the English*
trounce EG *Australia trounced France by 60 points to 4.*

variation NOUN
a change from the normal or usual pattern
EG *a variation of the same route*
alteration EG *some alterations in your diet*

a b c d e f g h i j k l m n o p q r s t u **v** w x y z

A B C D E F G H I J K L M N O P Q R S T U V W X Y Z

change EG *a change of attitude*
departure EG *Her new novel is a departure from her previous work.*
deviation EG *Deviation from the norm is not tolerated.*
difference EG *a noticeable difference in his behaviour*
diversion EG *a welcome diversion from the daily grind*

❶ variety NOUN
a number of different kinds of things
EG *a wide variety of readers*
array EG *an attractive array of bright colours*
assortment EG *an assortment of pets*
collection EG *a huge collection of books*
medley EG *a medley of vegetables*
mixture EG *a mixture of sweets*
range EG *a range of sun-care products*

WORD POWER

▷ **Synonyms**
cross section
miscellany
multiplicity

❷ variety NOUN
a particular type of something
EG *a new variety of celery*
category EG *There are three broad categories of soil.*
class EG *several classes of butterflies*
kind EG *different kinds of roses*
sort EG *several articles of this sort*
strain EG *a new strain of the virus*
type EG *What type of guns were they?*

various ADJECTIVE
of several different types
EG *trees of various sorts*
assorted EG *swimsuits in assorted colours*
different EG *different brands of drinks*
disparate EG *the disparate cultures of India*

diverse EG *Society is more diverse than ever before.*
miscellaneous EG *a hoard of miscellaneous junk*
sundry EG *sundry journalists and lawyers*

WORD POWER

▷ **Synonyms**
heterogeneous
manifold

❶ vary VERB
to change to something different
EG *weather patterns vary greatly*
alter EG *During the course of a day the light alters constantly.*
alternate EG *My moods alternate with alarming rapidity.*
change EG *My feelings haven't changed.*
fluctuate EG *Weight may fluctuate markedly.*

❷ vary VERB
to introduce changes in something
EG *Vary your routes as much as possible.*
alternate EG *Alternate the chunks of fish with chunks of vegetable.*
diversify EG *They decided to diversify their products.*
modify EG *The government refuses to modify its position.*

WORD POWER

▷ **Synonyms**
permutate
reorder

vast ADJECTIVE
extremely large
EG *farmers who own vast stretches of land*
colossal EG *a colossal statue*
enormous EG *The main bedroom is enormous.*
giant EG *a giant meteorite heading for the earth*
gigantic EG *a gigantic shopping mall*

great EG *a great hall as long as a church*
huge EG *a huge crowd*
immense EG *an immense castle*
massive EG *a massive theme park*

WORD POWER

▶ **Antonym**
tiny

---

verdict NOUN
a decision or opinion on something
EG *The doctor's verdict was that he was fine.*
conclusion EG *I've come to the conclusion that she's lying.*
decision EG *The editor's decision is final.*
finding EG *The court announced its findings.*
judgment EG *My judgment is that things are going to get worse.*
opinion EG *You should seek a medical opinion.*

very ADVERB
to a great degree
EG *very bad dreams*
deeply EG *I was deeply sorry to hear about your loss.*
extremely EG *My mobile phone is extremely useful.*
greatly EG *I was greatly relieved when he finally arrived.*
highly EG *Mr Singh was a highly successful salesman.*
really EG *I know her really well.*
terribly EG *I'm terribly sorry to bother you.*

WORD POWER

▷ **Synonyms**
exceedingly
profoundly
remarkably

---

❶ **veto** VERB
to forbid something
EG *Treasury officials vetoed the plans.*
ban EG *The authorities have banned the advertisement.*
forbid EG *Most airlines forbid the use of mobile phones on their planes.*
prohibit EG *The government intends to prohibit all trade with the country.*

❷ **veto** NOUN
the act of forbidding or power to forbid something
EG *Dr. Baker has the power of veto.*
ban EG *the arms ban on the Bosnian government*
prohibition EG *a prohibition on nuclear testing*

victory NOUN
a success in a battle or competition
EG *his 15th consecutive victory in a doubles final*
laurels EG *a former British champion took the laurels in this event*
success EG *league and cup successes*
superiority EG *United Nations air forces won air superiority.*
triumph EG *last year's Republican triumph in the elections*
win EG *eight wins in nine games*

WORD POWER

▶ **Antonym**
defeat

---

❶ **view** NOUN
a personal opinion
EG *his political views*
attitude EG *other people's attitudes towards you*
belief EG *people's beliefs about crime*
conviction EG *a firm conviction that things have improved*
feeling EG *It is my feeling that Klein is right.*
opinion EG *a favourable opinion of our neighbours*
point of view EG *an unusual point of view on the subject*

❷ **view** NOUN
the things you can see from a particular place
EG *There was a beautiful view from the*

a
b
c
d
e
f
g
h
i
j
k
l
m
n
o
p
q
r
s
t
u
v
w
x
y
z

A
B
C
D
E
F
G
H
I
J
K
L
M
N
O
P
Q
R
S
T
U
V
W
X
Y
Z

window.
aspect EG *the Yorkshire hills which give the cottage a lovely aspect*
landscape EG *Arizona's desert landscape*
panorama EG *a panorama of fertile valleys*
perspective EG *the aerial perspective of St Paul's Cathedral*
scene EG *Wright surveyed the scene from his chosen seat.*
spectacle EG *a sweeping spectacle of rugged peaks*

WORD POWER

▷ **Synonyms**
prospect
vista

---

❸ view VERB
to think of something in a particular way
EG *They viewed me with contempt.*
consider EG *We consider them to be our friends.*
deem FORMAL EG *His ideas were deemed unacceptable.*
judge EG *His work was judged unsatisfactory.*
regard EG *They regard the tax as unfair.*

viewpoint NOUN
an attitude towards something
EG *We all have our own personal viewpoints.*
attitude EG *other people's attitudes towards you*
belief EG *people's beliefs about crime*
conviction EG *a very personal, political conviction*
feeling EG *What are your feelings on this matter?*
opinion EG *a favourable opinion of our neighbours*
point of view EG *an unusual point of view on the subject*

❶ violence NOUN
behaviour which is intended to hurt

people
EG *Twenty people were killed in the violence.*
bloodshed EG *The government must avoid further bloodshed.*
brutality EG *the brutality of the war in Vietnam*
cruelty EG *Human beings are capable of such cruelty to each other.*
force EG *If you use any force, I shall inform the police.*
savagery EG *acts of vicious savagery*
terrorism EG *political terrorism in the 19th century*

❷ violence NOUN
force and energy
EG *Amy spoke with sudden violence.*
fervour EG *views he had put forward with fervour*
force EG *She expressed her feelings with some force.*
harshness EG *the harshness of her words*
intensity EG *His voice hoarsened with intensity.*
severity EG *the severity of her scoldings*
vehemence EG *Tweed was taken aback by her vehemence.*

❶ violent ADJECTIVE
intending to hurt or kill people
EG *violent criminals*
bloodthirsty EG *a bloodthirsty monster*
brutal EG *a brutal crime*
cruel EG *He is cruel towards animals.*
murderous EG *a murderous bank-robber*
savage EG *savage warriors*
vicious EG *He was a cruel and vicious man.*

WORD POWER

▶ **Antonym**
gentle

---

❷ violent ADJECTIVE
happening unexpectedly and with

great force
EG *violent storms*
powerful EG *He was caught by a powerful blow.*
raging EG *a raging flood*
rough EG *A wooden ship sank in rough seas.*
strong EG *strong winds and rain*
turbulent EG *the turbulent events of the century*
wild EG *the wild gales sweeping up from the channel*

WORD POWER

▷ **Synonyms**
tempestuous
tumultuous

❸ violent ADJECTIVE
said, felt, or done with great force
EG *the violent reaction to his plans*
acute EG *pain which grew more and more acute*
furious EG *a furious row*
intense EG *a look of intense dislike*
powerful EG *a powerful backlash against the government*
severe EG *a severe emotional shock*
strong EG *strong words*

WORD POWER

▷ **Synonyms**
forcible
passionate
vehement

❶ virtue NOUN
the quality of doing what is morally right
EG *He is a paragon of virtue.*
goodness EG *He has faith in human goodness.*
integrity EG *He was praised for his fairness and integrity.*
morality EG *standards of morality and justice in society*

WORD POWER

▷ **Synonyms**
probity
rectitude
righteousness

❷ virtue NOUN
an advantage something has
EG *the virtue of neatness*
advantage EG *the advantages of the new system*
asset EG *The one asset the job provided was contacts.*
attribute EG *a player with every attribute you could want*
merit EG *the merits of various football teams*
plus INFORMAL EG *The nutrients in milk have pluses and minuses.*
strength EG *the strengths and weaknesses of our position*

❸ virtue by virtue of PREPOSITION
because of
EG *The article stuck in my mind by virtue of one detail.*
as a result of EG *People will feel better as a result of their efforts.*
because of EG *She was promoted because of her experience.*
by dint of EG *He succeeds by dint of hard work.*
on account of EG *The city is popular with tourists on account of its many museums.*
thanks to EG *Thanks to recent research, new treatments are available.*

❶ visible ADJECTIVE
able to be seen
EG *The warning lights were clearly visible.*
clear EG *the clearest pictures ever of Pluto*
conspicuous EG *He felt more conspicuous than he'd have liked.*
distinguishable EG *colours just distinguishable in the dark*

a
b
c
d
e
f
g
h
i
j
k
l
m
n
o
p
q
r
s
t
u
v
w
x
y
z

in sight EG *There wasn't another vehicle in sight.*
observable EG *the observable part of the Universe*
perceptible EG *Daniel gave a barely perceptible nod.*

WORD POWER

▶ Antonym
invisible

2 visible ADJECTIVE
noticeable or evident
EG *There was little visible excitement.*
apparent EG *There is no apparent reason for the crime.*
evident EG *He ate with evident enjoyment.*
manifest EG *his manifest enthusiasm*
noticeable EG *subtle but noticeable changes*
obvious EG *There are obvious dangers.*
plain EG *It is plain a mistake has been made.*

WORD POWER

▷ Synonyms
conspicuous
discernible
patent

1 vision NOUN
a mental picture in which you imagine things
EG *my vision of the future*
conception EG *my conception of a garden*
daydream EG *He learned to escape into daydreams.*
dream EG *his dream of becoming a pilot*
fantasy EG *fantasies of romance and true love*
ideal EG *your ideal of a holiday*
image EG *an image in your mind of what you are looking for*

2 vision NOUN
the ability to imagine future

developments
EG *a total lack of vision and imagination*
foresight EG *They had the foresight to invest in technology.*
imagination EG *He had the imagination to foresee dangers.*
insight EG *the development of insight and understanding*
intuition EG *Her intuition told her something was wrong.*

3 vision NOUN
an experience in which you see things others cannot
EG *She was convinced her visions were real.*
apparition EG *One of the women was the apparition he had seen.*
hallucination EG *The drug can cause hallucinations.*
illusion EG *Perhaps the footprint was an illusion.*
mirage EG *The girl was a mirage, created by his troubled mind.*
phantom EG *People claimed to have seen the phantom.*
spectre EG *a spectre from the other world*

WORD POWER

▷ Synonyms
chimera
phantasm
wraith

1 visit VERB
to go to see and spend time with someone
EG *He wanted to visit his brother in Sydney.*
call on EG *Don't hesitate to call on me.*
go to see EG *I'll go to see him in the hospital.*
look up EG *She looked up friends she had not seen for a while.*

2 visit NOUN
a trip to see a person or place

EG *Helen had recently paid him a visit.*
call EG *He decided to pay a call on Tommy.*
stay EG *An experienced guide is provided during your stay.*
stop EG *The last stop in Mr Cook's tour was Paris.*

❶ vital ADJECTIVE
necessary or very important
EG *a blockade which cut off vital fuel supplies*
central EG *He is central to the whole project.*
critical EG *This decision will be critical to our future.*
crucial EG *the man who played a crucial role in the negotiations*
essential EG *It is essential that you see a doctor soon.*
important EG *the most important piece of evidence in the case*
indispensable EG *an indispensable piece of equipment*
necessary EG *the skills necessary for survival*
pivotal EG *He played a pivotal role in the match.*

❷ vital ADJECTIVE
energetic and full of life
EG *Old age has diminished a once vital person.*
active EG *an active youngster*
dynamic EG *a dynamic and exciting place*
energetic EG *She became a shadow of her happy, energetic self.*
lively EG *a beautiful, lively young girl*
spirited EG *the spirited heroine of this film*
sprightly EG *a sprightly old man*
vivacious EG *She is vivacious and charming.*

vomit VERB
to have food and drink come back up through the mouth
EG *Any product made from milk made him vomit.*

be sick EG *She was sick in the handbasin.*
bring up EG *Certain foods are difficult to bring up.*
chunder AUSTRALIAN AND NEW ZEALAND; SLANG EG *the time you chundered in the taxi*
heave EG *He gasped and heaved and vomited again.*
puke INFORMAL EG *They got drunk and puked out of the window.*
regurgitate EG *swallowing and regurgitating large quantities of water*

❶ vote NOUN
a decision made by allowing people to state their preference
EG *Do you think we should have a vote on that?*
ballot EG *The result of the ballot will be known soon.*
plebiscite FORMAL EG *A plebiscite made Hitler the Chancellor.*
polls EG *In 1945, Churchill was defeated at the polls.*
referendum EG *Estonia planned to hold a referendum on independence.*

❷ vote VERB
to indicate a choice or opinion
EG *It seems that many people would vote for the opposition.*
cast a vote EG *90% of those who cast a vote*
go to the polls EG *Voters are due to go to the polls on Sunday.*
opt EG *The mass of Spaniards opted for democracy.*
return EG *Members will be asked to return a vote for or against the motion.*

❸ vote VERB
to suggest that something should happen
EG *I vote that we all go to Holland.*
propose EG *I propose that we all try to get some sleep.*
recommend EG *I recommend that he be sent home early.*

a b c d e f g h i j k l m n o p q r s t u v w x y z

A
B
C
D
E
F
G
H
I
J
K
L
M
N
O
P
Q
R
S
T
U
V
W
X
Y
Z

suggest EG *I suggest we go round the table and introduce ourselves.*

❶ vulgar ADJECTIVE
socially unacceptable or offensive
EG *vulgar language*
coarse EG *coarse humour*
crude EG *crude pictures*
dirty EG *dirty jokes*
indecent EG *an indecent suggestion*
rude EG *a rude gesture*
uncouth EG *that oafish, uncouth person*

WORD POWER

▷ **Synonyms**
improper
ribald
unrefined

▶ **Antonym**
refined

❷ vulgar ADJECTIVE
showing a lack of taste or quality
EG *I think it's a very vulgar house.*
common EG *She could be a little common at times.*
flashy EG *flashy clothes*

gaudy EG *a gaudy purple-and-orange hat*
tasteless EG *a house with tasteless decor*
tawdry EG *a tawdry seaside town*

WORD POWER

▶ **Antonym**
sophisticated

vulnerable ADJECTIVE
weak and without protection
EG *vulnerable old people*
exposed EG *The west coast is very exposed to Atlantic winds.*
sensitive EG *Most people are highly sensitive to criticism.*
susceptible EG *an area that is susceptible to attack*
weak EG *He spoke up for the weak and defenceless.*

WORD POWER

▷ **Synonyms**
assailable
defenceless
unprotected

Ww

① **wait** VERB
to spend time before something happens
EG *Wait until we get there.*
linger EG *I lingered on for a few days until he arrived.*
pause EG *The crowd paused for a minute, wondering what to do next.*
remain EG *You'll have to remain in hospital for the time being.*
stand by EG *Ships are standing by to evacuate the people.*
stay EG *Stay here while I go for help.*

② **wait** NOUN
a period of time before something happens
EG *They faced a three-hour wait before they could leave.*
delay EG *The accident caused some delay.*
interval EG *a long interval when no-one spoke*
pause EG *There was a pause before he replied.*

wake VERB
to make or become conscious again after sleep
EG *It was still dark when he woke.*
awake EG *We were awoken by the doorbell.*
come to EG *When she came to she found it was raining.*
rouse EG *We roused him at seven so he would be on time.*
stir EG *She shook him and he started to stir.*
waken EG *wakened by the thunder*

① **walk** VERB
to go on foot
EG *I walked slowly along the road.*
→ see Word Study **walk**

② **walk** NOUN
a journey made by walking
EG *We'll have a quick walk while it's fine.*
hike EG *a long hike in the country*

march EG *a day's march north of their objective*
ramble EG *They went for a ramble through the woods.*
stroll EG *After dinner we took a stroll around the city.*
trek EG *He's on a trek across the Antarctic.*

WORD POWER

▷ **Synonyms**
constitutional
perambulation
saunter

③ **walk** NOUN
the way someone moves when walking
EG *Despite his gangling walk he was a good dancer.*
carriage EG *her regal carriage*
gait EG *an awkward gait*
pace EG *moving at a brisk pace down the road*
stride EG *He lengthened his stride to catch up with her.*

wander VERB
to move about in a casual way
EG *They wandered aimlessly around the village.*
cruise EG *A police car cruised by.*
drift EG *The balloon drifted slowly over the countryside.*
ramble EG *freedom to ramble across the moors*
range EG *They range widely in search of food.*
roam EG *Barefoot children roamed the streets.*
stroll EG *We strolled down the street, looking at the shops.*

① **want** VERB
to feel a desire for something
EG *I want a red car for a change.*
covet EG *He coveted his boss's job.*
crave EG *Sometimes she still craved chocolate.*

A
B
C
D
E
F
G
H
I
J
K
L
M
N
O
P
Q
R
S
T
U
V
W
X
Y
Z

desire EG *He could make them do whatever he desired.*
wish EG *I don't wish to know that.*

❷ want VERB
to need something
EG *My hair wants cutting.*
be deficient in EG *Their diet was deficient in vitamins.*
demand EG *The task of reconstruction demanded much sacrifice.*
lack EG *training to give him the skills he lacked*
need EG *My car needs servicing.*
require EG *He knows exactly what is required of him.*

❸ want NOUN
a lack of something
EG *becoming weak from want of rest*
absence EG *a complete absence of evidence*
deficiency EG *They did blood tests for signs of vitamin deficiency.*
lack EG *He got the job in spite of his lack of experience.*
scarcity EG *an increasing scarcity of water*
shortage EG *A shortage of funds is holding them back.*

WORD POWER

▷ **Synonyms**
dearth
insufficiency
paucity

▶ **Antonym**
abundance

❶ war NOUN
a period of armed conflict between countries
EG *The war dragged on for five years.*
combat EG *men who died in combat*
conflict EG *The conflict is bound to intensify.*
fighting EG *He was killed in the fighting which followed the treaty.*
hostilities EG *in case hostilities break out*
strife EG *The country was torn with strife.*
warfare EG *chemical warfare*

WORD POWER

▶ **Antonym**
peace

● **Related Words**
adjectives : belligerent, martial

❷ war VERB
to fight against something
EG *The two countries had been warring with each other for years.*
battle EG *Thousands of people battled with the police.*
clash EG *The two armies clashed at first light.*
combat EG *measures to combat smuggling*
fight EG *The tribe fought with its rivals.*

❶ warm ADJECTIVE
having some heat but not hot
EG *a warm spring day*
balmy EG *balmy summer evenings*
heated EG *a heated swimming pool*
lukewarm EG *Heat the milk until lukewarm.*
pleasant EG *After a chilly morning, the afternoon was very pleasant.*
tepid EG *a bath full of tepid water*

WORD POWER

▶ **Antonym**
cold

❷ warm ADJECTIVE
friendly and affectionate
EG *a warm and likable personality*
affectionate EG *with an affectionate glance at her children*
amiable EG *He was very amiable company.*
cordial EG *We were given a most cordial welcome.*

friendly EG *All her colleagues were very friendly.*
genial EG *a warm-hearted friend and genial host*
loving EG *He is a loving husband and father.*

WORD POWER

▶ **Antonym**
unfriendly

❸ warm VERB
to heat something gently
EG *The sun came out and warmed his back.*
heat EG *Heat the bread in the oven.*
heat up EG *The fire soon heated up the room.*
melt EG *He melted the butter in a small pan.*
thaw EG *Always thaw pastry thoroughly.*
warm up EG *You must begin gently to warm up the muscles.*

WORD POWER

▶ **Antonym**
cool

warn VERB
to give advance notice of something unpleasant
EG *I warned him about those loose tiles.*
alert EG *The siren alerted them to the danger.*
caution EG *Their reaction cautioned him against any further attempts.*
forewarn EG *We were forewarned of what to expect.*
notify EG *The weather forecast notified them of the coming storm.*

WORD POWER

▷ **Synonyms**
admonish
apprise

warning NOUN
something that tells people of possible danger
EG *advance warning of the attack*
alarm EG *They heard the fire alarm and ran to safety.*
alert EG *a security alert*
caution EG *a note of caution*
notice EG *three months' notice*
premonition EG *He had a premonition of bad news.*

WORD POWER

▷ **Synonyms**
augury
caveat
presage

wary ADJECTIVE
showing lack of trust in something
EG *She was wary of marriage.*
cautious EG *His experience has made him cautious.*
distrustful EG *Voters are deeply distrustful of all politicians.*
guarded EG *The boy gave him a guarded look.*
suspicious EG *He was rightly suspicious of their motives.*
vigilant EG *He warned the public to be vigilant.*

WORD POWER

▷ **Synonyms**
chary
circumspect
heedful

❶ wash VERB
to clean something with water
EG *He got a job washing dishes.*
bathe EG *She bathed her blistered feet.*
cleanse EG *the correct way to cleanse the skin*
launder EG *freshly laundered shirts*
rinse EG *Rinse several times in clear water.*
scrub EG *I was scrubbing the*

a
b
c
d
e
f
g
h
i
j
k
l
m
n
o
p
q
r
s
t
u
v
w
x
y
z

bathroom floor.

shampoo EG *You must shampoo your hair first.*

2 wash VERB

to carry something by the force of water

EG *washed ashore by the waves*

carry off EG *The debris was carried off on the tide.*

erode EG *Exposed soil is quickly eroded by wind and rain.*

sweep away EG *The floods swept away the houses by the river.*

1 waste VERB

to use too much of something unnecessarily

EG *I wouldn't waste my money on something like that.*

fritter away EG *He just fritters his time away.*

squander EG *He had squandered his chances of winning.*

throw away EG *You're throwing away a good opportunity.*

WORD POWER

▶ Antonym
save

2 waste NOUN

using something excessively or unnecessarily

EG *What a complete waste of money!*

extravagance EG *widespread tales of his extravagance*

misuse EG *This project is a misuse of public funds.*

squandering EG *a squandering of his valuable time*

WORD POWER

▷ Synonyms
dissipation
misapplication
prodigality

3 waste ADJECTIVE

not needed or wanted

EG *waste paper*

leftover EG *leftover pieces of fabric*

superfluous EG *She got rid of many superfluous belongings.*

unused EG *spoiled or unused ballot papers*

wasteful ADJECTIVE

using something in a careless or extravagant way

EG *wasteful duplication of effort*

extravagant EG *an extravagant lifestyle*

uneconomical EG *the uneconomical duplication of jobs*

WORD POWER

▷ Synonyms
improvident
profligate
spendthrift

▶ Antonym
thrifty

1 watch NOUN

a period of time when a guard is kept on something

EG *Keep a close watch on the prisoners.*

observation EG *In hospital she'll be under observation night and day.*

supervision EG *A toddler requires close supervision.*

surveillance EG *kept under constant surveillance*

WORD POWER

▷ Synonyms
vigilance
watchfulness

2 watch VERB

to look at something for some time

EG *I don't watch television very often.*

gaze at EG *gazing at herself in the mirror*

look at EG *They looked closely at the insects.*

observe EG *Researchers observed the behaviour of small children.*

pay attention EG *Pay attention or you won't know what to do.*
see EG *We went to see the semi-finals.*
view EG *The police have viewed the video recording of the incident.*

❸ watch VERB
to look after something
EG *You must watch the baby carefully.*
guard EG *They were guarded the whole time they were there.*
look after EG *I looked after her cat while she was away.*
mind EG *Can you mind the store for a couple of hours?*
take care of EG *Can you take care of the kids while I get my hair done?*

watch out VERB
to be careful or alert for something
EG *You have to watch out for snakes in the swamp.*
be alert EG *The bank is alert to the danger.*
be watchful EG *Be watchful for any warning signs.*
keep your eyes open EG *They kept their eyes open for any troublemakers.*
look out EG *What are the symptoms to look out for?*

waterfall NOUN

Types of waterfall
cascade
cataract
chute
fall
linn (*Scottish*)
rapids
torrent
white water

❶ wave VERB
to move or flap to and fro
EG *The doctor waved a piece of paper at him.*
brandish EG *He appeared brandishing a knife.*
flap EG *He flapped his hand at me to be quiet.*

flourish EG *He flourished his glass to emphasize the point.*
flutter EG *a fluttering white lace handkerchief*
shake EG *Shake the rugs well to air them.*

WORD POWER
▷ **Synonyms**
oscillate
undulate

❷ wave NOUN
a ridge of water on the surface of the sea
EG *the sound of the waves breaking on the shore*
breaker EG *The foaming breakers crashed on to the beach.*
ripple EG *gentle ripples on the surface of the lake*
swell EG *We bobbed gently on the swell of the incoming tide.*

❸ wave NOUN
an increase in a type of activity
EG *the crime wave*
flood EG *a flood of complaints about the programme*
movement EG *a growing movement towards democracy*
rush EG *He felt a sudden rush of panic at the thought.*
surge EG *the recent surge in inflation*
trend EG *This is a growing trend.*
upsurge EG *There was an upsurge of business confidence after the war.*

❶ way NOUN
a manner of doing something
EG *an excellent way of cooking meat*
approach EG *different approaches to gathering information*
manner EG *in a friendly manner*
means EG *The move is a means to fight crime.*
method EG *using the latest teaching methods*
procedure EG *He failed to follow the correct procedure when applying for a*

a b c d e f g h i j k l m n o p q r s t u v w x y z

visa.
technique EG *The tests were performed using a new technique.*

❷ way NOUN

the customs or behaviour of a person or group
EG *Their ways are certainly different.*
conduct EG *People judged him by his social skills and conduct.*
custom EG *an ancient Japanese custom*
manner EG *His manner was rather abrupt.*
practice EG *a public enquiry into bank practices*
style EG *Behaving like that isn't his style.*

WORD POWER

▷ **Synonyms**
idiosyncrasy
wont

❸ way NOUN

a route taken to a particular place
EG *I can't remember the way.*
channel EG *a safe channel avoiding the reefs*
course EG *The ship was on a course that followed the coastline.*
lane EG *the busiest shipping lanes in the world*
path EG *The lava annihilates everything in its path.*
road EG *the road into the village*
route EG *the most direct route to the town centre*

❶ weak ADJECTIVE

lacking in strength
EG *She had a weak heart.*
delicate EG *She was physically delicate and mentally unstable.*
faint EG *Feeling faint is one of the symptoms of angina.*
feeble EG *old and feeble and unable to walk far*
frail EG *in frail health*
puny EG *He was puny as a child but grew up to be a top athlete.*
sickly EG *a sickly baby with no resistance to illness*
wasted EG *muscles which were wasted through lack of use*

WORD POWER

▷ **Synonyms**
debilitated
decrepit
enervated
infirm

▶ **Antonym**
strong

❷ weak ADJECTIVE

likely to break or fail
EG *a weak economy*
deficient EG *The plane had a deficient landing system.*
faulty EG *The money will be used to repair faulty equipment.*
inadequate EG *inadequate safety measures*

❸ weak ADJECTIVE

easily influenced by other people
EG *He was a weak man who wouldn't stick his neck out.*
powerless EG *a powerless ruler governed by his advisers*
spineless EG *bureaucrats and spineless politicians*

WORD POWER

▷ **Synonyms**
indecisive
irresolute

▶ **Antonym**
resolute

weaken VERB

to make or become less strong
EG *His authority was weakened by their actions.*
diminish EG *to diminish the prestige of the monarchy*
fail EG *His strength began to fail after a few hours.*

flag EG *Her enthusiasm was in no way flagging.*
lessen EG *The drugs lessen the risk of an epidemic.*
reduce EG *Reduced consumer demand caused the company to collapse.*
sap EG *I was afraid the illness had sapped my strength.*
undermine EG *They were accused of trying to undermine the government.*
wane EG *His interest in sport began to wane.*

WORD POWER

▷ **Synonyms**
debilitate
enervate
mitigate

▶ **Antonym**
strengthen

❶ **weakness** NOUN
a lack of physical or moral strength
EG *His extreme weakness caused him to collapse.*
defect EG *a serious character defect*
flaw EG *His main flaw is his bad temper.*
fragility EG *They are at risk because of the fragility of their bones.*
frailty EG *the triumph of will over human frailty*
imperfection EG *He concedes that there are imperfections in the system.*
vulnerability EG *the extreme vulnerability of the young chicks*

WORD POWER

▷ **Synonyms**
Achilles' heel
debility
infirmity

▶ **Antonym**
strength

❷ **weakness** NOUN
a great liking for something
EG *a weakness for chocolate*
fondness EG *a fondness for good wine*
liking EG *a liking for tripe and onions*
passion EG *His other great passion was his motorbike.*
penchant EG *a stylish woman with a penchant for dark glasses*

WORD POWER

▷ **Synonyms**
partiality
predilection

▶ **Antonym**
dislike

❶ **wealth** NOUN
a large amount of money
EG *Economic reform brought them wealth.*
affluence EG *the trappings of affluence*
fortune EG *He made a fortune in the property boom.*
means EG *a person of means*
money EG *All that money brought nothing but sadness and misery.*
prosperity EG *Japan's economic prosperity*
riches EG *His Olympic medal brought him fame and riches.*
substance EG *run by local men of substance*

❷ **wealth** NOUN
a lot of something
EG *a wealth of information*
abundance EG *This area has an abundance of safe beaches.*
bounty EG *autumn's bounty of fruits and berries*
plenty EG *He grew up in a time of plenty.*
store EG *She dipped into her store of theatrical anecdotes.*

a
b
c
d
e
f
g
h
i
j
k
l
m
n
o
p
q
r
s
t
u
v
w
x
y
z

WORD POWER

▷ **Synonyms**
copiousness
cornucopia
plenitude
profusion

▶ **Antonym**
shortage

wealthy ADJECTIVE
having plenty of money
EG *She came from a very wealthy background.*
affluent EG *living in an affluent neighbourhood*
comfortable EG *from a stable, comfortable family*
opulent EG *Most of the cash went on supporting his opulent lifestyle.*
prosperous EG *The place looks more prosperous than ever.*
rich EG *I'm going to be very rich one day.*
well-to-do EG *a rather well-to-do family in the shipping business*

WORD POWER

▶ **Antonym**
poor

❶ **wear** VERB
to be dressed in something
EG *He was wearing a brown uniform.*
be clothed in EG *She was clothed in a flowered dress.*
be dressed in EG *The women were dressed in their finest attire.*
don EG *The police responded by donning riot gear.*
have on EG *I had my new shoes on that night.*
put on EG *He had to put on his glasses to read the paper.*
sport INFORMAL EG *sporting a red tie*

❷ **wear** VERB
to become worse in condition with use or age

EG *The old stone steps were worn in the middle.*
corrode EG *The underground pipes were badly corroded.*
erode EG *Exposed rock is quickly eroded by wind and rain.*
fray EG *fraying edges on the stair carpet*
rub EG *The inscription had been rubbed smooth by generations of hands.*
wash away EG *The topsoil had been washed away by the incessant rain.*

WORD POWER

▷ **Synonyms**
abrade
deteriorate

❸ **wear** NOUN
the type of use which causes something to be damaged
EG *The tyres showed signs of wear.*
corrosion EG *Zinc is used to protect other metals from corrosion.*
deterioration EG *The building is already showing signs of deterioration.*
erosion EG *erosion of the river valleys*
use EG *The carpet must be able to cope with heavy use.*

WORD POWER

▷ **Synonyms**
abrasion
attrition

wear out VERB
to make someone tired
EG *The past few days have really worn me out.*
exhaust EG *The long working day exhausted him.*
tire EG *If driving tires you, take the train.*
weary EG *wearied by the constant demands on his time*

weary ADJECTIVE
very tired

EG *She sank to the ground, too weary to walk another step.*
drained EG *He's always completely drained after a performance.*
exhausted EG *She was too exhausted and upset to talk.*
fatigued EG *Winter weather can leave you feeling fatigued.*
tired EG *He was too tired even to take a shower.*
tuckered out AUSTRALIAN AND NEW ZEALAND; INFORMAL EG *You must be tuckered out after that bus trip.*
worn out EG *He's just worn out after the long drive.*

weather NOUN

Types of weather
cloud
drought
frost
hail
haze
heatwave
ice
lightning
sunshine
thaw
thunder

Words used to describe the weather
balmy
blustery
breezy
clammy
clear
close
cloudy
cold
drizzly
dry
dull
fine
foggy
hot
humid
icy
mild

misty
muggy
overcast
rainy
showery
snowy
stormy
sultry
sunny
thundery
wet
windy

Words for rain and snow
drizzle
rain
shower
sleet
slush
snow

Words for storm
blizzard
hailstorm
snowstorm
squall
storm
tempest
thunderstorm

Words for wind
breeze
cyclone
gale
gust
hurricane
squall
tornado
typhoon
whirlwind
wind

Words for fog
fog
haar
haze
mist
smog

weird ADJECTIVE
strange or odd

A
B
C
D
E
F
G
H
I
J
K
L
M
N
O
P
Q
R
S
T
U
V
W
X
Y
Z

EG *I had such a weird dream last night.*
bizarre EG *his bizarre behaviour*
curious EG *What a curious thing to say!*
extraordinary EG *an extraordinary occurrence*
funny EG *There's something funny about him.*
odd EG *an odd coincidence*
singular FORMAL EG *I can't think where you got such a singular notion.*
strange EG *Didn't you notice anything strange about her?*
peculiar EG *It tasted very peculiar.*
queer EG *I think there's something queer going on here.*

WORD POWER

▶ **Antonym**
ordinary

weirdo NOUN; INFORMAL
a person who behaves in a strange way
EG *All the other kids thought I was a weirdo.*
crank INFORMAL EG *He kept quiet in case people thought he was a crank.*
eccentric EG *a local eccentric who wears shorts all year round*
freak INFORMAL EG *Barry's always been looked on as a bit of a freak.*
loony SLANG EG *I realize I must sound like a complete loony.*
nut SLANG EG *There's some nut out there with a gun.*
nutter BRITISH; SLANG EG *She was being stalked by a real nutter.*

❶ well ADVERB
in a satisfactory way
EG *The interview went well.*
satisfactorily EG *The system should work satisfactorily.*
smoothly EG *So far, the operation is going smoothly.*
splendidly EG *They have behaved splendidly.*

successfully EG *The changeover is working successfully.*

❷ well ADVERB
with skill and ability
EG *He draws well.*
ably EG *He was ably assisted by the other members of staff.*
admirably EG *dealing admirably with a difficult situation*
adequately EG *He speaks French very adequately.*
competently EG *They handled the situation very competently.*
effectively EG *In the first half he operated effectively in defence.*
efficiently EG *He works efficiently and accurately.*
expertly EG *Shopkeepers expertly rolled spices up in bay leaves.*
professionally EG *These tickets have been forged very professionally.*
skilfully EG *He skilfully exploited his company's strengths.*

WORD POWER

▷ **Synonyms**
adeptly
proficiently

▶ **Antonym**
badly

❸ well ADVERB
fully and with thoroughness
EG *They should be well washed and well dried.*
amply EG *I was amply rewarded for my trouble.*
closely EG *He studied the documents closely.*
completely EG *Make sure you defrost it completely.*
fully EG *The new system is now fully under way.*
highly EG *one of the most highly regarded authors*
meticulously EG *He had planned his trip meticulously.*
rigorously EG *Their duties have not*

been performed as rigorously as they might have been.
thoroughly EG *Add the oil and mix thoroughly.*

4 well ADVERB
in a kind way
EG *He treats his employees well.*
compassionately EG *He always acted compassionately towards her.*
considerately EG *I expect people to deal with me considerately and fairly.*
favourably EG *companies who treat men more favourably than women*
humanely EG *They treat their livestock humanely.*
kindly EG *Children are capable of behaving kindly.*
with consideration EG *He was treated with consideration and kindness.*

5 well ADJECTIVE
having good health
EG *I'm not very well today.*
blooming EG *She felt confident, blooming, and attractive.*
fit EG *He keeps himself really fit.*
healthy EG *Most people want to be healthy and happy.*
in good condition EG *He's in good condition for his age.*
in good health EG *He seemed to be in good health and spirits.*
robust EG *He's never been a very robust child.*
sound EG *a sound body*
strong EG *Eat well and you'll soon be strong again.*

WORD POWER

▷ **Synonyms**
able-bodied
hale
in fine fettle

▶ **Antonym**
sick

1 wet ADJECTIVE
covered in liquid

EG *Don't get your feet wet.*
damp EG *Her hair was still damp.*
drenched EG *getting drenched by icy water*
moist EG *The soil is reasonably moist after the September rain.*
saturated EG *The filter has been saturated with oil.*
soaked EG *soaked to the skin*
sodden EG *We took off our sodden clothes.*
waterlogged EG *The game was called off because the pitch was waterlogged.*

WORD POWER

▶ **Antonym**
dry

2 wet ADJECTIVE
in rainy weather conditions
EG *It was a miserable wet day.*
humid EG *hot and humid weather conditions*
misty EG *The air was cold and misty.*
rainy EG *The rainy season starts in December.*
showery EG *The day had been showery with sunny intervals.*

WORD POWER

▶ **Antonym**
dry

3 wet VERB
to put liquid on to something
EG *Wet the edges and stick them together.*
dampen EG *You must dampen the laundry before you iron it.*
irrigate EG *irrigated by a system of interconnected canals*
moisten EG *Take a sip of water to moisten your throat.*
soak EG *The water had soaked his jacket and shirt.*
spray EG *It can spray the whole field in half an hour.*

water EG *We have to water the plants when the weather is dry.*

WORD POWER

▷ **Synonyms**
drench
humidify
saturate

▶ **Antonym**
dry

whim NOUN
a sudden fancy for something
EG *We decided to go more or less on a whim.*
craze EG *the latest fitness craze*
fad INFORMAL EG *just a passing fad*
fancy EG *I had a fancy for some strawberries.*
impulse EG *He resisted the impulse to buy a new one.*
urge EG *He had an urge to open a shop of his own.*

WORD POWER

▷ **Synonyms**
caprice
vagary
whimsy

white NOUN OR ADJECTIVE

Shades of white
cream
ecru
ivory
magnolia
off-white
oyster white
pearl
snow-white

❶ whole ADJECTIVE
indicating all of something
EG *We spent the whole summer abroad.*
complete EG *The list filled a complete page.*
entire EG *There are only ten in the entire country.*
full EG *a full week's notice*
total EG *The evening was a total fiasco.*
uncut EG *the uncut version of the film*
undivided EG *He has my undivided loyalty.*

❷ whole NOUN
the full amount of something
EG *the whole of Asia*
aggregate EG *the aggregate of the individual scores*
all EG *All is not lost.*
everything EG *Everything that happened is my fault.*
lot EG *He lost the lot within five minutes.*
sum total EG *The small room contained the sum total of their possessions.*
total EG *The eventual total was far higher.*

❶ wicked ADJECTIVE
very bad or evil
EG *That was a wicked thing to do.*
atrocious EG *He had committed atrocious crimes against the refugees.*
bad EG *Please forgive our bad behaviour.*
depraved EG *the work of depraved criminals*
evil EG *the country's most evil terrorists*
sinful EG *"This is a sinful world", he said.*
vicious EG *He was a cruel and vicious man.*

WORD POWER

▷ **Synonyms**
egregious
iniquitous
nefarious

❷ wicked ADJECTIVE
mischievous in an amusing or attractive way
EG *She always felt wicked when eating*

chocolate.
impish EG *an impish sense of humour*
mischievous EG *like a mischievous child*
naughty EG *little boys using naughty words*

1 wide ADJECTIVE
measuring a large distance from side to side
EG *It should be wide enough to give plenty of working space.*
→ see Word Study **wide**

WORD POWER

► **Antonym**
narrow

2 wide ADJECTIVE
extensive in scope
EG *a wide range of colours*
→ see Word Study **wide**

WORD POWER

► **Antonym**
narrow

3 wide ADVERB
as far as possible
EG *Open wide!*
→ see Word Study **wide**

widespread ADJECTIVE
existing over a large area
EG *Food shortages are widespread.*
broad EG *The agreement won broad support among the people.*
common EG *the common view that treatment is ineffective*
extensive EG *The bomb caused extensive damage.*
pervasive EG *the pervasive influence of the army in national life*
prevalent EG *Smoking is becoming more prevalent among girls.*
rife EG *Bribery and corruption were rife in the industry.*

1 wild ADJECTIVE
not cultivated or domesticated
EG *a meadow of wild flowers*

fierce EG *Fierce hyenas scavenged for food after the kill.*
free EG *stunning pictures of wild and free animals*
natural EG *In the natural state this animal is not ferocious.*
uncultivated EG *developed from an uncultivated type of grass*
undomesticated EG *These cats lived wild and were completely undomesticated.*
untamed EG *the untamed horses of the Camargue*
warrigal AUSTRALIAN; LITERARY EG *a warrigal mare*

2 wild ADJECTIVE
in stormy conditions
EG *They were not deterred by the wild weather.*
howling EG *a howling gale*
raging EG *The trip involved crossing a raging torrent.*
rough EG *The two ships collided in rough seas.*
stormy EG *a dark and stormy night*
violent EG *That night they were hit by a violent storm.*

3 wild ADJECTIVE
without control or restraint
EG *wild with excitement*
boisterous EG *Most of the children were noisy and boisterous.*
rowdy EG *The television coverage revealed their rowdy behaviour.*
turbulent EG *five turbulent years of rows and reconciliations*
uncontrolled EG *His uncontrolled behaviour disturbed the entire group.*
wayward EG *wayward children with a history of emotional problems*

WORD POWER

▷ **Synonyms**
disorderly
riotous
uproarious

a
b
c
d
e
f
g
h
i
j
k
l
m
n
o
p
q
r
s
t
u
v
w
x
y
z

❶ will VERB
to leave something to someone when you die
EG *He had willed his fortune to his daughter.*
bequeath EG *She bequeathed her collection to the local museum.*
leave EG *Everything was left to the housekeeper.*
pass on EG *He passed on much of his estate to his eldest son.*

❷ will NOUN
the strong determination to achieve something
EG *the will to win*
determination EG *Determination has always been a part of his make-up.*
purpose EG *They are enthusiastic and have a sense of purpose.*
resolution EG *He began to form a resolution to clear his name.*
resolve EG *This will strengthen the public's resolve.*
willpower EG *succeeding by sheer willpower*

❸ will NOUN
what someone wants
EG *the will of the people*
choice EG *It's your choice.*
inclination EG *She showed no inclination to go.*
mind EG *You can go if you have a mind to do so.*
volition EG *a product of our volition*
wish EG *done against my wishes*

WORD POWER
● **Related Words**
adjective : voluntary

willing ADJECTIVE
ready and eager to do something
EG *a willing helper*
agreeable EG *We can go ahead if you are agreeable.*
eager EG *Children are eager to learn.*
game INFORMAL EG *He still had new ideas and was game to try them.*

happy EG *That's a risk I'm happy to take.*
prepared EG *I'm not prepared to take orders from her.*
ready EG *ready to die for their beliefs*

WORD POWER
▷ **Synonyms**
amenable
compliant
desirous

▶ **Antonym**
unwilling

❶ win VERB
to defeat your opponents
EG *The top four teams all won.*
be victorious EG *Despite the strong opposition she was victorious.*
come first EG *They unexpectedly came first this year.*
prevail EG *the votes he must win in order to prevail*
succeed EG *the skills and qualities needed to succeed*
triumph EG *a symbol of good triumphing over evil*

WORD POWER
▶ **Antonym**
lose

❷ win VERB
to succeed in obtaining something
EG *moves to win the support of the poor*
achieve EG *We have achieved our objective.*
attain EG *He's half-way to attaining his pilot's licence.*
gain EG *After three weeks the hostages finally gained their freedom.*
get EG *My entry got a commendation this year.*
secure EG *Her achievements helped secure her the job.*

❸ win NOUN
a victory in a contest

EG *a run of seven games without a win*
success EG *his success in the Monaco Grand Prix*
triumph EG *their World Cup triumph*
victory EG *the 3-1 victory over Switzerland*

WORD POWER

▶ **Antonym**
defeat

winner NOUN
a person who wins something
EG *The winners will be notified by post.*
champion EG *a former Olympic champion*
conqueror EG *This time they easily overcame their former conquerors.*
victor EG *He emerged as the victor by the second day.*

WORD POWER

▶ **Antonym**
loser

wisdom NOUN
judgment used to make sensible decisions
EG *the wisdom that comes from experience*
discernment EG *Her keen discernment made her an excellent collector.*
insight EG *a man of considerable insight and diplomatic skills*
judgment EG *He respected our judgment on this matter.*
knowledge EG *the quest for scientific knowledge*
reason EG *a conflict between emotion and reason*

WORD POWER

▷ **Synonyms**
astuteness
erudition
sagacity

▶ **Antonym**
foolishness

● **Related Words**
adjective : sagacious

wise ADJECTIVE
able to make use of experience and judgment
EG *a wise old man*
informed EG *an informed guess at his wealth*
judicious EG *the judicious use of military force*
perceptive EG *the words of a perceptive political commentator*
rational EG *You must look at both sides before you can reach a rational decision.*
sensible EG *The sensible thing is to leave them alone.*
shrewd EG *a shrewd deduction about what was going on*

WORD POWER

▶ **Antonym**
foolish

❶ **wish** NOUN
a desire for something
EG *She was sincere in her wish to make amends.*
desire EG *her desire for a child of her own*
hankering EG *She had always had a hankering to be an actress.*
hunger EG *a hunger for success*
longing EG *He felt a longing for familiar surroundings.*
urge EG *He had an urge to open a shop of his own.*
want EG *Supermarkets respond to the wants of their customers.*

❷ **wish** VERB
to want something
EG *We wished to return.*
desire EG *He was bored and desired to go home.*
hunger EG *She hungered for*

a
b
c
d
e
f
g
h
i
j
k
l
m
n
o
p
q
r
s
t
u
v
w
x
y
z

A
B
C
D
E
F
G
H
I
J
K
L
M
N
O
P
Q
R
S
T
U
V
W
X
Y
Z

adventure.
long EG *I'm longing for the holidays.*
thirst EG *thirsting for knowledge*
want EG *people who know exactly what they want in life*
yearn EG *The younger ones yearned to be part of a normal family.*

❶ withdraw VERB
to take something out
EG *He withdrew some money from the bank.*
draw out EG *I'll have to draw out some of my savings.*
extract EG *She extracted another dress from the wardrobe.*
remove EG *I removed the splinter from her finger.*
take out EG *There was a fee for taking out money from the account.*

❷ withdraw VERB
to back out of an activity
EG *They withdrew from the conference.*
back out EG *He backed out of the agreement.*
leave EG *Davis left the game to go to hospital.*
pull out EG *The general pulled out of the talks after two days.*
retire EG *The jury retired three hours ago.*
retreat EG *retreating from the harsh realities of life*

WORD POWER

▷ **Synonyms**
disengage
secede

wither VERB
to become weaker and fade away
EG *Will the company flourish or wither?*
decline EG *The church's influence has declined.*
droop EG *plants drooping in the heat*
fade EG *Prospects for peace have already started to fade.*
shrivel EG *They watched their crops*

shrivel and die in the drought.
wilt EG *The roses wilted the day after she bought them.*

WORD POWER

▷ **Synonyms**
atrophy
dessicate

❶ witness NOUN
someone who has seen something happen
EG *The police appealed for witnesses to come forward.*
bystander EG *Seven other innocent bystanders were injured.*
eyewitness EG *Eyewitnesses say the soldiers opened fire on the crowd.*
observer EG *A casual observer would not have noticed them.*
onlooker EG *a small crowd of onlookers*
spectator EG *carried out in full view of spectators*

❷ witness VERB
to see something happening
EG *Anyone who witnessed the attack should call the police.*
be present at EG *Many men are now present at the birth of their children.*
observe EG *We observed them setting up the machine gun.*
see EG *I saw him do it.*
watch EG *She had watched them drinking heavily before the accident.*

witty ADJECTIVE
amusing in a clever way
EG *He's so witty I could listen to him for hours.*
amusing EG *He provided an irreverent and amusing commentary to the film.*
brilliant EG *a brilliant after-dinner speaker*
clever EG *He raised some smiles with several clever lines.*
funny EG *a film packed with incredibly*

funny dialogue
humorous EG *a satirical and humorous parody*
sparkling EG *He's famous for his sparkling conversation.*

woman NOUN
an adult female human being
EG *women over 75 years old*
dame SLANG EG *Who does that dame think she is?*
female EG *The average young female is fairly affluent.*
girl EG *a night out with the girls*
lady EG *Your table is ready, ladies, so please come through.*
lass EG *a lass from the country*
sheila AUSTRALIAN AND NEW ZEALAND; INFORMAL EG *his role as a sheila in his own play*
vrou SOUTH AFRICAN EG *Have you met his vrou yet?*

WORD POWER

▶ **Antonym**
man

---

❶ **wonder** VERB
to think about something with curiosity
EG *I wondered what that noise was.*
ask oneself EG *You have to ask yourself what this really means.*
ponder EG *pondering how to improve the team*
puzzle EG *Researchers continue to puzzle over the origins of the disease.*
speculate EG *He refused to speculate about the contents of the letter.*

❷ **wonder** VERB
to be surprised and amazed
EG *He wondered at her anger.*
be amazed EG *Most of the cast were amazed by the play's success.*
be astonished EG *I was astonished to discover his true age.*
boggle EG *The mind boggles at what might be in store for us.*

marvel EG *We marvelled at her endless energy.*

❸ **wonder** NOUN
something that amazes people
EG *one of the wonders of nature*
marvel EG *a marvel of high technology*
miracle EG *It's a miracle no one was killed.*
phenomenon EG *a well-known geographical phenomenon*
spectacle EG *a spectacle not to be missed*

❶ **wonderful** ADJECTIVE
extremely good
EG *It's wonderful to see you.*
excellent EG *The recording quality is excellent.*
great INFORMAL EG *a great bunch of guys*
marvellous EG *What a marvellous time we had!*
superb EG *The hotel has a superb isolated location.*
tremendous EG *I thought it was a tremendous book.*

❷ **wonderful** ADJECTIVE
very impressive
EG *The sunset was a truly wonderful sight.*
amazing EG *containing some amazing special effects*
astounding EG *The results are quite astounding.*
incredible EG *The intensity of colour was incredible.*
magnificent EG *magnificent views across the valley*
remarkable EG *It was a remarkable achievement to complete the course.*

WORD POWER

▷ **Synonyms**
phenomenal
wondrous

---

a
b
c
d
e
f
g
h
i
j
k
l
m
n
o
p
q
r
s
t
u
v
w
x
y
z

A
B
C
D
E
F
G
H
I
J
K
L
M
N
O
P
Q
R
S
T
U
V
W
X
Y
Z

❶ word NOUN

WORD POWER

● **Related Words**
adjectives : lexical,
verbal

Parts of a word
capital letter
consonant
grapheme
letter
phoneme
prefix
suffix
syllable
vowel

❷ word NOUN
a remark
EG *I'd like to say a word of thanks to everyone who helped me.*
comment EG *He left without any further comment.*
remark EG *Apart from that one remark, he stayed quiet all evening.*
statement EG *Verity issued a brief statement to the press.*
utterance EG *a crowd of admirers who hung on his every utterance*

❸ word NOUN
a brief conversation
EG *James, could I have a quick word with you?*
chat EG *We need to have a chat about the arrangements some time.*
conversation EG *He recalled his brief conversation with the Queen.*
discussion EG *We had a very short discussion about what to do.*
talk EG *I bumped into him yesterday and we had a quick talk.*

❹ word NOUN
a message
EG *Since then we've had no word from them.*
announcement EG *There has been no formal announcement from either*

government.
bulletin EG *A spokesperson said no bulletin would be issued.*
communication EG *The ambassador brought a communication from the President.*
information EG *They will issue written information in due course.*
intelligence EG *He wanted to pass this intelligence on to her.*
message EG *Did he leave any message for me?*
news EG *Is there any news from the embassy?*

❺ word NOUN
a promise or guarantee
EG *He gave me his word that he would be there.*
assurance EG *Do I have your assurance that you'll take responsibility?*
oath EG *She gave her solemn oath not to tell anyone.*
pledge EG *He gave his personal pledge that he would help.*
promise EG *I'll support you - you have my promise on that.*
word of honour EG *I want your word of honour that you'll respect my anonymity.*

❶ work VERB
to do the tasks required of you
EG *I had to work twelve hours a day.*
labour EG *peasants labouring in the fields*
slave EG *slaving over a hot stove*
slog away EG *They are still slogging away at algebra.*
toil EG *Workers toiled long hours in the mills.*

WORD POWER

▶ **Antonym**
laze

❷ work NOUN
someone's job
EG *She's trying to find work.*

business EG *We have business to attend to first.*

craft EG *He learned his craft from an expert.*

employment EG *unable to find employment*

job EG *I got at a job at the sawmill.*

livelihood EG *fishermen who depend on the seas for their livelihood*

occupation EG *Please state your occupation.*

profession EG *a dentist by profession*

WORD POWER

▷ **Synonyms**
calling
métier
pursuit

---

❸ work NOUN
the tasks that have to be done
EG *Sometimes he had to take work home.*

assignment EG *written assignments and practical tests*

chore EG *We share the household chores.*

duty EG *My duty is to look after the animals.*

job EG *It turned out to be a bigger job than expected.*

task EG *catching up with administrative tasks*

yakka AUSTRALIAN AND NEW ZEALAND; INFORMAL EG *a decade of hard yakka on the land*

worker NOUN
a person who works
EG *seeking a reliable research worker*

craftsman EG *furniture made by a local craftsman*

employee EG *Many of its employees are women.*

labourer EG *a farm labourer*

workman EG *Workmen are building a steel fence.*

WORD POWER

▷ **Synonyms**
artisan
hand
proletarian

---

❶ work out VERB
to find the solution to something
EG *It took us some time to work out what was happening.*

calculate EG *First, calculate your monthly living expenses.*

figure out EG *You don't need to be a detective to figure that one out.*

resolve EG *They hoped the crisis could be quickly resolved.*

solve EG *We'll solve the case ourselves and surprise everyone.*

❷ work out VERB
to happen in a certain way
EG *Things didn't work out that way after all.*

develop EG *Wait and see how the situation develops.*

go EG *Did it all go well?*

happen EG *Things don't happen the way you want them to.*

turn out EG *Sometimes life doesn't turn out as we expect.*

❶ worn-out ADJECTIVE
no longer usable because of extreme wear
EG *a worn-out pair of shoes*

broken-down EG *Broken-down cars lined the road.*

tattered EG *tattered clothes*

threadbare EG *a square of threadbare carpet*

worn EG *Worn tyres cost lives.*

❷ worn-out ADJECTIVE
extremely tired
EG *You must be worn-out after the journey.*

exhausted EG *too exhausted to do any more*

fatigued EG *Winter weather can leave you feeling fatigued.*

a
b
c
d
e
f
g
h
i
j
k
l
m
n
o
p
q
r
s
t
u
v
w
x
y
z

A
B
C
D
E
F
G
H
I
J
K
L
M
N
O
P
Q
R
S
T
U
V
W
X
Y
Z

prostrate EG *He lay prostrate with exhaustion.*

tired EG *I need to rest because I'm tired.*

weary EG *a weary traveller*

worried ADJECTIVE
being anxious about something
EG *His parents were worried about his lack of progress.*

anxious EG *I was very anxious about her safety.*

bothered EG *I'm not bothered about it at all.*

concerned EG *a phone call from a concerned neighbour*

nervous EG *Consumers say they are nervous about their jobs.*

troubled EG *He was troubled by the lifestyle of his son.*

uneasy EG *an uneasy feeling that everything was going wrong*

WORD POWER

▷ **Synonyms**
overwrought
perturbed
unquiet

▶ **Antonym**
unconcerned

❶ **worry** VERB
to feel anxious about something
EG *Don't worry, it's bound to arrive soon.*

be anxious EG *They admitted they were still anxious about the situation.*

brood EG *constantly brooding about her family*

feel uneasy EG *I felt very uneasy at the lack of response.*

fret EG *You mustn't fret about someone else's problems.*

❷ **worry** VERB
to disturb someone with a problem
EG *I didn't want to worry the boys with this.*

bother EG *I hate to bother you again so soon.*

hassle INFORMAL EG *Then my boss started hassling me.*

pester EG *I wish they'd stop pestering me for an answer.*

plague EG *I'm not going to plague you with more questions.*

trouble EG *Don't trouble me while I'm working.*

WORD POWER

▷ **Synonyms**
harry
importune
perturb

❸ **worry** NOUN
a feeling of anxiety
EG *a major source of worry*

anxiety EG *anxieties about money*

apprehension EG *real anger and apprehension about the future*

concern EG *growing concern for the environment*

fear EG *His fears might be groundless.*

misgiving EG *She had some misgivings about what she was about to do.*

unease EG *a deep sense of unease about the coming interview*

worsen VERB
to become more difficult
EG *My relationship with my mother worsened.*

decline EG *Hourly output declined in the third quarter.*

degenerate EG *The whole tone of the campaign began to degenerate.*

deteriorate EG *The weather conditions are deteriorating.*

go downhill INFORMAL EG *Things have gone steadily downhill since he left.*

WORD POWER

▶ **Antonym**
improve

❶ **worship** VERB
to praise and revere something
EG *People go to church to pray and*

worship their god.
glorify EG *The monks devoted their days to glorifying God.*
honour EG *the Scout's promise to honour God*
praise EG *She asked the church to praise God.*
pray to EG *They prayed to their gods to bring them rain.*
venerate EG *the most venerated religious figure in the country*

WORD POWER

▷ **Synonyms**
deify
exalt
revere

▶ **Antonym**
dishonour

❷ worship VERB
to love and admire someone
EG *She had worshipped him from afar for years.*
adore EG *an adoring husband*
idolize EG *She idolized her father as she was growing up.*
love EG *He genuinely loved and cherished her.*

WORD POWER

▶ **Antonym**
despise

❸ worship NOUN
a feeling of love and admiration for something
EG *the worship of the ancient Roman gods*
admiration EG *Her eyes widened in admiration.*
adoration EG *He had been used to female adoration all his life.*
adulation EG *The book was received with adulation by the critics.*
devotion EG *flattered by his devotion*
homage EG *The emperor received the homage of every prince.*

praise EG *singing hymns in praise of their god*

WORD POWER

▷ **Synonyms**
deification
exaltation

Places of worship
altar
basilica
cathedral
chapel
church
gurdwara
meeting house
mosque
pagoda
shrine
synagogue
tabernacle
temple

worthless ADJECTIVE
having no real value or worth
EG *a worthless piece of junk*
meaningless EG *their sense of a meaningless existence*
paltry EG *a paltry amount*
poor EG *a poor reward for his effort*
trifling EG *We were paid a trifling sum.*
trivial EG *She would go to the doctor for any trivial complaint.*
useless EG *I felt useless and a failure.*
valueless EG *commercially valueless trees*

WORD POWER

▷ **Synonyms**
negligible
nugatory

▶ **Antonym**
valuable

write VERB
to record something in writing
EG *Write your name and address on a postcard and send it to us.*

a
b
c
d
e
f
g
h
i
j
k
l
m
n
o
p
q
r
s
t
u
v
w
x
y
z

A
B
C
D
E
F
G
H
I
J
K
L
M
N
O
P
Q
R
S
T
U
V
W
X
Y
Z

compose EG *Vivaldi composed many concertos.*
correspond EG *We corresponded for several years.*
inscribe EG *Their names were inscribed on the front of the pillar.*
record EG *Her letters record the domestic and social details of her life.*
take down EG *notes taken down in shorthand*

writing NOUN

Types of writing
autobiography
ballad
biography
column
dissertation
editorial
epitaph
essay
fable
feature
fiction
legend
letter
lyric
memoir
myth
narrative
non-fiction
novel
obituary
parable
play
poem
report
review
rhyme
riddle
script
story
thesis
verse

Styles used in writing
alliteration
cliché
idiom

metaphor
narrative
parody
pun
satire
simile

Features of writing
character
dialogue
imagery
motif
plot
setting
subplot
theme

❶ wrong ADJECTIVE
not correct or truthful
EG *That was the wrong answer.*
false EG *We don't know if the information is true or false.*
faulty EG *His diagnosis was faulty from the outset.*
incorrect EG *a decision based on figures which were incorrect*
mistaken EG *a mistaken view of the situation*
unsound EG *The thinking is good-hearted, but muddled and unsound.*
untrue EG *The remarks were completely untrue.*

WORD POWER

▷ **Synonyms**
erroneous
fallacious

▶ **Antonym**
right

❷ wrong ADJECTIVE
morally unacceptable
EG *It's wrong to hurt people.*
bad EG *I may be a thief but I'm not a bad person.*
crooked EG *crooked business deals*
evil EG *the country's most evil terrorists*

illegal EG *It is illegal to intercept radio messages.*
immoral EG *Many would consider such practices immoral.*
unfair EG *It was unfair that he should suffer so much.*
unjust EG *unjust treatment*

WORD POWER

▷ **Synonyms**
felonious
iniquitous
reprehensible
unethical

▶ **Antonym**
right

3 wrong NOUN
an unjust action
EG *the wrongs of our society*
abuse EG *controversy over human rights abuses*
crime EG *crimes against humanity*
grievance EG *He had a deep sense of grievance.*
injustice EG *A great injustice had been done to him in the past.*
sin EG *He admitted the many sins of his youth.*

a
b
c
d
e
f
g
h
i
j
k
l
m
n
o
p
q
r
s
t
u
v
w
x
y
z

Xx Yy Zz

A
B
C
D
E
F
G
H
I
J
K
L
M
N
O
P
Q
R
S
T
U
V
W
X
Y
Z

yellow NOUN OR ADJECTIVE

> **Shades of yellow**
> amber
> canary yellow
> champagne
> citrus yellow
> daffodil
> gold
> lemon
> mustard
> primrose
> saffron
> sand
> straw
> topaz

yes INTERJECTION
an expression used to agree with something or say it is true
EG *"Are you a friend of his?" - "Yes."*
aye SCOTTISH; INFORMAL EG *"Can I borrow this?" - "Aye, but I want it back."*
okay EG *"Will we leave now?" - "Okay, if you like."*
sure EG *"Can I come too?" - "Sure."*
ya SOUTH AFRICAN EG *"Are you a runaway?" - "Ya," the child replied.*
yeah INFORMAL EG *Yeah, I think we've met once.*

WORD POWER

▶ **Antonym**
no

yokel NOUN
a person who lives in the country
EG *a bunch of those yokels*
bushie *or* **bushy** AUSTRALIAN AND NEW ZEALAND; INFORMAL EG *"I'm a bit of a bushie at heart," she said.*
countryman EG *They are true old-fashioned countrymen.*

peasant EG *In rural Mexico a peasant is rarely without his machete.*

❶ young ADJECTIVE
not yet mature
EG *young people*
adolescent EG *He spent his adolescent years playing guitar.*
immature EG *an immature female whale*
infant EG *his infant daughter*
junior EG *a junior member of the family*
juvenile EG *a juvenile delinquent*
little EG *What were you like when you were little?*
youthful EG *the youthful stars of the film*

WORD POWER

▶ **Antonym**
old

❷ young PLURAL NOUN
the babies an animal has
EG *The hen may not be able to feed its young.*
babies EG *animals making nests for their babies*
brood EG *a hungry brood of fledglings*
family EG *a family of weasels*
litter EG *a litter of pups*
little ones EG *a family of elephants with their little ones*
offspring EG *female rats' offspring*

zero NOUN
nothing or the number 0
EG *I will now count from zero to ten.*
nil EG *They beat Argentina one-nil.*
nothing EG *Some weeks I earn nothing.*
nought EG *How many noughts are there in a million?*

Word Studies

bad

Bad is such a commonly-used word that it has come to lose much of its effectiveness. Depending on the sense and context of what you are saying, there are many other much more expressive substitutes which can be used instead.

● **having a harmful effect:**

Stress can be extremely **damaging** healthwise.
chemicals which have a **destructive** effect on the ozone layer
This could have a **detrimental** impact on the environment.
the **harmful** effects of radiation
illnesses caused by an **unhealthy** lifestyle
Some of the drug's side-effects are **unpleasant**.

● **making someone feel upset or uneasy:**

the **distressing** images shown in the film
We have just had some very **disturbing** news.
He's been having a **grim** time of it recently.
a sight which evoked **painful** memories
a very **traumatic** period in her life
an **unsettling** atmosphere
It must have been an **upsetting** experience.

● **causing physical pain:**

an **acute** attack of appendicitis
an **agonizing** way to die
She was in **excruciating** pain.
intense cramps
a **painful** back
He suffers from **serious** knee problems.
severe stomach pains
a **terrible** migraine

● **of poor quality:**

defective products which cause serious injury
a lack of exercise and a **deficient** diet
customers who take **faulty** goods back
Imperfect work will not be accepted.
protests over **inadequate** work conditions
the **inferior** quality of the recording
a **pathetic** excuse
an area with **poor** housing and high unemployment
a **sorry** state of affairs
I complained about the **unsatisfactory** service I had received.

● **lacking skill:**

the power to sack **incompetent** managers
an **inept** performance
a **poor** judge of character
He is **useless** at all sports.

● **having an evil character:**

the morally **corrupt** court of Charles the Second
the **criminal** actions of a few sick individuals
depraved and hardened criminals
the most **evil** man in history
people who believe gambling is **immoral**
behaviour considered **sinful** by society
Richard III, one of Shakespeare's most **villainous** characters
Snow White's **wicked** stepmother

*If you do something **wrong** you must take the consequences.*

● **of children: behaving badly:**

*I don't believe in smacking **disobedient** children.*
*a **mischievous** little scamp*
*You are a **naughty** boy for repeating what I told you.*
***undisciplined** pupils who disrupt classes*
*laws to penalise the parents of **unruly** kids*

● **of food:**

***mouldy** cheese*
*This meat's gone **off**.*
*butter which had gone **rancid** in the heat*
***rotten** eggs*
*The milk has gone **sour**.*

● **of language:**

*lyrics full of **obscene** content*
*I don't like to hear **offensive** language in the street.*
***rude** words*
*I can't bring myself to use such a **vulgar** expression.*

badly

Badly, like **bad**, can be avoided in favour of less commonly-used and more expressive alternatives.

● **in an inferior way:**

*He had been **inadequately** trained for the job.*
*a department which is run **ineptly***
*The event had been **poorly** organized.*
*housing which is ugly and **shoddily** built*
*an **unsatisfactorily** regulated system*

● **seriously:**

*I was **deeply** hurt by these comments.*
*Felicity looked **desperately** unhappy.*
*He was **gravely** ill following a heart*

operation.
*Four people have been **seriously** injured.*

● **cruelly:**

*marchers being **brutally** assaulted by riot police*
*He treated his wife **callously**.*
*He was **cruelly** tormented by his older brothers.*
*an old man who was **savagely** beaten by thugs*
*He struck me **viciously** across the face.*

best

There are a number of alternatives for the word **best** which will make your writing more interesting.

● **of the highest standard:**

the **finest** wines available
a **first-rate** musical performance
the **foremost** painter of his generation
the **greatest** film ever made
He has established himself as one of Britain's **leading** actors.
one of England's **outstanding** tennis players
her status as the **pre-eminent** pop act of her day
London's **principal** publishing houses
companies that offer **superlative** products
the **supreme** achievement of his career
one of the country's **top** athletes

● **most desirable:**

the **correct** thing to do in the circumstances
the **most desirable** outcome
the **most fitting** location for a house
Are you the **right** person for the job?

● **the preferred thing:**

a showcase for the **cream** of Scottish artists
the **elite** of the sporting world
Landlord, wine! And make it the **finest**!
the **pick** of the crop

better

WORD STUDIES

Like **best**, the word **better** can be replaced with a number of synonyms to add variety and interest to your written and spoken English.

● **of higher quality or worth:**

There is no **finer** place to live.

moving to a much **grander** house

Their eyes are now set on a **greater** prize.

We are trying to provide a **higher-quality** service.

This is a much **nicer** room than mine.

Owning property is **preferable** to renting.

His work is far **superior** to yours.

a film of **surpassing** quality

You should save your energies for a **worthier** cause.

● **of greater skill:**

He is acknowledged as the **greater** writer.

slopes suitable for the **more advanced** skiers

She is **more expert** at some things than others.

He is a **more skilful** player than the rest of the team.

There are lots of actors **more talented** than he is.

● **in improved health:**

I used to have insomnia but now I'm **cured**.

I'm a lot **fitter** now I've started jogging.

He had a back injury but now he's **fully recovered**.

I'm much **healthier** since I gave up smoking.

His symptoms are not **improving** despite the treatment.

She's **on the mend** now. (INFORMAL)

She's **recovering** after an attack of appendicitis.

He's slowly getting **stronger** after his accident.

I hope you're feeling **well** again soon.

big

A cautionary tale: a teacher was trying to get her class to substitute more interesting words for very commonly-used ones in their writing. She noticed that one boy had described a castle as "big" in his essay, and asked him to write the sentence again in a more creative way. He came back with the following: "I saw a castle which was big, and when I say big, I mean *big*."

● **in size:**

a **colossal** statue
an **enormous** building
The brontosaurus was a **gigantic** creature.
Her arrival caused a **great** commotion.
a **huge** birthday cake
an **immense** task
a **large** map of the world
a **massive** fireworks display
a **significant** difference
a **vast** football stadium

● **in importance:**

an **eminent** politician
My teachers had an **important** influence on me.

an **influential** figure in US foreign policy
one of Britain's **leading** screenwriters.
a **major** role in the company
a **powerful** businessman
the **principal** guest at the reception
a **prominent** jazz musician
the company in which he was a **significant** investor

● **of an issue or problem:**

The country was passing through a **grave** crisis.
the **momentous** decision to go to war
a **serious** disadvantage
the **urgent** need for major investment
a **weighty** problem

WORD STUDIES

The word **break** is often over-used. There are lots of more descriptive words which you can use to give additional information about how something breaks, so try to choose one of them instead.

● If something hard **cracks**, or you **crack** it, it becomes slightly damaged, with lines appearing on its surface:

*A gas main had **cracked** under my garden.*
*To get at the coconut flesh, **crack** the shell with a hammer.*

● If something **fractures**, or you **fracture** it, it gets a slight crack in it:

*One strut had **fractured** and had to be repaired.*
*You've **fractured** a rib.*

● If something **snaps**, or you **snap** it, it breaks suddenly, with a sharp cracking noise:

*A twig **snapped** under his foot.*
*She gripped the pipe in both hands, trying to **snap** it in half.*

● If something **splits**, or you **split** it, it breaks into two or more parts:

*In the severe gale, the ship **split** in two.*
*We **split** the boards down the middle.*

● If something **splinters**, or you **splinter** it, it breaks into thin, sharp pieces:

*The ruler **splintered** into pieces.*
*The stone hit the glass, **splintering** it.*

● If something **fragments**, or **is fragmented**, it breaks or separates into small parts:

*The rock began to **fragment** and crumble.*

● If something **crumbles**, or you **crumble** it, it breaks into many small pieces:

*Under the pressure, the flint **crumbled** into fragments.*
***Crumble** the cheese into a bowl.*

● If something **shatters**, it breaks into many small pieces:

*safety glass that won't **shatter** if it's hit*

● If something **disintegrates**, it breaks into many pieces and is destroyed:

*The car's windscreen **disintegrated** with the impact of the crash.*

● If you **smash** something, or it **smashes**, it breaks into many small pieces, often because it has been hit or dropped:

*Someone had **smashed** a bottle.*
*Two glasses fell off the table and **smashed** into pieces.*

● If you **wreck** or **demolish** something, you completely destroy it:

*The bridge was **wrecked** by the storms.*
*The hurricane **demolished** houses across the area.*

call

Depending on which sense of **call** you are thinking of, there are a number of words which you can substitute for it to make your language more interesting.

● **to give a name:**

*He decided to **christen** his first-born son Arthur.*
*The wood was **designated** an "area of natural beauty".*
*the man **dubbed** "the world's greatest living explorer"*
*They **named** their child Anthony.*

● **to describe as:**

*I **consider** myself an artist.*
*I'm not what you'd **describe as** an emotional person.*
*Do you **judge** this result a success?*
*He **referred to** her as a "bimbo".*
*a man widely **regarded** as a tyrant*
*prisoners **termed** as political*
*People will **think** us mad.*

● **to telephone:**

***Contact** us immediately if you have any new information.*
***Phone** me as soon as you get home.*
*I'll **ring** you tomorrow.*
*Please **telephone** to make an appointment.*

● **to say loudly:**

*"Dinner is served," he **announced**.*
*"Run, Forrest!" she **cried**.*
*She **cried out** to us as she disappeared from view.*

*He **shouted** to me from across the room.*
*"Ahoy there!" the captain **yelled** over to us.*

● **to send for someone:**

*Can someone please **fetch** a nurse?*
*The manager **sent for** the police at once.*
*I was **summoned** to the headmaster's office.*

● **to bring together:**

*They **assembled** the group for the closing ceremony.*
*The king has **convened** a council of elders.*
*He **gathered** us together in a small circle.*
*They **mustered** an army of over 10,000 men.*
*We have been **summoned** to a meeting this afternoon.*

● **to pay a visit:**

*I hate it when people just **drop in** without any warning.* (INFORMAL)
*Do **pop in** any time you're in the area.* (INFORMAL)
*I just thought I'd **stop by** on my way home.*

close

Close is another over-used word. Depending on whether you are talking about people or things which are close in *distance* or in *time*, the closeness of *personal relationships*, a closeness in *resemblance* between two things, or you are referring to a *description or translation*, you can use various other words as substitutes.

● **in distance:**

*Don't worry, help is **at hand**.*
*The fire spread to **adjacent** buildings.*
*the smell of hamburgers from the **adjoining** stall*
*Keep a pencil and paper **handy**.*
*The station is quite **near**.*
*I dashed into a **nearby** shop.*
*a man sitting at a **neighbouring** table*

● **in relationship:**

*We've got very **attached** to one another over the years.*
*a **dear** and valued companion*
*My parents were a deeply **devoted** couple.*
*I don't like men who try to get too **familiar**.*
*We gradually became very **friendly**.*
*one of my most **intimate** friends*
*They forged a **loving** relationship.*

● **in time:**

*My 30th birthday is **approaching**.*
*The time is **at hand** when we must take action.*

*Dawn is **coming**.*
*They now reckon a deal is **imminent**.*
*a sense of **impending** disaster*
*The day of reckoning is **near**.*

● **of a resemblance:**

*a vehicle with a **distinct** resemblance to a lunar buggy*
*There is a **marked** similarity between him and his brother.*
*a metal with **pronounced** similarities to lithium*
*prehistoric animals which bore a **strong** resemblance to horses*

● **of a description or translation:**

*an **accurate** description of her attacker*
*an **exact** translation of the phrase*
*a **faithful** rendition of the classic song*
*a **literal** interpretation of the words*
*Specify your requirements in **precise** detail.*
*a **strict** account of the events*

cry

There are a number of alternative words which you can use instead of **cry**, if you want to say a little more about how someone cries.

● If you **weep**, you cry. This is quite a literary word:

*The woman began to **weep** uncontrollably.*

● If you **whimper**, you make a low, unhappy sound as if you are about to cry:

*He huddled in a corner, **whimpering** with fear.*

● If you **sob**, you cry in a noisy way, with short breaths:

*Her sister broke down and began to **sob** into her handkerchief.*

● If you **blubber**, you cry noisily and in an unattractive way:

*To our surprise, he began to **blubber** like a child.*

● If you **howl** or **wail**, you cry with a long, loud noise:

*The baby was **howling** in the next room.*
*a mother **wailing** for her lost child*

● If you **bawl**, you cry very loudly:

*One of the toddlers was **bawling**.*

WORD STUDIES

There are many useful synonyms for the word **cut**. Different words are appropriate substitutes, depending on what it is that is being cut, what is being used to do the cutting, and how deep or extensive the cutting is.

● If you **nick** something, you make a small cut on its surface:

*He **nicked** his chin while he was shaving.*

● If you **score** something, you cut a line or lines on its surface:

*Lightly **score** the surface of the steaks with a cook's knife.*

● If you **pierce** something with a sharp object, or a sharp object **pierces** it, the object goes through it and makes a hole in it:

***Pierce** the skin of the potato with a fork.*
*One bullet had **pierced** his lung.*

● If something **penetrates** an object, it goes inside it or passes through it:

*a spider with fangs big enough to **penetrate** the skin*

● If you **slit** something, you make a long narrow cut in it:

*He began to **slit** open each envelope.*

● If you **gash** or **slash** something, you make a long, deep cut in it:

*He **gashed** his leg on the barbed wire.*
*She threatened to **slash** her wrists.*

● If you **clip** something, you cut small pieces from it in order to shape it:

*I saw an old man out **clipping** his hedge.*

● If you **trim** something, you cut off small amounts of it to make it look neater:

*I have my hair **trimmed** every eight weeks.*

● If you **pare** something, you cut off its skin or outer layer:

*She was sitting **paring** her nails with a pair of clippers.*

● If you **prune** a tree or bush, you cut off some of its branches:

*Apple trees can be **pruned** once they've lost their leaves.*

● If you **mow** grass, you cut it with a lawnmower:

*He **mowed** the lawn and did various other chores.*

● If you **snip** something, you cut it with scissors or shears:

*The hairdresser **snipped** off my split ends.*

● If you **split** or **divide** something, you cut it into two or more parts:

***Split** the planks down the middle.*
***Divide** the pastry into four equal parts.*

● If you **sever** something, you cut it off or cut right through it:

*He **severed** the tendon of his thumb in an industrial accident.*

● If you **saw** something, you cut it with a saw:

*Your father is **sawing** wood in the garden.*

● If you **hack** something, you cut it using rough strokes:

*Matthew desperately **hacked** through the straps.*

● If you **slice** something, you cut it into thin pieces:

*I **sliced** the beef into thin strips.*

● If you **chop** something, you cut it into pieces with strong downward movements of a knife or axe:

*You will need to **chop** the onions very finely.*

● If you **carve** an object, you make it by cutting it out of a substance such as wood or stone:

*He **carves** these figures from pine.*

● If you **carve** meat, you cut slices from it:

*Andrew began to **carve** the roast.*

● If you **hew** stone or wood, you cut it, perhaps with an axe. This is an old-fashioned word:

*He felled, peeled and **hewed** his own timber.*

● If you **hew** something out of stone or wood, you make it by cutting it from stone or wood:

*medieval monasteries **hewn** out of the rockface*

● If you **lop** something off, you cut it off with one quick stroke:

*Somebody has **lopped** the heads off our tulips.*

● If you **dock** an animal's tail, you cut it off:

*I think it is cruel to **dock** the tail of any animal.*

WORD STUDIES

WORD STUDIES

There are a number of more descriptive words which you can use instead of the basic **eat**, to say something about the way in which a person eats.

● If you **consume** something, you eat it. This is a formal word:

*Andrew would **consume** nearly a pound of cheese a day.*

● When an animal **feeds**, or **feeds on** something, it eats:

*After a few days the caterpillars stopped **feeding**.*
*Slugs **feed on** decaying plant material.*

● If you **swallow** something, you make it go from your mouth into your stomach:

*Snakes **swallow** their prey whole.*

● If you **snack**, you eat things between meals:

*Instead of **snacking** on crisps and chocolate, eat fruit.*

● If you **chew** something, you break it up with your teeth so that it is easier to swallow:

*I pulled out a filling while I was **chewing** a toffee.*

● If you **nibble** food, you eat it by biting very small pieces of it, perhaps because you are not very hungry:

*She **nibbled** at a piece of dry toast.*

● If you **munch** food, you eat it by chewing it slowly, thoroughly, and rather noisily:

*Luke **munched** his sandwiches appreciatively.*

● If you **stuff yourself**, you eat a lot of food:

*They'd **stuffed themselves** with sweets before dinner.*

● If you **gobble**, **guzzle**, **wolf (down)**, or **scoff** food, you eat it quickly and greedily. **Guzzle**, **wolf (down)**, and **scoff** are all informal words:

*Pete **gobbled** all the stew before anyone else arrived.*
*women who **guzzle** chocolate whenever they are unhappy*
*I was back in the changing room **wolfing** sandwiches.*
*She bought a hot dog from a stand and **wolfed** it down.*
*You greedy so-and-so! You've **scoffed** the lot!*

● If you **devour** something, you eat it quickly and eagerly:

*She **devoured** half an apple pie.*

end

End is a commonly over-used word. Depending on your context, you can use the following substitutes to add variety and interest to your writing.

● **of a period of time:**

The company made £100 million by the **close** of last year.
the **ending** of a great era
the **expiry** of his period of training
The college basketball season is nearing its **finish**.

● **of an event:**

the dramatic **climax** of the trial
the **close** of the festival
the **conclusion** of this fascinating tale
the remarkable **culmination** of a glittering career
a film with a tragic **ending**
a grand **finale** to the week-long celebrations
a disappointing **finish** to our adventures

● **the furthest part of something:**

We worked along the **boundaries** of the paths.
the landscape beyond the **bounds** of London
He fell off the **edge** of the cliff.
the western **extremity** of the continent
an area outside the official city **limits**

agricultural regions well beyond the forest **margin**

● **the point of something long or sharp:**

the southernmost **point** of the island
the **tip** of the knife

● **a leftover piece:**

a cigarette **butt**
Don't throw away all those trimmings and **leftovers**.
a doll made from **remnants** of fabric
scraps of spare material
a ticket **stub**
The **stump** of his left arm was bandaged.

● **the purpose of doing something:**

groups united by a common **aim**
We're all working towards the same **goal**.
He concealed his real **intentions**.
the stated **object** of the mission
the **objective** of all this effort
the true **purpose** of their visit
Are you here on holiday, or for business **reasons**?

fat

Some words used to describe a person who is overweight can be more hurtful or insulting than others. There are also words to describe varying degrees of being overweight.

● Someone who is **overweight** weighs more than is considered attractive. However, you can be just a little overweight as well as very overweight:

*Since having my baby, I feel slightly **overweight**.*

● If you say someone is **podgy**, you mean that they are slightly fat. This is an informal word:

*Eddie's getting a little **podgy** round the middle.*

● If you describe someone as **fleshy**, you mean that they are slightly too fat:

*He was well-built, but too **fleshy** to be an imposing figure.*

● A **chubby**, **tubby** or **stout** person is rather fat:

*I was greeted by a small, **chubby** man. He had been a short, **tubby** child who was taunted about his weight. a tall, **stout** man with gray hair*

● A **portly** person is rather fat. This word is mostly used to describe men:

*a **portly**, middle-aged man*

● You can use the word **plump** to describe someone who is rather fat or rounded, usually when you think this is a good quality:

*Maria was a pretty little thing, small and **plump** with a mass of dark curls.*

● If you describe a woman's figure as **rounded**, you mean that it is attractive because it is well-developed and not too thin:

*a beautiful woman with blue eyes and a full, **rounded** figure*

● A **roly-poly** person is pleasantly fat and round. This is an informal word:

*a short, **roly-poly** little woman with laughing eyes*

● If you describe a woman as **buxom**, you mean that she looks healthy and attractive and has a rounded body and big breasts:

*Melissa was a tall, **buxom** blonde.*

● If you describe someone as **obese**, you mean that they are extremely fat, perhaps to the point of being unhealthy:

***Obese** people tend to have higher blood pressure than lean people.*

● If you describe someone as **gross**, you mean that they are extremely fat and unattractive. This is a very insulting word to use:

*He tried to raise his **gross** body from the sofa.*

good

Like **bad**, the word **good** is used in so many ways to describe so many things that it has lost a great deal of its effectiveness. A wide range of synonyms is available to you for every context in which you might be tempted to use **good**; try to vary your language and vocabulary by choosing these instead.

● **in quality:**

an **acceptable** standard of education
The film has some **awesome** special effects. (SLANG)
We had an **excellent** meal.
a selection of **fine** wines
They played a **first-class** game.
a company offering a **first-rate** service
This is a **great** book.
I expect goods of a **satisfactory** quality at prices like these.
We stayed in a **splendid** hotel.
a **super** recipe (INFORMAL)
a **superb** selection of cheeses

● **of an experience:**

Her guests had an **agreeable** evening.
We spent a **delightful** few hours in the garden.
a very **enjoyable** trip
I had a **lovely** time in Paris.
We hope you have a **pleasant** stay.
The team has had a very **satisfactory** season.

● **having a beneficial effect:**

These changes could be **advantageous** for our business.
the **beneficial** effects of exercise
working under **favourable** conditions
training which produces **positive** results

● **morally virtuous:**

He showed **commendable** character in all his dealings with us.
No **decent** person would have said
such a thing.
an institution which prides itself on its **ethical** stance
just hard-working, **honest** citizens
An **honourable** person would have resigned.
They are law-abiding, morally **righteous** people.
a morally **upright** man
I try to live a **virtuous** life.
donating money to **worthy** causes

● **kind and thoughtful:**

a kindly and **benevolent** old man
She is too **charitable** to hurt his feelings.
He's **considerate** to his sisters.
I admire his **generous** and selfless nature.
a **gracious** and genial host
a **humane** and caring man
It's very **kind** of you to go to so much trouble.
donations from **kind-hearted** colleagues
At heart, he was a **kindly** soul.
an **obliging** fellow who is always glad to help
It was very **thoughtful** of him to offer.

● **skilled at something:**

a very **able** student
an **accomplished** pianist and composer
politicians who are **adept** at manipulating the press
She's a very **capable** nanny.
They are very **clever** at raising money

for charity.
a careful and **competent** worker
an **efficient** manager
inexperienced and **expert** cyclists
alike
I had a **first-rate** teacher.
a **proficient** driver
a **skilled** carpenter
the country's most **talented**
musicians

● **of behaviour:**

a school which rewards **disciplined**
behaviour
Elizabeth was a comparatively meek
and **docile** child.
a dutiful wife and three **obedient**
children
We expect **orderly** behaviour from our
pupils.
a polite and **well-behaved** boy
I was brought up to be **well-
mannered**.

● **of advice:**

Thank you for your thoughtful and
constructive input.
He made some very **helpful**
suggestions.
I need some **sound** advice.
I was given **practical** guidelines on

how to proceed.
some **useful** tips for beginners

● **of an idea:**

a **judicious** approach
a **practical** solution to the problem
a **prudent** strategy for economic
recovery
a **sensible** way out of our difficulties
a **wise** plan

● **of a price, sum of money,
amount or quantity:**

an **ample** supply of food
He has a **considerable** annual
income.
I had to pay a **fair** bit over the asking
price.
a **large** profit
A **reasonable** number of people
turned up.
She has been left a **substantial**
amount of money.

● **of a person's mood:**

He remained in **buoyant** spirits.
his unfailingly **cheerful** nature
the **genial** mood of the holidaymakers
She has a naturally **happy** disposition.
an **optimistic** frame of mind
He was in an unusually **sunny** mood.

great

There are a number of ways in which the word **great** can be used, depending on what you are referring to. But why not make your language more interesting and use one of the following instead?

● **in size:**

He lives in a **big** house.
a **colossal** tomb
a **huge** marquee in the grounds
a **large** pile of logs
They entered an **enormous** hall.
an **extensive** range of stock
a **gigantic** theme park
an **immense** building
a **stupendous** sum of money
It's a **tremendous** challenge
The fire destroyed a **vast** area of forest.

● **in degree:**

a job with a **high** degree of risk
driving at **excessive** speeds
I don't believe these **extravagant** claims.
a film containing **extreme** violence
tremendous strength

● **in importance:**

one of our **chief** problems
an **important** question
our **main** competitor
a **major** issue in the next election
a **momentous** occasion
Our **principal** aim
a **serious** deficiency in the system
This is a **significant** step towards peace.

● **in fame:**

the **celebrated** author of "Lord of the Rings"
a **distinguished** baritone
two **eminent** French scientists
the **famed** Australian actor
a **famous** artist

some of the world's most **illustrious** ballerinas
a **notable** chess player
Scotland's most **prominent** historian
the **renowned** heart surgeon

● **in skill:**

I had an **excellent** maths teacher.
slopes suitable only for **expert** skiers
a **masterly** display of teamwork
an **outstanding** cricketer
the most **skilful** snooker player in the world
a **skilled** boxer
He proved himself a **superb** goalkeeper.
a **superlative** thriller writer
a **talented** management team

● **in quality:**

a **beaut** place to live (AUSTRALIAN AND NEW ZEALAND)
He enjoys good food and **fine** wines.
an **excellent** pasta sauce
The room was full of **superb** works of art.
a **fantastic** firework display (INFORMAL)
They pride themselves on their **first-rate** service.
a **marvellous** rooftop restaurant (INFORMAL)
outstanding works of art
a **superb** staircase made from oak
It was a **terrific** party. (INFORMAL)
You've done a **tremendous** job. (INFORMAL)
I've had a **wonderful** time.

happy

Happy is another over-used word. You can vary your language by choosing one of the alternatives shown here.

● **displaying a cheerful nature or mood:**

a **cheerful** disposition
It's nice to see a **cheery** face round here for a change.
You're very **chirpy** today - has something nice happened? (INFORMAL)
Santa Claus is portrayed as a **jolly** fat man.
He broke into a **merry** laugh.
her unfailingly **sunny** nature

● **feeling joy at something:**

They seem **delighted** with their new home.
I was **ecstatic** to see Marianne again.
She was **elated** that she had won the lottery.
He is understandably **euphoric** over his success.
We're **glad** to be back.
He takes a **joyful** pride in his work.
They were **jubilant** over their election victory.
They were **overjoyed** to be reunited at last.
We're very **pleased** with the verdict.
I'm just **thrilled** to be playing again.
The team are **over the moon** with this result. (INFORMAL)

● **causing joy:**

I had the **agreeable** task of telling him the good news.
twenty years of **blissful** marriage
a truly **festive** occasion
We enjoyed a **gratifying** relationship.
A wedding is meant to be a **joyful** event.
the **joyous** news that he had been released
a **pleasurable** memory

● **willing to do something:**

She was **content** just to sit and watch.
I'm always **glad** to be of service.
I'll be **pleased** to take you there myself.
I'd be **prepared** to talk to him if you like.
He's **ready** to help anyone in trouble.
I'm **willing** to wait for you.

● **lucky:**

It was not an **auspicious** start to his new job.
a **convenient** outcome for all concerned
a **favourable** result
We're in a very **fortunate** situation.
It was a **lucky** chance that you were here.
It was hardly an **opportune** moment to bring the subject up.
his **timely** arrival

high

High is another word which has a number of meanings. Depending on just what you are describing as **high**, you have a whole range of substitutes to choose from to give your writing some added variety and expressiveness.

● **of a building, ceiling or mountain:**

an apartment in an **elevated** position overlooking the docks
lofty towers and spires
a 14th-century church with a **soaring** spire
the **steep** hill leading up to her house
a garden screened by **tall** walls
towering red sandstone cliffs

● **of an amount or degree:**

a state of **acute** anxiety
He was driving at **excessive** speed.
drinking **extraordinary** quantities of alcohol
acting under **extreme** emotional pressure
These products created a **great** level of interest.
There are **severe** penalties for drug smuggling.

● **of a cost or price:**

the **costly** premiums of private health insurance
The membership fee is too **dear** for me.
paying **expensive** prices for mediocre products
Their delivery charges are very **steep**.
(INFORMAL)

● **of a wind:**

a morning of **blustery** breezes
working in **extreme** wind and cold
There will be thunder and **squally** winds.
strong gusts of up to 60 miles per hour

the **violent** gales which have hit the North Sea

● **important:**

a **chief** position in the company
one of the country's most **eminent** scientists
He moves in **exalted** circles.
He held an **important** post in the government.
an **influential** place in the system
He is a **leading** figure in his field.
one of the most **powerful men** in Britain
her **pre-eminent** position among jazz singers
a host of **prominent** political figures
their **superior** status

● **of a voice or sound:**

A **high-pitched** cry split the air.
a **penetrating** whistle
a **piercing** note
a **shrill** scream
a **soprano** voice

● **of a person's spirits:**

They remain in **buoyant** spirits.
I've never seen him in such **cheerful** spirits.
that **elated** feeling you get when everything is going well
I was in an **exhilarated** frame of mind.
He is in one of his **exuberant** moods.
I felt **joyful** at the prospect of seeing him again.
We were all in a very **merry** mood.

hit

The word **hit** is often over-used. There are a number of more descriptive words which you can use to give additional information about the way in which something is hit, or how hard it is hit.

● If you **strike** someone or something, you hit them deliberately. This is a formal word:

*She stepped forward and **struck** him across the mouth.*

● If you **tap** something, you hit it with a quick light blow or series of blows:

***Tap** the egg gently with a teaspoon to crack the shell.*

● If you **pat** something or someone, you tap them lightly, usually with your hand held flat:

*"Don't worry about it," he said, **patting** me on the knee.*

● If you **rap** something, or **rap on** it, you hit it with a series of quick blows:

***rapping** the glass with the knuckles of his right hand*
*He **rapped on** the door with his cane.*

● If you **slap** or **smack** someone, you hit them with the palm of your hand:

*I **slapped** him hard across the face.*
*She **smacked** the child on the side of the head.*

● If you **swat** something such as an insect, you hit it with a quick, swinging movement using your hand or a flat object:

*Every time a fly came near, I **swatted** it with a newspaper.*

● If you **knock** someone or something, you hit it roughly, especially so that it falls or moves:

*She accidentally **knocked** the tin off the shelf.*

● If you **knock** something such as a door or window, you hit it, usually several times, to attract someone's attention:

*She went to his apartment and **knocked** the door loudly.*

● If you **beat** something, you hit it hard, usually several times or continuously for a period of time:

*a circle of men **beating** drums*

● If you **hammer** something, you hit it hard several times to make a noise:

*We had to **hammer** the door and shout to attract their attention.*

● If you **pound** something, you hit it with great force, usually loudly and repeatedly:

*He **pounded** the table with both fists.*

● If you **batter** someone or something, you hit them very hard, using your fists or a heavy object:

*He **battered** her round the head with a club.*

● If you **bang** something, you hit it hard, making a loud noise:

*We **banged** on the door and shouted to be let out.*

● If you **bang** a part of your body, you accidentally knock it against something and hurt it:

*She'd fainted and **banged** her head.*

● If you **belt** someone, you hit them very hard. This is an informal word:

*She drew back her fist and **belted** him right in the stomach.*

● If you **bash** someone or something, you hit them hard. This is an informal word:

*The chef was **bashed** over the head with a bottle.*

● If you **whack** someone or something, you hit them hard. This is an informal word:

*Someone **whacked** me with a baseball bat.*

● If you **wallop** someone or something, you hit them very hard, often causing a dull sound. This is an informal word:

*Once, she **walloped** me over the head with a frying pan.*

● If you **thump** someone or something, you hit them hard, usually with your fist:

*I'm warning you, if you don't shut up, I'll **thump** you.*

● If you **punch** someone or something, you hit them hard with your fist:

*After **punching** him on the chin, she ran off.*

laugh

There are a number of more interesting or creative words you can use in place of the basic verb **laugh**, if you want to say something about the way in which a person laughs.

● If you **chuckle**, you laugh quietly:

I chuckled to myself at the look on his face.

● If you **chortle**, you laugh in a pleased or amused way:

He sat there chortling at my predicament.

● If you **snigger**, you laugh in a quiet, sly way, perhaps at something rude or unkind:

two schoolboys who were telling dirty jokes and sniggering

● If you **giggle**, you laugh in a high-pitched way, because you are amused, nervous or embarrassed. This word is often used of *children* or *girls*:

They followed me around, giggling every time I spoke.

● If you **titter**, you give a short, nervous laugh, often at something rude or because you are embarrassed:

The audience began to titter as he came on dressed in drag.

● If you **cackle**, you laugh in a loud, harsh and unpleasant way, often at something bad which happens to someone else:

The old woman cackled in glee.

● If you **guffaw**, **howl**, or **roar**, you laugh very loudly because you think something is very funny:

They guffawed at me as I walked past.
The crowd howled at his antics.
He threw back his head and roared at this witticism.

little

Depending on what you are describing, you can choose from any of the following alternatives instead of the over-used word **little**.

● **of objects: in physical size:**

dainty sandwiches and cakes
He grows **dwarf** tulips.
a machine which resembles a **mini** laptop computer
a collection of **miniature** toy boats
minute particles of soil
a children's zoo with **pygmy** goats
dressed only in a **skimpy** bikini
They sat at a **small** table.
He tore the paper into **tiny** pieces.
Would you like a **wee** bit of cake?

● **of people: in height:**

a **dainty** Japanese girl
his **diminutive** stature
clothes specially designed for **petite** women
I was too **short** to reach the top shelf.
a short, **squat** figure
a **tiny** woman who only came up to his shoulder
He's only a **wee** guy, but he's strong.

● **in duration:**

There was a **brief** pause.
We only got a **fleeting** glimpse of his face.
He took a **hasty** peek at the list.
It was just a **momentary** lapse of memory.
She gave me a **quick** smile.
I need a **short** break.

● **in quantity:**

He's done **hardly any** work today.
There's **not much** difference between

them.
a **meagre** pay increase
a **measly** ration of food
a boring job with a **paltry** salary
He paid **scant** attention to his colleagues.

● **in age:**

my **baby** sister
a mother with her **infant** son
She has two **small** kids to support.
He was only a **young** child when his parents died.

● **in importance:**

an **insignificant** detail
a **minor** squabble
Their influence is **negligible**.
petty complaints
I don't want to bother him with such a **trifling** problem.
time wasted in discussing **trivial** matters
an **unimportant** event

● **a small amount:**

I wouldn't mind a **bit** of peace.
He spoke with a **dash** of bravado.
They only need a **fragment** of skin tissue to provide a DNA sample.
a delicate dish with just a **hint** of coriander
I only carry a **small amount** of cash.
Just a **spot** of milk for me, thanks.
There was a **touch** of irritation in his voice.
a **trace** of blood on the carpet

long

Try to vary your language by using one of these substitutes for **long**.

● **in physical extent:**

*The catfish has an **elongated** body.*
*an **extensive** list of products*
***lengthy** queues*

● **in duration:**

*an **extended** period of unemployment*
*the **interminable** debate about GM foods*

*a **lengthy** delay*
*a **lingering** death from cancer*
*the effects of a **long-drawn-out** war*
*A **prolonged** labour is dangerous for both mother and child.*
***protracted** negotiations over pay rises*
*Writing music is a **slow** process.*
*a **sustained** run of bad luck*

look

All of the following words mean **to look**, but each one has an extra shade of meaning which makes it a more expressive substitute for the word **look** in particular situations or contexts.

● If you **glance**, **peek**, or **peep** at something, you look at it quickly, and often secretly:

He glanced at his watch as she spoke.
She peeked at him through the curtains.
He peeped at me to see if I was watching him.

● If you **scan** something written or printed, you look at it quickly:

She scanned the advertisement pages of the newspapers.

● If you **eye** or **regard** someone or something, you look at them carefully:

The waiters eyed him with suspicion.
He regarded me curiously.

● If you **gaze** or **stare** at someone or something, you look at them steadily for a long time, for example because you find them interesting or because you are thinking about something else. **Staring** is often thought to be rude, but **gazing** is not:

She sat gazing into the fire for a long time.
They stared silently into each other's eyes.

● If you **observe** or **watch** someone or something, you look at them for a period of time to see what they are doing or what is happening:

A man was observing him from across the square.
I hate people watching me while I eat.

● If you **survey** or **view** someone or something, you look at the whole of them carefully:

He stood up and surveyed the crowd.
The mourners filed past to view the body.

● If you **examine**, **scrutinize**, or **study** something, you look at it very carefully, often to find out information from it:

He examined all the evidence.
He scrutinized her passport and stamped it.
We studied the menu for several minutes.

● If you **glare**, **glower**, or **scowl** at someone, you stare at them angrily:

He glared resentfully at me.
She stood glowering at me with her arms crossed.
She scowled at the two men as they came into the room.

● If you **peer** or **squint** at something, you try to see it more clearly by narrowing or screwing up your eyes as you look at it:

He was peering at me through the keyhole.
She squinted at the blackboard, trying to read what was on it.

● If you **gape** at someone or something, you look at them in surprise, usually with your mouth open:

*She was **gaping** at the wreckage, lost for words.*

● If you **goggle** at someone or something, you look at them with your eyes wide open, usually because you are surprised by them:

*He **goggled** at me in disbelief.*

● If you **ogle** someone, you look at them in a way that makes it very obvious that you find them attractive:

*I hate the way he **ogles** every woman who goes by.*

mark

Mark is rather a vague word. Depending on what you are referring to, there are a number of more interesting synonyms which you can use in its place.

● **a stain:**

an ink **blot**
A **line** of dirt ran across his face like a scar.
a lipstick **smudge** on his collar
He noticed a grease **spot** on his trousers.
a **stain** on the front of his shirt
A **streak** of mud smudged her cheek.

● **a damaged area:**

slight **blemishes** on her skin
He had ugly purple **blotches** all over his face.
Her face was dotted with cuts and **bruises**.
There was a tiny **dent** on the bonnet.
little **nicks** on his chin from shaving
a jagged **scar** on his forehead
a long **scratch** across the tabletop

● **a written or printed symbol:**

a jade pendant carved with Chinese **characters**
The company's **emblem** is a red diamond.
The box was stamped with the Papal **insignia**.
a multiplication **sign**

the date **stamp** on the front of the envelope
a flag bearing the **symbol** of the swastika

● **a characteristic of something:**

all the essential **attributes** of a good leader
a defining **characteristic** of the middle classes
the fundamental **features** of a democracy
the compassion that was the **hallmark** of his films
It is a **measure** of how much things have changed.
a **symptom** of depression
a common **trait** of all great athletes

● **an indication of something:**

a **gesture** of goodwill
an **indication** of his regard for the king
The shops closed as a **sign** of respect.
He wore black as a **symbol** of mourning.
The gifts were a **token** of our friendship.

move

Move is not a very expressive word. If you can use a more descriptive substitute to say something about the way in which a person or thing moves, it will give your writing variety and interest.

● When a person **crawls**, they move forwards on their hands and knees:

*As he tried to **crawl** away, he was kicked in the head.*

● When an insect **crawls** somewhere, it moves there quite slowly:

*I watched the moth **crawl** up the outside of the lampshade.*

● If a person or animal **creeps** somewhere, they move quietly and slowly:

*I tried to **creep** upstairs without being heard.*

● To **inch** somewhere means to move there very carefully and slowly:

*He began to **inch** along the ledge.*

● If you **edge** somewhere, you move very slowly in that direction:

*He **edged** closer to the telephone.*

● If a person or animal **slithers** somewhere, they move by sliding along the ground in an uneven way:

*Robert lost his footing and **slithered** down the bank.*
*The snake **slithered** into the water.*

● If you **wriggle** somewhere, for example through a small gap, you move there by twisting and turning your body:

*I **wriggled** through a gap in the fence.*

● When people or small animals **scamper** or **scuttle** somewhere, they move there quickly with small, light steps:

*The children got off the bus and **scampered** into the playground.*
*The crabs **scuttled** along the muddy bank.*

● When people or small animals **scurry** somewhere, they move there quickly and hurriedly, often because they are frightened:

*The attack began, sending residents **scurrying** for cover.*

● If you **hurry**, **race**, or **rush** somewhere, you go there as quickly as you can:

*Claire **hurried** along the road.*
*He **raced** across town to the hospital.*
*A schoolgirl **rushed** into a burning building to save a baby.*

● If you **hasten** somewhere, you hurry there. This is a literary word:

*He **hastened** along the corridor to Grace's room.*

● If you **hare off** somewhere, you go there very quickly. This is an informal British word:

*She **hared off** to ring the doctor.*

● If you **dash**, **dart**, or **shoot** somewhere, you run or go there quickly and suddenly:

*She jumped up and **dashed** out of the room.*

*The girl turned and **darted** away through the trees.*
*They had almost reached the boat when a figure **shot** past them.*

● If you say that someone or something **flies** in a particular direction, you are emphasizing that they move there with a lot of speed and force:

*I **flew** downstairs to answer the door.*

● If you **tear** somewhere, you move there very quickly, often in an uncontrolled or dangerous way:

*Without looking to left or right, he **tore** off down the road.*

● When you **run**, you move quickly because you are in a hurry to get somewhere:

*I excused myself and **ran** back to the telephone.*

● If you **jog**, you run slowly:

*She **jogged** off in the direction he had indicated.*

● If you **sprint**, you run as fast as you can over a short distance:

*The sergeant **sprinted** to the car.*

● If you **gallop**, you run somewhere very quickly:

*They were **galloping** round the garden playing football.*

● If a person or animal **bolts**, they suddenly start to run very fast, often because something has frightened them:

*I made some excuse and **bolted** towards the exit.*

● If a group of animals or people **stampede**, they run in a wild, uncontrolled way:

*The crowd **stampeded** out of the hall.*

WORD STUDIES

Depending on the sense of **new** which you mean, there are a number of alternatives which you can use to vary your writing and make it more interesting.

● **recently discovered or created:**

trial results of the company's most **advanced** drugs
all the **current** gossip on the stars
fresh footprints in the snow
a **ground-breaking** discovery
We review all the **latest** films.
modern technology
Lawson's most **recent** novel
an **ultra-modern** shopping mall
the most **up-to-date** computers
up-to-the-minute information

● **not used or owned before:**

I can't afford a **brand new** car.

He turned to a **fresh** page in his notebook.
shops selling **unused** wedding dresses and bridesmaids' dresses

● **unfamiliar:**

a completely **different** idea to attract the tourist market
a **novel** way to lose weight
an **original** idea
I was alone in a **strange** country.
the **unaccustomed** experience of having money to spend
I like visiting **unfamiliar** places.
This terrain is completely **unknown** to me.

nice

When you are writing or talking and you are going to use the word **nice**, try to think of a more descriptive and interesting word instead. Here are some ideas for words and phrases that you might use to describe different aspects of people and things.

● **of someone's appearance:**

*She's grown into an **attractive** young lady.*
*You're looking very **beautiful** tonight.*
*He's going out with a very **cute** girl.*
*I used to think he was **dishy** when I was younger.*
*Her son is **good-looking**, but very shy.*
*I think he's really **gorgeous**.*
*a very **handsome** young man*
*He married a **lovely** woman.*
*You look very **pretty** in that dress.*

● **of an object, place or view:**

*We found a **beautiful** little antique shop.*
*a **charming** little fishing village*
*a **delightful** place for a honeymoon*
*a **lovely** old English garden*
*a **pretty** room overlooking the courtyard*

● **of clothing:**

*a **chic** designer frock*
*That's a very **elegant** dress you're wearing.*
*a **fetching** outfit*
*I was wearing a **smart** navy-blue suit.*
*She always has such **stylish** clothes.*

● **of an event or occasion:**

*It's not a very **agreeable** way to spend your day off.*
*We had a **delightful** time.*
*The trip was much more **enjoyable** than I had expected.*
*Thanks for giving me such a **fantastic** party.*

*Have a **lovely** holiday!*
*It was a very **pleasant** experience.*
*the **pleasurable** sensation of getting into a warm bath*

● **of someone's personality:**

*I've always found him a very **amiable** man.*
*He's very **considerate** towards his sisters.*
*They aren't very **friendly** to strangers.*
*She is unfailingly **good-natured**.*
*I try to be **kind** to everyone.*
*a **kindly** old man*
*He was an immensely **likeable** chap.*
*That was a very **thoughtful** gesture.*

● **of food or drink:**

*An **appetizing** smell was coming from the kitchen.*
*We bought some **delectable** raspberries.*
*The food here is **delicious**.*
***luscious** peaches*
*a **mouthwatering** dessert*
*a café serving **tasty** dishes*

● **of the weather:**

*It was a **beautiful** morning.*
*I'll do the garden if the weather is **fine**.*
*It's a **glorious** day!*

● **of a room, flat or house:**

*I tried to make a **comfortable** home for my family.*
*a **cosy** parlour*
*a house with a **homely** atmosphere*
*This is a very **relaxing** room.*

Depending on the sense of **old** which you mean, there are a number of alternatives which you can use to vary your writing and make it more interesting.

● **having lived for a long time:**

an **aged** parent
her **ancient** grandparents
an **elderly** man
a **venerable** father-figure

● **in the past:**

relics of **ancient** cultures
rituals of a **bygone** civilization
his children from an **earlier** marriage
heroes of those **early** days of rock
his **ex**-wife
a **former** lover
Life was much harder in **olden** times.
the **one-time** president
a long list of **past** grievances
the **previous** tenants
They discovered his **prior** criminal
convictions.
harking back to those **remote** days of glory

● **out of date:**

antiquated teaching methods
archaic practices such as these
These buildings are very much **behind the times** in terms of design.
Some of the language sounds quite **dated** now.
These computers are **obsolete** almost before they're in the shops.
an **old-fashioned** style of writing
such **outdated** attitudes
working with **outmoded** equipment
a make of car that is now **out of date**
That kind of music is **passé**.

say

There are a number of more interesting or creative words you can use in place of the basic verbs **say**, **speak**, and **talk**, if you want to describe the way in which a person says something.

● If someone **utters** sounds or words, they say them. This is a literary word:

*They left without **uttering** a single word.*

● If you **comment** on something, you say something about it:

*He has refused to **comment** on these reports.*

● If you **remark** that something is the case, you say that it is the case:

*"I don't see you complaining," he **remarked**.*

● If you **state** something, you say it in a formal or definite way:

*Could you please **state** your name for the record?*

● If you **mention** something, you say something about it, usually briefly:

*He never **mentioned** that he was married.*

● If you **note** something, you mention it in order to bring people's attention to it:

*"It's already getting dark," he **noted**.*

● If you **observe** that something is the case, you make a comment about it, especially when it is something you have noticed or thought about a lot:

*"He's a very loyal friend," Daniel **observed**.*

● If you **point out** a fact or mistake, you tell someone about it or draw their attention to it:

*"You've not done so badly out of the deal," she **pointed out**.*

● If you **announce** something, you tell people about it publicly or officially:

*"We're engaged!" she **announced**.*

● If you **affirm** something, you state firmly that it is the case:

*"I'm staying right here," he **affirmed**.*

● If someone **asserts** a fact or belief, they state it firmly:

*"The facts are clear," the Prime Minister **asserted**.*

● If you **declare** that something is true, you say that it is true in a firm, deliberate way:

*"I'm absolutely thrilled with the result," he **declared**.*

● If you **add** something when you are speaking, you say something more:

*"Anyway, it serves you right," she **added** defiantly.*

● If you **interrupt**, you say something while someone else is speaking:

*"I don't think you quite understand," James **interrupted**.*

● If you **put in** a remark, you interrupt someone or add to what they have said with the remark:

"Not that it's any of your business," Helen **put in**.

● When people **chat**, they talk to each other in a friendly and informal way:

*We were just standing **chatting** in the corridor.*

● If you **converse** with someone, you talk to them. This is a formal word:

*They were **conversing** in German.*

● When people **natter**, they talk casually for a long time about unimportant things:

*Susan and her friend were still **nattering** when I left.*

● If you **gossip** with someone, you talk informally, especially about other people or events:

*We sat and **gossiped** well into the evening.*

● If you **explain** something, you give details about it so that it can be understood:

*"We weren't married at that point," she **explained**.*

● If you **ask** something, you say it in the form of a question because you want to know the answer:

*"How is Frank?" he **asked**.*

● If you **inquire** about something, you ask for information about it. This is a formal word:

*"Is something wrong?" he **inquired**.*

● To **query** or **question** means to ask a question:

*"Can I help you?" the assistant **queried**.*
*"What if something goes wrong?" he **questioned** anxiously.*

● When you **answer** or **reply** to someone who has just spoken, you say something back to them:

"When are you leaving?" she asked.
*"Tomorrow," he **answered**.*
"That's a nice outfit," he commented.
*"Thanks," she **replied**.*

● When you **respond** to something that has been said, you react to it by saying something yourself:

*"Are you well enough to carry on?" "Of course," she **responded** scornfully.*

● If you **riposte**, you make a quick, clever response to something that someone has just said. This is a formal word:

*"It's tough at the top," I said. "It's even tougher at the bottom," he **riposted**.*

● To **retort** means to reply angrily to someone. This is a formal word:

*"I don't agree," James said. "Who cares what you think?" she **retorted**.*

● If someone **babbles**, they talk in a confused or excited way:

*"I'm so excited I don't know what I'm doing," she **babbled**.*

● If you **chatter**, you talk quickly and excitedly about things which are not important:

*Everyone was **chattering** away in different languages.*

● If you **gabble**, you say things so quickly that it is difficult for people to understand you:

*Marcello sat on his knee and **gabbled** excitedly.*

● If you **prattle**, you talk a great deal about something unimportant:

*She was **prattling** on about this guy she had met the night before.*

● If someone **rambles**, they talk but do not make much sense because they keep going off the subject:

*an old man who **rambled** about his feud with his neighbours*

● If someone **breathes** something, they say it very quietly. This is a literary word:

*"Oh, thank God you're here," he **breathed**.*

● When you **whisper**, you say something very quietly, using your breath rather than your throat:

*"Keep your voice down," I **whispered**.*

● If you **hiss** something, you say it forcefully in a whisper:

*"Stay here and don't make a sound," he **hissed**.*

● If you **mumble**, you speak very quietly and not at all clearly, so that your words are hard to make out:

*"I didn't know I was meant to do it," she **mumbled**.*

● If you **murmur** something, you speak very quietly, so that not many people can hear you:

*"How convenient," I **murmured**.*

● If you **mutter**, you speak very quietly, often because you are complaining about something:

*"Oh great," he **muttered**, "That's all I need."*

● If you **croak** something, you say it in a low, rough voice:

*"Water!" he **croaked**.*

● If you **grunt** something, you say it in a low voice, often because you are annoyed or not interested:

*"Rubbish," I **grunted**, "You just didn't try hard enough."*

● If you **rasp** something, you say it in a harsh, unpleasant voice:

*"Get into the car," he **rasped**.*

● If you **wheeze** something, you say it with a whistling sound, for example because you cannot get your breath:

*"I'm really out of condition," I **wheezed**.*

● If you **gasp** something, you say it in a short, breathless way, especially because you are surprised, shocked, or in pain:

*"What do you mean?" she **gasped**.*

● If you **pant** something, you say it while breathing loudly and quickly with your mouth open because you have been doing something energetic:

*"Let me get my breath back," he **panted**, "I'm not as young as I used to be."*

● If you **groan** or **moan** something, you say it in a low voice, usually because you are unhappy or in pain:

*"My leg - I think it's broken," Eric **groaned**.*

"I can't stand it any longer," she **moaned**.

● When someone **growls** something, they say it in a low, rough, and angry voice:

"I ought to kill you for this," Sharpe **growled**.

● If you **snarl** something, you say it in a fierce, angry way:

"Get out of here," he **snarled**.

● If you **snap** at someone, you speak to them in a sharp, unfriendly way:

"Of course you can't have it," he **snapped**.

Some words used to describe a person who is **short** can be more hurtful or insulting than others.

● A **little** or **small** person is not large in physical size:

*She was too **little** to reach the books on the top shelf.*
*She is **small** for her age.*

● A **diminutive** person is very small:

*a **diminutive** figure standing at the entrance*

● A **tiny** person is extremely small:

*Though she was **tiny**, she had a loud voice.*

● If you describe a woman as **petite**, you are politely saying that she is

small and not fat. This is a complimentary word:

*a **petite** blonde woman*

● If you describe someone as **dumpy**, you mean they are short and fat. This is an uncomplimentary word:

*a **dumpy** woman in a baggy tracksuit*

● If you describe someone as **squat**, you mean that they are short and thick, usually in an unattractive way:

*Eddie was a short, **squat** fellow in his mid-forties.*

small

Depending on the sense of **small** which you mean, there are a number of alternatives which you can use to vary your writing and make it more interesting.

● **of things: in size:**

*We sat around a **little** table.*
*a **miniature** camera*
*wearing a pair of **minuscule** shorts*
*Only a **minute** amount is needed.*
*The living room is **tiny**.*

● **in area:**

*It's only a **little** distance from the station.*
*trying to squeeze through a **narrow** space*
*Plants, like animals, often have a **restricted** habitat.*

● **of a business:**

*He started with one **humble** corner shop.*
*The company started from **modest** beginnings.*
*a **small-scale** cheese industry*
*an **unpretentious** restaurant*

● **of people: in size:**

*a **diminutive** figure standing at the entrance*
*a **dumpy** woman in a baggy tracksuit*
*She was too **little** to reach the books on the top shelf.*
*a **petite** blonde woman*

*She is **small** for her age.*
*Eddie was a short, **squat** fellow in his mid-forties.*
*Though she was **tiny**, she had a loud voice.*

● **of people: young:**

*my **baby** sister*
*an **infant** prodigy*
*What did you look like when you were **little**?*
*a **young** child*

● **in importance:**

*a seemingly **inconsequential** event*
*an **insignificant** village in the hills*
*Fancy making such a fuss over such a **little** thing!*
*a **minor** detail*
*The impact of the strike will be **negligible**.*
*Rows would start over the most **petty** things.*
*It will only make a **slight** difference.*
*These are **trifling** objections.*
*Let's not get bogged down in **trivial** details.*
*a comparatively **unimportant** event*

strong

Strong is an over-used word. Depending on what you are referring to, there are many substitutes which you can use in its place to add variety and interest to your writing.

● **of a person: having powerful muscles:**

He was tall and **athletic**.
a **brawny** young rugby player
a big, **burly** man
Like most female athletes, she was lean and **muscular**.
a **powerful** bodybuilder
He was a bricklayer - a big, **strapping** fellow.
a fit, **well-built** runner

● **of a person: in good physical condition:**

She is positively **blooming** with health.
It won't be long till you're **fit** again.
She had a normal pregnancy and delivered a **healthy** child.
He's **in good condition** for his age.
He was never a **robust** child.
You need to be in **sound** physical condition to play this sport.

● **of a person: confident and courageous:**

You have to be **brave** for the children's sake.
a **courageous** leader
a **plucky** schoolgirl who battled leukaemia
You've always been **resilient** - I know you'll get over this.
He's attracted to feisty, **self-confident** women.
You have to be **tough** to survive in this business.

● **of an object: able to withstand rough treatment:**

made of **durable** plastic
hard-wearing cotton overalls
a **heavy-duty** canvas bag
reinforced concrete supports
a camera mounted on a **sturdy** tripod
a **substantial** boat with a powerful rigging
a **tough** vehicle designed for all terrains
You need a **well-built** fence all round the garden.

● **of feelings: great in degree or intensity:**

acute feelings of self-consciousness
an **ardent** admirer of his work
He harboured a **deep** resentment of me.
my **fervent** hope that things will get better
He inspires **fierce** loyalty in his friends.
an **intense** dislike of spiders
He has a **keen** interest in football.
I'm a **passionate** believer in animal rights.
his **profound** distrust of their motives
His announcement sparked off **vehement** criticism.
His plans met with **violent** hostility.
his **zealous** religious beliefs

● **of an argument: convincing or supported by a lot of evidence:**

There is a **compelling** case for higher spending on education.
It is, on first sight, a **convincing** theory.
Industry has produced some **effective** arguments against the tax.

There are **persuasive** reasons justifying the move.
a **sound** case for using organically-grown produce
the most **telling** condemnation of the system

● of a smell: very noticeable:

an **overpowering** aftershave
a **powerful** smell of ammonia
the **pungent** aroma of oregano

● of food or drink: having a powerful flavour:

a **hot** curry
the **overpowering** taste of chillis
a **piquant** sauce
a liqueur with a **powerful** aniseed flavour
I love the **sharp** taste of pickles.
Avoid **spicy** foods and alcohol.

● of a person's accent: very noticeable:

He has developed a **distinct** American drawl.
a **marked** West country accent
It took me a while to adjust to his **noticeable** southern accent.
the Cuban-born actor with the **unmistakeable** Latin accent

● of colours: very bright:

She always dresses in **bold** colours.
a room decorated in **bright** reds and blues
Brilliant jewel colours are in this season.
dressed in a **glaring** red Chanel dress and jacket
He likes shirts with **loud** patterns.

thin

Some words which you might use to describe someone who is **thin** are complimentary, some are neutral, and others are definitely uncomplimentary.

● A **slender** person is attractively thin and graceful:

*a tall, **slender** lady in a straw hat*

● A **slim** person has an attractively thin and well-shaped body:

*a pretty, **slim** girl with blue eyes*

● A **slight** person has a fairly thin and delicate-looking body:

*He is a **slight**, bespectacled, intellectual figure.*

● A **light** person does not weigh very much:

*You need to be **light** to be a dancer.*

● Someone who is **spare** is tall and not at all fat. This is a literary word:

*She was thin and **spare**, with a sharp, intelligent face.*

● If you describe someone as **lean**, you mean that they are thin but look strong and healthy:

*Like most athletes, she was **lean** and muscular.*

● If you say someone is **lanky**, you mean that they are tall and thin and move rather awkwardly:

*He had grown into a **lanky** teenager.*

● A **skinny** person is extremely thin, in a way that you find unattractive. This is an informal word:

*I don't think these **skinny** supermodels are at all sexy.*

● If you say a person is **scraggy** or **scrawny**, you mean that they look unattractive because they are so thin:

*a **scraggy**, shrill, neurotic woman*
*a **scrawny** child of fifteen*

● Someone who is **bony** has very little flesh covering their bones:

*a **bony** old woman dressed in black*

● If someone is **underweight**, they are too thin and therefore not healthy:

*Nearly a third of the girls were severely **underweight**.*

● A person or animal that is **emaciated** is very thin and weak from illness or lack of food:

*horrific television pictures of **emaciated** prisoners*

walk

There are a number of more interesting or creative words you can use in place of the basic verb **walk**, if you want to say something about the way in which a person walks.

● If you **step** in a particular direction, you move your foot in that direction:

*I **stepped** carefully over the piles of rubbish.*

● If you **tread** in a particular way, you walk in that way. This is rather a literary word:

*She **trod** carefully across the grass.*

● If you **amble** or **stroll**, you walk in a slow, relaxed way:

*We **ambled** along the beach hand in hand.*
*They **strolled** down the High Street, looking in shop windows.*

● If you **saunter**, you walk in a slow, casual way:

*He was **sauntering** along as if he had all the time in the world.*

● If you **wander**, you walk around in a casual way, often without intending to go anywhere in particular:

*Khachi was **wandering** aimlessly about in the garden.*

● If you **tiptoe**, you walk very quietly without putting your heels on the ground, so as not to be heard:

*She slipped out of bed and **tiptoed** to the window.*

● If you **toddle**, you walk unsteadily, with short quick steps. This word is

most often used of babies or small children:

*My daughter **toddles** around after me wherever I go.*

● If you **mince**, you walk with quick, small steps in a put-on, effeminate way:

*drag artists **mincing** around the stage in tight dresses and high heels*

● If you **pace**, you walk up and down a small area, usually because you are anxious or impatient:

*As he waited, he **paced** nervously around the room.*

● If you **stride**, you walk with quick, long steps:

*He turned abruptly and **strode** off down the corridor.*

● If you **march**, you walk quickly and in a determined way, perhaps because you are angry:

*She **marched** into the office and demanded to see the manager.*

● If you **stamp**, you put your feet down very hard when you walk, usually because you are angry:

*"I'm leaving!" he shouted as he **stamped** out of the room.*

● If you **flounce**, you walk quickly and with exaggerated movements, in a way that shows you are annoyed or upset about something:

*She **flounced** out of the room in a huff.*

● If you **stalk**, you walk in a stiff, proud, or angry way:

*He **stalked** out of the meeting, slamming the door.*

● If you **lurch**, you walk with sudden, jerky movements:

*He **lurched** around the room as if he was drunk.*

● If you **stagger** or **totter**, you walk very unsteadily, often because you are ill or drunk:

*He **staggered** home from the pub every night.*
*I had to **totter** around on crutches for six weeks.*

● If you **reel**, you walk about in an unsteady way as if you are going to fall:

*He lost his balance and **reeled** back.*

● If you **stumble**, you trip while you are walking and almost fall:

*I **stumbled** into the phone box and dialled 999.*

● If you **hike** or **ramble**, you walk some distance in the countryside for pleasure:

*They **hiked** along a remote trail.*
*a relaxing holiday spent **rambling** over the fells*

● If you **trek**, you make a journey across difficult country by walking:

*This year we're going **trekking** in Nepal.*

● You can also use **trek** to describe someone walking rather slowly and unwillingly, usually because they are tired:

*We **trekked** all round the shops looking for white shoes.*

● If you **plod**, **tramp**, or **trudge**, you walk slowly, with heavy steps, often because you are tired:

*He **plodded** about after me, looking bored.*
*They spent all day **tramping** through the snow.*
*We had to **trudge** all the way back up the hill.*

wide

There are a number of ways in which the word **wide** can be used, depending on what you are referring to. But you can make your language more interesting by using one of the following instead.

● **measuring a large distance from side to side:**

*a large woman with an **ample** bosom*
*He was wearing ridiculously **baggy** trousers.*
*His shoulders were **broad** and his waist narrow.*
*The park has swings and an **expansive** play area.*
*The grounds were more **extensive** than the town itself.*
*She was wearing a dress with a **full** skirt.*
*an **immense** body of water*
*This fish lives mainly in **large** rivers and lakes.*
*I like **roomy** jackets with big pockets.*
*The house has a **spacious** kitchen.*
*the long **sweeping** curve of the bay*
*The farmers there own **vast** stretches of land.*
*a **voluminous** trench coat*

● **extensive in scope:**

*There is **ample** scope here for the imagination.*
*A **broad** range of issues was discussed.*
*He has very **catholic** tastes in music.*

*a **comprehensive** guide to the region*
*He has an **encyclopedic** knowledge of the subject.*
*The author's treatment of the topic is **exhaustive**.*
*The question has received **extensive** press coverage.*
*the plan to introduce **far-ranging** reforms*
*an **immense** range of holiday activities*
*an **inclusive** survey*
*a **large** selection of goods at reasonable prices*
*a **vast** range of products*
*The aims of the redesign are **wide-ranging** but simple.*

● **as far as possible:**

*He opened the map out **completely** so we could see.*
*I could tell from his **dilated** pupils that he was on drugs.*
*Extend the aerial **fully**.*
*His mouth was **fully open** in astonishment.*
*Spread it **right out** to the edges.*

Subject Lists

Contents

ART

abstract
acrylic
charcoal
collage
collection
colour
crosshatch
dimension
display
easel
exhibition
foreground
frieze

gallery
highlight
illusion
impasto
kiln
landscape
palette
pastel
perspective
portrait
sketch
spectrum

DESIGN AND FOOD TECHNOLOGY

aesthetic
brief
carbohydrate
component
design
diet
evaluation
fabric
fibre
flour
flow chart
hygiene
ingredient
innovation
knife
knives
linen

machine
manufacture
mineral
natural
nutrition
polyester
portfolio
presentation
production
protein
recipe
sew
specification
tension
textile
vitamin

ENGLISH LITERATURE

POETRY

accented
alliteration
allusion
apostrophe
assonance
atmosphere
ballad
caesura
chorus
clause
clerihew
cliché
comparison
conjunction
connotation
consonant
couplet
dialogue
direct speech
effect
figurative
figure of speech
function
genre
haiku
hexameter
iambic foot
iambic pentameter
iambic rhythm
imagery
intention
limerick
metaphor
meter
monosyllable

monosyllabic
myth
narration
narrator
octave
ode
onomatopoeia
onomatopoeiac
pentameter
personification
playwright
poetic licence
quatrain
refrain
repetition
resolution
rhyme
rhyming couplet
rhythm
scanning
scene
sentimentality
sestet
simile
soliloquy
sonnet
stanza
stressed
structure
subordinate
syllable
synonym
tetrameter
tone
unaccented syllable
unstressed syllable
vocabulary
vowel

PROSE

advertise
advertisement
author
character
comma
exclamation
expectation
exposition
first person
flat character
grammar
impersonal narrator
introduction
intrusive narrator
irony
ironic
limited point of view

narrator
narrative voice
omniscient point of view
pamphlet
paragraph
plot
plural
prefix
preposition
punctuation
round character
second person
story
suffix
tabloid
third person
trait

GEOGRAPHY

ECONOMIC WORLD

arable farming
chemical fertiliser
commercial farming
factory farms
farming subsidies
fungicide
heavy industry
herbicide
human development index
life expectancy
light industry

migrant workers
mixed farming
natural resources
nonrenewable resources
organic farming
pastoral farming
renewable resources
shanty settlement
shifting cultivation
subsistence farming

ENVIRONMENTAL WORLD

biosphere
herbivore

organism
photosynthesis

GEOMORPHOLOGICAL PROCESSES

abrasion
alluvium
atmospheric depression
attrition
beach nourishment
biological weathering
chemical weathering
coastal flooding
confluence
corrasion
corrosion
deposition
drainage basin
erosion
flood plain

freeze-thaw
global warming
hurricane
igneous rock
metamorphic rock
metamorphosis
physical weathering
reefs
sedimentary rock
storm surge
typhoon
waterfall
wave-cut notch
wave-cut platform
weathering

THE PHYSICAL WORLD

acid lava
basic lava
composite volcano
compressional plate boundary
crater

destructive boundary
epicentre
lava
magma
Richter scale

seismograph
shield volcano
tectonic plates

tensional plate boundary
tsunami

POPULATION

conurbation
counter urbanisation
depopulation
dot map
internal migration

international migration
population density
population distribution
population pyramids
rural urban fringe

WEATHER AND CLIMATE

acid rain
altitude
anemometer
atmosphere
Beaufort scale
climate
condensation
convectional rainfall
deforestation
depression
drought
equatorial regions
evaporation
fossil fuels
frontal rain
greenhouse effect
hydrology
infiltration
isobar

isotherm
latitude
leeward side
meteorologist
millibars
ocean current
pollution
precipitation
rain gauge
relief rainfall
ultraviolet radiation
vegetation
water cycle
water table
water vapour
weather forecasters
windward side
wind speed

SUBJECT LISTS

HISTORY

agriculture
agricultural
bias
castle
cathedral
Catholic
chronology
chronological
citizen
civilisation
colony
colonisation
conflict
constitution
constitutional
contradict
contradiction
current
defence
disease
document
dynasty
economy
economical
emigration

government
immigrant
imperial
imperialism
independence
invasion
motive
parliament
politics
political
priest
propaganda
Protestant
rebel
rebellion
reign
religious
republic
revolt
revolution
siege
source
trade
traitor

INFORMATION AND COMMUNICATION TECHNOLOGY

binary
byte
cable
cartridge
CD-ROM
computer
connect
connection
cursor
data
database
delete
disk
document
electronic
graphic
hardware
icon
input
interactive
interface

internet
justify
keyboard
megabyte
memory
modem
module
monitor
multimedia
network
output
password
preview
processor
program
scanner
sensor
server
software
spreadsheet
virus

SUBJECT LISTS

INVESTIGATING WORDS

anomalous results
annotation
bias
classification
classify
control
controlling variables
data
database
data search
dependent/ independent variables
evaluate
evaluation
evidence
evidence of reaction
fair testing
insufficient data
line of best fit
predicting
prediction
quadrat sampling

qualitative data
qualitative observations
quantitative observations
reliability of results
reliable data
reliable evidence
repeat reading
sample
sample size
sampling
scientific method
secondary sources
sequence of events
spreadsheet
strength of evidence
sufficient data
survey
technique
theory
trial measurements
validity of conclusions

MATHEMATICS

ALGEBRA

▶ FORMULAE

area	perimeter
base	pi
circumference	radius
equation	subject
formulae	substitution
height	variable
hypotenuse	volume

▶ GRAPHS

constant	mapping
coordinates	one-dimensional
function	origin
gradient	parabola
graph	slope
horizontal	straight line
integers	two-dimensional
intersection	vertical
linear	

▶ LINEAR EQUATIONS

index	solution
inequality	simplify
inverse	

▶ SIMULTANEOUS EQUATIONS

linear	solving
sequence	unknown

NUMBERS

▶ ESTIMATION AND APPROXIMATION

omit	significant figure

▶ FRACTIONS

cancel	numerator
denominator	proper fractions

▶ INDICES

base number
index notation

powers
raise to a power

▶ MENTAL ARITHMETIC

cube
cuboid
decimals

expression
measures
ratio

▶ RATIOS AND PROPORTIONS

actual
enlarge
equivalent
initial

proportional
reduce
scale

▶ USING YOUR CALCULATOR

addition
amount
area of a circle
calculate
cube root
digit
divide
division
estimate
fraction
guess
minus
multiply

multiplication
negative
operations
percentage
positive
power
reciprocal
recurring
root
square
square root
subtraction

SHAPE, SPACE, AND MEASUREMENTS

▶ CIRCLES

perpendicular
quadrilateral
subtends

supplementary
symmetry

▶ CONSTRUCTION

pair of compasses
construction
diagonal
midpoint
polygon
protractor

radius
regular hexagon
regular pentagon
regular polygon
rhombus
vertex

SUBJECT LISTS

▶ LINES AND ANGLES

acute angle
adjacent angle
bisect
complementary angle
corresponding angle
degrees
interior angles

intersect
obtuse angle
parallel
reflex angle
right angle
supplementary angle

▶ LOCI

circle
equidistant
locus

loci
parallel lines

▶ MEASURES

abbreviation
accuracy
axis
capacity
compound
constant
conversion
cube
cuboid
cylinder
diameter
estimate
formula

imperial
kilogram
kilometre
length
litre
metre
parallelogram
prism
radius
trapezium
tonne
weight

▶ POLYGONS

decagon
exterior angle
heptagon
hexagon
nonagon

octagon
pentagon
polygon
regular polygon
triangle

▶ QUADRILATERALS

adjacent

isosceles

▶ SOLIDS

hexagon
isometric
octagon
parallelogram

pentagon
rectangle
rhombus
square

▶ TRANSFORMATION GEOMETRY

congruent shapes	similar
order of rotation	transformation
reflection	translation
rotation	

▶ TRIANGLES

equilateral	scalene
exterior	

HANDLING DATA

▶ COLLECTING DATA

continuous data	mean *or* arithmetic data
cumulative frequency	median
data	mode
frequency	range
frequency distribution table	tally
grouped data	tally table

▶ INTERPRETING DATA

bar chart *or* graph	hypothesis
census	pie chart *or* graph
cumulative frequency graph	quartile
cumulative graph	questionnaire
frequency polygon	survey
histogram	

▶ PROBABILITY

a certain chance	impossible
chance	likelihood scale
equally likely	likely
even	outcome
event	probability scale
favourable	unlikely outcome
fifty-fifty	

MUSIC

choir
chord
chromatic
composition
conductor
crotchet
dynamics
instrument
instrumental
interval
lyric
major
melody
minim
minor
musician
octave

orchestra
orchestral
ostinato
percussion
pitch
quaver
rhythm
scale
score
semibreve
synchronise
syncopation
tempo
ternary
timbre
triad
vocal

SUBJECT LISTS

PHYSICAL EDUCATION

active
activity
agile
agility
athletic
athlete
biceps
exercise
field
gym
gymnastics
hamstring
injury

league
medicine
mobile
mobility
muscle
personal
pitch
qualify
relay
squad
tactic
tournament
triceps

PHYSICAL, SOCIAL AND HEALTH EDUCATION

able
ability
achieve
achievement
addict
addiction
approve
approval
communication
control
dependant
dependency
discipline
discussion
effort
emotion
emotional
encourage
encouragement

gender
generous
generosity
involve
involvement
prefer
preference
pressure
racism
racist
reality
relationship
represent
representative
reward
sanction
sexism
sexist
stereotype

RELIGIOUS EDUCATION

baptism
Bible
biblical
Buddhist
Buddhism
burial
celebrate
celebration
ceremony
Christian
commandment
commitment
creation
disciple
faith
festival
funeral
Hindu
Hinduism
hymn
immoral
immorality
Islam
Israel
Judaism
Jewish

marriage
miracle
moral
morality
Muslim
parable
pilgrim
pilgrimage
pray
prayer
prejudice
prophet
religious
religion
shrine
sign
Sikh
Sikhism
special
spirit
spiritual
symbol
synagogue
temple
wedding
worship

SCIENCE

LIFE PROCESSES AND LIVING THINGS

▶ BREATHING

artery
bronchus
cilia
diaphragm
diffusion
emphysema
exhalation
exhale
haemoglobin
inhalation
inhale

lung cancer
lungs
mucus
nicotine
respiratory centre
respire
ribcage
tar
trachea
vein
ventilation

▶ CELL ACTIVITY

anabolism
cell membrane
cell wall
cells
cellular respiration
cellulose
cytoplasm
excretion
growth
joules
magnification
movement

multicellular
nucleus
nutrition
organ
protoplasm
reproduction
sensitivity
skin
tissue
unicellular
variable

▶ CIRCULATORY SYSTEM

blood vessel
coronary heart disease
heart
hypertension
oxygenated blood

plasma
red blood cells
stroke
white blood cells

▶ CLASSIFICATION

abdomen
amphibian
association
characteristics
class

classification
classify
confidence
correlation
database

environmental
family
identification
invertebrate
kingdom
leg
limb

mammal
phylum
reptile
segment
shell
taxonomic group
vertebrate

▶ HUMAN NUTRITION

absorption
anaemia
anorexia
bulimia
carbohydrate
catabolism
chemical digestion
deficiency of vitamins
digestion
defecation
enzymes

food
intestine
kwashiorkor
mechanical digestion
metabolism
obesity
propulsion
protein
take in or absorb
transport or translocation
villus

▶ HUMAN REPRODUCTION

adolescence
amniotic sac
baby
cervix
ejaculation
fallopian tube
foetus or fetus
gestation
hereditary
inherited
mammary glands
menopause
menstruation

national data
oviduct
ovulation
placenta
puberty
scrotum
semen
sexual intercourse
testis
umbilical cord
uterus
vagina

▶ INHERITANCE

addiction
breed
chromosome
clone
data set
embryo
family tree
fertilisation

gametes
gene
genetically modified
genetic information
hybrid
meiosis
mitosis
mutation

SUBJECT LISTS

ovum
purebred
selective breeding
sex cells

sperm
variation
variety
zygote

▶ MICROBES AND DISEASE

antibiotic
anti-microbial
bacteria
bronchitis
chickenpox
cholera
common cold
diphtheria
epidemic
food poisoning
fungi
German measles *or* rubella
glandular fever
immunisation
immunity
infection

infectious disease
inoculation
measles
meningitis
mumps
pathogen
pneumonia
salmonella *or* salmonellosis
tonsillitis
tuberculosis
vaccination
virus
viruses
whooping cough
yellow fever

▶ MOVEMENT

antagonistic muscles
endoskeleton
exoskeleton
fracture
joint

ligament
plaster cast
synovial joint
tendon

▶ PLANT NUTRITION AND GROWTH

chloroplast
compete
competition
fungicide
herbicide
insecticide
iodine solution
pesticide

pigment
soda lime
sodium bicarbonate
sodium hydroxide
toxin
weedkillers
yield

▶ PLANT REPRODUCTION

adapted feature
anther
calyx
carpel

chemical reaction
chlorophyll
clone
complete flower

corolla
cotyledon
filament
fruit
incomplete flower
metabolism
ovary
ovule

perfect flower
petal
pistil
pollen
pollination
stamen
stigma
vegetative

▶ PLANT RESPIRATION

aerobic respiration
anaerobic respiration
combustion
glucose *or* sugar

lactic acid
lime water
oxidation reaction

▶ THE SOLAR SYSTEM AND BEYOND

asteroid
eclipse
orbit

planet
rotate
satellite

▶ SOUND AND HEARING

alternative explanation
dynamics
frequency amplitude
loudness
noise pollution

pitch
temporary deafness
volume
wave

▶ VARIATION

continuous variation
discontinuous variation

family tree

LIVING THINGS AND THEIR ENVIRONMENT

▶ ADAPTATION

biosphere
hibernation
individual
migration

nocturnal
photosynthesis
phototropism
transpiration

▶ COMPETITION

carrying capacity
community
consumer
ecosystem
environment

evolution
extinct
habitat
natural selection
population

SUBJECT LISTS

population density
population size
predator

producer
species
variation

► ENVIRONMENTAL CHEMISTRY

air and water quality
catalytic converter

ozone depletion
vegetation cover

► FEEDING RELATIONSHIPS

availability of oxygen
autotrophic
carnivore
climatic
conifer
dormant
ecological pyramid
environmental conditions
fern
food chain
food web

herbivore
insulation
light intensity
mineral
omnivore
pesticide
prey
pyramid of numbers
stress
temperature sensor
transect

MATERIALS AND THEIR PROPERTIES

► ACIDS AND ALKALIS

acid rain
acid
alkali
base
caustic
corrosive
equation
harmful

hazard
hydrochloric acid
indicator
neutralisation
pH-scale
react
risk

► CHEMICAL CHANGES

anode
calcium carbonate
carbon
carbon dioxide
cathode
decompose
endothermic
exothermic
generalisation
hydrogen
line graph
methane

oxidation
oxidising agent
monomer
polymer
polymerisation
product
reactant
reducing agent
reduction
respiration
word equation
zinc

▶ GEOLOGICAL CHANGES

aligned
chemical weathering
crystal
erupt
fossil
granite
igneous rock
iron rich
lava
limestone
magma
metamorphic rock
millennia
millions of years

obsidian
onion skin peeling
physical weathering
porosity
porous
pumice
relative density
rock cycle
sandstone
sedimentary layer
sedimentary rock
sedimentation
shale
volcanic ash

▶ LIGHT

image
opaque
reflection

refraction
spectrum
transparent

▶ METALS AND NON-METALS

brittle
combustion reaction
copper carbonate
copper nitrate
copper sulfate
displacement reaction
electrical conductivity
lustre
magnesium nitrate
magnesium sulfate
malleable
metal oxide

nature
order of reactivity
potassium nitrate
react
reactivity
reactivity series
resonant
salt
thermal conductivity
visible change
zinc chloride

▶ PHYSICAL CHANGES

affect
alloy
attracted
boiling point
calcium chloride
chromatography
composition
conduction

conductor
contraction
convection
density
distillation
effect
expansion
filtration

gas pressure
heat (as energy)
insoluble
insulator
interpret
kinetic energy
melting point
mingling
miscible
mixing
mixture

model
particle
pure
radiation
saturated solution
sodium carbonate
solubility
solute
solvent
vibration

PHYSICAL PROCESSES

▶ ELECTRIC CURRENTS AND CIRCUITS

ammeter
ampere
battery
bulb *or* lamp
closed circuit
connecting wire
conventional current
electric current

electromotive force (EMF)
energy transfer
open circuit
parallel circuit
power supply
series circuit
switch

▶ ENERGY AND ELECTRICITY

chemical energy
conservation
dissipation
dynamo
electrical energy
electric generator

heat and light
movement as kinetic energy
position as potential energy
power station
sound

▶ FORCES AND MOTION

acceleration
accuracy
activity
air resistance
area
balanced forces
constant speed
counterbalance
distance
drag
energy
friction

force
fuel
gravitational attraction
hydraulic
lever
mass
moment
pivot
pneumatic
power
precision
pressure

principle of moments
resistance
revolve

speed
turning effect
upthrust

▶ MAGNETISM AND ITS EFFECTS

coil
core
electromagnet
magnetic field
magnetic field line
magnetic material
non-magnetic material
north pole
permanent magnet

precision
qualitative and quantitative
observation
range
relay
repeat
solenoid
South pole
temporary magnet

▶ STATIC ELECTRICITY

atom
chlorine
compound
electron
element
formula
molecule
negatively charged object
neutral object

neutron
positively charged object
products of reaction
proton
sodium
sodium chloride
state
symbol

Wordgames

SYNONYM PUZZLE

The clues are all headwords which appear in the thesaurus. The answers are all synonyms given for these headwords. When you have filled in the answers, you will find a hidden message in the vertical line.

Clues:

1 *sudden* (6)
2 *banish* (6)
3 *casual* (10)
4 *lack* (8)
5 *daring* (8)
6 *passionate* (9)

7 *tendency* (11)
8 *famous* (9)
9 *jail* (11)
10 *genius* (8)
11 *war* (11)
12 *helper* (8)

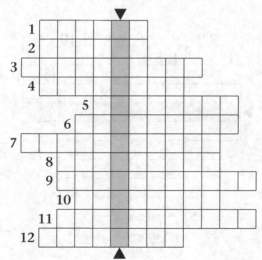

WORDGAMES

Further activities:

Try making your own puzzle like this, using your thesaurus to find your synonym clues.

Antonym Puzzle

Here is a word puzzle with a difference – the answers are all *antonyms* of the clues. When you have filled in the answers you will find a hidden message in the horizontal line.

Clues:

1 *approve* (4)
2 *straight* (7)
3 *safe* (9)
4 *temporary* (9)
5 *wasteful* (7)
6 *pessimistic* (10)

7 *changeable* (8)
8 *corrupt* (6)
9 *smart* (7)
10 *grace* (10)
11 *permit* (3)
12 *retreat* (7)

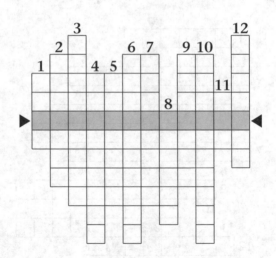

WORDGAMES

Further activities:

Try making your own puzzle like this using your thesaurus to find your antonym clues.

WORDSEARCH

Red Alert!

All the shades of red listed below can be found in the grid shown. They may read across, up or down, either forwards or backwards, but they are all in straight lines.

Two colours, which are not shades of red, can be made with the letters left over.

```
b  z  o  l  a  n  i  d  r  a  c
v  e  r  m  i  l  i  o  n  r  h
r  c  y  c  l  a  m  e  n  i  e
a  r  c  m  a  r  o  o  n  n  r
s  i  a  t  n  e  g  a  m  t  r
p  m  r  c  e  r  i  s  e  e  y
b  s  m  f  l  a  m  e  e  l  p
e  o  i  a  m  a  y  b  u  r  p
r  n  n  f  u  c  h  s  i  a  o
r  n  e  r  t  e  r  a  l  c  p
y  r  r  e  b  w  a  r  t  s  e
b  u  r  g  u  n  d  y  a  u  q
```

burgundy	crimson	poppy
cardinal	cyclamen	raspberry
carmine	flame	ruby
cerise	fuchsia	scarlet
cherry	magenta	strawberry
claret	maroon	vermilion

WORDGAMES

738

CODE GAME

In the boxes below, the letters of ten words have been replaced
by numbers.

A number represents the same letter each time. Try to crack the
code and find the ten words. Here is a clue: all the words you are
looking for have something to do with WEATHER.

1 | 1 | 2 | 3 | 4 | 5 | 6 | 7 |
    T   H   U

2 | 10 | 1 | 8 | 7 | 11 | 13 |

3 | 5 | 7 | 9 | 14 | 14 | 12 | 6 |

4 | 1 | 6 | 11 | 17 | 6 | 10 | 1 |

5 | 9 | 15 | 13 |

6 | 10 | 11 | 8 | 16 |

7 | 8 | 18 | 6 | 7 | 15 | 19 | 10 | 1 |

8 | 15 | 13 | 15 | 12 | 8 | 4 | 6 |

9 | 10 | 12 | 6 | 6 | 1 |

WORDGAMES

ANSWERS:

Synonym Puzzle:
1 abrupt
2 dispel
3 nonchalant
4 scarcity
5 fearless
6 emotional
7 inclination
8 legendary
9 incarcerate
10 virtuoso
11 hostilities
12 henchman   Hidden message: peace on earth

Antonym Puzzle:
1 veto
2 crooked
3 dangerous
4 permanent
5 thrifty
6 optimistic
7 constant
8 honest
9 scruffy
10 clumsiness
11 ban
12 advance   Hidden message: to err is human

WORDGAMES

Wordsearch:

```
b  z  o  l  a  n  i  d  r  a  c
v  e  r  m  i  l  i  o  n  r  h
r  c  y  c  l  a  m  e  n  i  e
a  r  c  m  a  r  o  o  n  n  r
s  i  a  t  n  e  g  a  m  t  r
p  m  r  c  e  r  i  s  e  e  y
b  s  m  f  l  a  m  e  l  l  p
e  o  i  a  m  a  y  b  u  r  o
r  n  n  f  u  c  h  s  i  a  p
r  n  e  r  t  e  r  a  l  c  e
y  r  r  e  b  w  a  r  t  s  q
b  u  r  g  u  n  d  y  a  u
```

The remaining letters make up two colours that aren't red: bronze, aquamarine

Code Game
1 thunder
2 stormy
3 drizzle
4 tempest
5 icy
6 smog
7 overcast
8 cyclone
9 sleet

Index

INDEX

INDEX

black-and-white → definite
blackball → exclude
blacklist → boycott
blain → boil
blame → accuse
blame → censure
blame → condemn
blame → fault
blame → responsibility
blameless → innocent
blameworthy → guilty
bland → tasteless
blandishment → flattery
blank → empty
blank → ignore
blank → space
blanket → layer
blaring → loud
blasé → casual
blast → attack
blast → bang
blast → explosion
blatant → clear
blatant → conspicuous
blatant → manifest
blatant → naked
blatant → obvious
blaze → burn
blaze → fire
blaze → glare
blazing → bright
blazon → advertise
bleached → light
bleak → cold
bleat → moan
blemish → fault
blemish → flaw
blemish → spot
blend → combination
blend → combine
blend → cross
blend → mix
blend → mixture
blend → union
blessed → holy
blessed → lucky
blessing → approval
blessing → sanction
blight → infect
blight → pest
bliss → ecstasy
bliss → heaven

bliss → joy
blister → boil
bloc → body
block → blockage
block → close
block → frustrate
block → hinder
block → impede
block → obstruct
block → plug
bloke → man
blond → fair
blond → light
blonde → fair
blonde → light
bloodshed → violence
bloodthirsty → violent
bloom → flourish
blooming → well
blossom → progress
blot → spot
blot → stain
blotch → spot
blow → bang
blow → disappointment
blow → hit
blow → shock
blow → sound
blow up → bomb
blow up → explode
bludge → scrounge
bludgeon → club
blue → argument
blue → dirty
blue → fight
blue → gloomy
blue → obscene
blue → sad
blue-pencil → delete
blueprint → design
blueprint → plan
bluff → blunt
bluff → con
blunder → err
blunder → error
blunder → mistake
blunder → slip
blunt → candid
blunt → direct
blunt → frank
blunt → straight
board → council
board → management

board → sign
boast → brag
boaster → braggart
bob → bounce
bob → float
bodeful → sinister
body → association
body → build
body → figure
body → organization
body politic → state
boggle → wonder
bogus → false
bogus → mock
bogus → phoney
boil → cook
boiling → hot
boisterous → rowdy
boisterous → wild
bold → brave
bold → daring
boldness → bravery
boldness → daring
boldness → impudence
bolster → reassure
bolster → strengthen
bolster → support
bolt → catch
bolt → dash
bolt → escape
bolt → flee
bolt → gobble
bolt → run
bolt → tear
bombard → bomb
bombardment → hail
bombastic → pretentious
bombshell → blow
bombshell → shock
bombshell → surprise
bona fide → authentic
bona fide → genuine
bona fide → real
bona fide → true
bond → association
bond → attachment
bond → connection
bond → link
bond → relation
bond → relationship
bond → stick
bond → tie

INDEX

conform → agree
conform → follow
conform to → suit
conformation →
structure
conformist →
conventional
confound → puzzle
confrontation → clash
confuse → cloud
confuse → mix up
confuse → muddle
confuse → puzzle
confuse with → mistake
confused → dazed
confused → garbled
confused → unclear
confusion → disorder
confusion → fuss
confusion → muddle
congeal → thicken
congealed → firm
congenial → compatible
congested → crowded
conglomeration →
mixture
congratulate → praise
congratulation → praise
congregate → assemble
congregate → crowd
congregate → gather
congregate → mass
congregate → meet
congregation →
gathering
congress → conference
congress → convention
congress → gathering
congress → hui
congress → meeting
congruence → similarity
congruent → compatible
congruous →
appropriate
congruous →
compatible
conjectural → uncertain
conjecture → guess
conjecture → suppose
conjecture → theory
conjunction → union
connect → associate
connect → attach

connect → join
connect → link
connection →
association
connection → bond
connection → contact
connection → link
connection → relation
connection →
relationship
connection → tie
connotation → meaning
conquer → beat
conquer → defeat
conquer → overcome
conquer → vanquish
conqueror → winner
conquest → defeat
conscience → principle
conscience-stricken →
guilty
conscience-stricken →
sorry
conscientious →
industrious
conscious → deliberate
conscious of → **aware** of
consciousness → sense
consecrate → bless
consecrated → holy
consent → blessing
consent → permission
consent to → accept
consent to → approve
consequence → effect
consequence → result
consequently →
therefore
conservationist →
green
conservative →
conventional
conservative → right-
wing
consider → contemplate
consider → feel
consider → judge
consider → ponder
consider → rate
consider → reckon
consider → regard
consider → think
consider → view

considerable →
extensive
considerable →
handsome
considerable →
respectable
considerable →
significant
considerably → far
considerate →
accommodating
considerate → kind
considerate →
thoughtful
considerate →
understanding
considerately → well
consideration → aspect
consideration → factor
consideration →
thought
consignment → load
consistency → texture
consistent →
compatible
consistent → logical
consistent → regular
consistent → steady
consolation → comfort
console → comfort
consolidate →
strengthen
consonant →
compatible
consort → associate
conspicuous → bold
conspicuous → clear
conspicuous → evident
conspicuous → manifest
conspicuous →
noticeable
conspicuous → obvious
conspicuous →
prominent
conspicuous → visible
conspiracy → plot
conspiratorial → secret
conspire → plot
constant → continual
constant → continuous
constant → devoted
constant → even
constant → loyal

INDEX

deafening → noisy
deal → administer
deal → agreement
deal → trade
deal in → sell
deal in → stock
deal with → handle
deal with → process
deal with → take care of
deal with → treat
dealer → trader
dealings → business
dear → cute
dear → expensive
dearest → beloved
dearest → favourite
dearth → lack
dearth → shortage
dearth → want
debacle → defeat
debar → exclude
debatable → doubtful
debate → argue
debate → deliberate
debate → discuss
debate → discussion
debauched → perverted
debauchery → excess
debilitate → weaken
debilitated → weak
debility → weakness
debris → garbage
debris → remains
debut → appearance
decamp → leave
decay → rot
decay → ruin
decayed → rotten
deceased → dead
deceased → late
deceit → dishonesty
deceit → fraud
deceit → lie
deceit → lying
deceitful → dishonest
deceitful → false
deceitful → insincere
deceitful → lying
deceitful → sneaky
deceitful → two-faced
deceive → cheat
deceive → con
deceive → dupe

deceive → fool
deceive → take in
deceive → trick
decelerate → slow (down)
decency → honour
decency → politeness
decent → respectable
deception → con
deception → fraud
deception → trick
decide → conclude
decide → determine
decide → resolve
decide → settle
decide on → select
decide on → settle
decide upon → pick
decided → definite
deciding → critical
decipher → crack
decipher → read
decipher → solve
decision → verdict
decisive → critical
decisive → crucial
deck → decorate
declaration → announcement
declaration → statement
declare → state
declination → slope
decline → decrease
decline → drop
decline → fail
decline → fall
decline → recession
decline → refuse
decline → reject
decline → wither
decline → worsen
declivity → slope
decompose → rot
decomposed → rotten
decorate → honour
decorated → fancy
decoration → ornament
decorous → fitting
decorum → ceremony
decoy → bait
decrease → abate
decrease → cut
decrease → decline

decrease → diminish
decrease → drop
decrease → fall
decrease → lessen
decrease → lower
decrease → reduce
decree → command
decree → law
decree → order
decree → rule
decrepit → weak
dedicate → bless
dedicated → devoted
deduce → conclude
deduce → reconstruct
deduct → subtract
deduction → conclusion
deed → achievement
deed → act
deed → action
deem → consider
deem → feel
deem → reckon
deem → think
deem → view
deep → extreme
deep → far
deep → heavy
deep → intense
deep → serious
deep → severe
deeply → very
defamation → slander
defame → slander
defeat → beat
defeat → failure
defeat → foil
defeat → subdue
defeat → vanquish
defect → fault
defect → flaw
defect → handicap
defect → hole
defect → weakness
defective → faulty
defective → imperfect
defence → safeguard
defenceless → helpless
defenceless → vulnerable
defend → champion
defend → guard
defend → justify

disavow >> dismissal

disavow → deny
discard → banish
discard → dispose of
discern → distinguish
discern → notice
discern → see
discern → spot
discern → tell
discern → understand
discernible → visible
discerning → acute
discerning → astute
discernment → wisdom
discharge → drain
discharge → dump
discharge → fire
discharge → free
discharge → release
discharge → sack
discharge → the **sack**
disciple → follower
discipline → field
discipline → punish
disclaim → deny
disclose → reveal
disclosure → news
discolour → fade
discolour → stain
discomfit → embarrass
discomfited →
embarrassed
discomfiture →
embarrassment
discomfort → pain
discompose → agitate
discompose → shake
discompose → upset
discomposed → uneasy
disconcert → embarrass
disconnect → separate
disconnected →
separate
disconsolate →
miserable
disconsolate → sad
disconsolate →
unhappy
discontinue → cease
discontinue → interrupt
discontinue → quit
discontinue → stop
discord → conflict
discount → ignore

discourse → discussion
discourse → lecture
discourse → speech
discourse → talk
discourteous → rude
discover → determine
discover → find
discover → hear
discover → learn
discover → observe
discover → see
discredit → disgrace
discredit → disprove
discredit → shame
discreditable →
disgraceful
discreet → tactful
discrepancy →
difference
discrete → different
discrete → individual
discrete → separate
discretion → freedom
discretion → tact
discretionary → flexible
discriminate →
distinguish
discriminating → fussy
discrimination →
injustice
discrimination →
prejudice
discussion → conference
discussion → word
disdain → contempt
disdain → scorn
disdainful → haughty
disdainful → scornful
disdainful → stuck-up
disdainful → superior
disease → disorder
disease → illness
disenchanted →
disappointed
disenchantment →
disappointment
disengage → withdraw
disfigured → deformed
disgrace → humble
disgrace → humiliate
disgrace → shame
disguised → invisible
disgust → horrify

disgust → horror
disgust → repel
disgust → shock
disgusting → nasty
dishearten →
discourage
disheartened →
disappointed
dishonest → corrupt
dishonest → crooked
dishonest → dubious
dishonest → insincere
dishonest → lying
dishonest → sneaky
dishonest → two-faced
dishonesty → corruption
dishonesty → lying
dishonour → disgrace
dishonour → shame
dishonourable →
crooked
dishonourable →
disgraceful
dishonourable →
shabby
disillusioned →
disappointed
disillusionment →
disappointment
disinclined → reluctant
disintegrate → erode
disinterested → fair
disinterested → neutral
dislike → animosity
dislike → disapprove
dislike → hate
dislike → hatred
dislike → resent
disliked → unpopular
disloyal → false
disloyal → treacherous
disloyal → two-faced
dismal → drab
dismal → gloomy
dismal → sad
dismay → horrify
dismay → panic
dismiss → banish
dismiss → discharge
dismiss → fire
dismiss → sack
dismissal → discharge
dismissal → the **sack**

distressed → upset
distressing → painful
distressing → tragic
distribute → circulate
district → area
district → local
district → region
district → territory
distrust → question
distrust → suspect
distrust → suspicion
distrustful → cynical
distrustful → suspicious
distrustful → wary
disturb → agitate
disturb → bother
disturb → concern
disturb → distress
disturb → shake
disturb → trouble
disturb → upset
disturbance → riot
disturbing → creepy
disunite → split
dither → hesitate
dive → descend
diverge → split
divergence → difference
divergence → split
divergent → different
divergent from → unlike
diverse → various
diversify → vary
diversion → escape
diversion → hobby
diversion → pastime
diversion → variation
divert → distract
divide → distribute
divide → separate
divide → share
divide → sort
divine → religious
division → compartment
division → department
division → section
division → split
divorce → separate
divorced → separate
divulge → reveal
dizzy → dazed
dizzy → faint
do → accomplish

do → achieve
do → commit
do → conduct
do → perform
do → practise
do → suit
do away with → abolish
do away with →
eliminate
do business → trade
do up → decorate
do up → renovate
do well → flourish
do well → succeed
do well → thrive
do wrong → sin
do your best → strive
do your utmost → strive
docile → meek
docile → passive
dock → land
doctrinal → religious
doctrine → belief
doctrine → principle
document → record
dodge → avoid
dodge → escape
dodge → manoeuvre
dodgy → suspect
dodgy → suspicious
dogged → determined
dogged → obstinate
dogged → stubborn
doggedness →
determination
doggedness → resolve
dogma → belief
dole out → distribute
doleful → sad
dolefulness → sadness
domain → field
domain → territory
domestic → home
dominance → advantage
dominance → hold
dominant → powerful
domination → influence
domineering → bossy
dominion → colony
dominion → power
dominion → territory
don → teacher
don → wear

donate → give
donate → present
donation → gift
donation → present
done → over
done → right
doom → condemn
door → entrance
door → entry
doorway → entrance
doorway → entry
dope → fool
dormancy → sleep
dosh → money
dote on → love
doting → devoted
doting → fond
doting → loving
double → lookalike
double-cross → betray
double-cross → deceive
doubt → question
doubt → suspect
doubt → suspicion
doubtful → dubious
doubtful → hesitant
doubtful → improbable
doubtful → suspect
doubtful → suspicious
doubtful → uncertain
doubtful →
unpredictable
doubtless → probably
dough → money
dovetail → fit
down → below
down → gloomy
down → miserable
down → pile
down → sad
down → unhappy
down at heel → shabby
down-to-earth →
realistic
down-to-earth →
sensible
down-to-earth → sound
downcast →
disappointed
downcast → miserable
downcast → sad
downfall → collapse
downfall → failure

dull → blunt
dull → boring
dull → cloudy
dull → dim
dull → dreary
dull → fade
dull → flat
dull → gloomy
dull → numb
dull → sleepy
dull → stuffy
dullness → boredom
dumb → dim
dumb → idiotic
dumb → silent
dumb → slow
dumbfound → amaze
dumbness → silence
dummy → mock
dummy → model
dump → discard
dump → dispose of
dump → get rid of
dunce → fool
dungeon → prison
dupe → cheat
dupe → con
dupe → deceive
dupe → fool
dupe → take in
dupe → trap
dupe → trick
duplicate → copy
duplicitous → false
duplicity → dishonesty
duplicity → fraud
duplicity → lying
durable → sturdy
durable → tough
duration → length
duration → term
duress → force
dusk → dark
dust → clean
dust → dirt
duty → function
duty → job
duty → part
duty → responsibility
duty → task
duty → tax
duty → work
dwell → inhabit

dwell → live
dwell on → stress
dwelling → home
dwelling → house
dwindle → decrease
dwindle → fall
dwindle → lessen
dwindle → shrink
dye → colour
dynamic → energetic
dynamic → vital
each → all
eager → enthusiastic
eager → impatient
eager → keen
eager → ready
eager → willing
eagerness →
enthusiasm
eagle-eyed → observant
earlier → before
earlier → first
earlier → previous
earliest → first
earmark → intend
earn → deserve
earn → gain
earn → merit
earnest → intense
earnest → serious
earnest → solemn
earnings → income
earnings → pay
earnings → profit
earth → dirt
earth → ground
earth → soil
ease → comfort
ease → moderate
easily offended →
sensitive
easily offended →
touchy
easily upset → sensitive
easy → comfortable
easy → fluent
easy → informal
easy → leisurely
easy → relaxed
easy → simple
easy → straightforward
easy to use → handy
easy-going → mild

eat away → erode
eavesdrop → hear
eavesdropping → nosy
ebb → abate
ebb → fall
eccentric → bizarre
eccentric → weirdo
echelon → rank
echo → repeat
eclipse → blot out
eclipse → outdo
eclipse → top
eco-friendly → green
ecological → green
economic → economical
economic → efficient
economic → financial
economical → cheap
economical → thrifty
economics → finance
economize → save
ecstasy → happiness
ecstasy → heaven
ecstasy → joy
edge → bank
edge → border
edge → ease
edge → outskirts
edge → side
edgy → nervous
edgy → restless
edgy → tense
edict → command
edict → law
edifice → building
edifice → structure
edit → revise
edit out → delete
edition → issue
educate → instruct
educate → teach
educate → train
education → knowledge
educator → teacher
eerie → creepy
eerie → scary
eerie → spooky
efface → remove
effect → accomplish
effect → bring
effect → cause
effect → influence
effect → result

exact → accurate
exact → correct
exact → faithful
exact → particular
exact → precise
exact → right
exact → strict
exacting → fussy
exacting → particular
exacting → stiff
exacting → tough
exactly → prompt
exaggerated → excessive
exalt → worship
exaltation → ecstasy
exaltation → joy
exaltation → worship
examination → check
examination → exam
examination → research
examination → review
examine → check
examine → contemplate
examine → inspect
examine → interrogate
examine → investigate
examine → question
examine → research
examine → scrutinize
examine → study
example → case
example → ideal
example → model
exasperate → irritate
excavate → dig
exceed → pass
exceed → top
exceeding → above
exceeding → over
exceedingly → very
excellence → merit
excellent → exceptional
excellent → fine
excellent → first-rate
excellent → marvellous
excellent → outstanding
excellent → splendid
excellent → superb
excellent → wonderful
except → but
except for → but

exception → qualification
exceptional → extreme
exceptional → first-rate
exceptional → outstanding
exceptional → particular
exceptional → rare
exceptional → singular
exceptional → special
exceptional → superior
exceptional → uncommon
exceptional → unusual
excerpt → extract
excerpt → passage
excess → extra
excessive → extreme
excessive → steep
excessively → too
exchange → change
exchange → substitute
exchange → swap
exchange views on → discuss
excise → duty
excise → remove
excise → tax
excite → thrill
excited → enthusiastic
excitement → bustle
excitement → enthusiasm
excitement → heat
excitement → passion
exciting → impressive
exclaim → cry
exclamation → cry
exclude → ban
exclude → boycott
exclude → forbid
exclude → omit
exclusive → posh
exclusive → private
exclusive → select
excoriate → criticize
excruciating → painful
excursion → drive
excursion → journey
excursion → ramble
excursion → trip
excuse → defence
excuse → forgive

excuse → grounds
excuse → justify
excuse yourself → decline
excused → exempt
execute → accomplish
execute → administer
execute → carry out
execute → conduct
execute → do
execute → kill
execute → perform
executive → manager
executive → official
exemplar → example
exemplar → model
exempt → immune
exemption → freedom
exercise → practice
exertion → effort
exertion → exercise
exertion → labour
exhaust → drain
exhaust → tax
exhaust → tire
exhaust → wear out
exhausted → tired
exhausted → weary
exhausted → worn-out
exhausting → hard
exhaustive → full
exhaustive → thorough
exhibit → bear
exhibition → fair
exhibition → show
exhilarating → exciting
exhort → press
exhort → urge
exiguous → meagre
exile → banish
exist → live
exist → occur
existence → life
exoneration → forgiveness
exorbitant → excessive
exorbitant → expensive
exorbitant → steep
exotic → foreign
exotic → strange
exotic → unfamiliar
expand → bulge
expand → elaborate

INDEX

extravagant → extreme
extravagant → fancy
extravagant →
ostentatious
extravagant → wasteful
extreme → acute
extreme → deep
extreme → drastic
extreme → intense
extreme → serious
extreme → severe
extreme → ultimate
extreme → uncommon
extremely → really
extremely → very
extremist → fanatic
extricate → release
exuberance →
happiness
exude → emit
exult → rejoice
exultation → joy
eye → inspect
eye → regard
eye-catching →
prominent
eyesight → sight
eyewitness → spectator
eyewitness → witness
fabric → cloth
fabric → material
fabric → substance
fabricate → build
fabricate → invent
fabricate → make
fabricate → make up
fabricate →
manufacture
fabrication → lie
fabrication → lying
fabrication → making
fabrication →
manufacture
facade → outside
face → brave
face → expression
face → front
face → look
face → outside
face down → prone
facility → capacity
facility → skill
facsimile → copy

facsimile → model
fact → reality
fact → truth
faction → movement
faction → party
faction → side
factor → aspect
factor → consideration
facts → information
factual → real
factual → right
factual → true
fad → craze
fad → fashion
fad → whim
faddish → fussy
fade → die out
fade → disappear
fade → vanish
fade → wither
fade away → die
fade away → vanish
fade out → die
faded → faint
faded → pale
fail → collapse
fail → neglect
fail → weaken
fail to notice → miss
fail to remember →
forget
failing → defect
failing → fault
failure → collapse
failure → crash
faint → dim
faint → slender
faint → soft
faint → weak
faint-hearted →
cowardly
faint-hearted → timid
fair → acceptable
fair → all right
fair → beautiful
fair → festival
fair → light
fair → market
fair → moderate
fair → reasonable
fair → respectable
fairly → pretty
fairly → quite

fairly → rather
fairness → justice
fairness → right
faith → belief
faith → confidence
faithful → accurate
faithful → devoted
faithful → exact
faithful → loyal
faithful → realistic
faithful → reliable
faithful → steadfast
faithful → trusty
faithfully → exactly
faithless → treacherous
fake → copy
fake → false
fake → fraud
fake → mock
fake → phoney
fake → pretend
fall → decline
fall → descend
fall → downfall
fall → drop
fall → ruin
fall → slope
fall apart → disintegrate
fall behind → lag
fall down → collapse
fall ill → develop
fall out → argue
fall out → quarrel
fall out → squabble
fall over → trip
fall through → fail
fall to → reach
fall to pieces →
disintegrate
fallacious → faulty
fallacious → wrong
fallacy → illusion
false → deceptive
false → fake
false → insincere
false → lying
false → mock
false → phoney
false → two-faced
false → untrue
false → wrong
falsehood → lie
falsify → misrepresent

fragment → bit
fragment → disintegrate
fragment → part
fragment → piece
fragmented → broken
fragrance → smell
fragrant → sweet
frail → fragile
frail → puny
frail → weak
frailty → weakness
frame → body
frame → build
frame of mind → humour
frame of mind → mood
frangible → fragile
frank → blunt
frank → candid
frank → direct
frank → natural
frank → open
frank → straight
frank → straightforward
frantic → furious
frantic → hysterical
frantic → upset
fraternity → association
fraternize → associate
fraud → con
fraud → corruption
fraud → fake
fraud → racket
fraudulence → dishonesty
fraudulent → corrupt
fraudulent → crooked
fraudulent → deceptive
fraudulent → dishonest
fray → quarrel
fray → wear
freak → curiosity
freak → weirdo
free → available
free → discharge
free → immune
free → independent
free → loose
free → release
free → spare
free → wild
free time → leisure
freedom → release

freeze → cool
freeze → harden
freeze → numb
freezing → cold
freight → load
frenetic → furious
frenzied → furious
frenzied → hysterical
frenzy → rage
frequency → rate
frequent → continual
frequently → often
fresh → original
fresh → recent
freshen → refresh
fret → fuss
fret → worry
fretful → cross
fretful → restless
friction → conflict
friend → china
friend → companion
friendliness → goodwill
friendly → cosy
friendly → favourable
friendly → pleasant
friendly → sociable
friendly → warm
friendship → goodwill
fright → alarm
fright → fear
fright → horror
fright → panic
fright → scare
frighten → alarm
frighten → scare
frightened → afraid
frightening → scary
frightening → spooky
frightful → awful
frightful → dreadful
frightful → terrible
frigid → cold
frigid → frozen
fringe → border
fringe → edge
fritter away → waste
frock → dress
frolic → play
from time to time → sometimes
front → face
front → head

frontage → front
frontier → border
froth → boil
froth → foam
frown → glare
frown on → disapprove
frowsty → stuffy
frozen → numb
frugal → economical
frugal → thrifty
frugality → economy
fruit → effect
fruitful → fertile
fruitful → productive
fruitless → in **vain**
fruitless → vain
frustrate → dash
frustrate → foil
frustrate → hamper
frustrate → hinder
fry → cook
fulfil → accomplish
fulfil → achieve
fulfil → carry out
fulfil → keep
fulfil → meet
fulfil → perform
fulfil → satisfy
full → abundant
full → busy
full → complete
full → crowded
full → thorough
full → whole
full of life → alive
full-grown → mature
fully → quite
fully → well
fully-fledged → mature
fume → rage
fuming → furious
fuming → mad
fun → entertainment
function → act
function → behave
function → go
function → job
function → part
function → party
function → purpose
functional → practical
functionary → official
fund → bank

generative → fertile
generative → productive
generic → general
generous → handsome
generous → noble
genesis → origin
genial → friendly
genial → warm
genius → talent
genre → class
genre → kind
genteel → polite
genteel → posh
genteel → refined
gentle → leisurely
gentle → mild
gentle → soft
gentle → tender
gentleman → man
gentlemanly → refined
gentleness → kindness
genuine → actual
genuine → authentic
genuine → dinkum
genuine → natural
genuine → real
genuine → right
genuine → serious
genuine → sincere
genuine → true
germ-free → pure
germ-free → sterile
germane → appropriate
germane → relevant
germinate → grow
gesticulate → signal
gesture → signal
get → acquire
get → develop
get → earn
get → extract
get → grow
get → obtain
get → receive
get → secure
get → see
get → take in
get → understand
get → win
get a move on → hurry
get across → convey
get as far as → reach
get away → escape

get back → recover
get back at → retaliate
get better → recover
get certified → qualify
get even → revenge
get even with → retaliate
get going → start
get hold of → contact
get hold of → obtain
get in the way → impede
get in touch with → contact
get off your chest → reveal
get on → do
get on someone's nerves → annoy
get on someone's nerves → bother
get on someone's nerves → pester
get out of → dodge
get rid of → dispose of
get rid of → dump
get rid of → eliminate
get rid of → remove
get smaller → shrink
get the better of → overcome
get the hang of → master
get the impression → sense
get through → pass
get to → reach
get to the bottom of → solve
get together → meet
get under way → proceed
get under way → start
get well → recover
get your hands on → obtain
get your own back → retaliate
get your own back → revenge
get-together → gathering
get-together → meeting

get-together → party
ghastly → awful
ghastly → dreadful
ghost → spirit
ghostly → spooky
giant → huge
giant → immense
giant → large
giant → vast
gibberish → garbage
gidday → hello
giddy → dizzy
giddy → faint
gift → blessing
gift → capacity
gift → present
gift → talent
gigantic → colossal
gigantic → enormous
gigantic → immense
gigantic → large
gigantic → vast
giggle → laugh
girl → female
girl → woman
girlish → female
gist → meaning
give → grant
give → hand down
give → issue
give → present
give → spare
give → supply
give a kick → thrill
give a talk → lecture
give a wide berth to → avoid
give back → return
give in → submit
give in → surrender
give leave → allow
give off → discharge
give off → emit
give out → emit
give out → fail
give out → issue
give permission → let
give prominence to → feature
give rise to → cause
give rise to → occasion
give someone a fright → scare

goggle → stare
gone → absent
gone → over
good → benefit
good → favourable
good → kind
good → respectable
good → sound
good afternoon → gidday
good afternoon → hello
good condition → health
good enough → acceptable
good enough → satisfactory
good evening → gidday
good evening → hello
good for you → beneficial
good for you → healthy
good manners → courtesy
good morning → gidday
good morning → hello
good sense → common sense
good turn → favour
good-for-nothing → lazy
good-humoured → cheery
good-looking → cute
good-looking → handsome
goodness → honour
goodness → virtue
goods → product
goods → stock
goodwill → friendship
gorge → abyss
gorge → fill
gorgeous → beautiful
gorgeous → cute
gorgeous → splendid
gossamer → fine
gossip → chat
gossip → rumour
gouge → dig
govern → control
govern → determine
govern → guide
govern → lead
govern → rule

government → control
governor → chief
governor → ruler
gown → dress
grab → grasp
grab → seize
grace → courtesy
grace → favour
grace → polish
graciousness → courtesy
grade → class
grade → classify
grade → kind
grade → level
grade → quality
grade → rank
grade → sort
gradient → slope
gradient → tilt
gradual → slow
gradually → slowly
graduate → pass
graduate → qualify
grain → bit
grain → finish
grand → impressive
grand → splendid
grandeur → glory
grandiloquent → pretentious
grandiose → grand
grandiose → ostentatious
grandiose → pompous
grant → admit
grant → allow
grant → give
grant → permit
grant → present
graphic → colourful
grapple → fight
grasp → command
grasp → comprehend
grasp → grab
grasp → grip
grasp → handle
grasp → hold
grasp → learn
grasp → master
grasp → realize
grasp → see
grasp → seize

grasp → take in
grasp → understand
grasp → understanding
grasping → greedy
grass on → inform on
grate → scrape
gratified → proud
gratify → satisfy
gratis → free
grave → acute
grave → critical
grave → deep
grave → grim
grave → heavy
grave → serious
grave → severe
grave → solemn
grave → tomb
graze → scrape
graze → touch
great → acute
great → brilliant
great → deep
great → excellent
great → extensive
great → extreme
great → grand
great → intense
great → large
great → outstanding
great → splendid
great → uncommon
great → vast
great → wonderful
great deal → plenty
greatest → foremost
greatest → supreme
greatest → ultimate
greatly → very
greedy → selfish
green → field
green → ignorant
green → inexperienced
greet → receive
gregarious → sociable
grenade → bomb
grey → dim
grey → drab
grief → misery
grief → pain
grief → regret
grief → sorrow
grief-stricken → sad**

INDEX

INDEX

INDEX

missive → note
mist → cloud
mistake → confuse
mistake → error
mistake → miss
mistake → mix-up
mistake → slip
mistaken → false
mistaken → untrue
mistaken → wrong
mistress → teacher
mistrust → suspect
mistrust → suspicion
misty → wet
misunderstanding → mix-up
misuse → waste
mitigate → weaken
mix → associate
mix → blend
mix → combination
mix → combine
mix → mixture
mix up → confuse
mix up → muddle
mix up with → mistake
mixture → blend
mixture → combination
mixture → cross
mixture → union
mixture → variety
moan → complain
moan → grumble
moan → lament
mob → crowd
mob → jam
mob → mass
mob violence → riot
mock → imitate
mock → make **fun** of
mock → tease
mock-up → model
mockery → scorn
mode → fashion
mode → manner
mode → method
mode → style
model → design
model → example
model → ideal
model → make
model → shape
moderate → change

moderate → modest
moderate → reasonable
moderately → quite
modernize → renovate
modest → homely
modest → humble
modest → low
modest → reasonable
modification → change
modification → qualification
modify → adapt
modify → change
modify → vary
modish → smart
modus operandi → system
moggie → cat
moggy → cat
moist → damp
moist → wet
moisten → wet
moisture → damp
moke → horse
mollify → calm
mollify → humour
mollify → pacify
mollycoddle → spoil
molten → liquid
moment → instant
moment → minute
momentary → brief
momentary → short
momentary → temporary
momentous → critical
momentous → crucial
momentous → important
momentous → serious
momentum → speed
monarch → king
monarch → ruler
monetary → economic
monetary → financial
money → financial
money → wealth
money-making → economic
mongrel → dog
monitor → observe
monotonous → boring
monotonous → dreary

monotonous → dull
monotonous → flat
monotony → boredom
monster → savage
monumental → grand
mood → humour
moody → sulky
moor → secure
moot → raise
moral → message
morality → right
morality → virtue
morals → principle
morals → standards
mordacious → sarcastic
mordant → sarcastic
more → extra
more than → over
moreover → also
moreover → too
moron → fool
moron → idiot
moronic → idiotic
moronic → stupid
morose → down
morose → moody
mortal → deadly
mortal → fatal
mortal → individual
mortgage → loan
mortification → embarrassment
mortification → shame
mortified → ashamed
mortified → embarrassed
mortify → embarrass
mortify → shame
most → majority
most → maximum
most important → foremost
most recent → last
mostly → mainly
mother → parent
motif → pattern
motion → movement
motion → question
motion → signal
motionless → quiet
motionless → still
motivate → drive
motivate → prompt

nasty → disagreeable
nasty → horrible
nasty → spiteful
nasty → unkind
nasty → unpleasant
nation → land
nation → public
nation → race
nation → state
national → home
native → home
native → inhabitant
native → local
native → natural
natter → chat
natty → smart
natural → automatic
natural → informal
natural → wild
naturalistic → realistic
nature → character
nature → essence
nature → personality
naughty → wicked
nausea → disgust
nauseate → disgust
nauseate → shock
nauseating → disgusting
nauseous → crook
nauseous → queasy
nauseous → sick
navigate → manoeuvre
ne plus ultra → peak
ne'er-do-well → failure
near → beside
near → immediate
near → imminent
near at hand → near
nearby → handy
nearby → near
nearest → next
nearly → about
nearly → almost
neat → handy
neat → orderly
neat → smart
neat → tidy
nebulous → vague
necessary → basic
necessary → vital
necessitate → demand
necessitate → involve
necessities → essentials

necessity → requirement
neck and neck → even
necromancy → magic
need → demand
need → distress
need → require
need → requirement
need → want
needle → irritate
needle → tease
needless → excessive
needless → unnecessary
nefarious → criminal
nefarious → crooked
nefarious → wicked
negate → counteract
negate → reverse
neglect → fail
neglect → ignore
neglect → overlook
neglected → derelict
neglectful → careless
negligible → minute
negligible → slight
negligible → tiny
negligible → trivial
negligible → worthless
negotiate → manoeuvre
neighbourhood → area
neighbourhood → local
neighbourhood → surroundings
neighbouring → next
nemesis → fate
neophyte → recruit
nepotism → favouritism
nerve → cheek
nerve → courage
nerve → daring
nerve → impudence
nerve-racking → tense
nervous → afraid
nervous → anxious
nervous → dubious
nervous → tense
nervous → timid
nervous → uneasy
nervous → worried
nervousness → alarm
nervousness → anxiety
net → earn
net → trap

neutral → impersonal
neutralize → counteract
new → extra
new → inexperienced
new → modern
new → original
new → recent
new → strange
new → unfamiliar
news → information
news → word
next to → beside
next to → near
next world → heaven
nib → point
nibble → bite
nice → agreeable
nice → pleasant
niceties → ceremony
nicety → detail
nick → arrest
nick → jail
nick → prison
nick → steal
nickname → name
nigh → near
nightmare → hell
nightmare → ordeal
nil → zero
nimble → agile
nip → bite
nip something in the bud → stop
nirvana → heaven
no-hoper → failure
nobleman → noble
nod → signal
node → bump
noise → racket
noise → sound
noiseless → quiet
noisome → smelly
noisy → loud
noisy → rowdy
nomination → appointment
nominee → candidate
non-polluting → green
non-specific → broad
nonaligned → neutral
nonchalant → careless
nonchalant → casual

object to → resent
objection → complaint
objection → disagreement
objection → grumble
objection → protest
objectionable → disagreeable
objectionable → offensive
objectionable → unpleasant
objective → aim
objective → goal
objective → intention
objective → object
obligate → force
obligation → bond
obligation → duty
obligation → responsibility
obligatory → compulsory
oblige → force
oblige → make
oblige → require
obliged → supposed
obliging → accommodating
oblique → indirect
obliterate → blot out
obliterate → destroy
obliteration → destruction
oblivious → ignorant
oblivious → preoccupied
oblivious → unaware
oblivious → unconscious
obloquy → slander
obnoxious → disagreeable
obnoxious → disgusting
obnoxious → hateful
obnoxious → unpleasant
obscene → crude
obscene → naughty
obscure → blot out
obscure → cover
obscure → dim
obscure → unknown
obsequiousness → flattery
observable → visible

observance → ceremony
observant → alert
observant → sharp
observation → comment
observation → remark
observation → watch
observe → comment
observe → discern
observe → follow
observe → note
observe → notice
observe → obey
observe → practise
observe → remark
observe → see
observe → spot
observe → watch
observe → witness
observer → spectator
observer → witness
obsessed → crazy
obsession → complex
obsessive → fanatical
obsolescent → old-fashioned
obsolete → old-fashioned
obsolete → out of date
obstacle → barrier
obstacle → difficulty
obstacle → handicap
obstinate → stubborn
obstreperous → difficult
obstreperous → rowdy
obstruct → bar
obstruct → block
obstruct → close
obstruct → delay
obstruct → hamper
obstruct → impede
obstruct → interfere
obstruction → barrier
obstruction → blockage
obstruction → delay
obstruction → obstacle
obtain → acquire
obtain → buy
obtain → earn
obtain → extract
obtain → gain
obtain → get
obtain → secure
obtrusive → pushy

obtuse → dim
obtuse → dumb
obtuse → slow
obtuse → stupid
obtuseness → stupidity
obverse → opposite
obvious → clear
obvious → conspicuous
obvious → evident
obvious → logical
obvious → manifest
obvious → noticeable
obvious → plain
obvious → prominent
obvious → visible
occasion → bring
occasion → case
occasion → chance
occasion → create
occasion → incident
occasional → irregular
occasionally → sometimes
occultism → magic
occupant → inhabitant
occupation → job
occupation → profession
occupation → trade
occupation → work
occupied → active
occupied → busy
occupy → busy
occupy → inhabit
occupy → invade
occupy → possess
occur → come
occur → happen
occur → take **place**
occurrence → case
occurrence → incident
odd → bizarre
odd → curious
odd → extraordinary
odd → funny
odd → occasional
odd → peculiar
odd → strange
odd → weird
oddity → curiosity
odds → chance
odds → possibility
odds → probability
odds and ends → junk

opportunity → turn
oppose → contest
oppose → disagree
oppose → object
oppose → protest
oppose → resist
opposed → different
opposed → opposite
opposite → reverse
opposition → competition
opposition → competitor
opposition → conflict
opposition → disagreement
opposition → objection
oppress → bully
oppress → persecute
oppression → abuse
oppressive → stuffy
oppressive → unbearable
oppressor → bully
opt → vote
opt for → choose
opt for → pick
opt for → select
option → choice
opulence → luxury
opulent → luxurious
opulent → rich
opulent → wealthy
oral → exam
oration → speech
oration → talk
orb → ball
orchestra → band
orchestrate → conduct
orchestrate → stage
ordain → impose
ordain → order
ordeal → experience
ordeal → hell
order → arrange
order → command
order → instruct
order → require
order → routine
order → rule
order → sequence
order → tell
orderly → neat
orderly → tidy

ordinance → law
ordinance → rule
ordinary → common
ordinary → conventional
ordinary → everyday
ordinary → humble
ordinary → natural
ordinary → normal
ordinary → regular
ordinary → routine
organization → body
organization → business
organization → firm
organization → movement
organization → society
organization → structure
organize → arrange
organize → book
organize → conduct
organize → group
organize → set up
organize → stage
organized → efficient
organized → ready
organizing → organization
origin → beginning
origin → cause
origin → source
origin → stock
original → first
original → individual
originality → imagination
originate → begin
originate → create
originate → invent
originate → start
originator → source
ornament → decorate
ornamented → fancy
ornate → elaborate
ornate → fancy
orthodox → conventional
orthodox → proper
orthodox → standard
oscillate → shake
oscillate → wave
ostensible → probable
ostentatious → flashy
ostentatious → gaudy

ostentatious → pompous
ostentatious → pretentious
ostentatious → vain
other than → but
other than → except
others → remainder
others → rest
oust → overthrow
out loud → aloud
out of danger → safe
out of date → old-fashioned
out of harm's way → safe
out of shape → crooked
out of the ordinary → exceptional
out of the ordinary → uncommon
out of the question → impossible
out of your mind → insane
out-and-out → total
out-and-out → utter
out-of-the-way → distant
out-of-the-way → lonely
out-of-the-way → strange
outback → country
outbreak → burst
outbreak → rash
outcome → result
outcry → protest
outdated → old-fashioned
outdated → out of date
outdo → beat
outdo → pass
outdo → top
outdoor → outside
outdoors → country
outer → outside
outfit → clothes
outfit → organization
outfit → provide
outfit → set
outgoing → sociable
outing → trip
outlandish → bizarre
outlandish → eccentric

INDEX

reference → mention
referendum → vote
refine → perfect
refine → polish
refined → fine
refined → polite
refined → sophisticated
refinement → polish
reflect → consider
reflect → deliberate
reflect → ponder
reflect → think
reflect on → contemplate
reflection → thought
reflective → thoughtful
reflex → automatic
reform → change
reform → correct
reform → improve
reform → transform
refractory → difficult
refractory → obstinate
refractory → stubborn
refrain → abstain
refrain from → avoid
refrain from → boycott
refresh someone's memory → remind
refreshing → cool
refreshment → food
refrigerate → cool
refuge → retreat
refuge → shelter
refund → compensate
refund → repay
refund → return
refurbish → renovate
refurbish → restore
refuse → decline
refuse → deny
refuse → garbage
refuse → junk
refuse → reject
refuse → resist
refuse → rubbish
refuse → trash
refute → deny
refute → disprove
regain → recover
regal → royal
regard → admiration
regard → esteem

regard → rate
regard → respect
regard → view
regard as → consider
regarding → about
regardless of → despite
regardless of → in spite of
regenerate → reconstruct
region → area
region → land
regional → local
register → list
register → note
register → record
regret → disappointment
regret → sorrow
regretful → guilty
regretful → sorry
regular → average
regular → constant
regular → continual
regular → conventional
regular → even
regular → formal
regular → normal
regular → orderly
regular → ordinary
regular → routine
regular → standard
regular → steady
regular → typical
regular → usual
regularity → order
regulation → law
regulation → restriction
regulation → rule
regulations → bureaucracy
regurgitate → vomit
rehabilitate → reform
rehabilitation → reform
rehearsal → practice
rehearse → practise
reheat → heat
reign → rule
reimburse → compensate
reimburse → pay
reimburse → repay
reimburse → return

reimbursement → compensation
reimbursement → pay
rein → restrain
reinforce → augment
reinforce → strengthen
reinforce → supplement
reinforce → support
reinstate → restore
reintroduce → restore
reiterate → repeat
reject → boycott
reject → deny
reject → refuse
reject → renounce
rejoice → celebrate
rejoin → reply
rejoinder → answer
rejoinder → reply
rejuvenate → refresh
rekindle → revive
relate → connect
relate to → identify with
relating to → about
relation → bond
relation → connection
relations → family
relations → kin
relationship → affair
relationship → association
relationship → connection
relationship → link
relationship → relation
relationship → tie
relative → relation
relatively → rather
relatives → family
relatives → kin
relax → calm
relax → ease
relax → lift
relax → moderate
relax → outspan
relax → rest
relaxation → ease
relaxation → leisure
relaxation → rest
relaxed → calm
relaxed → casual
relaxed → comfortable
relaxed → cool

replica → copy
replica → model
replication → copy
reply → answer
report → announcement
report → feature
report → item
report → review
report → statement
repose → lie
repose → peace
repose → sleep
repository → container
repository → store
reprehensible → wrong
representation → model
representation → symbol
representational → realistic
representative → official
representative → substitute
representative → typical
repress → contain
repress → suppress
repressed → pent-up
reprimand → caution
reprimand → lecture
reprimand → scold
reprisal → revenge
reproach → censure
reproduce → breed
reproduce → copy
reproduction → copy
reproduction → fake
reprove → scold
republic → state
repudiate → deny
repudiate → reject
repugnance → horror
repugnant → disgusting
repulse → repel
repulsion → disgust
repulsive → unpleasant
reputable → honest
reputable → respectable
reputation → fame
reputation → name
repute → reputation

reputed → supposed
request → appeal
require → demand
require → expect
require → involve
require → need
require → take
require → want
required → compulsory
required → necessary
required → supposed
requirement → condition
requirement → standard
requisite → compulsory
requisite → condition
requisite → necessary
reschedule → put off
rescind → abolish
rescind → cancel
rescind → lift
rescind → reverse
rescue → save
research → investigate
research → study
resemblance → similarity
resent → envy
resentful → bitter
resentful → jealous
resentful → sulky
resentment → animosity
resentment → envy
resentment → hostility
reservation → qualification
reserve → bank
reserve → book
reserve → fund
reserve → hoard
reserve → save
reserve → stock
reserve → stockpile
reserve → store
reserve → supply
reserved → cold
reserved → distant
reserved → remote
reserved → secretive
reservoir → bank
reservoir → fund
reservoir → stock

reservoir → store
reside → inhabit
reside → live
residence → home
residence → house
resident → inhabitant
resident → local
residue → remains
resign → quit
resigned → passive
resilient → tough
resist → oppose
resist → rebel
resist → repel
resistance → defence
resistance → opposition
resistant → immune
resolute → determined
resolute → firm
resolute → serious
resolute → steadfast
resolution → decision
resolution → determination
resolution → resolve
resolution → will
resolve → decide
resolve → determination
resolve → determine
resolve → intend
resolve → settle
resolve → solve
resolve → will
resolve → work out
resolved → serious
resonant → deep
resonate → ring
resounding → loud
respect → admiration
respect → admire
respect → appreciate
respect → approval
respect → approve
respect → consider
respect → consideration
respect → detail
respect → esteem
respect → value
respectable → decent
respectful → polite
respite → break
respite → rest
resplendent → bright

INDEX

INDEX

submerge → flood
submission → surrender
submission → tender
submissive → meek
submissive → obedient
submissive → passive
submit → give in
submit → nominate
submit → pose
submit → subject
submit → surrender
subordinate → inferior
subordinate → junior
subsequent → next
subsequently → after
subsequently → next
subservient → obedient
subside → abate
subside → decrease
subside → fall
subsidize → fund
subsidy → grant
subsistence → food
substance → essence
substance → material
substance → matter
substance → stuff
substance → wealth
substantial → solid
substantial → sturdy
substantiate → confirm
substantiate → prove
substantiation → proof
substitute → change
substitute → replacement
subterfuge → trick
subtle → fine
subvert → undermine
succeed → flourish
succeed → follow
succeed → pass
succeed → replace
succeed → triumph
succeed → win
succeed in → manage
succeeding → next
success → triumph
success → victory
success → win
successfully → well
succession → sequence
succession → series

successor → replacement
succinct → concise
succinct → short
succumb → develop
succumb → give in
succumb → surrender
sudden → abrupt
sudden → quick
sudden → sharp
suffer → bear
suffer → endure
suffer → feel
suffer → receive
suffer → undergo
sufferer → patient
suffering → distress
suffice → do
sufficient → adequate
sufficient → ample
sufficient → satisfactory
sugary → sweet
suggest → advise
suggest → hint
suggest → nominate
suggest → raise
suggest → vote
suggestible → impressionable
suggestion → advice
suggestion → hint
suggestion → idea
suggestion → indication
suggestion → trace
suit → blend
suit → flatter
suit → match
suitable → appropriate
suitable → favourable
suitable → fitting
suitable → proper
suitable → right
sulky → grumpy
sulky → moody
sullen → grumpy
sullen → moody
sullen → sulky
sully → soil
sultry → stuffy
sum → count
sum → quantity
sum → total
sum total → whole

summarize → outline
summarize → sum up
summary → outline
summing-up → summary
summit → peak
summit → top
sumptuous → luxurious
sumptuousness → luxury
sunder → separate
sunder → tear
sundry → several
sundry → various
sunken → low
sunny → cheery
sup → drink
superabundance → excess
superb → brilliant
superb → excellent
superb → first-rate
superb → marvellous
superb → outstanding
superb → splendid
superb → wonderful
supercilious → scornful
supercilious → superior
superciliousness → pride
superfluity → excess
superfluous → excess
superfluous → spare
superfluous → waste
superintend → supervise
superintendence → control
superior → prime
superior → select
superior → senior
superior → smug
superior → superb
superiority → advantage
superiority → victory
superlative → first-rate
superlative → incomparable
superlative → superb
supermarket → shop
supernatural → spooky
supernumerary → spare
supersede → follow
supersede → replace
superstar → celebrity

INDEX

swap → change
swap → exchange
swap → substitute
swarm → crawl
swarm → crowd
swarthy → dark
sway → hold
sway → influence
sway → mana
sway → persuade
sweep → blow
sweep → flourish
sweep → stretch
sweep away → wash
sweeping → broad
sweeping → extensive
sweeping → general
sweet → lovable
sweet-smelling → fragrant
sweet-smelling → sweet
sweet-tempered → gentle
sweetened → sweet
sweetie → sweet
swell → bulge
swell → expand
swell → increase
swell → wave
swelling → boil
swelling → bulge
swelling → bump
swelling → lump
swerve → curve
swerve → dodge
swift → brief
swift → fast
swift → hasty
swift → prompt
swift → quick
swift → sudden
swiftly → fast
swiftly → quickly
swiftness → speed
swig → drink
swindle → cheat
swindle → con
swindle → rob
swindler → crook
swine → pig
swing → swerve
swipe → steal
switch → exchange

switch → substitute
switch → swap
swivel → turn
swollen-headed → conceited
swoon → faint
swot → study
swotting → study
sycophancy → flattery
sylphlike → slender
symbol → sign
symbolize → represent
symmetry → order
sympathetic → compassionate
sympathetic → favourable
sympathetic → sorry
sympathetic → understanding
sympathize with → pity
sympathy → pity
symposium → conference
symptom → sign
symptomatic → characteristic
syndicate → association
syndicate → ring
synod → council
synopsis → outline
synopsis → summary
synthesis → union
synthesize → combine
system → plan
system → procedure
system → process
system → routine
systematize → arrange
systematize → classify
table → submit
tabulate → classify
tabulate → list
taciturn → silent
taciturnity → silence
tackle → equipment
tackle → stuff
tacky → flashy
tacky → gaudy
tacky → sticky
tacky → tasteless
tact → consideration
tactic → manoeuvre

tactless → thoughtless
tag → label
taint → infect
taint → pollute
take → accept
take → bear
take → bring
take → capture
take → carry
take → choose
take → demand
take → receive
take → select
take → steal
take a break → pause
take a chance → gamble
take a dim view of → disapprove
take a nap → sleep
take a stand against → oppose
take a trip → travel
take aback → surprise
take advantage of → impose on
take advantage of → profit
take after → resemble
take away → remove
take away → subtract
take care of → deal
take care of → handle
take care of → look after
take care of → mind
take care of → process
take care of → tend
take care of → watch
take cover → shelter
take down → lower
take down → write
take exception to → disapprove
take flight → flee
take for → mistake
take fright → fear
take from → subtract
take in → absorb
take in → admit
take in → comprehend
take in → deceive
take in → grasp
take in → involve

take in >> telling

variety → breed
variety → choice
variety → form
variety → kind
variety → range
variety → sort
variety → type
various → several
vary → range
vast → broad
vast → colossal
vast → enormous
vast → extensive
vast → huge
vast → immense
vast → large
vast → spacious
vastness → size
vault → jump
vault → leap
vault → tomb
veer → swerve
vehemence → heat
vehemence → strength
vehemence → violence
vehement → intense
vehement → violent
vehicle → automobile
vehicle → car
vehicle → medium
velocity → rate
velocity → speed
venal → corrupt
venality → corruption
vend → sell
venerate → admire
venerate → respect
venerate → treasure
venerate → worship
venerated → holy
veneration → esteem
vengeance → revenge
venom → poison
venom → spite
venomous → poisonous
venomous → spiteful
vent → opening
venture → business
venture → dare
venture → enterprise
venture → gamble
venture → undertaking
veracious → right

verbal → oral
verbalize → express
verdict → conclusion
verdict → decision
verdict → judgment
verge → side
verification → proof
verified → actual
verify → confirm
verify → determine
verify → prove
verisimilar → probable
vérité → realistic
verity → principle
vernacular → colloquial
vernacular → language
versed in → familiar
versus → against
vertical → sheer
vertical → steep
vertical → straight
vertiginous → faint
verve → energy
very → precise
very → really
very much → far
vessel → container
vestige → trace
vestiges → remains
vet → inspect
veteran → practical
veto → forbid
vex → annoy
vexation → anger
vexation → care
vexation → nuisance
viable → economic
viable → possible
vibrant → colourful
vibrate → shake
vice → evil
vicious → cruel
vicious → malicious
vicious → savage
vicious → violent
vicious → wicked
viciousness → cruelty
victor → champion
victor → winner
victory → success
victory → triumph
victory → win
victuals → food

vie → compete
vie with → play
view → belief
view → feeling
view → idea
view → judgment
view → observe
view → opinion
view → outlook
view → regard
view → scene
view → scenery
view → thought
view → watch
viewpoint → opinion
vigilance → watch
vigilant → alert
vigilant → observant
vigilant → wary
vigorous → energetic
vigorous → powerful
vigour → drive
vigour → energy
vigour → power
vigour → spirit
vigour → strength
vile → disgusting
vile → evil
vile → nasty
vilify → attack
vilify → slander
villain → criminal
villain → crook
vindicate → justify
vindictive → spiteful
violate → break
violate → disobey
violate → intrude
violate → invade
violated → broken
violation → breach
violation → crime
violent → rude
violent → savage
violent → wild
VIP → celebrity
virginal → innocent
virtually → nearly
virtue → merit
virtue → right
virtue → value
virtuoso → fundi
virtuoso → genius